Pattern van den Gridegts van Oudgestis Kerk op Staten Eiland un ao: 1714 Anno Dom: 1751.

Dan'l Carteret, Fecit

(Engraved from a tracing made by R. M. Bayles, from the original sketch.)

PLAN OF OLD REFORMED CHURCH, AT PORT RICHMOND, S. I.

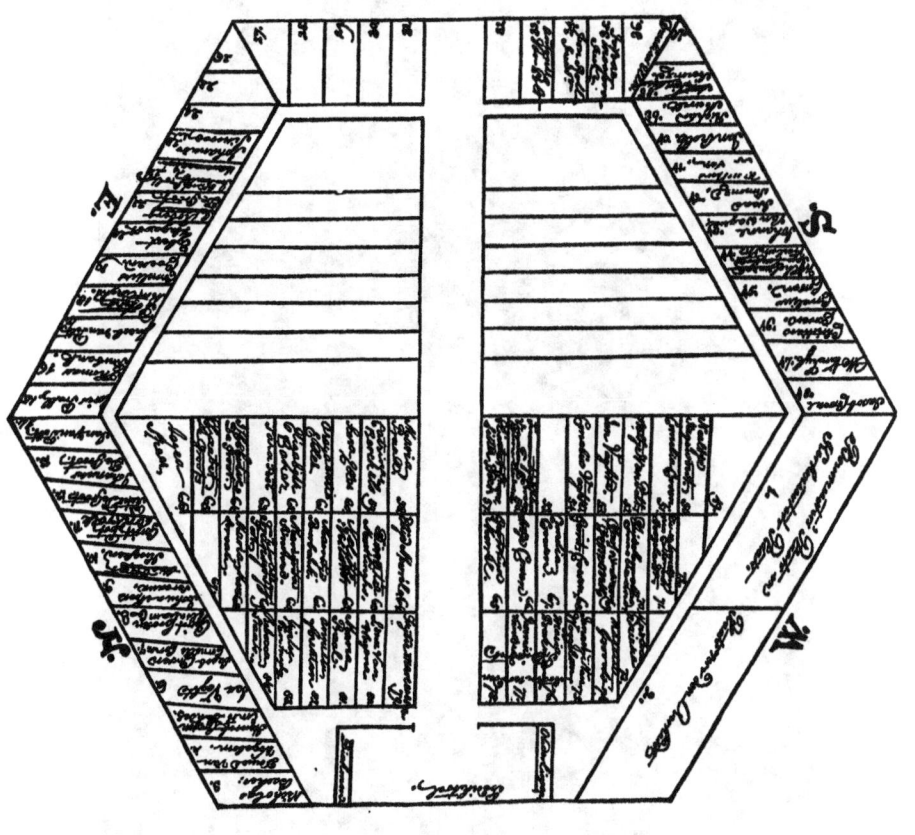

Melatiah E. Dwight

Staten Island Church Records

OFFICERS AND COMMITTEES OF THE SOCIETY FOR 1909

President,	Clarence Winthrop Bowen
First Vice-President,	William Bradhurst Osgood Field
Second Vice-President,	Tobias Alexander Wright
Secretary,	Henry Russell Drowne
Treasurer,	Hopper Striker Mott
Librarian,	John Reynolds Totten
Historian,	William Austin Macy, M.D.
Necrologist,	Richard Henry Greene
Registrar of Pedigrees,	Winchester Fitch

Executive Committee

John Reynolds Totten, *Chairman*

George Austin Morrison, Jr.
William Bradhurst Osgood Field
William Isaac Walker
Henry Pierson Gibson

Trustees

Henry Russell Drowne
George Austin Morrison, Jr.
Howland Pell
Warner Van Norden
Archer Milton Huntington
Gen. James Grant Wilson
John Reynolds Totten
Ellsworth Eliot, M.D.
Hopper Striker Mott
Henry Pierson Gibson
Ellsworth Everett Dwight
Clarence Winthrop Bowen
William Isaac Walker
Tobias Alexander Wright
William Bradhurst Osgood Field

Committee on Publication

George Austin Morrison, Jr.

Tobias Alexander Wright
Hopper Striker Mott
Richard Henry Greene
E. Doubleday Harris
J. Henry Lea
Josiah Collins Pumpelly

COLLECTIONS

OF THE

NEW YORK GENEALOGICAL AND BIOGRAPHICAL SOCIETY

VOL IV

Staten Island Church Records

CLEARFIELD

Originally published
New York, 1909

Reprinted for
Clearfield Company, Inc. by
Genealogical Publishing Co., Inc.
Baltimore, Maryland
2002

International Standard Book Number: 0-8063-5158-6

Made in the United States of America

Note: Our original copy of this work did not include any text pages 1–8.

TO THE MEMORY OF
Rev. Melatiah Everett Dwight, M.D., D.D.
THROUGH WHOSE ADVICE AND BY WHOSE GENEROUS
ASSISTANCE THESE RECORDS ARE PRESERVED
THIS VOLUME IS GRATEFULLY
Dedicated
BY THE NEW YORK GENEALOGICAL AND
BIOGRAPHICAL SOCIETY

INTRODUCTION

THE Publication Committee of the New York Genealogical and Biographical Society have selected the Staten Island Church Records for the fourth volume of the Society's publications, considering them next in importance to those of the Reformed Dutch Church of New Amsterdam and New York, previously published. As the membership of these early Staten Island churches was made up largely of people from Long Island, Manhattan Island, and the section just west of the Hudson River, opposite the latter island, now in the State of New Jersey, these records will prove exceedingly important and interesting to the descendants of the early settlers of these localities. They form a vital link in the historic-genealogical chain that leads from past ages in the old world down to the present time in the new.

While in many cases the names of the descendants of these early settlers are not only spelled differently, and the pronunciation so changed as to almost defy recognition by those unlearned in the peculiar characteristics of Dutch nomenclature, the genealogical student has little trouble in tracing the gradual changes and identifying the family connections from one generation to another.

During the period covered by these statistics the Dutch settlers especially were so closely identified with the Church that the baptismal records contain the names of a majority of the children born to Dutch parents, accompanied by the names of many witnesses, so that in presenting these vital statistics the committee believe they are blazing the trail and rendering the search for emigrant ancestors less difficult to thousands scattered over this continent.

For the history of these churches the editor has for his authority in large measure Mr. Ira K. Morris' exhaustive *History of Staten Island*, and through the courtesy of Mr. Morris most of the illustrations were obtained.

The Reformed Dutch Churches

During the Dutch Colonial Government there was a settlement of French Vaudois, or Waldensians, at Stony Brook (now a part of the New Dorp neighborhood), on Staten Island. There was a Huguenot settlement on the Island a short time afterward (located at Fresh Kill, now Green Ridge), parties of this sect having fled from Holland to escape persecution, and having come over to New Netherlands in company with their new friends.

The Waldensians formed the first permanent settlement on Staten Island, that of Stony Brook, Oude Dorp (Old Town), a Dutch Village (Arrochar Park now occupying the site), having been three times destroyed by the Indians. The Waldensian Church at Stony Brook was built sometime between the years 1657 and 1668. It was the first Waldensian Church on the North American continent, and the first church of any denomination on Staten Island.

Dominie Drisius, a pastor of the Dutch Church in New York (then New Amsterdam), from 1652 to 1682, preached regularly once a month to the Waldensians on Staten Island, from about 1660 onward. He preached in both the French and Dutch languages. The descendants of these Waldensians and Huguenots are still numerous on Staten Island, and bear some of the oldest and most honored names. They are prominent in all denominations.

Later, a church edifice was erected at Cucklestown (now Richmond, the County seat), in which the Presbyterians, Dutch Reformed and Episcopalians worshipped. This structure was burned by the British during the Revolution.

Hollanders having settled along the North Shore of the Island, they erected a church edifice at what is now Port Richmond, about 1680. Services were conducted in the Dutch language. There is no record to prove that either of the churches here mentioned had a pastor of its own. Dominie Selyns, pastor of Brooklyn, Bushwick and Gravesend, also preached in these churches at stated times.

During the years 1682 and 1683, Dominie Taschemaker, from the University of Utrecht, supplied the churches on the Island. He removed to Schenectady, and perished there in a massacre by the French and Indians, in February, 1690.

The Rev. Pierre Daille, who came to America in 1683, and was a colleague of Dominie Selyns, frequently preached to the Huguenots on Staten Island.

The church at Stony Brook was supplied, from 1687 to 1689, by Laurentius Van der Bosch. According to the records, "he was suspended from the ministry by Dominie Selyns and others, who could not wait the slow process of sending their proceedings to be reviewed by the authorities in Holland." The inference is warranted that this church, though composed of Frenchmen, was under the jurisdiction of the Church of Holland, and was, therefore, *ipso facto*, a Reformed Dutch Church.

There appear to have been no pastors regularly stationed on Staten Island for three years from 1694. Supplies came from New York, Long Island and New Jersey.

Governor Hunter executed a grant to the Reformed Protestant Dutch Church, in 1714, to build a new church edifice on the North Shore, undoubtedly on the site of the one which stood there thirty-four years previous.

The date of the organization of this church is not positively known. It is evident, however, from the title page of an old baptismal record that it must have been at a very early period. It is as follows:

"Register Boek Van De—namen Der Kinderen Dewelck Gedoopt Bennen Op Staten Eylandt—Beginne Van Het Jaer Anno 1696." (Translation: "Register book of the—names of children which have been baptized on Staten Island, beginning from the year 1696.") The first Sunday school organized in America, about 1812, was connected with this church.

The North Side Church and the Church at Bergen, New Jersey, united, in 1750, in a call on Petrus de Wint. His credentials, however, proved to have been forgeries, and he was dismissed in 1752. Then the two churches united in a call upon William Jackson, a student in the care of Rev. John Frelinghuysen of Raritan, New Jersey. He was sent to Holland to complete his studies, and on his return, in 1757, was installed as pastor. He had the reputation of a preacher scarcely inferior to that of Whitfield. The church edifices were not large enough to accommodate his auditors, and services were frequently held in the open air. After a pastorate of thirty-two years he became insane. He was the last minister who preached to these congregations in the Dutch language.

The Rev. Peter Stryker was ordained minister of the Reformed Dutch Church on the North Side in 1790-4. In 1792 the church was incorporated under the laws of the State of New York by the title of "The Reformed Protestant Dutch Church" on Staten Island. The names of the corporators were Peter Stryker, Hendrick Garretson, John Van Pelt, Wilhelmus Vreeland, John Garretson, William Merrel, Peter Haughwout, Abraham Prall and Nicholas Haughwout.

The old edifice was also classed "a rebel church," and was destroyed by the British soldiery during the Revolution. Another church was erected and completed in the spring of 1787. It finally proved inadequate to the necessities of the congregation, and was demolished to make room for the present edifice, which was built upon the same site and dedicated in February, 1846.

In 1797, the Rev. Thomas Kirby became the pastor. He remained for three years.

The Rev. Peter I. Van Pelt was ordained as pastor on May 16, 1802, and continued so until 1835. He was succeeded that year by the Rev. James Brownlee, who served for fifty-five years.

The Rev. Alfred H. Demarest was appointed Dr. Brownlee's successor in 1890, and served until 1901, when he was succeeded by the Rev. J. Frederic Berg, the present pastor.

The Reformed Dutch Church in Richmond, destroyed during the Revolution, was rebuilt through the efforts of the Rev. Dr. Van Pelt in 1808. He occupied its pulpit until 1853, and was succeeded, in 1854, when it became an independent church, by the Rev. Thomas R. G. Peck, and in turn, the Rev. Erskine N. White, the Rev. Jacob Fehrmann, the Rev. J. H. Sinclair and the Rev. F. M. Kip.

Through the efforts of the Hon. Daniel D. Tompkins, Vice-President of the United States, a Dutch Reformed Church was established at Tompkinsville. It was dedicated in 1818. Dr. Van Pelt occupied its pulpit until 1823, when it became an independent charge. The Rev. John Miller then became its pastor, and was succeeded in 1847 by the Rev.

Alexander R. Thompson, and he by the Rev. Philip M. Brett, in 1851. He died in the following year. He was succeeded by the Rev. Edward Hitchcock, and he by the Rev. William T. Enyard.

In the course of a few years the congregation erected an edifice on Brighton Heights, and the old structure was utilized for business purposes. It was finally demolished in the summer of 1908.

In 1850, the Church of the Huguenots was organized by members of the Reformed Dutch Church in Richmond, because of the great distance of the latter place from their homes. Many changes have occurred among those who have guided the affairs of this church. It is at present presided over by the Rev. David Junor.

THE MORAVIAN CHURCH

The history of the people who established the Moravian Churches in America having been fully published in *"A History of Bethlehem, Pennsylvania,"* by Bishop Levering, President of the Moravian Historical Society, a simple outline sketch of the branch on Staten Island is deemed sufficient here. These people had much in common with the Puritans of New England, but were infinitely broader and more tolerant in their religious views of those of other faiths, and ever ready to co-operate with and welcome to their United Brotherhood all who called themselves Christians.

Captain Nicholas Garrison, so far as authentic information goes, was the first of the denomination of Christians called Moravian, or United Brethren, on Staten Island. He commanded the ship *Irene*, sailing between Georgia and New York.

The Rev. David Bruce, a very zealous Christian, was sent by the Moravian authorities to visit the scattered flocks in New York, and on Staten and Long Islands. It is conceded that he was the first Moravian preacher who ever officiated as such on Staten Island.

The ship commanded by Captain Garrison was built for the service of the Moravians, on Staten Island, between the years 1745 and 1748, under the direction of Abraham Boemper and Timothy Horsfield, agents for the Moravian Church in New York. It was launched on May 29, 1748, and registered in the name of Mr. Henry Antes. The cost was defrayed almost entirely by Bishop Spangenberg from a legacy left him by Thomas Noble, a New York merchant.

The vessel remained in the service of the Moravian Church for nine years, in the course of which it crossed the Atlantic twenty-four times, sailing between New York and London, or Amsterdam, and made one voyage to Greenland. It put to sea for the last time on November 20, 1757, in command of Captain Christian Jacobson. Ten days later it was captured by a French privateer, and given to a prize crew to be taken to Louisberg; but owing to ignorance of navigation on the part of those to whom it had been entrusted, was totally wrecked on January 12, 1758, off the coast of Cape Breton, and its passengers had narrow escape with their lives. Captain Christian Jacobson returned to his home at New Dorp, on Staten Island, and was murdered in his own house, still standing on New Dorp lane, by British soldiers.

During his sojourn in America, between December, 1741, and January, 1743, Count Zinzendorf extended the influence and enlarged the membership of the Moravian denomination on Staten Island and the surrounding country. Religious intercourse remained unbroken from that time on between this place and Bethlehem, Pa.

The arrival of the first colony of Moravians was in June, 1742. Their evangelists entered earnestly into the work without delay. Among these were the brethren Bruce, Almers, Gambold, Neisser, Utley, Rice and Wade.

The Moravian Society in New York met for worship at the house of Thomas Noble between 1742 and 1746. After that time at the house of Henry Van Vleek, which became headquarters for Moravian ministers in the city.

In the early part of the year 1748, when there were fifty persons attached to the Brethren in the city, and the adjoining islands, an ineffectual effort was made to secure the use of the Lutheran Church in New York for stated services. A hall was rented for the purpose.

Abraham Boemper, Henry Van Vleek, William Edmonds, John Kingston, Jeremiah Burnet and Jannitje Boelen of New York; Timothy and Mary Horsfield, William and

Charity Cornwell and Jaques and Jacomyntje Cortelyou of Long Island; and Jacobus and Veltje Van Der Bilt of Staten Island, are mentioned in September, 1747, as being most active members of the triple Moravian Society in the Province of New York.

About a dozen different Moravian clergymen came occasionally to Staten Island to officiate between the years 1742 and 1763. There were only three communicant members on the Island in 1756; they were Jacobus Vanderbilt and his wife, Vettje or Neiltje, and the widow Elizabeth Inyard. Religious services were held in a school house that stood near the site of the Moravian Church at New Dorp.

In 1762, Richard Connor, Stephen Martino, Jun., Tunis Egbert, Jacob Vander Bilt, Aaron Cortelyou, Mathias Enyard, John Baty, Cornelius Cortelyou, Cornelius Vander Bilt, Cornelius Van Deventer, Stephen Martino, Mary Stillwell, Cornelius Martino and Peter Perine applied to the church authorities at Bethlehem, Pennsylvania, for the establishment of a Moravian Church on Staten Island. Consequently, on July 7, 1763, the cornerstone of a church and parsonage was laid, and on December 7 following, the church was consecrated.

The building was set on fire by British soldiers during the Revolution, but was saved from destruction by members of the congregation. It is still standing, a short distance from its original site, and was recently thoroughly renovated and remodelled.

For several years after the organization of this Society, the congregation was supplied with preachers from New York. They were David Bruce in 1742; Richard Utley in 1747; John Wade in 1749; Owen Rice in 1750; Abraham Reinke, Jasper Payne, Owen Rice and Abraham Rudmeyer in 1754; Richard Utley in 1755; Jacob Rogers in 1756; Thomas Yarrel in 1757; George Selle in 1761, and Thomas Yarrel in 1762. The first regularly settled pastor of this church, however, was the Rev. Hector Gambold, from 1763 to 1784. He was succeeded that year by James Birkly, and he by E. Thorpe, who served until 1787; then followed Frederick Moehring, from 1787 to 1793; James Birkly again, from 1794 to 1797; Frederick Moehring again, from 1797 to 1803;

Nathaniel Brown, from 1803 until his death in 1813; John C. Bechler, from 1813 to 1817; George A. Hartman, from 1817 to 1837; Ambrose Rondthaler, from 1837 to 1839; H. G. Clauder, from 1839 to 1852; Bernhard de Schweinitz, from 1852 to 1854; Amadeus A. Reinke, from 1854 to 1860; Edwin T. Senseman, from 1860 to 1862; Eugene Leibert, from 1862 to 1867; Francis F. Hagen, from 1867 to 1870; William L. Lennert, from 1870 to 1876; William H. Vogler, from 1876 to 1892; William H. Rice, from 1892 to 1897; William H. Oerter, from 1897 to 1904; F. E. Grunert, from 1904 to the present.

The Moravian Society at New Dorp was incorporated on April 15, 1808. The present church edifice was consecrated on May 15, 1845.

Three other Moravian Churches have been established on the Island—at Castleton Corners, Stapleton and Giffords—all under the supervision of the mother church at New Dorp.

Commodore Cornelius Vanderbilt made munificient donations to this church. His son, William H., also was very liberal in his dealings with the church. The Vanderbilt Mausoleum is located in a beautiful park on the north side of the cemetery.

St. Andrew's Protestant Episcopal Church

At the time of the organization of this church, its members worshiped in the Reformed Dutch Church, at Cucklestown (Richmond). It is a matter of record that divine service, after the manner of the Church of England, was held here prior to 1704. If marriage or baptismal records were kept prior to 1752, however, they are not in evidence. In October of 1704, the Rev. William Vesey, rector of Trinity Church, New York, in reporting the state of religion in Richmond County to the Society for the propogation of the Gospel in foreign parts, in London, says: "There was a tax of £40 per annum levied upon the people for the support of the minister, and that they desired to have a minister sent to them, as well as some further encouragement from the Society."

Governor Fletcher succeeded, in 1693, in having the Episcopal Church established by law throughout the Colony, to be supported by general taxation. This law remained in force until the Revolution, so that all non-Episcopalians, beside supporting their own churches, were obliged to contribute toward the support of the Episcopal Church. The law, however, became in a great degree inoperative in Richmond County after the munificent bequest of Judge Duxbury became available.*

The Rev. John Talbot was sent to Staten Island as a missionary in 1706. He was succeeded in 1710 by the Rev. Eneas McKensie. The church was built in 1713. It was a plain stone structure, a portion of the original walls still standing in the present structure. The Church Charter, usually known as "Queen Anne's Charter," begins as follows:

"Anne, by the grace of God, Queen of Great Britain, France, Ireland, Defender of the Faith, &c. To all whom these presents shall come, greeting:—Whereas our loving Subjects, the Reverend Eneas MacKenzie, Minister of Staten Island, Richmond County, Ellis Duxbury, Thomas Harmer, Augistin Graham, Joseph Arrowsmith, Lambert Garritson, Nathaniel Brittain, William Tillier, Richard Merrill, John Morgan and Alexander Stewart, all freeholders, and of the principal inhabitants of the said Island in Communion of the Church of England, as by Law established, by their petition presented unto our Trusty and Wellbeloved Robert Hunter, Esq., Captain Generall and Governour in Chief of our province of New York, in behelf of themselves and all other the Inhabitants of the said Island in Communion of the Church of England, as by Law established, and their Suc-

---

* In 1718, Ellis Duxbury bequeathed an extensive and valuable tract of land to the rector of St. Andrew's Church, and in case of voidance or vacancy, to his widow, until a successor is instituted, and for no other purpose whatever. Ellis Duxbury came to Staten Island at an early date. He was Judge of Richmond County for nineteen years, and several times member of the Colonial Assembly. His will, bequeathing the property, was dated May 5, 1718, and proved October 22 of the same year. The property was a plantation of two hundred acres, situated on the north-east extremity of the Island, and consequently the point of land at New Brighton was for many years known as "Duxbury's Point," and sometimes as "The Gliebe." It was bequeathed to the Minister, Church-wardens and Vestry of St. Andrew's Church. The property upon which the Quarantine Hospital stood, at Tompkinsville, was a part of this bequest. Being a devise to a religious incorporation, it was void by law; but as the title of the church was never disputed, and as the State by several acts incidentally recognized its validity, to say nothing of a possession of almost two centuries, the title long ago became unimpeachable.

cessors have sett forth that by the charitable and voluntary contributions of pious and well asserted Christians, and the blessing of Almighty God favouring their weak endeavours, there is now erected, built and finished neer the middle part of the said Island, a decent and convenient stone church for the service and worship of God, according to the Discipline of the Church of England, as by Law Established," etc. The Document ends thus: "And Witness our said worthy and well-beloved Robert Hunter, Esq., Captain Generall and Governeur in Chief of our said province of New York and province of New Jersey, and the Territories depending on them in America, And our Admirall of the same, pr in councill at ffort Ann in New York the Twenty ninth day of June in the Twelfth of our Reign, Anno Dm. 1713."

Queen Anne also presented the church with prayer books, pulpit cover and a silver communion service, with her name inscribed on them. Portions of these valuable relics are still in the possession of the rector of St. Andrew's.

The Rev. Richard Charlton became rector of St. Andrew's in 1747. His eldest daughter was connected by marriage to the Dongan family, and another daughter was the wife of Dr. Richard Bailey, who was the first Health Officer of the Port of New York, and died in 1801. His grave is located near the main entrance to St. Andrew's Church. Dr. Charlton's ministry continued until 1779, when he died and was buried under the church. He was also chaplain of Lieutenant-Colonel Christopher Billopp's Battalion of Staten Island Loyalists. It was during the pastorate of Dr. Charlton that the records published in this volume were begun. He was succeeded by the Rev. Mr. Barker.

In 1774, Henry Holland, Esq., a resident of Staten Island, and managing a mercantile business in New York, presented St. Andrew's Church with a bell, which for want of a belfry, was hung for several years in a tree.

Chaplain Field, of the Seventy-seventh Regiment of the British line, became rector of St. Andrew's in May, 1780. The regiment was serving at Richmond. Two weeks later occurred his first baptism. The record says:

"John Simonson, son of Isaac Simonson and Elizabeth his wife, was born on the 4th December, 1779, baptized by Mr. Field on Sunday, May 14, 1780."

In 1782, Mr. Field died. His remains were borne to the grave by the soldiers with whom he had served, and interred under the church.

Throughout the Revolution, divine service was generally suspended in all the churches of Staten Island but St. Andrew's, the Island being in constant possession of the British; the Dutch Church, however, kept their Baptismal Records as appear in this volume.

From 1783 to 1788, the Rev. John H. Rowland served as rector. He died in Nova Scotia in 1795. He was succeeded by the Rev. Richard Channing Moore in 1788, who served until 1808. In 1814, Dr. Moore became Bishop of Virginia and rector of the Monumental Church of Richmond, in that State. He built Trinity Chapel, on the North Shore, in 1802; it is now known as the Church of the Ascension. He died on November 11, 1841.

The Rev. David Moore succeeded his father as rector of St. Andrew's in 1808, and continued in that position for forty-eight years.

The Rev. Theodore Irving, LL.D., became rector in 1857, and resigned in 1864. He was succeeded, in 1865, by the Rev. C. W. Bolton. His successor, in 1875, was the Rev. Kingston Goddard, D.D. Dr. Goddard died on October 24, 1875, and was succeeded by the Rev. Thomas S. Yocom, D.D., on June 15, 1876. Dr. Yocom died in 1904, and his successor, installed in 1905, is the Rev. Charles Sumner Burch, Archdeacon of Richmond.

St. Andrew's celebrated its bi-centennial in November, 1908, on which occasion tablets in memory of Queen Anne and other benefactors of the church were unveiled.

Two sharp battles were fought around this church during the Revolution. It was occupied as a British hospital a considerable portion of that period.

From a pencil sketch in possession of the Dutch Reformed Church, Port Richmond.

THE REFORMED PROTESTANT DUTCH CHURCH

of Port Richmond, S. I.—Second Structure—Erected in 1787 to take the place of one destroyed by the British during the Revolution; demolished in 1845

RECORDS

OF THE

Dutch Reformed Church of Port Richmond, S. I.

BAPTISMS FROM 1696 TO 1772

United Brethren Congregation, commonly called Moravian Church, S. I.

BIRTHS AND BAPTISMS: 1749 TO 1853
MARRIAGES: . . . . 1764 TO 1863
DEATHS AND BURIALS: 1758 TO 1828

St. Andrews Church, Richmond, S. I.

BIRTHS AND BAPTISMS FROM 1752 TO 1795
MARRIAGES FROM 1754 TO 1808

With Portrait of Rev. Melatiah Everett Dwight, M.D., D.D.

EDITED BY
TOBIAS ALEXANDER WRIGHT

NEW YORK
PRINTED FOR THE SOCIETY
1909

EDITION OF 100 COPIES
Serial No. 70

Note: Our original copy of this work did not include any text pages 1–8.

RECORDS OF THE REFORMED DUTCH CHURCH OF PORT RICHMOND, STATEN ISLAND, N. Y.

BAPTISMS.

DATE	PARENTS	CHILD	WITNESSES
1696.			
	Theunis Van Pelt	Marritie	Jan Van Pelt Marritie Parrat
	Ephraim Thealer	Jan	Jan Pieterszen Woggelom Hendricka Strockelf (or Itrockelf)
May 5.	Ephraim Thealer	Margrietie	Seger Gerrissen Elisabet Ariesmet
	Derck Kroessen	Nickasa	Cornelis Vielen Caatye Bogardus
	Thomas Morgen	Abraham	Arent Praal Tryntie Barents
	Lambert Janszen	Winnifret	Jan Wauterzen Tryntie Hendricksen
	Lambert Gerritzen	Daniel	Thomas Morgen Grietje Gerritzen
	Jores Hooghlandt	Marytie	Johannes Richgau Elisabeth Wappelrie
	Johan Staats	Cornelia	Pieter Staats Cornelia Corssen
	Hendrick Van Pelt	Annetie	Jan Van Pelt Marytie Parra
Sept. 7.	Mattheus De Decker	Johannes	Barent Teyszen Maghdalena Teyszen
1698.			
	Hendrick Van Dyck	Annetie	Thomas Possel Jannetie Pauwelzen
	Thomas Possel.	Jan	Pieter Staats Grytie Woggelum
	Pieter Praal	Arent C.	Thomas Stillewel Frenck Stillewel
Sept. 7.	Lambert Janzen	Aafye	Jacob Janzen
	Thomas Morgen	Martha	Lammert Gerritzen Susanna Gerritzen
b. Sept. 28. bap. Dec.	Henderyck Kroesen	Maritje	Dirrick Kroesen Kathareina Staats
1700.			
	Cornelis Neefies	Metye	
	Daughters of Ryck Hendrickzen	Elisabeth Femmetye Marytie	Weyntie Rycken Ledey Waacker

DATE	PARENTS	CHILD	WITNESSES
1700.			
June 20.	Johan Staats	Annetye	
1701.			
March 25.	Hendrick Van Pelt	Aeltie	Hendrick Van Pelt Leydia Bendel
	Jacob Corssen	Suster	Christiaan Corssen Blandiena Woggelum
	Jeems Lesck	Jan	Thomas Morgen Mary Morgen
	Jacob Jansen	Jacobus	Lambert Janzen Reyne Janzen
	Pieter Rycken	Johanes	Johannes Machgielzen Neeltie Machgielzen
Oct. 22.	Stoffel Van Santen	Stoffel	Jacob Corssen and wife
	Derck Claassen	Femmetye	Tyssen and Elyner Morgen
	Derck Kroessen	Derck	Niclaes Backer Blandyena Bogardus
March 25.	Barent Symessen	Wyntie	Mattheus Decker Eva Decker
	Andrys Andryssen	Andrys	Gerrit Vechten Maghdalena Vechten
1703.			
April 20.	Marcus Du Secoy	Gabriel	Antony Thyssen Katteleyn De Sceen
	Derck Claassen	Hendrickie	Johan Pu and wife
	Jacob Wouters	Cornelis	Thomas Sutten (or Lutten) Susanna Du Secoy
	Pieter Rycken	Hendricus	Femmetie Rycken
b. May 20. bap. June	Henderyck Kroesen	Gerret	Jacob Crosse Trintje Backers
Aug. 4.	Barent Christoffelsen	Niclaes	Stoffel Christoffelsen Tryntie Barents
1703 or 1705.			
Oct. 23.	Jarels Morgen	Margrietye	Matthys Sween Sara Morgen Francyntye Morgen
1705.			
	Pieter Praal	Abraham	Arent Praal, Jr. Styntie Christoffels
b. May 28. bap. Aug. 2.	Cornelis Tyssen	Elisabeth	Leenert Smack Sara Smack
Oct. 2.	Abraham Van Tuil	Geertruyt	Nies Teunisse Isaack F. Van Tuil Lena Teunisse

DATE	PARENTS	CHILD	WITNESSES
1706.			
	Stoffel Van Santen	Josua	Johan Corsson
			Aeltye Laroe
	Josua Bosch	Samuel	Casper Smyet
			Maria Smyet
1707 or 1706.			
April 23.	Johannes Van Pelt	Blandyena	Syemen Laroy
			Blandyena Laroy
1706.			
April 23.	Pieter Rycken	Pieter	Jacobus Kreven
			Annetye Kreven
	Derck Claassen	Jacobus	Jacobus Classen
			Magdalena Claassen
	Barent Christoffelsen	Catharyna	Hans Christoffelzen
			Mary Praal
1707.			
	Matthys Sweem	Magdaleen	Barent Sweem and wife
	Barent Symessen	Johannes	Pieter Rycken and wife
	Evert Mesker	Neeltie	Ryck Ryckszen
			Elisabeth Sweem
July 3.	Joseph Bastido	Rosanna	Louis de Bois
			Eva Morgin
	Jacob Jansen	Wyntie	Lambert Janzen and wife
	Thomas Sotten	Jan	Isaak Simesson
April 22.	Jacob Jansen	Johanna	Jan Van Pelt and wife
Oct. 21.	Jacob Corssen	Jacob	Pieter Vyle
			Antie Corszen
April 22.	Jores Bouman	Elisabeth	Andrys Bouman
			Henders Bouman
	Joseph Bastido	Louys	Jan De Pue and wife
Oct. 22.	Johan Staats	Rebecca	Hendrick Kroesen
July 23.	Harmen Mesker	Johannes	Pieter Rycke
			Femmetie Rycke
	Harmen Mesker	Neeltie	Gillis Iniaart and wife
—— 22.	Cornelis Neefies	Cornelis	Cornelis Jorissen
			Neeltie Jorissen
April 22.	Evert Mesker	Hendrickie	Pieter Ricken and wife
	Cobus Creven	Elsie	Jan Iniaart
			Trintie Iniaart
	Cobus Claazen	Femmetie	Abraham Goolder and wife

DATE	PARENTS	CHILD	WITNESSES
1707.			
April 22.	Thomas Berbanck	Aeltie	Barent Marlin
			Fytie Jansz
	Lambert Wels	Lambert	Evert Van Namen
	Nicolaas Backer	Tryntie	Gerrit Kroesen and sister Neeltie
	Johan Woggelum	Christyntien	Barent Slecht
			Henders Bouman
23.	Joseph Britten	Jeams	Jeams Hanzen and wife
	Johannes Richau	Jacob	Isaack Karbet
			Maria Karbet
	Johannes Van Campen	Martha	Thys Sween
			Saraatie Sween
	Pieter Wynantse	Pieter	Jores Hooghlandt
			Hylletie Slechts
July 23.	Johannes Smack	Annetie	Leendert Smack
			Maria Sweem
30.	Derck Kroessen	Hendrick	Chrystiaan Korssen
			Sara Bogardus
Oct. 21.	Hendricus Backer	Nicolaas	Johannes Van Pelt
			Sara Van Pelt
	Jan Clerck	Dorote	Daniel De Hart
			Catalyntie De Hart
	Jan Dorlandt	Lambert	Lambert Dorlandt
			Helena Dorlandt
	Pieter Praal	Antie	Aert Simonzen
			Antie Simonzon
	Pieter Van Pelt	Jan	Jan Teunis Van Pelt
			Maria Van Pelt
	Abraham Staats	Isaak	Harmen Joreszen
			Neeltie Joreszen
	Mattheus De Decker	Abraham	Theunis Egberts
			Elisabeth Sweem
22.	Paul Richau	Daniel	Antoni Sweens
			Neeltie Sweens
	Johan Pue	Elisabeth	
	Daniel De Hart	Daniel	Jacob Van Pelt
			Grytie Clerck
	Barent Slecht	Johan	Johan Woggelom
			Blandina Woggelom
	Beniamin Carenton	Margriete	Adam Morgen
			Eva Morgen
1708.			
April 1.	Richart Merrel	Elsje	Johan Magels
			Blandyna Korsse
20.	Barent Christoffelsen	Rebecca	Christiaan Korszen and wife
	Aert Simoszen	Simon	Christoffel Christoffelzen
			Geertruy Simonsen

DATE	PARENTS	CHILD	WITNESSES
1708.			
April 20.	Abraham Leeck	Joseph	Barent Marlin and wife
	Johannes Richau	Isaack	Ahasuerus Van Engelen
			Anna Corbet
	Jan Maklies	Margriet	Jan Waglom and wife
	Jarels Morgen	Sarah	Pieter Praal and wife
	Johannes Sweem	Annetie	Barent Sweem
			Mary Belveel
	Johannes Van Pelt	Simon	Pieter Van Pelt and wife
	Pieter Staats	Edmond	Harmen Jorissen
			Annaatie Staats
b. Sept. 7.	Henderyck Kroesen	Cornelis	Jan Staats
Oct.			Antje Crorse
Oct. 11.	Nicolaas Britten	William	Nicolaes Britten
			Rachel Stilwel
19.	Hendrick Kroesen	Cornelis	Johan Staats and wife Catharina
b. Oct. 11.	Ryk Ryken	Femmetie	Johannes Rycken
Oct. 19.			Femmetie Rycken
	Isaac Bellin	Daniel	Pieter Praal and wife
b. Sept. 1.			Maria
1709.			
April 19.	Barent Slecht	Cornelis	Adriaen Van Wogelom
			Elisabeth Corssen
	Donckin Oliver	Margarietie	Egbert Hagewout
			Aeltie Hagewout
	Jan Clerck	Dorothea	Johannes Van Pelt
			Sara Van Pelt
	Jacob Jans	Jacobus	Simon Dey
			Maria Dey
	Lambert Wouters	Sara	Evert Van Namen
			Sara Jans
	Hendrick Van Campen	Laurens	Laurens Van Campen
22.	Evert Van Namen	Joseph	Engelbart Van Namen
			Aeltie Janz
Sept. 22.	Abraham Van Tuil	Elena	Hendrick Hendricksen
			Elena Hendricksen
	Jores Bouman	Johanna	Johannes Nevius
			Elsie Bouman
	Isaac Van Tuyl	Catharyntie	Abraham Van Tuyl
			Maria Laackman
	Richart Merrel	Richard	Christiaen Corssen
			Lena Dorlant
b. Oct. 22.	Ahasuerus Van Engelen	Rachel	Johan Staats
			Catharina Staats

DATE	PARENTS	CHILD	WITNESSES
1710.			
	Michiel De Jeen	Antoni	Johannes Van der Huven
			Magdalena Claassen
	Aert Simonsen	Hans	Hans Christoffel
			Maria Praal
	Barent Symessen	Aron	Michiel De Jeen
			Martha Jaddin
	Barent Christoffelzen	Maria	Aert Simessen
			Antie Simessen
	Johannes Van Pelt	Cathalyn	Daniel De Hart
			Cathalina De Hart
July 24.	Harmen Bouman	Joris	Willem Bouman
			Henders Bouman
25.	Abraham Leeck	Margariet	Engelbart Van Namen
			Feitie Hofte
	No parents	Mary Gennens	
		Sara Gennens	
	Pieter Van Pelt	Samuel	Jan Van Pelt
			Nenne Van Pelt
	Pieter Praal	Isaac	Jan Van Woggelom, Jr and wife Blandina
1711.			
April 17.	Mattheus De Decker	Elisabeth	Jacobus Dye and wife
	Daniel De Hart	Saartie	Johannes Van Pelt and wife Sara
	Hendrick Van Campen	Lammert	Johannes Van Campen and wife Mary
	Johannes Richau	Mary	Isaac Corbet and wife Martha
	Jan Clerck	Jan	Jan Van Pelt
			Cathalyntie De Hart
	Johannes Van Campen	Christina	Pieter Praal and wife Mary
	Jan Dorlandt	Joris	Willem Bouman
			Tryntie Bouman
	Johannes Sweem	Magdalena	Aron Praal, Jr.
			Elisabeth Sweem
	Jacob Van Pelt	Jan	Jan Theunissen and wife Mary
	Joris Nevius	Cornelis	Cornelis Nevius and wife Eechie
	Jan Vechten	Nicolaes	Gerrit Vechten and wife Magdaleentie
	Pieter Rycken	Abraham	Abraham Rycke
			Cathalyntie Decker
July 26.	Joseph Bastido	Bastido	Donckin Oliver
			Mary Oliver

DATE	PARENTS	CHILD	WITNESSES
1711.			
July 26.	Johannes Smack	Marytie	Isebrant Van Kleef and wife Jannetie
	Johan Woggelum	Suster	Adriaen Van Woggelom
			Elsie Merrel
Oct. 23.	Abraham Talor	Ephrum	Ephraim Talor
			Margriet Talor
	Aert Simoszen	Aert	Barent Simessen
			Styntie Christoffel
	Gerrit Kroese	Cornelis	Hendrick Croese
b. Sept. 18.			Aagie Nevius
	Johannes Nevius	Cornelis	Gerrit Van Wagene
			Tryntie Nevius
	Jacob Wouters	Beniamin	Hendrick Maarlin
			Antie Wouters
	Harmen Bouman	Tryntie	Johan Staats and wife Catharina
Oct. 23.	Ryk Ryken	Lena	Adriaen Schouten
			Marytie Schouten
1713 or 1715.			
	Daniel De Hart	Matthys	Jan Van Pelt
			Cornelia Mourits
1713.			
b. April 4.	Henderyck Kroesen	Neelje	Christjaen Crorse
April 22.			Lysebet Korse
July 13.	Egbert Egbertsen	Abraham	Theunis Egberts
			Antie de Sien
14.	Aert Simoszen	Aert	Barent Christoffel and wife Anna
	Hendrick Jansen	Marytie	Tys Jansen
			Rebecca Cool
	Jan Clerck	Sara	Pieter Van Pelt and wife Sara
	Jan Crossen	Elisabeth	
	Johannes Nevius	Gerrit	Joris Nevius and wife
	Lambert Gerritzen	Lambert	Hans Christoffel and wife Susanna
Oct. 21.	Rem Van de Bilt	Hilletie	Jacob Van de Bilt
			Femmetie Adriaenssen
1714.			
May 4.	Beniamin Corssen	Cornelis	Jacob Corssen
			Antie Corssen
	Egbert Hagewout	Derckie	Pieter Hagewout, Sr.
			Tryntie Backer
	Harmen Bouman	Jacob	Pieter Staats
			Elizabeth Staats

DATE	PARENTS	CHILD	WITNESSES
1714.			
May 4.	Joseph Bastido	Jan	Johan Simes
			Catharina De Pue
	Joost Van Pelt	Catharina	Jan Van Pelt
			Catharina Hooghland
	Stieven Tietelo	Hieronimus	Hieronymus De Syen
			Catharina De Syen
	Pieter Staats	Pieter	Abraham Metzelaer and wife Agnietie
	Ryk Ryken	Sofia	Johannes Van Cleef
			Sofia Van Cleef
July 14.	Pieter Rycken	Isaac	Beniamin Crorssen
			Blandina Corssen
27.	Cobus Creven	Johannes	Jan Maklies and wife Eytie
	Johan Pue	Moses	Thomas Barbanck
	Rut Vanden Bergh	Geesie	Gidie Van Campen
			Styntie Christoffel
Oct. 19.	Johannes Sweem	Antie	David Laforsie
			Antie Willemsen
	Harmen Mesker	Abraham	Abraham Rycke
			Cathalyntie Decker
1715 or 1713.			
	Joris Nevius	Margrietie	Jan Mangelsen
			Tryntie Nevius
1715.			
	Joris Nevius	Jan	Gerrit Croesen
			Marytie Nevius
	Willem Breetstede	Andries	Johan Staats
			Catharina Staats
	Jacob Van Pelt	Marytie	Aert Van Pelt and wid. of Pieter Hagewout
	Johannes Sweem	Tys	Johannes Van Campen
			Saara Van Namen
	Hendrick Van Campen	Aeltie	Giedie Van Campen
			Elsie Van Campen
	Hendrick Van Campen	Hendrick	Cornelis Egmont
			Marytie Van Campen
	Johannes Richau	Antie	Pieter Wynant
			Marytie Carbet
	Hendrick Kroesen	Neeltie	Christiaen Corssen
			Elisabeth Corssen
April 19.	Johannes Van Pelt	Simon	Pieter Van Pelt and wife
	Johannes Sweem	Martha	Simon Van Namen
			Sara Van Namen
	Jacob Van Pelt	Derckie	Pieter Hagewout, Jr.
			Geertie Hagewout

DATE	PARENTS	CHILD	WITNESSES
1715.			
April 19.	Isebrant Van Cleef	Beniamin	Rem Van der Bilt Aeltie Byvanck
	Jan Macklies	Cornelis	Gerrit Croesen Adriaetie Croesen
	Richard Merrel	Richard	Adriaan Van Wogelom Bennetie Ryke
	Willem Breetstede	Johannes	Johan Staats and wife Catharina Staats
	Mattheus De Decker	Mattheus	Pieter De Decker Catharina Decker
	Evert Mesker	Mattheus	Mattheus Decker and wife
	Engelbart Lot	Elisabeth	Abraham Ryken Metie Titsoer
	Abraham Leeck	Abraham	Abraham Meerling Elisabeth Bridges
	Jan Macklies	Eytie	Jan Dorlant and wife Barber
	Abraham Metzelaer	Jacobus	Jan Veghte and wife Cornelia
	Cornelis Bouman	Neeltie	Abraham Metselaer and wife
	Daniel De Hart	Elisabeth	Jan Clerck Elisabeth Niewenhuisen
b. May 21. June 6.	Aron Praal, Jr.	Elisabeth	Pieter Staats and wife Elisabeth
b. May 27.	Abraham Egbertsen	Abraham	Theunis Egberts and wife
b. May 21.	Johannes Van Campen	Arent	Johannes Sweem and wife Martha
June 6.	Joseph Carrinton	Jannetie	Abraham Metzelaer and wife Agnietie
Oct. 18. b. Sept. 8.	Gerrit Kroesen	Dirrick	Joris Neeftjes Cathareyntje Kroesen
	Tunis Exbersen	Susanna	
	Johannes Swame	Albert	Willem Seymensen Elybet
	Willem Swame	Magyel	Hendreck Willemsen Maritje Wyllemit
	Reick Reyken	Elisabet	Tammus Smyt Elesabet Reyken
Nov. 23.	Pieter Van Pelt	Willem	Johannes Van Pelt and wife
	Johannes Ryke	Abraham	Aabram Ryke Elysebet Ryke
	Abraam Taylor	Maregriet	Jacob Van Pelt and wife Aeltje
	Pieter Telburgh	Johannes	Willem Bouman and wife

DATE	PARENTS	CHILD	WITNESSES
1715.			
March 20. b. Jan. 1, 1715-6.	Jan Veghte	Gerret	Jan Staats and wife Catryna
1716.			
March 20.	Joost Van Pelt	Joost	Derck Hoogelant Elisebet Hogelant
	Andries Bouman	Andries	Barent Merlengh Katje Haste or Hafte
May 21.	Arey Van Woglom	Jan	Benyamen Korssen and wife Blandyna Corssen
	Machgyel Due Seen	Valentyen	Abram Meslur and wife Angenetye
June 12.	Steven Vetyto	Petrus	Fellip Cosie Maria Magdalena Durlyet
	Tyes Jansen	Beletye	Johannes Jansen Aeltje Jansen
	Sande Semson	Tabeta	Jan Semson and wife
Aug. 13.	Barent Christefer	Ane Catryn Barent	Jan Van Pelt and wife Aeltje Aert Symesen and wife Aentje
	Benjamin Corssen	Maria	Christjaan Corssen Elysebet Corssen
	Pieter Marlyngh	Isack	Henderyck Merlingh and the child's mother
Oct. 30.	Symon Van Amen	Saertie	Aront Prael, Jr., and wife Aentie
	Hendrick Kroesen	Cornelya	Benjamin Korssen and wife Blandyna Korsen
1717.			
April 16.	Pieter Van Pelt	Samuel	Jan Van Pelt and wife Altje
	Johannes Van Pelt	Petrus	Harme Jorusen and wife Neeltje
	Jacob Van Pelt	Pieter	Pieter Hagewout and wife Neeltje
17.	Aron Paraal	Haron	Symon Van Namen and wife Sartje
	Jan Dorlant	Isack	Benjamin Crorsson and wife Blandyna
	Gydeon Van Campen	Gerrit	Bastjan Elesen Cersteyntjes Christfeer
	Hendryck Van Campen	Johanes	Claas Backer Marytje Van Campen

DATE	PARENTS	CHILD	WITNESSES
1717.			
June 18.	Aert Symensen	Christoffel	Christoffel Christfeer and wife Styntje Christfeer
b. April 14.	Engelbart Lot	Pieter	Lowys de Bo Margita Wolffers
	Joseph Bastido	Maria	Lowys de Bo, Jr. Pieternel Bottelaar
June 19. b. May 7.	Jorius Neftjes	Eechtje	Johannes Neftjes and wife Antje
Aug. —.	Daniel De Hart	Samuel	James Helpets and wife Marytje Helpertsse
13.	Pieter Rycke	Jacob	Arme Rycke and wife Marytje Ryck
Sept. 8.	Cornelis Oenaert	Annetje	Willem Bouwman and wife
	Valeteyn Presser	Pieter	Pieter Van Pelt and wife Sara
	Joost Van Pelt	Johannes	Sarel Teller and wife Aerjaenje Tellers
Oct. 22. b. Sept. 17.	Johan Vechten	Catharyna	Benjamyn Korsen Antje Staats
b. Dec. 22. April 1, 1718.	Ery Dey	Johannes	Johannes Van Pelt and wife
	Cornelis Egmont	Altje	Louwerens Van Crampens and wife
April 1. b. Sept. 12, 1717.	Cobus Creven	Gillis	Gydon Van Campen and wife
1718.			
April 1.	Andries Bouman	Jorius	Johannis Afte Hendryektje Bouman
b. Jan. 12.	Gerret Kroesen	A son (no name)	Johannes Van Nieuwenhuysen Marytje Neeftjes
	Jacob Corssen	Benjamin	Douw Van Woglom Marytje Kroesen
	Johannes Sweem	Lysabet	Altje Paraels
	Pieter Hagewout	Pieter	Jacob Van Pelt Altje Van Pelt
	Pieter Tylborgh	Jorius	Benjamyn Crorsse Marytje Boumans
May 18.	Abram Talor	Altje	Jan Macklies and wife
b. Apl. 24.	Johannes Van Namen	Pieter	Pieter Van Pelt and wife Sartje
May 22.	Thys Jansz	Maria	Johannes Zweem Mary Milers
	Ryk Hendrickz	Symon	Thomas Jansz

DATE	PARENTS	CHILD	WITNESSES
1718.			
	Ledy Henricks Ad data reprehen- sione Patri and Testibus privata	Jan	Elysabet Obedye Susanna Winters
June 1.	Pieter Martlings Antje Vielen	Petrus	Benjamin Corssen Marytje Martlings
8.	Jan Claasz	Francyntje	Jeroen de Chene
b. Jan. 5, 1717–8.	Maria de Chene		Catlina de Chene
June 15.	Harme Bouman Neeltje Staats	Cornelis	Pieter Metzelaar Agneta Staats
July 20.	Cornelis Brees Sara Schilmans	Cornelis	Cornelis Jansz Susanna du Tes
	Eduard Jones Catharina Dekkers	Eduard	Barent Symonsz Eva Messeker
	Johannes Sweems, Sr. Jannetje La Forge	Jan	Adriaan La Forge Mary Merchen
27.	Samuel Olivier Catharina du Puy	Catharina	
Aug. 3.	Benjamin Corssen Blandina Vile	Benjamin	Hendrick Croesen Cornelia Corssen
	Evert Van Namen Wyntje Benhem	Maria	Jan Jennes Maria Jansz
10.	Teunis Egbertsen Jannetje du Chesne	Teunis	Jean Gareau Marie Auder
13.	Jacob Gramo	Johannes	Pieter Tilburgh and wife Mettje
17.	Abraham Ryke Anneken Oliver	Femmetje	Isaak Merling Susanna Oliver
	Symon Van Namen Sara Praal	Aaron	Stoffel Christopher Elsje Dorlant
24.	Barent Symonssen Apollonia Messe- ker	Maria	Cornelis Jansz Wyntje Symons
Sept. 14.	Gerrit Rosen Judith Toers	Nicolaas	Aaron Toers Pietertje Toers
	Johannes Neul Geertje Hagewout	Dirkje	Abraham Tailor Harmpje Hagewout
	Pieter Ceilo Blandina Van Pelt	Elsje	Pieter Van Pelt Jacob Van Pelt Aaltje Hagewout
21.	Pieter Dekker Susanna Hetseel (or Hetfeel)	Maria	Eduard Jones Eva Dekker
Oct. 19.	Samuel Burnet, dec. Antje Mangels Ral	Samuel	Theunis Egbertsz F.————
	Thomas Leake Jannetje Stryker	Thomas	Cornelis Stryker Gerritje Stryker

DATE	PARENTS	CHILD	WITNESSES
1718.			
26.	Jacob Grameaux Dirkje Van Tilburgh	Catharina	Jacobus Creven Antje Iniaart
Nov. 2.	Charles Messiel Marytje	Elisabet	David La Forge
	Teunis Bogaart Catharina Hegeman	Isaak	Isaak Hegeman
23.	Johannes Huysman Christina Hoppe	Anna	Paulus Hoppe Anna Huysman
Jan. 11, 1718-19.	Barent Christopher Anna Cathrina Stilwel	Susanna	Pieter ——— Elisabeth Arrow
Jan. 18, 1718-19.	Willem Breetstede Christina Bouwman	Andries	Willem Jorisz Bouwman Metje Bouwman
Jan. 25.	Jan Van Pelt Aaltje Hoogelant	Sara	Joh. Hogelant Femmetje Denys
March 1.	Joh. Sweems, son of Anthony Mary Rus	Jacobus	Jacobus Biebaut Rachel Sweem
	Lambert Gerritsz, Jr. Lysbet Sweem	Magdalena	Jan du Puy Susanna du Puy
15.	Ryk Ryken Willempje Clement	Henricus	Hierome de Chesne Catlyn Canon
1719. April 12.	Engelbert Van Namen Marytje de Camp	Johannes	Stoffel Christopher Christina de Camp
	Charles Gerritsz	Charles	Ary Schout Marya Van Pelt
	Hendrik Van Pelt Margrietje de Hart	Catlyntje	Johannes Van Pelt Daniel De Hart Catlyntje Van Pelt
19.	Matthys Sweem Catharina Mangels Ral	Anthony	Anthony Thysz Sweem Neeltje Jansz
	Joh. Van der Hoeven Anna Sweem	Lea	Johannes Sweem, Jr. Lea Sweem
	Johannes Jansz Johanna Stol	Johannes	Henrik Jansz Antje Jans
May 7.	Charles Ellens Marytje de Camp	Johannes	Laurens de Camp, Loco Past. Nicolaas Bakkers Catharina Vlierboom
29.	Hendrick Janszen Abigail Britton	Matthys	Jan du Puy Neeltje Jans

DATE		PARENTS	CHILD	WITNESSES
1719.				
	31.	Obadias Winter Susanna du Puy	Frans	Symon Bogaart Margrietje Ten Eik
June	7.	Gideon de Camp Hendrikje Elles	Laurens	Laurens de Camp Aaltje Mandeveil
b. May 18.		Johannes Van Pelt Sara Leroy	Johannes	Jan Van Pelt Aaltje Hooglant
July	26.	Rem Van der Beek Dorothea Coteleau	Jan	Petrus Simson Sophia Vander Beek
Aug.	2.	Hendrik de Camp Maria Lackes or La Mes	David	Bastiaan Elles Hendrikje Elles
	9.	Hendrik Van Leeuwen Geurtje Coteleau	Frederyk	Rem Vander Beek Dorethe Cateleau
	30.	Johannes Metselaar Cathryna Neefjes	Aafje Abraham (twins)	Joris Neefjes Lodewyk Metselaar Aagje Bouman Agneta Staats
Sept.	6.	Willem Stilwell Sara Pareyn	Willem Daniel (twins)	Johannes Sweem, Sr. Daniel Pareyn Elisabeth Parein Maria Sweem
	13.	Joris Neefjes Willempje Borkelo	Johannes	Jan Mangels Ral Sara Neefjes
Oct.	11.	Johannes Praal	Aaltje	Pieter Praal Aaltje Gerrits
		Thomas Barbanck Marritje Martling	Maria	Isaak Martlingh Anna Van Namen
	18.	Joseph Bastido Judith Ryke	Pieter	
		Thomas Greegs Lena Du Puy	Martinus	Jan du Puy Susanna du Puy
		Simon Bogaart Margrietje Ten Eik	Elisabet	Jacobus Krankheit Catharina Hegemans
		Willem Sweem Marya Lageler	Johannes	Abraham Manez Maria Sweem
Nov.	8	Eduard Jones Catharina Dekkers	Mattheus	Pieter Dekkers Neeltje Dekkers
		Jan Veghten Cornelia Staats	Johannes	Cornelius Van Sant- voord Maria Staats
		Jacob Van Pelt Aaltje Hagewout	Catlyntje	Pieter Van Pelt Sara Bogardus
	15.	Jan Stilwell Elisabeth Parein	Johannes	Johannes Sweem, Sr. Jannetje La Forge
	29.	Francois Bodin Maria Dey	Jean	Jean Journay Sara Dey
		Philip Casier Catharina Hooglant	Philip	Hans Hansen Maria Hoogland

DATE	PARENTS	CHILD	WITNESSES
1719.			
Dec. 25.	Ary Van Woglum Celia Preyer	Johanna	Jacob Corssen Hilletje Van Woglum
26.	Pieter Hagewout Neeltje Bakkers	Nicolaas	Nicolaas Bakker Cornelia Corssen
Feb. 7, 1719–20.	Abraham Van Tuyl Femmetje Denysz	Otto.	Jacob Van der Bilt Elisabet Hooghlant
	Henry Day Maria Van Pelt	Samuel	Jacob Van Pelt Aaltje Hagewout
Feb. 14.	Arent Praal, Jr. Antje Staats	Anna	Abraham Staats Agneta Staats
	Jacobus Egbertsen Catharina Dey	Maria	Jan Bisonet Sara Dey
March 6.	Corn. V. Santvoord Anna Staats	Maria Catharina	Jan Staats Catharina Corssen
	Johannes Neul Geertje Hagewout	Henrik	Jacob Van Pelt Aaltje Hagewout
13.	Jan Cocheau Elisabet Jackson	Abraham	Barent Symonsz Apolonia Messeker
1720.			
March 27.	Henrik Slecht Catharina Wynants	Maria	Pieter Wynants Hilletje Woglum
	Jacob Van der Bilt Neeltje Denys	Hilletje	Gozen Adriaansz Femmetje Van der Bilt
	Samuel Kierstede Lydia Dey	Samuel	Jacobus Egberts Catharina Dey
	Wynandt Wynandts Ann Cole	Pieter	Pieter Wynandts Anna Maria Richau
	Pieter Andrevet Rebecca Cole	Rebecca	Cornelis Jansen Mary Cole
April 3.	Jacobus Creaven Antje Iniaart	Anna	Carel Iniaart Marya Gleave
	Jan Dorlant Barbara Aukes	Harmpje Eva (twins)	Lambert Dorlant Richard Merl Elsje Dorlant Harmpje Ryke
10.	Abraham Egbertsen Francyntje Parain	Johannes	Jean Bodin Marie La Tourette
	Egbert Egbertse Francyntje de Chene	Isaak	Thomas Kasper Francyntje Mangels Ral
17.	Ary Schouten Maria Van Pelt	Adriaan	Jan Van Pelt Aaltje Hooglant
	Johannes Slecht Catharina Berger	Cornelia Catharina (twins)	Jacob Corssen Jacob Berger Brechtje Berger Elsje Berger

DATE	PARENTS	CHILD	WITNESSES.
1720.			
May 1.	Isaack Van Tuyl Sara Lakerman	Catharina	Abrah. Lakerman Antje Van Tuyl
15.	Cornelis Bouwman Antje Staats	Neeltje	Arent Praal, Jr., and wife Antje Staats
June 5.	John Jennes Antje Wouters	Sara	Evert Van Namen Jenneken Van Namen
12.	Isaak Symons Antje Vand^r Bilt	Jeremias	Jan Veghte Cornelia Staats
19.	Matthys Jansz Elisabet Ward	Matthys	Robert Frost Sara Usselton
26.	John Whithead (Secund Adjurationem) Elisabet Bakker	John (Extra Conjugium)	Nicolaas Bakker
	Pieter Martlings Antje Vilen	Barent	Barent Martlings Sara Van Namen
July 17.	John Richaud Amy Carber	Lea	Pieter Wynants Hilletje Van Woglum
24.	Pieter Dekker Susanna Hetseel or Hetfeel	Johannes	Nicolaas Du Puy Neeltje Dekker
Aug. 7.	Cornelis Woinat Tryntje Bouwman	Hendrikje	Willem Breedstede Elsje Bouwman
21.	Abraham Tailor Harmpje Hagewout	Rachel	Johannes Neul Rachel Hagewout
Oct. 9.	Michiel du Chene Susanna Van der Hoeven	Cornelis	Gerrit du Chene Anna du Chene
16.	Jan Hagewout Elisabet Hooghlant	Aaltje	Jacob Van Pelt Aaltje Hagewout
	Jan Van Pelt Aaltje Hooghlant	Catlyntje	Barent Christopher Marrytje Hooglant
Dec. 11.	Dirk Cadmus Jannetje Van Hoorn	Frederyk	Hendrik Ligget Antje Vile
	Pieter Van Tilburgh Metje Bouwman	Willem	Willem Breestede Christina Bouwman
18.	Teunis Bogaart Catharina Hegeman	Adriaan	Gozen Adriaans Femmetje Van der Bilt
26.	Jaques Coteleau Jacomyntje Van Pelt	Debora	Pieter Coteleau Dorothe Coteleau
Jan. 1, 1720-1.	Hendrik Van Pelt Margrietje De Hart	Hendrik	Jan De Hart Anna De Hart
	Richard Merl Elsje Dorlant	Lambert	William Mackeleen Elisabet Merl

DATE	PARENTS	CHILD	WITNESSES
1720-1.			
Jan. 1.	William Mackelien Elisabet Merl	Maria	Richard Merl Elsje Dorlant
	Johannes Van Pelt Sara Le Roy	Sara	Jan Van Pelt Aaltje Hooglant
8.	Auke Jansz Catharina Sebering	Isaak	Rem Van der Beek Isaak Balin
15.	Abraham Ryke Anneke Oliver	Abraham	Aart Symonsz Geertruyd Symons
	Johannes Huysman Christina Hoppe	Rachel	Christoffel Christopher Christina De Camp
	Jan Jurks Agnietje Staats	Johanna	Harmen Bouman Neeltje Staats
1721.			
April 30.	Cornelis Egmont Elsje de Camp	Femmetje	Gideon de Camp Hendrikje Elles
May 7.	Thomas Greegs Lena du Puy	Pieternelle	Nicolas dupuy Neeltje Dekkers
21.	Hendrik de Camp Maria La Mes	Gideon	Jacob Bakker Catharyna Vlierboom
28.	Rem Van der Beek Dorothea Coteleau	Rem	Jacques Coteleau Jacomyntje Van Pelt
June 11.	Lambert Van Dyk Marritje Hogelant	Henricus	Jan Van Pelt Aaltje Hogelant
July 2.	Lambert Gerritz, Jr. Lysbet Sweem	Nicolaas	Nicolaas du Puy Catharina Christopher
16.	Jacobus Biebaut Maria Sweems	Jacobus	Michel de Chene Susanna Van der Hoeven
23.	Corn. V. Santvoord Anna Staats	Anna	Do. Bernardus Freeman, V. D. M. on Long Island Margaretha Van Schayk, both repres. by Jan Staats and Catharina Corssen
Aug. 6.	Johannes Haften Marytje Johannesz	Jacob	Johannes Symons Catharina Beauvois
	Jacob de Garemeaux Dirkje Van Tilburgh	Anna Catharina	Abraham Taylor Harmpje Hagewout
13.	Willem Breetstede Christina Bouwman	Engeltje	Jacob Van der Bilt Elsje Bouwman
Sept. 3.	Dirk Hogelant Maria Slot	Jenneke	Johannes Hooglant Catharina Richaud

DATE	PARENTS	CHILD	WITNESSES
1721.			
Oct. 8.	Gozen Adriaansz Femmetje Van der Bilt	Hilletje	Jacob Van der Bilt Neeltje Denys
	Jacobus Egbertsen Catharina Dey	Teunis	Henrik Van Lawa Geurtje Coteleau
	Engelbert Van Namen Marytje de Camp	Sara Maria (twins)	Joh. Van Namen Joh. De Camp Maria Van Pelt Maria Praal
15.	Joris Neefjes Willempje Borkelo	Margarietje	Johs Metzelaar Jannetje Borkelo
	Johannes Metzelaar Cathryna Neefjes	Harmpje	Pieter Metzelaar Maria Neefjes
Dec. 10.	Aart Van Pelt Christina Immet	Maria	Jacob Van Pelt Maria Para
24.	Johannes Neul Geertje Hagewout	Margareta	Pieter Hagewout Neeltje Bakkers
Jan. 7, 1721-2.	Henrik Slecht Catharina Wynants	Hilletje	Ary Van Woglum Celia Preyer
	Jaques Hervan Charite Bries	Sara	Cornelis Jansen Catharina Simons
14.	Philip Cazier Catharina Hooglant	Catharina	Rem Van der Beek Dorothea Coteleau
Feb. 25.	Baay Spier Catalyntje Hasten or Haften	Sytje	Johannes Hasten or Haften Geesje Els
	Syrah Tites Aaltje Webs	Cornelis	Barent Martling Antje Vand' Bilt
	Pieter Hagewout Neeltje Bakkers	Dirkje	Abraham Taylor Harmpje Hagewout
March 18.	Johannes Van der Hoeven Anna Sweem	Cornelius	Michel du Chene Susanna Van der Hoeven
	Willem Sweem Marie Lageler	Cornelius	Pierre Manin Elisabet Sweem
1722.			
April 15.	Isaak Martling Anna Van Name	Anna	Thomas Barbank Sara V. Namen representing Ahasuerus Van Engelen Rebecca Van Namen
22.	Eduard Jones Catharina Dekkers	Abigail	Nicolas Lazilier Esther Lakeman
29.	Fredrik Bergen Gerritje Veghte	Gerritje	Gerrit Veghte Gerritje Wisselpenning

DATE	PARENTS	CHILD	WITNESSES
1722.			
May 20.	Egbert Egbertszen Francyntje du Chene	Johannes	Marytje Claassen
	Johannes Preyer Maria Ral	Anna	Ary Van Woggelum Catharina Sweem
	Jacob Ryt Anna Ral	Maria	Jannetje du Chene
	Thomas Greegs Lena Dupuy	Anna	Barent Christopher
June 3.	Ary Van Woglum Celia Preyer	Anna	Johannes Preyer Maria Ral
	Israel du Secoy Geertruydt Van Deventer	Anna	Abraham Lakeman Anna Van Tuyl
17.	Abraham Egbertsen Francyntje Parain	Elisabet	Matthieu La Roue Catharina La Roue
	Matthys Jansz Elisabet Ward	Rachel	John Miller Mary Miller
July 8.	Isak Symonsz Antje Vand' Bilt	Maria	Johannes Hasten Marytje Johannesz
	Pieter Metzelaar Maria Neefjes	Harmpje	Johannes Metzelaar Tryntje Neefjes
Aug. 5.	Aart Symons Margriet Daniels	Anna	Benjamin Corssen Blandina Vile
12.	Samuel Oliver Catharina du Puy	Petronella	Nicolas du Puy
19.	Pieter Martlings Antje Vilen	Debora	Jacob Corssen patrem representans Douwe Van Woglum Rebecca Corssen
26.	Jan Andrevet Leah Sweem	Neeltje	Johannes Sweem Anna Sweem
Sept. 9.	Henrik Bries Dina du Cecoy	Henrik	Cornelius Bries Sarah Bries
Oct. 14.	Pieter Ceilo Blandina Van Pelt	Pieter	Pieter Van Pelt Sara Bogardus
28.	Jacob Bennet Elisabet Brouwer	Aaltje	Philippe Cazier Catharina Hooghland
Nov. 4.	Jaques Corteleau Jacomyntje Van Pelt	Pieter	Rem Van der Beek Dorethe Coteleau
11.	Jan Van Voorhees Neeltje Neefjes	Femmetje Willempje (twins)	Jan Stevens Van Voorhees Pieter Neefjes Femmetje Auke Willempje Luyster
25.	Abraham Tailor Harmpje Hagewout	Aaltje	Pieter Hagewout Neeltje Bakkers

DATE	PARENTS	CHILD	WITNESSES
1722.			
Dec. 23.	Jacobus Craven Antje Iniaart	Christina	Joris Neefjes Willemtje Borkelo
30.	Simon Bogaart Margrietje Ten Eyk	Margareta	Teunis Bogaart Celia Preyer
Feb. 3, 1722-3.	Jacob Van der Bilt Neeltje Denys	Jacobus	Abraham V. Tuyl Femmetje Denys
Feb. 17.	Jacob Preyer Lea Beekman	Andries	Ary Van Woglum Celia Preyer
	Robert Frost Sara Usselton	Usselton	Matthys Jansz
March 8.	Corn. Van Sant- voord Anna Staats	Cornelius	Jan Veghte Cornelia Staats
1723.			
April 14.	Lambert Van Dyk Marritje Hooglant	Elisabet	Daniel Hogelant Elisabet Hogelant
	Samuel Kierstede Lydia Deny	Johannes	Francois Bodin Maria Deny
21.	Teunis Bogaart Catharina Hege- man	Abraham	Koert Van Voorhees Maria Hegeman
May 23.	Jan Jurks Agnietje Staats	Pieter	Cornelius Van Sant- voord Anna Staats
26.	Abraham Manez Anna Jansen	Abraham	Pieter Manez Elisabet Sweem
	Cornelis Wynant Maria Cole	Elisabet	Abraham Cole Hilletje Woglum
	Obadias Holmes Susanna dupuy	Joseph	Joseph Holmes Elisabet du Puy
June 2.	Rem Van der Beek Dorothea Coteleau	Jaques	Jan Hegeman Martha Van der Beek
July 14.	Jacobus Egbertzen Catharina Deny	Johannes	James Deny, Jr. Anna Deny
21.	Johannes Metze- laar Cathryna Neefjes	Cornelis	Pieter Bouman Sara Neefjes
	Cornelis Egmont Elsje de Camp	Zeger	Zeger Gerritzen Jannetje Faas
Aug. 25.	Johannes Sweem Mary Perine	Elisabet	Obadias Winter and wife Susanna de Puy
	Lambert Gerrit- zen, Jr. Lysbet Sweem	Abraham	Catharina Gerritzen
Sept. 15.	Abraham Gray Ariaantje Aartsen	Isaak	Joris Neefjes
22.	Job du Secoy Sarah Denis	Johannes	Israel du Secoy Geertruyd Van De- venter

DATE	PARENTS	CHILD	WITNESSES
1723.			
Sept. 22.	Pieter Barbarie Elisabet du Secoy	Abraham	Teunis Coevert Dina du Secoy
Nov. 24.	Jacob de Grameaux Dirkje Van Tilburgh	Matthys	Ab. de Grameaux Maria Bouman
	Cornelius Corssen Jannetje Boskerk	Maria	Gerrit Croesen Neeltje Corssen
Dec. 8.	Gerrit Croesen, son of Henrik Geertruyd Van Tuyl	Henrik	Henrik Croese Cornelia Corssen
22.	Thomas Stilwell Sara Van Namen	Thomas	Barent Martling Dina Van Namen
25.	Pieter Andrevet Rebecca Cole	Elisabet	Abraham Cole Hilletje Van Woglum
Jan. 12, 1723-4.	Joris Neefjes Willempje Borkelo	Pieter	Bastiaan Elles Tryntje Neefjes
Feb. 2.	Johannes Van der Hoeven Anna Sweem	Lea	Jacobus Biebaut Marya Sweem
23.	Elias Burger Susanna Whitman	Nathan	
March 15.	Philip Cazier Catharina Hooghlant	Dirk	Albert Rykman Maria Kip
1724.			
April 6.	Cornelis Janszen Sara Manbrut	Sara	Antony Van Pelt Lady Manbrut
	Isaak Van Tuyl Sara Lakerman	Geertruyd	Nicolas Lageler Esther Lakerman
	Nicolaas du Puy Neeltje Dekker	Catharina	Eduard Jones Catharina Dekkers
19.	Thomas Greegs Lena Dupuy	John	Francois Bodin Maria Dey
May 17.	Jaques Hervan Geertje Bries	Cornelis	Jan Andrevet Leah Sweem
	Jan Andrevet Leah Sweem	Leah	Jaques Hervan Geertje or Geestje Bries
24.	Pieter Dekker Susanna Hetseel or Hetfeel	Susanna	Abraham Crochon Catharina Gerritzen
June 7.	Henry Day Maria Van Pelt	Petrus	Jan Van Pelt Aaltje Hogelant
	Pieter Metzelaar Maria Neefjes	Cornelius	Lodewyk Metzelaar Aaghje Neefjes
July 19.	Douwe Van Wogelum Jannetje Staats	Zuster	Benjamin Corssen Blandina Vile

DATE	PARENTS	CHILD	WITNESSES
1724.			
	Dirk Cadmus Jannetje Van Hoorn	Rutgert	Jan Van Hoorn Antje Van Hoorn
26.	Aart Symons Margriet Daniels	Daniel	Catharina Symons
Aug. 16.	Tites Tites Blandina Van Pelt	Aaltje	Johannes Van Pelt Aaltje Web
30.	Bastiaan Elles Sara Neefjes	Catharina	Nicolaas Bakker Tryntje Vleereboom
	Gedeon de Camp Hendrikje Elles	Bastiaan	Zeger Gerritsen Jannetje Faas
Sept. 13.	Richard Merl Elsje Dorlant	Susanna	Joris Neefjes Willempje Borkulo
20.	Arent Praal, Jr. Antje Staats	Pieter	Nicolas Lageler Esther Lakeman
27.	Jacob Van Pelt Aaltje Hagewout	Catlyntje	Joh. Huysman Lea Hagewout
Dec. 13.	Johannes Neefjes Antje Gerritz	Pieter	Bastiaan Elles Sara Neefjes
	Henrik Slecht Catharina Wynants	Barent	Barent Slecht Catharina Richaud
20.	Jacob Bennet Elisabet Brouwer	Juriaan	Fredrik Bergen Gerritje Veghte
1724-5.			
Jan. 10.	Isak Martling Anna Van Namen	Aaltje	Thomas Barbank Anna Barbank representing Marritje Martling
24.	Jan Veghte Cornelia Staats	Jannetje	Douwe Van Woggelum Jannetje Staats
31.	Henrik Bries Dina du Secoy	Sara	Gabriel du Secoy Sara Schilman
Feb. 7.	Thomas Morgan Magdalena Staats	Elisabet	Pieter Dekker Susanna Hetfeel
14.	Samuel Kierstede Lydia Deny	Lydia	
21.	Simon Van Namen Sara Praal	Moses	Maria Sweem
March 14.	Jacobus Biebaut Maria Sweem	Maria	Johannes Van der Hoeven Anna Sweem
	Jaques Egbertzen Catharina Deny	Laurens	Gosen Adriaansz Femmetje Van der Bilt
	Wynant Wynants Ann Cole	Abraham	Abraham Cole Geertruyd Van Deventer
21.	Johannes Hasten Marytje Johannesz	Johannes	Benjamin Hasten Antje Van der Bilt

DATE	PARENTS	CHILD	WITNESSES
1724-5.			
March 21,	Corn. V. Santvoord Anna Staats	Staats	Douwe V. Woggelum Maria Staats
1725.			
March 28.	Teunis Bogaart Catharina Hegeman	Maria	Folkert Folkertzen Maria Bogaart repres. by Symon Bogaart and Margrietje Ten Eyk
29.	Johannes Van Namen Marytje Van Pelt	Sara	Pieter Van Pelt Sara Bogardus
	Willem Stibs Catlyna De Hart	Willem	Henrik Van Pelt Tryntje Vlierboom
April 18.	Teunis Coevert Femmetje Van der Schure	Femmetje	Henry Janszen Marie Manez
May 2.	Symon Symonsz Maria Woertman	Antje	Isak Symonsz Antje Vand^r Bilt
9.	Jan Van Voorhees Neeltje Neefjes	Jacobus	
	Charles Morgan Sara Lorton (Rutan?)	Maria	Henry Day Maria Morgan
30.	Obadias Holmes Susanna du Puy	Susanna	Thomas Greegs Lena du Puy
June 6.	Peiter Ceilo Blandina Van Pelt	Cornelia	Jacob de Gramo Dirkje Van Tilburg
12.	Gerrit Jacobusz Anna Van Nes	Rachel	Isak Van Nes Tryntje Jacobusz
27.	Ary Van Woglum Celia Preyer	Andries	Jacob Preyer Margrietje Ten Eyk
July 4.	Abraham Tailor Harmpje Hagewout	Pieter	Jan Barbank Lea Hagewout
	Philip Merril Elisabet Bakker	Catharina Susanna (twins)	Jacob Bakker Tryntje Vleereboom Pieter Hagewout Neeltje Bakker
Aug. 8.	Pieter Mariez Mary Brooks	Maria	Jean Miller Maria Coevert
13.	Cornelius Corssen Jannetje Boskerk	Pieter	Pieter Bouwman Antje Croesen
29.	Jan Dorlant Barbara Aukes	Abraham	Jan Veghte Cornelia Staats
Sept. 19.	Stephen Wood Geertje Winter	Jannetje	Obadias Winter Susanna du Puy
26.	Jacobus Craven Antje Iniaart	Esther	Thomas Craven, Jr. Neeltje Craven
	Fredrick Bergen Gerritje Veghte	Henrik	Jacob Corssen Sara Bergen

DATE	PARENTS	CHILD	WITNESSES
1725.			
Oct. 10.	Jan Jurks Agnietje Staats	Rachel	Lodewyk Metzelaar Antje Meszelaar
Nov. 7.	Bastiaan Elles Sara Neefjes	Cornelius	Joris Neefjes Aaghje Bouwman
Dec. 12.	Johannes Preyer Maria Rall	Andries	Jacob Preyer Lea Beekman
	Jean Seguin Elisabet Hooper	Jonas	Jaques Seguin Martha Hooper
	Thomas Greegs Lena du Puy	Maria	
25.	Jacob Van der Bilt Neeltje Denys	Magdalena	
	Johannes Richaud Amy Carbet	Rachel	Ary Van Woggelum Celia Preyer
	Cornelis Wynant Maria Cole	Maria	Pieter Wynant Anna Maria Richaud
26.	Johannes Metze- laar Cathryna Neefjes	Cornelis Sara (twins)	Bastiaan Elles Sara Neefjes
1725-6. Jan. 1,	Pieter Andrevet Rebecca Cole	Elisabet Anna (twins)	Henrik Slecht Cathryna Wynants Cornelis Janszen Lea Sweem
2.	Cornelis Egmont Elsje de Camp	Christoffel	Laurens de Camp Christyntje de Camp
30.	Elias Stilwell Anna Barbank	Thomas	Thomas Barbank Marietje Martlingh repres. by Anna Van Namen
	Joris Neefjes Willempje Borkelo	Aaghje	Jacobus Craven Antje Iniaart
Feb. 13.	Hendrik de Camp Maria La Mes	Christoffel	Laurens de Camp Loca Patris Cornelis Egmont Christyntje de Camp
20.	Cornelis Janszen Sara Mambrut	Maria	Jaques Seguin Lady Mambrut matern. representans
March 6.	Johannes Wimmer Wyntje Symons	Maria	Barent Symons Apollonia Messeker
20.	Henrik Slecht Catharina Wynants	Jacob	Peter Wynants Celia Preyer repres. Anna Maria Richaud
1726. April 10.	Tites Tites Blandina Van Pelt	Sara	Jacob Van Pelt Sara Le Roy
	Philippe Cazier Catharina Hoogh- lant	Jacobus	Jacobus Kierstede Sara Norby

DATE	PARENTS	CHILD	WITNESSES
1726.			
April 24.	Jean La Tourette Marie Mersereaux	David	David La Tourette Martha Mersereaux
May 19.	Simon Bogaart Margrietje Ten Eyk	Simon	
29.	Jaques Coteleau Jacomyntje Van Pelt	Neeltje	
	Jacob Wright Antje Rol	Susanna	
	Johannes Van der Hoeven Anna Sweem	Elisabeth	Anthony Sweem
30.	Henry Day Maria Van Pelt	Maria	Tites Tites Mary Morgan
	Thomas Janszen Antje Van Pelt	Thomas	Johannes Van Name Sara Bogardus
June 12.	Jacob Garamaux Dirkje Van Tilburgh	Metje	Johannes Metzelaar Tryntje Neefjes
26.	Nicolaas Gerritson Christina V. Woggelum	Nicolaas	Douwe V. Woggelum Cathrina Gerritson
	Pieter Metzelaar Maria Neefjes	Aaghje	Pr Bouman Neeltje Staats
27.	Nicolaas du Puy Neeltje Dekkers	Johannes	Pieter Dekkers Susanna Hetseel or Hetfeel
July 3.	Johannes Dekker Maria Sweem	Maria	Charles Dekker Lena Sweem
17.	Jan Janssen Jannetje Glascou	Elisabet	Thomas Janssen Mary Janssen
19.	Abraham Zutphen Marytje Borkelo	Abraham	
31.	Jacob Preyer Lea Beekman	Johanna	Symon Symonsz Maria Woersman
Aug. 14.	Eduard Jones Catharina Dekkers	Eduard	Zeger Dekkers Maria Sweem
28.	Isak Caspers Elisabet Lisk	Casparus	Hans Rol Anna Bouwman
Sept. 4.	Johannes Huysman Wyntje Symons	Anna	Harme Bouwman Neeltje Staats
18.	John Merril Geertruyd Symonsz	Geertruyd	
	Douwe Van Woggelum Jannetje Staats	Jan	Jan Staats Catharina Corssen
Oct. 9.	Nicolaas du Puy Neeltje Dekkers	Mattheus	Charles Dekkers Elisabet du Puy

DATE		PARENTS	CHILD	WITNESSES
1726.				
Oct.	9.	Wynant Wynants Ann Cole	Jacob	Henrik Slecht Catharina Wynants
		Teunis Van Pelt Marie Drageau	Anthony	Jan Van Pelt Susanna La Tourette
	16.	Aart Symons Margriet Daniels	Susanna	Zeger Gerritsz Jannetje Vlierboom
		Pieter Hagewout Neeltje Bakkers	Egbert	Philip Merril Elisabet Bakker
	23.	Pieter Dekker Susanna Hetseel or Hetfeel	Sara	
Nov.	27.	Nicolaas Christopher Christina Bouman	Barent	Joh. Christopher Styntje deCamp
Dec.	11.	Charles Morgan, Jr. Sara Rutan	Thomas	Thomas Morgan Magdalena Staats
	18.	Albert Rykman Catharina Christopher	Rebecca	Philippe Casier Maria Kip
1726-7.				
Feb.	12.	Thomas Morgan Magdalena Staats	Magdalena	
	19.	Jacobus Biebaut Maria Sweem	Elisabet	
	24.	Phillip Merril Elisabet Bakker	Phillip	Philippe Casier Catharina Houghlant
		Pieter Van Tilburgh Metje Bouwman	Henricus	Corn. Woinat Tryntje Bouwman, repres. by Hendrikje Bouwman
	26.	Johan Henrich Facker Anna Maria Jäger	Catharina	
		Cornelius Corssen Jannetje Boskerk	Christiaan	Christiaan Corssen Cornelia Corssen
1727.				
April	9.	Symon Symonsz Maria Woertman	Marritje	Jacob Preyer Lea Beekman
May	21.	Jacob Bennet Elisabet Brouwer	Elisabet	Abraham Brouwer, Jr.
June	4.	Abraham Zutphen Marytje Borkelo	Maria	
June	18.	Obadias Holmes Susanna duPuy	Johannes	Nicolas duPuy Neeltje Dekkers
	25.	Woodhul Tourneur Anna Lawrence	Benjamin	Jan Van Pelt Aaltje Hooglant
		Jan Veghte Cornelia Staats	Henrik	Rebecca Staats
July	9.	Pieter Ceilo Blandina Van Pelt	Sara	Johannes Van Pelt Sara Le Roy

DATE	PARENTS	CHILD	WITNESSES
1727.			
July 16.	Hendrik Janszen Francyntje Parein	Henrik	Symon Symonsz Maria Woertman
Aug. 13.	Jacob Van Dyk Catharina Van Brunt	Catharina	Tryntje Van Dyk
Oct. 1.	Bastiaan Elles Sara Neefjes	Aagtje	Matthys Iniaart Tryntje Neefjes
8.	Hendrik Van Leeuwen Geurtje Coteleau	Lena	
15.	Jacob Van Pelt Aaltje Hagewout	Jan	Abraham Taylor Harmpje Hagewout
	Gideon de Camp Henrikje Elles	Gideon	Cornelis Egmont Elsje DeCamp
22.	Matthys Sweem Catharina Mangels Rol	Jannetje	Johannes Sweem
Dec. 24.	Stephen Wood Geertje Winter	Steven Obadia (twins)	Obadia Winter Susanna de Puy Pieter Cailo
1727–8.			Blandina Van Pelt
Jan. 21.	John Lisk Rachel Hagewout	Jacob	Pieter Hagewout Neeltje Bakker
	Rem Van der Beek Dorothea Coteleau	Dorothea	
28.	Nicolaas Gerritzen Christina V. Woggelum	Susanna	Jannetje Staats
Feb. 11.	Johannes Metzelaar Tryntje Neefjes	Johannes	Geertruyd Metzelaar
18.	Johannes Van der Hoeve Anna Sweem	Johannes	
	Cornelis Wynant Mary Cole	Cornelius	Wynant Wynant Martha Hooper
Feb. 18.	Charles Dekker Lena Sweem	Charles	
25.	Douwe Van Woggelum Jannetje Staats	Jan Staats	Jan Veghte Cornelia Staats
March 3.	Pierre La Tourette Marianne Mersereaux	Daniel	Jean Bodin Elisabet Mersereaux
	Jaques Seguin Lady Mambrut	Sara	Jean Seguin Sara Mambrut
17.	Henrik Slecht Catharina Wynants	Jan	Jan Slecht
24.	Elias Stilwell Anna Barbank	Daniel	Jan Barbank Lea Hagewout

DATE	PARENTS	CHILD	WITNESSES
1727–8.			
March 24.	Jan Van Voorhees Neeltje Neefjes	Roelof	
	Tites Titusz Blandina Van Pelt	Maria	Henry Day Maria Van Pelt
1728.			
April 21.	Johannes Dekker Maria Sweem	Sara	Simon Van Namen
22.	Matthys Van Brakel Rachel Jansz	Rachel	
	Johannes Sweem Mary Row	Rachel	Lea Sweem
	James Botler Sara Pereine	Anna	Joh. Sweem
	Wynant Wynants Ann Cole	Daniel	Pieter Wynants Hilletje Woggelum
	Hendrik Janszen Francyntje Parein	Belitje	Johannes Sweem
28.	Jan Jurks Agnietje Staats	Catharina	Pieter Hagewout Neeltje Bakker
May 5.	Anthony Sweem Anna Brooks	Maria	Johannes Sweem Marytje Borkelo
26.	Johannes Huysman Wyntje Symons	Pieter	Aart Symons Margrieta Daniels
	Jacob deGramo Dirkje Van Tilburgh	Agneta	
June 10.	Pieter Dekker Susanna Hetseel or Hetfeel	Mattheus	Catlina Dekker
30.	Thomas Johnson Anna Bouwman	Casparus	Elisabet Lisk
July 14.	Aart Symons Margriet Daniels	Barent	
28.	André Escord Catline Richaud	Esther	Isaac Richaud Esther Escord
Aug. 11.	Henry Day Maria Van Pelt	Simon	Simon Van Namen Sara Praal
18.	Benjamin Haste or Hafte Jannetje Johannis	Jacob	Isaak Simonsz Cathrina Beauvois
Sept. 8.	Jean La Tourette Marie Mersereaux	Marie	Paul Mersereaux Esther La Tourette
13.	Gerrit Croesen, son of Henrik Geertruyd Van Tuyl	Femmetje	Ab. Van Tuyl Femmetje DeNys
Oct. 13.	Josue Mersereaux Marie Corssen	Josua	
	Fredrik Sharman Margreta Winter	Jacob	Abadia Winter, repres. Jacob Price or Prue

DATE	PARENTS	CHILD	WITNESSES
1728.			
Oct. 20.	Johannes Richaud Amy Corbet	Elsje	Daniel Escord Elisabeth Miller
	Johannes Preyer Maria Rall	Jannetje	Hans Ral Elisabet Strickhousz
Nov. 10.	Jan Janszen Mayke Verkerk	Elsje	
24.	Philip Merril Elisabet Bakker	Nicolaus	Jaques Egbertsz Catharina Bakker
	Nicolaas Bosch Elisabet Drenkwater	Eduard	Nathanael Drenkwater · Margriet Drenkwater
Dec. 8.	Jan Barbank Lea Hagewout	Thomas	Thomas Barbank Marretje Martlingh, repres. by the child's mother
22.	Corn. V. Santvoord Anna Staats	Jacoba	Christiaan Corssen Jannetje Staats
	Pieter Hagewout Neeltje Bakkers	Neeltje	Jacobus Bakker Rebecca Staats
25.	Cornelis Janszen Sara Mambrut	Rachel	Estienne Mersereaux Marie Mersereaux
	Jacob Van der Bilt Neeltje Denys	Johannes	
1729.			
—— —.	Henry Wright	Henricus	Barent Martling
1728-9.	Aaltje Martlings		Dina V. Name
Jan. 1.	Jacob Bergen Maria Croesen	Cornelia	Henrik Croesen Cornelia Corssen
12.	Pieter Ceilo Blandina Van Pelt	Daniel	Joh. Van Namen Marytje Van Pelt
19.	Simon Bogaart Margrietje Ten Eyk	Gysbert	Henrik Slecht Catharina Wynants
Feb. 23.	Cornelis Corssen Jannetje Van Boskerk	Cornelius	Frans Gerbrants Neeltje Corssen, repres. by Antje Croesen
March 2.	Teunis Bogaart Catharina Hegeman	Cornelius	
9.	Daniel Van Winkel Jannetje Vreelant	Aaghje	Jacob Van Wageninge Lea Jurriaans
	Thomas Morgan Magdalena Staats	Pieter	Aart Symons Margriet Daniels
16.	Symon Symonsz Maria Woertman	Maria	
23.	Jaques Egbertszen Cathrina Bakker	Nicolaas	
1729.			
April 6.	Abraham Tailor Harmpje Hagewout	Ephraim	John Day Frankje More

DATE	PARENTS	CHILD	WITNESSES
1729.			
April 7.	Jan Andrevet Leah Sweem	Jan	
20.	Abraham Manez Sarah du Chine	Petrus	
	Louis Guineau Anna Ciseau	Susanna	Jannetje Glascow
May 4.	Johannis Wynants Lena Bird	Cathryntje	Henrik Slecht Cathryna Wynants
11.	Jan Philip Simsembach Ule Catharina Pikkerling	Aaltje	Pieter Bouwman Antje Van Pe
	Anthony Fountain Belitje Byvank	Antje	
15.	Jacobus Biebaut Marytje Sweem	Petrus	
25.	Jan Van Pelt, son of Anthony Susanna La Tourette	Jan Susanna (twins)	Teunis Van Pelt Helena Van P. Corn. Dorlant Sara Van Pelt
26.	Frans Gerbrantsz Neeltje Corssen	Elisabet	Cornelis Corssen Antje Croesen
	Jacob Bennet Elisabet Brouwer	Willem	
June 1.	Johannis Johnson Jannetje Glascow	Albert	Albert Janszen Marytje Force both repres. by the parents
July 27.	Adriaan Van Woggelum Celia Preyer	Adriaan	
Aug. 24.	Jacobus Bakker Rebecca Staats	Catharina	Jan Staats Catharina Corssen
	Thomas Lisk Catlyntje Van Pelt	Sara	Pieter Bouwman Blandina Van Pelt
31.	Hendrik Janszen, dec^d. Francyntje Parein	Esther b. after her father's death	Esther Berville
Sept. 14.	Nicolaas Gerritzon Christina Van Woggelum	Jan	Jan Van Woggelum, repres. by the father
Oct. 26.	Abraham Zutphen Marytje Borkelo	Antje	
26.	Albert Rykman, dec^d. Cathrina Christopher	Albert (Posthumus)	Barent Christopher Cathrina Hogelant
	Cornelis Dorlant Saartje Van Pelt	Anthony	Jan Van Pelt Susanna La Tourette

DATE	PARENTS	CHILD	WITNESSES
1729-30.			
Jan. 4.	Andre Escord Catline Richaud	Maria	Pieter Wynants Catharina Wynants
	Nicolaas duPuy Neeltje Dekkers	Nicolaas	
Feb. 1.	Jan Winter Martha Puy	Jesias	Susanna duPuy
8.	Jacob Van Dyk Catharina Van Brunt	Catharina	
15.	JohannesHuysman Wyntje Simons	Aart	Bastiaan Ellis Sara Neefjes
	John Day Anne More	William	
March 6.	Titus Titusz Blandina Van Pelt	Syrah	Corn. Eghmont Elsje deCamp
29.	Benjamin Haste Jannetje Johannis	Johannes	Symon Symonsz Martha Symonsz
1730.			
30.	Matthys Van Brakel Rachel Jansz	Maria	
April 5.	Zeger Dekker Elizabet duPuy	Eva	
	Charles Dekker Lena Sweem	Matthys	Barent Sweem Maria Canon
May 24.	Lambert Gerritzen Lysbet Sweem	Elisabet	
29.	Josue de Mersereaux Maria Corssen	Jacob	Jacob Corssen Elisabet Vile
	Johannes Dekker Maria Sweem	Matthys	Simon Van Namen
31.	Charles Petit Anne Parliez	Elisabet	Jean Seguin Dorcas Seguin
June 7.	John Jones Rachel Van Engelen	Maria	Jan Van Pelt, son of Tony Lena Van Pelt
	Matthys Iniaart Elisabet Gerritzen	Matthys	Bastiaan Ellis Tryntje Vlierboom
	Arent Praal Marytje Bouwman	Willem Jorisze	Willem Jorisze Bouwman Maria Praal
28.	Douwe Van Woggelum Jannetje Staats	Cornelius	Jan Staats Catharina Corssen
	Charles Morgan Sara Rutan	Abraham	
July 19.	Fredrik Sharman Margreta Winter	Thomas	Susanna Winter

DATE	PARENTS	CHILD	WITNESSES
1730.			
Aug. 23.	Aart Symons Margriet Daniels	Cornelius	Cornelius Van Santvoord Anna Staats
	Philippe Cazier Catharina Hooghlant	Petrus	Peter Van Ranst Sara Van Ranst
Oct. 25.	Abraham Manez Sarah duChene	Antje	
11.	Pierre La Tourette Marianne Mersereaux	David Jaques (twins)	Jaques de Riveaux Marie La Tourette Esther La Tourette
1730-31. Jan. 17.	Phillip Merril Elisabet Bakker	Mary	Richard Merril Elsje Dorlant
24.	Jean La Tourette Marie Mersereaux	Henricus	Josue Mersereaux Maria Corssen
	Johannes Van der Hoeven Anna Sweem	Anthony	Lea Sweem
31.	Bastiaan Elles Sara Neefjes	Sara	Zeger Gerritze Jannetje Vlierboom, repres. by Neeltje Staats
Feb. 14.	Teunis Van Pelt Marie Drageau	Johannes	Adriaan Van Woggelum Lena Van Pelt
21.	Isaak Martling Anna Van Namen	Johannes	Barent Martling Dina Van Namen
	Cornelis Corssen Jannetje Van Boskerk	Cornelius	Cornelis Croesen Helena Van Tuyl
28.	Abraham Yates Hester Drinkwater	Joseph	Nicholas Gerritzen Christina Van Woggelum
	Jean Mersereaux Elisabet Creage(?)	Josua	Josua Mersereaux Maria Corssen
March 14.	Pieter Hagewout Neeltje Bakker	Jacobus	Cornelius Van Santvoord Anna Staats
	Pieter Ceilo Blandina Van Pelt	Wilhelmus	Joh. Van Namen, Loco Patris Jan Van Pelt, son of Pieter
21.	Isaac Gerritzen Maria Christopher	Christopher	Hans Christopher Geertje Stillwell
1731. March 26.	Joseph Lake Aaltje Barbank	Abraham	Jan Barbank Lea Hagewout
	Thomas Lisk Catlyntje Van Pelt	Margriet	Pieter Bouwman, loca Patris Johannes Van Namen Antje Van Pelt

DATE	PARENTS	CHILD	WITNESSES
1731.			
April 11.	Symon Symonsz Maria Woertman	Simon	
	Jean Grondin Marguerite du Bois	Pieter	Esther du Bois
25.	Jan Van Pelt, son of Jan Tryntje Bouwman	Maria	Pieter Bouwman Neeltje Staats
May 23.	Isak Lakerman Catharina Christopher	Louis	Hans Christopher Lena Van Pelt
June 7	Daniel Stilwell Maria Poillon	Francyntje	David La Tourette Catline Poillon
	Jaques Egberszen Catharina Bakker	Pieter	Pieter Hagewout Neeltje Bakker
13.	George Personet Jannetje Mangels	Jannetje	Jannetje DuChene
	Stephen Wood Jemima Mott	Richard	Tony Van Pelt
July 4.	Laurens More Sara Mambrut	Elisabet	Hilletje More
11.	Niers Johnson Sara Morgan	Francyntje	Charles Morgan Sara Rutan
18.	Jean Mersereaux Elisabet do.	Daniel	Paul Mersereaux Maria do.
Aug. 1.	John Thorp Apollonia Heermans	Abigail	
	Denys Van Tuyl Neeltje Croesen	Abraham	Femmetje Denysz Middelzwa ——
	Timothy Thorp Margrietje Heermans	Margreta	
8.	Adriaan Van Woggelum Celitje Preyer	Abraham	Johannes Preyer Hilletye Van Woggelum
29.	Matthys Janszen Geertje Wynants	Wynant	Pieter Wynants Anna Van Gelder
Sept. 5.	Jan Philip Sumsenbach Ule Catharina Pikkerling	Christoffel	Susanna Merl
23.	Jacob Bergen Maria Croesen	Jacob	
26.	Nicolaas Christopher Christina Bouwman	Anna Catharina	Nicolaas Gerritsze Maria Christopher
Oct. 10.	Johannes De Groot Elisabet Sikkels	Robbert	Zacharias Sikkels Ariaantje
	Cornelis Croesen Helena Van Tuyl	Henrik	Henrik Croesen Cornelia Corssen

DATE	PARENTS	CHILD	WITNESSES
1731.			
Oct. 10.	Thomas Morgan Magdalena Staats	Thomas	Christina Van Woggelom
24.	Jacob Van der Bilt Neeltje Denys	Cornelius	
	Abraham Zutphen Marytje Borkelo	Jannetje	
31.	Dirk Cadmus Jannetje Van Hoorn	Cathrina	Jacobus Van Wageningen Lea Van Wageningen
Nov. 7.	Barent Sweem Marie Canon	Johannes	
21.	Samuel Couwenhoven Sara Drinkwater	Maria	Matthys Iniaart Elizabet Gerritzen
	Nicolaas Bosch Elisabet Drinkwater	Margareta	
Dec. 5.	John Lion Maria Harmensz Bouwman	Neeltje	Jan Van Pelt, son of Jan Tryntje Bouwman
25.	Jacob de Gramo Dirkje Van Tilburgh	Jacob	
1731–2.			
Jan. 1.	Johannes Huysman Wyntje Symons	Margareta	Fredrik Bergen Gerritje Veghte
16.	Jan Barbank Lea Hagewout	Maria	Abraham Taylor Harmpje Hagewout
	Pieter Bouwman Elsje Van Pelt	Harmen	Harmen Bouwman Marie Parein
	Teunis Tiebout Margrietje Drinkwater	Marytje	Jannetje Borkelo
Feb. 13.	Jacob Van Dyk Catharina Van Brunt	Zacheus	
	Simon Bogaart Margrietje TenEyk	Sarah	
14.	Jacob Preyer Lea Beekman	Pieter	Johannes Preyer Marytje Mangels Rol
	Jan Winter Martha Baile	Maria	
March 12.	Fredrik Bergen Gerritje Veghte	Elsje	Bastiaan Ellis Sara Neefjes
19.	Jean Seguin Elisabet Hooper	Jaques	
	Johannes Wynants Magdalena Bird	Pieter	

DATE	PARENTS	CHILD	WITNESSES
1731-2.			
March 19.	Jaques Seguin Lady Mambru	Jean	Laurens More Marie Mersereaux
	Benjamin Haste Jannitje Johannis	Benjamin	
	David La Tourette	Jaques	
1732.	Catharine Poillon		
26.	Matthew Skane Jannetje Tites	Pieter	
	Josue Mersereaux Maria Corssen	Johannes	Jacob Corssen, Jr. Maria Van Pelt
	Pieter Dekker Susanna Hetfeel	Eva	
April 9.	James Butler Sara Parein	Jan	Matthew Sweem
	Nathanael Britton Esther Belleville	Sara	Sara Parein
10.	John Jones Rachel Van Engelen	Elisabet	
16.	Jan Van Voorhees Neeltje Neefjes	Neeltje	
	Hans Christopher Jane Arrowsmith	Johannes	Barent Christopher Catharina Christopher
June 4.	Abraham Manez Sara duChesne	Maria	
July 30.	Charles Morgan Sara Rutan	Charles	Jan Rol Jannetje Borkelo
Aug. 6.	Gerrit Croesen, son of Henrik Geertruyd VanTuyl	Abraham	Abraham Van Tuyl Femmetje Denys
13.	Nicolaas Gerritzen Christina Van Woggelum	Lambert	Elizabet Gerritzen
Sept. 24.	Jacob Bennet Elisabet Brouwer	Cornelius	Jan Rol, Jr. —— Merril
Oct. 22.	Cornelius Corssen Jannetje Van Boskerk	Jacobus	Jacobus Bakker Maria Staats
29.	Charles Dekker Lena Sweem	Magdalena	Sara Van Namen
	Nicolaas duPuy Neeltje Dekker	Moses	
Dec. 17.	Matthys Iniaart Elisabet Gerritzen	Gilles	Zeger Gerritzen Jannetje Vlierboom
	Isaak Symons Neeltje Coteleau	Isaak	
1733. —— —.	Estienne Mersereaux Anne Michel	Daniel	Pierre Roseaux Marie Mersereaux

DATE	PARENTS	CHILD	WITNESSES
1732-3.			
Jan. 14.	Teunis Tiebout Margrietje Drinkwater	Teunis	Jannetje Staats
Feb. 11.	Johannes Symons Dina Van Leeuwen	Antje	
March 18.	Johannes Preyer Marytje Roll	Catharina	Celia Preyer
1733.			
April 8.	Philip Merril Elisabet Bakker	Elisabet	Mathys Iniaart Elisabet Gerritszen
	Zeger Dekker Susanna Jones	Eva	
15.	Jan Van Pelt, son of Anthony Susanna La Tourette	Anthony	
July 15.	Symon Symonsz Maria Woertman	Cornelia	
29.	Cornelis Croesen Helena Van Tuyl	Abraham	Abraham Van Tuyl Femmetje Denys
Oct. 7.	Arent Praal Marytje Bouwman	Henricus	
	Corn. V. Santvoord Anna Staats	Zeger	Mr. Jan Schuyler Miss or Mrs. Sara Walters
1733.			
Nov. 4.	Jaques Egbertsz Catharina Bakker	Susanna	Tryntje Vliereboom
18.	Pieter Martlings Marytje Andries	Catharina	Daniel Van Winkel Jannetje Vreelant
Dec. 16.	Willem Janszen Lena Van Gelder	Femmetje	Nathanael Janszen Annaatje Van Gelder
1733-4.			
Jan. 13.	Johannes Huysman Wyntje Symons	Johannes	Catharina Symons
	Johan Philip Zumsenbach Ule Cathrine Pikkerling	Christina	Rachel Van Engelen
	Pieter Hagewout Neeltje Bakker	Geertruyd	Gerrit Croesen Geertruyd Van Tuyl
20.	Josua Mersereaux Maria Corssen	Elisabet	
Feb. 24.	Jacob Van der Bilt Neeltje Denysz	Antje	
March 3.	Samuel Kouwenhoven Sarah Drinkwater	Samuel	

DATE	PARENTS	CHILD	WITNESSES
1733–1734.			
March 24.	Pierre La Tourette Mariamne Mersereaux	Marie Susanne	
1734.			
April 7.	John Lion Maria Bouwman	Maria	Pieter Bouwman Elsje Van Pelt
	Nicolaas Veghte Neeltje Van Tuyl	Jan	Jan Veghte Cornelia Staats
14.	Jacob Van Dyk Catharina Van Brunt	Cornelius	
	Hans Christopher Jane Arrowsmith	Barent	
15.	Jacob De Gramo Dirkje Van Tilburgh	Dirkje	Gerrit Croesen Geertruyd Van Tuyl,
	Titus Titusz Blandina Van Pelt	Antje	
21.	Matthys Sweem Catharina Mangels Rol	Matthias	Michiel du Chene Hester Canon
June 3.	John Gold Antje Wynants	Marytje	
2.	Abraham Van Tuyl, son of Isak. Marytje Van Pelt	Jan	Jan Van Pelt Aaltje Byvank
3.	Teunis Van Pelt Maria Drageau	Maria	Nicolas Lazelier Esther Lakeman
	Jean Parlie Abigail Jones	Eduard	Nicolas Laselier Esther Lakerman
30.	Jacobus Bakker Rebecca Staats	Nicolaas	Henrik Croesen Cornelia Corssen
July 7.	Laurens More Sara Mambrut	Johannes	
Aug. 4.	Aart Symons Margriet Daniels	Isaak	Alida Hegeman
Sept. 1.	John Jennes —— Johnson	Elsje	Lambt. Jennes Wyntje Johnson
	David La Tourette Catherine Poillon	Marie	Judith Bodin
8.	Denys Van Tuyl Neeltje Croesen	Denys	
	Nicolaas Bosch Elisabet Drinkwater	Barent	
1734–5.			
Jan. 1.	Estienne Mersereaux Anna Mitchel	Marie	Marie Mersereaux

DATE	PARENTS	CHILD	WITNESSES
1734-5.			
March 9.	John Jones Rachel Van Engelen	Johannes	John Merril, Jr. Elisabet Mackleen
	Cornelius Corssen Jannetje Van Boskerk	Daniel	Daniel Corssen Cornelia Croesen
	Philip Merril Elisabet Bakker	Neeltje	
16.	Charles Dekker Lena Sweem	Mattheus	
1735.			
April 6.	Clement Hooper Mary Stilwell	Rachel	Philip Hooper Marie Mersereaux
7.	Charles Morgan Sara Rutan	Thomas	Zeger Dekker Susanna Jones
	Pieter Dekker Susanna Hetfield	Abraham	
13.	Richard Lean Sara Johnson	Jacob	John Jennes, Jr. Mary Johnson
May 4.	Matthys Iniaart Elisabet Gerritzen	Susanna	
	Jan Van Tuyl	Abraham	Abraham Van Tuyl, son of Isaack
11.	Arent Praal Marytje Bouwman	Henderske	
	Adam Clendenny Eva Johnson	Patience	
	Joseph Leak Aaltje Barbank	Maria	Thomas Barbank Maria Barbank
June 8.	James Butler Sara Parain	Sara	
	Thomas Simon Maria Johnson	Thomas	Thomas Johnson Catherina Simon
22.	Eneas Johnson Sara Morgan	Esther	
	Johannes Symons Dina Van Leeuwen	Isak	
Aug. 17.	George Personet Jannetje Mangels	Johannes	
Sept. 14.	Hans Symons Antje Van Pelt	Annatje	
21.	Richard Stilwell Jenneke Van Namen	Nicolas	
28.	Symon Hanszen [or] Symons Helena Sweem	Isaak	
Oct. 5.	John Gold Antje Wynants	Jan	Henrik Slecht Cathrina Wynants

DATE	PARENTS	CHILD	WITNESSES
1735.			
Nov. 16.	Pieter Ceilo Blandina Van Pelt	Johannes Maria (twins)	Jan Van Pelt, Pr's son Symon Van Pelt Jannetje Adams Mary Adams
18.	Dirk Cadmus Jannetje Van Hoorn	Andries	Jacob Gerritsz Van Wageningen Lea Gerritszen
1735–6.			
Feb. 1.	Johannes de Groot Elisabet Sikkel	Johannes	Abraham Sikkel Claasje Sikkel
29.	Johannes Johnson Jannetje Glascow	Thomas	
	Johannes Slecht Elisabet Van Engelen	Elisabet	Fredrik Bergen Gerritje Veghte
	Johannes Huysman Wyntje Symons	Dirk	
1736.			
March 28.	Jan Van Pelt, son of Pieter Jannetje Adams	Antje	Willem Van Pelt Grietje Van Pelt
	Johan Philip Zumsenbach Ule Catharine Pikkerling	Hanna	Joh. De Groot Elisabet Zikkel
	Jan Barbank Leah Hagewout	Geertje	Dirkje Van Pelt
	Lucas Barbank Martha Baile	Maria	
April 4.	Abraham Manez Sarah du Chesne	Catherine	
	Daniel Stilwell Marie Poillon	Daniel	Judith Bodin
	Jan Van Pelt, son of Anthony Susanna La Tourette	Joost	
18.	Jaques Egbertsen Cathrina Bakker	Abraham	Matthys Iniaart Elizabet Gerritzen
26.	Cornelius Van Cleef Sara Mashal	Jan	
	Pierre La Tourette Mariamne Mersereaux	Elisabet	
May 2.	Titus Titusz Blandina Van Pelt	Marytje	
June 3.	Rem Van der Beek Dorothea Coteleau	Lena	

DATE	PARENTS	CHILD	WITNESSES
1736.			
June 13.	Jean Parliez Abigail Jones	Pieter	Pieter Parliez Marie Parliez
27.	Douwe Van Woglum Jannetje Staats	Catharina	Jan Mangel Rol Christina Van Woglum
	Cornelis Gerritzen Aaltje Van Winkel	Daniel	Daniel Van Winkel Jannetje Vreelant
July 18.	Thomas Morgan Magdalena Staats	Annatje	
Aug. 1.	Symon Symonsz, son of Aart Sara Van Pelt	Anna	Aart Symons Margareta Daniels
8.	Cornelis Croesen Helena Van Tuyl	Cornelius	
	Hans Christopher Jane Arrowsmith	Joseph	Mary Christopher
Sept. 19.	Cornelius Corssen Jannetje Van Boskerk	Catharina	Cornelius Van Santvoord Anna Staats
Oct. 3.	Johannes Symons Dina Van Leeuwen	Geertje	
	Pieter Hagewout Neeltje Bakker	Margreta	
10.	Richard Lean Sarah Johnson	John	
31.	Richard Merril, son of Thomas Jenne Gewan	Annatie	Richard Merril Elsje Dorlant
	John Day Hanna More	Johannes	
1736-7.			
Feb. 13.	Willem Janszen Lena Van Gelder	Henricus	
1737.			
May 8.	Thomas Wilmot Elisabet Mersereaux	Thomas	Paul Mersereaux Marie Mersereaux
19.	Teunis Van Pelt Marie Drageau	Joost	
	Jacob Vandr Bilt Neeltje Denys	Femmetje	
July 31.	Daniel Stilwell Catherina Lazilier	Catharina	Ida Stillwell
Sept. 4.	Jacob Bergen Maria Croesen	Cornelia	Henrik Croesen Cornelia Corssen
18.	Tÿs Sweem Catharina Merril	Geertruyd	John Merril, Jr. Geertruyd Symons
	John Jones Rachel Van Engelen	Rachel	

DATE	PARENTS	CHILD	WITNESSES
1737.			
Oct. 23.	Roelof Van Voorhes —— Coteleau	Maria	
Dec. 11.	Louis duBois, Jr. Catharina Van Brunt	Samuel	Symon Bogaart Judith Bodin
1737–8.			
Jan. 1.	Richard Merril, son of Thomas Jenne Gewan	Margareta	Aart Symons Margriet Daniels
	Johannes Huysman	Maria	Abraham Praal Alida Hegeman
1738.	Wyntje Simons		
March 26.	Daniel Stilwell Marie Poillon	Jaques	Judith Bodin
	Abraham Manez Sarah du Chesne	Rachel	
Aug. 12.	Nicolaas Gerritzen Christina Van Woggelum	Zeger	Anna Staats
20.	Jaques Egbertzen Catharina Bakker	Elisabet	Elisabeth Bakker, repres. by Catharina Egbertsen
	Laurens More Sara Mambrut	Rachel	
Sept. 23.	Cornelius Corssen Jannetje Van Boskerk	Antje	
17.	Johannes Van Tuyl Belitje Byvank	Johannes	
Oct. 8.	Joseph Walderon Aafje Heilaken	Jacobus	Daniel Van Winkel Jannetje Vreelant
Nov. 5.	Elisee Gulledet Magdalaine Gendron	Esther	
19.	Teunis Van Pelt Marie Drageau	Teunis	
	Nathanael Johnson Sophia Van Gelder	Henricus	Henricus Van Gelder Anna Van Gelder
1738–9.			
Jan. 1.	Thomas Milbourn Anna Preyer	Francyntje	
7.	Hans Symons Antje Van Pelt	Maria	
21.	Hendrick Van der Hoef Eva Slot	Gerrit	Johannes DeGroot Elisabet Zikkels
	Johannes Cavelier Catlyntje Andriessen	Cornelia Antje (twins)	Dirk Caddemus Teunis Andriessen Jannetje Van Hoorn

DATE	PARENTS	CHILD	WITNESSES
1739.			
Feb. 25.	Jacob Roseau Susanne Merril	Petrus	John Brown Susanna Roseaux
March 4.	Denys Van Tuyl (decd) Neeltje Croesen	Neeltje	(Posthumus: born after her father's death)
18.	Tys Sweem Catharina Merril	Johannes	Jacob Roseau Susanna Merril
	Willem Janszen Lena Van Gelder	Wynant	
25.	Joh. Dekkers Marytje Sweem	Eva	
1739.			
April 23.	Matthys Iniaart Elisabet Gerritzen	Catharina	Christina Van Woggelum
	Pieter Bouwman Elsje Van Pelt	Pieter	
June 3.	Pierre Drageau Elisabet Gewan	Margrietje	
Aug. 5.	Michiel Vreelant Janneke VanHouten	Michiel	Ite or Isa Sips Antje Van Wagenen
26.	Jean Canon Maria Egberts	Catharina	Catharina Egberts
	Nicolas duPuy Neeltje Dekkers	Aaron	
Sept. 9.	Johannes Symons Dina Van Lawa	Aaltje	
16.	Carel Nyts Rebecca Winter	Carel	Obadiah Winter Geertje Winter
	Thomas Morgan Magdalena Staats	Sara	
30.	Hans Christopher Jane Arrowsmith	Richard	
Nov. 4.	Thomas Lisk Catlyntje Van Pelt	Sara	Petrus Van Pelt Sara Van Pelt
	Symon Symons son of Aart Sara Van Pelt	Aaltje	Jan Van Pelt Aaltje Hogelant
18.	Abraham VanTuyl Metje Vreelant	Femmetje	Femmetje Denys
25.	Daniel Stilwell Catherine Lazelier	Richard	Cornelius Van Santvoord, V. D. M. Esther Lazelier
Dec. 9.	Barent du Puy Elsje Poillon	Elsje	
	Johannes Huysman Wyntje Simons	Abraham	Christoffel Simons Cathrina Verschuur
	Johan Adam Schmit Maria Margareta Staat	Catharina	Philip Zimsenbach Ule Catharina Pikkerling

DATE	PARENTS	CHILD	WITNESSES
1739.			
Dec. 23.	Jacob Corssen, Jr. Cornelia Croesen	Maria	Josue Mersereaux Maria Corrsen
	Niers Johnson Sara Morgan	Sara	
1739-40.			
Jan. 20.	Pierre Parlier Martha duBois	Petrus	Louis duBois, Jr. Catharina Van Brunt
1740.			
March 30.	Abraham Manez Sara du Chesne	Sara	
	Daniel Crocheron Maria Du Puy	Abraham	Barent Sweem
	John Jones Rachel Van Engelen	Lucretia	
April 20.	John Brown Susanna Roseau	Maria	Jacob Roseau Susanna Merril
May 25.	Estienne Mersereaux Anne Mitchel	Richard	
26.	Tites Titesz Blandina Van Pelt	Teunis	Symon Van Pelt (Loco Patris)
	Jan Ral, Jr. Fytje Van Boskerk	Fytje	Douwe Van Woggelum Jannetje Staats
June 15.	Nicolaas Gerritzen Christina V. Woggelum	Blandina	
July 13.	Nicolaas Bosch Elisabet Drinkwater	Nicolaas	
Aug. 27.	Gerrit Croesen Claasje Brinkerhof	Cornelia	Henrik Croesen Cornelia Corssen
1741.			
May 7.	Abraham VanTuyl Metje Vrielandt	Machiel	Magiel Vrelandt Jenneke Vrelandt
	Jan Kanon Maria Egberts	Abraham	Maria Kanon
	Charles Decker Helena Sweem	Eva	
	Peter Decker Susanna Hetfeath	Jacob	
Aug. 18.	Johannes Brestede Trintie Hagewout	Jan	Jacob Corsen Marytie Staats
Sept. 14.	Tam Lisk Kadlyna Van Peldt	Maryya	Maria Ryte
	Jan Merrel Aeltie Bennit	Jan	Jan Bennit Aeltie Bennit

DATE	PARENTS	CHILD	WITNESSES
1741.			
b. May 10.			
1742.	Isaac ——	Catharina	
bap.	Maria ——		
April 13.			
	Lucas Barrabank	Catharina	
	Martha Baely		
	Barend de Pu	Johannes	
	Elsje Peljoung?		
	Jan Van Pelt	William	Hendrik Veltman
	Jannetje Adams		Rebecca Staats wife of Jacob Bakker
	Simon Simonsse	Van Pelt	Jan Van Pelt and
	Sara Van Pelt		wife Aaltje Hooglant
June 9.	Johannes Symonsse	Johannes	Jacob Corsse, Jr.
	Suster Corsse		Marytje Corsse, wife of Josua Masjero
Sept. 14.	Jan Van Pelt	Treintje	Harmen Bouman
	Maria Bouman		Maria Bouman
	Douwen Van Woglom	Antje	Hendereck Veltman Johanna Van Santvord
	Jannetje Staats		
	Pieter Bouman	Neeltje	Jan Van Pelt
	Elsje Van Pelt		
	Jacob Bouman	Neeltje	Harmen Bouman
	Maria Williams		Maria Weliams
	Nicklas Gerresen	Zeger	
	Crestina Van Woglom		
1743.			
April 18.	Jacob Corsen	Cornelia	Hendereck Croesen
	Cornelia Croesen		Cornelia Corsen
	Gerret Croesen	Maria	Henderick Blenkerhof
	Claesje Blenkerhof		Geesje Blenkerhof
	Josua Mossero	Elisabet	
	Maria Corsen		
	Mathies Exjard	Elisabet	Johannes Degroot
	Elisabet Gerresen		Elisabet Van Sekelen
	Petures Van Pelt	Maria	Cornelis Bouman
	Barbera Houlte		Aeltje Teitus
	Simon Vanpelt	Maria	Maria Bouman
	Maria Adams		
19.	Cristofel Simesen	Cristofel	
	Catrina Van Schuure		
	Johannes Post	Abraham	Jacob Backer
	Antje Huisman		Rabecka Staats
	Frances Gerrebrats	France	Cornelus Corsen
	Nieltje Corsen		Nieltje Backer

DATE	PARENTS	CHILD	WITNESSES
1743.			
April 19.	Jacob Roose	Weintje	
	Susanna Merril		Geertruy Seimensen
	Johannes Decker	Johannes	Peter Decker
	Nence Merril		Susanna Jons
	Mateis Swem	Maties	Jan Van Pelt
	Catrina Merrel		Susanna Tocet
	Richard Merrell	Annatje	Anatje Seimesen
	Jannetje Gouns		
	Ragel Willemsen	Hester	Johannes Van Pelt
			Barbara Houltje
June 7.	Hans Simonson	Blandena	
	Antje Van Pelt		
	Mateus Jones	Catrina	
	Margrietje Gowen		
Aug. 16.	Johannes Brestede	Pieter	
	Treintje Hagewout		
	Jan Burbanck	Jan	
	Sara or Leea Hagewout		
	Abraham Van Tuyl	Femmetje	
	Metje Freelant		
30.	Walter Clindenne	Maria	
	Pieternel Olfer		
Oct. 11.	Peter Marteling	Johannes	Peter Marteling, Sr.
	Annatje Hegeman		Susanna Gerresen
	Jacus Egberts	Catrina	Elisabet Merrell
	Trintje Backer		
	Johannes Huisman	Elisabet	
1744.	Weintje Seimesen		
April 17.	Wellim Elsewart	Antje	Cornelis Corsci ...
	Rabecca Stillwel	Mareitje	Jannetje Corsen
	Jan Jennens	Aentje	
	Aeltje Marteling		Aentje Jennius
	Jan Van Pelt	Jannetje	Seymon Van Pelt and
	Jannetje Adams		wife
	Abram Egbertse	Elisabet	The parents
	Elisabet Gerresen		
	Symen Symonsen	Art	The parents
	Sara Van Pelt		
May 21.	Carel Mackleen	Elisabet	Cornelus Corsen
	Maria Corsen		Jannetje Corsen
	Isaak Pral	Petrus	The parents
	Maria Dubois		
Sept. 18.	Jan Veltman	Maria	Gerret Croesen
	Jannetje Jurcks		Claesie Croesen
	Joseph Rolph	Cornelia	
	Neeltje Croesen		
	Nicolaes Gerresen	Abraham	
	Cristina Van Wogelom		

54

DATE	PARENTS	CHILD	WITNESSES
1745.			
May 6.	Lammert Jennens Annatje Marteling	Sara	Sara Jennens
	Jacob Bergen Grietje Bennet	Grietje	
	Jacob Resor? Susanna Merrel	Susanna	Jan Van Pelt Susanna Van Pelt
	Jan Merrel Aeltje Bennet	Sara	Geertruy Merrel
	Walter Clendenne Nieltje Ollefer	Johannes	
	Jan Van Pelt, Jr. Catrina Bouman	Nieltje	Bastejan Elles Saara Elles
	Nicklas Bos. Elisabet Drinkwater	Antje	
	Matties Swem Catrina Merrel	Martinus	
	Cristefel Simesen Catrina Van Seuren	Catrina	Catrina Simesen
	Cornelus Bouman Aeltje Titus	Aeltje	`Gerret Post and wife
	Jan Merrel Aeltje Bennet	Seimon	
	Tomas Lisk Catlintje Van Pelt	Martha	
	Jan Jones Ragel Van Engelen	———	
June 18.	Jan Van Derbeck Annatje Marteno	Doritje	Doritje Vanderbeck
	Abraham Rigga Annatje Van Woglom	Ragel	Arie Van Woglom Beelletje V. Woglom
	Father's name evidently omitted by mistake. A space was left open for it.		
	Sara Van Namen	Incres	
Aug. 6.	Seimen Van —— Maria Adames	Sara	Johannes Van Pelt and wife
	John Lawrance Derkje Van Pelt	Willem	Daniel De Hart Saara Beek
	Barent Marteling Susanna Gerresen	Maria	Peter Marteling and wife
	Baltes De Hart Maria Phillipel	Vereltje	Jan Van Pelt Geisbertje Durlant
Dec. 12.	Teunes Egbertse Peternel Depey	Johnnes	
	Cornelus Van Wagenen Hellena Bon	Antje	Johnanes Gerresen Margreta Sep
	Lodewik Metchel Ragel Sayler	Elsse or Eesse	

Staten Island, the 22d of April, 1746. Baptismal Register since the Ministration of Johannes Post.

DATE	PARENTS	CHILD	WITNESSES
1746.			
April 22.	Pieter Martlings Anna Heeveman	Pieter	Pieter Martling Maria Andries
	John Jennens Aeltye Martlings	John, alias Jan	John Jennens Anna Johnson
	John Burbanck Lea Hagewout	Abraham	
	Jan Veldtman Jannetye Jurks	Jan	
	Johannes Huysman Wyntye Symonson	Catherina	
	Basteyaan Elles Sara Neefyes	Maria	
	Jan Canon Maria Egberts	Elizabeth	
	Josua Mascire Maria Corsen	Rachel	
	Jan Van Pelt Jane Adams	Maria	Gerrit Post Francyntje Poulson
	Matthys Inyard Elizabeth Gerretse	Nicklaes	
	Johannes Brestede Catharina Hage- wouyt	Eckbert	Elizabeth Backer
May 20.	Joseph Ralph Neeltye Croese	Abraham	
	Johannes Symen- son Antye Van Pelt	Johannes	Johannes Van Pelt Sophya Slager
	Joseph Juwson Senne or Nenne Johnson	Joseph	
June 17.	Christoffel Symon- se Catharina Van Sheure	Symon	
	Nathaniel Johnson Mary Cole	Wynant	Mary Cole
Sept. 16.	Isack Prael Maria deBaa	Altye	
	Samuel Teeler Suster Waggelom	David	
	Frans Gerrtbratse Neeltye Corsen	Daniel	Antye Kroese Daniel Corsen
	Baltus Dehart Mary Phillipse	Catalyna	Daniel DeHart Derckye Vanpelt
	Thomas Leisk Catlyna Van Pelt	Antye	

DATE	PARENTS	CHILD	WITNESSES
1746.			
Sept. 16.	Cornelius Van Wagenen Helena Bon	Maragrita	
	Otto Van Tuyl Wyntje Boskerk	Abraham	Mateeus
	Seymon Seymonse Sara Van Pelt	Maria	
	Pieter Van Pelt Barbara Hoolten	Johannes	Johannis Van Pelt Sophya Slager
	Matthys Sweem Catharina Merrel	Benyamen	Elizabeth Sweem.
1748.			
April 26.	Christophel Hoogelandt Jannetye Veghten	Cornelia	
	Pieter Maertlings Jannetye Heereman	Johannes	
	Jan Van Pelt, son of Pieter Jane Adams	Maragritye	Maragrietye Van Pelt
	John Decker Anna Merrell	Richerd	
	Christophel Symonson Catharina Van Schuure	Nicholaes	
	Joseph Ralph Neeltje Kroese	Benyamen	
	Johannes Post Anna Huysman	Adriaen	Gerret Post, Jr. Clara Post
July 19.	Isaac Praal Maria Dubaa	Maragritye	
	Johannes Huysman Wyntye Symensse	Jemynna	
	Samuel Van Pelt Maria Falkenborgh	Pieter	Pieter Zielofs Blandina Zielofs
	Symon Symonson Sarah Van Pelt.	Elizabeth	
	Aron Van Namen Maria Macklean	Aron	
	John Canone Maria Egberts	Jacobus	
	Joseph Juwson Wenne Johnson	Enne	
Oct. 11.	Gerret Kroese Claesye Blinckerof	Claesye	
	Lambert Jenners Anna Martlinghs	Maria	Marya Jenners

DATE	PARENTS	CHILD	WITNESSES
1748.			
Oct. 11.	Johannes Van Wagene Elsye Berge	Johannes	
1747.			
April 22.	Jacus Egberts Catrina Backers	Antye	Agbert Hagewout Maria Gaelledet
	John Jones Rachel Van Engelen	Isaac	
	Mattheus Decker Elstye Merrill	Elstye	Elstye Merrill
	John Merrill Antje Merrill	Joida	
	Walter Clendenne Peternella Oliver	Jacob	
	Lewis Mitchell Rachel Tyler	Harmentye	Thomas Burbank Harmentje Tayler
	Johannis Merrill Aaltye Bennet	Richard	Elstye Merrill
June 10.	Jacob Bergen Margrietye Bennet	Gerretye	Frederick Bergen Gerretye Veghte
	Jan Laarens Caatye Bakker	Jacob	Jacobus Backer Rabecca Staats
	Symon Van Pelt Malli Adams	Jennie	Jan Van Pelt Jane Adams
	Thomas Stillwell Debora Martlings	Elias	Nickolaas Stilwell Maria Smith
	Andries Pryor Helena Dorlandt	Jan	Susanna Van Pelt
Oct. 13.	Tunis Egbertse Pieternalla dePuy	Abraham	
	Barent dePuy Elsje Poilyon	Elizabeth	
	Antony Van Peldt Jannetye Symonse	Maria	Johannes Van Pelt
	Charles McClean Maria Corsen	Jannetye	Aron Van Namen Mary McClean
	Jacob Corsen, Jr. Cornelia Croese	Jacob	Jacob Corsen
	Abraham Berkelau Catrina Ellis	Cornelius	Jan Rol Jannetje Berkelau
	Barent Martlinghs Susanna ? Gerritse	Jannety	
1748.			
Dec. 17.	Pieter Van Pelt Barbara Hoelten	Barbara	
	John Jenner Aaltye Martlinghs	Willem	Willem Jenner Sarah Jenner
	Jan Veltman Jannetje Jurks	Geertruyt	John Penhooren Geertruyt

DATE	PARENTS	CHILD	WITNESSES
1748.			
Dec. 17.	William Richardson Anne Fisher	Margret	
	Walter Clendenne Pieternella Oliver	Cathelyna	
1749.			
May 3.	Simon Simonsen Helena Sweem	Jeremyah	
	John Merrell Anna Merrell	Geertruyt	Geertruyt Merrell
	John Laarens Catherina Backer	Jan	
	Jacob Bergen Maragreta Bennet	Adriaen	
May 23.	Matthys Sweem Catherina Merrell	Catherina	
	Symon Van Pelt Maria Adams	Peterus	Peterus Van Pelt Barbera Hoolten
	Charles Rollens Susanna Merrell	Philip	Philip Merrell Catharina Merrell
	Joachim Stillewel Anna Jenners	Richard	Aeltye Jenners
	Hans Symonse Anna Van Pelt	Wyntye	
Sept. 19.	Cherles Makleen Marytje Corsen	Willem	Corneles Corsen Jannetye Boskerck
Nov. 7.	Jacus Ecbers Catharina Backer	Benyamen	Catharina Brestede
	Teunis Egbertsen Pieternelle depu	Barent	
	Barent Mertlings, Jr. Susanna Gerretse	Barent	Barent Meertlings, Sr. Elizabet Gerretse
	Lewis Mitchel Rachel Teeler	Joannis	Pieter M. Aeltye T.
	Joseph Ralph Neeltje Kroesen	Elizabeth	Cornelius —— (torn)
1750.			
May 20.	Samuel Dehart Abigael Jones	Samuel	John —— (torn) Catharina ——
	Jan Van Pelt Jane Adams	Samuel	Blandien —— (torn)
	Pieter Meerlings, Jr. Anne Heereman	Abraham	Pieter Mer-lings Catharina Merlings.
	Barent Depue Elsye Pailyon	Martha	
July 30.	Pieter D Grood Claertye Post	Elizabeth	Johannes —— Elizabeth
	Antony Van Pelt Jenneke Seymense	Elizabeth	Jacob Cor—— Palli Seym——

DATE	PARENTS	CHILD	WITNESSES
1750.			
July 30.	Joseph Juessen Wynty Clindinne	Eefye	

The date of the baptism of the following children could not be ascertained. The leaf was loose in the book, and the year of baptism had been torn or worn away. It is about 1750.

	—— Van Pelt —— Valkenburgh	Jannetye	
Oct. 6.	—— ——monse —— ——rem or eem	Vredrick	
	—— ——non	Abraham	
no year	—— ——es —— Van Pelt	Safya	Safya Van Pelt
	—— ——indinne	Rachel	Malli Clindinne
1751?			
July 28.	——am Berkelo	Gerret	Basteaan Elles
no year	——na Elles		Sara Neefyes
	—— Clindinne	Walteris	
	——nelle Alver		
	—— Veltman	Hendrik	
	——ety Jurks		
1750.			
Oct. 31.	Jacob Marsero Fitye Rol	Mareya	Josewa Marsero Mareya Corsen
1751.			
July 28.	Johannes Post Antye Huysman	Leya	Pieter D Grood Sara Elis
	John Laarns Kaetye Backer	Antye	
	Aron Van Namen Mary Mackleen	Rachel	
	Joachim Stilwil Antye Jinnes	Jan	
	Isaak Prael Marya debaa	Lowies	
	Charles Deckker Helena Sweem	Marya	
	Mathys Sweem Chatarina Merril	Isaak	
	Pieter Hagewout Aeltye Bennet	Neeltye	Neeltye Backer
	Abraham Egbertse Elizabet Gerretse	Hester	Hester Gerretse
Aug. 25.	Pieter D Grood Claerty Post	Gerret	Gerrit Post, Sr. Franscyntje Poulse
	Jacob Corsen, Jr. Cornelia Croesen or Crorsen	Neelty	

DATE	PARENTS	CHILD	WITNESSES
1752.			
June 24.	Gerret Croesen Claesye Blinckerhof	Hendrick	
	Barent Meerlings Susanna Gerretse	Antye	
	Willem Jinnes Jannetye Gerretse	Antye	Antye Jinnes
	Jan Stilwil Helena Van Namen	Eleyas	
	Joris Katmus Jannetje Vreland	Jenneke	Helmog Vrelant Neeltye Van Hoorn
	Hendrik Van Wagene Palli Seymense	Marregrietye	
	Pieter Hagewout Aeltye Bennet	Pieter	Nicklaas Hagewout Neeltye Hagewout
July 24.	David Kanon Aeltje Prael	Sara	
	Jacob Reso Susanna Merrel	Geertruy	
	Cornelius Van Wagenen Helena Bon	Catharina	Manes Van Wagenen Annaetye Van Wagenen
Sept. 17.	Helmig Vreland Neeltye Van Hoorn	Johannes	Otto Van Tuyl Tryntje Boskerk
	Pieter Meerlings, Jr. Annaetje Heereman	Benyaman	Josua Massero Malli Corsen
	Thomas Stillewil Debera Meerlings	Annaetje	
Oct. 1.	Joh. Jenners Aeltje Meerlings	Elsye	Johannes Merlings Elsye Jenners
Nov. 26.	John Laarns Catharina Backer	Catharina	
	Daniel Seymonse Mareytye Decker	Sara	
1753.			
May 2.	Pieter D Grood Claertye Post	Johannes	Johannes D Grood Elizabeth Sikkelse
	Abraham Joons Jannetye Peestnet	Jannetye	
	Walter Clindinne Pieternella Alver	Pieternelle	
	Pieter Hagewout Aeltye Bennet	Annaetye	
	Matheus Swem Catharina Merrel	Susanna	

DATE		PARENTS	CHILD	WITNESSES
1753.				
May	2.	Christoffel Sey-monse	Antye	
		Catharina Van Schuere		
		David Kanon	Marytye	
		Aeltye Prael		
Nov.	7.	Petrus Van Pelt	Jacob	
		Barbara Hulten		
		John Johnson	Pieter	
		Cornelia Ceilo		
		Jan Veldtman	Jannetje	
		Jannitje Jurks		Geertruyda Veldtman
		Jan Merrill	Wyntie	
		Anna Merrill		Geertruida Simonze
		Hendrick Van Wagenen	Annatje	
		Maria Simonze		
		Daniel Corsen	Richard	Gerardus Beekman
		Maria Stilwell		Maria Beekman, repres. by Neeltje Corsen
		Daniel Corsen	Daniel	Cornelius Corsen
		Maria Stilwell		Anna Croesen
		Charles McLean	Maria	
		Maria Corsen		
1754.				
Jan.	13.	Thomas Doghety	Maria	
		Sara Van Naame		Maria Van Pelt
May	2.	Wellem Sinnis	Lammert	
		Yannetye Gerretse		Elsye Sinnis
		Sara Dey	Jan	Marya Adams
		Merya Sinnis	Isack	John Sinnis
		Symon Symeson	Johennis	
		Sara Ven Pelt		
June	9.	Daneel Symeson	———	
		Molly Decker		
Aug.	7.	Pieter Sielof	Blandiena	
		Marya Van Pelt		
		Jacob Korsen	Liesabet	Maria Korson
		Cornelia Kroeson		
		Gerrit Post	Gerrit	Gerrit Post
		Sara Ellis		Frntcintye Poulse
Nov.	2.	Beniemin Praal	Abraham	Abraham Praal
		Sara Sweem		Alida Praal
		Abraham Beckelo	Cattriena	Cornelus Ellas
		Cattriena Elis		Egye Ellis
		Jacob Resoo	Catriena	Catriena Merl
		Susanna Merel		
		Davit Cornon	Aront	
		Aaltye Praal		

DATE	PARENTS	CHILD	WITNESSES
1754.			
Nov. 3.	Helmis Vrelant Neeltye Vanhoren	Machgiel	Joris Kadmis Jannitye Vrelant
	Antoni Founten Anaatje Gerretson	Antoni	
	Nettenel Bos Jannetye Post	Eliesebeth	Pieter Degroot Klaart Post
	Nettenel Laakerman Mareytye Merel	Susanna	Geertruy Merel
	Barent Depue Elsye Puelyon	Johannes	
4.	Aart Symenson Fransintye Morgon	Fransintye	Margrietye Simonson
1755.			
Feb. 16.	John Van Pelt Maria Joons	Susanna	John Van Pelt
	Adriaan Ryerse Hester Debaa	Luwes	
	Tammes Stillwel Nensy Founten	Antoni	
	Aron Van Namen Maria Macleen	Antye	
	Walter Clindinne Nelli Allever	Joseph	
	Hendrik Van Wagenne Maria Simonse	Johannes	
	Cornelis Van Wagenne Lena Bon	Lena	
July 27.	Pieter DeGroot Claartye Post	Cattriena	
	John Schinnis Aeltje Maerling	Susanna	Susanna
	John Lerns Kaatye Backer	Necclos	Necclos Backers
	Pieter Hagewout Altye Bnnet	Grietye	Egbert Hagewout Grietye Hagewout
	Daneel Silof Henne Klerre or Kleeve	Saartye	Elsye Silof
	Willim Spree Cattriena Maerling	Edwort	
	Cherls Mechleen Maria Corson	Cttriena	Cattriena Corson
Oct. 2.	John Merrel Anna Merrel	Sara	
	Pieter Johnson Malli Cister	Johnneton	

DATE	PARENTS	CHILD	WITNESSES
1755.			
Oct. 2.	Rem Symeson Geertruy Boskerk	Marretye	
5.	Douwe Corson Janntye Conein	Ragel	
12.	Pieter Van Pelt Barber Houlten	David	John Veltman Jannetye Jurk
Dec. 18.	Gerret Kroeson Klaasye Blincrof	Geertruy	
	Symon Symeson Sara Van Pelt	Eevert	
1756.			
March —.	Antoni Founten Anaatye Gerretson	Maragriet- ye	
Oct. 31.	Nicclos Backer Liesabet Foret	Jacob	
	Matteus Hus Cattrena Hus	Mary Mig- len	Stofel Simeson
	Tammas Merel Eva Yoons	Annaetye	
	Jeams Clendenny Rebecka Jonson	Jeams	
	Nettenel Laaker- man	Nettenel	
1757.	Mareytye Merel		
Sept. 11.	John Lerns Kaaty Backer	Mareia	Danal Lerns Fanny Lerns
25.	Richard Sandars Ragel	Hanna	Hehanna Kink—
Nov. 20.	Symon Symonson Sara Vanpelt	Sara	Otto Van Tuil. Catriena Boskerck
	Antoni Founten Anaatye Gerritson	Johannis	Johannis Gerretson
1758.			
Jan. 1.	John Marel Anna Marel	John	
29.	Davit Cornon Aaltye Praal	Davit	
Feb. 6.	Willim Spree Cattriena Maerling	Caty	Johannes Maar
12.	Antony Brat Neeltye Haage- wout	Catriena	Catriena Haagewout
26.	Naclos Backer Liesabet Latoret	Mary	
	Daniel Symenson Mally Dacker	Abraham	
	Nattenal Laacer- man Marya Marel	Isak	

DATE	PARENTS	CHILD	WITNESSES
1758.			
March 12.	Gerrit Post	Abraham	Abraham Berkelo
	Sara Ellis		Cattriena Ellis
	Pieter Haagewout	Necclos	Necclos Haagewout
	Altye Bennet		Geertruy Haagewout
	Johnnis Symonson	Geertruy	
	Antye Vanpelt	Maria	Geertruy Marel ?
July 21.	Conradus Vanderbeeck	Liesabet	Burger Vanderbeeck
	Catlyntje Lisse or Lisk		Annetye Massalaar
25.	Pieter DeGroot	Geertruy	
	Claartye Post		
Sept. 17.	Daniel Corsen	Cornelius	Daniel Corsen
	Liesebeth Bogert		Mareia Stillwel
	Abraham Kroeson	Geertruy	
	Antye Symonson		
	John Yennes	Mareya	
	Altye Merling		
	Netteniel Bos	Gerret	Pieter Post
	Jannetye Post		Maria Post
1759.			
March 4.	Denil Marsero	John	
	Cornelia Vanderbilt		
June 24.	Cornelis Symonson	Barant	
	Liesebet Depue		
	Walter Cleninne	Antye	
	Nelli Alever		
Aug. 26.	Tammes Merel	Tammes	
	Eva Yoons		
	David Cornon	Andries	
	Aaltye Praal		
	Danel Silof	Danel	
	Henne Klac		
	Cornelius Ellis	Saara	Basteaan Ellis
	Leena Vanderbilt		Saara Neefye
	Peater Van pelt	Sara	
	Barber ——		
	Cornelius Kroeson	Cornelius	
	Beelitye Degroot		
	Sammual Dangek	Andro	
	Jenny Rgt		
	Peater Cornon	Danal	
	Mally Stebs		
Nov. 4.	Christeyaan Gerrebrans	Neeltye	
	Marya Post		
	Johannis Gerritson	Maragrietye	
	Marritye Demot		

DATE	PARENTS	CHILD	WITNESSES
1759.			
Dec. 23.	Antony Founten Annaetje Gerritson	Cornelus	
1760.			
Jan. 1.	Antony Brat Neety Haagewout	Neeltye	
	John Marssero Marya Praal	Marya	
	Antony Van Pelt Jenneke Symeson	Sara	
Feb. 10.	John Larns Caatye Backer	Richard	
March 23.	Aron Van Namen Maria Macleen	Mosis	
25.	Willim Spree Cattriena Maarling	———	
April 20.	Peter Haagewout Aaltye Bennit	Wynant	
June 14.	Abraham Kroeson Antye Symonson	Johannes	Johannes Symonson
Oct. 5.	Richard Sandars Ragel	Sara	
	Charcels Dacer Maccy Maral	Marya	
	John Sweem Cornelia Bergen	Marya	
1763.			
March 25.	Gerrit Post Sara Ellis	Lea	Sara Ellis
1765.			
Oct. 6.	Johannis Huisman Antye Merling	Baarent	Pieter Merling Jannitye Merling
1766.			
Aug. 26.	Beniemen Praal Sara Sweem	Johannis	
Oct. 5.	Andru Coolter Mary Clendenny	Willim	
1767.			
Feb. 8.	Hanry Fialan Eghye Vanwinkel	Daniel	Matteis Everse and wife
1768.			
Oct. 9.	John Mecereau Mary Prall	All lada	
Dec. 4.	Abraham Skirmen Alizabeth	Peggy	
1772.			
March 8.	John Vanpelt Catherine Lawrence	Mary	
	Egbert Haugwout Elener Garebrantz	Danniel	
	Hennis Merril Cherrity Merril	Anney	

The following is an acc[t] of the Children that were Baptised by the Rev[d] W[m]. Jackson in the presence of me while or since I was chosen by the Church to act as Clerk of the Reformed Protestant Dutch Church at the North Side of Staten Island & kept by me.
A. Ryersz.

DATE		PARENTS	CHILD	WITNESSES
1786.				
July	9.	John Simonson Maricha Crusen	Abraham	
	23.	Aris Ryersz Sarah Stout?	Hannah	
Aug.	6.	Nicholas Houghwout	Mary	
		Peter Housman	Elizabeth	
Oct.	29.	John Van Pelt	Barbara	
		David Jaques	Elizabeth	
		John Buskirk	Sarah	

In the New Church at the North Side of Staten Island.

1787.				
May	27.	Abrm Rolph	Abraham	
		Jacob Van Derbilt	Jacob	
July	1.	Christian Vroome, Sr.	Elizabeth	
Sept.	2.	John Tysen, Jr.	John	
		John Garrison	Aulchie	
		Corn Corsen, Jr.	Cornelius	
	16.	John Segoine	Elizabeth	
	30.	Garrit Bush	Mary	
Oct.	28.	Peter Brasted	Abraham	
		W— Houghwout	Isaac	
Nov.	11.	Benjamin Swaime	Matthew	
		Richard Myers	Elizabeth	
1788.				
Feb.	—.	Israel Decker	Sarah	
June	7.	Peter Houghwout	Daniel	
	8.	Richard Merrill	Richard	
		Joshua Mersereaux, Jr.	Harmanus	
Aug.	3.	Jacob Mersereaux, Esq.	Peter	
	17.	Thomas Merrell, sawmill	John	
Sept.	14.	Peter Prall, Jr.	Abraham	
		John Christopher	Charity	
Oct.	26.	Capt. Richard Decker	Richard	
		Aaron Miller	Hendrick	
Dec.	7.	Peter Housman	Nancy	
1789.				
May	10.	John Kruse	Elizabeth	

DATE	PARENTS	CHILD	WITNESSES
1789.			
June 7.	Garret Ellis	Abraham	
July 5.	Samuel Styversant	Christian	
Aug. 2.	Jno Tysen, Jr. Deacon	Cornelia	
30.	Isaac Simonson, Deacon	Elizabeth	
	Richard Corsen	Catharina	
	Garret Bush	Elizabeth	
Oct. 11.	Austin Barton	Joseph	

1790.	Children bapt. by the Rev. Peter Stryker.		
Oct. 17.	Aris Ryersz	David	
	Jacob Mercereaux, Esq.	Garret	
	John Bushkirk	{ John { Cornelius	
	Cornelius Corsen	Yannetye	
Oct. 24.	Edward Dehart	Jacob	
31.	Jacob Vreeland	Derrick	
Nov. 7.	Christian Vroome	William White	
	Johannes Merrill, Jr.	Magdalen	
Nov. 11.	Thursday afternoon, after Mr. Stryker was ordained or rather installed in our Church by Mr. Livingston.		
b. July 31, ba. Nov. 14, 1790.	Abraham Post	Miriam	

Found on a loose piece of paper neither date nor year upon it.

	Christopher Simonson	Wouter	
	Chathrine Van Schuren		
	Johannis Simonson	Aart?	Art Simonson and wife Margrit
	Anna Van Peldt		
	Lambert Jenoure?	Antie	John Jenner
	Anna Marlin		Anna Jenner
	Joseph Lake	Clace?	
	Altie Lake		
	France Garribrance	Nailtie	
	Naile Corsen		
	Abraman Prall	Abraham	
	Aeleda Heheman		
	Tousseway? Moserow	Baules? or Paules?	Paul Merserue
	Mary Corsen		

WALDENSIAN CHURCH, STONY BROOK, 1658
The First Church on Staten Island

OLD MORAVIAN CHURCH AND PARSONAGE, NEW DORP, S. I.

PRESENT MORAVIAN CHURCH, NEW DORP, S. I., DEDICATED 1845

UNITED BRETHREN CONGREGATION,

COMMONLY CALLED MORAVIAN CHURCH.

List of Pastors of the United Brethren Congregation, commonly called Moravian Church, on Staten Island, New York, from 1747 to 1892:

1747.	RICHARD UTLEY.
1749.	JOHN WADE.
1750.	OWEN RICE.
1754.	JASPER PAYNE, RICHARD UTLEY.
1756.	JACOB ROGERS.
1757.	THOMAS YARREL.
1761.	GEORGE SELLE.
1763.	HECTOR GAMBOLD.
1784.	JAMES BIRKBY, E. THORPE.
1787.	FREDERICK MOERING.
1794.	JAMES BIRKBY.
1798.	FREDERICK MOERING.
1803.	NATHANIEL BROWN, d. 11 July, 1813.
1813.	JOHN C. BECHLER.
1817.	G. A. HARTMAN, left 3 May, 1837.
4 May, 1837.	A. RONDSHALER, to 1839.
26 May, 1839.	HENRY G. CLAUDER, to 17 May, 1852.
18 May, 1852.	BERNARD E. SCHWEINITZ, to June, 1854.
17 Sept., 1854.	A. A. RINKE, to 14 Oct., 1860.
23 Oct., 1860.	EDWIN T. SINSEMAN, to 1 Sept., 1862.
10 Sept., 1862.	EUGENE LEIBERT.
25 June, 1867.	FRANCIS F. HAGEN, to 1 July, 1870.
6 Aug., 1870.	WM. L. LENNERT, to 1 Aug., 1876.
1 Aug., 1876.	WM. H. VOGLER, to Oct., 1892.
17 Nov., 1892.	WM. HENRY RICE, gr.-gr.-grandson of Rev. Owen Rice.

RECORDS OF THE UNITED BRETHREN CONGREGATION, COMMONLY CALLED MORAVIAN CHURCH, STATEN ISLAND, N. Y.

BAPTISMS AND BIRTHS.

ABBREVIATIONS.

Sr.—Sister—A Communicant.   M. M.—Married Man.   M. W.—Married Woman.
Br.—Brother—A Communicant.   S. M.—Single Man.   S. W.—Single Woman.
Wid.—Widow.

DATE	PARENTS	CHILD	BY WHOM BAPTISED
1749.			
Feb. 11.	Tunis Egbert	Catharine	Rev. Dr. John Wade
Jan. 25.*	Anne Egbert		
Nov. 11.	Stephen Martino	Sarah	" "
Oct. 1.*	Anne Martino		
1750.			
Feb. 7.*	Jacob Vanderbilt	Jacob	" "
Jan. 17.	Mary Vanderbilt† (Spragg)		
1751.			
May 12.	Stephen Martino	Hannah	Rev. Owen Rice
1750. Oct. 12.	Elizabeth Martino		
1751.			
May 12.*	Teunis Egbert	John	" "
Feb. 27.	Anne Egbert		
d. Oct. 31, 1830.			
1752.			
July 6.	Richard Connor	Anne	" "
Jan. 3.*	Catharine Connor		
July 6.	Jacob Vanderbilt	John	" "
May 20.*	Mary Vanderbilt		
	Aaron Cortelyou	Peter	" "
Dec. 10.	Elizabeth Cortelyou		
1754.			
Sept. 1.	Stephen Martino	Elizabeth	Rev. Jasper Payne
Feb. 11.	Elizabeth Martino		
March 17.	Tunis Egbert	James	" "
Feb. 16.	Anne Egbert		
Sept. 1.	Richard Connor	Catharine	" "
April 16.	Catharine Connor		
Sept. 1.	Jacob Vanderbilt	Dorothy	" "
July 29.	Mary Vanderbilt		
1755.			
Feb. 9.	Cornelius Cortelyou	Eleanor	Rev. Richard Utely
1754. Dec. 27.	Sara Cortelyou		

* New Style.
† Jacob Vanderbilt's marriage to Mary Spragg is recorded in Trenton, N. J., but does not appear in this church record.

DATE	PARENTS	CHILD	BY WHOM BAPTISED
1755.			
Feb. 9.	Christopher Gar-	Mary	Rev. Richard Utely
Jan. 29.	rison		
	Phebe Garrison		
1756.			
Oct. 2.	Tunis Egbert	Edward	Rev. Jacob Rogers
March 8.	Anne Egbert		
1757.			
Aug. 3.	Jacob Vanderbilt	Oliver	Rev. Thomas Yarrel
June 16.	Mary Vanderbilt		
Oct. 19.	Cornelius Cortelyou	Martha	" "
Aug. 15.	Sara Cortelyou		
1758.			
March 17.	William Ward	Anne	" "
Nov. 1.	Charity Ward		
1758.			
April 5.	Richard Connor	Sara	" "
1757.	Catharine Connor		
Nov. 21.			
1758.			
April 5.	Cornelius Vander-	Phebe	" "
March 1.	bilt		
	Eleanor Vanderbilt		
1759.			
May 1.	Tunis Egbert	Tunis	" "
Jan. 11.	Anne Egbert		
May 1.	Peter Perine	Daniel	" "
Feb. 8.	Catharine Perine		
1760.			
June 25.	Cornelius Vander-	Jacob	" "
May 11.	bilt		
	Eleanor Vanderbilt		
Dec. 5.	Cornelius Cortelyou	Jacob	" "
Aug. 26.	Sara Cortelyou		
1761.			
May 3.	Peter Perine	Elias	Rev. George Selle
Feb. 10.	Catharine Perine		
May 3.	Richard Connor	Elizabeth	" "
March 3.	Catharine Connor		
1762.			
April 25.	Jacob Vanderbilt	Joseph	" "
1761.	Mary Vanderbilt		
Sept. 16.			
1762.			
April 25.	Tunis Egbert	Elizabeth	" "
1761.	Anne Egbert		
July 8.			
1763.			
March 24.	John Beatty	Anne	Rev. Thomas Yarrel
1762.	Anna Beatty		
Nov. 29.			

DATE	PARENTS	CHILD	BY WHOM BAPTISED
1763.			
March 24.	CorneliusCortelyou	Mary	Rev. Thomes Yarrel
March 23.	Sara Cortelyou		
Sept. 22.	Abraham Vande-	Elizabeth	Rev. Hector Gambold
Aug. 28.	venter		
	Mary Vandeventer		
Dec. 7.	Peter Perine	Peter	" "
Oct. 26.	Catharine Perine		
1764.			
Jan. 22.	Richard Connor	Richard	" "
1763.	Catharine Connor		
Dec. 27.			
1764.			
April 22.	Simon Cortelyou	Agnes	" "
March 10.	Sara Cortelyou		
Sept. 23.	Jacob Vanderbilt	Cornelius	" "
Aug. 28.	Mary Vanderbilt		
Oct. 14.	Peter Colon	Peter	" "
Sept. 7.	Mary Colon		
Oct. 14.	James Colon	James	" "
Oct. 8.	Catharine Colon		
1765.			
Feb. 17.	John Macky	Joseph	" "
1764.	Ann Macky		
Nov. 19.			
1765.			
May 12.	Tunis Egbert	Abraham	" "
March 31.	Anne Egbert		
Oct. 20.	Simon Cortelyou	Hannah	" "
Sept. 20.	Sarah Cortelyou		
1766.			
Nov. 3.	Peter Colon	David	" "
Oct. 5.	Mary Colon		
Nov. 9.	Stephen Martinoe	Benajah	" "
Oct. 5.	Elizabeth Martinoe		
1767.			
Jan. 20.	Christian Jacobson	Catharine	" "
Jan. 9.	Anne Jacobson		
March 1.	John Beatty	Charity	" "
Jan. 17.	Ann Beatty		
April 5.	Peter Perine	Abraham	" "
Feb. 28.	Catharine Perine		
May 12.	James Colon	Daniel	
May 4.	Catharine Colon		
d. the 17.			
June 21.	Simon Cortelyou	Sara	" "
May 13.	Sarah Cortelyou		
1768.			
July 10.	John Wendel	Anne Mary	" "
June 9.	Aletta Wendel		

DATE	PARENTS	CHILD	BY WHOM BAPTISED
1768.			
July 17.	James Colon	Margaret	
July 4.	Catharine Colon		
Nov. 13.	Nicholas Enyard	Mathias	Rev. Hector Gambold
Aug. 16.	Jemima Enyard		
1769.			
Jan. 26.	CorneliusCortelyou	Peter	" "
1768.	Sara Cortelyou		
Dec. 27.			
1769.			
Feb. 8.	Jacques Cortelyou	Peter	" "
1768.	Mary Cortelyou		
Nov. 28.			
1769.			
Feb. 8.	Simon Cortelyou	Peter	" "
Jan. 21.	Sara Cortelyou		
July 4.	James De Young	Daniel	" "
June 10.	Anne Connor		
Oct. 8.	Peter Colon	James	" "
Sept. 7.	Mary Colon		
1770.			
June 7.	Nicholas Enyard	Timothy	" "
April 13.	Jemima Enyard		
June 24.	John Wendel	Charity	" "
May 21.	Aletta Wendel		
July 8.	Christian Jacobsen	John Van-	" "
June 25.	Anne Jacobsen	deventer	
Nov. 18.	James Colon	Elizabeth	" "
Nov. 12.	Catharine Colon		
1771.			
July 4.	Peter Perine	Elizabeth	" "
June 5.	Catharine Perine		
July 11.	Christian Jacobson	Elizabeth	" "
July 5.	Ann Jacobson		
Nov. 21.	William Lake	William	" "
Sept. 13.	Dorothy Vanderbilt		
1772.			
March 22.	Nicholas Enyard	Elias	" "
Jan. 21.	Jemima Enyard		
April 19.	Peter Colon	Elizabeth	" "
March 13.	Mary Colon		
July 26.	John Wendel	Anne	" "
July 7.	Aletta Wendel		
1773.			
May 16.	George Colon	Mary	" "
April 17.	Mary Colon		
Sept. 19.	James Colon	Catharine	" "
Aug. 19.	Catharine Colon		

DATE	PARENTS	CHILD	BY WHOM BAPTISED
1774.			
Feb. 27.	Nicholas Enyard	Nicholas	Rev. Hector Gambold
1773.	Jemima Enyard		
Dec. 21.			
1774.			
May 8.	Edward Beatty	Sarah	" "
April 15.	Eleanor Beatty		
June 12.	Jacob Vanderbilt	Jacob	" "
Feb. 4.	Catharine Vanderbilt		
1775.			
Jan. 2.	Jacques Cortelyou	Timothy	" "
1774.	Sarah Cortelyou	Townsend	
Nov. 19.			
1775.			
Feb. 26.	Peter Perine	Mathias	" "
Jan. 26.	Catharine Perine		
April 16.	George Colon	Jane	" "
March 10.	Mary Colon		
Oct. 1.	Nicholas Enyard	Elisabeth	" "
July 21.	Jemima Enyard		
Oct. 15.	Peter Colon	Mary Magdalen	" "
Aug. 27.	Mary Colen		
Dec. 28.	Lewis Reyerse	Adrian	" "
Nov. 8.	Catharine Reyerse		
1776.			
Feb. 25.	James Colon	Helena	" "
Jan. 25.	Catharine Colon		
May 30.	Edward Beatty	John	" "
May 11.	Eleanor Beatty		
1775.			
Dec. 15.	George Barnes	Anne	" "
Oct. 9.	Dorothy Barnes		
1777.			
Jan. 19.	Jacob Vanderbilt	Jacob	" "
1776.	Catharine Vanderbilt		
Sept. 2.			
1777.			
March 30.	Benjamin Marlin	John	" "
1776.	Anne Marlin		
Nov. 30.			
1777.			
April 2.	William Van Pelt	Jane	" "
Jan. 29.	Alice Van Pelt		
May 25.	John Wendel	Thomas	
April 26.	Aletta Wendel		" "
Sept. 28.	George Colon	Rebekah	
Aug. 7.	Mary Colon		" "
1778.			
March 14.	Christopher Curtis	Christopher	" "
Jan. 11.	Eve Curtis		

DATE	PARENTS	CHILD	BY WHOM BAPTISED
1778.			
March 15.	Nicholas Enyard	Daniel	Rev. Hector Gambold
Jan. 21.	Jemima Enyard		
April 5.	James Egbert	Catharine	" "
Feb. 27.	Elizabeth Egbert		
May 3.	James Colon	Mary Mag-	" "
April 12.	Catharine Colon	dalen	
June 21.	Lewis Reyerson	Catharine	" "
May 24.	Catharine Reyerson		
1779.			
April 25.	Peter Hagewout	Elisabeth	" "
Feb. 18.	Mary Hagewout		
April 21.	Edward Beatty	Mary	" "
Feb. 22.	Eleanor Beatty		
June 20.	Peter Perine	James	" "
May 18.	Catharine Perine		
Oct. 20.	George Colon	Peter	" "
Oct. 8.	Mary Colon		
	James Egbert	Stephen	" "
Sept. 24.	Elizabeth Egbert		
Nov. 29.	Moses Egbert	Tunis	" "
Nov. 9.	Catharina Egbert		
1780.			
May 14.	Nicholas Enyard	Susanna	" "
b. & bap.	Jemima Enyard		
July 5.	Anthony Niel	Anthony	" "
April 24.	Mary Niel		
Nov. 6.	Edward Beatty	Cornelius	" "
Oct. 9.	Eleanor Beatty		
Nov. 12.	Peter Hagewout	Peter	" "
Oct. 6.	Mary Hagewout		
Nov. 29.	Lewis Reyerson	Phebe	" "
Oct. 20.	Catharine Reyerson		
1781.			
June 25.	George Barnes	George	" "
Jan. 1.	Dorothy Barnes		
July 8.	Nathaniel Britton	Nathaniel	" "
June 5.	Catharine Britton		
Aug. 19.	Simon Cortelyou	Mary	" "
July 18.	Sarah Cortelyou		
Sept. 2.	James Colon	Jonah	" "
Aug. 17.	Catharine Colon		
1782.			
May 5.	Peter Hagewout	Stephen	" "
March 15.	Mary Hagewout		
May 26.	Benjamin Marlin	Peter	" "
March 28.	Ann Marlin		
June 23.	Anthony Niel	Jacob	" "
May 8.	Mary Niel		
Sept. 8.	James Egbert	James	" "
Aug. 20.	Elisabeth Egbert		

DATE	PARENTS	CHILD	BY WHOM BAPTISED
1782.			
Oct. 20.	Lewis Reyerse	Richard	Rev. Hector Gambold
Sept. 10.	Catharine Reyerse		
Nov. 3.	Daniel Perine	Joseph	" "
Sept. 15.	Lucy Perine		
1783.			
March 4.	John Lysk	Isaac	" "
1782.	Sarah Lysk		
Aug. 8.			
1783.			
March 13.	George Colon	George	" "
Jan. 24.	Mary Colon		
March 13.	Edward Beatty	William	" "
Feb. 10.	Eleanor Beatty		
April 20.	Edward Egbert	Cornelius	" "
March 29.	Mary Egbert	Cortelyou	
1784.			
May 2.	Peter Hagewout	Nicholas	" "
Feb. 5.	Mary Hagewout		
May 4.	Nathaniel Johnson	Charles	" "
Oct. 26.	Eleanor Johnson	Garrison	
May 4.	Daniel Perine	Catharine	" "
April 5.	Lucy Perine		
June 15.	John Egbert	Joseph	Rev. Jas. B. Birkby
May 5.	Mary Egbert		
July 27.	Jeams Colong	Anne	" "
July 21.	Catran Colong		
Aug. 3.	Elizabeth Vanpelt	Jeams	" "
March 26.			
Oct. 25.	John Van Pelt	Ann	" "
	Judy Van Pelt		
Dec. 5.	Barent Simonson	John Beatty	Rev. E. Thorp
Nov. 1.	Ann Simonson		
Dec. 12.	Henry Barger	Jacob	" "
Oct. 27.	Mary Barger		
1785.			
March 20.	George Colong	Catharine	" "
Jan. 29.	Mary Colong		
d. Sept. 4, 1818.			
April 10.	John Dorset	Catharine	" "
Same day.	Martha Dorset		
May 25.	John Dorset, a married Man		Rev. John Ellwein, on
Jan. 10,			Staten Island
1752,* in Monmouth Co., East Jersey			
1785.			
Nov. 6.	James Burdine	Ann	Rev. E. Thorp
Sept. 18.	Elizabeth Burdine		
Nov. 6.	Edward Beatty	Jacob	" "
Oct. 8.	Eleanor Beatty		

* Old Style.

DATE	PARENTS	CHILD	BY WHOM BAPTISED
1785.			
Nov. 21.	Lucy Perine wife of Daniel		Rev. James Birkby
April 15, 1761.	Perine		"on her sick bed"
d. Jan. 1, 1787.			
1786.			
April 16.	John Egbert	Ann	Rev. E. Thorp
Feb. 13.	Mary Egbert		
April 16.	Edward Egbert	Tunis	" "
March 15.	Mary Egbert		
Nov. 2.	Barnabas Sprong	Citie	" "
Sept. 11.	Jane Sprong		
Dec. 17.	Daniel Periene	Lucia	" "
Nov. 22.	Lucia Periene		
Dec. 31.	Henry Barger	David	" "
Nov. 16.	Mary Barger		

BAPTISMS BY REV. FREDERIC MOERING.

DATE	PARENTS	CHILD	SPONSORS
1787.			
Aug. 19.	John Dorset	Cornelius	Edw. Beatty, Edw. Eg-
July 28.	Martha Dorset	Cortelyou	bert, Sarah Cortelyou, Eleanor Beaty
Aug. 23.	Stephen Wood	Richard	Bap. at parents' house
June 24.	Mary Wood	Webb	
Sept. 9.	George Colon	James	James & Cathrine Colon, John Dorset
Aug. 13.	Mary Colon		
d. Jan. 3, 1875.			
Sept. 30.	James Burdine	Dorcas	James & Cathrine Colon, Sarah Boillon
Sept. 6.	Elisabeth Burdine		
Dec. 26.	Peter Perine	Martha	
1787.	Susanna ——		
April 16.			
1786.			
1788.			
Feb. 4.	Cornelius Van der Bilt	Mary	John & Martha Dorset, Doroth. Garrison
1787.			
Dec. 21.	Phebe Van der Bilt		
1788.			
April 13.	John Gerritson	John	Richard Connor, Senr., Lewis & Cathrine Ryerse, Sarah Buillon
March 15.	Elizabeth Gerritson		
April 20.	Edward Beatty	Bittje	Lewis & Cathrine Ryerse, Mary Salome Moering
April 2.	Eleonor Beatty		
April 27.	John Egbert	Lucy	Lewis & Cathrine Ryerse, Salome Moering, Sarah Cortelyou
March 4.	Mary Egbert		
May 11.	Cornelius Bedell	Christian	Israel Bedell, Lewis & Cathrine Ryerse, Salome Moering
May 5.	Elizabeth Bedell	Jacobsen	

DATE	PARENTS	CHILD	SPONSORS
1788.			
Aug. 10.	Peter Perine	Charles	James Colon, George
July 15.	Sussanna Perine		& Mary Colon
Oct. 13.	Peter Haughwort	Aletta	Bap. in parents' house
Oct. 7.	Mary Haughwort		
Nov. 28.	Stephen Martino	Elizabeth	
	Eleonor Martino		
Nov. 30.	Edward Egbert	Sarah	John & Martha Dorset,
Oct. 18.	Mary Egbert		Salome Moering,
d. in 1872.			Sarah Cortelyou
Dec. 21.	Henry Barger	Mary	Lewis & Cathrine
Nov. 17.	Mary Barger		Ryerse
1789.			
Feb. 15.	John Jacobsen	Ann	
1788.	Hilletje Jacobsen		
Dec. 30.			
d. in 1848.			
1789.			
July 19.	Niclas Burgher	Mathias	
July 10.	Cathrine Burgher		
Oct. 18.	Cornelius Van der	Jacob	
Aug. 28.	Bilt	Bap. at home	
	Phebe Van der Bilt		
Nov. 8.	James Burdine	John	James & Cathrine Col-
Sept. 29.	Elizabeth		an, John Dorset
Dec. 6.	John Gerritson	Cathrine	Lewis & Cathrine
Oct. 28.	Elizabeth Gerritson	Conor	Ryerse, Sr. Salome
			Moering.
1790.			
Jan. 9.	John Skerret	Elizabeth	
1789.	Mary Skerret		
Dec. 10.			
1790.			
Jan. 3.	John Egbert	John	Br. Lewis Ryerse, Br.
1789.	Mary Egbert		James Colon, Sr.
Dec. 1.			Salome Moering
1790.			
Feb. 28.	Jacob Cortelyou	Cornelius	John & Martha Dorset,
Feb. 4.	Elizabeth Cortelyou		James Colon
March 27.	John Martino	Charity	Bap. in parents' house
1789.	Jane Martino		
Oct. 1.			
1790.			
April 25.	Georg Colon	David	Edward & Eleonor
March 17.	Mary Colon		Beatty, James Colon
July 6.	John Baker	John Wan-	
June 23.	Charity Baker	del	
Aug. 2.	Peter Perine	John	
1789.	Mary Perine		
Nov. 2.			

Baptism by Rev. John Ettwin.

DATE	PARENTS	CHILD	SPONSORS
1790.			
Aug. 29.	John Dorset	Sarah	Edw. & Eleonor Beatty,
Aug. 26.	Martha Dorset		Salome Moering,
			Sarah Cortelyou

Baptisms by Rev. Frederic Moering.

DATE	PARENTS	CHILD	SPONSORS
Sept. 16.	William Skerret	Hannah	
April 3.	Mary Skerret		
Oct. 31.	John Gerritson	Richard	Rich^d. Conor, Lewis &
Oct. 8.	Elizabeth Gerritson	Conor	Cathrine Ryerse,
			Salome Moering
Nov. 7.	Peter Perine	Sarah	
Sept. 27.	Sussana Perine		
Dec. 27.	Samuel Smith	Abel	Bap. in parents' house
Aug. 25.	Elizabeth Smith		
1791.			
Jan. 2.	John Jacobsen	Cathrine	
1790.	Hilletje Jacobsen		
Nov. 8.			
1791.			
Jan. 11.	Richard Skerret	Thomas	
1790.	Elizabeth Skerret		
Jan. 16.			
1791			
March 25.	Jeremy Hero	John	
1790.	Hannah Hero		
Aug. 30.			
1791.			
March 25.	James Mott	Samuel	
Feb. 10.	Appolona Mott		
May 9.	John Martino	Stephan	
	Jane Martino		
May 29.	Abraham Egbert	Abraham	Edward & Mary Egbert
April 26.	Ann Egbert		
May 29.	Edward Beatty	Eleonor	Lewis & Cathrine
May 6.	Eleonor Beatty		Ryerse
June 20.	Peter Mitchel	Sussanna	
Feb. 19.	Mary Mitchel		
Aug. 28.	Niclas Burgher	John	
July 25.	Cathrine Burgher		
Oct. 27.	Stephen Martino	Ann	
May 14.	Eleonor Martino		
Nov. 6.	James Burdine	Tunis	John & Martha Dorset,
Sept. 29.	Elizabeth Burdine		James Colon
1792.			
Feb. 12.	Peter Perine	Peter	
1791.	Mary Perine		
Oct. 21.			

DATE	PARENTS	CHILD	SPONSORS
1792.			
Feb. 19.	John Egbert	Tunis	
Jan. 15.	Mary Egbert		
May 7.	Cornelius Van der Bilt	Charlotte	
	Phebe Van der Bilt		
May 27.	Robert Dunn	Ann	
April 11.	Bittje Dunn		
	Tunis Egbert	Ann	
June 8.	Ann Egbert		
Aug. 5.	John Van der Bilt	John	
July 2.	Elizabeth Van der Bilt		
Sept. 24.	Richard Conor	Cathrine	Lewis Ryerse, Salome Moering, Mary Claussen
Aug. 10.	Sophia Conor d. Aug. 8, 1878, aged 86 yrs.		
Sept. 24.	John Baker	Joseph	
Aug. 13.	Charity Baker		
Oct. 12.	Joseph Stilwell	Joseph	
July 1.	Susanna Stilwell		
Nov. 25.	John Jacobsen	John	
Oct. 11.	Hilletje Jacobsen	Christian	
	Ab^m. Egbert	Tunis	
Nov. 7.	Ann Egbert		
Nov. 30.	Richard Syloy	Oliver Taylor	
Oct. 20.	Hester Syloy		
1793.			
Feb. 3.	John Garritson	Mary	
Jan. 6.	Elizabeth Garritson		
June 9.	Niclas Burgher	Mary Ann	Edward & Mary Egbert, Sr. Moering
	Cathrine Burgher		
	Jacob Cortelyou	Elizabeth	
March 9.	Elizabeth Cortelyou		
July 7.	Cornelius Bedell	John Van Deventer	John Jacobsen & Hilletje
May 19.	Elizabeth Bedell		
	Henry Barger	John	
Aug. 10.	Mary Barger		
Sept. 15.	Peter Perine	Silas	Peter Perine, Senr., Edward & Mary Egbert
	Mary Perine		
Sept. 27.	Stephan Martino	John	
March 22.	Eleonor Martino		
Oct. 13.	John Dorsitt	John	Edward & Eleonor Beatty, Edw. Egbert
Sept. 23.	Martha Dorsitt		

BAPTISMS BY REV. JAMES BIRKBY

1794.			
Feb. 27.	James Moore	James	James Perine, father & mother of the child
	Catharine Moore		

DATE	PARENTS	CHILD	SPONSORS
1794.			
March 9.	John Egbert	Samuel	Jas. Collon, Edward & Mary Egbert
Jan. 18.	Mary Egbert		
d. 29 Jan., 1825.			
May 14.	Jeremiah Aroe	William	Richard & Mary Skerret
1792 Feb. 25.	Hannah Aroe		
1794.			
May 14.	Peter Mitchel	Mary	Richard & Mary Skerret
1793. Oct. 19.	Mary Mitchel		
1794.			
May 14.	John Skerret	Rachel	Richard & Mary Skerret
1793. Nov. 26.	Mary Skerret		

"b. March 31, 1794, James Bodine & bap. by Rev. J. Birkby, who forgot to enter his name."

1794.			
March 9.	Tunis Egbert Ann Egbert	John	
June 22.	James Lewis Rebecca Lewis	Mary	
June 22.	John Vanderbilt Elizabeth Vanderbilt	Oliver	
June 15. May 19.	Edward Beaty Eleonor Beaty	Edward	
Dec. 7. Oct. 18.	John Jacobson Hilletje Jacobson	Peter	Bap. at their house at New Dorp
Dec. 16. May 27.	Cornelius Van der Bilt Phebe Van der Bilt	Cornelius*	John Hauseman, John Gerritson, P h e b e Van der Bilt
1795.			
Jan. 26. 1794. Dec. 26.	Daniel Guihon Phebe Guihon	Henry Garritson	Henry Garritson, Daniel Guihon, Betsey Garritson

b. Jan. 25, 1775, Eleonor Baker "Forgotten to enter in place"

1795.			
Feb. 15. Jan. 19.	Ab^m. Egbert Ann Egbert	John	Edward & Mary Egbert & the father
April 12. April 6.	Edward Egbert Mary Egbert	Ann	Edward Beatty, Edward Egbert, Sarah Cortelyou
July 12. May 17.	Richard Connor Sophia Connor	Richard	Edw. Beatty, John Dorset, Rich^d. Connor, Margaret Dorset, Eleonor Beatty
July 27. Feb. 7.	Richard Skerrit Elizabeth Skerrit	Elizabeth	Richard Skerrit, S^r., Rich^d. Skerrit, J^r., Mary Skerrit

* Bap. at John Garritson's house.

DATE	PARENTS	CHILD	SPONSORS
1795.			
July 27.	Jaˢ. Mott	Susanna	Edwᵈ. & Abᵐ. Egbert,
June 21.	"Applican" Mott		Elizabeth Skerrit
Aug. 2.	Henry Miller	Thomas	Edward Beatty, John
July 5.	Mary Miller		Dorsett, Martha Dorsett
Aug. 9.	Peter Perine, Jʳ.	Catharine	John Dorsett, Sarah Cortelyou, Martha Dorsett
Aug. 13.	Mr. & Mrs. Ratbon of N. York	Catharine	James Burdine, Betsey Burdine, Martha Dorsett
July 27.	James Mott	Sussanna	
June 21.	Appalian Mott		
July 27.	Richard Skerrit	Elizabeth	
1793. Feb.	Elizabeth Skerrit		
1795.			
Sept. 20.	John Garritson	Jacob	John Garritson, Jaˢ. Collon, Mary Miller
Aug. 24.	Betsey Garritson		
Oct. 25.	Benjamin Joyce	William	Edw. Beatty, James Perine, Anna Birkby, Rebecca Bokee
Sept. 29.	Mary Joyce		
	Benjamin Martino	Hanah	Baptised at home Benjamin & Eliz. Martino
	Hanah Martino		
Dec. 6.	Nicholas Burgher	David	Nicholas Burgher, Nicholas Stilwell, Frances Stilwell
Nov. 18.	Catharine Burgher		
Dec. 10.	Richard Skerrit	Abraham & Richard	Richᵈ. & Mary Skerrit & the parents
1794. Dec. 29.	Anna Skerrit		
1795.			
Dec. 25.	Peter Cortelyou	Cornelius	John & Martha Dorsett, Sarah Cortelyou
Nov. 15.	Amey Cortelyou		
1796.			
Jan. 10.	Nicholas Enyard	Abraham	Tunis & Ann Egbert, the grandmother Enyard
1795. Nov. 17.	Mary Enyard		
1796.			
Jan. 2.	Isaac Seymerson	"Abilgale"	George & Dorothy Barnes, Hannah Barnes
1795. Oct. 15.	Elizabeth Seymerson		
1796. March 8.	Isaac Butler	Daniel	Baptized in parents' house "a few hours before his departure"
Between 4 & 5 yrs. old.			
March 8.	Isaac Butler	Sarah	Bap. at home—ill with measles & expected to die
About 2 yrs. old.			

DATE	PARENTS	CHILD	SPONSORS
1796.			
March 21.	Ruben Symerson Phebe Symerson	Barnet	
March 21.	Walther Dungin Abigal Dungin	Sarah	
April 7. March 21.	Jacob Cortelyou ElizabethCortelyou	Sarah	John & Martha Dorsett, Sarah Cortelyou
May 1. 1794. Oct. 7.	Daniel Noble bap. at home.	Daniel	Jacob Cortelyou & the parents
1796.			
May 29. Jan. 9.	John Britain Rachel Britain	Patience	Tunis & Ann Egbert
June 19.	John Mitchell Mary Mitchell	John & Mary	At old Mr. Skerrit's house
July 10.	Jeremiah Aroe Hannah Aroe	Samuel	John Dorsett, Richard Skerrit
July 31.	James Lewis Rebecca Lewis	Billijah 'dau.'	Jas. Collon, Eleanor Beatty
Oct. 30. Sept. 14.	John Egbert Mary Egbert	Edward	Edw. Beatty, John Dorsett, Sarah Cortelyou, Elizabeth Bodine
1797.			
Jan. 20. 1796. Nov. 20.	John Van der Bilt Elisabeth Van der Bilt	Essabel	Jas. Collon, Cathrine Collon, Sarah Cortelyou
1797.			
Feb. 19. Jan. 21.	Abraham Egbert Ann Egbert	Stephen	Jas. & Cath. Collon, John Dorsett, Sarah Cortelyou
April 9. March 14.	John Garritson Elizabeth Garritson	James Birkby	Henry Miller, John Garritson, Rich^d. Connor, Hannah Birkby, Eliz. Garritson
April 20. Jan. 20.	William Hilliard Sarah Hilliard	Anna Maria	John & Martha Dorset, Sarah Cortelyou
April 30. March 25.	Hugh Gibson Sarah Gibson	Elizabeth	Henry Miller, Martha Dorsett, Sarah Cortelyou
March 26.	John Jacobson Hilletje Jacobson	Eliza	
July 12.	James Bodine Elizabeth Bodine	Edward	Edward Egbert, Ab^m. Egbert
Sept. 3.	Br. & Sr. Barrager	Henry	Edw. Beatty, John Dorsett, Elleonor Beatty, Martha Dorsett
Oct. 23. Sept. 17.		Nicolas Stilwell	Nicholas Burgher, Ann Burgher, Catharine Burgher

DATE	PARENTS	CHILD	SPONSORS
1797.			
Nov. 2.	James Egbert	Sally	Jas. Egbert, Eliz. Egbert, Sr. Birkby
Sept. 10.	Elizabeth Egbert		
Nov. 19.	Daniel De Young	Ann Elizabeth	Daniel De Young, Elizabeth Garritson, Martha Dorset
Sept. 1.	Fanny De Young		
Nov. 19.	Richard Connor	Mary	Richard Connor, Hannah Birkby, Sarah Cortelyou
Sept. 29.	Sophia Connor		
Nov. 27.	Isaac Symerson	Dorothy Barnes	Parents & grandmother
Nov. 17.	Elizabeth Symerson		
Nov. 28.	Ruben Symerson	Daniel	Ruben Symerson, Walther Dungin, Mrs. Dungin
Aug. 26.	Sarah Symerson		
Nov. 27.	Benjamin Martino	Elizabeth	Benijah Martino, Elizabeth Martino, Hannah Martino
Oct. 31.	Hannah Martino		
Dec. 3.	John Britton	John	Tunis & Ann Egbert, James Collon
Oct. 1.	Rachel Britton		
1798.			
Feb. 17.	James Moore	Ann Maria	Bap. by Rev. Frederic Moering
1797.	Cathrine Moore		
Oct. 14.			
1798.			
April 4.	Stephen Martino	Abraham	
March 13.	Eleonor Martino		
May 13.	Br. Edward Beatty	Eleonor	Br. John Dorsett, Sr. Martha Dorsett, Sr. Christine Moering
April 20.	Sr. Eleonor Beatty		
May 20.	Peter Van Pelt	Georg	Jas. & Cathrine Colon, Georg Colon, the child's grandfather
April 6.	Mary Van Pelt		
Whitsunday, May 27.	Amos Rooke, a married man, brought up a Quaker, b. in Philadelphia Co.		Edward Beatty & John Dorsett
1753. March 17.			
1798.			
May 27.	Peter Cortelyou	Sarah Ann	John & Martha Dorsett, Frances Stilwell
May 3.	Amey Cortelyou		
June 11.	Cornelius Van der Bilt	Phebe	Sarah Cortelyou, Eleonor Johnson
Jan. 19.	Phebe Van der Bilt		
June 24.	John Baker	Peter Wandel	James Colon, Edward Egbert, Christine Moering
April 23.	Charity Baker		
Aug. 17.	Richard Skerret	Ruth	
1797.	Elizabeth Skerret		
Dec. 23.			

DATE	PARENTS	CHILD	SPONSORS
1798.			
Aug. 17.	James Skerret, Junr.	William	
1797.	Ann Skerret		
April 23.			
1798.			
Sept. 16.	Br. John Dorset	Peter	Edward Beatty, James
Aug. 27.	Sr. Martha Dorset		& Cathrine Colon
Oct. 17.	John Beatty	John William	
Same day.	Elizabeth Beatty		
Dec. 22.	Walter Dungin	Thomas	
1797.	Abigail Dungin		
Dec. 26.			
1799.			
March 29.	Abraham Egbert	Cornelius	
Jan. 5.	Ann Egbert		
March 30.	John Jacobson	Hilletje	
March 24.	Hilletje Jacobson	Sleik	
April 14.	John Egbert	Thomas	
Feb. 22.	Mary Egbert	Holmes	
May 5.	Daniel Guyon	Daniel	
March 31.	Frances Guyon		
May 19.	James Lewis	Jane	
March 30.	Rebecca Lewis		
Oct. 6.	James Burdine	William	
Aug. 16.	Margret Burdine		
Oct. 6.	John Gerritson	Abraham	
Sept. 8.	Elizabeth Gerritson	Crocheron	
Nov. 24.	Jacob Lezier	Eleonor	
Oct. 10.	Sarah Lezier	Maria	
May 13.	Ruben Seymourson	John	Bap. at parents' house
	Sarah Seymourson		
Dec. 22.	Niclas Burgher	Frances	
Oct. 25.	Cathrine Burgher	Stilwell	
1800.			
Feb. 10.	John Merlin	Abraham	
1799.	Cathrine Merlin		
Sept. 7.			
1800.			
March 12.	Jacob Cortelyou	Gertry	George Colon, Sarah
Feb. 8.	Elizabeth Cortelyou	Martha	Cortelyou, Martha Dorset
June 1.	John Jacobson	Israel	John & Ann Bedell,
April 9.	Hilletje Jacobson	Bedell	Sr. Christine Moering
June 8.	Walter Dungan	Cornelia	Edward Beatty,
March 17.	Abigail Dungan		Eleonor Beatty, Christine Moering
June 8.	Richard Conor	Elizabeth	John & Elizabeth Gerritson Martha Dorsett
April 22.	Sophia Conor		

DATE	PARENTS	CHILD	SPONSORS
1800.			
June 8.	Tunis Egbert	Patience	John Dorsett, Elizabeth Egbert, Chr. Moering
May 9.	Ann Egbert		
Aug. 3.	James Moore	Daniel	Edward & Eleon. Beatty, John Dorsett, Martha Dorsett
1799.	Cathrine Moore		
Nov. 5.			
1800.			
Aug. 31.	John Beatty	Edward	Edw. & Eleon. Beatty, Sarah Cortelyou
July 29.	Elizabeth Beatty		
Sept. 17.	John Britton	Peter	Bap. by Rev. James Birkby
1799.	Rachel Britton		
Oct. 10.			
1800.			
Oct. 5.	Abraham Egbert	Mary Van der Beak	John Dorsett, Mary Van der Beak, Eliz. Gerritson
Aug. 24.	Ann Egbert		
July 1.	Taylor Villette, Judith Villette, of New York	Judith	Br. James Perrine, the mother's father, Sr. Christine Moering
Oct. 26.	Daniel Guyon	Richard Conor	Edward Beatty, Elizabeth Gerritson, C. Moering
Aug. 21.	Frances Guyon		
Oct. 26.	Stephan Martino	Mary	James Colon, Senr., Eliz. Martino, Christina Moering
June 13.	Eleonor Martino		
Nov. 14.	Cornelius Vanderbilt	Jane	Christina Moering, Sarah Cortelyou
Aug. 1.	Phebe Vanderbilt		
Dec. 24.	James Skerret, Junr.	Elizabeth	
April 5.	Ann Skerret		
Dec. 10.	Edward Beatty	James	James Colon, Senr., John & Martha Dorset
Nov. 16.	Eleonor Beatty		
1801.			
Feb. 20.	Amos Rooke	Frederick Moering	John Dorsett, James Perine, Christina Moering, Cathrine Colon
1798.	Martha Rooke		
Feb. 26.			
1801.			
Feb. 20.	Amos Rooke	Cathrine	Same sponsors as other child
1799.	Martha Rooke		
May 19.			
1801.			
Feb. 22.	Peter Cortelyou	Elizabeth	John & Martha Dorsett, Sarah Cortelyou
Jan. 24.	Amy Cortelyou		
1801.			
April 3.	Benajah Martino	Stephan	
1800.	Hannah Martino		
Oct. 29.			

DATE	PARENTS	CHILD	SPONSORS
1801.			
April 5.	James Bodine	Andrew	
Jan. 17.	Margret Bodine		
May 3.	John Baker	Jeremiah	James & Cathrine
March.	Charity Baker		Colon, John Dorsett
July 19.	John Dorsett	Eleonor	Edward & Eleonor
July 13.	Martha Dorsett	Mary	Beatty, Sarah Cortelyou
Sept. 17.	Reuben Simonson	Margret	
May 11.	Jane Simonson		
Sept. 20.	Niclas Burgher	Ann	Edward & Eleonor
Aug. 26.	Cathrine Burgher		Beatty, Christine Moering
Sept. 22.	Peter Colon	George	
June 11.	Hannah Colon		
Oct. 11.	John Vanderbilt	Edward	Edward & Eleonor
Sept. 1.	Elizabeth Vanderbilt		Beatty, James Perine, Sarah Cortelyou
1802.			
Jan. 11.	James Lewis	James Colon	
1801.	Rebecca Lewis	& David	
Dec. 6.		Colon	
1802.			
Feb. 8.	Daniel Guyon	Abraham	
1801.	Frances Guyon		
Dec. 24.			
1802.			
Feb. 21.	John Gerritson	Elizabeth	James Perine, Christine Moering, Sarah Cortelyou
Jan. 20.	Elizabeth Gerritson		
March 21.	John Egbert	Cornelius	James Colon, Senr., James Bodine, Sarah Cortelyou
Jan. 29.	Mary Egbert		
March 22.	Jacob Lezier	Cornelius	Edward & Eleanor Beatty, Christine Moering
March 6.	Sarah Lezier		
March 28.	John Jacobson	Cornelius	John & Cathrine Bedell, James Perine
Feb. 6.	Hillethay Jacobson	Van deventer	
1802.			
May 30.	John Britton	James	
1801.	Rachel Britton		
Dec. 28.			
1802.			
May 9.	James Moore	Catherine	
March 30.	Catherine Moore	Morgan	
Nov. 8.	James Skerret	James	
April 22.	Ann Skerret		

DATE	PARENTS	CHILD	SPONSORS
1802.			
Dec. 12.	Abraham Egbert	James	James Egbert, Edward Beatty, Elizabeth Egbert
Nov. 7.	Ann Egbert		
Dec. 12.	Peter Cortelyou	Lorenz Hilliard	James Egbert, Edward & Eleonor Beatty
Nov. 7.	Amy Cortelyou		
Nov. 14.	John Beatty	Ann	
Oct. 7.	Elizabeth Beatty		
1803.			
March 20.	James Bodine	Elizabeth	
1802.	Margaret Bodine		
Oct. 2.			
1803.			
April 3.	Richard Conor	Jonathan	Edward Beatty, John Dorset, Elizabeth Garritson, Sr. Moering
1802.	Sophia Conor		
Dec. 28.			

1803.   BAPTISMS BY REV. NATHANIEL BROWN.

May 22.	Peter Colon, farmer	Peter	Br. George Colon, child's g'father, Br Henry Miller, married man, Sr. Sarah Cortelyou, widow Sr. Martha Dorsett married
Feb. 22.	Hannah [Lewis, maiden name]		
July 17.	Stephen Martino, farmer	Peter	Br. John Dorset, m. m. Br. Amos Rooke, m m., Br. Niclas Stilwell, s. m.
1802.			
Sept. 5.	Eleonora [Haughwort]		
1803.			
Aug. 21.	Cornelius Egbert, fisherman	Mary Ann	Br. Edward Egberts m. m., Sr. Sarah Egberts, m. w., child's grandparents, Sr MarthaDorsett, m.w
May 8.	Hannah [Houseman]		
Sept. 5.	Andrew Gauthier, merchant, of N.Y.	Thomas	Mr. Thomas Hamersly, Widow Eliza Guthrie & the child's father, all from New York
Aug. 25.	Martha [Buninger]		

Bap. at Bergen Point, N. J., to which place the parents fled some time before on account yellow fever in N. Y. Child died soon after Baptism and was buried at Bergen Point

Aug. 24.	John Barton of N.Y.	William	Br. Henry Miller & his wife, by maiden name Barton, & the gr.-mother
1802.	Ann [Ruebottom], deceased		
Dec. 29.			
d. Aug. 26.	Bap. in Br. Miller's house		

DATE	PARENTS	CHILD	SPONSORS
1803.			
Sept. 7. July 29.	Nicholas Burgher Catharine [Swaim]	Jane	The father Nicholas Burgher, Br. Nicholas Stilwell, s. m., the mother of child
Oct. 1. July 25.	Reuben Symonson, farmer Jane [Decker]	Jane	The father & mother & Rev. Nath¹. Brown
Nov. 24. Sept. 25.	Benajah Martino Hanna [Decker]	Benjamin	The parents & Rev. Nath¹. Brown
Dec. 18. Oct. 26.	Daniel Guyon Frances [Garritson]	Sara	The parents & Sr. Ann C. F. Brown, m. w.
1804.			
Jan. 15. 1803. Nov. 3.	John Vanderbilt, farmer, Elizabeth [Taylor], both Society members	Sarah	Br. Edward Beatty & wife Eleonora, Sr. Sara Cortelyou, wid.
1804.			
March 3. Jan. 4.	Cornelius Vanderbilt, ferryman Phebe [Hand]	Eleonora	Sr. Eleonora Beatty, m. w., the mother Sr. Phebe Vanderbilt, Sr. Sarah Cortelyou, wid.
April 8. Feb. 10.	John Beatty, miller Elizabeth [Lake]	Eleonora	Br. Edward Beatty, Sr. Eleonora Beatty, grandparents, Sr. Sarah Cortelyou, gr.-grandmother
April 15. March 1.	Br. John Jacobsen, farmer Hilletje [Bedell]	Maria	Mr. John Bedell, grandfather, & his wife, Sr. Ann Cath. F. Brown
Whitsunday, May 20. May 11.	Jacob Loziers Sara [Beatty]	Edward	Br. Edward Beatty, gr.-father, Br. John Dorset, m. m., Sr. Eleon Beatty, Sr. Martha Dorset

Bap. by Rev. Geo. Henry Loskilla, Bishop of the United Brethren, on his visitation

June 13.	Mr. Isaac Butler	Catharine	The parents & Rev. Nath¹. Brown
June 13. March 23.	John Skerret, blacksmith Catharine [Perine]	Maria	The father Mr. John Skerret, the aunt Mrs. Skerret, & Rev. Nath¹. Brown
Sept. 1. June 28.	Charles Dey, farmer Mary [M'Ginnis]	Lewis	The parents & Br. Nath¹. Brown

DATE	PARENTS	CHILD	SPONSORS
1804.			
Oct. 7. Sept. 27.	Br. John Garritson Sr. Elis. [Conner], deceased	Hermanns	The father, Br. Richard Connor & wife Sr. Sophia
Oct. 28. Aug. 1.	Walter Dungan, merchant Abigail [Symonson]	Ruth	The father Br. W. Dungan, the mother, Sr. Ann C. F. Brown, m. w., Sr. Eleanora Beatty
Dec. 24. Oct. 7.	John Burbank, fisherman Ann [Egbert]	Ann	Br. Nath¹. Brown, child's gr.-mother, Sr. Mary Egbert, & the child's mother Ann Egbert
1805.			
Jan. 13. 1804. Oct. 29.	John Britton Rachel Britton	Sarah	Br. Edward Beatty, Sr. Eleonora Beatty, Sr. Ann Egbert, wife of Tunis
1705.			
Jan. 17. 1804 April 5. 1805.	James Moore Catherine Moore	David Mercerau	Rev. Nath¹. Brown, Mr. James Moore, the father, Mrs. Cath. Moore, the mother
Jan. 24. 1804. Nov. 8. 1805.	Anthony Riders Mary Riders	William	Br. George Colon, m. m., Mr. Anthony Rider, the father, Mrs. Mary Rider, the mother
March 31. Feb. 7.	Br. Abraham Egbert Sr. Ann Egbert	Edward	Br. Edward Beatty & the child's parents
March 31. March 9.	Br. Jacob Cortelyou Elizabeth Cortelyou	Jacob	Br. John V. D. Jacobson, m. m., the child's parents
March 31. March 18.	Rev. Nathaniel Brown Ann Catharine Frederica Brown Bap. by Rev. N. Brown	Caroline	Br. George Henry Loskiel in Bethlehem, in his place stood Rev. N. Brown, the father, Br. Henry Tenbrook, in his place Br. Edward Beatty, Sr. Mary Magd. Loskiel in her pl. wid. Sarah Cortelyou, Sr. Tenbrook, in N. Y., in her pl. Sr. Eleonor Beatty, Sr. Ann Rosina Kliestin, s. w., of Bethlehem, in her place Sr. Martha Dorset

DATE	PARENTS	CHILD	SPONSORS
1805.			
April 28. March 13.	John Egbert Mary Egbert	Henry	Br. James Egbert, m. m., Br. Nicolas Stilwell, s. m., Sr. Elizabeth Egbert, m. w.
May 5. Jan. 19.	Richard Conner Sophia Connor	William	John Garritson, widower, the child's father Br. Rich^d. Conor, Sr. Ann C. F. Brown, Sr. Ann Egbert, wife of Teunis
May 12. 1804. Dec. 26. 1805.	William Barton, ferryman at Amboy Lucy [Egbert]	John	Br. Tunis Egbert & his wife Sr. Mary Egbert, child's gr.-mother, widow Sr. Sara Cortelyou
May 23. May 5.	Br. Reuben Symonson, farmer & carpenter Jane [Decker]	Hannah	The child's father & mother, Mr. Jacob Symonson, m. m., Mrs. Hetty Symonson, m. w.
May 19. Feb.	James Bodine, farmer Margaret [Oakley]	Israel	Br. Edward Beatty, Br. James Bodine, the father, Sr. Eleonor Beatty
June 2. April 7.	James Skerrit, fisherman Ann ——	John Garritson	Br. John Dorset, Sr Sara Cortelyou, Sr. Martha Dorset
June 9. April 25.	John Beatty, miller Elizabeth Lake	Cornelius	Br. Edw. Beatty, grandfather of child, Br. John Beatty, the father, wid. Sarah Cortelyou, gr.-grandmother of child, Sr. Eleanor Beatty, gr.-mother
Aug. 18. April 5.	Francis, daughter of Silvy and ——		Br. Edw. Beatty, Sr. Eleon Beaty, Sr. Sara Cortelyou
Sept. 22.	Nicolas Burgher, farmer Catharine [Swaim]	Catharine	Br. Edward Beatty, Sr. Eleonora Beatty, Sr. Sara Cortelyou, wid.
Sept. 25. June 5.	Jeremia Aroe, farmer —— [Skerrit]	Sarah	The parents of the child & the brother Richard Aroe
Sept. 25. Aug. 23.	Richard Aroe, farmer Elisabeth [Stilwell]	Joseph	Same sponsors as above. Bap. in house of John Vanderbilt

DATE	PARENTS	CHILD	SPONSORS
1805.			
Oct. 7. April 7.	Stephen Martino, farmer & weaver Eleonore [Haughworth]	Cornelius	The child's father & mother & Br. Nath¹. Brown
Oct. 15. June 23.	Peter Colon Hannah Lewis	Mary	Br. Ruben Symonson, m. m., Sr. Sara Cortelyou, wid., Sr. Ann Egbert, wife of Tunis
Nov. 3. Oct. 4.	Isaac Barton, carpenter Catharine [Colon]	James	Br. John Dorset, m. m., Br. Jacob Cortelyou, m. m , Sr. Sarah Cortelyou, wid., Sr. Martha Dorset
Nov. 9. Oct. 31.	Peter Cortelyou Amy [Hilliard]	Peter Lochman	Br. John Dorset, md., Br. Jacob Cortelyou, md., Sr. Martha Dorset, md.
Dec. 1. Oct. 22.	Daniel Guyon, carpenter & farmer Frances [Garritson]	Cornelius	Br. Edward Beatty, md., Sr. Eleonor Beatty, md, Sr. Sara Cortelyou, wid.
Dec. 15.	John Skerrit, blacksmith Catharine [Perine]	Lucy Ann	Br. Edward Beatty, Sr. Eleanor Beatty, Sr. Sara Cortelyou
1806.			
April 27. Feb. 19.	John Vanderbilt, farmer Elizabeth Taylor	Jacob	Br. Edward Beatty, Br. Nath¹. Brown, Sr. Eleanor Beatty
Aug. 3. Feb. 26.	James Bodine, farmer Margreth [Oakly]	Margreth	Br. James Bodine, the father, Br. Edw. Beatty, Sr. Marg. Bodine, the mother
July 26. May 18.	Mr. James Moore Catharine [Perine]	John	Br. Nath¹. Brown, the child's father & mother
June 15. May 12.	Jacob Lozier, mason Sara [Beatty]	William	Br. Edward Beatty, the gr.-father, Sr. Eleonore Beatty, grandmother, Br. Nathaniel Brown
Sept. 26. Aug. 24.	Isaac Burbank, oysterman Sara [Egbert]	Mary Ann	Br. Edward Beatty, Sr. Sara Cortelyou, gr.-grandmother of child, Sr. Eleonor Beatty
Aug. 31. July 26.	Cornelius Beatty, storekeeper Ann [Jacobson]	John Jacobson	Br. Edward Beatty, the gr.-father, Sr. Eleon. Beatty, Sr. Martha Dorset, md.

DATE	PARENTS	CHILD	SPONSORS
1806.			
Nov. 8.	John Burbank, farmer & fisherman	Mary	Br. Edward Beatty, Sr. Eleon. Beatty, Sr. Ann Egbert, Ab^m.'s wife
July 17.	Ann [Egbert]		
Nov. 23.	John Jacobson, farmer	Bedell	Mr. John Bedell, the ch. gr.-father, John Jacobson, the father, the grandmother Mrs. Bedell, the mother of ch., Sr. Ann Cath. Frederica Brown
Oct. 9.	Hilletje [Bedell]		
Nov. 30.	Joseph Egbert, farmer	John	Br. John Egbert, gr.-father, Br. James Egbert, md., Sr. Mary Egbert, gr.-mother
	Jane [Merlin]		
Dec. 27.	Reuben Simonson, farmer	Mathias Decker	Br. Reuben Simonson, the ch.'s father, Sr. Jane Simonson, the mother, Br. Nathl. Brown
Nov. 21.	Jane [Decker]		
Dec. 27.	Charles Dey, farmer	David	The child's father & mother Mr. Chas. Dey & Mrs. Mary Dey, & Br. Nathl. Brown
Sept. 17.	Mary [M'Ginnis]		
1807.			
Feb. 28.	William Beatty, tanner & currier	Henry Barger	Br. Edw. Beatty, gr.-father, Sr. Eleon. Beatty, gr.-mother, wid. Mary Barger, gr.-mother, & the father. Bap. in gr.-parent's house
Same day.	Mary [Barger]		
May 10.	Abraham Egbert, farmer & weaver	Joseph	Br. John Dorset, Sr. Martha Dorset, Br. James Egbert
April 10.	Ann [Martino]		
May 31.	Benajah Martino, farmer & weaver	Gabriel	Br. Edw. Beatty, Sr, Sarah Cortelyou, wid., & child's father Br. Benajah Martino
March 25.	Hanna Decker		
June 14.	John, a md. man, blacksmith, eldest son of —— Marsh		Br. Edw. Beatty, Br. James Egbert
1774.			
Nov. 29, at Amboy, N. J.	The bap. was administered by Rev. John Renatus Verbeck, here on a visit from Berthelsdorf, Germany, the present residence of Directors of the Brethrens' Congregations.		

DATE	PARENTS	CHILD	SPONSORS
1807.			
June 21.	John Britton, boats-	Abraham &	Br. Tunis Egbert, Sr.
April 28.	man	Ann	A. C. F. Brown, Sr.
	Rachel [Burbank]		Ann Egbert, & the
Bap. at parent's house near Quarantine.			child's parents
June 21.	Michael Marsack,	Harvey	Same as above & at
1806.	boatsman		same time & place
Sept. 29.	—— [Jennings], his wife		
1807.			
July 26.	John Egbert, far-	William	Br. James Egbert, Br.
	mer & weaver		Tunis Egbert, Sr.
	Mary [Holmes]		Elis. Egbert, Sr.
			Ann Egbert
July 31.	Nicolas Burgher	Elizabeth	Br. Edw. Beatty, Sr.
Sept. 6.	Catharine Swaim		Eleonora Beatty, Sr.
			Ann Burgher, gr.-mother, from N. Y.
Sept. 16.	James Skerrit,	Ann	Jacob Cortelyou, William Beatty, the
April 6.	waterman & cop-		mother of ch. & gr.-
	persmith		mother, Mrs. Skerrit
	Ann [Garrison]		
Dec. 27.	Richard Connor,	Sophia Ann	Sr. Ann Egbert, &
Oct. 6.	surveyor, currier		child's parents
	& farmer		
	Sophia [Clauson]		
Oct. 7.	Cornelius Vander-	Jacob	Br. Nath¹. Brown, Dor-
Sept. 2.	bilt, ferryman &		othy Swaime, md.,
	farmer		Eleonore Johnson,
1808.	Phebe [Hand]		wid.
March 8.	John Skerrit,	Catharine	Br. Amos Rooks, gr.-
Feb. 15.	weaver & fisher-	Elizabeth	father, Martha
	man		Rooks, gr.-mother,
	Frances [Rooks]		& child's parents
Bap. at parent's house at the Narrows			
March 8.	Elijah Cribbs	Richard	Br. Abraham Binning-
1807.	Magdalen [M'Lean]		er from N. Y., Br.
June 26.			Nathaniel Brown,
1808.			the child's mother
March 8.	Richard Silvy, fish-	Hester	Same as above
1807.	erman		
Aug. 28.	Hester [Taylor]		
1808.			
March 19.	Charles Simonson,	Cornelius	Br. Nath¹. Brown,
1807.	farmer		Phebe Vanderbilt,
Oct. 3.	Mary Vanderbilt		gr.-mother, & child's
Ch. bap. in gr.-parent's C. Vanderbilt's			mother
Ferry House.			
1808.			
March 28.	Abraham Egbert,	Eliza Ann	Br. Nath¹. Brown, Br.
Feb. 11.	shoemaker		John Marsh, & child's
	Mary, his wife		mother

DATE	PARENTS	CHILD	SPONSORS
1808.			
April 3.	George W. Ingra-	George	Br. N. Brown, Br. John
1807.	ham, pilot	Washing-	Marsh, Sr. Phebe
Feb. 2.	Elizabeth, his wife	ton	Vanderbilt, & child's mother
1808.			
May 8.	Peter Breasted,	John Wil-	Br. N. Brown, Br. Ab^m.
1807.	blacksmith	liam	Bieninger fr. N. Y.,
Aug. 30.	Sara [Cribbs]		Sr. Frances Stilwell, s. w.
1808.			
May 19.	James Bodine, far-	Abraham	Br. Bodine, ch.'s father,
1807.	mer		Br. Constantine Mil-
Dec. 23.	Margaret Oakley		ler, wid., from Penn., & child's mother Sr. Bodine
1808.			
May 29.	Jacob Vanhorne, of N. Y. Mary [Wood]	Sarah Egbert	Br. N. Brown, Mrs. Charles Dey & child's mother
July 16.	Joseph Egbert,	Elizabeth	Br. Ab^m. Egbert, Br.
May 14.	oysterman & farmer Jane [Merlin]		James Egbert, Sr. Ann Egbert, Ab^m.'s wife
July 16.	Cornelius Beatty, storekeeper Ann [Jacobson]	Catharine Eleonore	Br. Edw. Beatty, gr.-father, Sr. Eleonore Beatty, gr.-mother, Sr. Frances Stilwell, s. w.
July 24.	John Burbank,	Abraham	Ab^m. Burbank, gr.-
March 6.	oysterman & farmer Ann [Egbert]		father, & child's parents
Aug. 31.	Cornelius Egbert,	Elizabeth	Br. John Dorset, Sr.
March 6.	weaver & farmer Naatje [Houseman]		Martha Dorset, Sr. Sara Cortelyou, wid., Mrs. N. Egbert, ch.'s mother
Nov. 27.	William Drury,	John	Br. N. Brown, Sr. Ann
Sept. 17.	sailor Susanna [Stilwell]		Brown, ch.'s mother Mrs. Drury, ch.'s gr.-mother Mrs. Sus. Stilwell
Aug. 14.	Michael Marsack,	Mary Mar-	Br. Ab^m. Egbert, Br.
July 28.	boatman Rachel [Jennings]	garet	John Britton, Mrs. Jennings, the ch.'s gr.-mother
1809.			
Jan. 1.	John Skerrit, black-	Joseph	Br. N. Brown, Sr.
1808.	smith		Eleon. Beatty, the
Nov. 13.	Catharine [Perine]		child's mother

DATE	PARENTS	CHILD	SPONSORS
1809. Jan. 9. 1808. Dec. 2.	Daniel Guyon, carpenter & farmer Elizabeth, his wife, late Young, maiden name Clawson	Sophia Catharine	Br. N. Brown, the child's parents, Dan¹. & Eliz. Guyon
Bap. in parent's house at the Manor			
1809. Feb. 12. Jan. 13.	Abraham Egbert, weaver & farmer Ann Martino, his wife	Ann	Br. Abᵐ. Egbert. the father of ch., Sr. Ann Egbert, the mother, Sr. Ann C. F. Brown, Marg. Lewis, s. w.
April 9.	John Vanderbilt, farmer & shoemaker Elizabeth [Taylor]	Cornelius	Br. Edw. Beatty, Br. N. Brown, Sr. Ann C.F. Brown & child's mother
April 17. 1808. Aug. 28.	Henry Roy Dunham, seaman Eve [Skerrit], both of N. Y.	Henry Roy	Br. N. Brown, Cath. Skerrit, md., Eve Dunham, the mother
1809. June 4. April 14.	John Britton, boatsman Rachel [Burbank]	Lovina	Sr. Ann Egbert & the child's parents
June 4. March 25.	Abraham Van Pelt, shoemaker Mary [Fountain]	Amy	Sr. Eleonore Beatty & the child's parents
July 31. 1808. Dec. 13.	Stephen Martino, farmer & weaver Eleonore Haughwout	Catharine Hanna	Br. Nath¹. Brown & the child's parents
1809. Aug. 30. April 6.	Charles Dey Mary [M'Ginny]	Uzal M'Ginny	Br. Nath¹. Brown & child's parents
Sept 3. July 16.	John V. D. Jacobson, farmer Hilletje [Bedell]	Abraham Van Deventer	The parents of the child, Corn. Beatty, the brother-in-law, Mrs. Ann Beatty, the sister
Sept. 17. July 11.	Reuben Simonson, farmer Jane [Decker]	Lena	Br. Edward Beatty, Sr. Eleonore Beatty & child's parents
March 26. Jan. 28.	Jacob Lozier, mason Sarah [Beatty]	Henry Cruse	Br. Edward Beatty, Sr. Eleonor Beatty & child's mother
July 3. May 1.	John Beatty, miller Elizabeth [Lake]	Daniel Lake	Br. Edw. Beaty, Sr. Eleon. Beatty, gr.-parents, & the ch.'s parents

DATE	PARENTS	CHILD	SPONSORS
1809. Sept. 10. 1808. Oct. 15.	James Moore, tailor Catharine [Perine]	Elizabeth	Sr. Eleonore Beatty & the child's parents
1809. Oct. 29.	Nicolas Burgher, farmer Catharine [Swaim]	James	Br. Nath¹. Brown & child's parents
Nov. 12. Aug. 6.	Richard Skerrit, Jr., coppersmith Ann [Garrison]	Thomas	The gr.-mother, Mrs. Skerrit, the mother, Br. Nath¹. Brown
Nov. 16. Aug. 12.	Charles Simonson, carpenter & farmer Mary [Vanderbilt]	Phebe Ann	Br. Nath¹. Brown & child's parents
Nov. 16. April 24.	George Washington Ingraham, pilot Elizabeth, his wife	Eliza Margaret Rider	Br. N. Brown, Sr. Mary Simonson, md., & child's mother
Nov. 16. Aug. 12.	Richard Silvy, farmer & fisherman Hester [Taylor]	William	Br. N. Brown, Br. Chaˢ. Simonson, Hester Silvy, the mother
1810. Jan. 7. 1809. Nov. 24.	William Beatty, tanner & currier Mary [Barger]	William	Br. Edw. Beatty, the gr.-father, Sr. Eleon. Beatty, gr.-mother, & child's parents
1810. April 10. March 18.	Cornelius Beatty, storekeeper Ann [Jacobson]	Edward Christian	Br. N. Brown, Sr. Eleon. Beatty, gr.-mother, H. Jacobson, gr.-mother, & child's mother
July 19. June 25.	David Proll, farmer & weaver Catharine [Dorset]	Catharine Mary	The child's parents, the gr.-mother Martha Dorset, the gr.-mother Sarah Cortelyou
Sept. 2. July 7.	Barnet Simonson, farmer Sarah [Romeyn]	Sarah	Br. B. Simonson, the father, Sr. Sarah Simonson, the mother, widow Romeyn, the gr.-mother
Sept. 2. July 8.	Moses Wood, turner Catharine [Colon]	Ruth Mary	The child's parents & Sr. —— Leonard, md., from N. Y.
Sept. 2. 1809. Sept. 5.	Richard Connor, farmer, currier & surveyor Sophia [Clauson]	Daniel	Br. Edward Beatty, Sr. Eleon. Beatty, Sr. Ann C. F. Brown, & ch.'s father

DATE	PARENTS	CHILD	SPONSORS
1810. Oct. 28. 1809. Nov. 15.	William Barton, oysterman, at Amboy Lucy [Egbert]	Mary Ann	Br. Nath¹. Brown, the gr.-mother, Mary Egbert, Sr. Jane Egbert, md.
1811. Feb. 8. 1810. Aug. 27.	Abraham Simonson Ann [Praull]	Elizabeth Hilliard	Br. & Sr. Peter & Amy Cortelyou & the child's parents. Baptized in John Dorset's house
1811. Feb. 25. Jan. 31.	Reuben Simonson, farmer Hanna [Decker]	Abigail Ann	Br. Reuben Simonson, the father, Hanna Simonson, the mother, Br. Barnet Simonson, md., Sr. A. C. F. Brown, md.
March 7. Feb. 15.	Amos Rooks, wheelwright & carpenter Mary [Skerrit], deceased	Mary	The father A. Rooks, wid., Bro. Nath¹. Brown, Sr. Frances Skerrit, md. Bap. in gr.-parent's house
March 7. Jan. 23.	John Jennings, waterman Catharine [Skerrit]	William	The parents of child & Br. Nath¹. Brown
March 8. Jan. 11.	William Drury, seaman Susan [Stilwell]	Joseph	Mr. Jos. Stilwell, gr.-father, Mrs. Sus. Stilwell, gr.-mother, & child's mother
March 8. 1809. Aug. 5.	Odissa Shay, seaman Appolonia [late Mott, nee Skerrit]	Henry	Jos. Stilwell, md., Susan Stilwell, md., & child's mother Bp. in Mr. Jos. Stillwell's house
1811. March 19. 1810. Nov. 20.	John Britton, boatsman Rachel [Burbank]	Dorcas	Br. Nath¹. Brown & child's parents
1811. March 19. 1810. Nov. 20.	Michael Marsac, boatsman Rachel [Jennings]	Olive Ann	Mr. John Britton & wife, Mrs. Rachel Britton, & child's mother Mrs. R. Marsac
1811. March 19. Feb. 24.	John De Forest, seaman Charlotte [Vanderbilt], his w	Gerardus	Br. Nath¹. Brown, Mrs. Phebe Vanderbilt, the gr.-mother, & Mrs. Ch. De Forest, the ch.'s mother

DATE	PARENTS	CHILD	SPONSORS
1811.			
May 19.	Abraham Egbert, farmer Ann [Martino], his wife	Hertje [daughter]	The parents Br. Ab^m. & Sr. Ann Egbert, Sr. Frances Stilwell, s. w., Sr. Ann, wife Tunis Egbert
March 28.			
March 19. 1808.	William M'Lean, carpenter Isabella [Wreath], his wife	Lydia Ann	Br. N. Brown, Mrs. M'Lean, ch.'s mother, Mrs. Debora V. Duzer
Dec. 11. 1810.		Charles Simonson	
Dec. 29.			Same as above & his sister Lydia Ann
1811.			
May 6. 1810.	Abraham Merril, farmer Elizabeth [Martino] his wife	Mahala	The parents & the gr.-mother Mrs. Eleonor Martino
April 11. 1811.			
July. 28. Feb. 24.	Abraham Van Pelt, shoemaker Mary [Fountain], his wife	Sarah	Br. N. Brown, Sr. A. C. F. Brown & child's mother
Aug. 4. May 12.	Isaac Burbank, farmer Sarah [Egbert], his wife	Edward Egbert	Br. N. Brown, Sr. A. C. F. Brown, Sara Burbank, the mother
Aug. 25. 1810. Dec. 19, in Jersey.	Charles Egbert, Christina [Pelec], his wife, from Jersey	John James	The child's parents & Sara Egbert, wid., the gr.-mother in whose house the baptism was ministered
1811.			
Sept. 15. May 19.	Joseph Silvy, laborer Elizabeth [Skerrit],	Eliza	Br. N. Brown, Sr. A. C. F. Brown & ch.'s mother
Aug. 14. Aug. 13.	John M'Kinlay, schoolmaster Lydia [Rea], his wife Both lately from Ireland	William	The father of child & his brother Wm. M'Kinlay from Philadelphia, & his wife

So far an extract was made and sent to Europe to the U. C. Conf.

1812.			
Jan. 13. 1811. in Dec. 1812.	Joseph Egbert, farmer & weaver Jane [Merlin], his wife	Mary	The parents & gr.-mother Mary Egbert
Feb. 20. 1810. Nov. 27.	Jacob Lozier, mason Sara [Beatty], his wife	John Beatty	Br. Nathl. Brown, Jacob Cortelyou, md., gr. gr.-mother of ch. Sara Cortelyou Bp. in John Dorset's house

DATE	PARENTS	CHILD	SPONSORS
1812.			
March 5. Jan. 11, in N. Y. d. March 8.	John Peters, seaman Sara [Pennycant], his wife	Abigail Ann	The mother, Mrs. Susan Stilwell, Mrs. Steward, at whose house the baptism was performed
March 25. Jan. 5.	James Skerrit, waterman & coppersmith Ann [Garrison], his wife	Mary	Br. Nath¹. Brown, the mother & the gr.-mother Mrs. Skerrit
	From the Quarantine on St. Island		
April 12. March 25.	Richard Connor, farmer & surveyor Sophia [Clawson], his wife	Jane	Br. N. Brown, the ch. father R. Connor, the ch.'s aunt Elis. Guyon
May 1. 1811. Nov. 9.	Richard Harcourt, Rosetta [M'Dewil], both from Ireland and employed at Quarantine	Daniel	The child's father, Br. John Vanderbilt & ch's mother
1812. May. 10. Feb. 19.	John Vanderbilt, employed at Quarantine Elizabeth [Taylor], his wife	Jacob	The parents & Br. Edwᵈ. Beatty
May 17. April 24.	Cornelius Beatty, storekeeper in N. Y. Ann [Jacobson], his wife	Alfred Eberhard, William Montgomery, twins	Br. Edw. Beatty, gr.-father, Br. John Jacobson, gr.-father, Sr. Eleonor Beatty, gr.-mother, Sr. Hilletje Jacobson, gr.-mother, Sr. Ann C. F. Brown
June 30. May 2.	William Beatty, tanner & currier Mary [Barger], his wife	Eleonore Maria	Br. Edw. Beatty, gr.-father, Sr. Eleon. Beatty, gr.-mother, & the child's mother
July 30. May 10.	John Skerrit, blacksmith Catharine [Perine], his wife	Catharine	Br. N. Brown & child's parents
Sept. 13. 1811. Feb. 1. 1812.	Abraham Aston, clerk in N. Y. Ann [Colon], his wife	Isaac	The ch.'s mother, Br. Dan¹. Guyon, md., George Colon, wid.
Sept. 13. Aug. 1.	Moses Wood, turner Catharine [Colon], his wife	Abraham Aston	Geo. Colon, wid., Br. Dan¹. Guyon, md., & his wife Elizabeth, child's mother

DATE	PARENTS	CHILD	SPONSORS
1812.			
Dec. 17. Sept. 30. In the house	Thomas Skerrit, weaver Martha [Cribbs], his wife	Lucy Ann	Br. N. Brown & wife, Sr. A. C. F. Brown, & child's mother Martha Skerrit
Dec. 20. Sept. 19. In ch.	Michael Marsac, boatman Rachel [Jennings], his wife	Henry	Br. Edward Beatty, Sr. Eleon. Beatty, & child's mother
1813. Jan. 7. 1812. Aug. 31.	Stephen Wood, wheelwright Ann [Bodine]	James	Br. Ab^m. Egbert & child's parents
1813. Feb. 23. 1812. Sept. 30. At parent's house	John Bird, waterman Susan [Mitchell],	Peter Duindam	Br. N. Brown, Mrs. Mary Mott & child's mother
1813. Feb. 23. 1812. Feb. 25.	Stephen Mott, laborer Mary [Mitchell],	James	Same sponsors as Preceding. Bap. by Rev. N. Brown
1813. Feb. 23. Jan. 5.	David Barger, blacksmith Sarah [Cortelyou], his wife	Mary	The child's parents, Bro. Edwd. Beatty Bp. by Rev. N. Brown
Feb. 28. Jan. 30.	Jacob Beatty, saddler & harnessmaker Elizabeth [Cortelyou]	Jacob Cortelyou	The gr.-father Br. Edw. Beatty, the gr.-mother Sr. Eleon. Beatty, & the child's father Bp. by Rev. N. Brown
Aug. 5. May 19.	John Jacobson, farmer Hilletje [Bedell], his wife	Matilda	Child's father, Cath. Bedell, the gr.-mother, Sr. Mortimer
Aug. 5. July 9.	Abraham Egbert, farmer & weaver Ann [Martino], his w.	Benjamin, the 13th ch.	No sponsors given in the memorandum left by Bro. Mortimer, minister of the Un. Bros. Ch. at N. Y., & who bap. here during Br. Brown's absence
Aug. 5. July 9.	John Deforest Charlotte [Vanderbilt], his wife	Phebe Ann	Bap. by Rev. Benj. Mortimer. No sponsors given

DATE	PARENTS	CHILD	SPONSORS
1813.			
Aug. 5.	Cornelius Johnson	Charles	Bap. by Rev. Benj. Mortimer. No sponsors given
July 9.	Elizabeth [Corsen], his wife		
June 15.	Richard Silvy	Jane	The mother & gr.-mother & Sr. Ann Brown. Bap. by Rev. N. Brown
March 19.	"Rachel" [Hester?]		
Aug. 25.	David Prawl	Sarah Ann	Bap. by Rev. Benj. Mortimer
July 7.	Catharine, his wife		
June 24.	William M'Lean	Joseph Lake	Bap. by Rev. N. Brown & sponsors not mentioned
Feb. 1.	Isabella, his wife		

BAPTISMS BY REV. JOHN C. BECHLER.

Oct. 24.	John Beatty, miller	Margaret	Br. Edw. Beatty, gr.-father, Sr. Eleon. Beatty, gr.-mother, Sr. Augusta Henr. Bechler, md. Bap. at parent's house
Aug. 27.	Elizabeth [Lake], his wife	Eliza, 7th ch., 3d dau.	
1814.			
June 12.	Reuben Simonson, farmer	Jane, 10th ch, 6th dau.	The child's parents, Br. Barnet Simonson. Bap. at parents' house
May 19.	Jane Decker, his wife		
June 18.	Richard Connor, farmer & surveyor	Abraham Van Vechten, 11th ch. & 5th son	Mrs. Clawson, gr.-mother, the child's father, the child's nurse, Mrs. Mersereau
1813.			
Aug. 28.	Sophia [Clawson], his wife		
1814.			
June 26.	John Skerret, blacksmith	Christiana	Child's mother, Edw. Beatty, md., Ann Egbert, Tunis' wife
April 7.	Catharine [Perine], his wife		
June 26.	Joseph Mellington, shoemaker	Ann Eliza, 1st ch.	Bap. at home, quarter mile from Church the father & John Vanderbilt, md.
June 23.	Lucy [Crips], his wife		
June 26.	Susan Drury [Stillwell], maiden name	John Jeremiah, 3d ch. & 3d son	Bap. at same time & place as above & same sponsors
March 10.			

DATE	PARENTS	CHILD	SPONSORS
1814.			
July 3. June 26.	Rev. John C. Bechler, Pastor of Ch. at Staten Island Augusta Henrietta [Cunow], his wife	Julius Theodore, 2d ch., 1st son	Br. & Sr. Edw. & Eleon. Beatty, Br. & Sr. John & Elizabeth Vanderbilt, standing for Charles Fr. & Dorothea S. Seidel of Nazarath, Penn., John & Hilletje Jacobson, for Br. & Sr. Henry D. & Anna Mar. Smith of Nazareth, Penn.
Aug. 28. July 19.	Moses Wood, turner Catharine [Colon], his wife	Jacob Clendenne, 3d ch., 2d son	Br. Edw. Beatty & his wife Sr. Eleon. Beatty, Br. Reuben Simonson, md.
Sept. 5. March 26.	Cornelius Beatty, at present Tavern keeper at the Narrows near Pt. Richmond Ann [Jacobson], his wife	Hellethah Ann	Br. Edw. Beatty, gr.-father, Sr. Eleon. Beatty, gr.-mother, Helletje Jacobson, gr.-mother
Sept. 20. 1813. Oct. 23, in Bethlehem Township, N. J.	Charles Egbert, shoemaker Christiana [Pels], his wife	Sarah Ann, 2d ch., 1st dau.	Sarah Egbert, wid., gr.-mother of child, in whose house it was baptized, & the child's father, C. Egbert
1814.			
Dec. 3. July 8.	James Scherret Ann [Garretson], his wife	Esther, 10th ch., 4th dau.	John C. Bechler, md., Sarah Cortelyou, wid., Martha Dorsett, md.
1815.			
Jan. 12. 1814. Dec. 9.	John Decker, waterman Ann [Egbert], his wife, Edward's dau.	Jane, 1st ch.	John Dorsett, md., Sarah Burbank, md., & the child's mother
1815.			
Feb. 7. 1814. Nov. 7.	Cornelius Vanderbilt, Junr., son of Com. V. Sophia [Johnson]	Phebe Jane	Rev. J. C. Bechler, the ch.'s mother, Jane Fountain, md. Bap. at house of C. Vanderbilt, Jr., near Van Duyer's Ferry

DATE	PARENTS	CHILD	SPONSORS
1815.			
Feb. 11. Jan. 8.	John Vanderbilt, Jr. [son of John] Celia [Story], his wife	Elizabeth, 1st child	John Vanderbilt, md., ch.'s gr.-father, Abm. Egbert, md., Ann Egbert, wife of Abm.
May 7. Jan. 18.	John Beatty Elizabeth Lake, his wife	Alfred, 8th ch., 5th son	Edw. Beatty, the gr.-father, John Beatty, the father, Aug. Henr. Bechler, md.
July 30. May 31.	William Beatty, tanner & currier Mary Barger, his wife	Emmeline	Bro. Edw. Beatty, the gr.-father, Sr. Eleon. Beatty, the gr.-mother, Sarah Lozier, md., the ch. aunt. Wm. Beatty resides at present in New York
Aug. 13. 1814. Aug. 28.	Richard Connor, farmer Sophia Clawson, his wife	Stephen Alexander, 12th ch., 6th son	Richard Connor, Senr., the ch.'s father, John Christian Jacobson, md., Miss Jemima Pearson
1815. Aug. 13. 1814. Dec. 15.	John Christian Jacobson, farmer Catharine Connor, his wife	Mary Luisa, 1st ch.	Richd. Connor, Senr., the ch.'s gr.-father, J. Chr. Jacobson, the father, Sr. Aug. Henr. Bechler, Jemima Pearson, unmd.
1815. Aug. 20. July 11.	Abraham Egbert, farmer & weaver Ann Martino, his wife	Catharine, 14th ch., 4th dau.	Br. Barnet Simonson, md., Sr. Eleon. Beatty, md., Sr. Ann Egbert, wife of Tunis
Nov. 5. Sept. 21.	Peter Wood, waterman Sarah Ann Cortelyou, his wife	Emmeline Hillyer, 1st ch.	Peter Cortelyou, gr.-father, Emma Cortelyou, gr.-mother, Elizabeth Cortelyou, md.
Nov. 5. Sept. 30.	Jacob Beatty, saddle & harness maker Elizabeth Cortelyou, his wife	William Lake, 2d ch.	Br. Peter Cortelyou, Sr. Amy Cortelyou, & ch.'s father
Nov. 26. Oct. 4.	John Vanderbilt, farmer Elizabeth, his wife	Richard Taylor, 8th son	Br. Edw. Beatty, Sr. Eleon Beatty, the child's father

DATE	PARENTS	CHILD	SPONSORS
1815.			
Nov. 26. Sept. 25.	Tunis Egbert, Abm's son, carpenter Isabella Vanderbilt, his wife	Abraham, 1st ch.	Br. Edw. Beatty, Br. John Vanderbilt, ch.'s gr.-father, Sr. Eleon. Beatty
Bap. in Ch. on Sunday, Dec. 10. Dec. 7.	Rev. John C. Bechler Augusta Henrietta [Cunow], his wife	Francis Eugenius, 3d ch., 2d son	Br. Edw. Beatty, md., Sr. Eleon. Beatty, md., Br. Nicholas Stilwell, unm., Sr. Francis Stilwell, unm.
Dec. 25. Dec. 14.	Joseph Mellington, shoemaker Lucy Crips, his wife	Joseph Henry, 2d ch., 1st son	Bap. at home, no sponsors given
Dec. 25. Sept. 11.	Thomas Skerrit Martha, his wife [Crips]	William Crips, 2d ch., 1st son	Bap. at house of Mr. Mellington. No sponsors given
Dec. 31. Nov. 15.	John De Forest [De Fries], waterman Charlotte Vanderbilt, his wife	John, 3d ch., 2d son	Jacob Beatty, md., Charles Simonson, md., Mary Simonson, md. Baptism in house of Mr. Jacob Beatty
Dec. 31. Oct. 9.	John Jacobson, farmer Hilletje Bedell, his wife	Lucretia, 14th ch., 7th dau.	Abm. Egbert, Senr., the ch.'s mother, Sr. Augusta Henr. Bechler, md.
1816. Jan. 3. 1815. Dec. 3.	David Praul, weaver Catharine Dorsett, his wife	Charlotte, 3d dau., 4th ch.	Br. J. C. Bechler, Sr. A. H. Bechler, Martha Dorsett, the ch.'s gr.-mother
1816. May 5. April 12.	Nathaniel H. Martin Sarah Dorsett, his wife	William Heard, 1st ch.	John Dorsett, Sen., the ch.'s gr.-father, Br. Edward & Sr. Eleon. Beatty. Baptism at house of John Dorsett, Sen., in presence of a number of relations
May 15. 1815. Nov. 9.	Reuben Simonson, farmer Jane Decker, his wife	Hylah, 11th ch., 7th dau.	The child's parents. Bap. at home
1816. June 21. 1815. July 11.	Stephen Wood, carpenter Ann Marsh, his wife	Elias Marsh, 1st ch.	Br. J.C. Bechler, Tunis Egbert, Senr., & his wife Ann Egbert

DATE	PARENTS	CHILD	SPONSORS
1816.			
June 10. 1815. Jan. 29.	James M'Lean, Capt. in U. S. service at Fort Tompkins, Staten Island Mary Ann Potter, his wife	James Potter, 1st ch.	The child was baptized by particular solicitation of the parents though being better than a year old, as he was near dissolution
1816. June 22. b. ———.	Oscar Fitz Patrick, Fort Tompkins.	youngest ch. of William Dustan at Bp. on Death-bed.	
July 21. in April.	Mathew Decker, waterman Ann Colon, his wife	Jane Maria, 1st ch.	Br. Edw. & Sr. Eleon. Beatty, child's mother
Aug. 2. 1815(?). Oct. 25.	Nicholas Crocheron, Junr. Ann Guyon, his wife	William Henry, 1st ch.	Rev. J. C. Bechler, Elizabeth Guyon, md., Mary Young, unmd. Bap. in house of Mr. Danl. Guyon
1816. Sept. 8. 1815. Nov. 22.	John Brittain Rachel Burbank, his wife	Jacob, 12th ch., 6th son	The parents of the child & Abm. Van Pelt, md.
1816. Sept. 8. April 4.	Abraham Van Pelt Mary Fountain, his wife	Henry, 3d ch., 1st son	The parents and John Brittain
Sept. 18. April 2.	Richerd Connor, farmer & surveyor Sophia Clawson, his wife	Henry Augustus, 13th ch., 7th son	Rev. J. C. Bechler, Sr. Aug. Henr. Bechler, the child's father
Sept. 29. Aug. 17.	Moses Wood, turner Catharine Colon, his wife	George Colon, 4th ch., 3d son	Br. Edw. & Sr. Eleon. Beatty, the child's father
Here on visit from N. Y.			
Oct. 10. July 28.	Cornelius Beatty Ann Jacobson, his wife	Elizabeth Cecilia, 3d dau.	John & Hellethan Jacobson, the ch.'s gr.-parents, the ch.'s mother. Bap. in house of John Jacobson, Esq.
Oct. 13. Aug. 17.	William Praul, farmer Ann Egbert, his wife	Tunis Augustus, 1st ch.	Tunis & Ann Egbert, gr.-parents, John Egbert, Junr., md., the uncle. Bap. in house of Tunis Egbert, Esq.
Oct. 13. Oct. 7.	John Egbert, Junr., [Tunis's son] Aletta Prawl, his wife	Abraham Prawl, 1st ch.	Tunis & Ann Egbert, the gr.-parents, Wm. Prawl, md., the uncle

DATE	PARENTS	CHILD	SPONSORS
1816.			
Dec. 29. Oct. 28.	John Decker Ann Egbert, his wife	Edward Egbert, 2d ch., 1st son	Br. Edward Beatty, Senr., Sr. Eleon. Beatty
1817.			
March 12. Jan. 8.	Richard Skerritt, Jr., shoemaker Mary Mott, his wife	Abraham, 1st ch.	The ch.'s father, Br. Nicholas Stillwell, unmd., Mary Johnson, md. Bp. at house of R. Skerrit, Jr., in presence of relations & neighbors
March 16. Jan. 10.	John Vanderbilt, Jr., Celia Story, his wife	Sarah Ann, 2d ch.	Br. Edw. & Sr. Eleon. Beatty, Sr. Elizabeth Vanderbilt, ch.'s gr.-mother
April 13. 1816. Dec. 5.	Oliver Vanderbilt, shoemaker, of N. Y. Esther Benson, his wife	Elizabeth, 1st ch.	Br. Edw. Beatty, Sr. Amy Cortelyou, Sr. Eliz. Vanderbilt, Senr., the ch.'s gr.-mother
1817.			
May 25. March 23.	Charles Egbert, shoemaker Christiana Pels, his wife	Eupheme, 2d dau.	Richard Conner, Senr., md., the ch.'s father, Catharina Smith, md.
Aug. 14. March 8.	Cornelius Vanderbilt, Jr. Sophia Johnson, his wife	Ethelinde, 2d ch.	Br. Edw. Beatty, Senr., Sr. Eleon. Beatty, the child's mother
Aug. 25. May 18.	Joseph Baker Susan Stilwell, his wife	Peter Vansal, 2d ch.	Rev. J. C. Bechler, the ch.'s mother, Mrs. Sarah Egbert, in whose house the bap. was performed
Sept. 17. Aug. 20.	John De Forest [De Fries] Charlotte [Vanderbilt], his wife	Cornelius Vanderbilt	Rev. J. C. Bechler, Sr. A. H. Bechler, Phoebe Vanderbilt, gr.-mother of child
Sept. 21. Sept. 1.	Peter Wood Sarah Ann Cortelyou, his wife	James, 2d ch., 1st son	Br. Edw. Beatty, Br. Peter Cortelyou, gr.-father, Sr. Amy Cortelyou, gr.-mother. Bap. in Br. Peter Cortelyou's house after a sermon preached there

Baptisms by Rev. G. A. Hartman.

DATE	PARENTS	CHILD	SPONSORS
1817.			
Nov. 27. Oct. 1.	Joseph Mellington, shoemaker Lucy Crips, his wife	Lenah Crips	Rachel Crips, gr.-mother of Ch., Elizabeth Crips, unmd., the aunt of ch., Nicholas Stillwell, unmd.
Dec. 23. Oct. 29.	Thomas Stewart Hannah Kitch, his wife [Abigail Keitch was her mother]	Sarah Jane	Rev. G. A. Hartman, Isabella S. Hartman
1818. Feb. 8. Jan. 1.	Jacob Beatty, saddle & harness maker Elizabeth Cortelyou, his wife	Edward, 3d ch., 3d son	Br. Edw. Beatty, gr.-father, Sr. —— Beatty, gr.-mother, Br. James Egbert, Senr. Bap. on Sunday before Church
Feb. 15. 1817. Nov. 22.	Tunis Egbert Isabella Vanderbilt, his wife	John Vanderbilt, 2d son	John Vanderbilt, gr.-father, Elizabeth Vanderbilt, gr.-mother, Ann Egbert, gr.-mother. Bp. at Ministar's house before ch. on Sunday
1818. April 27. b. not given, in neighborhood of Newton, Sussex Co., N. J.	John M'Kinlay Lydia, his wife	Lydia Jane	In presence of Ann Egbert this was performed by particular request of the mother who was born & educated at Granhill, Ireland
June 21. May 18.	Nathaniel Martin Sarah Dorsett, his wife	John	John Dorsett, the gr.-father, the gr.-mother
July 1. March 3.	Richard Connor, farmer & surveyor Sophia Clawson, his wife	Sarah Lovinia, 14th ch, 7th dau.	The parents of child
July 2. May 6.	Isaac Burbank Sarah Egbert, his wife	Sarah Jane, 3d ch., 2d dau.	The aunt, Ann Decker, Sarah Lozier, md.
July 22. June 20.	William Praul Ann Egbert, his wife	Henrietta	Tunis Egbert, the gr.-father, Sr. Ann Egbert, the gr.-mother, Miss Patience Egbert, the aunt. Bp. at house of Tunis Egbert, Esq.

DATE	PARENTS	CHILD	SPONSORS
1818.			
Dec. 9. An illigitimate child.	Caty Rook, now the wife of Charles Metsger of N. Y. City	Eliza Ann	Amos & Martin Rooks, the gr.-parents, the ch.'s mother
Dec. 13. Oct. 9.	Cornelius Beatty of N. Y. Ann Jacobson, his wife	Cornelius Augustus, 8 ch., 4th son	The father & the gr.-parents John V. D. and Hellethey Jacobson
Dec. 20. Sept. 23.	William Beattey Mary Barger, his wife	John Edward, 5th ch., 3d son	The ch.'s father, the gr.-father Br. Edw. Beattey, the aunt Sarah Lozier
1819.			
Jan. 6.	Mathew Decker Ann Colon, his wife	Catharine Wood	In presence of a number convened for Divine Service at house of Moses Wood
May 2. Feb. 27.	John Beatty Elizabeth Lake, his wife	Mary Lake	Eleon. Beattey, gr.-mother, Polly Beattey, Willm. Beattey, the uncle
June 6. April 15.	Oliver Vanderbilt Hetty Maria Benzaken, his wife	Christian Ann	Br. John Vanderbilt, Sr. Elizabeth Vanderbilt, the gr.-parents
Sept. 28. May 30.	Cornelius Vanderbilt, Jr., [son of Corn.], boatman Sophia, his wife	Elizabeth	Bp. by Rev. Benj. Mortimer of N. Y. Rev. G. A. Hartman absent
1820. Oct. 24. Oct. 11.	Jacob Beatty Eliza Beattey	Varansalaer	Br. Edw. Beatty, gr.-father, Mrs. Lozier & Mrs. Elizabeth Cortelyou & others
July 4. Feb. 5.	John Decker Ann Egbert, his wife	Mary Frances	Sr. Sally Burbank, Isaac Burbank, Eleon Beattey
1819. Dec. 15. Jan. 29.	Samuel Egbert Elizabeth Blake, his wife	Mary Jane, 1st ch.	None given
——— Oct. 11.	David Barager Sally Cortelyou, his wife	Henry, 2d ch., 1st son	Sr. Eleonor Beattey, Sr.
Dec. 21. 1818. Dec. 17.	James Scharret Ann Garritson, his wife	Daniel	In presence of Van Deventer Bedell & Mrs. Hartman
1819. Dec. 26. Oct. 12.	John Vanderbilt, Junr. Celia Story, his wife	John	In presence of Congregation in Church

DATE	PARENTS	CHILD	SPONSORS
1820.			
Jan 27. 1819. Oct. 19.	Joseph Baker Susan Stilwell, his wife	Joseph	In presence of Mrs. Dykman, Mrs. Sarah Egbert
1820. Jan. 28. 1819. in April.	Thomas Miller Maria Houghabout, his wife	Winant	The gr.-father Henry Miller, the gr.-mother, Elizabeth Miller & the ch.'s father
1820. March 24. Jan. 20.	James & Bett, belonging to Daniel Guyon, Esq.	Samuel, black	
April 24. March 4.	Michael Van Name Gertrude Martha Cortelyou, his wife	Edward	Edw. & Eleon. Beattey, Martha Dorsett
June 30. May 19.	Charles Egbert, now residing at N. Y. Christian Pels, his wife	Sussan	Bap. at his mother's dwelling on this Island.
July 3. Jan. 29.	Gerret Dykeman Ellen Lake, his wife	Eliza Cuszina	None given
July 30. May 16.	James Lewis Mary Stillwell, his wife	Sally Ann	Bap. at a lecture at the new school house near Mrs. John Scherrets
Aug. 7. July 9.	David Praul Catharine Dorsett, his wife	Emeline	John & Martha Dorsett, the gr.-parents
Oct. 22. 1815. Oct. 26. 1820.	Gerardus Dykman Ellen Lake, his wife	Richard	None given. Baptism in parent's dwelling
Oct. 22. 1818. Jan. 3. 1820.	Gerardus Dykman Ellen Lake, his wife	Gilbert	As above
Oct. 29.	Peter Wood Sarah Ann Cortelyou, his wife	Margaret Ann	Edw. & Eleon. Beattey & Miss Sarah Lozier
Nov. 5. 1821.	Tunis Egbert Isabella Vanderbilt, his wife	Elizabeth Ann	John & Elizabeth Vanderbilt, gr.-parents, Sr. Eleonor Beatty-Senr.
April 23. 1820. June 4.	Nicholas Cocheron Ann Guion, his wife	Emeline	Bap. at house of gr., father, Daniel Guyon in presence of Mrs. Sophia Connor & others

DATE	PARENTS	CHILD	SPONSORS
1821.			
June 3. March 3.	John Decker Ann Egbert, his wife	Sarah Ann	None given
July 8. March 29.	William Beattey Polly Barager, his wife	Edmund	Br. Edward & Sr. Eleonor Beattey, gr.-parents, Mr. John & Mrs. Betsey Beattey
April 29. March 31.	William Praul Ann Egbert, his wife	Edwin Theodor	Bp. at house of gr.-father Tunis Egbert, Esq.
May 21. 1820. Nov. 6. 1821.	Capt. Deforrest Charlotte Vanderbilt his wife	William Hand	Bp. in house of Mr. Edward Beatty & in his & his wife's presence
Sept. 12. Aug. 4.	John Scharret Catharine Perine, his wife	Benjamin Gryon	None given
Oct. 28. Feb. 10.	Abraham Stillwell Mary Scharret, his wife	Catharine Ann, 1st ch.	Bp. at house of Mrs. Thomas Steward at beginning of a lecture
Dec. 14. Nov. 6.	David Barger Sarah Cortelyou, his wife	Eliza Ann, 3d ch., 3d dau.	The parents & Sr. Eleonor Beatty
Dec. 27. 1820. Dec. 24.	Samuel Egbert Betsy Blake, his wife	Eliza Ann, 2d ch.	None given
1822.			
Jan. 2. 1821. May 9.	Cornelius Vanderbilt, Junr. Sophia Johnson, his wife	William Henry, 4th ch.	The gr.-father Cornelius Vanderbilt, Sen., and a sister of the father's
1822.			
March 31. Feb. 23.	Jacob Beatty Eliza Cortelyou. his wife	Isabella	Bp. in house of gr.-parents Edw. & Eleon. Beatty, in presence of number of friends
April 7. 1821. Oct. 24.	Joseph Baker Susan Stillwell, his wife	Letty Ann	Bp. at beginning of lecture at house of Thomas Steward
1822.			
Jan. 10.	Stephen Egbert Hannah Alston, his wife	Warren Alston	Bp. at house of gr.-father Mr. Abraham Egbert, Senr.
May 19. 1821. Dec. 3.	John Peterson Sarah Peterson	Mary Ann	Bp. at house of Thomas Steward, deceased at commencement of his funeral services

DATE	PARENTS	CHILD	SPONSORS
1822.			
May 19.	Colens M'Kinsay	John	Bp. as above same time & place
1821. Jan. 31.	Hannah M'Kinsay		
1822.			
June 25.	Hamilton M'Cauly	Robert Thompson	Bp. at dwelling of gr.-parent Mr. Thompson
1821. Sept. 4.	Margaret Thompson, his wife		
1822.			
July 26.	Charles Egbert	Peter	
1821. April 1.	Christianne Pels, his wife		
1822.			
Sept. 29.	Gerardus Dykeman	Mary Ann	Bp. at lecture at Mrs. Stewards
June 18.	Ellen Lake, his wife		
Oct. 1.	John Egbert	Eugene Mortimer	
Sept. 15.	Aletta Praul, his wife		
Oct. 2.	Edward Beattey, Jr.	Cynthia Jacobson 1st ch.	Bap. at house of his father Mr. John Beattey
Aug. 20.	Ann Denyse, his wife		
Oct. 17.	Tunis Egbert	Eliza Ann	Sponsors not given
Sept. 4.	Isabella Vandebilt, his wife		
Oct. 31.	Aaron Vanderbilt	Isaac	" " "
1821. Sept. 23.	Mary Simonson, his wife		
1822.			
Oct. 31.	John Vanderbilt, Jr.	Isabella	" " "
March 11.	Celia Story, his wife		
Dec. 29.	Cornelius Beattey	Maria Rebekah	" " "
Aug. 2.	Nancy Jacobson, his wife		
1823.			
March 24.	John Beattey Elizabeth Lake, his wife	Barzillor Burr	" " "
April 13.	Michael Van Namen	Sophia	" " "
Jan. 15.	Gertrude Martha [Cortelyou], his wife		
June 24.	Thomas Crips	Thomas	
1822. June 15.	Martha Crips		
1823.			
Sept. 2.	Capt. Deforest	Charlotte Jane	
1822. June 30.	Charlotte Vanderbilt, his wife		

DATE	PARENTS	CHILD	SPONSORS
1823.			
Oct. 15.	John Scharret	John & Mary	
1821.	Mary Swaim, his		
April 22.	wife		
1823,			
Oct. 15.	John Scharret	Peter Swaim	
June 9.	Mary Swaim, his wife		
Oct. 15.	Abraham Stilwell	Henry Edward Perine	Bp. at house of her brother John Scharret
June 16.	Mary Scharret, his wife		
Oct. 17.	Nicholas Crocheron Ann Guion	Frances Rebekah	
Oct. 18.	Daniel Mercereau	Ellen Maria	
July 18.	Ellen Maria Lozier, his wife		
Oct. 28.	William Praul	Maria Ann	
March 15.	Ann Egbert, his wife		
Oct. 28.	John Crocheron	William Henry	
July 3.	Patience Egbert, his wife		
1824.			
March 9.	John Vanduser	Abraham, 1st ch.	Bp. at house of the gr.-father John Vanderbilt
Jan. 28.	Sarah Vanderbilt, his wife		
March 14.	David Barger	John William	
1823.	Sally Cortelyou, his wife		
Nov. 9.			
1824.			
March 31.	Jacob Lozier	Catharine	
March 13.	Eliza Barnes, his wife	Eliza, 1st ch.	
April 14.	Samuel Egbert	Harriette	Bp. at house of gr.-father John Egbert, Sen.
1823.	Betsy Blake, his wife		
Feb. 26.			
1824.			
April 18.	John Decker	John Henry	
1823.	Ann Egbert, his wife		
Sept. 21.			
1824.			
April 20.	Capt. Moses Mills	John Newell	Bp. at parents' dwelling in City of N. York in presence of the mother & gr.-mother Mrs. Taylor
1823.	Mary, his wife		
Aug. 24.			
1824.			
July 19.	John Dorsett	Mary Jane	
Feb. 10.	Ellen Cropsy, his wife		

DATE	PARENTS	CHILD	SPONSORS
1824.			
Sept. 9.	Thomas Miller	Joseph	
1820.	Maria Haughwout,		
Nov. 25.	his wife		
1822.			
June 28.	Same parents	Mary Ann	
1824.			
Sept. 9.	Stephen Wood	Elizabeth	
March 26.	—— Marsh, his wife		
Sept. 12.	John Laza— (part	Catharine	
Feb. 7.	of name marked out)	Louise	
	Martha Ann Cropsy, his wife		
Oct. 10.	Richard Scharret	Mary Ann	Bp. at house of Mrs.
June 24.	Charity Stilwell, his wife		Steward
Oct. 20.	Jacob Beattey	Catharine	No sponsors given
Sept. 2.	Eliza Cortelyou, his wife	Eliza.	
Oct. 28.	Stephen Egbert	Ann	" " "
1822.			
June 28.	Hannah Alston, his wife		
1824.			
July 19.	Same parents	Abraham Martino	
Nov. 21.	Cornelius Vanderbilt, Jr.	Emily Elmira	" " "
1823.			
June 6.	Sophia Johnson, his wife		
1824.			
Nov. 25.	Jonathan Merrel	Eliza Ann	" " "
1819.	Maria Egbert, his wife		
Oct. 24.			
1821.			
Sept. 20.	Same parents	Catharina	
1824.			
June 11.	Same parents	Lafayette	
Dec. 6.	Edward Vanderbilt	Elizabeth	" " "
Sept. 6.	Mary Ann Egbert, his wife	Ann	
1825.			
Jan. 30.	Joseph Baker	James Bradly	" " "
1824.	Susan Stillwell, his wife		
Aug. 13.			
1825.			
Feb. 1.	Nicholas Crocheron	Ann Elizabeth	Daniel & Elizabeth Guion, the grandparents
1824.	Ann Guion, his wife		
Sept. 29.			
1825.			
April 4.	David Praul	Alfred Cortelyou	
March 4.	Catharine Dorsett, his wife		

DATE	PARENTS	CHILD	SPONSORS
1825.			
April 10.	Vincent Bodine	Isaac Bur-	"The gr.-parents"
Jan. 26.	Mary Ann Burbank, his wife	bank	
April 27.	John Egbert	Rachel	The parents & gr.-mother
1824.	Lydia, his wife	Ann, 2d ch.	
Dec. 5.			
1825.			
May 3.	Charles Egbert	Richard	The gr.-mother Sarah Egbert, Miss Jane Henderson
March 2.	Christiana Pels, his wife		
May 29.	Thomas Scharret	Joseph	None given
1824.	Martha Crips, his wife		
Oct. 30.			
1825.			
July 18.	Richard Connor	George, 1st ch.	" "
July 9.	Sarah Egbert, his wife		
Aug. 14.	Ann, a black woman, residing at Edward Beatty's	Jane Conosen, Mary Ann, black	
Aug. 15.	Richard Decker	Freeman Degroat, 1st ch.	None given
1824.	Elizabeth Egbert, his wife		
Sept. 15.			
1825.			
Aug. 26.	William Beatty	Hiram Eugene	Now residing at N. Y., at house of John Beatty
April 19.	Polly Barger, his wife		
Sept. 25.	Tunis Egbert	Isabella Sarah Catharine	
March 14.	Isabella Vanderbilt, his wife		
Oct. 2.	Aaron Vanderbilt	Mary Elizabeth	Bp. on Sabbath day
1823.	—— Simonson, his wife		
Dec. 28.			
1825.			
Nov. 2.	Cornelius Vanderbilt of New Brunswick, N. J. Sophia Johnson, his wife	Sophia Johnson	Bp. at house of gr.-father Corn. Vanderbilt, Senr.
March 9.			
Nov. 2.	Gerardus Deforrest	Julia Selina	Bp. at house of gr.-father Corn. Vanderbilt
May 25.	Charlotte Vanderbilt, his wife		
Dec. 22.	Gerardus Dykeman	Rachel	
April 28.	Ellen Lake, his wife		
Dec. 26.	Michael Van Name Gertrude Martha Cortelyou, his wife	Eliza Augusta	

DATE	PARENTS	CHILD	SPONSORS
1826.			
Jan. 1.	Lawrence Cortel-	Sarah Ann,	Bp. at house of gr.-
1825.	you of N. Y.	1st ch.	father Peter Cor-
Dec. 2.	Elizabeth Heckel, his wife		telyou at Freshkill
1826.			
Jan. 7.	Jacob Lozier, Jr.	Amanda	None given. Bp. at
1825.	Eliza Barnes, his	Augusta	Parsonage
Sept. 5.	wife		
1826.			
Jan. 13.	John Scharrot	Augustus	Bp. at parent's dwel-
1825.	Catharine Perine,	Eugene	ling
Sept. 28.	his wife		
1826.			
May 1.	Jonathan Merrell	Martha	Bp. at parent's dwel-
March 13.	Maria Egbert, his wife	Lavinia	ling
May 4.	John Vanduser	John Van-	Bp. at Parsonage
Jan. 16.	Sarah Vanderbilt, his wife	derbilt	
May 6.	John Decker	Elizabeth	" "
Jan. 14.	Ann Egbert, his wife		
May 20.	James Egbert	MarthaAnn	At parent's house
1815.	—— Merrell, his		
Oct. 16.	wife		
1819.			
March 15.		Richard	
1820.		Edmund	
Dec. 25.		Wesly	
1823.			
April 7.		Barzillai	
1825.			
Nov. 25.	All children of above parents	Hannah Mary	
1826.			
June 23.	John Dorsett	Amanda	At parent's dwelling
May 14.	Ellen Cropsy, his wife	Elizabeth	
July 5.	Oliver Decker	Mary Eliza-	Bp. in house of the
1823.	Hannah Simonson,	beth	gr.-father Barnet
Aug. 8.	his wife		Simonson
1824.			
Dec. 21.	Same parents	Isaac Si-	
1826.		monson	
Aug. 14.	Peter La Forge	Elizabeth	Bp. at house of Reu-
May 21.	Elizabeth Dongan, his wife	Ann Don- gan	ben Simonson
Aug. 29.	Edward Vanderbilt	Hannah	Bp. at house of her
Feb. 26.	Maria Ann Egbert, his wife	Maria	mother Mrs. Hannah Egbert

DATE	PARENTS	CHILD	SPONSORS
1826.			
Oct. 15. Sept. 2.	John Tooker Maria Jacobson, his wife	Julia Eliza	Bp. at house of gr.-father John V. D. Jacobson. Miss Eliza Jacobson, Capt. Benson Seaman, Miss Julia Seaman of N. Y.
Nov. 11. Oct. 19.	Jacob Beattey Eliza Cortleyou, his wife	Ellen Gertrude	None given
Nov. 28. Sept. 24.	Michael Marsac Rachel Jennings, his wife	George Adolphus Hartman	
Dec. 14. 1825. July 20. 1826.	Cornelius Egbert Maria Depui, his wife	Nicholas Depui	Bp. at his mother's at the Blazing Star
Dec. 25. Oct. 7. 1827.	Aaron Vanderbilt Mary Simonson, his wife	Benjamin Simonson	Bp. at house of the gr.-father John Vanderbilt
Jan. 2. 1826. Dec. 14. 1827.	Vincent Bodine Mary Ann Burbank, his wife	Jacob, 2d child	Bp. at house of the gr.-father Isaac Burbank
Feb. 13. 1825. June 23. 1827.	James Phanot Jane Jennings, his wife	James	Bp. at the house of Michael Marsac near Quaratine
Feb. 14. 1826. Jan. 29. 1827.	Cornelius Coursen Elsy Arrow, his wife	Susan Ann Reed	
March 4. Jan. 24.	Cornelius Egberts Catharine Lake, his wife	Cornelius, 1st ch.	Bp. at Dorsett's house
March 17. 1826. Nov. 15. 1827.	Charles Metzger Catharine Rook, his wife	Matthew William Reeves	Bp. at house of gr.-father Amos Rook
March 17. 1826. July 5. 1827.	Joshua Warren Catharine, his wife	Phebe Ann Glazier	Bp. at same time & place
March 24. 1826. April 26. 1827.	Moses Decker Lenah Depuy, his wife	Barnet Depuy	Bp. in house of gr.-father Nicholas Depuy
March 29. 1825. Sept. 23.	Samuel Coddington Catharine Jacobson, his wife	Sidny Fitz Randolph	Bp. at house of the parents in New York

DATE	PARENTS	CHILD	SPONSORS
1827. April 9. 1826. Jan. 13.	William Bodine Rosanna Mattes, his wife	George Washington James	Bp. at house of gr.-father James Bodine
1827. April 9. 1821. June 16.	Daniel D. Coursen Catharine Van Pelt, his wife	Mary Jane	
1823. Oct. 21.		Sarah Ann	
1825. Jan. 21. 1826. Dec. 15. 1827.	All children of above parents	Cornelius Van Name Stephen Kittletass	Bap. in the parent's house
April 20. 1826. Nov. 25.	William Beatty, residing at N. Y. Polly Barger, his wife.	Mary Elizabeth	Baptism at house of Mr. Dorsett
1827. Aug. 2. March 24.	Nicholas Crocheron Ann Guyon, his wife	Franklin Guyon	
Aug. 8. 1826. Oct. 4.	Andrew Bodine Polly Housman, his wife	William Alfred Housman	Bp. at house of gr.-father, James Bodine, Senr.
1827. Aug. 8. Jan. 7.	Abraham Housman Mergrett Bodine, his wife	Elizabeth, 1st ch.	Bp. as above
Aug. 27. Feb. 11.	Richard Connor Sally Egbert, his wife	Oscar Theodore, 2d ch.	Bp. in parents' house
Oct. 28. Oct. 15. 1828.	James Gilbert Abigail Ann Black, his wife	Hannah Jane, 1st ch.	At Mrs. Steward's at beginning of Lecture
Jan. 29. 1827. Dec. 1.	Richard Johnson Susan Van Pelt, his wife	Richard Taylor,	"bap. while very sick"
Jan. 29. 1827. Oct. 18.	John Cocheron Patience Egbert, his wife	Selina Theresa	In Minister's house, Edward Taylor, sponsor
1828. Feb. 3. 1827. May 24.	Abraham Martino Ann Simonson, his wife	Raymond	Bp. at beginning of a Lecture at gr.-mothers' Mrs. Martino
1828. March 28. 1827. Dec. 28.	William Bodine Rosanna Mattes, his wife	William Oakly	Bp. at a Lecture at the house of gr.-parents James Bodine

DATE	PARENTS	CHILD	SPONSORS
1828. March 31. 1827. Oct. 20.	John Dorsett Ellen Cropsy, his wife	John William Beattey	
1828. April 2. 1827. Oct. 17.	Tunis Egbert Isabella Vanderbilt, his wife	Mary Precilla	Bp. at gr.-father's John Vanderbilt, Senr.
1828. April 2. 1827. Dec. 23.	John Van Duser Sarah Vanderbilt, his wife	Isaac Housman	Bp. at John Vanderbilt's Sen.
1828. April 2. Feb. 13.	Cornelius Vanderbilt Eliza Martling, his wife	Sarah Elizabeth	Bp. at same time & place
April 8. 1827. Nov. 3.	John Deforrest Charlotte Vanderbilt, his wife	Charles Simonson	
1828. April 24. 1827. Nov. 30.	Oliver Decker Joannah Simonson, his wife	Sarah Ann	Bp. at house of gr.-father Barnet Simonson
1828. May 17. Jan. 24.	Peter Dorset Eliza Lewis, his wife	Susan Maria Mersereau	
May 28. 1824. Dec. 1.	Bedel Jacobson [mother not given]	Israel Vandevender	
1827. Feb. 11.	Bedell Jacobson	Warren Alston	
1828. May 28. 1827. June 22.	Thomas Sharrot Martha Crips, his wife	Stephen	Bp. in church
June 15. 1825. Feb. 28. b. in 1826.	John D. Waters Lucretia Stillwell, his wife Same parents	William Helen	Bp. at Schoolhouse near John Sharrot's in South quarter " "
1828. June 26. 1827. May 8.	Cornelius Vanderbilt of N. Brunswick, N. J. Sophia Johnson, his wife	Maria Louisa	Bp. at house of gr.-father Cornelius Vanderbilt, Senr.

DATE	PARENTS	CHILD	SPONSORS
1828.			
July 8.	Cornelius Beattey	Maria Eliz-	Bp. at home of gr.-
March 12.	of N. Y.	abeth	father John Beattey
	Mary Ann Allen, his wife		
July 24.	John Egbert from	Catharine	
1827.	the Quarantine	Maria	
Nov. 20.	Lydia Sequin, his		
1828.	wife		
Aug. 17.	John M. Black	John Wil-	Bp. at Mrs. Steward's
1826.	Rachel King, his	liam	
March 14.	wife		
1828.			
Aug. 17.	Richard Sharrott	Abraham	
Jan. 20.	Charity Stilwill, his wife		
Oct. 26.	John Vanderbilt	Ellen	Bp. in church after
March 31.	Celia Story, his wife		service
Oct. 26.	Aaron Vanderbilt	Sarah	In church
Aug. 3.	Mary Simonson, his wife	Catharine	
Nov. 29.	Cornelius Egbert	Catharine	Bp. at house of her
May 31.	Catharine Lake, his wife	Maria	mother
Dec. 5.	Richard White	John	Bp. at house of
1826.	Rebeckah Dey, his		Michael Marsac
May 8.	wife		
1828.			
Dec. 5.	James Sharrot	Abraham	Bp. as above
1827.	Jane Jennings, his		
May 3.	wife		
1828.			
Dec. 5.	Michael Marsac	George	" "
July 18.	Rachel Jennings,	Adolphus	
1829.	his wife	Hartman	
Jan. 6.	Jacob Beattey	Sarah Ann	In Minister's dwelling
1828.	Eliza, his wife		
Nov. 28.			
1829.			
Jan. 17.	Daniel Butler	Cornelius	In parents' dwelling
Feb. 23.	Eliza Egbert, his wife	Egbert, 1st ch.	
Feb. 15.	Stephen McIntosh	Harry	Bp. at gr.-father's
1828.	Mary Marsac, his	Augustus,	Michael Marsac
Aug. 12.	wife	1st ch.	
1829.			
May 17.	David Moore	William	Bp. at Lecture at Mrs.
1828.	Mary Ann Barton,	Augustus	Martino's in the
Dec. 31.	his wife		Manor

DATE	PARENTS	CHILD	SPONSORS
1829.			
May 31.	Vincent Bodine	Vincent	In parents' house
Feb. 26.	Mary Ann Burbank, his wife		
June 12.	Joseph Mount	Alicia Ann	Bp. in Minister's dwelling in presence of Mrs. Coddington and her daughter Ann
1826.	Isabella, his wife		
Sept. 6.			
1829.			
June 12.	Joseph Egbert	Joseph	
b. 1822.	Jane Holmes, his wife	Thomas	
1829.			
June 24.	John Davis	James	
1828.	Susan Sharrott, his wife		
Nov. 17.			
1829.			
June 30.	Cornelius Coursen & his wife	William Blake	
1828.			
May 28.			
1829.			
Aug. 16.	Abraham Martino	Elizabeth Merrell	
June 6.	Ann Simonson, his wife		
Sept. 14.	Capt. Cornelius Vanderbilt	Frances Lavinia	Bp. in parents' house in New York
1828.			
Dec. 8.	Sophia, his wife		
1829.			
Sept. 10.	James Gilbert	James Thomas Steward	
July 22.	Abby Ann Black, his wife		
Sept. 10.	Abraham Sharrot	Benjamin Housman	
1828.	Margaret Housman, his wife		
Aug. 16.			
1829.			
Oct. 18.	John Sharrot	Lenah Ann	Bp. in dwelling of parents
1825.	Maria Swaim, his wife		
March 3.			
1826.			
b. Nov. 3.	Same parents	Alfred	
1829.			
Oct. 18.	Jeremiah Sharrot	Susan Ann	Bp. in John Sharrot's house
1825.	Lenah Swaim, his wife		
June 19.			

DATE	PARENTS	CHILD	SPONSORS
1827.			
b. Nov. 24.	Same parents	John William	" "
1829.			
Oct. 18.	Joseph Baker, deceased	Ellen Eliza	" "
1826.			
Aug. 6.	Susan, his wife		
1829.			
Oct. 23.	John Van Duser	Jacob Taylor	
Aug. 22.	Sarah Vanderbilt, his wife		
Oct. 23.	Jacob Lozier	Mary Ann	
Aug. 17.	Eliza Barnes, his wife		
July 5.	Benson Seaman	Henry John	Bp. at house of gr.-mother
March 8.	Eliza Jacobson, his wife		
Aug. 27.	John Burton	Margaret Jane	
1819.	Louise, his wife		
Nov. 17.			
1821.			
b. June 13.		William	
1823.			
b. Aug. 30.		Ellen Thomas	
1827.			
b. Nov. 24.		Sarah Rumrill	
1829.			
b. Aug. 4.	All ch. of John & Louise Burton	Louise	
1830.			
Jan. 14.	Cornelius Vanderbilt, Jr.	Hetty Maria	Bp. at house of parents
1829.			
Dec. 16.	Eliza Martling, his wife		
1830.			
Jan. 14.	William Crips	James Butler	At same place
1829.	Jane Butler, his wife		
Aug. 8.			
1830.			
Jan. 14.	Daniel Coursen	Catharine Jones Martling	" "
1828.	Catharine Van Pelt, his wife		
July 26.			
1830.			
May 7.	Isaac Swift	John William	
1829.	Eliza Bodine, his wife		
Sept. 23.			

DATE	PARENTS	CHILD	SPONSORS
1830.			
June 27.	Richard Johnson	Tunis Van Pelt	Bp. in Ch. after service. Present were the gr.-father Peter V. Pelt, Eliza C. Hartman, Mrs. Ann Egbert, wid. of Tunis
1829. Sept. 18.	Susan Van Pelt, his wife		
1830.			
June 29.	Tunis Egbert	Frances Lavinia	Bp. at parents' home
March 6.	Isabella Vanderbilt, his wife		
July 1.	Jacob Cortelyou	William Cuberly, 1st ch.	
March 13.	Mary Winant, his wife		
Sept. 20.	Thomas Sharrot	John Davis	
April 25.	Martha, his wife		
Sept. 20. June 1.	Benjamin Housman Eliza Sharrot, his wife	John William	
Oct. 21.	Edward Vanderbilt	John Edward	
April 19.	Mary Ann Egbert, his wife		
Oct. 24.	Edward Beattey [John's son]	Eliza Alexander	
1824. April 22.	Ann Denyse, his wife		
1826. b. Oct. 7.		Henrietta Mieks	
1828. b. Feb. 20.		Annethie Vooris	
1830. b. Aug. 5.	All children of E. & Ann Beattey	Eleanor Louise	
Oct. 24.	Cornelius Beattey [John's son], from N. York	Jane Ann	Bp. at house of his brother Edward, where a considerable number of persons had convened
Sept. 19.	Mary Ann Allen, his wife		
1831. Jan. 31.	Godfrey Crawbuck	James Franklin Beattey	Bp. at house of James Beattey
1821.	Mary Ross, his wife		
Oct. 10.			
1831. March 13.	John D. Waters	Ann	Bp. at parents' house
1830. Oct. 2.	Lucretia Stilwell, his wife		
1831. March 20.	Edward Egbert	Mary Josephine	
1827. June 20.	Hannah Price, his wife		
1829. b. Sept. 18.	Same parents	Letty Ann Lake	

DATE	PARENTS	CHILD	SPONSORS
1831. March 29. 1830. Sept. 23.	David Moore Mary, his wife [Barton]	John Henry	
1831. April 3. 1830. Dec. 30.	Abraham Garretson Eliza Sanders, his wife	Hermanus	
1831. May 15. 1803. Jan. 15.	Ann Marsh, wife of James Beattey		Bp. in a particular meeting after the Public Service on the Lord's day, by the Right Revd. J. D. Anders, Bishop of the U. Br. Ch. Here from Bethlehem, Penn.
1831. June 19. Feb. 6.	John Sharrot Mary Swaim, his wife	Washington	
June 19. 1830. July 23.	Jeremiah Sharrot Lenah Swaim, his wife	David	Bp. at house of his brother John Sharrot
1831. June 19. 1830. Dec. 9.	William Johnson Catharina Wood, maiden name Sharrot	William Henry, illegitimate	
1831. June 19. 1830. Jan. 22.	Vincent Butler Martha Ann Swaim, his wife	William Fountain	
1831. June 19. Jan. 26.	Vincent Butler Martha Ann Swaim, his wife	Sarah Elizabeth	
June 21. March 1.	Peter Dorset Eliza Lewis, his wife	Ellen Elizabeth	
July 13. 1829. March 25.	John N. Tooker Maria Jacobson, his wife	Ann Matilda	
1831. July 13. 1829. Feb. 22.	Bedell Jacobson Sarah Ann Alston, his wife	John Bedell	
1831. July 13. March 4.	Capt. Benson Seaman Eliza Jacobson, his wife	Ann Elizabeth	

DATE	PARENTS	CHILD	SPONSORS
1831.			
July 14.	Richard Decker	Jane Eliza	
1829.	Eliza Egbert, his		
July 23.	wife		
1831.			
July 30.	Abraham Prall	Edward	
May 29.	Isabella Beattey, his wife	Beattey	
Aug. 17.	Abraham Stilwell	Abraham	Bp. in their dwelling
1830.	Mary, his wife		on the north side
Dec. 25.			
1831.			
Aug. 19.	Nicholas Crocheron	Lenah Ara-	
1830.	Ann, his wife	minta	
Sept. 7.			
1831.			
Aug. 20.	Jacob Cortelyou	Frances	
March 20.	Mary Winant, his wife		
Aug. 28.	William Egbert	John Wil-	
Aug. 12.	Mary Ann Lake, his wife	liam	
Aug. 28.	Cornelius Egbert	Annet Lake	
1830.	Catharine Lake, his		
Dec. 16.	wife		
1831.			
Sept. 8.	Michael Marsac	Catharine	
Jan. 3.	Rachel, his wife	Eliza Sassenberg	
Sept. 8.	Stephen McIntosh	Elizabeth	
July 11.	Mary, his wife	Letitia	
Sept. 25.	Richard Conner	Crowel	
1830.	Sally Egbert, his	Mundy	
Nov. 21.	wife		
1831.			
Oct. 15.	William Bodine of	Margaret	Bp. in house of gr.-
1830.	Warwick Co.,	Jane	father James Bo-
Feb. 25.	Virginia Rosanna, his wife		dine
1831.			
Oct. 19.	Joseph Christopher	John Milton	
April 26.	Maria Martino, his wife		
Nov. 20.	Edward Egbert	Elizabeth	
Sept. 18.	Hannah Price, his wife		
Nov. 20.	Abraham Martino	Ellen Maria	
Sept. 23.	Ann Simonson, his wife		
Nov. 20.	Andrew Decker	Tunis	
Aug. 2.	Patience, his wife	Augustus	

DATE	PARENTS	CHILD	SPONSORS
1831. Dec. 4. 1830. Aug. 13.	Israel B. Jacobson Ann Cuberly, his wife	Elizabeth Emelia	
1831. Dec. 25. Sept. 4.	John Jacobson, late from England, a miner at work in the iron mines near our church Mary, his wife	John	
1832. Jan. 23. 1830. Aug. 14.	Lockman Cortelyou of N. York Nelly, his wife	Maria	Bp. in house of gr.-parents
1832. March 11. 1831. July 8.	Charles Waller Mary Burgher, his wife	Catharine Elizabeth Burgher	
1832. March 21. 1830. Dec. 29.	Capt. Cornelius Vanderbilt Sophia Johnson, his wife	Cornelius Jeremiah	Bp. at parent's house in N. York
1832. April 10. 1831. July 27.	Daniel Mersereau Ellen, his wife	John Edward Winant	Bp. at house of parents at Tompkinsville
1832. April 12. 1822. March 13.	James Romer —— Stilwell, his wife	Joseph Lake	Bp. at house of James Beattey at a Lecture
1824. b. April 8.		Isaac Parlee	" "
1826. b. Sept. 25.		Mary Louise	" "
1831. b. Dec. 16. 1832.	All children of J. Romer & wife	Margaret Jane	" "
April 24. 1831. Nov. 27.	Jacob Lozier Eliza Barnes, his wife	Elmira	Bp. in dwelling of parents at Tompkinsville
1832. June 7. 1831. Jan. 21.	Henry Perine Sarah, his wife [Stilwell?]	Emma Elizabeth Cortelyou	Bp. at James Beattey
1832. July 5. 1830. Oct. 23.	William Winning Ann, his wife	Ann Louise	Bp. at house of Stephen McIntosh
1832. b. March 1.	Same parents	George William	

DATE	PARENTS	CHILD	SPONSORS
1831.			
b. Sept. 4.	Richard White Rebekah, his wife	Mary Louise	Bp. in house of parents
1832. July 25. June 1.	John Egbert, of New York Aletta, his wife	Ann Rebekah	Bp. in house of Andrew Decker
July 30. 1831. Nov. 20.	James Gilbert Abby Ann, his wife	Sarah Ann Matilda	At house of parents
1832. July 30. 1831. April 15.	William Henry King of N. Y. Nancy, his wife	Mary Ann	
1832. Oct. 12. Jan. 24.	Cornelius Vanderbilt Eliza, his wife	Cornelius Taylor	
Oct. 14. 1830. Jan. 11.	Isaac Simonson Abby Jane his wife	Daniel D.	
1831. b. June 21.	Same parents	Sarah Eliza	
1832. Oct. 16. Feb. 17.	John Egbert Lydia Egbert	Lydia Eliza	
Oct. 16. Oct. 8.	Matthias Jones Julia Ann Jones	Isabella M'Lean	
Oct. 24. 1830. March 19.	Aaron Vanderbilt Mary Vanderbilt	Margarett Metcalf	Bp. in parents' dwelling at Tompkinsville
1831. b. Nov. 5.	Same parents	Jacob	
1832. Oct. 24. March 23.	John Van Duser Sarah Van Duser	Oliver Vanderbilt	Bp. as above
Oct. 24. April 10.	Samuel Coddington of N. Y. Catharine Jacobson, his wife	Catharine Helenah	Bp. in Minister's dwelling
Nov. 18. 1831. Aug. 7.	Abraham Sharrot Margaret Housman, his wife	Mary Ann	Bp. at house of Mrs. Steward
1832. Nov. 25. May 1.	Abraham Garretson Eliza Sanders, his wife	Henry Davis	Bp. in their dwelling
Nov. 25. April 11.	Richard Johnson Else Sanders, his wife	Eliza Ann	At same time as above

DATE	PARENTS	CHILD	SPONSORS
1832.			
Dec. 2.	David Moore	George Washington	Bp. at house of Edward Bodine at a lecture
May 3.	Mary Barton, his wife		
1833.			
Jan. 6.	Benjamin Housman	James Edward	On Lord's Day at beginning of service
1832.			
April 23.	Elizabeth Sharrot, his wife		
1833.			
March 8.	Matthias Burgher	Alfred & James, *twins*	Bp. in parents' dwelling
1829.	Hannah, his wife		
Dec. 26.			
1833.			
March 19.	William Bodine	Abraham	Bp. at gr.-father's James Bodine
1832.	Rosanna, his wife		
July 5.			
1833.			
March 19.	Isaac Swift	Margaret Elizabeth	At same place as above
1832.	Eliza Bodine, his wife		
March 19.			
1833.			
April 10.	Stephen Martling	Sarah Catharine	In minister's dwelling
1832.	Mary Burbank, his wife		
Dec. 16.			
1833.			
April 15.	Jonathan Merrels	Julia	In their dwelling
1832.	Maria, his wife		
March 25.			
1833.			
April 19.	John Van Pelt & wife	John Christopher	In dwelling of parents
1823.			
Nov. 21.			
1825.			
b. Oct. 26.	" "	Peter	" "
1828.			
b. Oct. 16.	" "	George Washington	" "
1831.			
b. Oct. 14.	Same parents as above	Tunis	" "
1833.			
April 18.	Joseph Sharrot	William Henry	Bp. in gr.-parents dwelling
1832.	Cornelia Mersereau, his wife		
Oct. 26.			
1833.			
May 19.	Richard Conner	Elizabeth Sophia	In his dwelling
1832.	Sarah Egbert, his wife		
Sept. 11.			
1833.			
July 6.	John Lovet, late from England	William Thomas	In Church
Feb. 3.	Elizabeth, his wife		
1831.			
b. June 10.		Edmund John	

DATE	PARENTS	CHILD	SPONSORS
1833.			
July 28. April 23.	Tunis Egbert Isabella Vanderbilt, his wife	Jane Louise	Bp. in church on Lord's day
Aug. 26. Feb. 4.	Thomas Scharot & his wife	Mary Elizabeth	At Parsonage
Oct. 4. 1832. Sept. 23.	Capt. Cornelius Vanderbilt Sophia Johnson, his wife	George Washington	At parents' dwelling
1833.			
Oct. 9. Sept. 23.	David Barger Sally Cortelyou, his wife	James Guion	At parent's dwelling
Oct. 24. March 29.	Abraham Stillwell Mary Sharot, his wife	John William	At house of parents' on north side
Nov. 17. Feb. 10.	Edward Beatty Ann Denyce, his wife	John	At dwelling of gr.-parents
Dec. 1. 1827. Oct. 11 1830.	Richard Johnson Elsie Sanders, his wife	Peter Augustus	At house of Abraham Garretson
b. Feb. 11.	Same parents	Andrew	
1833.			
Dec. 29. Aug. 29.	Cornelius Egbert Catharine Lake, his wife	Emeline	In their dwelling
1834.			
Feb. 17. 1833. Feb. 23.	Jacob Cortelyou Mary Cortelyou	Jacob Winant	In Minister's dwelling
1834.			
Feb. 26. 1830. April 11.	George Avery of New York Catharine Avery	George Washington	
1833.			
b. Aug. 2.	Same parents	Julia Simpson	
1834.			
April 8. Jan. 29.	Richard Johnson Elsie Sanders, his wife	Mary Catharine	Bp. at house of her sister Mrs. Garretson
April 9. 1833. Jan. 7.	Stephen McIntosh Mary Marsac, his wife	John Williams	Bp. at parents' hoese
1834.			
April 17. Jan. 4.	Joseph Sharrot Cornelia Mersereau, his wife	Joseph Willson	" "

DATE	PARENTS	CHILD	SPONSORS
1834.			
May 13.	John Lovet	James	Bp. at parents' house
Feb. 22.	Elizabeth Lovet	Henry	
June 15.	John Jackson	George William	" "
May 21.	Mary Jackson		At Lecture there
June 15.	Benjamin Housman	Joseph Egbert	" "
Feb. 21.	Eliza Housman		
June 15.	Abraham Housman	Mary Louisa	" "
1833.			
Oct. 15.	Catherine Housman		
1834.			
June 18.	Andrew Decker	Lawrence Hillyer Lafayette	At Minister's dwelling
April 30.	Patience Egbert, his wife		
June 22.	Henry Perine	Mary Matilda	Bp. at Lecture at South side Schoolhouse near James Lewis
1833.	Sally Stilwell, his wife		
Aug. 12.			
1834.			
July 20.	Cornelius Vanderbilt, deceased	John	Bp. at house of gr.-father Mr. John Vanderbilt
Jan. 19.	Eliza Martling, his wife		
Aug. 24.	Abraham Garretson	Edgar Eugene	
June 23.	Eliza Sanders, his wife		
Oct. 15.	Daniel Butler	Sarah Elizabeth	Bp. at Minister's house
April 17.	Eliza Egbert, his wife		
Oct. 27.	Edward Burbank	Isaac	At house of gr.-parents
May 2.	Jane Britton		
Nov. 5.	Capt. Cornelius Vanderbilt	Mary Alicia	Bp. at his residence in N. Y. City
1833.			
April 25.	Sophia, his wife [Johnson]		
1834.			
Nov. 12.	Edward Egbert	Hannah Jane	In parents' house
Feb. 22.	Hannah Price, his wife		
Nov. 12.	Edward Johnson	Mary Catharine	
July 6.	Mary Housman, his wife		
1835.			
Jan. 5.	Jacob Burckert	Johann Valentine	Bp. at parents' house, Tompkinsville. Sponsors were, Valentine Cornelius & Johann Spries
1834.	Terresia Schultzebach, his wife		
Sept. 4.			

DATE	PARENTS	CHILD	SPONSORS
1835. March 4. 1834. July 25.	Richard Connor Sarah Egbert, his wife	James Egbert	Bp. in the sick room at the request of the mother who lay at the point of death. A number of friends were present
1835. June 1. March 25.	John Egbert Lydia Seguine, his wife	Sarah Adeline	In parents's house
June 21. 1830. Nov. 6. 1832.	William Crips of Bergen, N. J. Jane Butler, his wife	Catharine Fountain	Bp. at house of gr.-father James Butler
b. Nov. 26.	" "	Isaac Butler	
1834. b. Dec. 17.	Same parents	Charity Butler	Bp. as above
1835. Aug. 19. 1829. Oct. 20.	Abraham Herman Halle from Germany, now living on the Island	Eugene Benhornean	
1833. b. April 19.	Sarah, his wife Same parents	La Fayette Matthias	
1835. Sept. 1. 1833. Dec. 18.	James Gilbert Abbey Ann, his wife	Maria	In house of gr.-mother Mrs. Steward
1835. Sept. 9. 1834. Oct. 4.	Michael Marsac Rachel Jennings, his wife	Harvy Washington Edgar	In parents' house
1835. Sept. 19. July 7.	William Beattey Elizabeth Simonson, his wife	William Henry	In minister's dwelling
Sept. 4. 1834. Dec. 23.	Isaac Swift Eliza Bodine, his wife	James Bodine	In house of gr.-father James Bodine
1835. Sept. 27. 1834. Jan. 7.	"Joseph Peat or Paterman" Hannah, his wife	Lydia	At house of Mrs. Mc-Keese at a Lecture
1835. Oct. 1. July 21.	Peter Dorset Eliza Lewis, his wife	Isaac Lewis	In parents' house
Oct. 1. July 11.	John Romer Catharine Lewis, his wife	Mary Ann	At same place

DATE	PARENTS	CHILD	SPONSORS
1836. Feb. 21. 1835. Dec. 2.	Abraham Miller Jane Simonson, his wife	Jane Anna	In Minister's dwelling
1836. March 9. 1835. Sept. 15.	John Egbert Elizabeth Simonson, his wife	Ann Lavinia	" "
1836. March 15. 1835. Dec. 13.	Richard Decker Eliza Egbert, his wife	Angeline	In parent's house
1836. March 23. 1835. Oct. 23.	Jacob Burkert Teresa, his wife	Ferdinand Jacob	At Tompkinsville in their dwelling
1836. July 24. 1835. Oct. 2.	Anthony Y. Steward Mary, his wife	Archibald Douglas	At gr.-mother's house
1836. Aug. 18. 1835. Oct. 15.	Stephen Martling Mary Ann, his wife	Mary Elizabeth	In gr.-father's house
1836. Sept. 1. April 30.	Israel O. Dissasway Lucretia Jacobson, his wife	Israel Fitz-randolph	
Sept. 11. March 21.	Joseph Pateman Hannah, his wife	Ann Caroline	At Mrs. McKeese
1836. Sept. 13. April 25.	John Egbert of New York Aletta Prall	Daniel Mersereau	In the church
Sept. 17. April 3.	Jocob Cortelyou Mary, his wife	Charlotte Ann	In parents' house
Oct. 29. Jan. 31.	Edward Johnson —— Housman, his wife	Eliza Ann	
Nov. 3. March 12.	James Gilbert Abbey Ann, his wife	Hannah Jane	In gr.-mother's dwelling
Nov. 7. July 4.	Abraham Garretson Eliza Sanders, his wife	Abraham Crocheron	In parents' house
Nov. 22. Oct. 2.	Edward Beattey Ann, his wife	Ann Louisa	In parents house
Dec. 12. Aug. 1.	Abraham Bodine Abbey Ann Kinsey, his wife	Tunis	In parents' house

DATE	PARENTS	CHILD	SPONSORS
1836. Dec. 24.	Lawrence H. Cortelyou Eliza, his wife	Theodore Hartman	In min. Dwelling
1837. Jan. 2. 1836. May 18.	James Thompson Charity Romer, his wife	Mary Elizabeth	Bp. at a Wedding party at gr.-father's house
1837. Jan. 2. 1836. Jan. 4.	James Romer Sarah Maria Lewis, his wife	Fanny Ann	At same time & place
1837. Jan. 13. 1835. Feb. 22.	John Van Pelt Susan Van Pelt, his wife	Mary Elizabeth	In the West quarter
1837. Jan. 18. 1836. Aug. 23.	Capt. Cornelius Vanderbilt Sophia Johnson, his wife	Catharine Juliette	In parents' dwelling at New York
1837. Jan. 18. 1834. Nov. 7.	James Madison Cross Phoebe Jane Vanbilt, his wife	Cornelius Vanderbilt	At same time as above
1837. Jan. 18. 1836. Sept. 1.	James Madison Cross Phoebe Jane Vanderbilt, his wife	William Harrison	At Capt. Corn. Vanderbilt's, N. York
1837. Jan. 18. 1835. Feb. 26.	Daniel Bicknel Allen Ethelinde Vanderbilt, his wife	William Barton	Same as above
1837. b. Jan. 18. 1836. Nov. 14.	Same parents	Jacob Hand	Same as above
1837. March 26. Feb. 19.	John Romer Catharine Rachel Lewis, his wife	Emeline	At Peter Dorsett's house
April 14. 1836. Nov. 18.	Lewis Cave of N. York Emeline Wood, his wife	Caroline, 1st ch.	In Min.'s dwelling
1837. April 20. 1835. Feb. 6.	Samuel Coddington Catharine Jacobson, his wife	Samuel Franklin	In parents' house
1837. April 25. 1836. Dec. 19.	Isaac Swift Eliza Bodine, his wife	Jeremiah	

Thus far Record is by Br. Hartman, 3 May, 1837.

DATE	PARENTS	CHILD	SPONSORS
1837.	BAPTISMS BY REV. A. RONDSHALER.		
July 23. 1835. Nov. 19.	Johann T. Shaber & wife, maiden name Shaber	Catharine Margaretha	The parents
1837. Aug. 16. 1836. Feb. 2.	John Van Duzer Sarah Vanderbilt, his wife	Daniel Theodore	Bp. at parents' house, Tompkinsville
1837. Sept. 2. 1829. May 1.	Howard Vooris Mary Rhine, his wife	Mary Elizabeth	In house of Cornelius Vanderbilt, the girl's step-father
1834. b. April 1.	Same as above	Julia Parmer	
1837. Sept. 2. July 27.	Cornelius Vanderbilt Mary, his wife, late Vooris, maiden n. Rhine	Elijah Rhine	
Oct. 13. June 7.	Johann Ruppinger Catharine Friederica Rengaten, his wife	Catharine Friederica	Christian & Barbara Mann, Johannes & Maria Essig
Dec. 25. 1835. June 3.	John Widsworth Elizabeth Widsworth	Margaretha Ann	The parents
1837. Dec. 25. July 1.	Leonard Fountain Mary Widsworth, his wife	Elizabeth Ann	The gr.-parents John & Elizabeth Widsworth, & Mary Fountain, the mother
1838. Feb. 1. 1837. May 26.	Carl Auguste Frende Augusta Caroline Rudinger, his wife	Mary Blanche	
May 9. 1837. Oct. 1.	Abraham E. Miller Jane Simonson, his wife	George Albert	
1838. Dec. 25. 1835. April 25.	William Egbert Mary Ann Lake, his wife	Catharine Ann	

DATE	PARENTS	CHILD	SPONSORS
1838. Dec. 9. July 2.	Cornelius Egbert Catharine Lake, his wife	Henrietta	

"During the Year 1838 Br. Ronshaler baptized several children belonging to other churches, these were of course entered in the church book of their respective churches."

1839. March 21. 1838. Nov. 16.	Jacob Burckerdt Teresa Schutzen- bach, his wife	Anthon Friederich	
1839. Jan. 6. 1838. Nov. 30.	Ambr. Rondshaler Matilda Caroline Busse, his wife	Edward Henry	
1839. March 21. 1837. Aug. 31.	Isaac Butler Martha Swain, his wife	Mary Cath.	
1839. March 21. 1837. Sept. 6.	William Crips Jane Butler, his wife	John	
1839. March 26. 1837. May 12.	Oliver Vanderbilt Catharine Ann, his wife	Sarah Louisa	
1838. Feb. 9. 1837. Oct. 8.	John Egbert Lydia Seguine, his wife	John	
1839. March 26. 1838. Sept. 23.	John Van Duzer Sarah Vanderbilt, his wife	Daniel Theodore	

1839.
March 31.
Feb. 25.
	Cornelius Vander-
	  bilt
	Mary, his wife, late
	  Vooris [nee Rhine]
		Oliver H.	

March 18. 1838. Sept. 10.	James Thompson Charity Rome, his wife	Samuel Lewis Ryess	Bp. in house of John Baker, the uncle of child
1839. April 23. 1838. Sept. 26.	Daniel Butler Elisabeth Egbert, his wife	Tunis Eg- bert	Bp. in house of Mr. Edw. Vanderbilt

DATE	PARENTS	CHILD	SPONSORS
1839.			
April 23.	Edward Johnson	John Ed-	Bp. as above
1838.	Hannah Housman,	ward	
March 22.	his wife		
1839.			
April 23.	Edward Vanderbilt	Cornelius	Bp. as above
1838.	Mary Ann Egbert,	Egbert	
July 7.	his wife		
1839.			
April 28.	Ferdinand Thun	Margaretha	Martin and Sophia
Jan. 14.	Jacobina Small, his wife		Schmidt
April 29.	Anthony Y. Stewart	Sarah Eliz-	
1838.	Mary Lipincott, his	abeth	
March 3.	wife		
1839.			
April 29.	James Gilbert	Elizabeth	
1838.	Abigail Black, his	Frances	
Sept. 4.	wife		

BAPTISMS BY H. G. CLAUDER.

DATE	PARENTS	CHILD	SPONSORS
1839.			
June 9.	Lawrence H. Cor-	Eugene	The parents
1838.	telyou	Augustus	
Dec. 2.	Eliza Hekel, his wife		
1839.			
Sept. 26.	Joseph Sharrott	David Mer-	
1838.	Cornelia Mer-	cereau	
April 16.	cereau, his wife		
1839.			
Oct. 11.	William Egbert	Mary Eliza-	Bp. in house of parents
March 21.	Mary Elizabeth Lake, his wife	beth	in North Quarter. Sponsors, parents & gr.-mother
Nov. 10.	Abraham Bodine	Abraham	Bp. at parsonage,
Feb. 28.	Abby Kinsy, his wife	Brown	parents sponsors
Dec. 18.	Edward Egbert	Ester Ellen	The parents
1837.	Hannah Price, his		
Aug. 31.	wife		
1839.			
b. July 10.	Same parents	Caroline Atkins	The parents & Miss Atkins of N. York
1840.			
Jan. 28.	John Baker	James	James Romer & wife,
	Eliza Romer, his wife	Henry	gr.-parents, at whose house baptism took place

DATE	PARENTS	CHILD	SPONSORS
1840.			
Arpil 23. 1839. Sept. 22.	Moses Alston Sarah Ann Decker, his wife	Sarah Ann	Bp. at house of gr.-mother Sr. Ann Decker at Long Neck
1840. June 21. 1839. Sept. 6.	Peter Hibbets from N. Y. Catharine Merrile	Euphemia	Parents & gr.-mother sponsors
1840. Aug. 16.	Johann Martin Lutz Christina Rokere, his wife	Christiana	Gallus Gahner of N.Y., Catharina Lutz & the parents
Aug. 29. 1839. Sept. 7.	Jacob Frederic Jakle of Wurtemburg, Germany Eva Maria Sicking	Carolina Louise	
1840. Oct. 1. 1837. Oct. 25. 1839. b. Dec. 1.	James Romer, Jr. Sarah Maria Lewis, his wife Same parents	Sarah Jane James Isaac	The gr.-parents James Romer, Sr., & his wife, at whose house ch. was bap.
1840. Oct. 18. Aug. 31.	Cornelius Vanderbilt Mary Rhine, his wife	Lydia Ann	The parents
Nov. 18. 1841.	Edward Beatty Ann Denice, his wife	Ellenor Louisa	The parents
Jan. 8. 1839. April 10. 1841.	Capt. Cornelius Vanderbilt Sophia Johnson, his wife	George Washington	The parents, ch. bap. at house of parents at Quarantine
April 11. Feb. 21.	Rev. H. G. Clauder Charlott Elizabeth Ruede, his wife	Henry Theophilus, 4th son	John Gottlieb Herman, Anna Pauline Herman of Bethlehem, Pa., Louisa C. Kranisch, single, Lydia Benzien, single, both of Bethlehem, Pa.
April 11. Feb. 21.	Rev. H. G. Clauder Charlotte Elizabeth Ruede, his wife	Charlotte Jane, 4th dau., twin of Henry Theop.	Chas. A. Bleck & Sophia, his wife of N. Y., Lawrence H. & wife Eliza Cortelyou of S. I., Sr. Jane Matilda Cargile, single, of N. Y.

DATE	PARENTS	CHILD	SPONSORS
1841. June 27. 1840. Dec. 21.	John Vanduzer Sarah Vanderbilt, his wife	Elisabeth Ann	Bp. in house of John Vanderbilt
1841. June 27. 1840. Dec. 3.	Jacob Van Duzer Mary Holden, his wife	Mary Louisa	" "
1841. June 30. 1840. Sept. 8.	Oliver Vanderbilt Catharine Morris, his wife	Edward Ward	Mrs. Ward of N. Y., & the parents. Bp. at parents' house at Quarantine
1841. Oct. 18. 1840. July 28.	(James) Thompson, ship carpenter at Quarantine Charity Romer, his wife	Joseph Lake	James & Ann Romer
1841. Nov. 7.	Adam Fugel, Catharine Thum, his wife, both of Wurtemberg, Germany, now at Castleton	Hans Jorg	Hans Jorg Fritz & wife, Maria Wolfen & the parents
Dec. 25. Nov. 30. 1842.	Lawrence H. Cortelyou Eliza Hekkel, his wife	David Hekkel	The parents. Living at Freshkill
Jan. 2.	Abraham Bodine Abby, his wife	Sarah Ann Kinsey	The parents
Jan. 16. 1841. July 4.	Martin Schmidt, a German farmer now near Capt. Connor's Wife not given	Louis	The parents, Louis Göntz, single
1842. Jan. 30. 1839. April 19. 1841. h. July 24.	Edward Burbank Jane Britton, his wife	Edward Egbert. Sarah Ann	The gr.-parents Isaac & Sarah Burbank, at whose house ch. was bap.
1842. Feb. 8.	Joseph Decker Sarah, his wife	Amanda Malvina	The parents
March 6. Jan. 4.	Ferdinand Thum Jacobina "	Christina	Adam Wagener, Christina Bisbalin, his wife
March 18. 1841. July 25.	Paul Schmidt Catharine Miller, his wife	Eliza Barrett	The parents, residing at Factoryville

DATE	PARENTS	CHILD	SPONSORS
1842.			
March 27.	Anthony Stewart	William	The parents
March 8.	Mary "	Thomas	
1840.			
b. March 28.	Same parents	Julia Ann	
1842.			
March 27.	William Neats, wheelwright Di., his wife	John Richard Shelton	Bp. at house of Anthony Stewart
July 24.	Joseph Sharrott	Catharine	The parents. Bp. at
1840.	Cornelia Mer-	Eliza	minister's
Oct. 6.	sereau, his wife		
1842.			
Aug. 1.	William Egbert	Henry	The parents, residing
1841.	Catharine, his wife		on North Side
June 3.			
1842.			
Sept. 2.	Theodore O. Sier-	Marianne	The ch. was evidently
Aug. 19.	sina	Emily	near its last & was
	Meda Lenting, his wife		bp. in house of parents
Sept. 5.	John Baker	Mary Ellen	Bp. in house of E.
Jan. 3.	Eliza Romer, his wife		Johnson
Sept. —.	Edward Johnson	Richard	" "
March 11.	Hannah Housman, his wife		
Nov. 18.	Wm. Neats, wheel-	Sarah Fran-	The parents
Aug. 30.	wright at Northside, & wife	ces	
Sept. 18.	Wm. De Groot	Lenah Ann	The parents, living at
1840.	Mary Sharrott, his		North side
Sept. 18.	wife		
1842.			
Oct. 9.	Philip Leiser	Ernst Franz	The parents, living at
1840.	Hetwig, his wife		Factoryville
July 29.			
1842.			
Oct. 28.	James Gibett of	James	Both this ch. & fol-
1841.	N. Y.	Augustus	lowing bp. in ch. on
Jan. 20.	Abigail Ann Black, his wife		S. Island
1842.			
Oct. 28.	Wm. Julin, residing at 80 Oliver St., N. Y. Sarah Jane Stewart, his wife	James Thomas	
Nov. 6.	Daniel Butler	Daniel	
March 7.	Eliza "		

DATE	PARENTS	CHILD	SPONSORS
1842.			
Nov. 28. Aug. 28.	Abraham Garrettson Eliza Sanders, his wife	John Jacob	
Dec. 10. 1841. Dec. 14.	Barney Hughes & wife	George Washington	Residing in Jersey City where he has a situation in R. R. office
1843. Jan. 17.	James Brittain Frances Oakly, his wife	Elizabeth Ann Violetta Harriet Amanda	Grocer & shoemaker in this vicinity
	All ch. of same parents	Mary Theresia	
May 16. Feb. 11.	John Rathyen Anna Rotsen, his wife	Mathin, inf. son	Bootmaker at Pt. Richmond
June 18.	Robert Sommers, carpenter Susan Ann "	Robert Gray	Parents sponsors
July 22. 1840. Sept. 11.	John G. Lake Violetta Spear, his wife	Mary Gifford	Bp. at house of John G. Lake. Parents sponsors
1843. b. Jan. 19.	Same parents	Adriana Britton	
Sept. 10.	Adam Fugel Catharine Thum, his wife	Michael	
Sept. 27.	T. O. Siersina Meda "	Unatais	
Oct. 20. Sept. 30.	Wm. Julin, residing in N. Y. Sarah Jane Steward	Hanna Ann Elizabeth	
	Richard Housman, Jr., & wife Martha, late Butler, nee Swaim	Alfred	This ch. & one above bp. in house of widow Steward
Nov. 12. May 16.	J. Thompson Charity Romer, his wife	James	Ship carpenter at Tompkinsville
1844. Jan. 6.	James Pollworth, farmer near the Blackhorse, from Berkshire, Scotland	William & Peter	
Jan. 31. 1843. Jan. 7.	Edward Egbert Hannah Price, his wife	Henrietta Prall	Bp. at house of Joseph Lake, Manor

DATE	PARENTS	CHILD	SPONSORS
1844.			
Feb. 4. 1843. Nov. 20.	H. G. Clauder Charlotte Elizabeth Ruede, his wife	Sarah Adelaide	Rev. D. Bigler & Adelaide, his wife, maiden name Finauf, of N. Y., Br. Isaac Burbank, Sr. Burbank, nee Egbert, Sr. Lydia Rice, wid., of Bethlehem
1844. March 31. Feb. 29.	Anthony Stewart, brushmaker Mary "	Samuel "	Bp. at Parents' house near Abr. Egbert's. The parents & Br. & Sr. Clauder
April 14. 1838. July 30. 1841. b. July 28.	Capt. Jacob H. Vanderbilt, residing at Tompkinsville Maria Banta, his wife Same parents	Ellen Jacob Ellis	Bp. in presence of Mrs. Charlotte Deforest Egbert & Miss Phoebe Vanderbilt
1844. April 28. Jan. —.	Peter Cozine Hannah Maria Vanbilt, his wife	James Edward	The parents & Eliza Ann Vanderbilt
May 5. March 16.	James Wood Emily Britton	Mary Ann	Bp. in church
May 26. 1842. Dec. 14. 1844.	George Schmidt, tailor & draper at Tompkinsville Barbara Heusler, his wife	Magdalena	The parents & Magda. Schmidt, single, dau. of Martin Schmidt
July 6. May 8.	Alexander Boyd, laborer at Col. Connors Rebecca McNab, his wife	Margaret Ann, Rebecca Jane, twins	
1844. Aug. 5.	Joseph Romer Jane Moore, his wife	Sarah Jane	Bp. in house of Br. John Sharrott. Parents sponsors
Sept. 10. 1839. b. 29 Sept. 1844. b. March 5. 1839. b. July 25. 1841. b. Dec. 19. 1844. b. May 26.	Oliver R. Martin Sarah Ann Vanderbilt, his wife Same parents Henry Flagler Isabella Vanderbilt, his wife Henry & Isabella Flagler	Sarah Ann Oliver Rollin John Walter Constance Maria Isabella	These five children are gr.-grandchildren of Br. John & Elizabeth Vanderbilt & baptized at their house

DATE	PARENTS	CHILD	SPONSORS
1844.			
Sept. 15.	Abraham Bodine	Jacob	
April 8.	Abby Ann Kinsy, his wife	Howard	
Sept. 23.	Paul Schmidt,	Catharine	
Jan. 6.	laborer at Factoryville Catharine Schmidt	Christiana	
Oct. 13.	Robert Summers, carpenter in this vicinity Susan Ann Stilwell	Albert	
Nov. 8.	James Armstrong	Amelia	
Oct. 7.	of Ireland, farmer & laborer, residing on this Island Rose, his wife		
Nov. 16.	Augustus Saddler	Mary Eliza-	The mother, Sr. D.
June 16.	of Port Richmond Ann Eliza	beth	Neat, Sr. Ann Neat
Dec. 29.	Cornelius Egbert	Louisa	Parents & gr.-mother
June 25.	Catharine Lake, his wife		
1845.			
March 4.	Ernst Senne,	Charles	The parents & August
1844.	Gesine Schiegel,	Henry	Senne, single
Dec. 28.	his wife, both of Germany	Augustus	
1845.			
March 30.	T. O. Siersema	PhoebeAnn	The parents
1844.	Meda Leiting, his		
Oct. 10.	wife		
1845.			
May 21.	Wandel Baker	Susan &	
	Betsy Haughwout, his wife	Mary	
June 8.	George W. Blake	EmilyAnna	
Jan. 16.	Mary Ann Wood, his wife	Christopher	
June 17.	Barney Hughes of	Ellen Jane	Bp. in parents' dwelling. Parents sponsors
1843.	Jersey City		
Dec. 30.			
1845.			
July 13.	Joseph Corron	Alfred	
1843.	Jane Burgher, his		
May 31.	wife		
1845.	Ch. of above parents	Nicolas	
July 13.	Abraham Stewart Mary Ann Burger, his wife	Mathias Burger	

DATE	PARENTS	CHILD	SPONSORS
1845.			
July 24. April 1.	John Baker, mason, near Pt. Richmond Elizabeth Romer	John William	
Aug. 24. 1844. Nov. 21. 1845.	William Wilson, residing in N. Y. Catharine Ann Noble, his wife	Abraham Noble	The parents & gr.-parents, Abr. Noble
Sept. 25. 1841. Jan. 25. 1842.	Jacob Fred. Jackle at Factoryville Eva Maria Jackle	Maria Catharine	
b. Dec. 28. 1845. b. 16 Jan.	All ch. of above parents	Emma Amalia Jacob Frederick	
Nov. 17. July 1.	Mathias Swaim Margaret Jane Egbert, his wife	George Abraham	The parents
Nov. 20. June 17.	James G. Britten Frances Oakley, his wife	George Washington Oakley	The parents
Nov. 23. July 19.	John Mills of Tompkinsville Eliza Egbert, his wife	Moses Newel	The parents & gr.-mother Mrs. Mary Mills
Nov. 23. 1842. Nov. 26. 1845. b. 17 May.	Robert Johnston, seaman at Tompkinsville Adaline Holden, his wife Same parents	Clara Holden Robert Clyde	The mother & her sister Mrs. Jacob Vanduzer
Dec. 30. April 20.	Richard Conner, Junr. Ann Smith, his wife	Dewitt Clinton	The parents
1846. Feb. 5.	Oliver Vanderbilt, of Tompkinsville Elizabeth Morris, his wife	James Oliver	
Jan. 9. 1845. Oct. 21. 1846.	John Rathyen at Port Richmond Anna Rothen, his wife	Henry	The parents & Henry Gans
Feb. 11. 1842. March 1. 1845. b. 14 June.	Thomas Holmes Egbert Elizabeth Ann Merril, his wife Same parents	John Merril Elizabeth Mary	Bp. at parents' house, North side

DATE	PARENTS	CHILD	SPONSORS
1846. March 27. 1845. Nov. 25.	Adam Fugel of Wurtemberg, Germany, now at Factoryville, Staten Island Catharine Shum, his wife	Maria Catharine Barbara	
1846. April 8. 1845. Nov. 6.	T. O. Siersema, residing near Edw. Bodine's in the Manor Meda Lenting, his wife	John Theodore	The parents & John Siersema, unmd.
1846. May 24. 1845. Sept. 1.	William Winant, carpenter Hannah Burger, his wife	George Henry Tyson	
1846. June 7. Jan. 25. April 2.	Oliver R. Martin at Port Richmond Sarah Martin	ChauncySt. John Georg Cortelyou	The gr.-parents, Br. John & Priscilla Vanderbilt
Aug. 16. Jan. 18.	Robert Summers Susan Ann Stillwell, his wife	George James	
Aug. 19. 1845. Oct. 2. 1846.	John Perine, of New York Rebecca Jane Lewis, his wife	Richard Taylor	The gr.-mother, at whose house ch. was bap.
Aug. 19. 1844. March 25.	James Romer Sarah Maria Lewis, his wife	Mary Elizabeth	
1845. b. July 22.	Same parents	Thomas Simpson	
1846. Aug. 30. July 21.	Alexander Boyd, laborer Rebecca McNab, his wife	Mary	
Aug. 31. Jan. 23.	Abr. S. Egbert, hackman Eliza Bird, his wife	Henrietta	Bp. at house of Mrs. Lydia Egbert, Tompkinsville
Aug. 31. April 15. 1845. b. 22 Oct.	Wm. Vroome Catharine Maria Egbert, his wife Jacob Arnold, shoemaker, & wife Susan Ann, late Bird nee Perine	Georgianna MariaLouisa	

DATE	PARENTS	CHILD	SPONSORS
1846.			
Oct. 11. April 12.	Paul Schmidt, laborer, Catharine, his wife, both from Germany	Jacob Edward	Parents & Jacob Stoll
b.April 22.	John Kirtche Elizabeth	Henry	The parents. Both these reside at Factoryville
Oct. 20. June 30.	William Maines Ellen Baker, his wife	David Wooley	Residing at North shore
Oct. 25. 1845. Oct. 24.	John V. Vanduzer, Junr. Frances Louisa Roff, his wife	Sarah Catharina	The parents & Sr. Sarah Vanduzer
1846. Nov. 4. Oct. 16.	Abraham Bodine Abby Kinsy, his wife	James Edward	The parents, at whose house at 4 corners the ch. was bap.
Nov. 7. Oct. 16.	David Mersereau of Richmond Anneke Lake, his wife	Marieta Gifford, 1st ch.	
Nov. 22. Oct. 15.	Henry G. Clauder Charlotte Elizabeth, his wife	Ottelia Virginia	Bp. in ch. on Sunday by her father
Dec. 6. July 6.	William Julin, sailor Sarah Jane, his wife	Catharine Maria Stewart	Bp. at house of Anthony Stewart
Dec. 6. Oct. 11.	Anthony Stewart Mary "	George Anthony	" "
1847. Feb. 5. 1846. Dec. 4.	Ernst Senne Kissine Schiegel, his wife	Louisa Margaretha Christiana	Living at Northfield when baptism was administered
1847. April 4.	John Mills of Tompkinsville Eliza Ann Mills	Mary Elizabeth Vanderbilt	
April 25. 1846. Oct. 12.	William Wilson, residing in N. Y. Catharine Noble, his wife	Grace Noble	
1847. July 23. May —.	Abraham Vanduzer, residing at Quarantine Eliza Vanderbilt, his wife	Sarah Elizabeth	

DATE	PARENTS	CHILD	SPONSORS
1847.			
Oct. 3.	Joseph Decker, blacksmith Sarah Fitzgerald, his wife	Theodore Hampton	
July 25.			
1848.			
April 9. 1844.	George Fritz at Factoryville Anna Maria Wolf, his wife	Henrietta Elisabeth	Conrad Barton, Elisabeth Schlect
Jan. 13.			
1848.			
April 23. March 6.	Peter Cozine Hanna Maria Vanderbilt, his wife	Mary Priscilla	
July 30. 1847. Aug. 31.	John Biaron, formerly of Easton, Pa., now at Factoryville Caroline Weidenmiller, his wife	Henry	
1848.			
Aug. 3. June 7.	Raymond Augustus Dominge of N. Y. Ellen, his wife	Ellen Matilda	Bp. at parsonage in presence of the gr.-mother Mrs. Dunham
Aug. 17. July 15.	John Rathyen of Port Richmond Ann Rathyen	Anna	
Sept. 17. 1844. Aug. 18. 1848.	Jacob Schneider, at Factoryville Maria Clara Schneider	Anna Emilia	
Sept. 28. 1847. June 8. 1848.	Isaac M. Brown Mary Romer, his wife	Charles Henry	Bp. at dwelling of Br. James Romer at North side
Oct. 6. Aug. 22.	Wm. Vroome, residing at Quarantine Catharine Maria Egbert, his wife	Maria Louise	Bothe these ch. bap. at the house & in the presence of their gr.-mother Lydia Egbert
Oct. 6. 1847. Nov. 28. 1848.	Abrm. S. Egbert of Tompkinsville Eliza Bird, his wife	Madora	
Oct. 15. Sept. 20.	Thomas Sharrott Mary Elizabeth Voorhis, his wife	Thomas Howard	The parents & gr.-mother Mrs. Mary Vanderbilt, at whose house ch. was bap.
1849.			
Jan. 21. 1848. Dec. 24.	Louis Geiser, Maria Kollman, his wife, natives of Germany, now at Pt. Richmond	Johannes	John Walter, single, the parents

DATE	PARENTS	CHILD	SPONSORS
1849.			
April 8.	Paul Schmidt of	George	The parents, George
1848.	Factoryville	Sommers	Sommers, Margt.
Nov. 13.	Catharine Schmidt	Marks	Baltzer
1849.			
b. Jan. 29.	Adam Fugel	John	The parents, John
	Catharine Fugel		Schlect, Ros. Rapp
	These two ch. were bp. at D. Ref. Ch. at Pt. Richmond, by H. G. Clauder		
July 29.	Ernst Senne,	Amalia	Aike Marg. Schiegel,
April 26.	Gesiene Senne, Germans	Sophie Matilda	Sophie Lange, Louise Senne
	Bp. in D. Ref. Ch. at Pt. Richmond		
July 29.	Theodore Siersema	Frederick	
	Meda Siersema	Henry	
July 29.	John Mills, carpenter	Gilbert Tunis Egbert	
	Eliza Ann Egbert, his wife, deceased		
Aug. 30.	Abraham S. Egbert,	William St.	
April 3.	coachman, son of John, residing at Tompkinsville	Clair	
	Eliza Bird, his wife		
Sept. 6.	Mathias Burger	John	
1847.	Hetty Vanderbilt,		
Dec. 11.	his wife		
1849.			
Sept. 9.	John Rathyen,	Anna	The parents, Anna
Aug. 3.	Anna, his wife, Germans at Port Richmond		Reiners, mother, Anna Reiners, daughter
Sept. 9.	Wm. Mains	Elizabeth	
April 23.	Ellen Baker, his wife	Virginia	
Oct. 21.	John Housman &	Martha	Residing near 4 Corners
1845.	his wife Susan	Jane	
Aug. 29.	Ann [Houghwout]		
1849.			
Oct. 21.	Abraham Bodine	Benjamin	This ch. & above one
Jan. 7.	Abby Ann "	JohiaKinsy	were bap. at house of Abr. Bodine
Nov. 18.	Johann Fisher,	Johann	The father & John
May 13.	Christina Rothfus, his wife, Germans		Rothfus, single
Dec. 17.	Benjamin Lydle &	Gilbert Osborne	Residing at Richmond
1843.	wife Ann, late		
Aug. 24.	Pierson, formerly		
1849.	Fredericks		
b. June 30.		Wm. Wallace	
1847.	All ch. of above		
b. Nov. 21.	parents	Mary Elizabeth	

DATE	PARENTS	CHILD	SPONSORS
1849.			
Dec. 24.	John Johnson, boot & shoemaker at Quarantine	Anna Maria	Christian Block, Anna Mary Leating
1838. Jan. 31.			
1850. Jan. 7.	Adelaide Eggers, his wife		
1843. May 17.	Wm. Egbert at Grantville Mary Ann Lake, his wife	Joseph	
1848. b. March 6.	Son of same parents both members of our congregation	Wesley	
1850. March 31.	Henry Prall of Port Richmond	William Henry	
1849. Sept. 27.	Elizabeth Neats, his wife		
1850. March 31.	Wm. Neats at Port Richmond	Lester Palmer	
1849. Sept. 27.	Di Neats		
1850. March 31.	Anthony Stewart, brushmaker	Mary Alina	
1849. Nov. 25.	Mary Stewart		
1850. June 5.	John Vanduzer Louisa Roff, his wife	Ellen Louisa	
1847. Oct. 6.			
1849. b. Dec. 24.	Abrm. Vanduzer Eliza Ann Vanduzer	Sarah Elizabeth	Both these ch. bp. at house of Sr. Sarah Vanduzer at Tompkinsville
1850. July 7. April 12.	Christian Block Rebecca Kniep, his wife	Henry Christn. Ludwig	
Aug. 11. April 30.	Wm. B. Seawood at Pt. Richmond Ann Neats, his wife	Eva Harrison	The parents & Miss Elizabeth H. Palmer of N. Y.
Sept. 11. May 8.	John Bieran of Factoryville Caroline Weidmuller, his wife	Elizabeth	
Oct. 20. Aug. 15.	James B. Wood Emily Britton, his wife	Henrietta	
Jan. 6.	"Garrit Vroome, a *single* young man & [son of Christopher Vroom] Maria Housman *his wife* was baptized into the death of Jesus"		
Jan. 20.	Mathias Burger, md., son of Mathias Burger & Hannah, his wife		

DATE	PARENTS	CHILD	SPONSORS
1849.			
Nov. 18.	Martha Hauseman, late Butler, nee Swaim, wid.		
1850.			
Dec. 15.	John Christian,	Heinrich,	
Aug. 30.	Margaret Ahrens, Germans at Port Richmond	infant	
Nov. 10	John Simonson Catharine, his wife	Catharine, & Ellen, wife of John V. Egbert	
Dec. 29.	John Schlect,	Catharine	Paul & Cath. Schmidt
May 7.	Rosina Raff, his wife, Germans, near Factoryville		
1851.			
Jan. 12.	John V. Egbert	Louisa Sidney	
1844.	Ellen [Simonson], his wife		
July 11.			
1847.	Same parents	John Simonson	
b. Nov. 3.			
1851.			
Jan. 26.	John Düringer, miller	John Henry	The parents, John Herman Kniper, first mate on steamer Washington, & Heinrich Ohl
1850.			
Sept. 16.	Nancy Lubers, his wife		
1851.			
April 13.	Christopher Vroome & wife	Mary Ann	
1830.			
April 13.	—— Housman		
1851.			
June 21.	John V. Egbert	Abraham	
Jan. 31.	Ellen Simonson	Tunis	
June 26.	John Oldfield, residing in Troy, formerly in N. York Martha Levinia Merril, his wife	George	
1847.			
Sept. 16.			
1851.			
b. July 7.	Same parents	Egbert	
June 29.	John Hatsche & his wife, at Factoryville	Elizabeth Georgiana	Elizabeth Schmidt, George Hatsche
Aug. 26.	August Kiesele, Tompkinsville Louisa Julia Dimpfel	Louisa	John Lambert, Eliza Schoenberg, George Louis Dimpfel, Augustus Plessing, Elizabeth Dimpfel, Emilie Plessing
1845.			
b. Sept. 12.			
1847.			
b. April 28.		Emilie	
1849.			
b. Sept 18.		Lilia	
1851.	All ch. of above parents	Augusta Eliza Anna	
b. July 22.			

DATE	PARENTS	CHILD	SPONSORS
1851.			
Oct. 5.	Carl Christian Friderick Deinmann Louise Johanna Catarina Reuter, his wife	Friderica Dorotea Cicilia	Germans now living at New Brighton
Nov. 6. Oct. 10.	Benjamin Lydle & wife Ann, late Pierson, nee Fredericks of Richmond	George Washington	
1852.			
Jan. 23 Jan. 1.	Adam Fügel Catharine Thum, his wife	Nathan	
Feb. 8. 1851. Oct. 25.	Heinrich Weidmuller Eliza Gerd, his wife	Carl Heinrich Christian	Germans, now at Port Richmond. Carl Etsch, Heinrich Kaus, Christina Hützel
1852. March 3. 1847. b. April 27. 1845. b. Feb. 3. 1849. b. Jan. 7. 1850. b. Nov. 27.	George Ebbits Serena Downs, his wife All ch. of above parents	George Patten Ann Wright Lucy Harriet	
1852. April 4. 1851. Nov. 29.	Dietrich Senne & wife Dorothea Krumdick	August Ernst Wilhelm Christian	Living near 4 Corners. Christian Schiegel, August Senne, Ernst Senne, Friedrich Lange
1852. April 4. Jan. 4.	Ernst Senne Gesine Schiegel, his wife	Diedrich Friedrich Christian August	Johann. Chr. Schiegel, Diedrich Senne, Friedrich Senne, Friedrich Lange, August Senne
April 23. 1849. b. Sept. 5. 1851. b. Feb. 12.	Charles Lewis Moelich Catharine Ann Hausman, dau. of Isaac, his wife Same parents	Charles Frederick Elizabeth Augusta	Both ch. bap. at house of Isaac Housman

DATE	PARENTS	CHILD	SPONSORS
1852. April 29. Jan. 9.	Abraham Vanduzer Eliza Ann, his wife	John Housman	
1851. b. Jan. 6.	John Vanduzer Francis Louisa Roff, his wife	Peter Winant	
b. July 10. 1852.	Jacob Vanduzer Margaret, his wife	Eveline	
b. March 23.	Isaac Vanduzer Mary, his wife	Isaac Oliver	These 4 bap. at house of Sr. Sarah Vanduzer at Tompkinsville
May 2. 1851. April 22.	Wm. Vroome Catharine Egbert, his wife	Ann Eliza	Living at Tompkinsville. Bp. at house of Sr. Vroome near 4 Corners
1852. May 2. March 13.	Wm. Seawood Ann Neats, his wife	Elizabeth Frances	At Port Richmond

BAPTISMS BY BERNARD E. SCHWEINITZ.

DATE	PARENTS	CHILD	SPONSORS
1852. July 25. Feb. 8.	Daniel Eidam Margarita Neterman, his wife	Elizabeth	Germans in Factoryville. Bp. in D. Ref. Ch. at Port Richmond
Sept. 1.	Friedrich A. Dreyer of Brooklyn Augusta Henriette Schmidt, his wife	Carl Bruno	Bp. at house of gr.-father, Dr. Schmidt
Sept. 5. 1851. Nov. 22.	Andrew Soner Clara Wagner, his wife	Anna Maria Clara	Germans at Factoryville. Baptism at Mr. Rathyen's house in Port Richmond
1852. Sept. 10. 1851. Aug. 28.	Joseph Jacobsmyer Anna, his wife	Johann Christian	Germans near Port Richmond. Bap. at parent's house when very sick
1852. Oct. 3. 1850. June 24.	James Hausman Catherine Bauer, his wife	Theodore Adam	Living at Factoryville
1852. Oct. 3. 1850. Feb. 27.	Jacob Fried'k Jackel Eva Maria Sekinger, his wife	Magdalena Rosina	Living at Factoryville. Bp. at house of James Housman
1852. Oct. 3. Sept. 9.	Thomas Sharrot Mary Elizabeth Voorhis, his wife	Alfred	Bp. at house of gr.-mother Mrs. Mary Vanderbilt

DATE	PARENTS	CHILD	SPONSORS
1852. Oct. 17. June 5 or 11.	Paul Schmidt Catharine Müller, his wife	Carl Henry	
Oct. 17. July 31.	Reinhart Koch Anna Catharina Walter, his wife	Anna Maria	Both Bp. in D. Ref. Ch. at Port Richmond
Nov. 28. 1850. b. Nov. 3.	Adolph Levando Emma Schmidt, his wife	Joseph	Bp. at Factoryville
1852. b. Sept 21.	Same parents	Elisabeth	" "
Dec. 1. 1850. b. April 22.	Bernard Alfrenk Anna Myers, his wife	William Henry	Bp. at parents' dwelling near Mariner's Harbor
1851. b. 11 Oct.	Same parents	John Frederick	
1852. Dec. 12. Dec. 14.	Christian Bloch Rebecca Knief, his wife	Louise Marie	Bp. at D. Ref. Ch. at Port Richmond
Dec. 14.	Sarah Rodgers, wife of Capt. W. Cole		Bp. at her home where she was confined by consumption
Dec. 14. 1844. Nov. 30.	Capt. W. Cole Sarah Rodgers, his wife	Jonah Rodgers	
1853. Jan 9. 1852. June 20.	Jacob Mauer Catharine Kebel, his wife	John Jacob	
1853. March 6. 1852. Sept. 13.	Johann Heinrich Knoch Martha Elisabetha Penhart, his wife	Johanna Henerika Juliana	Bp. in Ch. at Port Port Richmond
1853. March 13. 1852. Sept. 29.	Robert Summers Susan Ann Stilwell, his wife	Sylvester	
1853. March 27. Feb. 23.	B. E. Schweinitz Marie Ottilie Goepp, his wife	Paul Bernhard	Sr. Mary Connelz of Bethlehem, Pa., (absent), Br. L. H. Cortelyou & Eliza, his wife, Mr. & Mrs. Dettmar Basse of Brooklyn, N. Y., Br. John F. Bigler of N.Y.

DATE	PARENTS	CHILD	SPONSORS
1853.			
March 27.	Heinrich Jansen Eden	Heinrich Jansen	Bp. in Ch. at Port Richmond
Feb. 1.	Cathrina Behrens, his wife		
May 8.	Edward Holzhalb	Bertha	Bp. in Ch. at Port Richmond
1852.	Bertha Holzhalb,		
Dec. 28.	nee Motzer		
1853.			
June 19.	John Ahrens	Anna Maria	Anna Hattof, Maria Alsguth. Bp. in Port Richmond
1852.	Margretha Als-		
July 21.	guth, his wife		
1853.			
July 17.	Albert Hulsebas	Gesina Car-olina	Bp. in Ch. at Port Richmond
April 20.	Fredericka Caro-lina Feust, his wife		
May 15.	Daniel Torrance &	Alfred	
1852.	wife Sophia J.		
Nov. 6.	Vanderbilt, dau. of Corn. Vander-		
1853.	bilt of N. Y.		
May 22.	Jacob Salbacher	Bertha	Bp. at parents' house at 4 Corners
1851.	Barbara Shelling		
Dec. 6.			
1853.			
Aug. 8.	Louis Ettlinger	Adolph	Germans
June 25.	Charlotte Abel, his wife		
Sept. 2.	Maria Egbert [nee Simonson], wife of Jacob Egbert of Tomp-kinsville		On her dying bed
Sept. 25.	James Burger	Maria Ottilia	
March 27.	Maria Jane Noble, his wife		
Nov. 20.	James Coyne	Harriet Matilda	Both members of our church
July 6.	Harriet Matilda Thompson, his wife		
Nov. 28.	Benjamin Lydle	Josephine	Bp. at Richmond in house of parents
Nov. 18.	Ann [Nancy] Fred-ericks, his wife		
Dec. 2.	Cornelius P. Bird	Cornelia	At Tompkinsville in presence of ch's. mother & gr.-mother Lydia Eg-bert
1852.	Lydia Eliza Egbert,		
April 12.	his wife		
1853.			
Dec. 9.	Abraham S. Egbert	Cornelius Bird	Bp. at parents' house at Vanderbilt Land-ing
1852.	Mary Eliza Bird,		
May 31.	his wife		
1853.			
Nov. 12.	Same parents	John	

DATE	PARENTS	CHILD	SPONSORS
1853. Dec. 11. 1854.	John Simonson of Clifton	Catharine	
Jan. 15. 1852. Nov. 30.	Joshua Mercereau Sarah Ann Perine, his wife	Stephen Henry	Living on South side
1854. March 13. Feb. 8.	John Godfried Gebhardt Catharine Christina Ehrhardt, his wife	John Godfried	Germans. Godfried W. Gebhardt & his wife
March 13. Feb. 21.	George Barth Elisabeth Schmidt, his wife	John	Natives of Germany, now of New Brighton Conn. Bp. at house of gr.-father John Schmidt, who was sponsor with his wife Catharine Galmer

BAPTISMS BY A. A. REINKE.

DATE	PARENTS	CHILD	SPONSORS
1854. Sept. 25. Aug. 8.	John V. Egbert Ellen Simonson, his wife	Lemont Williams	Living near Bound Brook, N. Jersey. Bp. at Parsonage
Oct. 15. Aug. 22.	James Wilson Sharrott Agnes Caroline, his wife	Cornelia Frances	Bp. at house of gr.-parents
1855. Jan. 7. 1854. July 17.	Robert Sommers Sarah A. Stilwell, his wife	Lavina	
1855. April 11. 1854. Feb. 2.	William Vroome Catharine Maria Egbert, his wife	Wm. Emmett	
1855. June 20. 1854. Dec. 12.	Abraham Van Duzer Elizabeth Ann Van Duzer	Mary Emma	Bp. at house of Mrs. S. Van Duzer
1855. June 20. 1853. Jan. 14.	John Van Duzer Louisa Roff, his wife	Peter Winant	" " "
1855. June 20. 1854. July 22.	Isaac Van Duzer Mary, his wife	Jacob Theodore	Bp. at house of Mrs. S. Van Duzer
1855. June 20. 1853. Nov. 4.	Jacob Van Duzer Margaret Van Duzer	John Jacob	" " "

DATE	PARENTS	CHILD	SPONSORS
1855.			
July 1.	Jns. Pearce	Mary Jane	Both lately arrived
March 28.	Matilda Lunt, his wife		from London, Eng.
Aug. 20.	Jno. Schmidt	Catharine	Near Bull'shead
March 7.	Catharine Eulner, his wife	Margaret	
Sept. 30.	James Wood Emily Britton, his wife	William Henry	
1856.			
Jan. 1.	James Coyn & his wife Harriet Matilda Thompson	James	
1855.			
July 19.			
1856.			
April 13.	Cornelius P. Bird Lydia Eliza Egbert, his wife	Jane Louisa	Bp. at house of Mr. Wm. Vroome in Tompkinsville
1855.			
Sept. 23.			
1856.			
April 17.	Garry Vroome Mary Elizabeth Martling, his wife	Mary Anna	Bp. at house of Mr. Christopher Vroome at Centreville
Feb. 23.			
April 27.	Jacob Frettert Maria Steker, his wife	Frederick Jacob Magdalena	
March 26.			
Sept. 9.	Jacob Van Duzer Margaret Van Duzer	Wm. Oliver	Bp. at house of Mrs. Sarah Van Duzer at Quarantine
1855.			
Oct. 16.			
1856.			
Sept. 28.	George M. Root Anna M. Van Duzer, his wife	Elliott Aymar	
1854.			
July 15.			
1856.			
Oct. 26.	Peter Hirschle Francesca Weber, his wife	Heinrich	
Sept. 2.			
1857.			
April 3.	Robert Barnes Louisa Ketteltas, his wife	George & Elizabeth, twins	Bp. at house of parents in presence of gr.-parents & sisters
April 1.			
April 7.	Peter Anderson Waglom Margaret Stilwell, his wife	Margaret Anna	Bp. at parents' house in presence of —— S. Summers & S. Mersereau
1855.			
May 25.			
1857.			
April 12. Easter.	Anna, wife of Joseph Egbert, bap. in Ch. on occasion of the confirmation of Sarah L. Cortelyou, Elizabeth Simonson & Br. N. Britton.		
April 26.	Jacob Herman Garretson of Centreville Elizabeth Egbert, his wife	Mary Ida	
1856.			
Jan. 11.			

DATE	PARENTS	CHILD	SPONSORS
1857. April 26. 1856. July 27.	Alexander Littell Hannah Jane Egbert, his wife	Ada Louise	
1857. April 18. 1856. b. Oct. 6.	James Baker Elizabeth Burningham, his wife	Julia Ann	Bp. at house of gr.-mother
b. not given.	Ch. of above parents	Sarah Elizabeth Joanna	
1857. Sept. 1. 1856. July 18.	Jno. Housman Susan Haughwout, his wife	Egbert Haughwout	
1857. Sept. 27. 1856. b. March 22.	George Vroome Elizabeth Taylor, his wife	Maria Ann	Bp. in parents' house at Centreville
1857. b. March 27.		Leonora Walker	
Sept. 17. 1847. b. July 9.	Jno. W. Burbank Anna Egbert, his wife	John Alfred	Both ch. bap. in sick room of the mother, in presence of witnesses
1850. b. April 9.	Same parents	Anna	
1857. Oct. 1. May 23.	Jacob Van Duzer Margaret Van Duzer	Lilian	Bp. at home of Mrs. Sarah Van Duzer
Oct. 1. 1856. Oct. 10.	Isaac Van Duzer Mary Van Duzer	Daniel Clyde	
1857. Oct. 15.	Geo. M. Root Anna M. Van Duzer, his wife	Pierre Vanderbilt	
Dec. 2. 1847. b. Sept. 20.	Isaac Romer —— Noble, his wife	Emma Jane	At house of parents in New Dorp
1854. b. May 14.		Mary Matilda	
1857. b. Feb. 21.	Ch. of above parents	Catharine Ann Elting	
1858. Jan. 25. 1849. March 6.	Geo. Washington Blake Mary Ann Wood, his wife	Geo. Washington	

DATE	PARENTS	CHILD	SPONSORS
1858.			
Feb. 2.	Henry Hilton	Edward	Bp. in house of parents
1850.	Ellen Banker, his	Banker	in 9th St., N. York
b. March 25.	wife		
1852.			
b. Jan. 10.		William McMurray	
1854.			
b. April 21.		Cornelia	
1856.			
b. Jan. 13.		Josephine	
1857.			
b. June 12.	All ch. of above parents	Henry Graham	" " "
1858.			
April 4.	Isaac Swift of Centreville and ——	Sarah & Emma	Bp. in Ch. at confirmation of Henrietta and Emeline Egbert, Catharine Vroom & Mrs. Julia Luby
May 23.	Abm. Egbert Ann Egbert	Catharine Hannah	Of New Dorp
Sept. 26.	Edward Wood	Mary	Bp. at house of gr.-
1857.	Catharine Maria	Augusta	parents Cornelius
Aug. 23.	Egbert, his wife		Egberts
1858.			
Sept. 28.	Wm. H'y Smith	Mary Elizabeth	Colored
1855.	Garrettson		
Sept. 26.	Diana Spicer		
1858.			
Sept. 28.	Thomas Spicer	Ann Eliza	Colored
April 4.	Matilda Catharine Spicer		
1857.			
b. in Aug.	John Garrettson Jane Spicer	Margaret Ann	Colored
1858.			
Dec. 8.	Lawrence H. Bogart Sarah Catharine	James Walnut	Bp. at home of Stephen Martling after the wedding of Mr. Jas.
1857.	Bogart		Vreeland to Miss
b. April 30.	Same parents	Stephen Martling	[E. or C.] Martling
1858.			
Dec. 20.	Edward M. Johnson, gardener at Mr. W. H. Newman's Margaret Johnson	John	Bp. at parents' house on Mr. Newman's grounds
May 30.			

DATE	PARENTS	CHILD	SPONSORS
1859.			
Feb. 27.	Amandens A.	Edward	Bp. at Parsonage.
Feb. 5.	Reinke Ellen Elizabeth Rece, his wife	Jacob	Bp. by Rev. Alexander R. Thompson of D. Ref. Ch. at Stapleton. Sponsors—Br. & Sr. Cortelyou, Br. & Sr. Coyne, Br. Clement L. Reinke
Feb. 23. 1858. Sept. 1.	Abraham Sharrott Hannah Jane Sharrott	Jno. William	
1859. April 17. 1858. April 11.	William Vroome Catharine Egbert, his wife	Christopher	Bp. at house of Br. Garry Vroome
.	Garret Vroome Elizabeth Martling, his wife	Sarah Elizabeth	" " "
1859. July 14. April 18.	Cornelius P. Bird Lydia Eliza Egbert, his wife	Susan Ann	
July 14. 1858. Sept. 24.	Benjamin Simonson Adeline Egbert, his wife	Helen Melissa	Both bp. in house of gr.-mother Lydia Egbert
1859. July 21. 1858. April 17.	Abraham Van Duzer Elizabeth Ann Vanderbilt, his wife	Edward Vanderbilt	
1859. Oct. 2. 1858. April 29.		Ann Lyle	Bp. at parents' house
1859. Oct. 16. 1858. Jan. 17.	Alexander Littell Jane Littell	Emma Laura	Bp. at School house at Centreville after evening service
1859. Nov. 3. Sept. 3.	James Cubberly Frances Crocheron, his wife	Walter Inman	
Nov. 14. 1855. b. Dec. 25.	Samuel Farrow Catharine Elizabeth Farrow	Lucy Ann	Bp. at house of mother Sharrott, S. side
1858. b. July 25.	Same parents	Ida Lucretia	
1859. Nov. 20. 1858. Oct. 18.	Robert Summers Susan Summers	Emily Etta	

DATE	PARENTS	CHILD	SPONSORS
1859.			
Dec. 1.	Henry Hilton	Alexander	Bp. at their house in
July 25.	Ellen Hilton	Stewart	E. 28th St., N. Y.
1860.			
Jan. 23.	George Vroome married son of Christopher		
Feb. 5.	Edward M. Johnson	Jane	Bp. at parents' house
1859.	Margaret Johnson		at Mr. Newman's
Oct. 2.			
1860.			
April 20.	Jacob Van Duzer	Percival	Bp. at house of Mrs.
1859.	Margaret Van		Sarah Van Duzer
July 25.	Duzer		
1860.			
May 28.	George Vroome	Louis	Bp. at parents' home
1859.	Elizabeth Taylor,	Taylor	at Centreville
July 4.	his wife		
1860.			
June 24.	Thomas Luby	Mary	Bp. at Parsonage
Jan. 15.	Julia Luby	Elizabeth	
Sept. 9.	John Kadlitz	Cora	Residing near Br.
April 2.	Elizabeth Kadlitz		Summers
Sept. 26.	James Vreeland	Jennie	
1859.	Elizabeth Martling,	Martling	
Dec. 21.	his wife		
1860.			
Oct. 8.	Wm. F. Butler	Adelaide	
Jan. 25.	Leah Elizabeth Johnson his wife		
Oct. 10.	Peter Anderson	Caroline	
1859.	Waglom		
July 22.	Margaret Stilwell, his wife		
1860.			
Oct. 13.	Robert Barnes	Sarah	
1859.	Mary Louisa Barnes	Louisa	
April 8.			

BAPTISMS BY E. T. SINSEMAN.

1860.			
Nov. 17.	David Colon	David Ben-	Bp. at house of gr.-
1852.	Sarah Ann Colon	net	parents
July 12.			
1860.			
Dec. 27.	Alexander Littell	Clara	Bp. at house of Mr.
Jan. 25.	Hannah Jane Littell	Adelaide	Edward Egbert at Centreville
b.Aug.23.	Edm. Crocheron	Leah Stout-	
	Lucretia Crocheron	enborough	
1861.			
Feb. 11.	August Brunholer	Carl August	
Jan. 30.	Elizabeth Brunholer		

DATE	PARENTS	CHILD	SPONSORS
1861.			
March 6.	John Brindley Frances Brindley	John Tunis Frances	Bp. in sick-chamber of mother at Tompkinsville
1859. b. Aug. 3.	All ch. of above parents	Belle William H.	
1861. April 10. Jan. 19.	Edward Johnson Margaret Johnson	Elizabeth Secord	
Oct. 2. 1853. b. Nov. 11.	John Vanderbilt Sarah Vanderbilt	Eva Louisa	Bp. at house of Mr. Jacob Van Duzer in Tompkinsville
1855. b. Feb. 20. 1861.	Same parents	Charles Henry	
b. Feb. 23.	Jacob Van Duzer Margareth Van Duzer	Priscilla	" " "
1860. b. Nov. 12.	Isaac Van Duzer Mary Van Duzer	Henry Carey	" " "
1861. b. March 2.	Abraham Van Duzer Elizabeth Van Duzer	Eliza Ann	" " "
May 12.	Bradley Woad Elizabeth Woad	Agnes	
Nov. 7. 1860. Oct. 25.	Albert Vroome Caroline Vroome	Martha Jane	Bp. at house ot Will. Vroome, Centreville Sponsor, Maria Vroome
b. Nov. 24.	Benjamin Simonson Sarah Adeline Simonson	Ecford Webb	Lydia Egbert
1861. b. Feb. 9. 1862.	William Vroome Catharine Vroome	Lydia	
Jan. 9. 1860. Sept. 10. 1862.	John Housman Susan Ann Housman	Caroline Houghwout	
April 1. 1861. Aug. 12. 1862.	James Coyne Harriet Coyne	Margaret	
April 13. 1861. Dec. 11. 1862.	William Taylor Emeline Taylor	Josephine Adelaid	
April 19. 1861. Sept. 17.	John Radlitz Elizabeth Radlitz	Ada Medora	

DATE	PARENTS	CHILD	SPONSORS
1862.			
July 1. 1858. Nov. 11.	John Vanderbilt Eliza Vanderbilt	John William	Bp. at house of Mr. Thomas Sharrott
1862.			
July 1. 1860. Dec. 19.	"Mary Clara, dau. of Eliza Vanderbilt & Henrietta Vanderbilt [Thus in original Ch. book]	"	" " "
1862.			
July 1. 1861. March 23.	Oliver Vanderbilt Sarah Vanderbilt	Ann Amelia	" " "
1862.			
July 1. 1861. Nov. 25.	Joseph Housman Lydia Housman	Mary Elizabeth	" " "
1862.			
July 4. June 16.	Carl Sebastian Kirch Christine Kirch	John Henry	Mathew Oelmann, Anton Rappeneker
July 6. March 21.	Edwin T. Senseman Sarah Lueders, his wife	William Ormsby	Thomas Lueders, Elenore Lueders
July 29. June 30.	William Johnson Charlotte Johnson	William	
Aug. 1. July 26.	Robert Barnes Mary Louisa Barnes	Frederic	
Aug. 6. Jan. 27.	George L. Reader Cath. Reader	Christopher Vroome	Bp. at gr.-parents' house
Aug. 11. 1861. Dec. 21.	George W. Vroom Elizabeth S. Vroom	Eliza Taylor	
1862.			
Aug. 11. March 6.	Peter Heal Emma Heal	Eliza Swift	Bp. at Mrs. Swifts' house
Oct. 19. Aug. 22.	John Theodor. Zorn Esther Ruth Eliza Zorn	Georgiana Theodora Jacobina	Bp. by Eugene Leibert. Sponsors: Sarah Leibert. Miss Alvina Schuman, Theodore Kleinknecht, by proxy
Oct. 28. Sept. 29.	Christian Knoesel, Mr. Banker's farmer Salome Knoesel	Catharina, sick child	Charles Wolf, Catharine Rose. Bp. in parents' house at Freshkill by Eugene Leibert

MARRIAGES.
BY REV. H. GAMBOLD.

1764. Dec. 27.	David Burger Anne Stilwell	In presence of about 30 persons in her mother's house at Old Town
1766. March 4.	Christian Jacobson Anne Vandeventer	
1771. Nov. 17.	George Colon Mary Limner	
1773. June 29.	Edward Beatty Eleanor Cortelyou	
1774. July 17.	Nathaniel Britton Catharine Colon	
1775. Jan. 15.	Lewis Ryerze Catharine Connor	
1777. Aug. 3.	James Egbert Elisabeth Martinoe	
Dec. 28.	Jacob Wood Elisabeth Nichols John Buskirk Jane Blaw	
1778. Jan. 21.	Peter Selif Elisabeth Beglo	
Jan. 30.	"Peter Guyon [or Deyoung]" Catharine Ketteltass	
April 5.	Peter Haughwout Mary Martinoe	
April 5.	Cornelius Dugan Aletta Cousine	
May 20.	Stephen Wood Alice Simerson	
June 17.	Albert Journey Mary Perine	
Aug. 9.	Hezekiah Rickow Sarah Dennys	
Aug. 20.	Benjamin Appleby Sarah Van Pelt	
Aug. 26.	Jonathan Gage Elizabeth Medes	
Aug. 27.	Tucker Tabor Jane Love	
June 7.	John Bachus —— Brock	
Aug. 30.	Thomas Robinson Alice Hill	
Sept. 6.	Gager Freeman Catharine Simeson	
Sept. 11.	Elihu Wolly Sara Vansise	
Sept. 15.	Thomas Parker Eleanor Smith	

1778.		Joseph Sylva
Dec.	20.	Susanna Mitchell
Dec.	20.	Isaac Decker
		Ally Burbank
1779.		John Lisk
Jan.	1.	Sara Decker
Jan.	6.	John Dunham
		Elisabeth Oliver
Feb.	3.	Lewis Dunham
		Catharine Slegt
Feb.	9.	Joseph Beers
		Mary Barton
Feb.	28.	Abraham Bowlby
		Sara Lake
May	5.	Christopher Hevler
		Elizabeth Bront
May	9.	James Johnson
		Mary Wood
May	16.	Reuben Rickow
		Ann Thorn
May	17.	William Carroll
		Mary Chambers
May	26.	William Jeacocks
		Hannah Garrison
June	12.	Benjamin Prall
		Margaret Simonson
June	21.	Thomas Trot
		Sophia Romer
Oct.	18.	Thomas Batten
		Mary Hinslif
Oct.	31.	Nathaniel Britton
		Sarah Pugh
Nov.	7.	Daniel De Hart
		Elisabeth Mersereau
1780.		Stephen Mercereau
Jan.	23.	Sara White
Jan.	23.	William Biggs
		Hannah Beard
1779.		Peter Rednor
Nov.	20.	———
1780.		Robert Mesy
Feb.	13.	Margaret Daily
March	2.	Stephen Wood
		Joice Boyes
March	14.	John Innes
		Eleanor Smith
April	9.	Jonah Colon
		Elizabeth Zeller
May	6.	William Ellison
		Ann Hughs
May	8.	Hezekiah Marks
		Eleanor Callahoun

1780. John Britt
May 15. Catharine Hemmium
May 16. Jesse Tabor
 Elizabeth Wood
May 31. William Beser
 Eleanor Elland
July 3. John Fortunate
 Sarah Britton
July 16. John Hughs
 Ann Dobson
July 23. Rulof Jacobus
 Lydia Van Syle
Aug. 25. John Williams
 Tryphena Gold
Aug. 31. Jacob Long
 Eliz. Fleming
1781. John Tyson
Jan. 3. Mary Housman
Jan. 16. Eliphalet Jones
 Elizabeth Bogart
Feb. 16. Jesse Keen
 Margaret Henly
Feb. 25. John Mersereau
 Judith Poillon
March 15. William Reed
 Elizabeth Waters
March 25. Daniel Lewis
 Elizabeth Handlin
April 4. Richard Webb
 Dorcas Bardine
April 3. Joseph Stackhouse
 Sarah Anderson
April 15. Nicholas Journeay
 Ann Garretson
April 22. David Leaforge
 Catharine Seguine
April 29. John Wood
 Caturey Ridgway
May 12. Ashley Bowen
 Sarah Palmer
May 13. Barney Slack
 Mary Cole
May 30. Henry Parlee
 Rebeka Cole
June 3. John Guyon
 Sara Ward
June 3. Thomas Craddock
 Sarah Bedel
June 3. William Granger
 Sarah Stuart
June 10. Myles Gardner
 Eleanor Strickland

1781.		Amos Rooke
June	13.	Martha Mersereau
June	18.	John Mersereau
		Mary Taylor
June	18.	James Mitchel
		Margaret Wilson
Aug.	13.	John Segoin
		Catharine Jennins
Aug.	15.	Joseph Leake
		Frances Egbert
Aug.	15.	Peter Price
		Mary Spann
Sept.	2.	Henry Miller
		Elisabeth Garrison
Sept.	5.	Daniel Storer
		Catharine Androvette
Oct.	7.	Daniel Perine
		Lucy Holmes
Oct.	21.	John Garretson
		Martha Codmas
Nov.	8.	John Kruse
		Jemima Simonson
Nov.	20.	Peter Saunders
		Letta Skinner
Nov.	30.	Edmund Warner
		Jane Fitchet
Dec.	4.	Edward Egbert
		Mary Cortelyou
Dec.	6.	Henry Priester
		Elizabeth Romer
Dec.	18.	Adam Smith
		Hannah Barclay
Dec.	20.	William Thorn
		Anne Rickow
1782.		Duncan Kennedy
Jan.	14.	Mary Mann
Feb.	14.	Lewis Frazur
		Catharine Thorn
March	12.	John Egbert
		Mary Holmes
March	22.	Jonathan Parker
		Mary Paterson
April	8.	George McLeland
		Margery Teague
April	14.	Cornelius Mersereau
		Aultje Amerman
April	22.	Simon Meyer
		Ann Bush
April	23.	George Grey
		Mary Eldridge
April	28.	Peter Perine
		Ann Palmer

1782.		Peter Prall
May	19.	Elizabeth Ridgway
June	9.	Moses Van Namur
		Mary Legrange
June	12.	—— Telston
		Susan Newland
June	12.	John Ferris
		Mary Stilwell
June	13.	Richard Hately
		Mary Cole
June	23.	Peter Boost
		Mary Van Namer
June	3.	Jacob Vanderbilt
		Rachel Dennis
July	14.	Hugh Doyle
		Elisabeth Chambers
July	24.	Charles Murphy
		Catharine McBride
Sept.	14.	William Allen
		Martha Grimma
Oct.	7.	William Van Pelt
		Sarah Saunders
Oct.	9.	Isaac Baldwin
		Frances Kelly
Nov.	3.	Asher Codington
		Judith Taylor
Nov.	10.	James Butler
		Frances Butler
Nov.	24.	Abraham Stilwell
		Ann Ward
Dec.	1.	Thomas Gerrand
		Esther Smith
Dec.	1.	Garret Bush
		Elizabeth Van Namur
1783.		Henry Sleight
Jan.	23.	Catharine Butler
March	18.	John Wandel
		Susannah Latterette
March	25.	Elias Van Winkel
		Lucy Price
April	15.	William Alexander
		Jane Allen
April	16.	Jacob Crocheron
		Ann Morgan
May	14.	Henry Barger
		Mary Tysen
June	11.	Daniel Ross
		Desire Bigilow
Aug.	7.	Abraham Lake
		Patience Berbank, widow
Aug.	10.	Laurence Cripps
		Susanna Fountain

1783.		Roger Flinn
Aug.	12.	Johanna Barnes
Aug.	29.	John Ayre
		Elizabeth Smith
Aug.	30.	Zenophon Jewet
		Gertrude Garritson
Sept.	2.	George Adkens
		Abigail Ogles
Sept.	9.	Abraham Long
		Ann Rambel
Sept.	17.	Anthony Fountain
		Martha Crips
Sept.	25.	Nicholas Britton
		Judith Johnson
Oct.	6.	John Ingham
		Margaret Calcraft
Oct.	15.	Barent Simonson
		Anne Beatty
Oct.	26.	Austin Barton
		Rebeka Burbank
Nov.	19.	"John Byvank or Burbank"
		Elisabeth Decker
Dec.	28.	Timothy Wood
		Mary Blake
1784.		Joakim Stilwell
Feb.	15.	Susanna Scarret
Feb.	18.	John Van Pelt
		Judith Durant
Feb.	17.	Cornelius Fountain
		Elisabeth Vandeventer
May	7.	John Dorset
		Martha Cortelyou

By Rev. Jas. Birkby.

1784.		James Burdine
Aug.	3.	Elisabeth Egbert

By Rev. Frederick Moering.

1787.		John Garrison
May	31.	Elizabeth Connor
Sept.	20.	Cornelius Bedell
		Elizabeth Jacobson
1788.		John Jacobson
July	2.	Hilletje Bedell
Nov.	16.	Samuel Egbert
		Cathrine Smith
Nov.	17.	John Martino
		Jane Christopher
Dec.	17.	Jacob Cortelyou
		Elizabeth Corsen

1789.   Abraham Egbert
May 31.   Ann Martino
Dec. 23.   John Baker
            Charity Wandel
1790.   Samuel Smith
Jan. 3.   Elizabeth Perine
Jan. 16.   Francis Post
            Experience Marshall
Feb. 21.   Daniel Corsen
            Rebecca Martino
April 7.   Peter Fountain
            Claushea Spears
1791.   Richard Conor, Junr.
May 19.   Sophia Clausen
July 6.   Tunis Egbert
            Ann Burbank
Sept. 25.   Stephen Ketteltas
            Ardrae Britton
Oct. 30.   John Van der Bilt
            Elizabeth Taylor
1792.   Joseph Moore
Jan. 26.   Johanna Ward
Jan. 26.   William Williams
            Sarah Hooper
Feb. 19.   John White
            Mary Lockerman
March 25.   Elisha Kribbs
            Magdalene McLean
1793.   Benajah Martino
Feb. 4.   Hannah Decker

BY REV. JAS. BIRKBY.

1793.   James Lewis
Nov. 5.   Rebecca Collong
1794.   Jeremiah Baker
Feb. 2.   Sarah Butler
Feb. 3.   John Marshall
            Sussanna Swaim
Feb. 6.   Zedick Vincnant
            Catherine Sefurde [or Lefurde]
Feb. 25.   Vincent Fountain
            Alice Jinnings
April 1.   Richard S. Cary
            Judith Bard
June 5.   Matthew Decker
            Mary Latterete
Sept. 25.   Isaac Symerson
            Elizabeth Barnes
1795.   John Britton
Jan. 1.   Rachel Burbank

"in 1794." Rubin Symerson
Phoebe Decker
1795. Antony Fountain
Feb. 17. Phoebe Thomson
Feb. 19. Matthias Enyard
Sarah Decker
March 5. Peter Cortelyou
Amey Hilliyard
March 22. Richard Decker
Mary Ann Kinsey
Aug. 3. Thomas Vanderbilt
Williga Symerson, from the north side
1796. Christopher Parkinson
Sept. 24. Phoebe Garritson. Md. at house of Henry Garritson, Esq.
Oct. 23. Edward Egbert
Sarah Phrol. Md. in the church
1797. Jacob Lossier
May 2. Sarah Beatty. In church
June 22. John Chroson
Catharine Ryerss. Md. at the house on north side
Oct. 22. Henry Miller
Elizabeth Barton

By Rev. Frederick Moering.

Dec. 28. John Beatty
Elizabeth Lake
1798. Abraham Decker
Jan. 20. Cathrine Kinsey
Sept. 2. James Burdine, widower
Margret Oakley
Sept. 2. Robert Anderson of N. Y.
Mary Sargent
Nov. 10. Niclas Depew of N. Y.
Sussanna Seymourson of Staten Island
1799. Daniel Lake
Jan. 17. Ann Lockerman
Feb. 28. John Merlin
Cathrine Mitchel
March 19. Niclas Depuy
Cathrine Decker
Aug. 4. Ord. Housman
Mary Morgan
Dec. 21. Mathew Stevenson
Anne Drake
1800. Daniel Froom
Jan. 19. Martha Baker
April 14. George Colon
Billetje Lewis, widow
Sept. 9. John Morrel
Jane Jones

1800.	Daniel Jones
Sept. 21.	Elizabeth Christopher
Oct. 16.	Robert Journey
	Sarah Cole
Nov. 20.	Peter Van Pelt
	Cathrine Glendinen
1801.	George Shingles, single
May 3.	Jemima Bredsted, single
June 21.	David Vanamour [Van Namur?]
	Elizabeth Mercereau
Aug. 11.	Mathew Bennet
	Rachel Burbank
Aug. 23.	Jacob Bantea, single
	Elizabeth Wood, single
Aug. 29.	Nathaniel Frome, single
	Mary Barton, single
Sept. 22.	Abraham Mitchel, single
	Margret Decker, single
Oct. 14.	Gerrit Post, single
	Margret Mercereau, single
Nov. 16.	Aaron Simonson, single
	Elizabeth Mercereau, single
Nov. 21.	James Warren, single
	Elizabeth Mercereau, single
Dec. 3.	John Corsen, single
	Sussanna Enyard, single
Nov. 29.	Richard Van Pelt, single
	Elizabeth Donats, single
Dec. 6.	Niclas Bush, single
	Cathrine Van Pelt, single
1802.	Cornelius Egbert, single
July 28.	Naatje Housman, single
Sept. 4.	John Burbank, single
	Ann Egbert, single, dau. of John Egbert, Senr.
Nov. 9.	Joseph Skerret, single
	Elizabeth Lockerman, single
Dec. 27.	Jeremy Baker, single
	Deborah Hatfield, single
1803.	John Hatfield, single. Md. by Rev. N. Brown, no min-
Oct. 1.	ister of any other church then on the Island
	Catharine Bogart, widow, by maiden n. Van Pelt

By Rev. Nathaniel Brown.

1803.	Peter Mitchel, widower
Oct. 16.	Sarah Baker, widow
Dec. 5.	John Skerret, single
	Catharine Perine, single
1804.	William Barton, single, son of Austin Barton & Re-
March 4.	becca, his wife, m. n. Burbank
	Lucy Egbert, dau. of John Egbert & Mary, his wife, by m. n. Holmes

1804.	John Journeay, single
March 29.	——, single, from New York
Aug. 4.	Charles Symonson, single
	Mary Vanderbilt, eldest dau. of Br. Cornelius & Sr. Phebe Vanderbilt
Aug. 18.	Abraham Symonson, single
	Phebe Locker
Oct. 6.	Peter Cozine, single
	Susanna Butler, single
Nov. 24.	Richard Aroe, single
	Elizabeth Stilwell, single
Dec. 23.	John Skerret, single
	Francis, by maiden name Rooks, widow
1805.	Isaac Barton, single, son of Joseph Barton
Feb. 2.	Catharine Colon, dau. of James Colon, Sr., deceased
April 1.	Nicolas Vancleve, single
	Mary Terret
Feb. 12.	James Murray, single
	Susan Skerret, dau. of Richard Skerret
April 14.	Isaac Burbank, single, son of Abm. Burbank
	Sarah Egbert, eldest dau. of Mary, dec., & Edwd. Egbert
	Tunis Egbert, single, youngest son of Edward & Mary Egbert, dec.
	Sarah Barton, dau. of Joseph Barton
June 9.	Jeffries Alston, single
	Sarah Decker
Sept. 22.	—— Morgan, single
	Francis Wynand, single
Oct. 2.	Abner Johnson, single
	Salome Hedding
Oct. 13.	Cornelius Beatty, second son of Edw. & Eleanore Beatty
	Ann Jacobson, eldest dau. of John & Hilletje Jacobson
Oct. 20 or 28.	Richard Taylor, single
	Dinah Swaim, single
Oct. 23.	Ozias Alnsley, widower
	Elizabeth Johnson, widow
Nov. 9.	Joseph Lake, single
	—— Morgan, single
Dec. 22.	Michael Marsac, single
	Rachel Jinnings, single
1806.	Daniel Stilwell, single
Jan. 16.	Hanna Skerrett, single
March 2.	John Decker, single
	Mary Van Norman, single
March 2.	William Morgan, single
	Sabina Decker, single
March 22.	Jacob Breasted, single
	Lavina Totten, single

1806.		William Beatty, single
June	22.	Mary Barger, single
July	6.	Richard Bedell, widower
		Hanna Van Pelt, widow, m. n. Pepperill
Aug.	7.	Peter Breasted, single
		Sara Crips, single
Aug.	12.	Abraham Lisk, single
		Jane Wandel, single
Oct.	23.	James Colon, single
		Charity Johnson, single
1807.		Abraham Hooper, single
Feb.	10.	Charity Stilwell, single, dau. of Abraham & Ann Stilwell. Md. in minister's house, in presence of John Marsh, John Dorset & others
April 30.		James Romer, single
		Mary Stilwell, single, dau. of Abm. & Ann Stillwell. Md. in presence of above & some others
June	28.	Daniel Lake, widower, son of Joseph Lake & wife
		Ann Flitcher, single. Md. in ch. in presence of Corn. Perine & Mary Fountain & others
Aug.	9.	Peter Van Pelt, widower. Md. in church in presence of James Skerrit, his sister & others
		Martha Wood, single
Aug.	1.	Cornelius Christopher, single. Md. in church in presence of their neighbors
		Sarah Pew, single
Oct.	11.	John De Fries [De Forest?], single
		Charlotte Vanderbilt, single, dau. of Corn. Vanderbilt & Phebe, his wife. Md. in church in presence of a number of people
Oct.	11.	Jack & Margaret, Blacks, md. by consent of their respective owners
Dec.	19.	William Drury, single, from Scotland
		Susan Stilwell, single, dau. of Joshua Stilwell & Susan Skerrit, his wife. Md. in minister's dwelling in presence of Danl. Guyon & some of Bride's relations
Dec.	22.	Barnet Depew, single
		Sarah Decker, single, dau. of Israel Decker & his wife. Md. in presence of bride's father & others in minister's house
1808.		—— Depew, single, brother of above
Jan.	23.	Elisabeth Decker, single. Md. in church in presence of Moses Wood & others
March 12.		Daniel Guyon, widower, son of James Guyon & Ann Connor, dec.
		Elisabeth Young, widow, maiden n. Clawson. Md. at house of Richd. Connor, in his presence & his wife's Sophia Connor & her brother Reuben Clawson

1808. March 13.		John Fountain, single, son of Anthony Fountain & his first wife
		Margaret Holmes, single. Md. in church in presence of his Bro. Anthony, his uncle & aunt H. Crusers & others
July	7.	Joseph Mersereau, single
		Sara Bedell, single, dau. of Richd. Bedell & his first wife whose maiden name was Elnesly. Md. in church in presence of Joseph Barton & others
July	9.	John Decker, single
		Mary Burbank, single, dau. of Abm. Burbank & wife. Md. in church in presence of John Burbank & others
July	16.	David Praul, single, father dec.
		Catharine Dorsett, single, eldest dau. of John & Martha Dorsett. Md. in house of John Dorsett in presence of Bride's parents & others
Aug.	20.	John Jennings, single
		Catharine Skerret, single, dau. of Richard Skerret. Md. in church in presence of some near neighbors
Sept.	11.	Abraham Van Pelt, single
		Mary Fountain, single, dau. of Vincent Fountain & wife. Md. in church in presence of some neighbors
Dec.	2.	Odissa Shay, single
		Appolonia Mott, widow, m. n. Skerret. Md. in ch. in in presence of N. Froome, his wife & others
1809. April	1.	Abraham Decker, single, son of Col. Decker & his wife
		Ann Martino, single, third dau. of Steph. Martino & Elen., his wife. Md. in ch. in presence of bride's bro. & sister & neighbors
Oct.	22.	John Burbank, widower, son of Abm. & his wife
		Ann Decker, single, dau. of Mathias & his wife. Md. in presence of Mr. Simonson & some neighbors in church
Nov.	5.	David Decker, single, son of Mathias & his wife
		Catharine Decker, single, dau. of Mathias. Md. in presence of Mr. Taylor, Mr. Wood & others in church
Dec.	10.	Abraham Simonson, single
		Ann Prall, single. Md. in church in presence of several neighbors from the Neck
Dec.	14.	Hosea Alexander Rozeau, single, son of Peter Rozeau, Esq., & Mary, his wife
		Mary Morgan, single, dau. of Jesse & Cath. Morgan. Md. at Mr. Jesse Morgan's house in West Quarter in presence of parents of both parties & other relations
Dec.	23.	Stephen Wood, single, son of Stephen Wood & his wife
		Ann Bodine, single, dau. of James Bodine. Md. in church in presence of friends and relations

1810.	Abraham Merril, single
Jan. 14.	Elisabeth Martino, single, dau. of Stephen Martino & Eleon., his wife. Md. in presence of some of their friends here in the laborers' room
Jan. 27.	John Simonson, single, son of Simonson, dec. Catharine Garretson, single, dau. of John, in whose house she was md. in presence of a number of friends & relations
Feb. 22.	Lewis R. Marsh, single, lawyer, son of Ralph Marsh & Jennet, his wife Margaret P. Dubois, single, dau. of Lewis Dubois & Elis his wife. Md. here in the laborer's house
March 10.	William Squires, single, son of —— Squires Taylor [tailor?] & wife Lena Merril, single. Md. in minister's house in presence of bridegroom's sister & others
March 31.	John Decker, single Elisabeth Van Pelt, single. Md. in presence of neighbors in minister's house
Aug. 19.	Robert Marsh, single, from Jersey State, son of Christopher Marsh & Ann, his wife Rhoda Marsh, single, dau. of John Marsh & wife of Staten Island. Md. in West Quarter at Bride's parents' house, both parents and some relations being present
Sept. 27.	Moses Van Pelt, single Mary Upton, single. Md. in minister's dwelling, Peter Colon & some neighbors present
Sept. 29.	Isaac Lewis, widower, son of late Lewis & Billetje, his wife [now Colon] Rachel Marshall, single, both of Staten Island. Md. in in church in presence of neighbors
Oct. 14.	John M'Cullagh, single, from N. Y. Sarah Gibson, single. Md. in minister's dwelling in presence of bride's father & brother from here & others from N. Y.
Dec. 19.	Joseph Sylvy, single Elizabeth Skerret, single, dau. of Richard Skerret, both of St. Island. Md. here in presence of relations
1811. Feb. 16.	Anthony Fountain, single, son of Anthony Fountain & 1st wife [née Journey] Ann Egbert, single, dau. of James Egbert & Elizabeth, his wife, deceased. Md. in house of Br. James Egbert, he & family being present
Feb. 28.	Abraham Winant, single Hettie Dubois, single. Md. here in church in presence of Br. Bunninger from N. Y., & some neighbors
April 9.	Nathaniel Bodine, single, son of John Bodine & Stat. Island Maria Garretson, single, dau. of John Garretson & 1st wife, Elisabeth, née Conner. Md. at house of bride's father in presence of parents & other relations

1811.		Francis Morse, single, from England
May —.		Mary Pew, single, dau. —— Pew, dec. & wife of St. Island. Md. in presence of some of bride's relations in minister's dwelling
June 29.		Thomas Skerret, single, son of Richard & his wife of St. Island
		Martha Crips, single. Md. in presence of their brother & sister here in church
June 29.		Stephen Mott, single, son of John Mott & Appolonia, his wife, née Skerret, of St. Island
		Mary Mitchel, single, dau. of Peter Mitchell of St. Island & his wife, née Skerret. Md. at same time as above
Sept. 18.		Patrick Currant, single, from Ireland
		Jane Hunter, widow. Md. in presence of some neighbors from Quarantine ground
Oct. 28.		James Egbert, son of James Egbert & Elizabeth, his wife, maiden name Martino
		Sarah Merril, dau. of John Merril & wife of Staten Island. Md. in presence of neighbors
Nov. 23.		Aron Van Pelt, single, son of Van Pelt & wife of St. Island
		Sara Praul, single, dau. of John Praul & his wife, whose m. n. was Hilliard. Md. at church in presence of relations
Dec. 23.		Abraham Brasted, single, son of John Brasted of Staten Island, & wife Willempje Bratt
		Elsea Silvy, single, dau. of Joseph Griggs de Silva & Susan, his wife. Md. in presence of relations
1812. Jan. 2.		Cornelis Johnson, single, son of Nath. Johnson, dec., of S. Island, & his wife Eleonore, m. n. Vanderbilt
		Elizabeth Corsen, single, of Staten Island. Md. in presence of relations
Jan. 28.		Abraham Van Houten, single, from Elizabethtown, N. Jersey
		Catharine Grandine, single. Md. in presence of relations
Jan. 29.		David Barger, single, son of Henry Barger & wife Mary, by m. n. Tysen, both decd.
		Sara Cortelyou, single, second dau. of Jacob Cortelyou & wife Elisabeth, m. n. Corsen. Md. in house of bride's parents, they & relations present
May 2.		Jacob Beatty, single, son of Edward Beatty & Eleonore, his wife, m. n. Cortelyou
		Eliza Cortelyou, single, oldest dau. of Jacob & Elisabeth Cortelyou. Md. in church in presence of most of the neighbors
May 10.		Stephen Martino, single, son of Stephen & his wife, m. n. Haughwout
		Charity Christopher, single, dau. of Peter Christopher & wife. Md. in presence of some relations

1812.	John Bird, single, son of Anthony Bird ·
May 28.	Susan Mitchel, single, dau. of Peter Mitchel & his first wife, dec. Md. in presence of some of their neighbors from Quarantine
May 25.	John Fountain, single, son of Vincent Fountain & wife Jane Housman, single, dau. of Abm. Housman & his wife. Md. here in presence of some relations
Sept. 6.	John Decker, single, son of Barnet Decker & his wife Ann Jones, single, dau. of J. Jones, dec., & his wife now a widow. Md. in presence of some friends from Quarantine
Sept. 18.	Mathias Jones, single, son of Jones, dec., & Catharine, his wife Juliana Sylvy, single, dau. of Jas. & Susan Sylvy. Md. as above
Oct. 10.	Jacob Housman, single, son of Abm. Housman Lena Cruse, single. Md. in presence of some friends from North side of Island
Nov. 1.	John Baker, single, son of Andrew & Catharine Baker of Germany Elizabeth Prickett, also from Germany. Md. in presence of some friends
Dec. 17.	William Winant, single Hannah Decker, single, dau. of Jacob Decker from the Manor. In presence of some neighbors.
1813. Jan. —.	John Lake, single Sarah Prickett, single. Md. here in the house
Feb. 8.	John Sebring, single, son of Widow Eliza Sebring of N. Y. Eliz. Taylor, single. Both from North Side of Island. Md. in presence of some neighbors
June 20.	Peter Post, single, son of Francis & Experience Post Catharine Merrill, dau. of John & Frances Merrill
June 27.	Isaac Housman, son of Abm. & Jane Housman Frances Van Namur, dau. of Aaron & Mary Van Namur
Nov. 24.	John Christian Jacobson, single, 21 yrs., eldest son of John V. D. Jacobson, farmer on St. Island, & Hilletje, his wife. m. n. Bedell Catharine Connor, eldest dau. of Richard Connor, Esq., & Sophia, his wife, by m. n., Clawson. This marriage was by Rev. John C. Bechler at house of Richard Connor, Esq., in presence of friends & relations

BY REV. J. C. BECHLER.

1813. Dec. 8.	Jesse Laforge, single Catharine Pryor, single
1814. Feb. 26.	John Decker, single, about 22 yrs., a waterman Ann Egbert, single, youngest dau. of late Edward Egbert. Md. in house of Mr. Isaac Burbank in the Manor in presence of some friends

1814. March 25. James, } Blacks, belonging to Mr. Garrettson
Mary, } Blacks, belonging to Mr. Edw. Perine. With consent of their masters

April 30. Sam, } Blacks, belonging to Mr. Richd. Corson
Mary, } Blacks, belonging to Mr. John Garrettson. With consent of their masters

May 8. Simon, } Blacks, belonging to Mr. Abm. Fountain
Sally, } Blacks, Mr. Ketteltas. With consent of their masters

Oct. 1. Cesar & Saran, both about 22, belonging to Mr. Richd. Freeling

Oct. 23. John Bodine, son of Vincent Bodine, farmer
Elisabeth Martino, dau. of Benajah Martino, at whose house they were md. in presence of number of friends

Oct. 26. Daniel Decker, single, son of Mathias & Mary Ann Decker
Mary Lewis, dau. of James & Rebecca Lewis. Md. in presence of friends

Nov. 12. Henry Seguine, single, weaver, son of John & Rachel Seguine
Patience Brittain, dau. of John & Rachel Brittain. Md. at parsonage in presence of friends

Dec. 26. Arthur Burbank, son of Abm. & Lena
Mary Ann Enyard, dau. of Mathias & Sarah

1815. Jan. 1. Matthew Decker, single, son of Matthew & Mary Decker
Ann Colon, single, dau. of —— & Jane Colon

Jan. 3. William Decker, single, son of Barnet & Hannah Decker
Rebekkah Ammeman, dau. of John & Elizabeth Ammeman

Feb. 4. Peter Wood, single, son of James Wood
Sarah Ann Cortelyou, dau. of Peter & Amy Cortelyou

Feb. 11. Tunis Egbert, single, carpenter, son of Abm. & Ann Egbert
Isabella Vanderbilt, single, dau. of John & Elizabeth Vanderbilt

Feb. 12. Stephen Wood, single, farmer & carpenter, son of late Joseph Wood & Ann, his wife
Ann Marsh, single, dau. of Richd. & Sarah Marsh

Feb. 20. Jesse Wynant, single, son of George & Elizabeth Wynant
Catharine Wright, single dau. of Joshua & Catharine Wright

March 26. Nathaniel H. Martin, single, son of Benjamin & Abigail Martin of N. Jersey
Sarah Dorsett, single, second dau. John & Marth Dorsett, at whose house they were married

1815.	Benjamin Sibell, single, son of John & Sarah Sibell
April 16.	Frances Wynant, single, dau. of Daniel & Sarah Wynant, all of this Island. Md. at Parsonage
April 16.	Aaron Saffin, son of William Saffin
	Mary Wynant, single, dau. of Daniel & Sarah Wynant
May 13.	Joseph Lockman, widower
	Locky Cears, single, dau. of Elias & Jane Cears, both decd
May 27.	Thomas Miller, son of Henry Miller, weaver, & wife decd.
	Mary Haughwout, dau. of Wynant Haughwout, Esq., & Mary, his wife
Aug. 12.	Nicholas Crocheron, single, 19(?) yrs., son of Nicholas Crocheron, Esq., & Ann, his wife
	Ann Elizabeth Guyon, single, near 18 yrs., dau. of Danl. Guyon, Esq., & Frances his 1st wife. Md. at house of Danl. Guyon in the Neck
Oct. 4.	Tom. a negro of Mr. John Fountain's, about 23
	Sal, " of Mr. Barnt Lake, " 18. With consent of masters in writing
Oct. 7.	Richard Skerrit, 21 yrs., son of James & Ann Skerret
	Mary Mott, dau. of James & Appolonia Mott. Md. in house of Mrs. Appolonia Mott
Oct. 9.	James Sharp, son of Wm. & Elizabeth Sharp. A young man living on North side of Island
	Jane Cruser, dau. of John & Jemima Cruser of this Island. Md. at Parsonage
Nov. 22.	William Stillwell, single, son of Abraham & Ann Stilwell
	Lavina Simonson, single, dau. of Silas & Ann Simonson
Dec. 9.	Matthias Haughwout, son of Francis & Hester Haughwout
	Susan Ann Roff, dau. of Joseph & Catharina Roff
Dec. 23.	Abraham Egbert, tanner & currier, son of Abraham & Ann Egbert
	Ann Burbank, dau. of Jacob & Ann Burbank
Oct. 26.	William Prawl, farmer, son of Danl. Prawl
	Ann Egbert, dau. of Tunis & Ann Egbert
1816. Jan. 7.	Thomas, } Blacks, belonging to Mr. John Seguine Eliza, } belonging to Mr. Jeremiah Simonson
March 30.	Tunis Egbert, single, blacksmith, son of John & Mary Egbert
	Margaret Crocheron, single, dau. of Richard & Jane Crocheron
May 4.	William Blake, single, about 21 yrs., eldest son of William & Ann Blake
	Elizabeth Wood, single, dau. of Timothy & Mary Wood

1816. June 2. Abraham Noble, single, weaver, son of Daniel Noble, dec., & Esther
Catharine Morgan, single, dau. of William Morgan, dec., & Mary, his wife. Md. in presence of friends & relations

" Tom, } Blacks, belonging to Mr. Henry Crouse
Ana, } belonging to Mr. Nichs. Burgher

June 8. Cornelius Sleight, son of Jacob & Jane Sleight
Mary Ann Butler, dau. of Nathaniel & Sophia Butler

Oct. 6. Lewis Ryerze, son of Orris Ryerze, dec., & Sarah, his wife
Catharine Decker, dau. of Richard & Mary Ann Decker

Oct. 20. Abraham Merrill, single, blacksmith, son of Abm. & Mary Merrill
Eleonor Merrill, single, dau. of John & Elizabeth Merrill. Md. in the church

Oct. 31. Oliver Decker, single, son of Abm. Decker & Mary, his wife, decd.
Hannah Simonson, single, dau. of Barnet & Sarah Simonson in whose house they were married

Dec. 2. Gerrit Post, single, son of Abraham and Mary Post
Elizabeth Blake, single, eldest dau. of Wm. & Ann Blake

Dec. 23. Jacob Van Pelt, single, son of Samuel, decd., & Sarah Ann Van Pelt
Mary Simonson, single, dau. of Joseph & Rebecca Simonson, in presence of witnesses

1817. Jan. 1. John Blake, single, son of William & Ann Blake
Mary Van Name, dau. of Aaron & Cath. Van Name. Md. in presence of friends at Parsonage

March 29. Egbert Merrill, single, son of John & Elizabeth Merrill of this Island
Mary Jones, dau. of Abm. Jones, decd., & Mary, his wife. Md. at Parsonage in presence of friends

April 20. Michael Van Name (or Namur), single, son of Moses, decd., & Mary Van Name (or Namur)
Gertrude Martha Cortelyou, youngest dau. of Jacob, decd., & Elizabeth Cortelyou. Md. at house of mother in presence of friends.

June 11. Samuel Coddington, single, son of David Coddington & Elizabeth, his wife, m. n. Randolph
Catharine Jacobson, single, dau. of John V. D. Jacobson, Esq., & Hilletje Bedell, his wife. Md. at parents' house

July 7. John Winant, single, from North side of Island, son of Simon & Sarah Winant
Martha ——, dau. of Barnet & Mary Jones, a widow

Aug. 27. Jeremiah Winant, son of John & Sarah Winant
Ann Crocheron, single, dau. of John, decd., & Sophia Crocheron. Md. at Parsonage

By Rev. G. A. Hartman.

1817.
Nov. 15. — Samuel Egbert, single, son of John & Mary, his wife, m. n. Holmes
Betsey Blake, dau. of John & Polly Blake

Dec. 13. — Peter Sisk, single, son of John & Sarah Sisk, m. n. Decker
Mary Wright, single, dau. of Thomas & Cath. Wright, m. n. Blake. Md. at Parsonage.

Dec. 25. — Elias Butler, single, son of John Butler and Polly Kingston, his wife
Charlotte Van Pelt, single, dau. of Samuel V. Pelt & his wife, Sally, by m. n. Housman. In presence of a few friends at the Parsonage

1818.
Jan. 31. — Joseph Lake, single, son of Joseph & Maria Lake, m. n. Coursen
Ann Jane Tuthill, dau. of Israel & Elizabeth Tuthill, by m. n. Janer. Md. at parsonage in presence of John Locker & Maria V. Namur

March 8. — Terrence R. Ryers, single, son of Orris & Sarah Ryers
Ellen H. Decker, single, dau. of Matthias & Lydia Decker

April 18. — Abraham Seguine, single, son of John & Rachel Seguine
Elizabeth Simonson, single, dau. of Joseph & Rebecca Simonson. Md. at parsonage in presence of Wm. H. Fountain & Lydia Seguine

May 11. — Saul, } Blacks, belonging to Peter Decker
Louisa, } free woman. Md. in Ch. by permission in writing from Mr. Decker

Aug. 23. — Peter Van Pelt, single, son of David & Ann Van Pelt
Rachel Haughabout, single, dau. of Peter, dec., & Hannah, his wife. Md. at Parsonage, John Selenf & Eliza Housman, witnesses

Sept. 8. — James Wood, widower, son of Abraham, decd., & Ruth, his wife
Esther Prue, single, dau. of Revd. Elias & Esther Prue. Md. at Parsonage. All of this Island

Dec. 15. — James Egbert, Sen., widower, son of Tunis & Ann Egbert
Martha Egbert, m. n. Burbank, widow of Abraham Egbert, shoemaker. Md. at bride's residence in presence of their children & others

Dec. 26. — Jacob Harzen, single, of Elizabethtown, N. Jersey, son of Cornelius & Ann Harzan of York Island
Margaretta Perine, single, dau. of Abm. & Sarah Perine, at whose house they were md. in presence of friends

1819.
Jan. 7. Jonothon Merril, single, son of Richard Merril & Martha, his wife, m. n. Hooper
Maria Egbert, single, dau. of James Egbert, Sen., & wife Elizabeth, by m. n. Martinse. Md. at house of Bride's parents in presence of friends

Oct. 2. Vincent Fountain, single, son of Vincent & Else Fountain
Catharine Butler, single, dau. of Isaac & Cath. Butler, both decd. Md. at Parsonage in presence of bride's brother Vincent Butler

Oct. 12. Abraham Tyson, single, son of Richard Tyson, widower
Ann Housman, single, dau. of Aaron Housman & wife Mary, by m. n. Morgan. Md. at Parsonage in presence of Richard Johnson, Rebecca Courson. By Rev. Benj. Mortimer of N. Y.

Oct. 25. Richard Tyson, widower
Elizabeth Cortelyou, widow. Md. at her dwelling. No other parties present but the clergyman, G. A. Hartman

Dec. 14. John Davis, son of John Davis, decd., & Sally, his wife
Jane Wood, dau. of Richd. & Cath. Wood. Md. in presence of Peter Johnson & Lucy Rodgers

Dec. 14. George Van Pelt, son of Peter & Mary Van Pelt
Ann Moore, dau. of James & Catharine Moore. In presence of John Van Pelt & James Moore, brothers to bride & bridegroom

1820.
Jan. 1. Abraham Van Duser, single, son of Daniel V. Duzer & Ann, his wife
Jane Vanderbilt, single, dau. of Cornelius Vanderbilt & Phebe, his wife. Md. at Parsonage, number of friends present

Jan. 4. Robert Wilson, free colored man
Nellie Simonson, free colored woman, etc.

Jan. 22. Moses Decker, single, son of Samuel Decker & Rebecca, his wife, by m. n. Decker
Lenah Pugh, single, dau. of Nicholas Pugh & Caty, his wife, by m. n. Decker. Md. in presence of Lydia Decker & James, bro. of bridegroom

March 18. Abraham Stilwill, son of Abraham & Caty Stilwill, dec., N. side of Island
Mary Scharret, dau. of John & Mary Sharret. In presence of Nicholas Daniels, Gitty Stilwill and Susan Ann Sharret

May 12. Daniel Jones, son of Barent Jones & Mary, his wife
Jane Banta, dau. of Jacob & Eliza Banta. Md. at Parsonage in presence of Bedell Johnston & Jane Wood

April 3. John, } Blacks, belonging to Mr. Abm. Praul
Charity, } belonging to Mrs. Ryersz

1820. May 14.	Thomas Johnston, } Blacks, Sally Peterson, }	belonging to John Fountain free, residing with Mr. Dubois

May 20. James Scharrot, son of James & Hannah Scharrot
Jane Jennings, dau. of Lambert Jennings & Mary, his wife, decd. Md. at Parsonage in pres. of Richd. Johnston, Nancy White

May 24. David Cannon, son of Thomas & Betsy Cannon
Margaret Cannon, dau. of Isaac & Elizabeth Cannon. Md. at Parsonage

June 3. Harry, } Blacks, belonging to Jesse Oakley
Tenor, } belonging to Mary Seguine. By permission of their masters

June 15. James Moore, single, son of James & Catharine Moore, m. n. Perine
Sarah Cannon, single, dau. of John & Ann Cannon. Md. at Parsonage in pres. of Joseph Shaddock & Martha Ann Taylor

July 4. Daniel Martling, single, son of Benjm. Martling & Elizabeth, his wife
Mary Blake, single, dau. of Edwd. Blake & Mary, his wife. Md. at house of Daniel Guyon, Esq., in presence of James Salter & Ann Martling

Nov. 5. John Egbert, single, son of Abraham & Nancy Egbert, m. n. Martinoe
Lydia Seguine, single, dau. of John Seguine & Rachel, his wife, m. n. Mitchell. In pres. of Abm. Bird & Lenah Perine

Nov. 18. John Cannon, single, son of John & Ann Cannon
Dinah Swaim, dau. of John & Martha Swaim. Md. at house of Mr. Martinus Swaim near Richmond

Nov. 26. Daniel Wood, single, son of Stephen Wood & Diodema, his wife, m. n. Housman
Deborah Mott, single, dau. of James & Appolonia Mott, by m. n. Scharrot. Md. at mother's house in presence of John Scharrot & Susan Ann Scharrot

Dec. 6. John Goodheart, single, residing near Woodbridge, N. Jersey, son of Christopher Goodheart & Sophia, his wife
Tabitha Merril, dau. of Richard Merril & Marth, his wife, m. n. Hooper

1821. March 22. Daniel Buskirk, son of Philip Buskirk & Phebe, his wife, m. n. Tucker
Hannah Cannon, dau. of Andrew Cannon & Polly, his wife, m. n. Wright. Md. at Parsonage in presence of Benjamin Bedell & Judah Wright

June 3. Aaron Johnson, single, son of Daniel & Margaret Johnson
Elisabeth Praul, single, dau. of Peter & Abigail Praul. In presence of James Colon & wife, the sister of Mrs. Johnson

1821. June 23.		Peter Burbank, single, son of Abraham Burbank & Lenah, his wife
		Hannah Butler, single, dau. of James Butler & Catharine, his wife. In presence of Newton Post & Eliza Herrington
June 23.		Newton Post, single, son of Francis Post & Experience, his wife, decd.
		Eliza Herrington, single, dau. of William Herrington & Betsey, his wife. Md. at Parsonage, in pres. of Peter Burbank & Hannah, his wife
July 21.		Thomas, ⎱ Blacks, belonging to Col. Nicholas Burger Maria, ⎰ belonging to Mr. Denyse D. Denyse. Md. by consent of their masters
Sept. 26.		Cornelius Van Name (or Namur), son of Aaron Van Name & wife Catharina, by m. n. Bartholew
		Rebekah Coursen, single, dau. of Danl. Coursen & his wife Rebekah, m. n. Martinoe. Md. at Parsonage in pres. of Abraham Martling & Mary Courson
Oct. 31.		Peter Woglom, single, son of Simon Woglom & wife Elisabeth, m. n. Dubois
		Susan Simonson, single, dau. of Arthur Simonson & Harriet, his wife, m. n. Prickett. Md. at Parsonage
Oct. 18.		Jacob Johnson, single, son of Jacob Johnson & Betsey, his w., m. n. Haughabout
		Ann Burbank, single, dau. of John Burbank & his wife Ann, m. n. Egbert
Dec. 8.		Peter Post, son of Garrit Post & Winie, his wife, by m. n. Bush
		Mary Bartholew, dau. of John Bartholew, decd., & Mary, his wife, by m. n. Palmer. Md. at Parsonage
Dec. 19.		Jacob Rozeau Cropsy, single, son of Hermanus Cropsy & w. Elizabeth, m. n. Rozeau
		Elizabeth Cortelyou, dau. of Peter Cortelyou & Amy, his wife, m. n. Hilliard. Md. at bride's parents' house
Dec. 30.		Bill, belonging to Mr. Parkinson at Old town
		Dine, free Black. Md. by permission of master
1822. March 30.		Stacy D. Kenison, single, son of Stacy Kenison & Elizabeth, his wife, decd.
		Maria Bush, single, dau. of William & Ann Bush, m. n. Van Namur. Md. at parsonage
Aug. 28.		John Van Pelt, single, son of Peter Van Pelt & his wife, by m. n. Colon, dec.
		Susan Christopher, single, dau. of John & Elizabeth Christopher, in presence of Jacob van Cleef & Catharine Wood at Parsonage
Sept. 10.		John Crocheron, single, son of Abraham Crocheron & Jane Coursen, his wife
		Patience Egbert, dau. of Tunis & Ann Egbert, m. n. Burbank. Md. at Parsonage

1822. Oct. 2.		Capt. Moses Mills, son of Revd. John Mills & Jemimah, his wife Mrs. Mary Brintley, dau. of Oliver & Sarah Taylor. Md. at Parsonage
Nov. 3.		Anzell Hill, son of Ephraim & Sarah Hill Lenah Perine, dau. of Cornelius & Magdalen Perine at Quarantine. Md. at house of George Van Pelt in presence of Rev. Mr. Mortimer & number of friends
Nov. 30.		John Miers, son of Derick & Mary, his wife Martha Van Cleef, dau. of Daniel & Anletchy Van Cleef. Md. at Parsonage
Nov. 13.		Joshua Mercereau, single, son of Stephen & Elizabeth Mercereau Maria Sharrot, dau. of John & Catharine Sharrot, m. n. Perine. Md. at her father's house
Dec. 25.		James Johnson, widower, son of Edward & Polly Johnson, m. n. Sharrot Ann Martling, dau. of John & Cath. Martling. Md. at Parsonage
Dec. 26.	Thomas Jackson, Judy Crockeron, } Blacks,	belonging to Col. Burger. free. By his written permission.
1823. Jan. 2.		Merrel Hilliard, single, son of John Hilliard, Esq. Eliza Coursen, single, dau. of Richard Coursen & wife m. n. Egbert. In presence of father & friends
Jan. 2.	Harry Swaim, Eliza Barnes, } Blacks,	by permission of their respective masters, John V. D. Jacobson & Geo. Western Barnes, Esq.
Feb. 15.	Daniel Jackson, Mary Seely, } Colored,	by permission of their master Edward Perine
March 23.		John Van Duser, single, son of Daniel Van Duser & Ann, his wife Sarah Vanderbilt, single, dau. of John & Elizabeth Vanderbilt, m. n. Taylor. Md. in church
April 9.		Daniel Mersereau, single, son of Stephen Mersereau Ellen Maria Lozier, dau. of Jacob & Sarah Lozier, m. n. Beatty
May 11.		Jacob Van Cleef, son of Daniel & Letty Van Cleef Catharine Wood, single, dau. of Timothy Wood
May 17.		Jacob Bush, son of Nicholas Bush & Caty, dec. Mary Cairns, dau. of John & Harriet Cairns
May 17.		Aaron Drake Ellen Decker, dau. of Barnet & Catharine Decker
May 24.		Peter Van Pelt, single, son of Jacob & Catharine Van Pelt Elizabeth Decker, dau. of Barnet Decker & Catharine, his wife
June 4.		Aaron Saffin, widower, son of William Widow Eliza Foot, dau. of William & Sarah ——. Md. at Parsonage
June 8.		James Britton, son of John & Rachel Britton Frances Sylvy, Richard & Hester Sylvy. Md. at Parsonage

1823.		Jesse Paulus, single, son of Cornelius & Sophia Paulus
June	8.	Sarah Simonson, single, dau. of Joseph & Rebekah Simonson. Md. at Parsonage.
June	19.	John Wood, single, son of Stephen & Deina (or Demah?) Wood
		Mary Vroom, single, dau. of Christopher & Mary Vroom
July	19.	Edward Vanderbilt, single, son of John & Elizabeth Vanderbilt
		Mary Ann Egbert, single, dau. of Cornelius Egbert, dec. Md. at Parsonage
Oct.	4.	Ebenezer Davis, son of Ebenezer & Rachel Davis
		Elizabeth Merrell, dau. of Abraham & Ann Merrell. Md. at Parsonage
Oct.	18.	John Taylor, son of Abraham Taylor & Catharine, his wife
		Grace Thatcher, dau. of Charles & Elizabeth Thatcher, decd. Md. at Parsonage
Oct.	29.	John Dorsett, single, son of John and Martha Dorsett
		Ellen Connover Cropsy, dau. of Nichs. & —— Cropsy, m. n. Winant
Dec.	13.	Abraham Martling, son of John & Catharine Martling
		Elizabeth Wright, dau. of Thomas & Catharine, his wife
1824.		Richard Decker, single, son of Richard & Mary Ann,
Jan.	6.	his wife
		Eliza Egbert, dau. of Joseph & Jane Egbert, m. n. Martling
April	4.	Paris M. Davis, son of Richard & Sarah Moore Davis of N. Y.
		Eliza Jane Lake, dau. of Richard & Mary Lake of Staten Island. Md. at Parsonage in presence of Mrs. Price, the bride's sister & her husband
May	9.	Henry Kruser, son of John & Miami Kruser
		Ellen Simonson, dau. of Arthur & Mary Simonson. Md. at church
June	13.	Jacob Vreeland, single, son of George & Rebecca Vreeland
		Betsy Lockman, single, dau. of Joseph & Jane Lockman. Md. at Parsonage
June	16.	John Barron, single, son of Joseph & Fanny Barron of Woodbridge, N. J.
		Mary Connor, single, dau. of Richard Connor, Esq., & his wife Sophia, m. n. Clawson. Md. at bride's parents
June	22.	Vincent Bodine, single, son of Vincent Bodine, dec., & his wife, by m. n. Blake
		Mary Ann Burbank, single, dau. of Isaac & Sally Burbank, m. n. Egbert. Md. at Bride's parents
Aug.	15.	Abraham Bird, single, son of —— & Martha Bird
		Susan Ann Perine, dau. of Cornelius Perine & wife. Md. at Parsonage

1824.		Israel Decker, son of Israel & Leah, decd., Decker
Sept. 22.		Catharine Bartholen, dau. of John & Mary Bartholen. Md. at Parsonage in presence of Abraham Decker & Mary Coursen
Sept. 29.		Daniel Stilwell, single, from Long Island Hester Silvy, dau. of Richard & Hester Silvy, by m. n. Taylor. Md. at Bride's parents
Oct. 23.		Barnt Seaman, } Colored, belonging to Daniel W. Lake Margaret Price, } & md. by his permission
Nov. 18.		Edward Barnes, single, son of John & Margrett Barnes Maria Merrill, single, dau. of Mr. Abraham Merrill. Md. at Parsonage
Dec. 11.		Cornelius Egbert, single, son of Abraham, dec., Egbert & Nancy, his wife, m. n. Martinoe Maria De Pugh, dau. of Nicholas & Catharine De Pugh. Md. in presence of friends
Dec. 18.		Daniel Simonson, son of John & Phebe Simonson Sally Ann De Pugh, dau. of Abraham & Mary De Pugh. Md. in presence of Capt. Edward Perine & Mrs. Eliza C. Hartman
		Daniel Jackson, } belonging to Mr. Edward } Colored, Perine Ann ——, } widow, belonging to Mr. Edward Beatty. By consent of their masters
		Charles, } Colored, a freeman Sarah, } residing at James Egbert, Jr.
1825. Jan. 6.		Richard Connor, single, son of Richard Connor, Esq., & Sophia, his wife, by m. n. Clawson Sarah Egbert, single, dau. of Janes Egbert & Elizabeth, his wife, m. n. Martino. Md. at Bride's parents in presence of friends
Jan. 8.		Matthew Decker, single, son of Abraham Decker, decd., & Catharine, his wife Eliza Cole, single, dau. of Richard Cole & Ann, his wife, both decd. Md. at house of Joseph Egbert in presence of friends
March 17.		John Wood, widower, parents deceased Catharine Jacobson, widow, dau. of Richard & Sophia Conner, m. n. Clawson. Md. at Mr. Conners in presence of friends
March 23.		James Garretson, } free, Colored. Ann Winet, }
April 7.		Abel Cannon, son of John & Ann Cannon Catharine Moore, dau. of James & Catharine Moore. Md. at Parsonage
April 17.		John Davis, single, of Mass., son of Jacob Davis & Harriott (Reed), his wife Susan Ann Scharrot, dau. of John Scharrot & Mary, his wife. Md. at house of Abm. Stilwell, North side

1825.
June 5. Cornelius Egbert, son of John Egbert & Mary (Holmes), his wife
Catharine Lake, dau. of Barnet Lake, decd., & Cath., his wife. Md. at the bride's mother's

June 16. Lawrence Crips, and aged widower
Polly Lake, single, dau. of William Lake. Md. at Parsonage

July 2. Henry Garretson, } Colored, free
Mary Lawrence, } belonging to Mr. Simon Perine

July 16. Thomas Disosway, } Colored, both free, residing with
Diana Clarkson, } Hermanus Guion, Esqr.

July 30. Abraham Decker, single, son of Israel & Rachel Decker
Catharine Maria Pryor, single, dau. of Andrew & Elizabeth Pryor

July 31. Cornelius Marston, son of John & Deborah Marston
Mary Butler, dau. of James & Catharine Butler. Md. at Parsonage. In presence of John Laferge & Matilda Marston

Sept. 4. George Avery, son of Geo. Avery, decd., & Grace, his wife
Catharine Crips, dau. of James & Sally Crips. Md. at Parsonage in pres. of Lewis Mitchell & Ann Simonson

Nov. 1. John N. Tooker, single
Maria Jacobson, dau. of John V. D. Jacobson, Esqr., & Hilletje, his wife. Md. at house of Mr. Jacobson in presence of large number of friends

Nov. 20. John Merrell, single, son of Abm. Merrell, dec., & Ann, his wife
Margarett Housman, single, dau. of Abm. Housman & Hester, his wife. Md. at Parsonage

Nov. 27. William Ross, son of William Ross
Margrett Simonsen, dau. of Reuben & Jane Simonson, m. n. Decker. Md. at Parsonage

Nov. 30. Abraham Housman, son of Abraham Housman & wife
Margarett Bodine, dau. of James Bodine & Margarett, his wife. Md. at house of Mr. Bodine

Dec. 15. Barzillai Burr, of New Jersey
Ann Beatty, dau. of John & Elizabeth Beatty. Md. at house of Mr. Beatty

1826.
March 18. Garret Ellis, son of Garret & Mary Ellis
Susan Butler, dau. of Nathaniel, decd., & Sophia Butler, his wife

April 2. Edward Merrell, single, son of John & Elizabeth Merrel
Catharine Shields, single, dau. of Thomas & Ann Shields. Md. at house of Mr. Bogart in the Manor

June 14. Gabriel Martino, son of Benajah & Hannah Martino, m. n. Decker
Eliza Catharine Martling, dau. of John & Dorcas Martling, by m. n. Laforge. Md. at house of parents

1826. July 27.	James McLaughlin, single Caroline Jaques, residing on North side of Island. Md. at Parsonage in presence of John M. Tooker & Israel Jacobson
Aug. 5.	Samuel Johnson, ⎫ ⎬ Colored, Hagar Thomas, ⎭ by permission of his master, Judge Mercereau / free
Aug. 16.	Benjamin Praul Ellen Beatty, dau. of Edward & Eleanor, dec., Beatty. Md. at Parsonage
Oct. 11.	John La Forge, son of David La Forge, dec., & Gertrude, his wife, m. n. Martling Cornelia Simonson, dau. of John Simonson, dec., & Nancy, his wife. Md. at Parsonage
Nov. 21.	Walter Wendel, single, son of Peter & Sarah Wandel Ann De Puy, dau. of John & Ann DePuy. Md. at Parsonage
1827. Jan. 6.	Ellis Mundy, son of Joshua & Phebe Mundy Sarah Ann Egbert, dau. of Tunis Egbert & Sarah, his wife, m. n. Barton, in whose house she was md.
Feb. 5.	Stephen McIntosh, son of Charles & Margarett McIntosh Mary M. Marsac, dau. of Michael & Rachel Marsac, m. n. Jennings, in whose house she was md.
Feb. 18.	Richard Johnson, son of James & Phebe Johnson Susan Van Pelt, dau. of Peter & Margaret Van Pelt
March 24.	David Wood, son of James Wood, dec., & Elizabeth, his wife Eliza De Puy, dau. of Nicholas & Cath. De Puy. Md. at Mr. De Puy's in presence of friends
March 24.	Winant Haughabout, son of Peter & Ellen Haughabout Sarah Britton, dau. of John & Rachel Britton. Md. in church in presence of friends
March 29.	Capt. Benson Seaman, son of Wm. & Elizabeth Seaman of N. Y. Eliza Jacobson, dau. of John V. D. Jacobson, dec., & Helletje, his wife. Md. at house of Samuel Coddington at N. Y.
April 22.	Nathan Decker, son of John & his wife, dec. Mary Ann Bedell, dau. of James & Esther Bedell. Md. at Parsonage
April 22.	Israel De Puy, son of Nicholas & Elizabeth, his wife, dec. Eliza Ann Decker, dau. of Abm. & Mary Decker, dec. Md. at Parsonage at same time as above
May 6.	Matthew De Pugh, son of John De Pugh & Ann, his wife, dec. Maria Simonson, dau. of John & Phebe Simonson. Md. at Parsonage in pres. of Walter Wendel & his wife

1827. John Merrell, son of Thomas Merrell, dec., & Mag-
June 23. dalen, his wife
  Elizabeth Davis, widow, dau. of Abraham Merrell, dec., & Ann, his wife. Md. in presence of number of friends

Aug. 2. Adam A. Doyle, formerly of Chambersburgh, Penna., son of Robert Doyle, dec., & Elizabeth, his wife
  Catharine Merrell, dau. of John T. Merrell & Eliza, his wife. Md. at Parsonage

Aug. 22. Daniel Butler, son of Isaac & Catharine Butler
  Eliza Egbert, dau. of Cornelius Egbert, decd. Md. at Parsonage

Oct. 17. James Mussentine, of Philadelphia, son of John & Margaret Mussentine, dec.
  Catharine La Forge, widow, dau. of John & Susan Pryor. Md. at the Parsonage

Nov. 24. John Decker, son of John & Martha Decker
  Sarah Alston, dau. of Japhet & Sarah Alston. In presence of Abm. Decker & Eliza Christopher

Dec. 10. James Beatty, son of Edward & Eleanor Beatty, dec.
  Ann M. Bryant, dau. of David & Jane Bryant. Md. at house of the mother in N. Y.

Dec. 23. Cornelius Vanderbilt, son of John & Betsy Vanderbilt
  Eliza Martling, dau. of Benjamin & Elizabeth Martling, both dec. Md. at Parsonage

Dec. 31. Peter Van Pelt, son of Richd. Van Pelt, dec., & Elisabeth, his wife
  Betsy Butler, dau. of James & Catharine Butler. Md. in presence of friends at Parsonage

1828. David Moore, single, son of James & Catharine Moore,
Jan. 15. m. n. Perine
  Mary Ann Barton, single, dau. of —— Barton & Lucy, his wife, m. n. Egbert. Md. at house of her gr.-father John Egbert

Feb. 14. Israel Wood, son of William Wood, dec., & his wife
  Mary Parker, dau. of Nathaniel & Sally Parker. Md. at parents' house

March 6. John Freeman, } Colored
  Mary Prue,

May 11. George W. Chambers, son of Wm. & Mary Chambers, dec.
  Hannah Simonson, dau. of John & Ann Simonson. Md. at Parsonage in presence of friends

May 18. Lewis Mitchel, single, son of Peter Mitchel & Sarah, his wife
  Mary Boram, John & Sarah Boram, both dec. Md. at Parsonage

May 18. Abraham Sharrot, son of John & Mary Sharrot
  Margaret Housman, dau. of Benjamin & Letty Housman

1828.	Benjamin Price, son of Elias Price & Esther, his wife
Aug. 3.	Jane Blake, dau. of John & Mary Blake. Md. in presence of a number of friends
Aug. 10.	Joseph R. Heath, widower, from N. Y., son of Simon A. Heath & Eliza, his wife
	Sarah Egbert, widow, dau. of Richard & Martha Merrell
Sept. 7.	James Sharrot, Senr., son of Richard Sharrot, Senr., gatekeeper at Quarantine
	Mrs. Van Cleef, widow. Md. at Parsonage, a number of friends being present
Sept. 11.	Abraham Praul, single
	Isabella Beatty, dau. of Edward & Eleanor Beatty, both decd. Md. at house of Benjamin Praul
Nov. 29.	William Egbert, son of John Egbert, Senr., & his wife, decd.
	Mary Ann Lake, daug. of Widow Catharine Lake at whose house the marriage took place
Dec. 14.	Elias Price, single, son of David Price & Ruth Ellen, his wife
	Polly Menee, dau. of Peter Menee & Sally, his wife
Dec. 31.	Charles D. Wood, widower, son of James & Ann Wood
	Elizabeth Jones, single, dau. of Abm. Jones, dec., & Elsy, his wife
1829. Feb. 18.	James Wood, single, at the Long Neck, son of John & Mary Wood
	Abbey Ann Simonson, single, dau. of Reuben Simonson & Jane, his wife. At whose house they were married
March 2.	William Winnings, widower, from N. Y., son of Wm. & Isabella Winnings, dec.
	Ann Simonson, dau. of Joseph & Rebekah Simonson. Md. at Parsonage in presence of friends
May 30.	Joseph Bedillion, } Colored, formerly of N. Jersey Eliza Peterson, } formerly at G. W. Barnes
May 30.	Aaron Fardon, } Colored, at Judge Seguine's Hannah Jackson, } sister to Bedillion's wife
Nov. 15.	John W. Burbank, single, son of Jacob & Ann Burbank, by m. n. Wandell
	Gertrude Egbert, single, dau. of Abm. Egbert, dec., & Ann Martha, his wife. Md. in minister's dwelling
Dec. 30.	Stephen Squire, widower
	Martha Egbert, widow. In presence of Moses Egbert & wife in whose house they were married
Dec. 25.	John Emmot to Maria Andee, Colored, living at Mr. Parkinson's
1830. Feb. 3.	Abraham Garretson, single, son of Col. John Garretson & Elizabeth, his wife, m. n. Conner
	Eliza Sanders, single, dau. of Peter & Eliza Sanders. In presence of Peter Dorsett & Jane M. Betts

1830. May 4.		Joseph Christopher, single, son of Joseph & Elizabeth Christopher
		Maria Martino, single, dau. of Stephen Martino, dec., & Eleanor, his wife. In presence of Holmes Egbert, Ellen Haughabout & Eliza C. Hartman
May 26.		Daniel Mersereau, single, son of Daniel & Ann Mersereau
		Lucretia (Christiana?) Sharrot, single, dau. of John & Catharine Sharrot
July 15.		Augustus Luckenbach, age 24, single, son of Samuel & Sarah Luckenbach of Bethlehem, Penn.
		Matilda Jacobson, 17 yrs., dau. of John V. D. Jacobson & Hilletje, his wife. Md. at house of Samuel Coddington, Esq., in presence of number of friends
Oct. 24.		Joseph Egbert, single, son of Abm. Egbert, dec., & Ann, his wife
		Eliza Fountain, single, dau. of Anthony Fountain, Jr., & Nancy, his wife. Md. at church
Nov. 10.		Andrew B. Decker, single, son of Jeseph Decker & Catharina, his wife
		Patience Crocheron, widow, m. n. Egbert. Md. at house of her mother, Mrs. Ann Egbert
1831. March 22.		James Beatty, son of Thomas & Susan Beatty of N. J.
		Maria Housman, dau. of Richard & Judith Housman of this island. Present, Edwd. Johnson, Jr., & Maria Housman
June 16.		Mathias Decker, son of David Decker & Catharine, his wife, m. n. Decker
		Jane Decker, dau. of John Decker, dec., & Ann, his wife. Md. at house of bride's mother
June 18.		John Simonson, widower, son of Arthur & Mary Simonson
		Rachel Baker, dau. of Jeremiah & Debby Ann Baker. In presence of Wm. S. Brown & Mary Burbank
Aug. 14.		Charles Barbour, single, son of Edward & Margrett Barbour
		Eliza Christopher, single, dau. of John Christopher & Elizabeth, his wife, both dec.
Oct. 8.		James Simonson, son of Abm. Simonson, dec., & Susannah, his wife
		Catharine Butler, single, dau. of James Butler & Cath., his wife, dec. In presence of Eliza Ann Morgan & Jacob Mersereau
1832. March 15.		Stephen Martling, son of Garret Martling & Mary Wood, his wife
		Mary Ann Bodine, widow, m. n. Burbank. In presence of Br. Edward & Nathan Housman
		Barnt Siebern, wid., to Delia Jackson, Colored
Oct. 14.		Abraham M. Steward, single, son of Thomas Steward, dec., & Hannah, his wife
		Mary Ann Burgher, single, dau. of Mathias Burgher & wife. In presence of Jacob Garretson & Margaret Ann Tyson

1833. May 26.	John C. Thompsen, son of John E. Thompsen, dec., grocer of Tompkinsville, & Mary Lake Elizabeth Johnson, dau. of Anthony & Fanny Johnson. In presence of Ephraim & Addria Johnson
July 17.	Edward Burbank, single, son of Isaac & Sally Burbank, by m. n. Egbert Jane Britton, single, dau. of Nathaniel & Mary Britton, m. n. Bodine
Aug. 1.	John Burgher, single, son of Mathias & Hannah Burgher, m. n. Tyson Elizabeth Stilwell, single, dau. of Daniel & Hannah Stilwell. Md. in presence of friends
Dec. 29.	Abraham Bodine, son of James & Margaret Bodine, dec. Abby Ann Kinsy, dau. of Benjamin & Susan Ann Kinsy. In presence of John Kinsy, her brother, & of Ann Merrel. Md. in church
1834. Jan. 8.	Edward Johnson, single, son of Edward & Mary Johnson, m. n. Sharrot Hannah Housman, dau. of Richard & Judith Housman. Md. at Parsonage in presence of Jeremiah & Judith Turner
Jan. 12.	Daniel Haughwout, single, son of Francis & Esther Haughwout Jane Jones, dau. of Abm. & Alice Jones. At parsonage in pres. of Jacob Winant, Presilla Jones
Feb. 13.	Capt. Jacob H. Vanderbilt, son of Cornelius Vanderbilt, dec., late of this Island Euphemia M. Banta, dau. of Wiart Banta, dec., & Sylva, his wife, of N. Y., where they were md. in presence of friends
May 21.	Samuel Lesher. Both from Germany now at Tompkinsville Elizabeth Nedicker.
May 26.	Leonhart Wilhelmin. Both from Germany now at Tompkinsville Catharine Maurer.
June 22.	Elias Price, son of Rev. Elias Price of Methodist Ch. & Hester his wife Mary Ann Lake, dau. of Joseph & Mary Lake
Aug. 13.	James Thompson, son of Robert Thompson & Susan, his wife, dec. Charity Guyon Romer, dau. of James & Mary Romer. Md. at parent's house in presence of friends
Sept. 27.	Jacob Housman, son of Benjamin Housman & Mary, his wife Susan Robbins, dau. of Nathaniel Robbins, dec., & Mary, his wife. In presence of John & Mary Ann Haughabout
Nov. 4.	Dennis Sullivan, single Elizabeth Vanderbilt, dau. of Capt. John Vanderbilt & Celia, his wife. Md. in presence of friends in dwelling of her parents at "town Point," New Jersey
Nov. 19.	James Egbert, son of James Egbert, dec., & Sally, his wife Eliza Decker, dau. of Abm., dec., & Ann, his wife

1834. William Francis Post, single, son of Francis Post, dec.,
Nov. 19.   & Sarah, his wife
            Martha Ann Egbert, dau. of James Egbert, dec., &
              Sally, his wife. Md. at Parsonage
Dec. 26. George Lentz.   Both from Germany now at Tomp-
            Magdalen Jacky.   kinsville
Dec. 30. Israel O. Dissasway, single, son of Israel R. Dissasway
            & Ann, his wife
            Lucretia Jacobson, youngest dau. of John V. D. Jacob-
              son, & Hellethay, his wife, both dec. Md. in presence
              of friends
1835.   William Townsend, single, son of John & Sarah
June 14.   Townsend
            Dorcas L. Martling, single, dau. of Peter & Elizabeth
              Martling. Md. at dwelling of bride's parents in pres.
              of friends
March 26. Tunis A. Egbert, widower, son of Abraham & Ann
            Egbert, dec.
            Charlotte De Foreest, widow, m. n. Vanderbilt. In
              presence of Mrs. Catharine Prall & Eliza C. Hartman
Sept. 3. Abraham Lockman, single, son of Richard Lockman &
            Catharina, his wife, dec.
            Matilda Britton, single, dau. of Cornelius Britton &
              Jane, his wife, dec. Md. in presence of Hamilton &
              Ann Britton, in Parsonage
Oct. 12. Oliver Martin, single, son of Moses Martin, dec., &
            Nancy, his wife
            Sarah Ann Vanderbilt, single, dau. of Capt. John &
              Presilla Vanderbilt of Elizabeth, Town Point, N. J.
              Md. in presence of a large number of friends
Oct. 14. Abraham Vanpelt, single, son of David & Ann Vanpelt
            Ellen Maria Dorset, single, dau. of John & Martha
              Dorset, both dec.
Nov. 1.   Abraham Tyson, single, son of Peter Tyson & Mary,
            his wife, dec.
            Elsie Jane Haughawout. Md. in presence of some
              friends in dwelling of minister
Nov. 23. James Livingston Lynch, single, son of James &
            Rachel Lynch
            Olivia Ann Marsac, dau. of Michael & Rachel Marsac.
              Md. at house of Bride's parents
Nov. 23. William Thomas, son of Thomas & Elizabeth Thomas, dec.
            Mary Ann Hilyer. At same time as above
Dec. 5.   Williamson Decker, son of Reuben & Maria Decker,
            both dec.
            Mary Bonnel, dau. of Enos & Rachel Bonnel. Md. in
              minister's dwelling in presence of John Baker &
              Eliza Bonnel
Dec. 16. Barnet Jones, son of Daniel & Elizabeth Jones
            Sarah Hatfield, dau. of James & Sarah Hatfield, both
              dec. In minister's dwelling in presence of Thomas
              Christopher & Elizabeth Jones

1835.		Charles Van Name, son of Aaron & Deborah Van Name
Dec.	17.	Catharine Decker, dau. of John & Elizabeth Decker. In dwelling of Minister, in presence of David Alston & Eliz. Decker
1836.		Henry Burbank, son of John & Ann Burbank
Jan.	20.	Elizabeth Alston, dau. of Japhet & Sarah Alston. In dwelling of Minister
Jan.	21.	Martinus S. Lake, son of Daniel & Catharine Lake
		Ann Eliza Parker, dau. of William & Ellen Parker
Feb.	9.	John Brooker, son of William & Lucy Brooker, dec.
		Catharine Simonson, dau. of Abraham & Margarett Simonson
June	12.	David Mersereau, single, son of Peter & Elizabeth Mersereau
		Ann Holmes, dau. of Samuel & Margaret Holmes. In presence of Sally Ann Perine
Sept.	4.	Moses Alston, son of Japhet & Sarah Alston
		Sarah Ann Decker, dau. of John Decker, dec., & Nancey, his wife. At ministers, in presence of friends
Sept.	25.	Isaac V. Snedieker, son of Abm. I. Snedieker & Sarah, his wife of N. Y.
		Margaret E. Beatty, dau. of John Beatty & Eliz., his wife, dec.
Nov.	5.	Isaac Butler, single, son of James Butler & Charity, decd., his wife
		Martha Butler, widow, dau. of John & Martha Swaim
Nov.	20.	David Decker, son of John & Martha Decker
		Mary Frances Decker, dau. of John Decker, dec., & Ann, his wife
Dec.	28.	John White, son of George & Jane White of N. Y.
		Evelina Thompson, dau. of Peter & Ellenor Thompson of this Island. Md. in house of Bride's parents
1837.		John J. Baker, son of Joseph Baker, dec., & Susan, his wife
Jan.	2.	
		Eliza Romer, dau. of James & Mary Romer, in whose house they were married
June	28.	James Van Cott
		Emeline Smith. Both from Jamaica, Long Island
Sept.	9.	Leonard Fountain, son of James & Mary Fountain
		Mary Wadsworth, dau. of John & Elisabeth Wadsworth
Sept.	11.	John Elmwood
		Sarah Wolfe
1838.		Ferdinand Thum, a German
Feb.	3.	Jacobina Small, dau. of Adam & Margaret Small
March	13.	Thomas Fitzgerald, son of Wm. & Mary Fitzgerald
		Frances Tubbs
June	11.	Jacob Walker, son of John & Maria Walker
		Gertrude Freeman, dau. of Mary & John Freeman
Oct.	14.	James Hatfield Merrel, son of Thomas & Sarah Merrel
		Susan Ann Scharret, dau. of Richard & Mary Scharret

By Rev. H. G. Clauder.

1839.
June 7. Joseph Egbert, widower, son of Abm. Egbert, dec., & Ann, his wife
Ann Downs, dau. of John Downs, dec., & Ann, his wife

Aug. 11. Philip Leiser, single, native of Prussia
Maria Hetwig Fries, single, native of Hesse Darmstadt. Md. at Parsonage

Dec. 31. Samuel Decker, single, son of Silvanus Decker
Margareth Ann Wood, single, dau. of Peter Wood. Md. at Parsonage

1840.
March 29. Thamas Holmes Egbert, single
Elisabeth Ann Merrill, dau of John T. & Elisabeth Merrill. Md. in minister's dwelling in presence of Edward & Hannah Egbert & Charlotte Elisabeth Clauder. All of Northfield

June 2. Joseph Lake, widower, residing at Northfield
Sr. Ann Prall, widow, m. n. Egbert, md. in minister's dwelling in presence of Andrew Decker & Charlotte E. Clauder

June 14. Richard Ditten, single
Jane Cannon. Both of Castleton. Md. in church in presence of Danl. Smith & Giddy Prall

Sept. 1. Theodore Onnis Siersema, single, lately from Holland, province of Cronen
Meda Lenting, of same country. Md. at their dwelling in presence of Mr. Ashman & wife, Mrs. Ed. Bodine & daughter

Sept. 13. Stephen Egbert, widower, carman in N. Y., son of Abm. Egbert, Sr., decd., of N. Y.
Abigail Simonson, dau. of Isaac & Elizabeth Simonson. In presence of Ann Egbert & Ann Eliza Egbert in minister's dwelling

Sept. 30. George W. Sprague, single, chairmaker in N. Y.
Sarah Maria Decker, single, dau. of Andrew Decker. Md. at house of bride's parents

Oct. 4. Richard Decker, son of John & Alcy Decker
Harriet Egbert, single, dau. of Saml. and Elisabeth Egbert, dec. Md. at parsonage in presence of Cornelius Egbert & wife

Oct. 18. Peter Cozine, single, residing at Northfield on this Island
Hannah Maria Vanderbilt, single, dau. of Edward & Mary Ann Vanderbilt. In pres. of Stephen Martling & Miss Sarah Jane Burbank

Dec. 22. Stephen Martling, widower, residing at Isaac Burbanks, son of Garret Martling & his wife Mary Wood
Sarah Jane Burbank, dau. of Isaac & Sarah Burbank. Md. at minister's in pres. Charlotte G. Clauder & Mrs. Nancy Egbert

1841. April 6.	William Loveridge, basket-maker of Gloucester, England Rebecca McLees, widow, m. n. Lewis, of Monmouth Co., N. J. Both now residents of Staten Island. Md. at ministers
July 11.	William Skarret, boatman, son of Thomas & Patty Skarret, dec. Sarah Ann, dau. of Danl. & Catharine Corson. Md. in presence of Nathan Britton
July 20.	Charles Adams, merchant of N. Y. Henrietta Cubberly, dau. of Isaac Cubberly of St. Island
Aug. 22.	Peter Van Pelt, son of Peter Van Pelt, at Quarantine Mary Kneeland, of Manchester, England. Md. in presence of Mr. Fountain here in minister's dwelling
Aug. 27.	Richard Tyson, son of John Tyson Elizabeth Housman, dau. of Richard Housman. Md. in presence of Nathan Housman, Abm. Bodine
Sept. 14.	Johann Wilhelm, single, native of Baden, Germany, residing at Factoryville Christina Frederika Kurrlin, single, native of Wurtemberg. Md. at minister's in presence of many friends
Sept. 26.	Nathan Housman, single, carpenter Catharine Blake, single, dau. of Richard Blake. All of Staten Id. Md. in minister's dwelling
Oct. 24.	John Randolph, single. Both now of Staten Island Emma Ann Hicks, single, formerly of Long Island. Md. at minister's dwelling
Nov. 9.	James Guyon, Junr., single, son of Harry Guyon, dec. Elizabeth Ann Coddington, eldest dau. of Saml. & Catharine Coddington. Md. at bride's parents in presence of many friends
Nov. 22.	James S. Lake, single, native of St. Island, son of Daniel Lake, dec. Jane J. Mercereau, dau. of Josua Mercereau, dec. Md. at minister's in presence of John Fountain, the stepfather of bride, & John Lake & others
Nov. 28.	Joseph McClymer, y. man, at Tompkinsville Elizabeth Millington. Md. in church after service, none of their friends being present
1842. Feb. 2.	Benjamin Y. Williams, single, oysterman Catharine Williams, widow of B. Williams' brother, dec., m. n. Stodhoff, formerly of Long Island. Md. at Parsonage
March 6.	Adam Wagener, single, native of Germany in Europe Christina Bubalin, native of Germany. Md. at house of Ferdinand Thum, near Col. Connors
April 11.	Joseph Lake, single, native of Staten Island Mrs. Sarah Hicks, widow, formerly of Long Island. Md. in presence of James Romer & w. Ann

1842. May 8.		Abraham Noble, widower, native of Staten Island Grace Gillesby, single, native of Ireland. Md. in minister's room in presence of Mrs. Corns. Egbert
June 14.		Louis Göntz, single, native of Germany, laborer Margareth Schmidt, single, her father a farmer & garden near Col. Connors at whose house they were md.
June 22.		Edward Barton, single, son of Col. Saml. Barton. Natives of Staten Island Miss Louisa Jacobson, single, dau. of Mrs. Cath. Woods, late Jacobson, m. n. Connor. Md. at residence of bride's mother in presence of many friends
July 4.		Alexander Boyd, laborer Rebecca McNab, cook & servt. at Mr. E. Taylor's. Both natives of Ireland. Md. at minister's dwelling
July 6.		Richard Stephenson, } colored Mary Ann Drake,
July 19.		Joseph A. Humphry, of Silvaton, Staten Island Hester Elten, dau. of Abm. & Sarah Sharrot of Tompkinsville. Md. at ministers in presence of some friends
July 25.		John Egbert, laborer at Mr. Reacy's Mary Room, from Ireland. Md. here in presence of bride's brother
Aug. 9.		John W. Burbank, widower, son of Jacob Burbank Sr. Ann Egbert, dau. of Abm. Egbert, Sr., deceased
Oct. 5.		Edward Egbert, single Susan Garretson Bodine. Both of this Island. Md. in presence of a few friends
Oct. 13.		William Po. Noble, from Newfield, Maine Miss Susan Housman, dau. wid. Ann Housman, residing in village of Tompkinsville. Md. at minister's in presence of John Egbert (hackman) & others
Oct. 13.		Richard Connor, Jr., widower, son of Richard & Sophia Connor Ann Smith, single, native of Antigna, where her father was a planter. Md. in church in presence of bride's sister & Charles Young
Nov. 20.		John E. Perine, widower, carman of N. Y., native of St. Island Sr. Rebecca Jane Lewis, dau. of Br. James Lewis. Md. in Parsonage Joshua Mercereau
Nov. 20.		Sr. Sarah Ann Perine. Both of N. Y.
Dec. 28.		David M. Mersereau, single, carpenter, native of St. Island, son of Daniel Mersereau Annette V. Lake, dau. of Daniel Lake, dec. Md. at Parsonage

1843. Feb. —. Joseph Romer, son of James & Ann Romer, dec.
Jane Moore, single, from West Quarter

May 24. John Vanderbilt Egbert, son of Tunis at Tompkinsville
Ellen Simonson, dau. of John & Cath. Simonson

Aug. 16. Nicolas Burger, single, son of Matthias & Hannah Burger
Catharine Eliza Noble, dau. of Edmd. Noble. Both of this Island. Md. in church in presence of friends

Oct. 5. Mathias Swaim, native of Staten Island, now a merchant at Port Leon, Florida, son of John Swaim, dec.
Margaret Jane Egbert, 2nd dau. of Br. Abm. Egbert, tanner, & Ann, his wife. Md. in ch. in presence of friends

1844. May 29. John Krohm, single, native of Germany, a baker at Stapleton
Susan Wright, single, of Town of Northfield, S. I. Md. at Parsonage in presence of Charlotte E. Clauder

Aug. 4. John Copes, mariner
Isabella S. C. Egbert, dau. of Tunis Egbert. Md. in presence of Abm. Egbert, Jr.

Sept. 9. Charles Henry Shaw, single, from N. Y. City
Louisa Fountain, dau. of wid. Clarissa Fountain. Md. at house of bride's mother

Oct. 23. William Winant, single, carpenter
Hannah Burger, single, dau. of Mathias & Hannah Burger. Md. at bride's residence

Dec. 11. Stephen H. Williams, single, of N. Y.
Sarah Brown, dau. of Joseph Brown, residing at Great Kill Beach. Md. at Bride's residence

Dec. 15. Daniel De Pugh, native of Staten Island
Elizabeth Decker, single. Md. in church

1845. Jan. 12. Cornelius Cole Eddy, grocer, of this Island
Mary Ross, a niece of Mrs. E. Pattons, at whose house the marriage took place

Jan. 15. William W. Stillwell, butcher
Cornelia Burger, dau. of Mathias & Hannah Burger. Md. in presence of Nicolas Burger & Mrs. Steward. Sister of the bride

Feb. 20. John H. Sprague, merchant of New York
Miss Henrietta Prall, dau. of Wm. Prall, dec., & Ann, by m. n. Egbert, now Lake. Md. at house of her stepfather, Br. Joseph Lake

May 21. William Maines
Ellen Baker, dau. of Widow Susan Baker. They were md. at ministers, in presence of the mother, Mrs. S. Baker, & brother Wandel Baker

1845. William D. Simonson
June 15. Jane Eliza Koss, dau. of Wm. Koss, sailmaker at Port Richmond. Md. in minister's room in presence of C. E. Clauder
June 18. William V. Vroom, carpenter; son of Christopher Vroom & Maria Housman, his wife
Catharine Maria Egbert, dau. of John Egbert, dec., & Lydia, m. n. Seguine, residing at Quarantine
Sept. 25. Abraham S. Egbert, son of John & Lydia Egbert of Tompkinsville
Mary Eliza Bird, single
Sept. 30. James Bradley, butcher of Tompkinsville
Ellen V. Vanderbilt, youngest dau. of Capt. John Vanderbilt & his wife Cecilia, residing at Elizabethport. Md. at house of bride's parents
Oct. 12. Abraham Van Duzer, son of John & Sarah Van Duzer, Tompkinsville
Eliza Ann Vanderbilt, dau. of Edward Vanderbilt. Md. in presence of Mrs. Clauder & the bride's brother, John R. Vanderbilt
Nov. 29. Thomas Charles Holmes, } colored
Mary Elizabeth Jay,
1846. John Barnes, single, farmer, in this vicinity
July 1. Rebecca Maria Egbert, dau. of Abm. Egbert, tanner, & Ann, his wife, m. n. Burbank
July 27. George A. Fall, house & sign painter of N. Y.
Mary Elizabeth Woodward, of N. Y. Md. at Parsonage in presence of Mrs. Clauder, Mrs. Rice of Bethlehem. Pa., Miss Amanda Cargill
Aug. 24. Isaac M. Brown, baker at Port Richmond
Mary Romer, dau. of James Romer. Md. at house of bride's father
Sept. 1. Mathias Burger, Junr.
Hetty Maria Vanderbilt, dau. of Cornelius Vanderbilt, dec.
Nov. 4. Edward Bodine, widower, son of James Bodine, deceased
Martha Ann Bedell, widow, formerly Decker. Md. at house of Abm. Bodine at 4 corners
Nov. 7. Emmett W. Hyde, y. m., of Rochester, N. Y.
Margaretta M. Lake, dau. of Danl. Lake, dec., of Richmond, S. I. Md. in presence of numerous friends
Dec. 20. Thomas Sharrot, single, son of Thomas Sharrot, dec.
Mary Elizabeth Voorhis, dau. of Widow Mary Vanderbilt, late Voorhis, formerly Rhine of New Brunswick
1847. John Oldfield.
Feb. 14. Martha Levinia Merril, of N. Y. City, dau. of Jonathan & Maria Merrell, m. n. Egbert. Md. in presence of C. E. Clauder here

1847. April 28.	George W. Wright Jane M. Bradley, of Tompkinsville, St. Island
July 19 or 29.	George W. Knox, of N. Y. Sarah Jane Mercereau, of Tompkinsville. Md. at Parsonage
Aug. 16.	Ludwig Velein Margaret Petersen. Germans. Now in service at Mr. Van Wagenen's, Clifton. Md. in Ch. Sunday afternoon
Sept. 13.	John Burger Margaret Ann Garrison. Both of Northfield, Staten Island. Md. at Parsonage in presence of bride's sister
1848. Jan. 7.	Jans Geritt Koninge Johanna Schumacker. Natives of Holland. At present living at T. O. Seisema's in the Manor. Witnesses were T. O. Seisema & Meda, his wife, m. n. Lenting
April 12.	Isaac H. Van Duzer, son of John & Sarah, at Quarantine Mary M. Yerks, formerly of Tarrytown, N. Y.
May 2.	Ernst Papst, native of Germany Marie Lingelbach, residing at Clifton. Md. here
June 17.	Thomas Scales Mary Ann Jenkinson. Natives of Ireland. Witness Miss Fanny Johnson
July 26.	Jacob Bodine, gr.-son of Isaac & Sarah Burbank Miss Harriet Emily Bodine, dau. of Nathl. Bodine, dec., & Maria, his wife, m. n. Garrettson. Md. in church in presence of many friends
Aug. 7.	Japheth Alston, widower Elizabeth Wood, widow, formerly De Pugh. Both residing in Northfield, S. I. Md. here
Sept. 17.	John Pforr, cabinetmaker of N. Y. Clara Catharina Margareth Schneider, dau. of Jacob Schneider, Maria Clara Schneider, of Factoryville
Oct. 4.	James B. Baker, son of Widow Susan Baker Elizabeth Bridget Burtingham, of Ireland. Lived lately at Br. John Vanderbilt's
Nov. 1.	William Henry Sharrot Sarah Elisabeth Vanderbilt, dau. of Corns. Vanderbilt, dec. Md. in church in presence of friends
Dec. 10.	William B. Seawood, native of Staten Island Sr. Ann Neats, dau. of Wm. & Dy Neats at Pt. Richmond.
Dec. 31.	Henry Prall, of Port Richmond Miss Elizabeth Neats, dau. of Wm. & Dy Neats
1849. Feb. 14.	Joseph McLean, widower, at Tompkinsville Sarah Mallen
Feb. 14.	John McKee, pilot at Tompkinsville Mary Murray

1849. Peter Van Pelt, fisherman, son of George Van Pelt
April 8. Mary Jane Lewis, dau. of Henry Lewis. Md. here in presence of widows Ann Decker & Ann Egbert
April 8. Johannes Schlect, a German
  Rossina Raff, a German. In D. Ref. Ch. at Port Richmond
April 15. James Hetherington, native of Ireland, now at Quarantine
  Catharine L. White. Md. here with two witnesses who came with them
April 22. William Hetherington, from Ireland, residing at Stapleton
  Miss Ann Cary, also of Ireland. Md. here in presence of Charlotte & Ann Eliza Clauder
April 29. John N. Crocheron, son of Nathan Crocheron, at Grantville, S. I.
  Mahala Selina Blake, dau. of Danl. & Ann Blake of Springville, L. I. Md. in presence of Charlotte E. Clauder
July 3. Robert J. C. Johnson
  Ann S. Baker. Witnesses Charlotte E. Clauder, George Winsor, Mrs. Winsor, P. Decker
Oct. 7. James Wilson
  Margaret Fitz Patrick
Dec. 1. George W. Corson, son of Richard Corson
  Miss Emeline Simonson, dau. of James Simonson of Northfield, Staten Island
Dec. 22. John R. Van Name
  Hanna Maria Cannon. Natives of Staten Island, residing at Northfield. Md. here
Dec. 24. Christian Block
  Rebecca Knief. Both lately from Hanover, Germany, & now living at Quarantine
1850. Benjamin Griffin
Jan. 15. Content Decker. Natives of this Island from Northfield. Md. in Parsonage
June 2. August Zilkens
  Anna Maria Graz. Germans. Md. at Port Richmond. Wit. J. Rathyen & others
Oct. 13. Frederick Wunsch
  Margareth Korneman. Germans. Md. in D. Ref. Ch. at Tompkinsville. Witness, Louis Hageman
Nov. 30. Theodor Rosenthal
  Catharine Müller, widow, m. n. Lamb. Both natives of Germany. Md. in Parsonage. 3 friends witnesses
Dec. 18. Frederick Adolph Dreyer, of N. Y. City
  Auguste Henriette Wilhelmina Schmidt. Md. at house of Bride's parents, Doct. Schmidt of Northfield
Dec. 21. Jacob Bauer, laborer. Md. here in presence of friends
  Margaret Erzer, widow of late Jäkle, m. n. Hoegel
1851. Heinrich Scharlach
Jan. 26. Friderika Wohlfahrt. Germans, now at Stapleton, S. I.

1851.   Gerd. Struss, from N. Y., native of Hanover, Germany
March 24. Margareta Lohmyer. Md. in presence of John Lenting
May 3.   Robert M. H. Jones
          Susan G. Perine, dau. of Simon Perine. Md. in presence
             of parents & Corns. Perine
May 8.   Heinrich August Senne, y. m., native of Germany
          Deborah Fitzinger, from Cape May, N. Jersey. Both
             residing in Williamsburgh, L. Island. Witnesses,
             August Senne, Fridrich Lange
July 6. Cornelius Bird
          Lydia Egbert, dau. of John & Lydia Egbert of Tomp-
             kinsville. Witnesses, Bride's sister & M. Seguine
Sept. 4. John E. Vanderbilt, son of Edward
          Sarah Julia Brindley. Md. in presence of John Brind-
             ley & wife
Oct. 16. John Hull Olmstead, M. D.
          Mary E. B. Perkins. Md. at residence of late Doct.
             Perkins, South side, in presence of many friends
Nov. 30. Jhns. Jansen Tyaden, native of Germany
          Louisa Antoinette Oym, of Oldenburg, Ger. Md. in
             presence of Albert Hulsebus of Pt. Richmond
1852.   James Anderton
March 21. Ellen Richardson, m. n. Bowman. Both from England.
             Md. at house of their friend Thomas Harrison
April 6. Edward Wood, son of John Wood of Chelsea
          Catharine Maria Egbert, dau. of Corns. & Catharine
             Egbert. Md. at her father's residence

By B. E. Schweinitz.

1852.   Friedrich Lange, widower, living at Four Corners
May 30.   Metha Struss. Both Germans. Md. at house of bride-
             groom
July 4. Heartwell Bellow, of N. Y.
          Elisabeth Cavelly, of N. Y. Md. at parsonage in
             presence of Mrs. James Burger & others
Sept. 1. Edwin Tyson, of Four Corners
          Jane Tyson, of Port Richmond. Md. at parsonage in
             presence of bride's sister, etc.
Sept. 5. Johanes Ochs
          Doratha Fey. Germans at Factoryville. Md. at house
             of Mr. Hatsche
Sept. 12. Lamont Williams, of Providence, R. Island
          Eliza Simonson, dau. of John Simonson, Esq., of Clifton.
             Witnesses, Mr. John Egbert & bride's sister
Nov. 30. John William Housman
          Hester Maria Burgher, m. n. Vanderbilt. Md. in
             presence of Wm. Sharret & friends
1853.   James Lockman, widower
March 26. Dorcas Britton, of Tompkinsville
April 3. Sydney Booram, of Centreville
          Mary Catharine Butler. Md. at Parsonage

1853. Johann Alfrank, widower, tailor of Tompkinsville
June 12. Gertrud Hutmacher, single. Md. in presence of Mr. & Mrs. Jean Jansen
June 28. Conrad Sinning, shoemaker in Stapleton, b. in Altenriette, Hessen Cassel, 24 May, 1831, son of Martin Sinning & wife, Sophia, m. n. Rinslard
Henriette Rosalie Gummert, of Berlin, b. 11 Feb., 1830, dau. of C. Gummert & wife Auguste, m. n. Patke. Md. at house of bride's uncle, Mr. Sabel, many friends present
Nov. 27. Warren D. Alston, of Chelsea, Staten Island, farmer, son of Warren Alston
Mary Elizabeth Freeman, dau. of Smith B. Freeman of Factoryville
Nov. 30. Daniel Wandell, Junr., of Southfield, S. I., son of David Wandall, farmer & blacksmith
Jane Elizabeth Garretson, of Southfield, S. I., dau. of James B. Garretson, at whose house they were md.
Dec. 7. Thomas Luby, of Rossville
Julia Palmer Voorhis, dau. of Mrs. M. Vanderbilt, late Voorhis, at whose house they were md.
1854. John Schmidt, Blacksmith, German
Jan. 3. Catharine Eulner, dau. of Valentine Eulner, of N. Y., & his wife Catharine. Md. in church in presence of G. Barth & his wife Elizabeth
April 23. John G. Simonson, son of John Simonson, Esq., of Clifton
Elizabeth Latimer, dau. of John Latimer, dec., of England. Md. here in presence of Miss C. Simonson & Mrs. Schweinitz
June 18. Lawrence Hilliard Bogart, son of Timothy Bogart of S. I.
Sarah Catharine Martling, dau. of Stephen Martling. Md. in church Sunday morning
Dec. 29. Jacob Herman Garretson
Elizabeth Egbert, dau. of Edward Egbert. Md. at Centreville in the evening at Mr. Egbert's house

By Rev. A. A. Reinke.

1854. Henry Britton
Sept. 11. Elizabeth Britton. Md. at Mrs. Jas. Britton's
Dec. 29. Garrett Vroome
Mary Elizabeth Martling. Md. at Parsonage
1855. Samuel Pharo
Jan. 1. Catharine Elizabeth Perine. Md. at Mr. Mersereau's near South Side school-house
Jan. 14. Alexander Littell
Hannah Jane Egbert. Md. at Parsonage in presence of their mothers

1855.		James T. Allen
Jan.	22.	Frances Louisa Smith. At the parsonage in presence of bride's mother
Feb.	14.	Varnum Slocum Mills Dorcas LaFarge Martling, of Centreville. Md. at church at 8½ P. M. in presence of witnesses
June	24.	Hiram Stillwell Frances Ann Johnson. Both of Castleton, North shore. Md. at Parsonage
July	1.	Jacob Egbert, of Tompkinsville Catharine Simonson, of Clifton
July	4.	J. A. Woodland, Stapleton, Staten Island Eliz. A. Turner,
Sept.	18.	Mr. Butler, of Quarantine Miss Milton, of Quarantine. Md. at Parsonage
Oct.	23.	John Lisk, of Egbertsville Miss Mary Ann Harrison. Md. at Mr. Harrison's
Dec.	31.	John Wm. Egbert, of Castleton Sarah Ann Wandell. Md. at Mr. Wandell's
1856.		Henry C. Raymond
June	9.	Eleanor Johnston. Md. at Parsonage
April	8.	Jacob Maree Catharine Koebel
June	15.	Christian Silberhorn, of Stapleton Paulina Seibert, of Stapleton. Md. at Parsonage
Nov.	19.	Henry N. Timolat, of N. Y. Violetta Britton, Staten Island. Md. at church
1857.		Charles Henry Winnett, of Tompkinsville
April	1.	Charlotte Jane Richardson, of Tompkinsville
May	21.	Julius C. Warner, of Macon, Georgia Mary E. Squier, of Southside. Md. at house of bride's father. Family & Mr. Wm. Moore, present
May	30.	Daniel Ditton, of Castleton Mary Ann Sharrot, of Toad Hill. Md. at house of bride's parents & in their presence
June	10.	Benjamin Simonson, pilot, of Richmond, S. I. Sarah Adeline Egbert, of Tompkinsville. Md. in house of bride's mother in presence of witnesses
Aug.	25.	William Henry Horton, } colored Phoebe Ann Tenbroeck, }
Nov.	15.	Thomas Jenkins, of Centreville Sarah Elizabeth Butler, of Prospect Hill, S. I. Md. at Parsonage Sunday evening
1858.		Lawrence ——
Jan.	7.	——. Md. in church in presence of friends
Feb.	3.	Joseph Housman, of Factoryville Lydia Vanderbilt, of New Dorp. Md. at house of bride's brother-in-law Mr. Thomas Sharrot. Friends present

1858. Feb. 4.	John Henry Petersen, } colored Maria Sayles,
Feb. 4.	William Henry Smith to Diana Spicer, colored
May 23.	Carl August Brumhuber, of Bavaria Catharina Elizabeth Schade, of Hesse Cassel. Md. in church on Whitsunday
June 30.	Oliver Vanderbilt Sarah Houseman. Md. at Parsonage
Aug. 25.	Jacob Britton, of Quarantine Lena Van Pelt, of Quarantine. Md. at Parsonage
Sept. 3.	John Daniel Mahkin Anna Maria Oehlmann. Md. at Parsonage in evening in presence of Mrs. Maines & others
Sept. 7.	John E. Woodland, livery stable keeper, of Stapleton Maria Ward, of Stapleton. Md. at parsonage in presence of Abm. Egbert
Oct. 2.	John D. Fink Miss Barbara W. Bogart, of Centreville. Md. at house of bride's father
Dec. 8.	James Vreeland, son of Jacob Vreeland & wife, Elizabeth Lockman Miss Elizabeth Martling, dau. of Stephen Martling, at whose house ceremony was performed
Dec. 23.	Wm. W. Hale Miss Elizabeth Blake. Md. at Parsonage in presence of Alb. Vroome & a lady
1859. Feb. 15.	Raymond Tysen Miss Louisa Barnes. Md. at bride's parents in presence of friends
Oct. 27.	Albert Vroome Caroline Lafarge. Md. at house of Mr. Harmen Tysen in presence of friends
Dec. 8.	John D. Sharrot Harriet Houseman. Md. at Parsonage at New Dorp
1860. Jan. 1.	John Stillwell, of Southfield Sarah Romer, of Westfield. Md. at Parsonage
June 1.	John Sharret, Toad Hill Ellen Freegard. New Dorp Parsonage. Md. at 7½ A. M., at parsonage
June 20.	Abraham S. Wood Emeline C. Tysen. Md. at Moravian Parsonage in presence of Mr. Tunis Butler, Miss Johnson & Mrs. M. Vanderbilt
June 25.	Eugene Swift Sarah Ann Burbank. Md. at house of Mr. S. Martling in presence of friends
Sept. 6.	David M. Colon, policeman of N. Y. City Catharine Hendricksen, of Williamsburg. Md. at Parsonage in presence of Mrs. James Colon
Sept. 11.	James E. Abbatt Catharine Adeline Tysen. Md. in church in presence of friends

1860.		William Taylor
Nov. 28.		Emeline Egbert. Md. at house of Mr. Corns. Egbert, bride's father, in presence of friends
Dec. 25.		George Lewis Reader
		Catharine Vroom. Md. at Mr. Christopher Vroom's, the bride's father
Dec. 27.		James Simonson
		Ellen Egbert. Md. at house of bride's father, Edward Egbert
1861.		William Balzer
Jan. 6.		Harriet Martling. Md. at Parsonage
Jan. 25.		William E. Emmons
		—— Seymore. Md. at Mr. Wobly's house near lighthouse
Jan. 28.		Peter Heal
		Emma Swift. Md. at house of bride's mother, in presence of relatives
April 10.		William Thompson
		Elizabeth T. Mallett. Md. at house of Mr. Taylor in Richmond
April 14.		Samuel L. Thompson
		Sarah Amelia Houseman. Md. at the Parsonage
May 12.		Elias Whitehead
		Elizabeth Summers. Md. at Church
Sept. 5.		Henry Armstrong
		Jane C. Johnson
Sept. 22.		William P. Alston
		Eveline Burbank. Md. at Mr. Burbanks at Centreville
Dec. 18.		Davis Carel Hapenny
		Susan Ann Cole. Md. at house of bride's parents, South side
1862.		Richard Blake Vroom
Feb. 2.		Eleanor Briggs. Md. at Parsonage in presence of Miss Elizabeth Vroom
Aug. 7.		John Luckert
		Jane R. Van Pelt. Md. at parsonage in presence of friends
Aug. 28.		John P. Conklin
		Marietta Egbert. Md. in church

BY REV. EUGENE LEIBERT.

1862.		Charles Perry Cole
Oct. 19.		Mary C. Burgher. Md. at Parsonage in presence of Mr. Burgher, Mr. Noble & several witnesses
Dec. 24.		Cornelius D. Guyon
		Mary L. Burgher. Md. in church in presence of large company
1863.		William Briggs, of Buffalo, N. Y.
Dec. 30.		Susan A. Boone. Md. in Parsonage in presence of John Phillips & Jemima Boone

Deaths and Burials.
Graveyard of Moravian Church at New Dorp.

Vandeventer, John, d. 16 Oct., 1758; 61 y.
Vanderbilt, Jacob, d. 14 Dec., 1760 (family says 1759).
Colon, Peter, son of Peter, d. 22 Nov., 1765; 14 m.
Vanderbilt, Jacob, d. 20 Oct., 1768; 45 y., 9 m., 14 d.
Connor, Anne, dau. of Richard Conor, d. 22 June, 1769; 18 y.
Allison, Mary Catharine, d. 1770; 5 m.
Vanderbilt, Nieltie, d. 9 Dec., 1770; 72 y.
Colon, James, son of Peter Colon, d. 23 April, 1771; 18 m.
Wendel, Thomas, son of John & Aletta Wendel, bur. 26 March, 1778; 11 m.
Colon, Mary Magdalen, d. 26 Oct., 1779; 70 y.
Egbert, Catharine, bur. 27 Nov., 1779; 31 y., 10 m.
Perine, Ann, wife of Peter, bur. 5 Feb., 1785.
Conor, Cathrine, wife of Richard Connor, Esq., d. 24 June, 1787; 62 y., 4 m.
Seymourson, Sr. Ann, wife of Bernard Seymourson of New York, d. 15 Sept,, 1788.
Haughwort, Mary, late Martino, wife of Peter Haughwort, d. 16 Oct., 1788.
Van Pelt, Ann, a child, dau. of John Van Pelt, d. 23 Oct., 1788.
Colon, Peter, widower, d. 10 Feb., 1789.
Limner, Owen, widower, d. 7 April, 1789.
Martino, Cathrine, single, d. 22 June, 1789.
Enyard, Sr. Sussanna, single, d. 21 Dec., 1789.
Enyard, Sr. Elizabeth, single, d. 2 Jan., 1890.
Poillon, Sarah, late Connor, widow, d. 21 Jan., 1790.
Egbert, child of Moses, at N. Y., d. 3 July, 1791.
Perine, Elizabeth, single, dau. of James Perine, d. 8 Aug., 1791.
Conor, Richard, Senr., widower, d. 1 Feb., 1792; 69 y.
Egbert, Sr. Ann, Senr., d. 16 Jan., 1792.
Ryersz, Sr. Cathrine, late Conor, d. 25 Feb., 1792.
Perine, Br. Daniel, md., d. 25 Nov., 1792.
Cortelyou, Cornelius, a child, d. 26 Jan., 1794.
Collon, David, a child, d. 22 May, 1794.
Egbert, Sr. Mary, late Cortelyou, md., d. 18 May, 1795.
Perine, Br. Peter, md., d. 24 March, 1796.
Miller, Sr. Mary, md., d. 2 Sept., 1796.
Ryersz, Adrian, young man, d. 16 Sept., 1796.
Perine, Lucy, a girl, d. 8 April, 1797.
Burgher, Mary Ann, a child, d. 29 Sept., 1797.
Martino, Sr. Elizabeth, md., m. n. Lee, wife of Stephen, d. 4 April, 1798; 76 y., 1 m., 9 d.
Colon, Sr. Mary, wife of George, m. n. Limner, d. 16 Dec., 1798, 47 y.
Egbert, Cathrine, single, dau. of James & Eliz. Egbert, d. 30 July, 1800; 22 y., 5 m.
Martino, Hannah, a child, dau. of Benjah & Hannah Martino, d. 4 Oct., 1800.
Colon, George, youth, son of Geo. & Mary, d. 1 Nov., 1800.

Martino, Stephen, widower, d. 9 May, 1801.
Martino, Stephen, a child, son of Benajah & Hannah Martino, d. 28 Jan., 1802.
Colon, Catharine, wife of James, d. 24 Feb., 1802.
Colon, Jane, single, d. 23 Nov., 1802.
Colon, Elizabeth, single, d. 30 Nov., 1802.
Lewis, Rebecca, late Colon, md., d. 4 April, 1803.
Colon, Jonas, single, son of James & Catharine Colon, dec., d. 22 April, 1803; 21 y., 8 m., some days.
Legier, Cornelius, child, son of Jacob Logier & Sarah, m. n. Beatty, d. 23 Sept., 1803; 1 y., 6 m., 8 d.
Lewis, Jane, little child, b. 19 May, 1799, dau. of James & Rebekah Lewis, late Colon, dec., d. 28 Sept., 1803, in her 6th y.
Colon, Br. James, widower, d. 9 Dec., 1803.
King, John, little boy, b. 15 Nov., son of —— King & ——, m. n. Morgan, bur. 6 Dec., 1803, at Richmond.
Burbank, little child, dau. of John Burbank, fisherman, & Ann, his w., m. n. Egbert, d. 19 Dec., 1803.
Symonson, John, child of Reuben, d. 31 May, 1804; 5 y.
Garritson, Elisabeth, m. n. Conner, d. 5 Oct., 1804; 43 y., 7 m.
Egbert, Edward, md., d. Friday, Oct. 12, 1804.

MORAVIAN CEMETERY AT NEW DORP.

Skerret, Maria Martha, dau. of John Skerret & Francis Rooks, his wife, d. 26 March, 1807; about 4 w.
Barton, Catharine, wife of Isaac Barton, dau. of James, dec., & Cath. Colon, dec.; she was md. 2 Feb., 1805, & had one ch. which lived a few months; d. 4 April, 1807; 33 y. & nearly 9 m.
Guyon, Francis, wife of Daniel Guyon, dau. of Hendrick Garritson. Her parents belonged to D. Ref. Ch. about 1795. She was m., had 4 sons and 2 daus., all living now; d. 3 Aug., 1807; about 35 y.
Vanderbeak, Mary, single, dau. of John Vanderbeak of Stat. Island & his wife Naatje Martinoe, both deceased; d. 24 Aug., 1807.
Vanderbilt, Jacob, a child, b. 19 Feb., 1806, son of John Vanderbilt & Elizabeth, his wife, m. n. Taylor, d. 29 May, 1808; 2 y. & little over 3 m.
Martino, Benjamin, a child, b. 25 Sept., 1803, son of Benajah Martino & his wife, by m. n. Decker, d. 15 Sept., 1808; almost 5 y. old.
Burbank, Ann, m. n. Egbert, b. 13 Feb., 1786, dau. John & Mary Egbert; md. John Burbank 4 Sept., 1802; had 4 children, eldest dead, 2 daus. & 1 son living; d. 23 Sept., 1808; 22 y. & near 9 m.
Colon, Hannah, wife of Peter, m. n. Lewis, dau. of —— Lewis & his wife Billetje (now Colon); leaves 2 sons & 1 dau.; d. 2 Oct., 1808.

Barger, Mary, wid. of Henry, m. n. Tyson, b. Aug., 1765; md. 14 May, 1783, Henry Barger, d. 24 Dec., 1804; dau. of —— Tyson & Mary, his wife; she had 5 chil., Jacob, David, Mary, John & Henry; 2 are md., & she has 2 gr.-children; d. 20 March, 1809.

Lozier, Henry Cruse, infant, b. 28 Jan., 1809, son of Jacob Lozier & Sarah, his wife, d. 5 Nov., 1809.

Ingraham, Eliza Margreth Rider, b. 24 April, 1809, dau. of Geo. Washington Ingraham & Elizabeth, his wife, d. 7 Feb., 1810.

Egbert, Elizebeth, wife of James Egbert, m. n. Martino, b. 11 Feb., 1754, dau. of Stephen & Eliz. Martinoe, dec.; md. James Egbert in 1777; had 3 sons, Stephen, Tunis & James, & 6 daus., Catharine, Eliz., Ann, Maria & Sara, one b. dead; Cath. dec., Stephen is md. & has 2 ch., they lived in N. Y.; d. 29 Sept., 1810; 56 y., near 8 m.

Martino, Catharine Hanna, child, b. 13 Dec., 1808, on Staten Island, dau. (youngest) of Stephen Martino & wife Eleanor, m. n. Haughwout, d. 25 Jan., 1811.

Egbert, John, single, b. 1 Dec., 1789, son of Br. John Egbert & Mary, his wife, m. n. Holmes, d. 28 April, 1811.

Conner, Sarah, a child not baptized, dau. of Richard Conner & wife Sophia, m. n. Clawson, d. 5 July, 1811; some m.

Egbert, Mary infant, b. last Dec., dau. of Joseph Egbert & wife Jane, by m. n. Merlin, d. 19 Jan., 1812; about 5 weeks old.

Egbert, an infant, dau. of Tunis Egbert & Sara, his wife, m. n. Barton, d. 31 March, 1812; about 5 weeks.

Beatty, Alfred Eberhard, infant, b. 24 April, 1812, son of Cornelius Beatty & Ann, his wife, by m. n. Jacobson; the parents moved to New York where he died, bur. 8 Aug., 1812.

Egbert, Tunis, single, b. 11 Dec., 1786, in N. Y., second son of James Egbert & wife Elizabeth, m. n. Martino; Tunis learned trade of chair making in N. J., worked here when he died; d. 24 Sept., 1812 (stone, 25 y., 9 m.).

Brown, Rev. Nathaniel, minister of the Brethren's Ch. on Staten Island, d. 11 July, 1813; 50 y., 1 d.

Egbert, Benjamin, infant, b. 9 July, 1813, son of Abraham Egbert, farmer, & Ann Martino, his wife, d. 2 Oct., 1813.

Egbert, Mary, wife of John, m. n. Holmes, b. in April, 1766, md. John Egbert, farmer & weaver, 12 March, 1782; had 12 children; d. 15 Oct., 1813; 47 y.

Mott, Samuel, b. 10 Feb., 1791, son of Mrs. Mott; he d. of a malignant fever on Sandy Hook; d. 10 Jan., 1814.

Barton, Tunis, infant, son of Wm. Barton, gr.-son of John Egbert, d. 2 Feb., 1814; 6 weeks.

Skerret, Elisabeth, wife of Richard Skerret, shoemaker in Castleton township; d. 19 Feb., 1814; 59½ y.

White, William, single, laborer, d. 6 March, 1814; 56 y.

Davis, Sarah, m. n. Knox, d. 6 March, 1814; brought over from N. Y. & interred here.

Scherret, Catharine Eliza, child, dau. of John Scherret & wife Frances Rooke; d. in N. Y., 12 March, 1814; 6 y., 22 d.

Beatty, Eleonore, child, dau. of Wm. Beatty, tanner & furrier, & Mary Barger, his wife, d. 26 Aug., 1814; 2 y., 3 m., 3 w.
Perine, Mary, wife of James, m. n. Stout, wife of James Perine, tailor, of this Island, d. 26 Oct., 1814; about 60 y.
Bedell, Elisabeth, wife of Cornelius, m. n. Jacobson, wife of Mr. Cornelius Bedell, farmer & miller, d. 24 Oct., 1814; 43 y., 3 m., 18 d.
Martinoe, Benajah, married, farmer, b. 5 Oct., 1766, d. 21 Nov., 1814; 48 y., 1 m., 16 d.
Barger, Catharine Mersereau, child, dau. of Jacob & Hannah Barger, d. 26 Nov. 1814; about 2 y.
Crips, William, married, shoemaker, d. 23 Jan., 1815; 62 y.
Egbert, Cornelius Cortelyou, md., son of Edwd. & Mary Egbert, d. 1 Aug., 1815; 32 y., 4 m., 3 d.
Makings, John, formerly seaman, later soldier in U. S. service, d. 6 Aug., 1815; 43 y.
Wood, Elizabeth, widow, b. 13 April, 1765; d. 30 Oct., 1815; buried at expense of county.
Stuart, William, child, b. 5 Jan., 1812, son of Thomas & Hannah Stuart, d. 18 Nov., 1815.
Egbert, Elizabeth, dau. of James & Elizabeth Egbert, communicant in this ch., d. 1 Feb., 1816; 31 y., 1 m., 3 w.
Fountain, William, child, son of Anthony Fountain & wife, m. n. Ann Egbert, d. 12 Feb., 1816; 2 y.
Dunn, Mary, wife of John Dunn of Richmond, d. 17 March, 1816, buried 19 March, 1816, by Methodist preacher; (stone, 37 y., 11 m.).
Egbert, Stephen, son of James & Elizabeth Egbert, b. 24 Sept., 1779, d. 1 April, 1816; 36 y., 6 m., 7 d.
McLean, Lake, single, d. — April, 1816.
Brasted, John, from N. York, buried 23 April, 1816 (stone, d. 22 April, 1816); 46 y. & 29 d.
McLean, James Potter, child, son of James & Mary Ann McLean, d. 14 June, 1816; 16 m., 2 w.
Dustan, Oscar Fitz Patrick, son of William Dustan, d. 25 June, 1816; 5 y.
Crips, Anthony, md., d. 4 July, 1816; about 22 y.
Dunn, Isabella, wife of Robert, m. n. Vanderbilt, d. July 5, 1816, at New York.
Butler, Isaac, married, farmer, d. 9 Aug., 1816; about 60 y.
Stillwell, Sarah, dau. of Daniel & Hannah Stilwell, d. 2 Nov., 1816; about 6 m., unbaptized.
Martling, Elizabeth, widow of Benjamin Merlin, d. 26 Nov. 1816.
Housman, ——, widow of Benjamin, d. 14 Dec., 1816.
Cortelyou, Jacob, md., member of Bros. church, d. Feb. 7, 1817 (stone, 56 y., 5 m., 12 d.).
McSwine, Sarah, widow, d. 2 April, 1817; 82 y.
Merrill, ——, son of Capt. Abm. Merrill, d. 18 July, 1817.
McSwine, Mary, single, d. 2 Aug., 1817; about 36 y.
Stilwell, John, single, d. 17 Jan., 1818.
Britton, John, single, from New York, son of John Britton waterman, near Quarantine, d. 19 Feb., 1818.

Martino, Benjamin, d. 26 May, 1818.
Drury, Joseph, son of Susan Baker by former husband, d. 28 May, 1818.
Conner, Sarah Lavinia, dau. of Richard Connor, Esq., & Sophia Clawson, his wife, d. 4 July, 1818.
Seguine, Sally Ann, dau. of Henry Seguine & Patience, his wife, m. n. Britton, d. 28 Aug., 1818.
Wood, Catharine, wife of Moses, m. n. Colon, dau. of George & Mary Colon, d. 4 Sept., 1818.
Hartman, Isabella Forker, wife of Rev. G. A. Hartman, m. n. Futton, d. 1 Nov., 1818; 27 y., 2 m., 27 d.
Rook, Frederick Moehring, son of George Rook, d. at house of gr.-father, Br. Amos Rook, 1 Dec., 1818.
Driskyl, Ann, wife of Daniel, d. 20 Dec., 1818.
Stilwell, Catharine, wife of Abraham, m. n. Housman, d. in April, 1818.
Jennings, James, child, son of John Jennings & wife Catharine, m. n. Scherret, d. 27 Jan., 1819; 11 m., 9 d.
Vroom, ——, a poor boy living at Anthony Fountain's, d. 2 March, 1819.
Crips, Lenah, wife of Elisha, d. 12 March, 1819.
Cortelyou, Sarah Sprague, widow of Cornelius Cortelyou (stone, b. 10 April, 1735), d. 20 March, 1819; 84 y. lacking 6 d.
Stilwell, Nicholas, single, d. 26 April, 1819; (stone, 72 y., 3 m., 19 d.)
Lisk, ——, wife of John Lisk, d. 24 May, 1819.
De Forrest, Hugh, son of Capt. Deforest, son-in-law of Cornelius Vanderbilt, Senr., d. 19 June, 1819.
Jacobson, John, Jr. (C. on stone), son of John V. D. Jacobson, Esq., d. 16 Sept., 1819 (stone, 26 y., 11 m., 5 d.).
Scherret, ——, a child of Thomas Scherret, d. 22 Sept., 1819.
Miller, Isaac, child, Thomas Miller & Maria, his wife, m. n. Haughabout, d. 22 Oct., 1819.
Perine, James, widower, d. 5 Dec., 1819.
Ryerz, Sarah, a widow, d. Dec. 28, 1819.
Marsh, ——, child of Robert & Rhoda Marsh, d. 14 Sept., 1819; buried on Episcopal ground.
Stilwell, Henry, son of Daniel and Hannah Stilwell, m. n. Sharrot, d. 1 July, 1819.
Simonson, William Gosen, son of Chas. & Mary Simonson, by m. n. Vanderbilt, d. 14 May, 1820.
Barager, Henry, son of David & Mary Cortelyou, his wife, d. 13 July, 1820.
Beattey, ——, son of John Beattey, Sr., & Bettsy, his wife, m. n. Lake, about one month & not yet baptized, d. 17 Dec., 1820.
Mott, James, son of Stephen & Mary, his wife, m. n. Mitchel, d. 15 Aug., 1821; 9 y., 5 m., 21 d.
Dye, Charles, son of John Dye, near Quarantine, d. 10 Sept., 1821; about 18 y.
White, John, d. 19 Sept., 1821 of yellow fever; buried in Episcopal ground; about 60 y.

Housman, Peter, son of Benjamin Housman, d. 13 Oct., 1821; 7 y., 9 m., 21 d.
Housman, Edward Perine, son of Benjamin Housman, d. 15 Oct., 1821; 5 y., 11 m., 6 d.
Egbert, Elizabeth Ann, youngest dau. of Tunis Egbert & Isabella, his wife, m. n. Vanderbilt, d. 29 Oct., 1821; 11 m., 24 d.
White, John, child of Richd. & Rebecca White, m. n. Dye, d. 3 Nov., 1821; about 3 weeks old.
Stillwill, Frances, single, a communicant in Bros. church, d. 26 Nov., 1821; 83 y., 5 m., 15 d.
McLean, William, d. 1 Jan., 1822, at the Quarantine.
Colon, George, born in Montpelliard County in Germany, 16 April, 1743, d. 23 Feb., 1822; 70 y., 10 m., 7 d.
Egbert, Abraham, d. 2 March, 1822, at Blazing Star Ferry (stone, 56 y., 11 m., 2 d.).
Beattey, Isabella, infant dau. of Jacob Beattey & Eliza, his wife, m. n. Cortelyou, d. 12 March, 1822; not quite 2 m.
Martino, Stephen, md., d. 17 April, 1822 (stone, 61 y., 25 d.).
Egbert, Warren Alston, son of Stephen Egbert & wife, m. n. Alston, d. 30 April, 1822.
Steward, Thomas, md., d. 17 May, 1822.
Sutlif, David, child, son of Valentine Sutlif of N. Y., & Penina, his wife, d. 18 July, 1822, at house of Christian Smith.
Parkinson, Mary Jane, child of Leonard Parkinson, d. 2 Aug., 1822, buried at Richmond.
Stilwell, Abraham, d. 11 Aug., 1822; aged.
Tucker, Abraham, d. 18 Aug., 1822; aged.
Bogart, Hannah Maria, dau. of Simon Bogart, d. 6 Sept., 1822, of yellow fever, buried at Richmond.
Dennis, Mahala, wife of Thomas, m. n. Russel, d. 12 Sept., 1822.
McLean, ——, child of William McLean, d. 28 Oct., 1822.
Stilwell, Susanna, wife of Joseph, d. 16 Dec., 1822.
Crips, ——, son of Lawrence & Susan, his wife, d. 30 Jan., 1823.
Thompson, Louis, d. 5 Feb., 1823.
Crips, ——, a single man, son of Lawrence & Susan Crips, d. 11 March, 1823.
Egbert, Sally Ann, dau. of Charles & Christiana Egbert, d. 10 May, 1823; about 9 y.
Van Pelt, George, md., d. 12 May, 1823; fell overboard on way from N. York here.
Beattey, William, son of Cornelius & Nancy Beattey, d. 26 June, 1823; about 11 y.
Britton, Fanny, md., d. 27 June, 1823, of yellow fever.
Clark, ——, child of Capt. Clark from Quarantine, d. 20 July, 1823.
Keetch, Abigail, d. 6 Feb., 1824; 98 y.
Vanderbilt, ——, child of Oliver & Hetty Vanderbilt, d. 24 March, 1824; d. soon after birth.
Lozier, Catharine Eliza, infant, child of Jacob & Eliza Lozier, d. 5 April, 1824.
Martino, Benjamin, d. 23 May 1824 (stone, 17 May, 1824); aged 82 y.
Crips, Susan, wife of Lawrence, d. 17 June, 1824.

Martino, Stephen Vanranssalear, child of Abraham Martino & Ann, his wife, d. 5 Sept., 1824.
Stilwell, Abraham, d. 12 Sept, 1824 (stone, Sept. 12, 1824, aged 74 y., 6 m., 12 d.).
Baker, ——, child of John & Sophia Baker, d. 23 Sept., 1824.
Stilwell, ——, child of Daniel Stilwell & w., m. n. Scharrot, d. 28 Sept., 1824.
Dunham, Amos, d. 9 Oct., 1824.
Lake, Daniel, d. 16, Nov., 1824, at house of Jesse Bedell at Freshkill.
Swaim, Dorothy, d. 4 Dec., 1824 (stone, 28 Nov., 1824); aged 71 y.
Garretson, ——, child of John Garretson, Jr., d. 9 Jan., 1825.
Egbert, Samuel, d. 19, Jan., 1825.
Martin, Charles, ch. of Revd. Mr. Martin of Baptist Ch., d. 20 April, 1825; about 4 y.
Little, ——, Mr., d. 17 July, 1825.
Beatty, Edward, Senr., d. 17 July, 1825; 82 y.
Lake, Daniel, single, d. 19 July, 1825; near 30 y.
Dorsett, Martha, d. 21 July, 1825; 69 y.
Conner, George, son of Richd. Conner & Sarah, his wife, m. n. Egbert, d. 26 July, 1825.
Burger, Ann, d. 5 Aug., 1825; in 90 y.
Marsh, Sarah, d. 12 Aug., 1825 (stone, w. of Richard, d. 11 Aug., in 77 y); typhus fever.
Praul, William, d. 17 Aug., 1825; typhus fever.
Beatty, Eleanor, d. 24 Aug., 1825; typhus fever.
Marsh, Richard, d. 20 Aug., 1825 (stone, in 82 y.); typhus fever.
Dunn, ——, Mrs., mother of Judge Dunn of this Island, d. 3 Sept., 1825.
Egbert, Henry Edward, infant, ch. of Edward Egbert & Hannah, his wife, m. n. Prue, d. 25 Sept., 1825.
McClyman, Louisa, infant, dau. of William & Elizabeth McClyman, d. 26 Sept., 1825.
Praul, David, d. 3 Oct., 1825 (stone, 'Prall,' in 57 y.); typhus fever.
Egbert, ——, a child of Tunis J. Egbert, d. 11 Oct., 1825.
Silvy, ——, a child of Frances Silvy, d. 15 Oct., 1825.
Black, Sarah Eliza, child of John & Rachel, his wife, d. 22 Oct., 1825.
Egbert, Tunis, Sr., d. 5 Nov., 1825.
Coursen, Hannah, d. 8 Nov., 1825; about 15 y.
Scharrot, Mary Ann, ch. of Richard & Charity Scharrot, d. 24 Nov., 1825.
Degroat, Henry, child of Patty Simonson, d. 5 Dec., 1825.
Housman, Abraham, d. ——, 1825.
Bodine, ——, a child of Nathaniel Bodine & Maria, his w., m. n., Garretson, d. 10 March, 1826.
Decker, John Henry, son of John Decker & Ann, his wife, m. n. Egbert, d. 23 March, 1826; 2 y., 6 m., 2 d.
Scharrot, Richard, Jr., single, son of Richard Scharrot & Elizabeth, his wife, m. n. Winters, d. 31 March, 1826.
Egbert, Charles, son of James & Sarah, his wife, m. n. Dey, d. 28 April, 1826.

Johnson, Peter, child of Peter & Hetty Johnson, m. n. Noble, d. 31 May, 1826.
Praul, Alfred Cortelyou, ch. of David Praul, dec., & wife, Catharine, d. 2 June, 1826; about 15 m.
Decker, Elizabeth, dau. of John & Ann Decker, d. 14 June, 1826; about 5 m.
Dorsett, Amanda Elizabeth, dau. of John & Ellen Dorsett, d. 24 June, 1826.
Guyon, Daniel, Esq., d. 29 July, 1826 (stone, 57 y., 1 m., 19 d.).
Egbert, Gertrude M., ch. of Edward & Hannah Egbert, d. 12 Aug., 1826; 10 m., 3 w., 4 d.
Decker, John, d. 19 Aug., 1826; 35 or 36 y.
Egbert, Margrett, child of Tunis, blacksmith, & Peggy, his wife, d. Sept. 20, 1826.
Sharrot, Mary, wife of Richard Sharrot, d. 3 Oct., 1826, of yellow fever.
Egbert, James, Jr., young, md., d. 4 Oct., 1826; typhus fever.
Lewis, James, single, b. Dec. 6, 1801, d. Oct. 10, 1826; 24 y., 10 m., 4 d.
Fowler, Abigail, wife of —— Fowler of N. Y., d. 14 Oct., 1826.
Sharrot, ——, wife of James, Sr., d. Oct. 19, 1826, at the Quarantine.
Simonson, Sophia, single, d. 29 Oct., 1826; buried at Richmond.
Wood, Polly, single, d. 1 Nov., 1826; buried at Richmond; aged.
Crips, Rachel, d. 2 Nov., 1826; aged.
Mersereau, ——, a child of Stephen, Jr., from Quarantine; d. 3 Nov., 1826; buried at Richmond.
Hooper, ——, d. 4 Nov., 1826; buried at Richmond.
Jacobson, John V. D., d. 11 Nov., 1826 (stone, 58 y.).
Moore, Plinkel Fleeson Glentworth, son of Rev. David Moore of Episcopal ch. on this Island, d. 1 Dec., 1826.
Dorsee, Evo, d. 28 Dec., 1826, at N. York (stone, d. 27 Dec., 37 y.).
Stilwell, Joseph, single, d. 5 Jan., 1827; buried from his brother Abraham Stilwell's.
Dye, John, d. 7 Jan., 1827; aged.
Fardon, Dr. Isaac, d. 7 March, 1827; typhus.
Egbert, Cornelius, child of Cornelius & Cath., m. n. Lake, d. 10 April, 1827.
Egbert, James, son of Abm., dec., & Ann, his wife, m. n. Martino, d. 26 April, 1827.
Jennings, James Lambert, ch. of John Jennings & Catharine, his wife, m. n. Sharrot, d. 11 May, 1827.
Carver, Peter D., ch. of William Carver & Catharine, his w., m. n. Braisted, d. 21 July, 1827.
Bodine, Isaac Burbank, ch. of Vincent & Mary Ann Bodine, m. n. Burbank, d. 6 Aug., 1827.
Barnes, George, d. 11 Aug., 1827, typhus fever; middle aged.
Thompson, Susan, md., d. 3 Sept., 1827.
Randolph, a Mr. (stone, Fitz Randolph, Hartshorn), from N. York d. 14 Sept., 1827 (stone, 13 Sept., 1827); 28 y.
Barnes, Bathia, single, d. 20 Sept., 1827; aged; for many years insane.

Vanderbilt, Benjamin Simonson, child of Aaron & Mary Vanderbilt, m. n. Simonson, d. 18 Oct., 1827.
Egbert, James, Sr., d. 19 Oct., 1827; about 73 y.
Fitzgerald, Margret Eliza, child of Michael Fitzgerald, d. 22 Oct., 1827; buried in Swaim family gr. at Richmond.
Lake, Catharine, single, dau. of Joseph Lake, d. 28 Oct., 1827.
Dye, John, d. 27 Dec., 1827; about 62 y.
Burtus, Gitty Ann, m. n. Stilwell, d. 2 Jan., 1828; about 23 or 24 y.
Sharrot, William, single, son of James Sharrot, Sr., at Quarantine, d. 16 Jan., 1828.
Johnson, Richard Taylor, ch. of Richard & Susan Johnson, d. 31 Jan., 1828.
Lewis, Sarah Ann, ch. of James & Mary Lewis, d. 3 Feb., 1828.
Stilwell, Marietta, ch. of Abraham & Mary Stilwell, d. 24 March, 1828; about 4 m.
Stilwell, Joseph, d. 4 July, 1828; near 80 y.
Garretson, Eliza, dau. of Major John Garretson & Catharine, his wife, dec., d. 12 Sept., 1828.
Lemphy, ——, a German, d. 18 Sept., 1828, at John Guion's.
Little, Margaret Eliza, wife of Richard D. Little, Esq., & dau. of John Dunn, Esq., & Mary Garritson, his wife, d. 19 Sept., 1828 (stone, 27 y., 8 m., 5 d.).
Wood, Nancy, m. n. Bodine, wife of Stephen Wood & dau. of James Bodine, d. 20 Sept., 1828.
Little, Emilie Teresa, child of Richd. D. Little, Esq., & his wife Margt. Eliza Dunn, d. 22 Sept., 1828; 9 m., 14 d.
Bodine, Sophia, dau. of Nathaniel & Maria Bodine, d. 23 Sept., 1828; about 14 y.
Jacobson, Israel Van Devender, ch. of Bedell Jacobson & Sarah, Ann, his wife, d. 28 Sept., 1828.
Allen, ——, a Mrs., d. 30 Aug., 1828; from the house of Mr. Pardee.
Dittens, ——, a child, d. 24 Aug., 1828; no minister attending.
Vanderbilt, Jacob, son of John Vanderbitt, Sr., & Elisabeth, his wife, m. n. Taylor, d. 19 Oct., 1828; lockjaw; about 17 y. (stone, 19 y., 8 m.).
Beattey, Edward, child of Jacob & Eliza Beattey, fell from a tree, d. 1 Dec., 1828; 10 or 11 y.
Barton, Lucy, dau. of John Egbert, Sr., d. 15 Dec., 1828.
Yates, Joseph, d. 23 Dec., 1828; quite aged.
Perine, ——, a child of John Perine & Lucy Ann, his wife, m. n. Sharrot, d. 8 Oct., 1828; child not yet baptized.
Beatty, William Addison, ch. of John Beatty & Hannah, of N. York, d. 31 Dec., 1828.
Dorset, John William Beatty, John Dorset & wife, Ellen Cropsy, parents, d. 5 Jan., 1829.
Baker, Joseph, d. 11 Jan., 1829; his body was afterwards removed to Baptist Church.
Miller, ——, a child of Thomas Miller & gr.-ch. of Henry Miller, weaver, d. 24 Jan., 1829.
Sequine, ——, child of Seguime, the son-in-law of John Britton at Quarantine, d. 27 Feb., 1829.

Sharrot, ——, child of James Sharrot, Jr., near Quarantine, d. 28 March, 1829.
Shay, Henry, single, d. 26 May, 1829.
Wood, Abbey Ann, wife of James Wood, m. n. Simonson, dau. of Reuben & Jane Simonson, d. 2 Sept., 1829; 18 y., 7 m., 3 d.
Crocheron, John, md., d. 5 Sept., 1829.
Egbert, Betsy, wid. of Samuel, Jr., d. 29 Oct., 1829.
Stillwell, Peter, brother of Abraham of N. side from whose house he was buried, d. 1 Nov., 1829.
Deforest, Capt. John, d. 22 April, 1829 (stone, d. 21 April, 1829, in 49 y.).
Romer, Catharine, unbaptized, child of James Romer & wife, d. 26 Jan., 1830.
Sharrot, Richard, Sr., d. 15 April, 1830; 81 y.; buried from his son James Sharrott's at Quarantine.
Gilbert, Hannah Jane, child of James & Abbey Ann, d. 6 May, 1830.
Lemory, ——, a child of widow Lemory, d. 1 July, 1830.
Resszeau, Mrs. Polly, widow of Judge Resszeau, d. 19 July, 1830; buried on Swaim family ground.
Butler, Cornelius Egbert, child of Daniel & Eliza Butler, m. n. Egbert, d. 13 Aug., 1830.
Vanderbilt, Richard Taylor, son of John, Sr., & Elizabeth Vanderbilt, d. 12 Aug., 1830; near 15 y. (stone, 14 y., 9 m., 8 d.); cold produced symptoms of lock jaw.
Dorset, Ellen C., wife of John Dorset, m. n. Cropsy, d. 27 Aug., 1830.
Williams, William, of Long Island, d. 13 Sept., 1830; 26 y.; buried at Richmond.
Britton, John, child of James & Marietta Britton, d. 8 Sept., 1830.
Merrell, Lafayette, ch. of Jonathan Merrell & Maria, his wife, m. n. Egbert, d. 10 Oct., 1830; about 6 y.
Bodine, Nathaniel, md., d. 31 Oct., 1830.
Egbert, John, Sr., d. 31 Oct., 1830; near 80 y.
Stilwell, Daniel, single, d. 31 Oct., 1830; about 40 y.; buried from house of his Br. Abraham, North side.
Wood, ——, widow of Saml., d. 7 Sept., 1830, buried at Richmond; died of yellow fever at Quarantine.
Bodine, a child of Vincent & Mary Ann Bodine, d. 27 Jan., 1831; lived but one hour.
Burgher, Catharine, wife of Col. Nicholas Burgher, d. 25 Jan., 1831.
Bodine, Vincent, son-in-law of Isaac Burbank, d. 10 Feb., 1831.
Rooke, Martha, wife of Amos Rooke, d. 24 Feb., 1831.
Simonson, Barnt, d. 8 March, 1831; aged.
Fardon, Eliza, widow of Dr. Isaac Fardon, d. 17 April, 1831, at New York.
Barger, ——, child of Henry Barger, d. 13 May, 1831; born dead.
Dunn, John W., son of Judge Dunn, dec., d. 30 June, 1831, at N. Y. (stone, in 24 y.).
Garretson, Hermanus, son of Abraham & Eliza Garretson, m. n., Sanders, d. 31 July, 1831.

Swift, ——, child of Isaac & Eliza, d. 1 Aug., 1831; unbaptized.
Wandel, Mary Elizabeth, child of Mr. Danl. Wandel, d. 8 Aug., 1831.
Prall, Edward Beatty, child of Abraham & Isabella Prall, m. n. Beatty, d. 9 Aug., 1831.
Vanderbilt, Hetty Maria, wife of Oliver Vanderbilt, d. 1 Sept., 1831.
Hill, Elizabeth, wife of David, dec., of Long Island, d. 18 Sept., 1831; buried from house of Mr. Doty.
Bodine, Margrett, wife of James, Sr., d. 1 Oct., 1831.
Kruzer, Henry, d. 1 Nov., 1831; aged; buried in Baptist gr. in the Clove; formerly a neighbor but late of N. J.
Clawson, Anna Maria, child of Daniel & Maria Clawson, d. 7 Nov., 1831; about 4 y.
Egbert, Moses, d. 13 Nov., 1831; in 90 y.
Miller, Elisabeth, wife of Henry Miller, m. n. Barton, d. 15 Nov., 1831.
Beatty, ——, child of Jacob Beatty & Eliza, m. n. Cortelyou, d. 3 Dec., 1831; about 1 d., unbaptized.
Beatty, Eliza, wife of Jacob, m. n. Cortelyou, d. 8 Dec., 1831.
Baker, Letty Ann, ch. of Joseph Baker, dec., & his wife Susan, d. 13 Dec., 1831; in Baptist gr.-yd.
Simonson, Sarah, widow of late Barnt Simonson, d. 12 Feb., 1832; 68 y.
Oblinis, Albert, ch. of Henry & Eliza, his wife, m. n. Burgher, d. 18 Feb., 1832.
Dorset, John, Sr., d. 7 March, 1832; aged (stone, 7 March, 1832, 80 y., 1 m., 27 d.).
Spong, Francis Maybury, child of Robert Spong & Mary, his wife, m. n. Johnson, d. 14 March, 1832.
Egbert, Eugene Mortimer, son of John & Aletta Egbert of New York, d. 14 March, 1832; about 9 y.
Cortelyou, Mary Frances, ch. of Jacob & Mary Cortelyou, d. 11 April, 1832.
Egbert, Sally, d. 18 April, 1832, at Tunis J. Egbert's; aged widow.
Gilbert, James Thomas Steward, child of James & Abby Ann Gilbert, d. 14 May, 1832.
Vanderbilt, Cornelius (Commodore's father), d. 20 May, 1832; 67 y., 9 m.
Dunn, Capt. Robert, of N. York, d. 13 June, 1832; 74 y.
Seguine, Henry, d. 20 July, 1832, of Asiatic cholera.
Innis, Mrs. Martha, wife of George, of N. Y., d. 11 Aug., 1832, of cholera at Capt. John Blake's on N. side (stone, 52 y., 11 m.).
Stilwell, Elizabeth, child, parents Daniel Stilwell & wife, Eliza, m. n. Crips, of Long Island, d. 11 Aug., 1832.
Butler, Sarah Elizabeth, child of Vincent Bulter & Martha Ann, his wife, m. n. Swaim, d. 14 Aug., 1832.
Simonson, Nathan Runnels, a child of Isaac Simonson, d. 20 Aug., 1832.
Cortelyou, ——, child, parents Lawrence & Eliza Cortelyou of N. Y., d. 2 Sept., 1832; not one hour old.

Christopher, Maria, wife of Joseph Christopher, d. 6 Sept., 1832.
Christopher, John Milton, her babe, in same grave, d. 6 Sept., 1832; both died of cholera.
Christopher, Joseph, the husband, d. 8 Sept., 1832; cholera.
Martino, Ellenor, the mother of Maria Christopher, d. 15 Sept., 1832; cholera.
Beatty, Jacob, widower, son of Edward Beatty, dec., d. 25 Sept., 1832, of cholera (stone, 25 Sept., 1832, 47 y.).
Haughabout, Peter Nicholas, child, d. 16 Oct., 1832; parents, James Haughabout & Clarisse, his wife, m. n. Johnson.
Smith, Mary Elizabeth, dau. of James & Mary Smith, d. 18 Oct., 1832, at Mr. Osborne's at Long Neck; about 8 m. old.
Littell, Ann Maria, m. n. Dunn, wife of Richd. D. Littell, d. 24 Dec., 1832; 34 y., 5 m.; (stone, dau. of John Dunn, Esq., & his w., Mary Garritson.)
Van Duser, Louisa, infant dau. of Daniel Van Duser & Ellen, his wife, m. n. Vanderbilt, d. 7 Jan., 1833; 7 m., 7 d.
Colored people whose names are not clear.
Johnson, Tunis Van Pelt, child of Richard Johnson & Susan, his wife, m. n. Van Pelt, d. 25 Feb., 1833.
Burgher, Alfred, a twin, a child of Matthias & Hannah Burgher, d. 13 March, 1833.
Jacobson, Helletha, widow of John V. D. Jacobson, d. 5 April, 1833.
Van Duser, Ellen, m. n. Vanderbilt, wife of Daniel C. Van Duser & dau. of Cornelius Vanderbilt, dec., d. 21 April, 1833.
Egbert, Ann, widow of Abraham Egbert, dec., d. 25 April, 1833.
Thompson, John E., d. 28 April, 1833, at Tompkinsville.
Siebern, Thomas, colored, d. 29 May, 1833.
Barger, Jacob, of N. Y., md., d. 12 Aug., 1833.
Mott, Stephen, son of Mrs. Mott or (Shay) at Quarantine, d. 30 Aug., 1833; said to have died of yellow fever.
Egbert, Isabella, wife of Tunis, m. n. Vanderbilt, daughter of John & Elizabeth Vanderbilt, d. 28 Sept. 1833.
Cortelyou, Josephine, child of Lawrence & Eliza Cortelyou of New York, d. 22 Nov., 1833.
Miller, Henry, d. 29 Nov., 1833; aged; a resident of this Island but formerly of Ireland, d. in N. Y.
Crocheron, Ann, wife of Nicholas Crocheron, m. n. Guyon, dau. of Daniel Guyon, dec., d. 28 Dec., 1833.
Miller, Mary Ann, grand-child of Br. Henry Miller, d. 5 July, 1833, at N. Y.
Vanderbilt, Eliza, wife of Cornelius, Jr., son of John, d. 29 Jan., 1834.
Lozier, Edward, single, d. 6 Feb., 1834.
Carver, ——, a child from N. Y., d. 6 Feb., 1834.
Beatty, Elizabeth, wife of John Beatty, Sr., d. 8 March, 1834.
Burbank, Mary Adeline, child of John & Gertrude Burbank, d. 22 March. 1834.
Butler, Catharine, dau. of James & Charity Butler, d. 24 March, 1834.

Bininger, Abraham, d. 11 April, 1834; an aged member of the Brs. Ch. in N. Y.
Little, ——, Mrs., mother of Derric Littell, d. 15 April, 1834.
Oblenis, Henry, md., d. 24 April, 1834.
Britton, James, child of James & Mariette Britton, d. 11 May, 1834; about 15 m.
Cortelyou, Emma, wife of Peter, d. 22 May, 1834; 63 y., 4 m., 6 d.
Beatty, Eleanor Louisa, child of Edward and Ann Beatty, d. 2 June, 1834.
Egbert, ——, a child of Stephen & Hannah, his wife, d. 7 June, 1834.
McSwaim, John, d. 1 July, 1834; in 67 year.
Egbert, Hannah, wife of Stephen, of N. Y., d. 2 July, 1834.
Spries, ——, a child of John, a German, at Quarantine, d. 5 July, 1834.
Seaman, ——, a child of Capt. Benson Seaman, d. 9 July, 1834.
Johnson, ——, a child of Peter, d. 26 July, 1834.
Jacobson, ——, a child of Bedell Jacobson, d. 2 Aug., 1834; unbaptized.
A German at Quarantine, d. 22 Aug., 1834; cholera.
Britton, Abraham, child of James & Marietta Britton, d. 5 Oct., 1834; 5 y., 5 m., 7 d.
Innis, John, son of Mr. George Innis of N. Y., d. 13 Oct., 1834.
Haughawout, Dorcas, wife of Nicholas, d. 18 Oct., 1834; buried in D. Ch. gr. on North side.
Burgher, ——, a child of James, d. 20 Oct., 1834.
Haughwout, James, son of Nicholas Haughwout, d. 8 Nov., 1834.
Beam, Eleanor, md., grand-daughter of Mrs. Eleanor Martino, d. 19 Nov., 1834, at N. Y.
Martino, Raymond, child of Abraham, d. 2 Dec., 1834.
Haughwout, Isaac Minton, son of Winant & Sarah Haughwout, d. 16 Dec., 1834.
McLean, Ann, wife of Cornelius, dec., d. 27 Dec., 1834; 79 y.
Britton, Mary, child of James & Mariette Britton, d. 20 Jan., 1835; 3 y., 6 m., 22 d.
Britton, John, child of Abm. & Catharine Britton, d. 5 Feb., 1835; 2 y., 11 m., 5 d.
Beatty, Cornelius, late of N. Y., son of Edward, dec., & Eleanor, dec., Beatty, both of this Island, d. 19 Feb., 1835.
Perine, William Oscar, a child of John & Lucy Perine of N. Y., d. 20 Feb., 1835.
Connor, Sarah, wife of Richard, Jr., d. 5 March, 1835.
Haughawout, Rachel Ann, child of Winant & Sarah Haughawout, d. 8 March, 1835; 4 y., 9 m., 5 d.
Moore, ——, a child of David & Mary Moore, d. 6 May, 1835; about 3 m.
Swaim, John, d. 31 July, 1835; 66 y.
Beatty, John, son of William & Polly Beatty of N. Y., d. 2 Aug., 1835.
Egbert, Henry, single, son of Mr. John Egbert, dec., d. about 19 Sept., 1835; he resided at Amboy, N. J.
Lake, Daniel, d. 6 Oct., 1835.

Simonson, Sarah Ann, dau. of Barnt & Sarah Simonson, dec., d. 13 Oct., 1835; she was member of Bap. Ch. in N. Y.
Mass, ——, a child of Francis & Lydia Mass., d. 14 Oct., 1835.
Burr, Barzillai, son-in-law of Br. John Beatty, d. 12 Nov., 1835; formerly of N. J., lately of N. Y.
Crips, Polly, wife of Lawrence, d. 19 Nov., 1835.
Lozier, ——, a child of Jacob & Eliza Lozier, d. 29 Nov., 1835.
Lozier, Mary Ann, child of above, d. 4 Dec., 1835.
Butler, Vincent, md., d. 30 March, 1835; about 32 y.
Beatty, Annethie Vooris, child of Edward & Ann Beatty, d. 2 Jan., 1836.
Halle, Lafayette Mathias, son of Abm. Herman Halle, d. 28 Jan., 1836.
Bodine, Rosanna, wife of William, d. 6 Feb., 1836.
Bodine, ——, a child of William, d. 8 Feb., 1836; buried with the mother.
Stilwell, Thomas, and aged man, d. 26 Feb., 1836; froze to death.
Mersereau, ——, a child of Joshua & Maria Mersereau, d. 7 March, 1836; 15 m., unbaptized.
Egbert, Eliza, wife of Joseph, d. 17 March, 1836.
Vanderbilt, Catharine, child of Capt. Oliver Vanderbilt, d. 20 April, 1836.
Vanderbilt, Oliver, child of Capt. Oliver Vanderbilt, d. 14 May, 1836; 15 m.
Butler, Charity, wife of James, d. 3 June, 1836 (stone, 46 y.).
Jacobson, ——, a child of Cornelius Jacobson of N. Y., d. 3 Aug., 1836.
Burgher, ——, a child of John, d. 8 Aug., 1836.
Squire, Mary Louisa, child of John Squire, d. 21 Aug., 1836; 3 m.
Dissosway, Israel Fitz Randolph, child of Israel & Lucretia Dissosway, d. 2 Sept., 1836; buried in Jacobson ground.
Egbert, ——, a child of Cornelius & Catharine, d. 30 Sept., 1836; about 12 w. old.
Perry, ——, Mrs., d. 15 Oct., 1836; a French or Swiss woman.
Broadhead, —— a child of Mr., d. 18 Oct., 1836.
Vanderbilt, George Washington, son of Capt. Cornelius Vanderbilt of N. Y., d. 16 Nov., 1836; about 4 y. old.
Frost, Caroline, dau. of Samuel, of N. Y., d. 30 Nov., 1836.
Steward, ——, a child of Abraham Steward of N. Y., d. 3 Dec., 1836; about 2 y.
McClennent, William, d. 12 Dec. 1836.
Lewis, Margaret, single, d. 9 Feb., 1837; aged.
Barger, Matilda, wife of Henry, dau. of Samuel Frost of N. Y., bur. 15 March, 1837.
Mozier, ——, a child of Mr., d. 29 March, 1837; residing in the Manor.
Barger, ——, infant child of Henry Barger & his wife, Matilda, dec., m. n. Frost, d. 2 April, 1837.
Jacobson, Elizabeth, wife of Cornelius, of N. Y., m. n. Housman, d. 2 April, 1837.
Swaim, Mott, d. 3 May, 1837.
Harvey, Sophia D., wife of R. Harvey of Brooklyn, m. n. Drinkwater, d. 15 May, 1837.

Connor, James Egbert, son of Richard Connor & Sarah, his wife, dec., d. 4 June, 1837.
Vance, James Wadsworth, son of Oliver and Sarah Vance, d. 12 July, 1837.
Lozier, Jacob, d. 29 July, 1837.
Van Duzer, Daniel Theodore, son of John & Sarah Van Duzer, d. 9 Sept., 1837.
Cropsy, Harmon, son of Harmon, d. 17 Oct., 1837.
De Forrest, John J., d. 1 Nov., 1837.
Innes, Jane, b. 25 Dec., 1837.
Martling, Garret, child of Stephen & Mary Ann, b. in Aug., 1837, d. 1 Jan., 1838.
Beatty, Louisa, dau. of Edward & Ann Beatty, d. 12 Jan., 1838.
Morgan, ——, Mrs., widow, d. 9 March, 1838.
Vanderbilt, Isabella, d. 6 April, 1838.
Innes, Mary, d. 7 April, 1838.
Bryant, Jane, d. 10 April, 1838.
Bodine, James, d. 13 May, 1838.
Martling, Mary Ann, wife of Stephen, d. 3 July, 1838.
McClennent, ——, an illegitimate ch. of Mrs. McClennent's, d. 15 June, 1838.
Burckhard, ch. of Jacob & Theresa Burckhardt, d. 15 Aug., 1838.
Morris, Elizabeth, d. 22 Sept., 1838.
Mercereau, Lucretia, dau. of Joshua & Maria Mercereau, d. 19 Sept., 1838.
Allen, Jacob Hand, d. 27 Oct., 1838.
Mercereau, Maria, d. 8 Nov., 1838.
Egbert, John d. 17 Jan., 1839 (stone, son of Joseph & Jane Egbert, 23 Jan, 1839, 35 y., 5m., 23 d.).
Peckman, ——, a child of Mr. H., d. 31 Jan., 1839.
Burbank, Isaac, son of Edward & Jane Burbank, d. 2 Feb., 1839.
Housman, Benjamin, d. 26 Feb., 1839.
Baker, ——, ch. of John & Eliza Baker, d. 17 March, 1839.
Butler, Isaac, son of James & Charity, his wife, d. 18 April, 1839 (stone, in 25 y.).
Perine, James, d. 22 April, 1839.
Burgher, ——, Col., at Quarantine, bur. 25 May, 1839.
Burgher, James L., of N. Y., d. 31 July, 1839.
Garretson, Col. John, old town, d. 13 Aug., 1839.
Burgher, Emeline, dau. of John, d. 20 Oct., 1839.
Sharrot, James, at Quarantine, d. 24 Dec., 1839.
De Forest, Gerardus, Tompkinsville, d. 29 Jan., 1840 (stone, 29 y., 5 d.).
Innes, Miss Martha, of N. Y., d. 18 March, 1840.
Brittain, Mary Etta, dau. of James Britton, of N. Y., d. 29 March, 1840.
Vanderbilt, Frederick Putnam, son of Jacob Vanderbilt of N. Y., d. 6 April, 1840 (stone, 9 w.).
Perine, ——, infant child of John & Lucy Ann Perine of N. Y., d. 18 Aug., 1840.
Burgher, Lydia, d. 1 Dec., 1840; bur. in Col. Burgher's family plot.

Burbank, Gertrude, d. 2 Dec., 1840.
Simonson, Cornelius, of N. Y., d. 11 Dec., 1840 (stone, 35 y., 2 m., 8 d., also Mary Osborn, his wife, b. 29 June, 1815, d. 8 Oct., 1883).
Whitsworth, ——, an infant ch. of John Whitsworth, Jr., bur. 16 Dec., 1840.
Egbert, Hannah, d. 24 Dec., 1840.
Whitworth, John, d. 27 Dec., 1840.
Simonson, John King, an infant son of Cornelius Simonson & Mary, d. 21 Jan., 1841 (stone, d. 13 Jan., 1 y., 9 m.).
Smith, John W., an Englishman, a native of London, d. 23 Jan., 1841 (stone, 57 y., 11 m., 23 d.).
Stilwell, Abraham, d. 9 Feb., 1841.
Steward, Sarah Elisab., infant dau. of Anthony & Mary Steward, d. 8 March, 1841.
Gildersleave, ——, d. 2 April, 1841.
Sharrott, William, d. 2 April, 1841.
Egbert, ——, Mrs., wife of Tunis, of N. Y., m. n. Barton, d. 7 May, 1841.
Dustan, ——, Major, d. 23 May, 1841 (stone, 81 y., 8 m., 8 d.).
Dugan, Mary, of N. Y., bur. 1 June, 1841.
Scharrott, Thomas, d. 5 June, 1841.
Britton, ——, infant of James & Mary Etta (or Ella) Britton, d. 6 June, 1841.
Scharrott, Mrs. Martha, wife of Thomas, dec., d. 20 June, 1841.
Vanderbilt, Cornelius, son of John, d. 22 June, 1841.
Hughes, James Cubberly, an infant child of Barry Hughes, d. 28 June, 1841.
White, ——, wife of Richard, d. 3 July, 1841.
Marlin, ——, wife of Benjamin, d. 20 Aug., 1841.
Perine, Lucy Ann, wife of John Perine, d. 20 Aug., 1841.
Thorn, Emily Augusta, infant, d. 25 Aug., 1841.
Housman, ——, a child of Richard, bur. 30 Sept., 1841.
Cripps, James, Senr., bur. 11 Oct., 1841.
Simonson, Emeline, d. 14 Oct., 1841.
Perine, Peter, of N. Y., d. — Sept., 1841.
Van Pelt, ——, infant of Br. Van Pelt of N. Y., d. — Oct., 1841.
Egbert, Jane, wife of Joseph, d. 27 Oct., 1841.
Gibson, Mr. A. C., of N. Y., d. 31 Oct., 1841 (stone, native of Scotland, 36 y.).
Winant, Mark, d. 20 Nov., 1841.
Vanderbilt, Mary, d. 27 Dec., 1841.
Fitz Randolph, an infant dau., d. 8 Feb., 1842.
Dunn, Edward, of N. Y., d. 7 Feb., 1842.
Waller, Jocelyn, of N. Y., d. 5 April, 1842; bur. in Col. Burgher's plot.
Sylva, Cornelius, d. 10 April, 1842.
Beatty, Ellenor Louise, infant dau. of E. Beatty, Jersey City, d. 20 April, 1842.
Dustan, William Saml., d. — May, 1842 (stone, 23 or 28 April, 40 y., 4 m., 25 d.).
Romer, Mary, d. 30 July, 1842.

Lake, Joseph, d. 18 Aug., 1842 (stone, 18 Aug., 1842, 38 y.).
Winant, Charles H., an infant, bur. 20 Aug., 1842.
Krapf, Conrad, d. 31 Aug., 1842.
Burgher, Robert, infant, from N. Y., bur. 5 Sept., 1842.
Dustan, Harriet Jean, d. 14 Sept., 1842.
Cortelyou, ——, infant ch. of Jacob, bur. 10 Sept., 1842.
Rook, Amos, Sen., d. 30 Sept., 1842; 89 y., 6 m., 13 d.
Egbert, Cornelius, bur. 13 Oct., 1842.
Lake, Catharine, Arthur's wife, bur. 15 Oct., 1842.
Fountain, ——, illegitimate child of Mary, bur. 16 Oct., 1842.
Egbert, John, of N. Y., bur. 26 Oct., 1842.
Cropsy, Nicholas, of N. Y., bur. 9 Nov., 1842.
Butler, James, d. 24 Dec., 1842; in 58 y.
Connor, Sophia, d. 14 Jan., 1843.
Cripps, ——, child of James, at Quarantine, d. 16 Jan., 1843.
Clark, ——, from Quarantine, d. — Feb., 1843.
Egbert, John, d. 17 March, 1843.
Martino, Angelina, bur. 6 April, 1843 (stone, dau. Abraham & Ann, d. 4 April, 1843, age 20 y., 6 m.).
Wood, ——, infant, James & Emily Wood, d. 7 April, 1843.
Bodine, Sarah Ann, infant of Abm., d. 19 May, 1843.
Swaim, Martha, d. 28 May, 1843.
Egbert, Alfred, of N. Y., d. 17 June, 1843.
Cortelyou, ——, infant ch. of Lockman Cortelyou, bur. 30 June, 1843.
Lake, Mary Gifford, infant, d. 26 July, 1843.
Britton, ——, child of James, of N. Y., pilot, bur. 29 July, 1843.
Lake, Adriana B., infant, d. 19 Sept., 1843.
Egbert, J. Holmes, d. 21 Sept., 1843.
Siersema, Unitas, infant, bur. 30 Sept., 1843.
Lawrence, Mary, of N. Y., bur. 8 Nov., 1843.
Merry, Harriet, of N. Y., d. 4 Jan., 1844.
Fountain, ——, Mrs., bur. 7 Feb., 1844.
Dunn, D. V., bur. 27 Feb., 1844 (stone, Dorothy Vanderbilt Dunn, d. 24 Feb., 38 y., 4 m., 1 d.).
Littell, ——, infant of Judge, bur. 29 Feb., 1844.
Broadhead, ——, Mrs., bur. 21 March, 1844.
Lewis, Mrs. Ann, bur. 22 March, 1844.
Spragg, ——, child of J., bur. 3 April, 1844.
Downes, ——, Mrs., bur. 11 April, 1844.
Turner, ——, a child, bur. 1 May, 1844.
Baker, ——, ch. of John Baker, bur. 14 May, 1844.
Connor, ——, infant son of R., bur. 24 May, 1844.
Lake, Mrs. Violetta B., d. 30 May, 1844.
Vanderbilt, Jacob Ellis, d. 2 June, 1844 (stone, 2 y., 10 m., 6 d.).
Schaber, Margaret, bur. 16 June, 1844.
Jackle, J. L., d. 19 Aug., 1844.
Sharrott, Thos. Jeff., bur. 22 Aug., 1844.
McLean, Mrs. Charles & infant, bur. 5 Sept., 1844.
Swaim, ——, inft. of Math., bur. 10 Sept., 1844.
Simonson, Reuben, d. 19 Sept., 1844.
Van Pelt, inf. dau. of Abrm. of N. Y., bur. 2 Oct., 1844.

McClynnon, ——, child of Joseph, bur. 1 Nov., 1844.
Cripps, Anthony, bur. 3 Nov. 1844.
Kettletas, Peter, d. 13 Jan., 1845 (stone, d. 12 Jan., 33 y., 11 m., his wife, Mary, b. 5 April, 1812, d. 25 Sept., 1887).
Garretson, Sr. Eliza, d. Jan. 30, bur. Feb. 1, 1845.
Miller, Isaac, of Jersey City, d. 2 April, 1845.
Morris, Elizabeth, a child, bur. April, 16, 1845.
Prince, Mary, bur. April 17, 1845, in Robt. Prince's ground.
Egbert, ——, inft. son of Holmes, bur. 26 April, 1845.
Burger, Joseph, of Texas, bur. 2 May, 1845.
Fountain, Abraham, of N. Y., bur. 22 May, 1845.
Siersema, Phoebe Ann, d. 26 May, 1845.
Hughes, George W., child, bur. 9 June, 1845, in same grave with Hughes' former ch.
Guebet, *alias* Gilbert, ——, a Frenchman, bur. 13 June, 1845.
Lewis, James, d. 15 June, 1845.
Mott, ——, Mrs.
Decker, ——, ch. of David.
Burger, Jacob, bur. 3 July, 1845.
Corson, Alfred, infant, bur. 17 July, 1845.
Braisted, Garret, bur. 22 July, 1845.
Cross, James, inft., bur. 26 July, 1845; in Vanderbilt ground.
Earle, James, bur. 29 July, 1845.
Simonson, Mrs. Mary, bur. 11 Aug., 1845 (stone, wife Charles M., in 57 y.).
Innis, George, of N. Y., bur. 12 Aug., 1845.
Kissam, M. A., of N. Y. (stone, Thomas M'Auley, d. 27 Aug., 1845, b. 28 Aug., 1823, son Rev. Samuel Kissam).
Rives, ——, Mrs., N. Y.
Saunders, ——, Mrs., d. 18 Sept., 1845.
Alston, Mrs. Sarah Ann, d. 19 Sept., 1845.
Stewart, Samuel, an inft., bur. Sept. 26, 1845.
McSwaim, Sarah, d. 27 Oct., 1845.
Squires, Martha, bur. 31 Oct., 1845.
Burger, ——, child of Step., bur. 23 Nov., 1845.
Mills, ——, child of John, bur. 11 Jan., 1846.
Swaim, Mathias, bur. 13 Jan., 1846.
Kinsey, Charles Cortland, bur. 20 Jan., 1846.
Egbert, Thos. Holmes, d. 21 Feb., bur. 23 Feb., 1846.
Burger, John, Jr., d. 22 Feb., 1846.
Britten, G. W. O., inft., d. 30 March, 1846.
Puillon, James, Jr., d. 27 March, 1846.
Fountain, ——, ch. of Abm., of N. Y., bur. 5 April, 1846.
Allen, ——, child of Mr., of N. Y., bur. 14 April, 1846, in Vanderbilt yard.
Beatty, Wm., Senr., of N. Y., bur. 6 June, 1846.
Anderson, ——, an inft., bur. 29 June, 1846.
Scott, Mary Caroline, bur. 13 July, 1846.
Kettletas, Stephen, d. 2 Aug., 1846 (stone, 81 y., 29 d.; Ann, wife Stephen Kettletas, b. 7 Aug., 1788, d. 28 Feb., 1864; his 1st wife d. 1813).

Littell, Eveline P., inft. dau. of Judge Richd. & Rebecca Littell, bur. 30 July, 1846; 10 w., 15 d.
Tonpet, Henrietta V., of N. Y., bur. 5 Aug., 1846.
Ebbet, ——, inft. of D. Ebbet, bur. 6 Aug., 1846.
Johnson, ——, inft. of D., bur. 15 Aug., 1846.
Stacy, ——, inft. of Mr., bur. 29 Sept., 1846.
Crips, Charles, bur. 24 Oct., 1846.
Dustan, Capt. Isaac of steamer Atlantic, bur. -9 Nov., 1846, in Simonson's ground.
Lozier, John, d. 16 Dec., 1846.
Sanders, Peter, d. 11 Jan., 1847.
Martino, ——, Miss, bur. — Feb., 1847 (stone, 10 Feb., 1847, Elizabeth, dau. Abraham & Nancy, 17 y., 8 m.).
Child of a foreigner, bur. 12 March, 1847.
Moore, Mary, bur. 21 March, 1847.
Bradly, Mrs. Ellen V., bur. 22 March, 1847.
Beatty, ——, inft. dau. of Edward, of N. Y., bur. 26 March, 1847.
Prine, Joseph (Sharrot's brother), bur. — April, 1847.
Reed, Susan P., of N. Y., bur. 22 April, 1847.
Corson, Leonard, of S. I., bur. 23 April, 1847.
Lake, ——, Mrs., widow, bur. 24 April, 1847.
Lozier, Jacob, d. 5 June, 1847.
Miller, George, of N. Y., bur. 23 June, 1847.
Kinsey, James P., of N. Y., d. 26 June, 1847.
Garretson, Jacob, Senr., of Clifton, bur. 15 July, 1847.
Vroom, Georgiana, bur. July 27, 1847.
Egbert, ——, inft. of Jac.
Sharrot, John, Blacksmith, d. 11 Aug., 1847 (stone, 63 y., 5 m., 12 d.).
Reed, ——, inft. of Susan P., dec., bur., 14 Aug., 1847.
Vanderbilt, Capt. John, d. 13 Aug., 1847 (stone, 55 y., 1 m., 11 d.).
Metcalf, ——, a child of Richard, bur. 10 Sept., 1847.
Turner, Jeremiah, bur. 19 Oct., 1847.
Merril, Maria, of N. Y., bur. 4 Dec., 1847.
Simonson, Josephine Vanderbilt, child of Ch. & Sarah A. (stone, d. 4 Dec., 1847); 2 y., 24 d.
Egbert, ——, child of T., a daughter, bur. ——, 1848.
Cripps, ——, wife of J.
Littell, Henrietta, inft. of Judge, dau. of Richd. & Rebecca, d. 12 Jan., 1848.
Tompson, ——, "old Mr."
Townsend, ——, ch. of Mr., of N. Y., bur. 4 Feb., 1848.
McSwain, Vincent, bur. 12 Feb., 1848.
Dening, Raymond P., d. 24 March, 1848.
Martin, ——, inft. dau. of Ol. R. & S., d. 15 April, 1848.
Beatty, Henry, inft., N. Y., d. 17 June, 1848.
Binninger, Catharine E., d. July 11, 1848.
Tiboux, ——, Mrs. (Phila.), d. 21 July, 1848.
Cross, John, d. 21 July, 1848.
Tyson, Elizabeth, late Cortelyou, d. 2 Aug., 1848.
Lake, —— (John), bur. Aug. 6 to 11, 3 children in one grave.
Borth, Johan, d. 16 Aug., 1848.
Rathyen, Anna, infant, d. 24 Aug., 1848.

Vanduzer, Sarah Elizabeth, d. 25 Aug., 1848.
Cortelyou, George Adolph, d. 26 Aug., 1848.
De Forrest, Julia, bur. 8 Sept., 1848 (stone, Julia Selina, b. 25 May, 1825, d. 8 Sept., 1848).
Housman, Richard, bur. 8 Sept., 1848.
Garretson, Catharine, wid. of Jacob, bur. 20 Sept., 1848.
Toupet, ——, inft. of Mr., bur. 22 Sept., 1848.
Townsend, ——, inft. of Mr. of N. Y., bur. 26 Sept., 1848.
Lake, Joseph, Jr. (John's), bur. 28 Sept., 1848.
Madden, John (Irish Catholic).
Racy, ——, child of Charle's, bur. 30 Sept., 1848.
Winant, ——, child of Wm., bur. 2 Oct., 1848.
Seguine, Rachel, bur. 3 Oct., 1848; 94 y.
Cummings, ——, Mrs. of N. Y., bur. 8 Oct., 1848.
Gasquoine, ——, child of H., of Clifton, bur. 9 Oct., 1848.
Lenting, John, bur. 6 Nov., 1848.
Garretson, Cornelius (Jacob's), bur. 17 Nov., 1848.
Smith, Frances, of N. Y., bur. 29 Nov., 1848.
Simonson, Chas. V., a child, N. Y., bur. 4 Dec., 1848 (stone, d. 3 Dec.; 13 y., 4 m., 24 d.).
Hibbits, Oscar, a child, N. Y., bur. — Dec., 1848.
Romer, Ann, bur. 16 Jan., 1849.
Randal, ——, ch. of John, bur. 18 Jan., 1849.
Jacobs, Wm. W., bur. 28 Jan., 1849; 47 y., 2 m.
Jemison, Sarah E., of N. Y., bur. 3 Feb., 1849; 4 y., 11 m.
Swift, Margaret, bur. 30 March, 1849.
Mills, Eliza Ann, m. n., Egbert, d. 9 April, 1849.
Cargill, Abraham, N. Y., bur. — June, 1849.
Van Pelt, George, bur. 24 June, 1849.
Stockdale, Charity, N. Y., bur. 26 June, 1849.
Boyd, ——, aged Irishman, bur. 9 July, 1849.
Boyd, Rebecca (Irish), bur. 18 July, 1849.
Quinty, Anthony, bur. 22 July, 1849.
Sharrot, Mary (Quarantine), bur. 14 July, 1849.
Stilwell, Harriet (Thom.'s), bur. 28 July, 1849.
Sharrot, ——, child of Wm., bur. 31 July, 1849.
Clauder, Charlotte Jane, a twin, daughter of Rev. H. G. Clauder, Pastor of ch., d. 3 Aug., 1849; 8 y., 5 m., 13 d.
Mosier, Charles, d. 10 Aug., 1849; 4 y.
Mosier, ——, Mrs., bur. 14 Aug., 1849.
Metcalf, ——, a child, bur. 19 Aug., 1849; 3d y.
Jacobs, Augusta, N. Y., bur. 28 Aug., 1849; 4½ m.
Stephenson, ——, a child of Mr., d. 5 Sept., 1849; 1 y.
Fountain, William, d. 31 Aug., 1849.
Summers, ——, a child of Robert, d. 29 Aug., 1849; 1 w.
Egbert, Abraham T., d. 13 Sept., 1849; 34 y.
Steers, John, Jr. (Charle's), d. 19 Sept., 1849; 17 y.
Steers, Thomas, d. 21 Sept., 1849.
Fountain, Catharine, bur. 24 Sept., 1849; 44 y.
Van Duzer, John, d. 4 Oct., 1849; 49 y.
Drake, Evelina A., bur. 11 Oct., 1849, in Mrs. C. Heath's ground; 24 y., 10 m.

Randolph, ——, child of John, bur. 23 Oct., 1849; 7 y.
Allen, Peter W., N. Y., bur. 27 Oct., 1849; 45 y.
Wandell, Peter S., d. 28 Oct., 1849; 48 y. (stone, b. 7 May, 1800, d. 28 Oct., 1849; also Elisa, wife Peter S. Wandell, b. 23 April, 1803, d. 14 Oct., 1893).
Egbert, ——, inft. son of Edwd., bur. 11 Nov., 1849; 1 y.
Bodine, Jacob H., bur. 6 Dec., 1849; 5 y., 8 m.
Bedel, Mrs. Jesse, d. 15 Jan., 1850; 70 y.
Smith, Sarah Ann, N. Y., bur. 25 Jan., 1850; 42 y. (stone, d. 20 Jan., 1850, b. 16 Aug., 1808); has mother & is next to Jeremiah Smith.
Simonson, Catharine, bur. 20 Feb., 1850; 61 y.
Kinsey, ——, Mrs. of N. Y., bur. 9 March, 1850.
Beatty, ——, child of Vanras, bur. 19 March, 1850.
Beatty, Mrs. Mary, bur. 20 March, 1850; 63 y.
Burbank, Isaac, d. 21 March, 1850; 68 y., 9 m., 8 d.
Latimer, John, Clifton, d. 3 April, 1850.
Bodine, Vincent, bur. 10 April, 1850, in Burbank ground ; 21 y., 1 m.
Hand, Patrick, bur. 3 May, 1850.
Winant, ——, gr.-ch. of Danl., bur. 12 May, 1850.
Rogers, ——, inft. of O. M., bur. 22 May, 1850.
Egbert, Richard, bur. 24 April, 1850; 85 y.
Britton, ——, infant son of D., bur. 29 May, 1850.
Burger, Mathias, d. 10 June, 1850; 24 y., 2 m.
Parker, Ann M., N. Y., bur. 18 June, 1850; 6 y., 6 m.
Copes, Francis, bur. 25 June, 1850; 2 y., 6 m.
Burns, ——, bur. 1 July, 1850; 31 y.
Merry, Julia, N. Y., bur. 2 July, 1850; 14 m.
Tucker, George, bur. 30 July, 1850.
Steers, William, infant, bur. 20 Sept., 1850; 11 m.
Cortelyou, Mary (Jacob), d. 28 Sept., 1850; 40 y.
Van Pelt, John, d. 17 Oct., 1850; 49 y., 11 m.
Smith, Sarah, of N. Y., d. 27 Nov., 1850; 62 y.
Baker, ——, infant of John L., bur. 30 Nov., 1850; 14 m.
Lange, Sophie, d. 2 Jan., 1851.
Pachtman, Charles, N. Y., d. 11 Jan., 1851; 30 y.
Swift, Isaac B., d. 10 Jan., 1851; 46 y.
Cripps, James, bur. 12 Feb., 1851; 21 y., 6 m.
Conner, Jane, bur. 27 Feb., 1851; 30 y.
Vanderbilt, John, Sr., bur. 27 March, 1851; 81 y., 5 m. (stone, 81 y., 7 m., 27 d.).
Neats, William, Sr., bur. 13 April, 1851; 50 y.
Torrence, Elliot, bur. 18 April, 1851; 14 m.
Van Allen, ——, Mrs., bur. 3 May, 1851.
Summers, John, Sr., bur. 12 May, 1851; 65 y.
Egbert, Abraham, Senr., bur. 19 June, 1851; 60 y.
Burger, John, Sr., bur. 20 June, 1851; 58 y.
Touppet, E. Louisa, bur. 24 June, 1851; 22 m.
Pfohl, Louisa T., Salem, N. C., bur. 27 June, 1851; 20 y.
Steers, ——, a child, bur. 29 June, 1851.
Humphreys, Asa, a child, bur. 4 July, 1851; 22 m.

Connor, ——, a child of V. V., bur. 17 July, 1851.
Lake, ——, Mrs., a widow, bur. 28 July, 1851; 69 y.
Vanderbilt, Dane Ellenwood, bur. 31 July, 1851, in Capt. Vanderbilt's ground; 1 y.
Bodine, John, of N. Y., bur. 3 Aug., 1851; 24 y., 9 m.
Senne, Christian, bur. 5 Aug., 1851; 81 y.
Dugan, ——, bur. ——, 1851; 56 y.
Laforge, ——, child, bur. 21 Aug., 1851.
Siersema, Frederick Henry, bur. 24 Aug., 1851; 2½ y.
Sprague, Sarah M. (Decker), bur. 30 Aug., 1851; 33 y.
Egbert, ——, infant of J., bur. 4 Sept., 1851; 18 m.
Stile, Isabella, bur. 2 Oct., 1851; 59 y.
Cripps, ——, inft. ch. of Wm., bur. 11 Sept., 1851.
Fountain, John V., bur. 5 Oct., 1851.
Vredenburg, ——, Mr., bur. 29 Oct., 1851.
Seguine, ——, ch., Quarantine, bur. 10 Nov., 1851; 5 m.
Lenting, John, Senr., bur. 23 Nov., 1851; 57 y.
Stacy, ——, at Clifton, bur. 15 Jan., 1852; 39 y.
Metcalf, ——, child, at Clifton, bur. ——, 1852; 10 y.
Corson, Catharine, bur. 8 Jan., 1852; 17 y.
Van Pelt, John, wheelwright, bur. 18 Jan., 1852; 55 y.
Connor, Mrs. A. V., bur. 8 March, 1852.
Medcalf, ——, child, bur. 15 March, 1852.
Sharrot, ——, child of Wm., bur. 16 March, 1852.
Bigler, Amelia H., N. Y., bur. 14 March, 1852; 6 y., 3 m.
Coddington, Ann, bur. 25 April, 1852.
Thiebault, John F., bur. 27 April, 1852; 31 y.
Vanderbilt, ——, child of Isaac, bur. 28 April, 1852.
Garretson, Mrs. Eliza, bur. 29 April, 1852.
Oldfield, ——, a child, bur. 15 May, 1852.
Jacobson, Abr., bur. 17 May, 1852.
Britton, John, bur. 31 May, 1852.
Coddington, Samuel, bur. 3 June, 1852.
Latimer, ——, Mrs., bur. 12 June, 1852.
Lewis, ——, Mrs., bur. 13 June, 1852.
Steel, John, bur. 18 June, 1852.
Basse, ——, child, bur. 28 June, 1852.
Taylor, James, bur. 14 July, 1852; 55 y.
Marks, ——, a child, bur. 16 July, 1852; 5 m.
McLean, ——, Mr., bur. 21 July, 1852; 39 y.
Cozine, Elizabeth Ann, bur. 28 July, 1852; 6 y.
Van Duzer, Peter W., bur. 29 July, 1852; 18 m.
Van Duzer, Evelina, bur. 11 Aug., 1852; 13 m.
Robinson, ——, child, Brooklyn, bur. 14 Aug., 1852.
Van Duzer, Sarah E., bur. 17 Aug., 1852; 3 y., 7 m.
Bedell, Jesse, bur. 30 Aug., 1852; 8 y.(?)
Wakeham, ——, Mrs., bur. 13 Oct., 1852; 24 y.
Jacobson, Elizabeth, bur. 19 Oct., 1852; 22 y.
Allen, ——, child, bur. Sept. ——, 1852.
Stilwell, J.,(?) bur. 9 Dec., 1852; 21 y.
Armstrong, Mrs. James, bur. 14 Dec., 1852.
Sharrot, Milvaise, bur. 21 Dec., 1852; 16 y.

Frost, Mrs. Samuel, Senr., bur. 27 Dec., 1852; 84 y.(?)
Root, ——, child, bur. 31 Dec., 1852.
Stilwell, Abraham, bur. 28 Jan., 1853; 40 y.
Cole, Sr. Sarah, d. 27 Jan., 1853; bur. at Woodrow M. C.
Jacobson, ——, a child, bur. 21 Feb., 1853.
Buck, ——, a dau. of Mrs., bur. 14 March, 1853.
Taylor, Mrs. Chas., bur. 4 April, 1853.
Alston, ——, child of Moses, bur. 6 April, 1853; 6 m.
Connor, Col. Richard, bur. 7 April, 1853; 89 y.
Van Pelt, William, bur. 9 April, 1853; 10 m.
Burgher, Mathias, bur. 10 April, 1853; 64 y.
Domingo, Raymond A., N. Y., bur. 12 May, 1853; 3 y.
Wagstaff, Mrs. Agnes, maiden name Bininger, bur. 9 June, 1853.
Wians, ——, daughter, bur. 27 June, 1853; 14 y., 10 m.
Jones, ——, a child, d. 4 July, 1853; 2 y., 6 m.
Simonson, Charles, Senr., d. 25 July, 1853 (stone, d. 26 July, in 73 y.),
Van Pelt, ——, a dau. of John, d. 2 Aug., 1853; 16 m.
Britton, ——, ch. of Abm., d. 7 Aug., 1853; in 7 y.
Clark, Ann B., d. 7 Aug., 1853; 4 y.
Egbert, Mrs. Maria, m. n. Simonson, bap. on sick bed, d. 2 Sept., 1853; 29 y.
Patterson, ——, a child, d. — Sept., 1853.
Vanderbilt, ——, a child, d. — Sept., 1853; 1 y.
Guyon, ——, Miss, d. 30 Sept., 1853; 18 y.
Lake, Sabina(?), m. n. Egbert, late Prall, d. 1 Oct., 1853; 63 y.
Sharrot, Thomas, son of David Sharrot, bur. 4 Oct., 1853; 5 y.
Sneeden, ——, a child, bur. 9 Oct., 1853.
Whitehead, ——, a child, bur. 11 Oct., 1853.
Fountain, ——, a child, d. 18 Oct., 1853; 7 w.
Sharrot, ——, a child of Daniel, d. 19 Oct., 1853.
Lake, ——, a son of James, d. 21 Oct., 1853; 2 y., 6 m.
Vredenburg, ——, Mr., d. 22 Oct., 1853.
Dugan, —— (sister), of N. Y., d. 21 Oct., 1853.
Smith, Thomas, bur. 27 Oct., 1853.
Martin, Mrs. Nancy, bur. 1 Nov., 1853.
Lake, ——, a child of James, bur. 1 Nov., 1853.
Cole, Capt. William, a born member of our church, bur. 2 Nov., 1853; 40 y.
Martino, Abraham, of Tompkinsville, d. 15 Nov., 1853; bur. 17 Nov., 1853; 62 y.(?) (stone, 54 y., 8 m., 2 d.).
Dittmer, ——, bur. 18 Nov., 1853.
Romer, ——, a child, bur. 3 Dec., 1853.
Heyer, ——, Miss, d. 16 Dec., 1853.
Maclain, Cornelius, bur. 22 Dec., 1853.
Germond, ——, a child, bur. 1 Jan., 1854; 1 yr.
Walker, illegitimate, mother's name Walker, bur. 15 Jan., 1854; 3 m.
Snedicker, Mrs. Mary, m. n. Beatty, bur. 23 Jan., 1854; 41 y.
Hansby, Mrs. Ann (this may be Abraham), bur. 23 Jan., 1854; 59 y.
Vanderbilt, Mrs. Phoebe, d. 22 Jan., 1854; 87 y.
—— (illegible), Ida, bur. 17 Jan., 1854; 2 y.

Lozier, Mrs. Sarah, bur. 29 Jan., 1854; 80 y.
Goodyear, ——, inft. dau., bur. 22 Feb., 1854; 8 m.
Patterson, ——, a child, bur. 5 March, 1854; 4 y.
Parker, ——, a child, of Factoryville, bur. 5 March, 1854.
Lake, Br. Joseph, a born member of our ch., d. 16 March, 1854; 81 y.
Roff, Mary, bur. 28 March, 1854; 1 y., 1 m.
Nedwell, Ann, N. Y., bur. 10 April, 1854; 12 y.
Brittain, James, d. 14 April, 1854 (stone, James Guyon Britton, d. 11 April, 1854; b. 25 Feb., 1808; same stone, Frances Oakley, w. of James Guyon Britton, b. 19 May, 1805; d. 30 May, 1883).
Tysen, Harriet, d. 15 April, 1854; 17 y.
Moore, James, d. 17 April, 1854; in 99 y. (This is a little uncertain.)
Maclain, ——, Miss, bur. 24 April, 1854.
Prince, Samuel, d. 24 April, 1854; 14 y., 5 d.
Townsend, William, d. — Feb., 1853. (Probably removed to this cemetery.)
Egbert, John, inft. son of A.
Wood, Mrs. Barbara, wife of John, d. 19 June, 1854.
Garretson, ——.
[Here is an interval between two pastors.]
McLean, ——.
Vanderbilt, ——, a child (stone, Cornelius E., son of Edward & Mary Ann, d. 19 July, 1854, 16 y., 12 d.).
Fountain, ——.
Tyson, ——.
Beatty, ——.
Britton, ——.
Randolph, ——.
Cripp, T——.
Cripps, ——, master, d. 18 Sept., 1854, of Cholera; 13 y.
Barnes, ——, Miss, d. 19 Sept., 1854.
Winant, ——, a child, d. 23 Sept., 1854; 6 m.
Braisted, Peter, from N. Y., d. 25 Sept., 1854; 60 y.
Wood, ——, child, from N. Y., d. 7 Oct., 1854; 2 m.
Decker, Mrs. Patience, d. 10 Oct., 1854; 54 y.
Sharrot, Cornelia Frances, d. 20 Oct., 1854; 2 m.
Egbert, ——, child of Jno., d. 6 Nov., 1854; 7 y.
Bininger, Mrs. Harriet, d. 14 Nov., 1854; 64 y.
Egbert, Ann, m. n. Burbank, d. 30 Nov., 1854; 60 y., 6 m., 27 d.
Humphreys, ——, Mrs., d. 20 Dec., 1854.
Moellich, Eliz. Augusta, d. 27 Jan., 1855; 3 y., 28 d.
Frost, Samuel, bur. 12 Feb., 1855; 80 y.(?)
Fountain, ——, Mr., bur. 12 Feb., 1855.
Lockman, ——, Mrs., d. 2 March, 1855.
Wandell, Mr. Henry D., d. 3 March, 1855; 22 y. (correct by stone).
Blake, ——, Mr., d. 9 March, 1855; 40 y.
Carlyle, Miss, d. 10 March, 1855; 18 y.
Ebbit, Mrs. Serena, d. 17 April, 1855; 31 y.
Moore, Richard, d. 24 April, 1855; 53 y.
Martin, Oliver.
Egbert, Mrs. Nancy.
Simonson, Charles Mc., d. 12 May, 1855; 43 y., 8 m.

Cargill, ——, Mrs.
Schmidt, C. C., M. D., d. June 13, 1855; 61 y., 3 m.
Cole, ——, ch. of John, Stapleton, d. 16 July, 1855; 1 y., 6 m.
Dugan, Thomas, d. 22 July, 1855; 60 y.
Beatty, ——, ch. of Mr., of L. Island, d. 13 Aug., 1855; 8 m.
Mills, Gilbert, d. 16 Aug., 1855; nearly 7 y.
Vanderbilt, ——, son of Jacob, d. 17 Aug., 1855; 2½ y.
Clemens, Magdalena, N. Y., d. 17 Aug., 1855; 9 m.
Colon, John, of Southfield, d. 1 Sept., 1855; 25 y.
Bodine, William, d. 7 Sept., 1855; 50 y.
Wood, Moses, bur. 11 Oct., 1855; 70 y.
Root, ——, a ch. of George, bur. 24 Oct., 1855.
Lockman, ——, Miss, bur. 24 Oct., 1855; 17 y.
Sprague, ——, Mrs., bur. 24 Oct., 1855; 50 y.
Garrettson, James B., d. 4 Nov., 1855; 60 y. (stone, 58 y., 7 m., 10 d.).
Baker, ——, ch., bur. 11 Nov., 1855; 2 w.
Ryers, Arris, d. 27 Nov., 1855; 78 y.
Noble, Abraham, d. 17 Dec., 1855; 68 y.
Simonson, Jane, d. 14 Jan., 1856; 85 y.
Winant, Wm., Senr., d. 31 Jan., 1856; 74 y.
Vroome, Wm. Emmet, d. 9 Feb., 1856; 2 y.
Fleming, D., Jr., d. 29 Feb., 1856; 7 y., 8 m.
Butler, ——, d. 4 March, 1856; 4 y.
Cole, M. Elizabeth, d. 5 March, 1856; 4 y.(?)
Thistle, Samuel, d. 10 March, 1856.
Egbert, ——, ch. of Jno., d. 12 March, 1856; 8 d.
Steers, Mrs. F., d. 13 March, 1856; 18 y.
A stranger buried in Mr. Fleming's lot, d. 7 April, 1856.
Stilwell, ——, Mr., d. 8 April, 1856; 74 y. (stone, Daniel Stilwell, 71 y., 7 m., 24 d. & wife Hannah, d. 20 June, 1870, 80 y., 2 m., 17 d.).
Cripps, Henry, d. 16 April, 1856; 40 y.
Simonson, Susan, d. 18 April, 1856; 39 y., 1 y., 16 d.
Boardman, ——, Mrs., d. — May, 1856; aged.
Fountain, Gideon, d. 6 May, 1856; 22 y.
Donaldson, Jno. A., d. 29 May, 1856; 64 y.; "Club House."
Miller, George, of N. Y., d. 30 June, 1856; 5 y.
Simonson, Emma Josephine, d. 8 Aug., 1856; 5 y., 5 m. (this record is all from stone, no mention in book, dau. of Chas. & Sarah).
Colon, Mary Jane, Southfield; 27 y.(?)
Ditton, ——, a child, bur. 18 Oct., 1856; 2 y., 10 m.
A small ch. in grave of Sarah McClynen, bur. 19 Oct., 1856.
Lake, ——, a ch. of James, bur. 28 Oct., 1856; 10 w.
Fountain, Wm. Austin, bur. 8 Nov., 1856; 37 y.
Egbert, Rachel Ann, bur. 11 Dec., 1856; 35 y.
Swaim, George, d. 19 Dec., 1856; 12 y.
Mesier, James, d. 19 Dec., 1856; 21 y.
Wandell, Sarah, d. 4 Jan., 1857; 84 y., 11 m., 12 d.
Blake, ——, d. 4 Jan., 1867; 30 y.
Van Pelt, Peter, d. 28 Jan., 1857; 88 y.
Cortelyou, Peter, d. 3 Feb., 1857; 88 y., 1 m., 16 d.

Kilburn, Margaret, d. 24 Feb., 1857; 47 y.
A ch. bur. in Miller's vault, d. 7 March, 1857.
Little, Emma West, d. 25 March, 1857; 15 y. (stone, b. 26 July, 1842); her stone is by that of Richd. & Rebecca Littell.
Garrettson, ——, a ch. of Jacob, d. 28 March, 1857; 15 m.
Barnes, ——, a ch. of Robert Barnes, d. 6 April, 1857; 7 d.
Vrome, Rachel Ann, d. 22 April, 1857; 5 w.
Boyd, Margaret, d. 15 April, 1857; 70 y.
Wandell, Peter, d. 17 April, 1857.
Baker, Susan, d. 9 June, 1857.
Baker, Josephine, "Jno.'s," d. 16 June, 1857; 21 m.
Cole, Joseph, d. 30 June, 1857; 55 y.
Baldwin, Reuben, d. 1 July, 1857; 11 y., 3 m.
Female friend of Mrs. Matthias, d. 2 July, 1857.
Egbert, Annette, d. 26 July, 1857; 27 y.
Cubberly, William Holland, d. 28 July, 1857; 13 y.
Mersereau, Sophia, d. 3 Aug., 1857; 4 y., 8 m.
Baker, ——, inft. dau. of Jno., d. 4 Aug., 1857; 6 w.
Jacobson, ——, child, d. 11 Aug., 1857; 9 m.
Randolph, ——, child, d. 16 Aug., 1857, at Quarantine; 6 m.
Bender, Annie, d. 22 Sept., 1857; 11 m.
Littell, Ada Louisa, d. 29 Sept., 1857; 14 m.
Egbert, Stephen, d. 6 Oct., 1857; 60 y., 10 m.
Decker, Ephraim, d. 7 Oct., 1857; 33 y.
Patterson, ——, child, d. 9 Oct., 1857, at Vanderbilt's Landing; 1½ y.(?)
Simonson, Isaac, d. 15 Oct., 1857; 56 y.
Lake, ——, child of Jas, d. 29 Oct., 1857; 6 m.
Craig, ——, Mrs., d. 15 Nov., 1857.
Ditton, D., d. 17 Nov., 1857.
Perine, H., d. 19 Nov., 1857.
Coyne, Beatus, d. 25 Nov., 1857.
Taylor, Mrs. Mary, d. 1 Dec., 1857; 66 y.
Houseman, ——, Mrs., d. 2 Dec., 1857; 82 y.
Townsend, Henry V., d. 19 Dec., 1857; 5 m.
Bird, Jane L., d. 21 Dec.. 1857; 2 y.
Lafarge, ——, child, girl, d. 4 Jan., 1858.
Maas, John, d. 5 Jan., 1858; 30 y.
Beatty(?), ——, child, J. City, d. 13 Jan., 1858; 2 d.
Luby, Henry, a child, d. 14 Jan., 1858; 1 y.
Sharrott, Mrs. Agnes, d. 22 Jan., 1858; 24 y., 5m.
Williams, Mr. Lamont, d. 25 Jan., 1858; 61 y., 6 m.
Barton, Col. Samuel, d. 29 Jan., 1858; 73 y. (stone, 72 y., 6 m.).
Stillwell, John, d. 30 Jan., 1858; 50 y.
Welsh, Richard, d. 14 Feb., 1858; 3 y.
Gaines, ——, a ch. of Wm., d. 13 Feb., 1858; 2 y.
Taylor, Edward R.(?), d. 14 Feb., 1858; 22 y.
Ditton, ——, a child, d. 24 Feb., 1858; 9 m.
Garrettson, Jacob, d. 4 March, 1858; 63 y.
Sharrot, ——, a child, d. 22 March, 1858; 5 y.
Simonson, Daniel, d. 23 March, 1858; 60 y., 6 m.
Cozine, Hannah M., d. 18 April, 1858; 32 y.

Freegard, ——, Mrs.
Sharrot, ——, child; of same parents as March 23.
Mersereau, Joshua; 63 y.
Jacobson, Israel, d. 25 June, 1858; 50 y.
Burgher, D., d. 4 July, 1858; 52 y.
Butler, ——, d. 4 July, 1858.
Seguine, ——, ch. of Mr. J., d. 30 July, 1858; 1 y., 4 m.
Randolph, ——, Mrs., d. 15 Aug., 1858.
Simonson; ——, Miss, d. 17 Aug., 1858, at Clifton; 53 y. (stone, Mary, dau. of Charles & Mary). Her mother would be only 17 if this is correct.
Weed, ——, Mr. d. 24 Aug., 1858; 64 y.
Garrettson, ——, ch. of Hiram, d. 14 Sept., 1858; 14 m.
Blake, ——, child, d. 18 Sep., 1858; 1 y.
Sharrott, Richard.
Kerr, Elizabeth W., d. 18 Oct., 1858; 8 m., 12 d.
De Hart, ——, Mrs., d. — Dec., 1858 (stone, M. De Hart, d. 4 Dec., in 76 y.).
Littell, ——, Judge, d. Jan. 11, 1859 (stone, Richard Dumont Littell, b. 16 July, 1790, d. 7 Jan., 1859; also, Rebecca, his relict, b. 10 Dec., 1810, d. 22 Feb., 1863).
Egbert, Mrs. Hannah, d. 22 Jan., 1859; 57 y.
Prince, Wm. Robert, d. 6 Feb., 1859; 43 y., 3 m.
Crocheron, ——, Mr., d. 7 Feb., 1859; 45 y.
Blake, ——, Mr., d. 10 Feb., 1859.
De Forest, John, 43 y.
Van Duzer, George, d. 18 Feb., 1859; 12 y. (stone, 11 y., 11 m., 15 son of Daniel C. & Julia V. Duzer).
Baldwin, Ella, d. 12 April, 1859; 9 m.
Clark, ——, Mr. (or Mrs.).
Snediker, ——, d. 21 April, 1859.
Bodine, John, d. 23 April, 1859; 60 y.
Gilbert, James, d. 6 May, 1859: 18 y., 3 m.
Clark, Mr. R., d. 7 May, 1859.
Littell, ——, d. 19 May, 1859.
Baker, ——, Mr. or Mrs., d. 21 May, 1859; in Methodist ground.
White, Pinkney, d. 3 June, 1859; 2 y.
White, Isabella, d. 22 Aug., 1858; 13 y. These two children d. at St. John's Rectory at Clifton; the father, Rev. John C. White
Deforest, John, b. 17 Nov., 1815, d. 27 Jan., 1859 (stone, no record of this in Ch. book).
Senseman, Lucinda Eliz., d. 15 May, 1859; 31 y.
Weed, ——, child, d. 5 July, 1859; 10 y.
Wolf, Maria Eliz., d. 7 July, 1859.
Caesar, P. W., d. 12 Aug., 1859; 9 m.
Seguine, ——, ch. of H'y, d. 13 Aug., 1859.
McLean, Anna, d. 29 Aug., 1859; 18 y.
Sharrot, ——, child of Wm., d. 29 Aug., 1859; 1 y.
Egbert, ——, child of Mr., of N. Y., d. 1 Sept., 1859; 4 y.
Ripley, ——, child of Mr., of Clifton, d. 3 Sept., 1859; 5 y.
Castree, Miss H., d. 7 Sept., 1859; 55 y.
Thistle, ——, Mrs., d. 18 Sept., 1859; 70 y.

Egbert, John, son of Joseph, d. 25 Sept., 1859; 17 y.
Hazard, Robert, d. 29 Sept., 1859.
Eisele, R., from N. Y., d. 1 Oct., 1859; no minister.
Martin, William, d. 3 Oct., 1859.
Sharrott, Benjamin T., d. 5 (6?) Nov., 1859 (stone, 38 y., 3 m., 2 d); he was christened "Benjamin Guyon."
Dissossway, ——, child, d. 14 Nov., 1859; 18 m.
Littell, Mary Eliza, d. 4 Dec., 1859; 17 y. (stone, Margaret Eliza, b. 23 April, 1824, d. 3 Dec., 1859).
Colon, George, d. 28 Dec., 1859.
Marsh, ——, child from Clifton, d. 30 Dec., 1859; 2 y., 4 m.
Carr, ——, Mrs., d. 5 Jan., 1860; buried in Vanderbilt's plot.
Kempton, ——, child, d. 17 Jan., 1860.
Caper, ——, Mr., of Brooklyn, d. 15 Jan., 1860.
Tysen, Mrs. Louisa, d. 21 Jan., 1860; 24 y.
Swift, John, d. 3 Feb., 1860; 30 y.
Martino, Cornelius, d. 13 Feb., 1860.
Ogle, ——, child, d. 15 Feb., 1860; 14 y.
Littell, ——, Hoboken, d. 19 Feb., 1860; 4 y., 8 m.
Barger, Mr. John, d. 2 March, 1860; 67 y.
Swift, John, d. 26 March, 1860; 26? y. (as there is another John Swift above, this seems like a mistake and there has been doubt about the age).
Post, Mrs. Susan, d. 15 April, 1860 (stone, Susan Martineau, wife of Peter Post, b. 21 Jan., 1837).
Van Duzer, Emma, d. 24 April, 1860; 4 y.
Lawson, Reinhalt Wesley, d. 17 July, 1860; 35 y.
Burgher, ——, child of James, d. 20 July, 1860.
Sharrot, ——, child of Abraham, d. 28 July, 1860.
Geibert, ——, master, d. 3 Aug., 1860.
Clark, ——, ch. of Dr. James, d. 15 Aug., 1860; 8 y.
Keyes, ——, child, d. 14 Sept., 1860.
Townsend, ——, child of Mr. E., d. 14 Sept., 1860.
Crocheron, James, d. 13 Sept., 1860; 60 y.
Racey, Miss Bessie, d. 25 Sept., 1860; 21 y.(?)
Bedell, Abrm., d. 1 Oct., 1860; 30 y.(?)
Kinsey, John, d. 12 Oct., 1860; 43 y.
Swift, Sarah.
Burgher, ——, ch. of Stephen, d. 23 Oct., 1860.
Cortelyou, Cornelius, d. 26 Oct., 1860; 8 m.
Smith, ——, Mrs., d. 28 Oct., 1860; 75 y.
Lewis, ——, colored, d. 5 Nov., 1860; 80 y.
Barton, Isaac, d. 8 Nov., 1860; 81 y.
Swift, Caroline, d. 9 Nov., 1860; 16 y.
Ostrander, Nathaniel, d. 12 Dec., 1860; 80 y., 9 d.
Wandell, Julia, dau. of Philip, d. 16 Dec., 1860; 5 y.
Swift, Mary, d. 18 Dec., 1860; 14 y.
Ketchum, ——, Mrs., d. 30 Dec., 1860.
Colon, David, d. 30 Dec., 1860; 32 y.
Davis, Maria, d. 11 Jan., 1861; 55 y.
Egbert, Shirley Morton, d. 23 Jan., 1861; 3 y.
Littell, Dunn, d. 26 Feb., 1861.

Gates, ——, child, d. 26 Feb., 1861.
Cole, ——, d. 28 Feb., 1861.
Blake, John, d. 9 March, 1861; 19 y.
Dugan, ——, d. 26 March, 1861.
Bardine, ——, child, d. 12 April, 1861; 8 m.
A servant of Mr. Jac. Vanderbilt, d. 4 May, 1861.
Doeller, Christine, d. 9 May, 1861; 26 y.(?)
Decker, ——, Mrs., d. 18 May, 1861.
More, David.
Brinley, Frances, d. 24 May, 1861; 29 y.
Sharrot, ——, Mrs.
Sherer, ——, Mrs., d. 2 June, 1861.
Swift, ——, a child.
Garrettson, Edwin, d. 1 July, 1861; 24 y.
Vroome, Lewis, d. 12 July, 1861; 1 y. (middle initial illegible).
Burgher, ——, child, d. 22 July, 1861; 2 y.
Burgher, Charles, d. 3 Aug., 1861; 4 y.
Luby, Mary Elizabeth, d. 6 Aug., 1861; 1 y., 7 m.
Vroome, ——, son of Gar., d. 14 Aug., 1861; 3 m. (this whole entry is uncertain, so illegible).
Clark, Binninger, d. 18 Aug., 1861; 22 y.
Ebbit, David, d. 22 Ang., 1861; 4 y.
Richards, ——, Mrs., d. — Sept., 1861.
—— (illegible).
Hyde, ——, child, N. Y., d. 21 Sept., 1861.
Delaree, ——, child, d. 23 Sept., 1861.
Patterson, ——, child of George, d. 24 Sept., 1861.
Seguine, Patience, bur. 28 Nov., 1861; 75 y. (stone, d. 28 Nov., 1861, wife of Henry Seguine, 65 y., 10 m., 11 d.).
Snedicker, Brasilla, d. 1 Dec., 1861; 20 y.
Fischt, Jane F., d. 27 Dec., 1861; 2 y.
Rogers, Ogden M., d. 26 Dec., 1861; 2 y.
Noble, Amanda, d. 4 Feb., 1862; 21 y.
Dustan, Sarah, d. 6 Feb., 1862; 91 y.
Stockdale, Sarah, d. 16 Feb., bur. 18 Feb., 1862; 63 y.
Cole, Catharine, d. 9 March, 1862; 79 y.
Sharrot, Joseph, d. 18 March, 1862; 53 y.
Metcalf, Richard, d. 21 March, 1862; 4 m.
McLynnon, Sarah E., d. 26 March, 1862; 4 y.
Barton, Joseph, d. 27 March, 1862; 81 y.
Wandell, Peter S., Junr., d. 14 May, 1862; 12 y.
Beatty, Edward, d. 8 June, 1862; 62 y.
Taege(?), ——, Mrs., d. 9 June, 1862; 25 y.
Hildreth, Will. H'y., d. 14 June, 1862; 1 y., 5 m.
Crocheron, ——, d. — June, 1862.
Beatty, Mary E., d. 7 July, 1862; 27 y.
Barnes, Frederick, d. 1 Aug., 1862; 6 d.
Johnson, William, d. 3 Aug., 1862; 1 m.
Beckwith, ——, a soldier belonging to 145 N. Y. Regt., d. 7 Sept., 1862.
Houseman, Mary Elizabeth, d. 17 Sept., 1862; 10 m.
Noble, Geo. Edward, d. 27 Sept., 1862; 9 m.

Kempton, Matilda L., d. 28 Sept., 1862; 2 y.
Folager, ——, d. 28 Oct., 1862; 7 y.
North, Mrs. Cath., late Heath, d. 28 Oct., 1862; bur. in John Heath's lot.
Scott, Mrs. Eleanor, d. 29 Oct., 1862; 58 y.
Britton, Mrs. Rachel, d. 30 Oct., 1862; 87 y.
Steers, ——, d. 25 Nov., 1862; 8 yrs.
Littell, Alexander, d. 24 Nov., 1862; about 34 y.
McLymon, Benj. D., d. 27 Nov., 1862; 36 y.
Braisted, Grace, d. 26 Nov., 1862; 4 y.
Simonson, John, d. 25 Nov., 1862; 80 y.
Egbert, Tunis, d. 5 Dec., 1862; 77 y.
Auten, Emilie, d. 6 Dec., 1862; 6 y.
Woods, Joseph, d. 16 Dec., 1862; 83 y.
Clark, ——, ch. of Dr., bur. 26 Dec., 1862.
Mayhew, ——, a child, bur. 29 Dec., 1862.

BURIALS ATTENDED BY MINISTERS OF BRETHREN CHURCH OF STATEN ISLAND BUT NOT BURIED ON THEIR GROUND.

Praul, Elizabeth, ch. of Benj. & Ellen, d. 31 Aug., 1828; bur. at Dutch Ch. on N. side.
Crocheron, Nancy, wife of Richard, Esq., d. 4 Sept., 1828; bur. at Richmond.
Wait, Ann, d. 5 Oct., 1828; bur. from house of Henry Miller on Burbank family plot.
Johnson, Eliza, ch. of James, dec., & Phoebe, his wife, d. 25 Oct., 1828; bur. at Richmond.
Mussantine, Laforge, a child, d. 27 March, 1829; bur. at Woodrow Methodist meeting.
Burton, Charles, son of John & Louisa, d. 18 Aug., 1829; about 4 y.; bur. in Episcopal gr. y'd.
Burbank, John, md., d. 23 Dec., 1829; bur. on family burying gr.
Clawson, Samuel, d. 21 Jan., 1814; 44 y.; bur. at Episcopal ground at Richmond.
Bedell, Elizabeth, wife of Cornelius, m. n. Jacobson, d. 24 Oct., 1814; 43 y., 3 m., 18 d.; Mr. Corn. Bedell, farmer & miller.
Marsh, John F., d. 21 Jan., 1815; 18 m.; he was son of L. R. Marsh, attorney-at-law in Richmond, S. I., & Margaret, his w., m. n. Dubois.
Brittain, Margaret Eliza, dau. of James & Violetta, b. 24 Feb., 1815, d. 20 May, 1815.
Bogart, John, d. 16 July, 1815; about 18 y.; bur. at Richmond, was drowned.
Garritson, Hendric, d. — Nov., 1818; 94 or 95 y.; bur. on Col. Garritson's farm.
Benjamin,——, wid. of late Capt., d. 18 May, 1819; bur. at Richmond.
Smack, Sarah, wife of Martin, d. 5 Sept., 1819; bur. at English Ch.
Marsh, ——, ch. of Robert & Rhoda, d. 14 Sept., 1819.
Fountain, ——, child, d. 11 Sept., 1819.
Vroome, Peter Houseman, son of Christopher & Maria, m. n. Houseman, d. 8 Jan., 1820; 7 m., 5 d.; bur. at Methodist gr. yd. on Neck.

Bedell, Vandeventer, single, son of Cornelius & Elizabeth Bedell, m. n. Jacobson, d. 9 June, 1820; 27 y., 21 d.
Jewson, Nancy, d. 22 Nov., 1820; aged; resided at her dau.-in-law's at house of Peter Decker.
Butler, Mary, dau. of Elias Butler at Quarantine, d. 27 Sept., 1821; 17 m.
Perine, Cornelius, son of Edwd. & Patience Perine, d. 29 Sept., 1821; 12 y., 3 m., 6 d.; bur. at Episcopal Ch. at Richmond.
Smith, Hetty, single, d. 19 May, 1823; bur. in Episcopal gr. yd. at Richmond.
Lake, William, Senr., of Southfield, d. 23 Oct., 1823; aged.
Cubberly, ——, an aged woman, d. 6 Aug., 1823.
Decker, John Hilliard, son of Mathias Decker & his wife, m. n. Hilliard, d. 14 Sept., 1824; about 16 m.
Butler, Samuel, son of Elias Butler at Quarantine, d. 18 Sept., 1824.
Lewis, ——, Mrs., wife of Jonathan, Esq., d. 31 July, 1825, at Freshkill; bur. at Richmond.
Decker, Frances, d. 15 Aug., 1825; bur. at Richmond.
Van Cleaf, Daniel, a young man, d. 14 Feb., 1826; bur. at Richmond.
Johnson, ——, a ch. of John, d. 2 Oct., 1826; bur. at Richmond.
Cairns, Margaret, a widow, d. 5 Feb., 1827; bur. at Richmond, S. I.
Blake, ——, a child of John, d. 27 March, 1827; bur. at N. Side Episcopal Ch.
Sharrot, John, d. 11 July, 1827; aged; hung himself.
Mersereau, Rebekah, single, d. 12 July, 1827; aged; bur. at Richmond.
Cropsy, Cornelius Cortleyou, child of Jacob & Elizabeth Cropsey, d. 23 July, 1827.
Barnes, Robert, child of Geo., dec., & wife, m. n. Holmes, d. 20 Aug., 1827.
Schenk, Holmes, d. 29 March, 1828, at N. Y.; bur. from Anthony Fountain, Sr., in Holme's family ground.

PERSONS RECEIVED INTO THE CONGREGATION.

1785, May 24. George and Mary Colong. First Communion June 11, 1786.
June 14. Cathrina Ryerss.
Aug. 23. Sarah Cortelyou. First Communion, Sept. 24, 1786.
1786, Feb. 26. Edward and Eleanor Beatty. First Communion Dec. 24, 1786.
June 5. Elizabeth Enyard.
John Dorset. First Communion June 11, 1786.
Sept. 26. Ann Egbert, wife of Tunis, Senr.
1787, April 15. Edward & Mary Egbert, md. pair.
Lewis Ryerss, also md.
Oct. 14. Nicolas Stilwell, single.
Martha Dorsett, md.
Frances Stilwell, single.
Dec. 26. Elizabeth Garrison, md.
Sarah Boillon, widow.
Susanna Enyard, single.
1788, March 24. Daniel Perine, widower.
July 6. Richard Conor, widower.
Aug. 13. Richard Sherret, Senr., md.
Owen Limner, widower.
1794, Jan. 15. Mary Egbert, md.
1798, May 27. Amos Rooke, md.
1804, April 1, Easter day. Reuben Symonson, md.
Ann Egbert, wife of Tunis.
1805, April 14, Easter. Abraham & Ann Egbert, married couple.
Aug. 18. John Egbert, md.
Dec. 15. Elizabeth Rickerte, "a great girl."
1806, Sept. 21. Batharine Barton, md.
1807, March 16. The negro York, slave of Br. & Sr. James & Elizabeth Egbert, was bap. by name of Peter
Nov. 16. Thomas Robin, slave of Mr. & Mrs. Taylor, also bap.

THOSE WHO PARTOOK OF COMMUNION FOR FIRST TIME.

1787, June 18. Cathrine Ryerss, late Conor.
1788, Jan. 20. Elizabeth Martino.
March 20. Br. Lewis Ryersz, single; Br. Nicolas Stilwell, & single Sr. Elizabeth.
May 18. Br. Edward & Sr. Mary Egbert, md. pair; Sr. Martha Dorset, md.; Sr. Frances Stilwell, single, & Sr. Susanna Enyard, single.
Aug. 13. Sr. Elizabeth Gerritson, md.
Sept. 28. Sr. Ann Egbert, md.
1789, April 9. Richard Conor, md.
1795, May 24. The md. pair, Henry & Mary Miller.
1801, Feb. 1. Br. Amos Rooke, md.
1805, Feb. 24. Sr. Ann Egbert, md., wife of Tunis, Jr.
April 11. Br. Reuben Symonson, md.
1806, Oct. 5. The md. pair, Abraham & Ann Egbert.
Dec. 6. The md. pair, John & Mary Egbert.

ST. ANDREW'S CHURCH.

RECORDS OF ST. ANDREW'S CHURCH IN RICHMOND, STATEN ISLAND.

BAPTISMS.

BORN	BAPTIZED	PARENTS	CHILD
	1752.		
	Aug. 9.	Charles Penny Dorothy, his wife	Daniel
	1753.		
	Aug. 5.	Lewis Grandine & wife	John
	Aug. 12.	Henry Butler & wife	Henry
	Aug. 12.	Peter Burbank & Martha, his wife	Joseph
	Sept. 23.	Nathaniel Britton & wife	Mary
	Oct. 7.	Jonathan Lewis & Mary, his wife	Sarah
	Oct. 7.	James Johnson & Mary, his wife	a child
	1754.		
	April 21.	John Lisk & Elizabeth, his wife	Marget
1753. Aug. 27.	1753. Oct. 14.	Thomas Taylor & Elizabeth his wife	Thomas
	1754.		
	April 21.	Richard Lawrence & wife	Mary
	April 21.	dau. of same	Sarah
	May 26.	Thomas Arrosmith & Mary, his wife	Mary
	May 26.	John Hylliard & Ester, his wife	Ester
	June 1.	Charles Penny & Dorothy, his wife	Hannah
	Sept. 1.	Anthony Stoutenborough & Mary, his wife	John
	Sept. 1.	John Simonson & Elizabeth, his wife	Elizabeth
	Sept. 15.	John Griffith & Hannah, his wife	Arthur
	Sept. 29.	John Marshal & Susannah, his wife	Martha
	Sept. 29.	Abraham Cole & Martha, his wife	Elizabeth
	Oct 13.	John Waglon & Catharine, his wife	Catharine
	Oct. 27.	Henry Marsh & Joannah, his wife	Elizabeth
	Nov. 10.	Daniel Crocheron & Mary, his wife	Nicholas
	Nov. 17.	Henry Ralley & Franky, his wife	Ann
	Dec. 8.	John Dupuy & Sarah, his wife	Sarah

BORN	BAPTIZED	PARENTS	CHILD
1754.	1755.		
Nov. 18.	Feb. 2.	John Pollion & Marget, his wife	Elizabeth
April 5.	May 11.	Andres Waglum & Nelly, his wife	Elizabeth
Dec. 3.	May 25.	Abraham Parley & Mary, his wife	Barnt
June 7.	June 29.	George Wood & Elizabeth his wife	John
1754.			
Nov. 1.	June 29.	John Silvester & Elizabeth, his wife	Ann
	Dec. 7.	John Dupuy & Sarah, his wife	John
	1756.		
	Jan. 18.	Joseph Beadle (or Beagle) & Catharine, his wife	John
1756.			
Jan. 16.	Feb. 29.	Joseph Yeates & Sarah, his wife	Abraham
Feb. 4.	April 11.	John Butler & Rachel, his wife	Mary
Feb. 23.	May 16.	James Pretch & Esther, his wife	Benjamin
1755.			
Dec. 5.	May 16.	Joseph Arysmith & Mary, his wife	Elizabeth
	May 23.	John Burdine & wife	Elizabeth
1754.			
May 22.	June 13.	James Latteret & Elizabeth, his wife	{ James { David
1756.			
April 6.			
April 16.		John Dubois & Esther, his wife	John
Jan. 27.	June 13.	Thomas Taylor & Elizabeth, his wife	John
1755.			
July 12.		John Morgan & Elizabeth, his wife	Charles
1756.			
April —.		James Seguine & Ells, his wife	Sarah
June 9.	Aug. 1.	Richard Lawrence & Mary, his wife	Leggett
July 15.	Sept. 19.	Charles Penny & Dorothy, his wife	Elizabeth
Aug. 29.	Sept. 26.	John Journey & Martha, his wife	Nicholas
Sept. 19.	Nov. 14.	John Hillird & Ester, his wife	Francis, dau.
1756.	1757.		
Nov. 4.	Jan. 2.	Abraham Cusheron & Jane Elizabeth, his wife	Johannah
Nov. 18.		John Foy & Mary, his wife	John
Nov. 20.		John Lecount & Katharine, his wife	John
	March 27.	Barnt Simonson & Abigail, his wife	Ort

BORN	BAPTIZED	PARENTS	CHILD
1755. March 11.	1757.	David Laforge & Mary, his wife	Rachel
1744. Nov. 5.		John Poillon & Marget, his wife	Mary
1746. March 2.		" "	Judith
1748. April 17.		" "	Ann
1750. April 27.		" "	Margret
1753. June 6.		" "	John
1756. Nov. 12.		All children of John Poillon & Marget, his wife	Sarah
1757. Feb. 7.		Zacharias Vandike & Ann, his wife	Jacob
March 7.		Augustus Dubois & Martha, his wife	Mary
Feb. 20.	March 27.	Jonathan Lewis & Mary, his wife	David
April 6.		Nathaniel Brittain & wife	Katharine
1752. Jan. 4.		John Journey & Martha, his wife	John
1753. Aug. 7.		" "	Martha
1755. March 8.		" "	Albert
1757. Feb. 21.		John Griffis & Hannah, his wife	John
April 13.		John Mushereau (Mersereau) & Charity, his wife	John
Feb. 16.		Paul Mushereau & Frances, his wife	Martha
1756. Sept. 19.		John Lisk & Mary, his wife	Thomas
1757. June 16.		Jacob Lazeleere & Alice, his wife	Daniel
1755. Feb. 11.		Daniel Garrison & Mary, his wife	Charles
1757. June 13.		" "	Jacob
Oct. 8.		Elexander Ogg & Margeret, his wife	Mary
1756. Sept. 25.		Anthony Fountain & Susanna, his wife	Charles
1757. Nov. 7.		Joseph Arysmith & Mary, his wife	Violetta
Nov. 2.		Joseph Bedgel & Katharine, his wife	Paul
		John Dupuy & Sarah, his wife	Nicholas

BORN	BAPTIZED	PARENTS	CHILD
1757.	1758.		
Nov. 30.		Abraham Parley & Mary, his wife	Peter
Dec. 9.		Cornelius Dissasway & Catharine, his wife	Ann
Sept. 30. 1755.		John Marshall & Susannah, his wife	Katharine
Dec. 26. 1746.		John Marshall & Susannah, his wife	Margaret & Frankey, dau.
April 4. 1749.		Daniel John & Hannah, his wife	Daniel
July 31. 1751.			Rees
Nov. 28. 1753.			Hannah
Dec. 4. 1755.			Moses
Nov. 24. 1758.			Jacob
Feb. 7. 1757.		All children of Daniel John & Hannah, his wife	Margaret
Oct. 27.		Joseph Yates & Sarah, his wife	Martha
Dec. 14.		Thomas Marshall & Sarah his wife	Martha
Dec. 10. 1758.		David Laforge & Mary, his wife	David
Feb. 19. 1757.		Henry Perine & Susan, his wife	Edward
Jan. 16. 1758.		John Silvester & Elizabeth, his wife	Francis (son)
July 17. 1754.		Barnt Simonson & Abigail, his wife	John
June 19. 1746.		Simon Bogart & Martha, his wife	Simon
Dec. 4. 1757.		" "	Mary
Feb. 22. 1758.		" "	Richard
Aug. 9.		Abraham Cushon, Jr., & Elizabeth, his wife	Jacob
April 21.		William Thomson & Mary, his wife	Samuel
Aug. 4.	Sept. 17.	James Latterette & Elizabeth, his wife	Sarah
Sept. 30.		Abraham Winant & Mary, his wife	Ann
Nov. 30.		Thomas Arysmith & Mary, his wife	Henry
Oct. 29.		Richard Lawrence & Mary, his wife	Elizabeth

BORN	BAPTIZED	PARENTS	CHILD
1759.			
Jan. 7.		John Gold & Katharine, his wife	John
March 27.		John Van Pelt & Margaret, his wife	Mary
Jan. 10.		Moses Dupuy & Leah, his wife	John
Jan. 20.		John Hilliard, Jr., & wife	Abraham
Jan. 20.		John Slack & Ann, his wife	Katharine
1758.			
Dec. 24.		James Seguine & Katharine, his wife	Henry
1759.			
March 22.		Jonathan Lewis & Mary, his wife	Katharine
March 13.		Jacob Lazeleer & Alice, his wife	Nicholas
1745.			
Aug. 22.		David Dye & Mary, his wife	Apha (dau.)
1759.			
March 12.		David Dye & Mary, his wife	Sarah
1748.			
Dec. 24.		William Hilliard & Dinah, his wife	Sarah
1756.			
Sept. 11.		" "	Mary
1752.			
April 14.		Patrick Corkin & Margaret, his wife	Peter
1759.			
June 12.		John Silvester & Elizabeth	Martha & Sarah
June 18.		John Foy & Mary, his wife	Francis (son)
March 22.		Richard Webb & Mary, his wife	Richard
May 8.		Henry Butler & Belleche, his wife	James
May 2.		Paul Mushereau & Francis, his wife	John
1752.			
May 15.		Leah Camp, widow	Naomi
1759.			
July 13.		John Latterette & Susannah, his wife	Mary
Aug. 6.		John Journey & Martha, his wife	William
July 5.		James Segan and Else, his wife	John & Jacob
1758.			
Oct. 19.		Thomas Butler & Mary, his wife	James
Oct. 29.		John Butler & Rachel, his wife	Daniel
1759.			
Oct. 24.		Daniel Drummond & Ann, his wife	Elexander
May 19.		James Pretchet & Ester, his wife	William

BORN	BAPTIZED	PARENTS	CHILD
1759.			
Jan. 14.		John More & Mary, his wife	John
1758.			
Oct. 6.		James Johnston & Mary, his wife	Dower (son)
1759.			
Aug. 28.		Anthony Van Pelt & Susannah, his wife	John
Sept. 9.		Anthony Stoutenborough & Mary, his wife	James
1758.			
Nov. 15.		John Dupuy & Sarah, his wife	Nicholas
1760.			
Jan. 17.		John Dupuy & Sarah, his wife	Jacob
Jan. 31.		Christian Smith & Ester, his wife	Isaac
Jan. 3.		Thomas Marshall & Sarah, his wife	John
May 10.		Daniel Winnens & Rachel, his wife	Daniel
June 6.		Peter Van Pelt & Phoebe (feeby), his wife	T u n i s (or Francis)
April 4.		James Johnson & Mary, his wife	Ann
July 20.		Richard Lawrence & Mary, his wife	Francis(dau.)
Aug. 8.		John Van Pelt & Margret, his wife	Tunis
		Henry Pereyn & Susannah, hie wife	Margret
May 4.		Roger Barnes & his wife	Richard
May 3.		John Seghong & Sarah, his wife	Elisha
1755.			
April 2.		Charles Vanscice & Cathrine, his wife	Joseph
1760.			
April 1.		" "	Sarah Dehart
1757.			
Aug. 14.		" "	Charles
1760.			
Sept. 13.		Charles Laforge & Elizabeth, his wife	A d r y o n g (Adrian?), son
Dec. 10.		James Segan (Seguine) & Elsie, his wife	James
Oct. 28.		Henry Johnson & Rachel, his wife	Henry
1761.			
Feb. 26.		Simon Hilliard & Sarah, his wife	Simon
March 1.		George Wood & Elisabeth, his wife	George
Feb. 28.		Samuel McSwain & Sarah, his wife	Catharine
Jan. 22.		Jonathan Lewis & Mary, his wife	James

BORN	BAPTIZED	PARENTS	CHILD
1761.			
April 2.		Lawrence Hilliard & Ann, his wife	Sarah
March 7.		Henry Taylor & Arriantie (or Amantica)	James
Feb. 1.		John Moor & Mary, his wife	Daniel
March 28.		John Meserow & Charity, his wife	Lowrance
June 14.		Matthew Hughes & Catharine, his wife	Martha
1760.			
April 29.		Joseph Morrel & Marthe, his wife	Thomas
Nov. 15.		Nathaniel Britton & Mary, his wife	Joseph
1761.			
June 26.		John Hilliard & Hester, his wife	Nathaniel
April 17.		Albert Rickeman & Mary, his wife	Katharine
July 1.		James Latterette & Elizabeth, his wife	Sarah
Aug. 9.		Abraham DeCoshorong & Elizabeth, his wife	Nicholas
Oct. 24.		Jeremiah Connor & Anny, his wife	Adam
July 4.		Paul Meshereau & Francis, his wife	Paul
Dec. 18.		John Journey & Martha, his wife	Katharine
Nov. 13.		Nicholas Stilwell & Esey, his wife	Katharine
Oct. 4.		Zachariah Vandick & Ann, his wife	Catharine
Oct. 22.		Jacob Ladeleer & Alice, his wife	Benjamin
1762.			
April 14.		Christopher Smith & Hester, his wife	Catharine
April 4.		Anthony Stoutenborough & Mary, his wife	Anthony
April 1.		John Foy & Mary, his wife	John
		James Butler & wife. Ch. bap. by Rev. Mr. Charlton	Eltey (son)
March 25.		Abraham Lakerman & Elizabeth, his wife	Sarah
	1762.		
May 11.	June 27.	Abraham Cole & Hannah, his wife	Ann
	June 3.	Daniel Van Clef & his wife	John
	July 18.	John Segain & Sarah, his wife. By Rev. Mr. Charlton	James
	July 18.	Daniel Stilwell & Ariaentie, his wife	Susannah
	July 25.	James Segain	Catharine

BORN	BAPTIZED	PARENTS	CHILD
	1762.		
	Aug. 22.	Daniel Garrison & Mary, his wife	Daniel
1762.			
June 21.		Paul Micheau & Mary, his wife	Paul
Aug. 7.		James Wood & Eve, his wife	Abraham
	Oct. 31.	John Bodine & Dorcas, his wife	Martha
	Oct. 31.	Samuel Tenicke	a daughter
	Oct. 31.	John Van Pelt & Margret, his wife	a son
	Oct. 31.	James Johnson	child
	Nov. 14.	James Poillon & Francis, his wife	John
	Nov. 14.	Henry Taylor & Judith, his wife	Daniel
1764.			
Oct. 23.		William Granger & Franca	William
1760.			
Oct. 19.		Joseph Bedell & Catrine	Mary
1763.			
Oct. 24.		" "	Joseph
1762.			
June 27.		Daniel Winant & Susannah, his wife	Ann
	1763.		
Oct. 23.	Jan. 23.	John Gold & Catharine, his wife	Peter
1763.			
Oct. 14.	Jan. 23.	Henry Johnsohn & Rachel, his wife	Rachel
1761.			
Sept. 30.		John Slact & Ann, his wife	Ann
1766.			
Nov. 30.		William & Ann Scobe	Elexander
1763.			
Jan. 27.	April 17.	John Poillon & Margret, his wife	Peter
Jan. —.		Jonathan Lewis & Mary, his wife	Mary
Jan. 4.		Henry Perine & Ann, his wife	Margret
April 3.		John Journey & Martha, his wife	Elizabeth
		John Morgan & Debrough	Jesse
Aug. 28.		Mathew Decker & Miriam, his wife	Israel
1764.	1764.		
March 20.	May 20.	John Moor & Mary, his wife	Larans
Feb. 4.	May 27.	John Seguyn & Sarah, his wife	Henry
April 23.	June 3.	Henry Taylor & Guda, his wife	Peter
March 22.		James Seguyn & Caty, his wife	Steven
May 10.		Anthony Van Pelt & Susanna, his wife	Susanna

BORN	BAPTIZED	PARENTS	CHILD
1764.			
April 12.		Daniel Vancleaf & Mattho, his wife	Daniel
April 3.		Jeremiah Stillwell & Yetty, his wife	Peter
1757.			
April 17.		James Howell & Elisabeth, his wife	Richard
1758.			
Dec. 20.			Susanna
1761.			
Feb. 15.		"Here is the age of four of James Howells chileren & Elizabeth's his wives"	Jams
1764.			
Feb. 16.			Elizabeth
	1764.		
June 2.	July 1.	John Halsted & Elizabeth, his wife	Elizabeth
April 26.		Abraham Johnson & Rachel, his wife	Mary
1763.			
Dec. 1.		Daniel Stilwell & Araienty (or Ann), his wife	Jeremiah
1764.			
May 22.	July 29.	Henry Prine & Susanna, his wife	Peter
1763.			
Jan. 16.	Aug. 27.	Joseph Morrel & Martha, his wife	Mary
1764.			
April 28.	Sept. 21.	John Chrips & Margret, his wife	William
Sept. 11.		Abraham Jones & Jene, his wife	John
Sept. 30.		John Latterette & Susanna, his wife	John
	Nov. 8.	Edward Blak & Anne, his wife	a child
	Nov. 4.	John Bedell & Hannah, his wife	Cornelius
	Nov. 4.	Silas Bedell & Febey, his wife	Hannah
Oct. 21.	Dec. 23.	Antony Stoutinbura & Mary, his wife	Mary
	1765.		
Nov. 26.	Jan. 13.	Nicolas Baker & Elizabeth, his wife	Catrin
1762.			
Nov. 1.		Richard Larrens & Mary, his wife	Anne
1764.			
Oct. 18.		" "	Elizabeth
Dec. 11.	Jan. 20.	James Lawtoret & Elizabet, his wife	John
1765.			
Feb. 6.	March 31.	Peter Cole & Susanna, his wife	Henry
Feb. 10.		John Van Pelt & Margret, his wife	John
Feb. 11.	April 14.	Dennice Vandelip & Martha, his wife	Elias

BORN	BAPTIZED	PARENTS	CHILD
1759.			
Oct. 26.		Capt. Drummoncts & Susan Grasbeek, his wife	Alexander
1765.			
Jan. 16.		" "	Mary
	1765.	Godparents, A. Waters & wife	
Jan. 24.	April 21.	Tenaton Lewis & Mary, his wife	Francis, dau.
1764.			
Aug. 23.		George Johnson & Nanne, his wife	George
1765.			
Dec. 13.	May 12.	Thomas Mashel & Sarah, his wife	Elcy
March 15.		Henry Johnson & Elizabeth, his wife	Nathaniel
1763.			
Dec. —.	July 21.	John Decker & Elizabeth, his wife	Nanne
1765.			
April —.		" "	Febey
May 28.	July 21.	John Journey & Martha, his wife	James
1736.			
April 12.	Aug. 4.	Mary Rolph, wife of Abraham	Swame
1765.			
March 6.		Abraham Swame & Mary, his wife	John Rolph
1742.			
April 10.	Aug. 18.	Larance Rolph, adult	
Jan. 22.		Patience Lake, his wife	
1765.			
Feb. 12.		Larance Rolph & Patience Lake, his wife	William Roberson
Aug. 9.	Oct. 13.	John Michaux & Sarah, his wife	Ann
June 25.		Abraham Winants & Mary, his wife	Mary
1763			
Nov. 8.		" "	Cornelas
1765.			
Aug. 7.		John Butler & Rachel, his wife	Sarah
Aug. 10.		Silas Totten & Charity, his wife	Joseph
Sept. 8.		Isaac Bogart & Rachel, his wife	Hannah
Oct. 4.		Richard Wood & Mary, his wife	Mary
Oct. 9.	Nov. 24.	Larrance Hillyer & Anne, his wife	Abram
Oct. 5.		Christian Smitt & Hester, his wife	Christian, son
July 9.	Dec. 15.	Lambert Merrell & Tabitha, his wife	Richard
	Dec. 15.	Samuel Britten & Mary, his wife	Patience
	1766.		
Oct. 4.	Jan. 3.	Daniel Winant & Lizabet, his wife	Rachel

BORN	BAPTIZED	PARENTS	CHILD
1765.	1766.		
July 6.		Peter Androvet & Caty, his wife	Peter
Oct. 28. 1762.		Peter Winant & Cristyan, his wife	Cornelous
May 9. 1765.		David Dye & Mary, his wife	Anne
April 13. 1766.		Children of David & Mary Dye	Elizabeth / John David
Jan. 5.		Benjamin Cots & Catrin, his wife	Daniel
Jan. 31.	March 16.	Jams Lawtoret & Elezebet, his wife	Johnaton
March 6.	April 6.	Abraham Cole & Hannah, his wife	Abraham
Feb. 1. 1765.		Henry Perine & Hannah, his wife	Abraham
Nov. 19. 1764.	April 13.	Moses Doutey & Anne, the mother	Rachel
April 4. 1766.	April 13.	Jacob Van Pelt & Elezebeth, the mother	Elezebeth
Feb. 19.		" "	Mary
Jan. 30.		Daniel Vanclef & Marta, the mother	Benjamine
March 22.	May 11.	Abraham Crocheron & Elezebet, the mother	Henry
March 22. 1765.		Nathaniel Brittain & Mary, the mother	Richard
Dec. 23. 1766.		David Laforge & Mary, the mother	Necolas
March 10.		Henry Taler & Judith, the mother	Alezebeth
April 14.		John Sugan & Sary, the mother	Catrin
Jan. 26. 1765.		John Wood & Margret, the mother	Mary
Sept. 12. 1766.		Peter Noe & Mary	Margret
April 5.		James Seguine & Catrin	James
April 10.		Edward & Elezebet Blake	Winety (dau.)
April 21.		William & Mary Blake	William
May 27. 1765.	July 13.	George Johnson & Nanne	George
April 4. 1766.		Joseph & Martha Morrell	John
June 3. 1765.		Moses & Ledde Dupuy	Necolas
Aug. 18. 1766.		Nathaniel & Eleanor Johnson	Nathaniel
	Aug. 3.	Christopher & Febe Garrison	Elener
July 30.		James & Lezebeth Howell	John
July 2.		Joseph Bedell & Catrine	Martha

BORN	BAPTIZED	PARENTS	CHILD
1765.	1766.		
June 14.		Benjamin & Mary Parker	John
Oc. 26.	Sept. 4.	Boude & Mary Vanderlip	Thomas
1766.			
March 11.		Henry & Rachel Johnson	Nathaniel
June 27.		John & Easters Dubois	Mary
Aug. 20.	Nov. 16.	James & Francis Polon	Adder
1765.			
Jan. 10.		Hamilton & Rachel Martin	Ann
1766.			
April 5.		Roger & Ann Barns	Margret
Nov. 9.		David & Elzebeth Lawtorette	Catrin
Oct. 30.		Jeremiah & Hettee Stillwell	Rebaco
1767.	1767(?.)		
Dec. 1.	Feb. 1.	Richard & Mary Laurence	Susanna
Jan. 1.		Capt. Drummond & Susan, the mother. God-parents were, Thomas Lynch, Mrs. Lynch, Mrs. Dongan	Jacobina
1766.	1767.		
Sept. 22.	March 25.	John & Margrit Crips	Willum
May 15.		Joseph & Elizabeth Silve	Nanne
1765.			
Dec. 22.		Doctor Frost & Tomagine, the mother	John Thomas
1766.			
Sept. 8.		Stephen & Ledy Mercereau	Sary
Dec. 24.		Thomas & Sarah Marshal	Elizabeth
1767.			
Feb. 1.		Benjamin & Sarah Lesalyear	Nicolas
Feb. 14.	May 17.	Jacob & Hannah Belew	Sarah
Jan. 3.		Lambert & Thalita (Tabitha) Merrell	Johnaton
May 13.	June 21.	John & Margret Van Pelt	James
April 29.		Jonathan & Mary Lewis	Elizabeth
March 17.	June 28.	John Journey & Martha, the	Mary
1766.			
Aug. 6.		John & Elizabeth Decker	Rubin
1767.			
June 5.		Henry & Hannah P r i n e (prob. Perine)	Henry
July 17.	Aug. 16.	James & Naomi Prine	Supfiah
Aug. 3.		Joseph Van Pelt & Elizabeth	James
July 18.		George & Dorety Barn	Elizabeth
1766.			
Nov. 26.		John & Dorcas Bodine	Vinsant
1767.			
Aug. 26.	Dec. 13.	Nathaniel Eleanor & Johnson	Jacob
	Dec. 30.	William Scobe, "a Dult"	
1766.			
Aug. 16.		Samuel & Nanne Lining	John
	1768.		
	Jan. 15.	Isaac Lacreman (Lakerman),	"a Dult"

BORN	BAPTIZED	PARENTS	CHILD
1768.	1768.		
Jan. 26.	March 20.	Isaac & Martha Lacreman	David
March 11.	April 10.	Jacob Van Pelt & Elizabeth	Mary
1767.			
Dec. 25.		Abraham Lacreman & ———.	Margaret
1768.			
Jan. 29.		John & Margaret Wood	John Grondain
1767.	April 8.	Richard Dongan & ———.	Thomas
Oct. 2.		Isaac & Rachel Bogart	Mary
1768.			
Feb. 24.		Silas Totten & Charity	Ephrahim
—— 14.	May 15.	Richard & Mary Wood	Mary
March 1.	June 19.	Edward & Elizabeth Blake	John
Feb. 20.		Henry & Judith Taylor	William
March 15.		John & Sarah Michan	John
March 23.		Henry & Balette Butler	Nathaniel
1752.			
Feb. 27.		Elizabeth, an adult dau. of Timothy Wood	
1750.			
June 15.	July 3.	Elizabeth, an adult dau. of Matthew Jones	
1768.			
July 28.	Aug. 28.	Daniel & Martha Vancleaf	Martha
March 2.		Daniel & Sarah Mac Swan	Elizabeth
Aug. 25.		Abraham & Elizabeth Egberts	Benjamin
1765.			
Dec. 9.	Oct. 9.	Matthew & Anastace Lisk	Elizabeth
1766.			
Dec. 7.		" "	Moses
Dec. 22.		Abraham Harris & Ann Lacreman	Margret
1768.			
Sept. 9.		James & Elizabeth Latterette	Elizabeth
June 7.		Nicolas & Sarah Lazaryear	Johanna
July 2.		Stephen & Ann Cole	Ann
	(bap.)	Mary, wife of Josua Mersereau	
Oct. 4.		"Paci" dau. of Josua & Mary Mersereau	
Nov. 30.		William & Ann Scoby	Alexander
Nov. 14.		Lawrance & Ann Hilyer	Elizabeth
Nov. 11.	1769.	Peter & Addie Burbank	Martha
Sept. 19.	Feb. 12.	Nathaniel & Mary Britton	William
Nov. 8.		Moses & Caty Egbert	Abraham
1759.			
June 4.		Edward & Ann Prine	Joseph
1761.			
May 24.		" "	Mary
1763.			
Nov. 23.		" "	Sarah
1766.			
July 6.		" "	Edward
1768.			
Nov. 29.		All children of above	Henry

BORN	BAPTIZED	PARENTS	CHILD
1769.	1769.		
Jan. 1.		Moses & Liddy Dupuy	Moses
1768.			
Nov. 4.	April —.	Lambert & Thalata Merrell	Elce
Oct. 11.		George & Dorothy Barns	John
1769.			
Jan. 10.		John & Martha Journeay	Ann
1766.			
Oct. 23.		William & Frances Granger	William
1769.			
March 16.	May 7.	George & Nanney Johnson	Jasper
March 15.		Anthony & Susanna Van Pelt	George
March 7.	June 4.	Paul & Mary Michau	Elizabeth
April 7.		Jonathan & Mary Lewis	Israel
1768.			
Dec. 11.		Abraham & Rachel Marshal	Mary
1769.			
May 2.		John & Caty Egberts	James
		Christopher Billopp & ——	John Willet
Mrrch 23.		Peter & Rebekah Mercereau	Sarah
1868.			
Feb. 26.		Richard Carbe(?) & Ann, his wife	Richard
1769.			
Nov. 16.	Dec. 24.	William & Mary Lake	William
Nov. 13.		John & Margaret Van Pelt	Peter
	1770.		
Oct. 2.	Jan. 1.	Nathaniel & Eleanor Johnson	Winant
1768.			
Dec. 13.		Thomas & Mary Butler	Catrin
1769.			
Nov. 17.		" "	Anthony
1768.			
Nov. 14.		Thomas & Tamer Frost	Elizabeth
1769.	1769.		
Nov. 20.	Dec. 8.	Capt. Drummond & Susanna. God-parents were, Monsr.	Susanna
1770.	1770.	Marquis De Conti & his wife	
Feb. 7.	April 8.	Richard & Mary Stillwell	Daniel
Jan. 31.		Stephen & Ann Cole	John
March 5.		Edward & Martha Jones	Barent
Jan. 15.	May 13.	Abraham & Margaret Crocheron	Daniel
April 13.		Henry & Nanne Crocheron	John
April 13.		Jacob & Elizabeth Van Pelt	Susanna
March 21.		Lambert & Tabitha Merrell	Tabitha
March 3.	July 1.	Abraham & Mary Winant	Elizabeth
May 6.		Silas & Charity Totten	Mary
May 5.		Josua & Mary Mercereau	Stephen
1764.			
March 20.		"Lidia Coade"	Mary

BORN	BAPTIZED	PARENTS	CHILD
1770.	1770.		
Jan. 29.		Abraham & Elizabeth Egberts	Sarah
March 6.		Benjamin & Sarah Drake	Elizabeth
April 8.	July 29.	Isaac & Easter Cole	Edward
July 1.	Sept. 1.	Abraham & Hannah Cole	John Bedell
Feb. 4.		Abraham & Ann "Parelee"	Abraham
June 9.	Oct. 7.	Winant & Mary Johnson	Winant
1769.			
March 30.		John & Dorcas Bodine	Nanne
1770.			
Sept. 18.		Richard & Easter Christopher	John Garrison
July 11.	Oct. 14.	John & Jude Write	John
Sept. 13,		Anthony & Mary Egberts	Reuben
on Thursday about ten in the morning			
July 5.		Henry & Belletie Butler	Sarah
Sept. 1.	Nov. 4.	Peter & Christian Winant	George
Sept. 23.		Daniel & Heletie Pethman	Daniel
Oct. 19.		Moses & Catrin Egberts	Ann
Aug. 24.	Dec. 2.	John & Sarah Micheau	Mary
Oct. 28.	Dec. 9.	Peter & Margret Pollon	John
Nov. 19.		Silas & Mary Bedell	Phoebe
1771.	1771.		
Jan. 22.	April 21.	James & Elizabeth Lawtorette	Catrin
1770.			
Nov. 16.		" "	Elisabeth
Oct. 14.		Isaac & Rachel Bogard	John
1771.			
March 25.	May 26.	William & Mary Lake	Barent
1770.			
Oct. 11.		Matthias & Mary Duboys	Mary
1773.	1773.		
April 12.	June 13.	David & Elizabeth Lattorette	Francis, dau.
1771.			
May 7.		Dowa & Margaret Johnson	Ann
April 7.		John & Catrin Bedell	Hyllite
	1771.		
	June 23.	John Wood, adult	
	June 23.	William & Sara Crips	Elizabeth
June 17.		Isaac & Jemima Roper	Elizabeth
1770.			
Sept. 20		Henry & Jude Taylor	John
Aug. 4.		William & Nanne Scobey	John
1772.			
Dec. 21.		" "	Liddie
1771.			
July 7.		Samuel & Mary Brittan	Addra (dau.)
	1771.		
June 10.	Aug. 4.	Joseph & Catrin Bedell	Catrin
Jan. 1.		George & Dorothy Barns	Roger

BORN	BAPTIZED	PARENTS	CHILD
1771.	1771..		
July 21.		Isaac & Matthew (Martha, Margaret?) Lacreman	Jacob
Aug. 7.		John & Martha Jurnee	Richard
Aug. 24.		Oliver & Sarah Taylor	Elizabeth
July 19.		Stephen & Catrin Bedell	David
Aug. 17.	Oct. 6.	George Johnson	Thomas
Aug. 27.		Peter & Becke Mercereau	Daniel
Aug. 5.		Lambert & Tabitha Merrel	Abraham
1770.			
Feb. 14.		James & Elizabeth Howell	Edward
1771.			
June 10.	Oct. 27.	Jacob & Elsey Lazalyear	Richard
July 26.		Edward & Ann Prine	Ann
Sept. 29.		Benjamin & Mary Parker	Ephraim
Sept. 11.		Stephen & Ann Cole	Stephen
Dec. 2.		Joseph & Elizabeth Van Pelt	Theunis
Nov. 11.		John & Catrine Egberts	Tunis & Eleanor
	1772.		
1772.	Jan. —.	Elisabeth Crips, adult	
Dec. 17.	March 22.	Winant & Mary Johnson	Suffiah
April 4.	April 12.	Abraham & Elisabetn Lacreman	Abraham
Dec. 26.		Henry & Nanny Crocheron	Henry
March 31.		Edward & Martha Jones	Abraham
Jan. 10.		Matthias & Mary Dubois	Lewis
March 6.		Peter & Margret Pollon	Peter
Dec. 15.	May 24.	John & Judith Wright	Judith
April 25,		Antony & Mary Egberts	Martha
"Saterday about ten in ye morning."			
	May 27.	William & Sarah Jennance	Eleanor
Feb. 18.		David & Mary Laforge	Cornelis
1751.			
July 17.		Son of Mattice Johnson	William Johnson, adult
1772.			
March 13.		John & Margrit Van Pelt	Margrit
Jan. 31.		John & Sara Seguine	Catrine
1771.			
Dec. 26.	Aug. 16.	John & Ann Simonson	Francis, dau.
	Sept. 6.	Josua & Mary Mercereau	Josua
1772.			
Aug. 30.		Richard & Easter Christopher	James Grover
Aug. 15.		Jonathan & Mary Lewis	Phoebe
Sept. 18.		Stephen & Mary Wood	Mary
1773.	1773.		
Nov. 7.	Dec. 12.	John Dubois & Mary Geffers	Catrin
1772.			
Sept. 24.	Jan. 10.	Abram & Hannah Cole	Susanna
Oct. 11.		William & Mary Lacreman	Sarah
Oct. 23.		Abram & Rachel Marshal	John

BORN	BAPTIZED	PARENTS	CHILD
1769.	1773.		
Nov. 15.	Jan. 24.	Abranam & Rachel Harris	Richard
1772.			
Nov. 4.	" "	" " "	David
Oct. 2.	April 4.	Edward & Elisabeth Blake	Edward
1773.			
Feb. 9.		Benjamin & Sarah Lazalyear	Jacob
Feb. 24.		Lambert & Tabita Merrell	Ann
1772.			
Nov. 24.	May 9.	Isaac & Margret Lacreman	William
Oct. or			
Nov. 25.		William & Mary Lake	Joseph
1773.			
March 4.		John & Geney Crocheron	Mary
May 6.		Egbert & Rachel Brasted	Egbert
April 9.		Silas & Mary Bedell	James
	July 13.	Anthony Burd, his wife & sister & 3 of his children	
March 26.	Aug. 1.	Abraham & Phoebe Decker	Noah
1772.	Aug. 1.	John & Margret Wood	Stephen
Dec. 5.		Benjamin & Sarah Drake	Francis, dau.
1773.			
July 2.		Matthew & Meryan Decker	Hannah
July 31.		Samuel & Mary Britton	Mary
June 28.		Barent & Elizabeth Slect	Barent
Oct. 23.		William & Mary Smith. John Hilliard, Jr., & Francis Hilliard, Godfather & Godmother	Susannah
	1774.		
Dec. 6.	Feb. 6.	John & Ann Simonson	John
1774.			
Feb. 17.	March 25.	Thomas & Tamer Frost	William Errell
1766.			
Sept. 8.		Stephen & Lidde Mercereau	Sarah
1768.			
Dec. 6.		" " "	Daniel
1774.			
Feb. 14.		" " "	Stephen
	March 25.	Lydia, wife of Stephen Mercereau, Jr.	
	" "	Mary, adult dau. of Stephen Wood	
Feb. 9.		Edward & Martha Jones	Margrit
Feb. 27.		Peter & Margrit Pollon	Elizabeth
March 29.		John & Mary Hillyar	Mary
March 22.		John & Juda Whrite	Andrew
April 13.		Winant & Mary Johnson	David
1772.			
Feb. 18.	Aug. 21.	Daniel & Martha Vancleaf	Sarah
1774.			
April 14.		" " "	Mary

BORN	BAPTIZED	PARENTS	CHILD
1774.			
May 18.		Abraham & Catrine Parlee	Martha
May 4.		Lambert & Tabitha Merrell	Jonathan
Aug. 23.		Henry & Nanne Crocheron	Jacob
July 29.		John & Hannah Winant	Elizabeth
Aug. 7, about 1 o'clock in the morning		Antony & Mary Egberts	Elener
Aug. 31.		John & Margret Van Pelt	Hannah
July 2.		Charles & Elizabeth Lafarge	Catrine
Oct. 18.		Joseph & "Ander" Cubberly	James
1775.	1775.		
Jan. 23.	March 26.	James & Susannah Guyon	Ann
Feb. 11.		John & Mary Dubois	Edward
Feb. 11.		Jonathan & Mary Lewis	Joseph
Feb. 5.		Stephen & Ann Cole	John
Sept. 20.		Daniel & Hilletie Petman	Catrin
Feb. 1.		Peter & Charity Winant	Isaac
April 8.		Daniel & Sarah Crocheron	Mary
March 6.		Richard & Mary Cole	Abram
April 10.		Abram & Phoebe Decker	Charles
April 20.		Benjamin & Sarah Drake	Rachel
May 21.		Stephen & Mary Wood	Elizabeth
March 28.		Silas & Mary Bedell	John
April 15, Saturday		William & Ann Scobe	Elizabeth
		Mary Wood, adult	
March 10.		Abram & Rachel Marshal	Martha
April 4.	June 5.	Nathaniel & Catrin Britton	Mary
1774.			
Nov. 11.		Thomas & Mary Powel	Elisabeth
	June 5.	Nathaniel Brittan } adults Nicholas Brittan Mary Susanna Adra	
1775.			
April 22.		James & Elizabeth Lautoret	Henry
March 13.		William & Mary Lake	Mary
		William Larance	two children
		Henry & Liddy Taylor	Abram
Jan. 19.		John & Francis Slact	Francis, dau.
Aug. 21.		William & Mary Smith. Godparents, Oliver Taylor & Sarah, his wife	John
April 6.		John & Cathrine Cole	Abraham
July 3.	Oct. 3.	Joseph & Elleanor George	Catarine
Oct. 7.	Nov. —.	Isaac & Martha Lacreman	Joseph
		Peter & Rebecka Mercereau	John
May 9.		Richard & Esther Christopher	Joseph
	1776.		
	March 11.	Olliver & Sarah Taylor	Frances
1776.		Steven & Catrin Bedell	child
Feb. 14.		Cornelius & Elisabeth Vancleaf	Hester

BORN	BAPTIZED	PARENTS	CHILD
	1776.	John & Mary Butler	Henry
	April 21.	James & Ann Walls. Sureties, George Shaw, Nathaniel Moor, Mary Shaw	George Nathaniel
1775. Oct. 28.		John & Martha Jeirnee	Ann
1776. Jan. 10.		Barent Martling & Nanne Jusen	Barent
	May 5.	Daniel & Loretta Duke. Sureties, Terence Kerin, Terence & Susanna Reilly	Daniel
Feb. 13.		Peter Polon & Margaret	Catrin
Feb. 10.		Edward & Elce Jones	Elce
April 18.	June 9.	John & Mary Hillyar	John
May 15.		John & Johannah Winant	Jacob
	July 19.	"A child of ye Army"	
	July 21.	"A child of ye Scotch"	Charles by name
	July 28.	Daniel Mac Daniel & Catrine	Dunkan
1771. Jan. 16.		Lawrence & Ann Hilyer	Emm
1773. Feb. 26.		" " "	William
1775. Sept. 3.		" " "	Margret
	1777. May 12.	Daniel Lake & Margret, his wife	Daniel
1776. Nov. 24.	Feb. 25.	Daniel & Elizabeth Corson. Bap. by Rev. Mr. Charlton	William Howe
Aug. 2.		William & Mary Lakerman	Susannah
	1779. March —.	John Write & wife	Mary

(In the corner of this entry is a word blotted and after it " 23 Nov., 1789.")

	Sept. 19.	James & Patience Wood, of the 37 Regt. 19 Foot	Elizabeth
1779. Dec. —.	1780. Sunday, May 11.	Isaac Simorson & Elizabeth. Bap. by Mr. Field	John
Dec. 3.	May 14.	Obadiah Jones & Mary, his wife	John
Aug. 5.		Henry Curshon & wife	Daniel
1778. Aug. 28.	May 14.	Edward & Martha Jones. Bap. by Mr. Field	Daniel
	June 11, 4 mos. old.	Joseph & Anna (De Silvee perhaps, name illegible)	Anna
	June 4.	Joseph Coberly	a child
1780. April 15.		Stephen Wood & Elce, his wife	Elisabeth

BORN	BAPTIZED	PARENTS	CHILD
	1780.		
	June 4.	Joseph Wood & Ann, his wife	Stephen Lawrence
	June 4.	James Wood & Ann, his wife	John
	June 4.	Matias Decker & Lidda, his wife	David
	June 18.	Abram Cole A Corporal of 22nd Regt.	Charity child
1779.			
May 19.	June 25.	William & Eliday Lake	Daniel
	June 25.	William Smith	Sarah
1780.			
Aug. 25.		Benjamin & Sarah Drake	Anna
July 24.		Charles Morgan & Catharine, his wife	David
June 15.		John Write & Judy, his wife	Hanna
1781.	1782.		
May 25.	Feb. 5.	John Bogart & Anna, his wife. Bap. by Mr. Howland	Mary
1782.			
May 17.		Joseph De Silva & Sarah, his wife	Elizabeth
1781.			
Nov. 19.		Jacob Vanderbilt & Rachel, his wife	Robert
1780.			
Sept. 28.		William Lake	John
1782.			
March 16.		William Lake	Sarah

"William Burbank entering Clerk of the Church of St. Andrews Begun May the 4th day in the year of our Lord 1783."

CHILDREN BAPTIZED BY REV. MR. ROLAND.

	1783.		
	June 2.	John Voke, Capt., & Mary, his wife	Christopher
	June 15.	Stephen Wood & Alice, his wife	John
	June 15.	Hery Corshong & Nancy, his wife	Richard
1783.			
Feb. 20.		James Wood & Nancy, his wife	Mary
July 29, b. about sunset	Aug. 17.	William Sharp	Samuel
Aug. 1.		John Lambert	Elizabeth
1784.			
Feb. 13.		Jacob Crocheron & Ann, his wife	Elizabeth
April 18.		Isaac Lakeman & Jane, his wife	Elizabeth Johnson
Feb. 3.		Richard Weeb & Noyche, his wife	Alchey
March 6.		Timothy Wood & Mary, his wife	John

BORN	BAPTIZED	PARENTS	CHILD
1783.			
June 20.		Peter Lefarge & Martha, his wife	Dorcas
1784.			
May 8.		Daniel Crocheron & Sarah, his wife	Catrine
July 6.		Robert Barnes & Elisabeth, his wife	Ann
June 23.		John Burbank & Elizabeth, his wife	Margaret
1783.			
Dec. 10.		Israel Bedell	Meriah
1784.			
Oct. 15.		Stephen Wood & Alice, his wife	Stephen
1785.			
March 22.		Henry Crocheron & Ann, his wife	Abraham
April 22.		John Crocheron & Fithy, his wife	Abraham
	1785.		
	June 5.	Stephen Wood & Mary, his wife	Stephen
Oct. 2.		James Scarret & Mary, his wife	a daughter
	Nov. 20.	Peter Winant & Ann, his wife	Daniel & Ann
1786.			
Feb. 7.		Edward Prine & Sarah, his wife	Edward
July 7.		James Latorette & Mary, his wife	David
June 3.		John Burbank & Elizabeth, wife	William
March 19.		Nathaniel Johnson & Nelly, his wife	Cornelius Vanderbilt
Sept. 1.		James Burbank & Nelly, his wife	Abraham
1787.			
Feb. 14.		Winant Winant & Ann, his wife	Mary
March 17.		John More & his wife	Mary
April 10.		David Laforge & Catharine, his wife	David
April 15.		Henry Crocheron & Ann, his wife	David
Oct. 6.		Abraham Crocheron & Mary	Eleanor
July 29.		Charles Morgan & Catrine, his wife	John
1788.			
June 9.		Daniel Crocheron	Daniel

"October 5th, 1788, the REVEREND RICHARD MOOR Begun Devine Serves at the Church of Saint Andrew."

	1788.		
1778.	Oct. 5.	John Pillion	Catharine
Dec. 15.		Stephen Wood & Eles, his wife	Mary

BORN	BAPTIZ	PARENTS	CHILD
1786.			
Nov. 4.		Stephen Wood & Eles, his wife	Cornelis
1788.			
Sept. 22.		" " "	Abraham
	1789.		
	Feb. 22.	John Pollion	James
	Feb. 22.	Mary Doty, adult dau. of Moses Doty	
	May 24.	William Heady, adult	
	May 24.	William Heady & Hester, his wife	Cathrine
1789.			
Feb. 23.		John Simonson & Ann, his wife	Stephen Bedell
	June 28.	Abraham Crocheron & Mary, his wife	Benjamin
	July 5.	Martha Baker, adult	
	July 5.	Daniel Mersereau & Susan, his wife	Ann
	July 15.	John Crocheron & Fithee, his wife	Sophia
July 10.		Barzillai Grover & Cristine, his wife	William
March 20.		John More & his wife	Peter Vanpelt
	Sept. 20.	Walter Dungan & Abigail, his wife	Abigail Simonson
	Sept. 20.	Vincent Wood	William Barber
Sept. 24.	Sept. 24.	Henry Crocheron & Ann, his wife	Reuben
	Sept. 24.	James Wood & Ann, his wife	Susannah
Sept. 6.		Peter Wandel & Sarah, his wife	Mathew
Aug. 6.		William Prine & Fanny, his wife	Mary
	Nov. 1.	Nicholas Journey & wife	Nicholas
1790.	1790.		
Jan. 6.	March 2.	Abraham Crocheron & Jane, his wife	Abraham

Peter Poillon entered as clerk, 9th May, 1790.

1790.	1790.		
April 2.	May 9.	Joseph & Catharine Decker	Hannah Bedell
1789.	May 16.	Catharine Dorsett, adult	
Aug. 16.		James & Anna Johnson	Ann
	May 15.	David & Catharine Laforge	Henry Seguine
	" "	Abram Manee & wife	Isaac
	" "	Thomas & Susan Butler	Maria
	" "	Charles Laforge & wife	Charles
	June 20.	Vincent & Jane Bodine	Martha
	June 27.	William & Miranda Perine	Peter

BORN	BAPTIZED	PARENTS	CHILD
1790.	1790.		
	July 7.	Peter & Ann Winant	Susannah
March 15.		Charles & Catharine Morgan	Mary
May 30.		Joseph & Catharine Lake	Patience
June 9.		Robert & Hester Barnes	Abraham Lakerman
June 29.		Isaac Lakerman & wife	Margrette
	Oct. 24.	John & Margrette Seguine	John
	" "	John & Susannah Latourette	Susannah
	Nov. 21.	Cornelius & Catharine Winants	Cornelia
1786.			
May 27.		John & Hester Williams	Rebecca
1790.			
Nov. 25.		" " "	William
	1791.		
	May 1.	Jacob & Audra Simonson	Elizabeth
1791.	June 26.	Daniel & Ann Mersereau	Cornelia
June 1.		Abraham & Mary Crocheron	Elizabeth
1790.			
Nov. 26.		Peter Laforge & his wife	a child
1791.			
Sept. 10.		James & Mary Scarret	James
Sept. 24.		John & Fanny Taylor	Oliver
Oct. 9.		Edward & Patience Perine	Mary
Oct. 24.		Jacob & Margaret Seguine	Catharine
Sept. 20.		Abraham & Sally Perine	Peter Razeau
1792.			
June 1.		Robert & Hester Barnes	Margaret
Dec. 12.		Stephen & Audra Kettletas	Elizabeth
	1793.		
	Oct. 27.	John & Margrette Seguine	Henry
	Nov. 3.	John & Margaret Poillon	Jacob
1795.	1796.		
Sept. 26.	Jan. 5.	Benjamin & Ann Taylor	Esther Pamela
	Jan. 6.	George & Ann Young	Thomas
Aug. 27.	Jan. 24.	Isaac & Jane Lakerman	Isaac
Sept. 26.		Richard & Catharine Wood	Mary

Marriages.

1754,	June	2.	Daniel Zeluff, Hannah Clarck
	Oct.	7.	John Slinsby, Joannah Skinner
	Oct.	24.	Peter Johnson, Mary Taylor
	Dec.	16.	William Morgan, Elizabeth Winter
	Dec.	17.	David Woodruff, Sarah Zeluff
1755,	May	28.	Peter Griffiths, Hannah Banson
	June	9.	Samuel Stilwell, Hannah Van Pelt
	June	16(?).	Peter Savary, Esther Garrison
	July	13.	Joseph Yates, Sarah Chysick
	July	13.	Jacob Cain, Franky Van Pelt
	March	8.	Barnt Simonson, Abigail Croshun
	April	25.	Samuel Denike, Jean Wright
1756,	Jan.	4.	Ephraim Taylor, Elizabeth Morgan
1757,	June	12.	James Mac Daniel, Freelove Lewis
	July	28.	Isaac Simonson, Elizabeth Wood
	Aug.	30.	Thomas Trott, Gizeburt Durland
	Sept.	15.	John Stilwell, Olly Taylor
1759,	June	14.	Isaac Pepperill, Hannah Johnson
1760,	Feb.	3.	Edward Newman, Hannah Griffis
1761,	Jan.	5.	John Crips, Martha Bety
1763,	——	—.	James Hilyear, Mary Frome
			John Goodman, Hannah Van Pelt
1764,	——	—.	Isaac Johnson, Ellender Bowman
1765,	Jan.	10.	Beniamin Hetfield, Nanne Merrel
1766,	Dec.	16.	Samuel Leyning, Nenney Powel
——,	Feb.	—.	Joseph Allason, Elizabeth Rineo
——,	March	28.	Joseph Silva, Elizabeth Kingston

Names of those Published.

1766,	May	25.	Cornelius Cole, Ann —yellard
	May	25.	Stephen Bedell, Catrin Latorett
	Nov.	9.	John Silvester, Hannah Simonson
1767,	Oct.	18.	Isaac Pritchet, Elizabeth Creed
	Oct.	25.	James Clark, Easter Crain
	Nov.	1.	John Baker, Ellender Creed
1768,	June	—.	John Degroat, Mary Larrance
	July	24.	Nicholas Imyard, Jemima Wood
1769,	Jan.	15.	Timothy Wood, Sarah Rezeau, wid.
	Nov.	5.	Andrew Brown, Jane Simson
	Nov.	5.	Benjamin Bouth, Ann Bush
1771,	April	28.	Moses Decker, Elizabeth Wood
	Aug.	18.	William Jannance, Sarah Kingston
1772,	March	—.	Isaac Johnson, Ploney Frome
1773,	Aug.	15.	John Radfort, Rebecca Plummer
1774,	Aug.	21.	Lambert Jenners, Mary Mitchel
	Oct.	26.	Richard Cole, Mary Spragg
	Aug.	13.	Abraham Mitchel, Susanna Janance
1775,	Nov.	12.	John Seguine, Rachel Mitchel
			Matthias Decker, Lidde Milburn
1776,	Jan.	28.	John Breasted, Elizabeth Grace

1776, Aug.   4. Abraham Prall, Sarah Cannon
      Aug.   4. William Merrell, Ann Merrell

REGISTER OF MARRIAGES COPIED BY REV. DAVID MOORE FROM HIS PRIVATE RECORDS FOR HIS SON RICHARD CHANNING MOORE.

1788, Oct.   —. Richard Lake, —— Simonson
                 John Ammerman, —— Bush
      Dec. 31. Peter Perine, Mary Beedle
1789, Jan. 14. Peter Androvet, Elizabeth Slack
      Jan. 18. Jacob Garretson, Catharine Simonson
                 John Slack, Elizabeth Wynant
      March —.   Peter Vandel, Sarah Vancleif
                 John Bauman, —— Decker
      April 5. Isaac Simonson, Elizabeth Bird
      June   7. Vincent Bedine, Jane Blake
      Oct.   6. Adrian Bancker, Elizabeth Decker
      Oct.   9. John Scarret, Mary Burbank
                 David Lewis, Susan Rezeau
      Dec. 20. Thomas Butler, Mary Herod
1790, Jan.   3. John Simonson, Alice Marshal
      Jan.   5. Matthias Swaim, Eleanor Clendenny
      Jan. 17. Abraham Poillon, Susan Cole
      Jan. 22. Jacob Simonson, Adrian Poillon
      Feb. 14. John Braisted, Nauche Marlin
      March 16. Samuel Lackerman, Catharine Crowel
      June   7. Edward Perine, Patience Mersereau
      July 14. Peter Wynant, Mary Wynant
      July 25. Reuben Decker, Mary Swaim
      Aug. 17. Michael Freeland, Mary Blake
      Aug. 24. Abraham Perine, Sarah Rezeau
      Sept. 6. Henry Mersereau, Elizabeth Laforge
      Oct.   3. Abraham Merril, Ann Merril
      Nov.   2. Mark Dissosway, Elizabeth Cortelyou
      Nov. 18. Abraham Waglum, Hannah Parlee
      Dec. 27. James Mott, Appolonia Scarret
1791, Jan. 26. Edward Perine, Adrian Guion
      Jan. 30. James Segang, Mary Guion
      April 24. Andrew Roomer, Susan Butler
      May   11. Abraham Jones, Ann Decker
      July   9. John McKay, Elizabeth Micheau
      Aug.   7. Lucius Chapin, Susan Rezeau
      Aug.   7. Isaac Decker, Margaret Jones
      Aug. 20. Peter Simonson, Ann Cole
      Sept. 8. William Van Brunt, Catharine Dissosway
      Sept. 29. John Swaim, Martha Housman
      Oct. 16. Richard Sylve, Hester Taylor
      Oct. 29. Jacob Slack, Jane Waglum
      Nov.   9. Nathaniel Johnson, Catharine Waglum
      Nov.   —. Thomas Crips, Mary Perine
      Dec.   6. Christina Smith, Catharine Egbert
1792, March 27. Edward Still, Ann Cubberly
      March 28. James Britton, Violetta Dissosway

1792,	April	29.	Richard Henderson, Mary Journeay
	July	5.	John Poillon, Elizabeth Segang
	Sept.	9.	Benjamin Taylor, Ann Decker
	Nov.	8.	Stephen Segang, Susanna Poillon
	Dec.	8.	George Van Pelt, Catharine Marlin
	Dec.	10.	Joseph Bush, Mary Johnson
1793,	Jan.	27.	John Hudson, Mary Everson
	Feb.	10.	John Crocheron, Hannah Houseman
	May	2.	John Barnes, Margaret Perine
	June	18.	Benjamin Schenck, Mary Holmes
	Aug.	5.	John Dixey, Susanna Vachereau
	Sept.	18.	Barnt Slack, Catharine Johnson
	Oct.	18.	Lawrence Brenan, Fanny Taylor
	Nov.	28.	James Bradish, Margaret Thompson
	Dec.	24.	Lewis Johnson, Phoebe Van Pelt
1794,	Jan.	22.	Daniel Prall, Ann Mersereau
	Feb.	3.	Stephen Wood, Damy Houseman
	Feb.	9.	Isaac Wood, Susan Lewis
	Feb.	12.	William Ralph, Mary Ann Wynant
	Feb.	12.	John Wood, Sarah Lackerman
	March	23.	John Johnson, Patty Bedell
	April	6.	Cornelius Lake, Susan Androvet
	April	6.	John Wynant, Sarah Decker
	June	2.	John Nicoll, Elizabeth Lisk
	July	25.	—— Scarret, —— Garretson
	Sept.	24.	Abraham Johnson, Jane Jennings
	Sept.	25.	Reuben Clason, Ann Lake
	Oct.	28.	Edward Haughwout, Ann Bogart
	Nov.	15.	George Wynant, Elizabeth Wynant
	Nov.	29.	Benjamin Parker, Phoebe Bedell
1795,	Jan.	7.	Richard Wood, Catharine Lackerman
	Jan.	21.	Henry Perine, Mary Wynant
	Jan.	27.	Lambert Bush, Mary Stilwell
	April	2.	Joseph Ralph, Catharine Wynant
	May	2.	William Barclay, Mary Van Clief
	June	13.	Benjamin Marlin, Anla Cosine
	July	28.	Jacob Johnson, Elizabeth Haughwout
	Aug.	15.	Lucas De Wine, Ann Marshall
	Dec.	16.	Robert De Groat, Elizabeth Betts
	Dec.	31.	—— Dempsey, —— Waglum
1796,	Jan.	6.	John Hillicker, Polly Betts
	Jan.	16.	Isaac Wynant, Patty Wynant
	Jan.	23.	David Johnson, Jane Wynant
	Feb.	10.	Joshua Waglum, Martha Cole
	Feb.	14.	Abraham Bond, Ann Wynant
	March	26.	Samuel Randolph, Mary McClean
	March	27.	Daniel Van Dusen, Ann Houseman
	May	3.	Peter Decker, Betsy Merril
	June	5.	Jacob Decker, Leah De Pugh
	Sept.	3.	John Marsh, Elizabeth Hooper
	Oct.	16.	Stephen Cole, Jane Mersereau
1797,	Feb.	22.	Jacob Crocheron, Mary Oakly

1797, April	1.	John Cole, Mary Wynant
May	24.	Samuel Britton, Polly La Torett
July	13.	Lewis Loper, Ann Micheau
July	15.	Isaac Woodward, Leanah Stillwell
July	16.	Isaac Parlee, Margaret Van Pelt
Aug.	3.	Daniel Crocheron, Elizabeth Wood
Sept.	11.	Charles Androvet, Margaret Slack
Oct.	10.	Ephraim Johnson, Catharine Laforge
Nov.	11.	Cornelius Cole, Francis Cole
Nov.	26.	Wynant Johnson, Catharine Guion
Dec.	3.	Andrew Cannon, Mary Wright
Dec.	5.	Peter Van Pelt, Mary Cologne
1798, Jan.	3.	Roger Barnes, Sally Lake
Jan.	20.	Joseph Lake, Elizabeth Van Pelt
July	19.	James Bedell, Hetty Packer
Aug.	12.	Abraham Auten, Jane Wynant
Aug.	30.	William Barclay, Patty Parlee
Sept.	5.	Jacob Mersereau, Mary Crocheron
Oct.	6.	Daniel Mersereau, Alida Lake
Oct.	14.	William Drake, Catharine Prickett
Nov.	29.	Daniel Crocheron, Jane Jones
1799, Jan.	20.	James Cubberly, Eleanor Ralph
June	1.	James Wood, —— Elston
June	22.	Samuel Holmes, Margaret Cole
Sept.	28.	John Simonson, Phoebe Wood
1800, Jan.	12.	John Guion, Elizabeth Butler
Feb.	8.	Daniel Mersereau, Elizabeth Wynant
April	13.	John Baker, Mary Lackerman
May	2.	—— Thompson, —— Lewis
June	19.	Henry Perine, Magdalen Simonson
June	28.	Andrew Spragg, Catharine Pryor
July	12.	Jacob Spragg, Margaret Wood
Aug.	7.	Moses Wynant, —— Wynant
Aug.	13.	Hery Segang, Jane Garretson
Aug.	10.	Abraham Bird, Elizabeth Swaim
Aug.	11.	John Hacher, Eliza Riker
Dec.	24.	Sylvanus Decker, Sarah Parker
1801, Jan.	7.	—— Mersereau, Deborah Britton
Feb.	—.	Isaac Lewis, —— Prall
April	—.	—— Baker, —— Wright
April	—.	Harmanus Bennett, Mary Segang
May	28.	Nicholas Crocheron, —— Wynant
June	2.	David Keisham, Hannah ——
June	21.	David Van Pelt, Hannah Wright
June	27.	Arthur Simonson, Harriot Pritchett
Oct.	1.	James Crips, Elis. Blake
Oct.	4.	Barney Egbert, Ann Taylor
Oct.	13.	Silas Reynolds, Rebecca Decker
Nov.	—.	—— Corson, Else Ayro
Dec.	13.	Peter Cortelyou, Sarah Van Pelt
Dec.	16.	Jeremiah Ayro, Jane Jennings
Dec.	19.	Daniel Wynant, Eliza Oakly

1801,	Dec.	22.	Isaac Jacques, Eliza Jones
	Dec.	24.	John Cole, Eliza Drake
1802,	Jan.	3.	John Marlin, Dorcas Laforge
	Jan.	14.	John Prall, Martha Latouretta
	Jan.	15.	James Campbell, Eliza Pew
	Feb.	17.	—— Laforge, —— Marlin
	April	28.	William Johnson, Catharine Marlin
	May	2.	Harmanus Guion, Eliza Holmes
	June	5.	Daniel Lake, Margaret Jackson
	July	—.	John Journeay, Patience Cole
	Aug.	21.	John Androvet, Ann Cole
	Nov.	21.	Stephen Mersereau, Lanah Wynant
	Nov.	28.	Abraham Jones, Else De Pugh
	Dec.	1.	James Guion, Ann Perine
	Dec.	5.	Matthew Decker, Francis Marlin
	Dec.	11.	Richare Lackerman, Catharine Lake
1803,	Jan.	18.	William Blake, Sarah Merrit
	March	2.	George Van Pelt, Ann Merril
			William King, Eliza Morgan
	March	31.	Daniel Lake, Mary Gifford
	July	5.	John Jones, —— Grandine
	Aug.	28.	George Barns, Sally Holmes
	Oct.	19.	John Seaman, Rebecca Benson
	Dec.	22.	Jacob Cole, Eliza Laforge
	Dec.	31.	John Mersereau, Ann Parlee
1804,	Jan.	4.	Peter Manne, Mary Pryor
	Jan.	7.	John Taylor, Sarah Yates
	Jan.	11.	Jesse Johnson, Rachel Totten
	Jan.	12.	Lewis DuBois, Jane Mersereau
	Jan.	21.	John Stevens, Lanah Lake
	March	31.	Cornelius Perine, Mary McClean
	April	21.	Richard Blake, Lydia Packer
	July	25.	S. Blake, —— Crocheron
	Aug.	11.	Saml. Marsh, Patty Seabrook
	Sept.	15.	John Laforge, Phoebe Bedell
	Oct.	13.	Isaac Decker, Elizabeth Christopher
	Oct.	31.	John Smart, Eleanor Wade
	Nov.	7.	John Van Dyke, Jane Seaman
	Dec.	11.	Joseph Totten, Mary Cubberly
	Dec.	23.	John Wood, Barbara Van Pelt
	Dec.	24.	John Fountain, Catharine Fountain
	Dec.	30.	Nathaniel Britton, Margaret Bedell
1805,	Feb.	20.	James Johnson, Letitia Totten
	March	5.	Stephen Segang, Margaret Guion
	Nov.	16.	Josselyn Shuttleworth, Mary Robinson
	Nov.	17.	William Cairns, Sarah McDavit
1806,	Jan.	12.	Joseph Bedell, Hetty Segang
	Feb.	8.	James Leforge, Catharine Wynant
	April	12.	Uriah Henderson, Addra Guyon
	June	3.	Amos Abrams, Mary Coddington
	Sept.	2.	Nic. Stilwell, Mary Micheau
	Dec.	11.	Charles Wood, Joanna Dongan

1806, Dec.	23.	John Garretson, Susan Lake
Dec.	25.	Jack & Phoebe, servants of Barnt Segang & D. Van Clief
Dec.	31.	Samuel Sharp, Sarah Squires
1807, Jan.	28.	Anthony Johnson, Fanny Oakly
Feb.	9.	Cornelius Britton, Jane Bedell
April	9.	Isaac Houseman, Hannah Perine
May	16.	Cornelius Guyon, Gitty Mercereau
June	4.	Robert Clements, Sarah Conyer
July	8.	David Laforge, Ann Johnson
July	9.	Jesse Wood, Cathrine Marshal
July	11.	John Pollard, Else Robins
Aug.	1.	Abm. Wynant, Mary Parlee
Sept.	8.	Thomas Wright, Susanna Johnson
Sept.	13.	Cornelius Perine, Maria Egbert
Sept.	19.	John Moore, Phoebe Johnson
Dec.	22.	Jacob Barger, Hannah Wynant
Dec.	27.	Harry & Sarah, servants of D. Crocheron & Wm. Journey
Dec.	29.	Joseph Journeay, Mary Wynant
1808, Jan.	8.	Daniel Butler, Elizabeth Pray
Feb.	6.	Ezra Ludlow, Rachel Seguine
March	9.	Stephen Bedell, Mary Donolly
April	—.	Wm. Mannee, Elizabeth Pryor
Oct.	8.	Abm. Mannee, Mary Waglum
Nov.	12.	David La Tourette, Phoebe Cole
Dec.	4.	Lawrence Hillyer, Ann Larzalere
Dec.	10.	Joshua Mercereau, Susan Story
Dec.	14.	Andrew Pryor, Catharine Aydee
Dec.	17.	Jacob Allen, Elizabeth Seguine
Dec.	24.	John Waglum, Lanah Pryor

MARRIAGES AT AMBOY DURING MY MINISTRY THERE, REV. D. MOORE.

1793, Dec.	29.	Andrew Smith, Maria Packer
1794, April	17.	John Halsted, —— Johnson
April	20.	Edward Ball, Susan Halstead
1795, May	17.	—— Dixon, Mary Johnson
Sept.	5.	Joseph Marsh, Ruth Smith
1796, Aug.	7.	Herry Bambridge, Sarah Truxton
1797, Jan.	12.	John Roe, Susan Stephens
1798, Dec.	27.	John Brown, Ann Segang
1800, Nov.	24.	Mr. Terrils black woman
1801, Jan.	8.	Richard Meade, Margaret Butler

OLD ST. ANDREWS CHURCH

PRESENT ST. ANDREWS CHURCH

INDEX

A

Aartsen, Ariaantje, 28
Abbatt, James E., 208
Abel, Charlotte, 156
Abrams, Amos, 272
Adames, Maria, 54
Adams, Charles, 199
  Jane, 55-58
  Jannetje, 47, 52, 53
  Malli, 57
  Maria, 52, 58
  Mary, 47
  Marya, 61
Adkens, George, 170
Adra, Mary Susanna, 262
Afte, Johannis, 19
Ahrens, Anna Maria, 156
  John, 156
  Margaret, 152
Adriaans, Gozen, 24
Adriaansz, Gosen, 30
  Gozen, 23, 26
  Hilletje, 26
Adriaenssen, Femmetie, 15
Alever, Nellie, 64
Alexander, William, 169
Alfrank, Johann, 206
Alfrenk, Bernard, 155
  John Frederick, 155
  William Henry, 155
Allason, Joseph, 268
Allen, ——, 227, 231
  mr., 227
  ——, mrs., 218
  Daniel, Bicknel, 136
  Jacob, 273
  Jacob Hand, 136, 224
  James T., 207
  Jane, 169
  Mary Ann, 123, 126
  Peter W., 230
  William, 169
  William Barton, 136
Allever, Nelli, 62
Allison, Mary Catharine, 210
Almers, br., vi
Alnsley, Ozias, 174
Alsguth, Margretha, 156
  Maria, 156
Alston, ——, 215, 232
  David, 197
  Elizabeth, 197
  Hannah, 114, 117

Alston, Japhet, 192, 197
  Japheth, 203
  Jeffries, 174
  Moses, 140, 197, 232
  Sarah, 192, 197
  Sarah Ann, 127, 140, 227
  Susan, 192
  Warren, 206
  Warren D., 206
  William P., 209
Alver, ——nelle, 59
  Pieternella, 60
Amerman, Aultje, 168
Ammeman, Elizabeth, 180
  John, 180
  Rebekkah, 180
Ammerman, John, 269
Ana, 182
Andee, Maria, 193
Anders, J. D., 127
Anderson, ——, 227
  Robert, 172
  Sarah, 167
Anderton, James, 205
Andrevet, Anna, 32
  Elisabet, 29, 32
  Jan, 27, 29, 38
  Leah, 29
  Neeltje, 27
  Pieter, 23, 29, 32
  Rebecca, 23
Andries, Maria, 55
  Marytje, 44
Andriessen, Catlyntje, 49
  Teunis, 49
Androvet, Caty, 255
  Charles, 271
  John, 272
  Peter, 255, 269
  Susan, 270
Androvette, Catharine, 168
Andryssen, Andrys, 10
Antes, Henry, vi
Appleby, Benjamin, 165
Ariesmet, Elisabeth, 9
Armstrong, Amelia, 145
  Henry, 209
  James, 145
  James, mrs., 231
  Rose, 145
Arnold, Jacob, 147
  Maria Louisa, 147
  Susan Ann Perine Bird, 147
Aroe, Hannah, 84, 86
  Jeremia, 94

Aroe, Jeremiah, 84, 86
  Joseph, 94
  Richard, 94, 174
  Samuel, 86
  Sarah, 94
  William, 84
Arrosmith, Mary, 245
  Thomas, 245
Arrow, Elisabeth, 21
  Elsy, 120
Arrowsmith, Jane, 43, 45, 48, 50
  Joseph, ix
Arysmith, Elizabeth, 246
  Henry, 248
  Joseph, 246, 247
  Mary, 246-248
  Thomas, 248
  Violetta, 247
Ashman, mr., 198
Aston, Abraham, 103
  Isaac, 103
Atkins, miss, 139
Auder, Marie, 20
Auke, Femmetje, 27
Aukes, Barbara, 23, 31
Auten, Abraham, 271
  Emilie, 239
Avery, Catharine, 132
  Geo., 190
  George, 132, 190
  George Washington, 132
  Grace, 190
  Julia Simpson, 132
Aydee, Catharine, 273
Ayre, John, 170
Ayro, Else, 271
  Jeremiah, 271

B

Baely, Martha, 52
Bachus, John, 165
Backer, Caatye, 65
  Catharina, 58, 60
  Catherina, 58
  Claas, 18
  Elizabeth, 55
  Jacob, 52, 63
  Jacobus, 57
  Kaaty, 63
  Kaatye, 62
  Kaetye, 59
  Mary, 63
  Neeltye, 59
  Nicclos, 63

Backer, Nicolaas, 12
  Nieltje, 52
  Niclaes, 10
  Niclos, 63
  Trintje, 53
  Tryntie, 12, 15
Backers, Catrina, 57
  Necclos, 62
  Trintje, 10
Baile, Martha, 42, 47
Bailey, Richard, x
Baker, ——, 216, 224, 226, 230, 234-236, 271
  Andrew, 179
  Ann S., 204
  Catharine, 179
  Catrin, 253
  Charity, 81, 83, 87, 90
  Debby Ann, 194
  Eleonor, 84
  Eliza, 224
  Elizabeth, 253
  Ellen, 148, 150, 201
  Ellen Eliza, 125
  James, 159
  James B., 203
  James Bradley, 117
  James Henry, 139
  Jeremiah, 90, 171
  Jeremy, 173
  Joanna, 159
  John, 81, 82, 87, 90, 138, 139, 142, 146, 171, 179, 196, 216, 224, 226, 268, 271
  John J., 197
  John L., 230
  John Wandel, 81
  John William, 146
  Josephine, 235
  Joseph, 83, 110, 113, 114, 117, 197, 215, 218, 220
  Jno., 235
  Julia Ann, 159
  Letty Ann, 114, 220
  Martha, 172, 266
  Mary, 145
  Mary Ellen, 142
  Nicolas, 253.
  Peter Vansal, 110
  Peter Wandel, 87
  Rachel, 194
  S., 201
  Sarah, 173
  Sarah Elizabeth, 159
  Sophia, 216
  Susan, 125, 145, 197, 201, 203, 214, 220, 235
  Wandel, 145, 201
Bakker, Caatye, 57
  Catharina, 37, 38, 41, 44, 49
  Cathrina, 37, 47

Bakker, Elisabet, 24, 31, 34, 37, 40, 44, 46
  Elisabeth, 49
  Jacob, 25, 31, 52
  Jacobus, 37, 38, 43, 45
  Neeltje, 31, 35-37, 40, 41, 44, 48
  Nicolaas, 23, 24, 30, 45
Bakkers, Neeltje, 23, 26, 27, 34
  Nicolaas, 21.
Baldwin, Ella, 236
  Isaac, 169
  Reuben, 235
Balin, Isaak, 25
Ball, Edward, 273
Baltzer, Margt, 150
Balzer, William, 209
Bambridge, Herry, 273
Bancker, Adrian, 269
Banker, mr., 164
  Ellen, 160
Benson, Hannah, 268
Banta, Eliza, 184
  Euphemia M., 195
  Jacob, 184
  Jane, 184
  Maria, 144
  Sylva, 195
  Wiart, 195
Bantea, Jacob, 173
Barager, David, 112, 214
  Henry, 112, 214
  Polly, 114
Barbarie, Abraham, 29
  Pieter, 29
Barbour, Charles, 194
  Edward, 194
  Margrett, 194
Barbanck, Maria, 22
  Thomas, 16, 22
Barbank, Aaltje, 40, 46
  Anna, 30, 32, 35
  Geertje, 47
  Jan, 31, 35, 37, 40, 42, 47
  Lucas, 47
  Maria, 42, 46, 47
  Thomas, 26, 30, 32, 37, 46
Barclay, Hannah, 168
  William, 270, 271
Bard, Judith, 171
Bardine, ——, 238
  Dorcas, 167
Barents, Tryntie, 9, 10
Barger, ——, 219, 223
  Catharine Mersereau, 213
  David, 80, 104, 114, 116, 132, 178, 212
  Eliza Ann, 114
  Hannah, 213

Barger, Henry, 79-81, 83, 169, 178, 212, 219, 223
  Jacob, 97, 212, 213, 221, 273
  James Guion, 132
  John, 83, 212, 237
  John William, 116
  Mary, 79-83, 100, 103, 104, 107, 112, 175, 212, 213
  Matilda, 223
  Polly, 118, 121
Barker, rev. mr., x
Barn, Dorety, 256
  Elizabeth, 256
  George, 256
Barnes, ——, 235
  miss, 235
  Abraham Lakerman, 267
  Ann, 265
  Anne, 77
  Bathia, 217
  Dorothy, 77, 78, 85, 258
  Edward, 189
  Elisabeth, 265
  Eliza, 116, 119, 125, 129, 187
  Elizabeth, 158, 171
  Frederic, 164
  Frederick, 238
  Geo., 240
  George, 77, 78, 85, 158, 217
  Geo. Western, 187
  G. W., 193
  Hannah, 85
  Hester, 267
  Johanna, 170
  John, 189, 202, 270
  Louisa, 208
  Margaret, 267
  Margrett, 189
  Mary Louisa, 162, 164
  Richard, 250
  Robert, 158, 162, 164, 235, 240, 265, 267
  Roger, 250, 271
  Sarah Louisa, 162
Barns, Ann, 256
  Dorothy, 259
  George, 258, 259, 272
  John, 258
  Margret, 256
  Roger, 256, 259
Barrabank, Catharina, 52
  Lucas, 52
Barrager, br., 86
  sr., 86
  Henry, 86
  Nicolas Stilwell, 86
Barron, Fanny, 188
  John, 188

279

Barron, Joseph, 188
Barth, Elizabeth, 206
  G., 206
  George, 157
  John, 157
Bartholen, Catharine, 189
  John, 189
  Mary, 189
Bartholew, Catharina, 186
  John, 186
  Mary, 186
Barton, ——, 192, 225
  Austin, 67, 170, 173
  Catharine, 211, 241
  Conrad, 149
  Edward, 200
  Elisabeth, 220
  Elizabeth, 172
  Isaac, 95, 174, 211, 237
  James, 95
  John, 91, 94
  Joseph, 67, 174, 176, 238
  Lucy, 218
  Mary, 127, 131, 166, 173
  Mary Ann, 101, 123, 192
  Saml, 200
  Samuel, 235
  Sara, 212
  Sarah, 174, 191
  Tunis, 212
  William, 91, 94, 101, 173
  Wm., 212
Basse, ——, 231
  Dettmar, 155
  Dettmar, mrs., 155
Bastido, Bastido, 14
  Jan, 16
  Joseph, 11, 14, 16, 19, 22
  Louys, 11
  Maria, 19
  Pieter, 22
  Rosanna, 11
Batten, Thomas, 166
Baty, John, vii
Bauer, Catherine, 154
  Jacob, 204
Bauman, John, 269
Beadle, Catharine, 246
  John, 246
  Joseph, 246
Beagle, Catharine, 246
  John, 246
  Joseph, 246
Beam, Eleanor, 222
Beard, Hannah, 166
Beattey, ——, 214
  Ann, 126, 175
  Ann Louisa, 135
  Annethie Vooris, 126
  Barzillor Burr, 115
  Betsey, 114
  Catharine Eliza, 117

Beattey, Cornelius, 115, 123, 126, 215
  Cynthia Jacobson, 115
  E., 126
  Edmund, 114
  Edw., 112, 113
  Edward, 114, 126, 135, 218
  Edward, jr., 115
  Eleanor Louise, 126
  Eleon, 112, 113
  Eleonor, 112, 114
  Eliza, 112, 123, 128
  Eliza Alexander, 126
  Ellen Gertrude, 120
  Hannah, 218
  Henrietta Mieks, 126
  Isabella, 128, 215
  Jacob, 112, 117, 120, 123, 215, 218
  James, 126, 127, 129
  Jane Ann, 126
  John, 114, 115, 123, 126, 218
  John, sr., 214
  John Edward, 112
  Maria Elizabeth, 123
  Maria Rebekah, 115
  Nancy, 215
  Polly, 112
  Sarah Ann, 123
  Vanransalaer, 112
  William, 112, 114, 134, 215
  William Addison, 218
  William Henry, 134
  Willm, 112
Beatty, ——, 111, 220, 228, 330, 233-235
  Alfred, 107
  Alfred Ebberhard, 103
  Alfred Eberhard, 212
  Ann, 75, 91, 99, 190, 212, 222-224
  Anna, 74
  Anne, 74, 170
  Annethie Vooris, 223
  Bittje, 80
  Catharine Eleonore, 98
  Charity, 75
  Corn., 99
  Cornelius, 78, 94, 95, 98, 100, 103, 106, 109, 112, 174, 222
  Cornelius Augustus, 112
  Daniel Lake, 99
  E., 225
  Edw., 80, 82, 84-86, 89, 94-112, 174
  Edward, 77-85, 87-94, 96, 99, 100, 104, 108, 110, 111, 114, 118, 132, 140, 165, 178, 189, 192-194, 216, 221-224, 228, 238, 241

Beatty, Edward, sr., 216
  Edward Christian, 100
  Edwd., 103, 104
  Eleanor, 77-79, 86, 94, 95, 191-193, 216, 222, 241
  Eleanor Louisa, 222
  Eleanora, 93
  Eleanore, 174
  Eleon., 89, 92, 95, 96, 98, 99, 100, 103, 110, 114
  Eleonor, 80-84, 87-91, 94, 95, 98, 103, 113, 114
  Eleonora, 92, 93, 97
  Eleonore, 95, 98-100, 213
  Eleonore Maria, 103
  Eliz., 197
  Eliza, 220
  Elizabeth, 88, 89, 190, 221
  Elizabeth Cecilia, 109
  Ellen, 191
  Ellenor Louisa, 140
  Ellenor Louise, 225
  Elleonor, 86
  Emmeline, 107
  Hellethah Ann, 106
  Henry, 228
  Henry Barger, 96
  Hiram Eugene, 118
  Isabella, 114, 193, 220
  Jacob, 79, 104, 107, 108, 111, 114, 178, 220, 221
  Jacob Cortelyou, 104
  James, 89, 92, 194
  John, 74, 75, 77, 88, 89, 91, 92, 94, 99, 105, 107, 112, 118, 132, 172, 190, 197, 222, 223
  John, sr., 221
  John William, 88
  John Jacobson, 95
  Louisa, 224
  Margaret E., 197
  Margaret Eliza, 105
  Mary, 78, 230, 232
  Mary E., 238
  Mary Elizabeth, 121
  Mary Lake, 112
  Polly, 222
  Sara, 92, 95, 102
  Sarah, 77, 99, 172, 189, 211
  Susan, 194
  Thomas, 194
  Vanras, 230
  William, 79, 96, 97, 100, 103, 107, 118, 121, 175, 222
  William Lake, 107
  William Montgomery, 103

Beatty, Wm., 107, 213
  Wm., sr., 227
Beaty, Edward, 84
  Eleanor, 80
  Eleon., 94
  Eleonor, 84
Beauvois, Catharina, 25
  Cathrina, 36
Bechler, A. H., 108, 110
  Aug. Henr., 107-109
  Augusta Henr., 105
  Francis Eugenius, 108
  J. C., 108, 110
  John C., viii, 71, 105, 106, 179
  Julius Theodore, 106
Beckelo, Abraham, 61
  Cattriena, 61
Beckwith, ——, 238
Bedel, Jesse, mrs., 230
  Sarah, 167
Bedell, mrs., 96
  Abrm., 237
  Ann, 88
  Benjamin, 185
  Cath., 104
  Cathrine, 90
  Catrin, 259, 260, 262
  Catrine, 252, 255
  Christian Jacobsen, 80
  Corn, 239
  Cornelius, 80, 83, 170, 213, 239, 240, 253
  David, 260
  Elisabeth, 213
  Elizabeth, 80, 83, 239, 240
  Esther, 191
  Febey, 253
  Hannah, 253
  Hilletje, 92, 96, 99, 104, 108, 170, 179, 182
  Hyllite, 259
  Israel, 80, 265
  James, 191, 261, 271
  Jane, 273
  Jesse, 216, 231
  John, 88, 90, 92, 96, 253, 259, 262
  John, Van Deventer 83
  Joseph, 252, 255, 259, 272
  Margaret, 272
  Martha, 255
  Martha Ann, 202
  Mary, 252, 259, 261, 262
  Mary Ann, 191
  Meriah, 265
  Patty, 270
  Phoebe, 259, 270, 272
  Richard, 175
  Richd., 176
  Sara, 176

Bedell, Silas, 253, 259, 261, 262
  Stephen, 260, 268, 273
  Steven, 262
  Vandeventer, 240
  Van Deventer, 112
Bedine, Vincent, 269
Bedgel, Joseph, 247
  Katharine, 247
  Paul, 247
Bedillion, ——, 193
  Joseph, 193
Beedle, Mary, 269
Beek, Saara, 54
Beekman, Gerardus, 61
  Lea, 28, 32, 33, 34, 42
  Maria, 61
Beers, Joseph, 166
Beglo, Elizabeth, 165
Behrens, Cathrina, 156
Beker, Jeremiah, 194
Belew, Hannah, 256
  Jacob, 256
  Sarah, 256
Bellin, Daniel, 13
  Isaac, 13
Belleville, Esther, 43
Bellow, Hartwell, 205
Belveel, Mary, 13
Benjamin, ——, 239
  capt., 239
  Corseen, 19
Bendel, Leydia, 10
Bender, Annie, 235
Benhem, Wyntje, 20
Bennet, Aaltje, 27
  Aaltye, 57
  Aeltje, 54
  Aeltye, 59, 60
  Altye, 64
  Cornelius, 43
  Elisabet, 34
  Grietje, 54
  Jacob, 27, 30, 34, 38, 43
  Juriaan, 30
  Maragreta, 58
  Margrietye, 57
  Mathew, 173
  Willem, 38
Bennett, Harmanus, 271
Bennit, Aaltye, 65
  Aeltie, 51
  Jan, 51
Benson, Esther, 110
  Rebecca, 272
Benzaken, Hetty Maria, 112
Benzien, Lydia, 140
Berbanck, Aeltie, 12
  Thomas, 12
Berbank, Patience, 169
Berg, Frederic, iv
Berge, Elsye, 57

Bergen, Adriaen, 58
  Cornelia, 37, 48, 65
  Elsje, 42
  Frederick, 57
  Fredrick, 31
  Fredrik, 26, 30, 42, 47
  Gerretye, 57
  Gerritje, 26
  Grietje, 54
  Henrik, 31
  Jacob, 37, 41, 48, 54, 57, 58
  Sara, 31
Berger, Brechtje, 23
  Catharina, 23
  Elsje, 23
  Jacob, 23
Berkelau, Abraham, 57
  Cornelius, 57
  Jannetje, 57
Berkelo, Abraham, 64
  ——am, 59
  Gerret, 59
Berville, Esther, 38
Beser, William, 167
Betts, Elizabeth, 270
  Jane M., 193
Bety, Martha, 268
Biaron, Henry, 149
  John, 149
Biebaut, Elisabet, 34
  Jacobus, 21, 25, 29, 30, 34, 38
  Maria, 30
  Petrus, 38
Bieninger, Abrm., 98
Bieran, Elizabeth, 151
  John, 151
Biggs, William, 166
Bigilow, Desire, 169
Bigler, Adelaide Finauf, 144
  Amelia H., 231
  D., 144
  John F., 155
Bill, negro, 186
Billopp, Christopher, x, 258
  John Willet, 258
Bininger, Abraham, 222
  Agnes, 232
  Harriet, 233
Binninger, Abraham, 97
  Catharine E., 228
Bird, Abraham, 188, 271
  Abm., 185
  Anthony, 179
  Cornelia, 156
  Cornelius P., 156, 158, 161, 205
  Eliza, 147, 149, 150
  Elizabeth, 269
  Jane L, 235

Bird, Jane Louisa, 158
  John, 104, 179
  Lena, 38
  Magdalena, 42
  Martha, 188
  Mary Eliza, 156, 202
  Peter Duindam, 104
  Susan Ann, 161
  Susan Ann Perine, 147
Birkby, sr., 87
  Anna, 85
  Hannah, 86, 87
  J., 84
  James, 71, 80, 83, 89
  Jas., 170, 171
  Jas. B., 79
Birkley, James, vii
Bisbalin, Christina, 141
Bisonet, Jan, 23
Boardman, ——, 234
Bodin, Francois, 22, 28, 29
  Jean, 22, 23, 35
  Judith, 45, 47, 49
Bodine, ——, 216, 219, 223
  br., 98
  sr., 98
  Abby, 141
  Abby Ann, 150
  Abm., 199, 202, 226
  Abr., 150
  Abraham, 98, 131, 135, 139, 141, 145, 148, 150, 195
  Abraham Brown, 139
  Andrew, 90, 121
  Ann, 104, 176
  Benjamin Johia Kinsy, 150
  Dorcas, 252, 256, 259
  Ed., mrs., 198
  Edw., 147
  Edward, 86, 131, 202
  Eliza, 125, 131, 134, 136
  Elizabeth, 86, 91
  George Washington James, 121
  Harriet Emily, 203
  Isaac Burbank, 118, 217
  Israel, 94
  Jacob, 120, 203
  Jacob H., 230
  Jacob Howard, 145
  James, 84, 86, 90, 91, 94, 95, 98, 121, 128, 131, 134, 176, 190, 195, 202, 218, 224
  James, sr., 121, 220
  James Edward, 148
  Jane, 266
  John, 177, 180, 231, 236, 252, 256, 259
  Marg., 95
  Margaret, 91, 195

Bodine, Margaret Jane, 128
  Margarett, 190
  Margret, 90
  Margreth, 95
  Margrett, 220
  Maria, 218
  Martha, 252, 266
  Mary, 195
  Mary Ann, 194, 217, 219
  Mergrett, 121
  Nancy, 218
  Nanne, 259
  Nathaniel, 177, 216, 218, 219
  Nathl., 203
  Rosanna, 128, 131, 223
  Sarah Ann, 226
  Sarah Ann Kinsey, 141
  Sophia, 218
  Susan Garretson, 200
  Tunis, 135
  Vincent, 118, 120, 124, 180, 188, 217, 219, 266
  Vinsant, 256
  William, 121, 128, 131, 223, 230, 234
  William Alfred Housman, 121
  William Oakly, 121
Boelen, Jannitje, vi
Boemper, Abraham, v, vi
Bogaart, Abraham, 28
  Adriaan, 24
  Cornelius, 37
  Elisabet, 22
  Gysbert, 37
  Isaak, 21
  Margareta, 28
  Maria, 31
  Sarah, 42
  Simon, 22, 28, 33, 37, 42
  Symon, 22, 31, 49
  Tunis, 21, 24, 28, 31, 37
Bogard, Isaac, 259
  John, 259
  Rachel, 259
Bogardus, Blandyena, 10
  Caaty, 9
  Sara, 12, 22, 27, 31, 33
Bogart, Ann, 270
  Anna, 264
  Barbara W., 208
  Elizabeth, 167
  Catharine, 173
  Hannah, 254
  Hannah Maria, 215
  Isaac, 254, 257
  James Walnut, 160
  John, 239, 264
  Lawrence H., 160
  Lawrence Hilliard, 206
  Martha, 248

Bogart, Mary, 248, 257, 264
  Rachel, 254, 257
  Richard, 248
  Sarah Catharine, 160
  Simon, 215, 248
  Stephen Mertling, 160
  Timothy, 206
Bogert, Liesebeth, 64
Boillon, Sarah, 80, 241
Bokee, Rebecca, 85
Bolton, C. W., xi
Bon, Helena, 56, 60
  Hellena, 54
  Lena, 62
Bond, Abraham, 270
Bonnel, Eliza, 196
  Enos, 196
  Mary, 196
  Rachel, 196
Boone, Jemima, 209
  Susan A., 209
Booram, Sydney, 205
Boost, Peter, 169
Boram, John, 192
  Mary, 192
  Sarah, 192
Borkelo, Jannetje, 26, 42, 43
  Marytje, 33, 34, 36, 38, 42
  Willempje, 22, 26, 29, 32
  Willemtje, 28
Borkulo, Willempje, 30
Borth, Johan, 228
Bos, Antje, 54
  Eliesebeth, 62
  Gerret, 64
  Nettenel, 62
  Netteniel, 64
  Nicklas, 54
Bosch, Barent, 45
  Eduard, 37
  Josua, 11
  Margareta, 42
  Nicolaas, 37, 42, 45, 51
  Samuel, 11
Boskerck, Catriena, 63
  Jannetye, 58
Boskerk, Geertruy, 63
  Jannetje, 29, 31, 34
  Tryntje, 60
  Wyntje, 56
Botler, Anna, 36
  James, 36
Bottlaar, Pieternel, 19
Bouman, Aagje, 22
  Aeltje, 54
  Andries, 18, 19
  Andrys, 11
  Catrina, 54
  Christina, 34
  Cornelis, 17, 20, 52

Bouman, Cornelus, 54
　Elisabeth, 11
　Elsie, 13
　Harme, 20
　Harmen, 14, 15, 25, 52
　Henders, 11, 12, 14
　Hendryektje, 19
　Jacob, 15, 52
　Johanna, 13
　Jores, 11, 13
　Joris, 14
　Jorius, 19
　Maria, 29, 52
　Neeltie, 17
　Neeltje, 52
　Pieter, 28, 52
　Pr., 33
　Tryntie, 14, 15
　Willem, 14, 17
Boumans, Marytje, 19
Bouth, Benjamin, 268
Bouwman, Aaghje, 32
　Anaa, 33, 36
　Christina, 21, 24, 25, 41
　Cornelis, 24.
　Elsje, 24, 25
　Harme, 33
　Harmen, 42
　Hendrikje, 34
　Maria, 45
　Maria Harmensz, 42
　Marytje, 39, 44, 46
　Metje, 21, 24, 34
　Neeltje, 24
　Pieter, 31, 38, 40-42, 45, 50
　Tryntje, 24, 34, 41, 42
　Willem, 19
　Willem Jorisz, 21
　Willem Jorisze, 39
Bowen, Ashley, 167
Bowlby, Abraham, 166
Bowman, Ellen, 205
　Ellender, 268
Boyd, ——, 229
　Alexander, 144, 147, 200
　Margaret, 235
　Margaret Ann, 144
　Mary, 147
　Rebecca, 229
　Rebecca Jane, 144
Boyes, Joice, 166
Black, Abby Ann, 124
　Abigail, 139
　Abigail Ann, 121, 142
　John, 216
　John M., 123
　John William, 123
　Rachel, 216
Blak, Anne, 253
　Edward, 253
Blake, ——, 188, 233, 234, 236, 240

Blake, Ann, 181, 182, 204
　Betsey, 183
　Betsy, 114, 116
　Cath., 183
　Catharine, 199
　Danl., 204
　Edward, 255, 257, 261
　Edwd., 185
　Elis., 271
　Elezebet, 255
　Elisabeth, 261
　Elizabeth, 112, 182, 208, 257
　Emily Anna Christopher, 145
　George W., 145
　Geo. Washington, 159
　Jane, 193, 269
　John, 182, 183, 193, 220, 238, 240, 257
　Mahala Selina, 204
　Mary, 170, 185, 193, 255, 269
　Polly, 183
　Richard, 199, 272
　S., 272
　Sarah Eliza, 216
　William, 181, 182, 255, 272
　Winety, 255
　Wm., 182
Blaw, Jane, 165
Bleck, Chas. A., 140
Blenkerhof, Claesje, 52
　Geesje, 52
　Henderick, 52
Blinckerof, Claesye, 56, 60
Blincrof, Klaasye, 63
Bloch, Louise Marie, 155
Block, Christian, 151, 155, 204
　Henry Christn. Ludwig, 151
Bnnet, Altye, 62
Bradish, James, 270
Bradley, James, 202
　Jane M., 203
Bradly, Ellen V., 228
Braisted, Catharine, 217
　Garret, 227
　Grace, 239
　John, 269
　Peter, 233
Brasted, Abraham, 66, 178
　Egbert, 261
　John, 178, 213
　Peter, 66
　Rachel, 261
Brat, Anthony, 63
　Antony, 65
　Catriena, 63
　Neeltye, 65
Bratt, Willempje, 178

Breasted, John, 98, 268
　Jacob, 174
　John William, 98
　Peter, 175
Bredsted, Jemima, 173
Breedstede, Willem, 24
Brees, Cornelis, 20
Breestede, Willem, 24
Breetstede, Andries, 16, 21
　Engeltje, 25
　Johannes, 17
　Willem, 16, 17, 21, 25
Brenan, Lawrence, 270
Brestede, Eckbert, 55
　Catharina, 58
　Jan, 51
　Johannes, 51, 53, 55
　Pieter, 53
Brett, Philip M., v
Bridges, Elisabeth, 17
Bries, Charite, 26
　Cornelius, 27
　Geertje, 29
　Geestje, 29
　Hendrik, 27, 30
　Sara, 30
　Sarah, 27
Briggs, Eleanor, 209
　William, 209
Brindley, Frances, 163
　Frances Belle, 163
　John, 163, 205
　John Tunis, 163
　Sarah Julia, 205
　William H., 163
Brinckerhof, Claasje, 51
Brinley, Frances, 238
Brintley, Mary, 187
Britt, John, 167
Britain, John, 86
　Patience, 86
　Rachel, 86
Brittain, Amanda, 143
　Elizabeth Ann, 143
　Harriet, 143
　Jacob, 109
　James, 143, 233, 239
　John, 109, 180
　Katharine, 247
　Margaret Eliza, 239
　Mary, 255
　Mary Etta, 224
　Mary Theresia, 143
　Nathaniel, ix, 247, 255, 262
　Necolas, 255
　Patience, 180
　Rachel, 180
　Violetta, 143, 239
Brittan, Addra, 259
　Mary, 259
　Nicholas, 262

Brittan, Samuel, 259
Britten, George Washington Oakley, 146
  G. W. O., 227
  James G., 146
  Jeams, 12
  Joseph, 12
  Mary, 254
  Nicolaas, 13
  Nicolaes, 13
  Patience, 254
  Samuel, 254
  William, 13
Britton, ——, 225, 226, 230, 232, 233
  Abigail, 21
  Abm., 222, 232
  Abraham, 97, 222
  Ann, 97, 196
  Ardrae, 171
  Catharine, 78, 222
  Catrin, 262
  Cornelius, 196, 273
  D., 230
  Deborah, 271
  Dorcas, 101, 205
  Elizabeth, 206
  Emily, 144, 151, 158
  Fanny, 215
  Frances Oakley, 233
  Hamilton, 196
  Henry, 206
  Jacob, 208
  James, 90, 187, 219, 222, 224-226, 269
  James Guyon, 233
  Jane, 133, 141, 195, 196
  Jas., mrs., 206
  John, 87, 89, 90, 93, 97-99, 101, 171, 187, 191, 213, 218, 219, 222, 231
  Joseph, 251
  Lovina, 99
  Marietta, 219, 222
  Mariette, 222
  Matilda, 196
  Mary, 195, 222, 245, 251, 257, 261, 262
  Mary Etta (Ella), 225
  N., 158
  Nathan, 199
  Nathanael, 43
  Nathaniel, 78, 165, 166, 195, 245, 251, 257, 262, 272
  Nicholas, 170
  Patience, 214
  Peter, 89
  Rachel, 87, 89, 90, 93, 101, 187, 191, 239
  Samuel, 261, 271
  Sara, 43
  Sarah, 93, 167, 191

Britton, Violetta, 207
  William, 257
Broadhead, ——, 223
  mr., 223
  ——, mrs., 226
Brock, ——, 165
Bront, Elizabeth, 166
Brooks, Anna, 36
  Mary, 31
Brooker, John, 197
  Lucy, 197
  William, 197
Brouwer, Abraham, jr., 34
  Elisabet, 27, 30, 34, 38, 43
Brown, A. C. F., 97, 101, 102, 104
  Andrew, 268
  Ann, 98, 105
  Ann Caroline, 93
  Ann Catharine Frederica, 93
  Ann Cath. F., 92
  Ann Cath. Frederica, 96
  Ann C. F., 92-94, 99, 100, 103
  Charles Henry, 149
  Isaac M., 149, 202
  John, 50, 51, 273
  Joseph, 201
  Maria, 51
  N., 93, 98-105, 173
  Nathl., 92, 93, 95-97, 99-103
  Nathaniel, viii, 71, 91, 93, 95, 97, 173, 212
  Sarah, 201
  Wm. S., 194
Brownlee, James, iv
Bruce, br., vi
  David, vii, x
Brumhuber, Carl August, 208
Brunholer, August, 162
  Carl August, 162
  Elizabeth, 162
Bryant, Ann M., 192
  David, 192
  Jane, 192, 224
Bubalin, Christina, 199
Buck, ——, 232
Buillon, Sarah, 80
Buninger, Martha, 91
Bunninger, br., 177
Burbanck, Abraham, 55
  Jan, 53
  John, 55
Burban, mr., 209
  sr., 144
  Abm., 98, 174, 176, 180
  Abraham, 98, 186, 265
  Addie, 257

Burbank, Ally, 166
  Ann, 93, 171, 181, 186, 197, 202, 211, 233
  Anna, 159
  Arthur, 180
  Edward, 133, 141, 195, 224
  Edward Egbert, 102, 141
  Elizabeth, 265
  Eveline, 209
  Gertrude, 221, 225
  Henry, 197
  Isaac, 95, 102, 111, 120, 141, 144, 174, 179, 188, 195, 198, 203, 219, 224, 230
  Jacob, 181, 193, 200
  James, 265
  Jane, 224
  John, 93, 96, 98, 170, 173, 176, 186, 197, 211, 221, 239, 265
  John Alfred, 159
  Jon W., 193, 200
  Joseph, 245
  Jno. W., 159
  Lena, 180
  Lenah, 186
  Margaret, 265
  Martha, 183, 245, 257
  Mary, 96, 131, 176, 194, 269
  Mary Adeline, 221
  Mary Ann, 95, 118, 120, 124, 188, 194, 217
  Nelly, 265
  Peter, 186, 245, 257
  Rachel, 97, 99, 101, 109, 171, 173
  Rebecca, 173
  Rebeka, 170
  Sally, 112, 295
  Sara, 102
  Sarah, 106, 141, 198, 203
  Sarah Ann, 141, 208
  Sarah Jane, 111, 198
  Thomas, 57
  William, 264, 265
Burch, Charles Sumner, xi
Burckerdt, Anthon Friederich, 138
  Jacob, 138
Burckhard, ——, 224
Burckhardt, Jacob, 224
  Theresa, 224
Burckert, Jacob, 133
  Johann Valentine, 133
Burd, Anthony, 261
Burdine, Ann, 79
  Betsey, 85
  Dorcas, 80

Burdine, Elisabeth, 80
  Elizabeth, 79, 81, 82, 246
  James, 79-82, 85, 88, 170, 172
  John, 81, 246
  Margret, 88
  Tunis, 82
  William, 88
Burger, ——, 227
  col., 187
  Ann, 216
  Cornelia, 201
  David, 165
  Elias, 29
  Hannah, 147, 151, 201
  Jacob, 227
  James, 156, 205
  John, 150, 203, 227, 230
  Joseph, 227
  Maria Ottilia, 156
  Mary Ann, 145
  Mathias, 150, 151, 201, 230
  Mathias, jr., 202
  Matthias, 201
  Nathan, 29
  Nicholas, 186
  Nicolas, 201
  Steph., 227
Burgher, ——, 222, 223, 237, 238
  col., 225
  ——, col., 224
  mr., 209
  Alfred, 131, 221
  Ann, 86, 90, 97
  Catharine, 85, 86, 94, 219
  Cathrine, 81-83, 88, 90
  Charles, 238
  D., 236
  David, 85
  Eliza, 220
  Elizabeth, 97
  Emeline, 224
  Frances Stilwell, 88
  Hannah, 131, 195, 221
  Hester Maria, 205
  James, 100, 131, 222, 237
  James L., 224
  Jane, 92, 145
  John, 82, 195, 223, 224
  Lydia, 224
  Mary, 129
  Mary Ann, 83, 194, 210
  Mary C., 209
  Mary L., 209
  Mathias, 81, 194, 195, 232
  Matthias, 131, 221
  Nicholas, 85, 86, 92, 219
  Nichs, 182
  Niclas, 81-83, 88, 90
  Nicolas, 94, 97, 100

Burgher, Robert, 226
  Stephen, 237
Burkert, Ferdinand Jacob, 135
  Jacob, 135
  Teresa, 135
Burnet, Samuel, 20
  Jeremiah, vi
Burningham, Elizabeth, 159
Burns, ——, 230
Burr, Barzillai, 190, 223
Burtingham, Elizabeth Bridget, 203
Burton, Charles, 239
  Ellen Thomas, 125
  John, 125, 239
  Louisa, 239
  Louise, 125
  Margaret Jane, 125
  Sarah Rumrill, 125
  William, 125
Burtus, Gitty Ann, 218
Bush, ——, 269
  Ann, 168, 268
  Caty, 187
  Elizabeth, 67
  Garret, 67, 169
  Garrit, 66
  Jacob, 187
  Joseph, 270
  Lambert, 270
  Maria, 186
  Mary, 66
  Nicholas, 187
  Niclas, 173
  William, 186
  Winie, 186
Bushkirk, Cornelius, 67
  John, 67
Buskirk, Daniel, 185
  John, 66, 165
  Philip, 185
  Sarah, 66
Busse, Matilda Caroline, 138
Butler, ——, 234, 236
  mr., 207
  Adelaide, 162
  Anthony, 258
  Balette, 257
  Belleche, 249
  Belletie, 259
  Betsy, 192
  Cath., 184, 194
  Catharine, 92, 169, 184, 186, 190, 192, 194, 221
  Catrin, 258
  Charity, 197, 221, 223, 224
  Cornelius Egbert, 123, 219

Butler, Daniel, 85, 123, 133, 138, 142, 192, 219, 249, 272
  Elizabeth, 271
  Elias, 183, 240
  Eliza, 142
  Eltey, 251
  Frances, 169
  Hannah, 186
  Henry, 245, 249, 257, 259, 263
  Isaac, 85, 92, 138, 184, 192, 197, 213, 224
  James, 43, 46, 134, 169, 186, 190, 192, 194, 197, 221, 223, 224, 226, 249, 251
  Jan, 43
  Jane, 125, 134, 138
  John, 183, 246, 249, 254, 263
  Maria, 266
  Margaret, 273
  Martha, 197
  Martha Ann, 220
  Martha Swaim, 143, 152
  Mary, 190, 240, 246, 249, 258, 263
  Mary Ann, 182
  Mary Cath., 138
  Mary Catharine, 205
  Nathaniel, 182, 190, 257
  Rachel, 246, 249, 254
  Samuel, 240
  Sara, 46
  Sarah, 85, 171, 254, 259
  Sarah Elizabeth, 127, 133, 207, 220
  Sophia, 182, 190
  Susan, 190, 266, 269
  Susanna, 174
  Thomas, 249, 258, 266, 269
  Tunis, 208
  Tunis Egbert, 138
  Vincent, 127, 184, 220, 223
  Wm. F., 162
Byvanck, Aeltie, 17
Byvank, Aaltje, 45
  Belitje, 38, 49
  John, 170

C

Caddemus, Dirk, 49
Cadmus, Andries, 47
  Cathrina, 42
  Dirk, 24, 30, 42, 47
  Frederyk, 24
  Rutgert, 30
Caesar, P. W., 236
Cailo, Pieter, 35

Cain, Jacob, 268
Cairns, Harriet, 187
  John, 187
  Margaret, 240
  Mary, 187
  William, 272
Calcraft, Margaret, 170
Callahoun, Eleanor, 166
Camp, Leah, 249
  Naomi, 249
Campbell, James, 272
Cannon, Abel, 189
  Andrew, 185, 271
  Ann, 185, 189
  Betsy, 185
  David, 185
  Elizabeth, 185
  Hanna Maria, 204
  Hannah, 185
  Isaac, 185
  Jane, 198
  John, 185, 189
  Margaret, 185
  Sarah 185, 269
  Thomas, 185
Canon, Catharina, 50
  Catlyn, 21
  Elizabeth, 55
  Hester, 45
  Jan, 55
  Jean, 50
  Maria, 39
  Marie, 42
Canone, Jacobus, 56
  John, 56
Caper, mr. ——, 237
Carbe, Ann, 258
  Richard, 258
Carber, Amy, 24
Carbet, Amy, 32
  Marytie, 16
Carenton, Beniamin, 12
  Margriete, 12
Cargile, Jane Matilda, 140
Cargill, mrs. ——, 234
  Abraham, 229
  Amanda, 202
Carlyle, miss, 233
Carr, ——, mrs., 23
Carrinton, Jannetie, 17
  Joseph 17
Carroll, William, 166
Carver, ——, 221
  Peter D., 217
  William, 217
Carry, Ann, 204
  Richard S., 171
Casier, Philip, 22
  Philippe, 34
Caspers, Casparus, 33
  Isak, 33
Castree, H., 236
Cateleau, Dorethe, 22

Cave, Caroline, 136
  Lewis, 136
Cavelier, Antje, 49
  Cornelia, 49
  Johannes, 49
Cavelly, Elisabeth, 205
Cazier, Catharina, 26
  Dirk, 29
  Jacobus, 32
  Petrus, 40
  Philip, 26, 29
  Philippe, 27, 32, 40
Cears, Elias, 181
  Jane, 181
  Locky, 181
Ceilo, Cornelia, 31, 61
  Daniel, 37
  Elsje, 20
  Johannes, 47
  Maria, 47
  Peiter, 31
  Pieter, 20, 27, 34, 37, 40, 47
  Sara, 34
  Wilhelmus, 40
Cesar, 180
Chambers, Elisabeth, 169
  George W. 192
  Mary, 166, 192
  Wm., 192
Chapin, Lucius, 269
Charity, negro, 184
Charles, negro, 189
Charlton, rev. mr., 251, 263
  Richard, x
Chrips, John, 253
  Margret, 253
  William, 253
Christefer, Ane Catryn Barent, 18
  Barent, 18
Christfeer, Cersteyntjes, 18
  Christoffel, 19
  Styntje, 19
Christian, Heinrich, 152
  John, 152
Christoffel, Anna, 15
  Barent, 15
  Hans, 14, 15
  Styntie, 15, 16
  Susanna, 15
Christoffels, Styntje, 10
Christoffelsen, Barent, 10-12
  Catharyna, 11
  Niclaes, 10
  Rebecca, 12
  Stoffel, 10
Christoffelzen, Barent, 14
  Christoffel, 12
  Hans, 11
  Maria, 14

Christopher, Anna Catharina, 41
  Barent, 21, 24, 27, 34, 38, 43, 45
  Catharina, 25, 34, 41, 43
  Cathrina, 38
  Charity, 66, 178
  Christoffel, 25
  Cornelius, 175
  Easter, 259, 260
  Eliza, 192, 194
  Elizabeth, 173, 186, 194, 272
  Esther, 262
  Hans, 40 41, 43, 45, 48 50
  James Grover, 260
  Jane, 170
  Joh., 34
  Johannes, 43
  John, 66, 186, 194
  John Garrison, 259
  John, Milton, 128, 221
  Joseph, 48, 128, 194, 221, 262
  Maria, 40, 41, 221
  Mary, 48
  Nicolaas, 34, 41
  Peter, 178
  Richard, 50, 259, 260, 262
  Stoffel, 20, 21
  Susan, 186
  Susanna, 21
  Thomas, 196
Chroson, John, 172
Chysick, Sarah, 268
Ciseau, Anna, 38
Cister, Malli, 62
Claassen, Derck, 10, 11
  Femmetye, 10
  Hendrickie, 10
  Jacobus, 11
  Magdalena, 11, 14
  Marytje, 27
Claasz, Francyntje, 20
  Jan, 20
Claazen, Cobus, 11
  Femmetie, 11
Clarck, Hannah, 268
Clark, ——, 215, 226, 236, 237, 239
  capt., 215
  Ann B., 232
  Binninger, 238
  James, 237, 268
  R., 236
Clarkson, Diana, 190
Clason, Reuben, 270
Classen, Jacobus, 11
Clauder, br., 144
  sr., 144
  mrs. 202,

Clauder, Ann Eliza, 204
  C. E., 202
  Charlotte, 204
  Charlotte E., 198, 201, 204
  Charlotte Elisabeth, 198
  Charlotte Elizabeth, 148
  Charlotte G, 198
  Charlotte Jane, 140, 229
  H. G., viii, 139, 140, 144, 150, 198, 229
  Henry G., 71, 148
  Henry Theophilus, 140
  Ottelia Virginia, 148
  Sarah Adelaide, 144
Clausen, Sophia, 171
Clauson, Sophia, 97, 100
Claussen, Mary, 83
Clawson, mrs., 105
  Anna Maria, 220
  Daniel, 220
  Elisabeth, 175
  Elizabeth, 99
  Maria, 220
  Reuben, 175
  Samuel, 239
  Sophia, 103, 105, 107, 109, 111, 179, 188, 189, 212, 214
Clemens, Magdalena, 234
Clement, Willempje, 21
Clements, Robert, 273
Clendenne, Cathelyna, 58
  Jacob, 57
  Johannes, 54
  Walter, 54, 57, 58
Clendenny, Adam, 46
  Eleanor, 269
  Jeams, 63
  Mary, 65
  Patience, 46
Cleninne, Antye, 64
  Walter, 64
Clerck, Dorote, 12
  Dorothea, 13
  Grytie, 12
  Jan, 12-15, 17
  Sara, 15
Clindenne, Maria, 53
  Walter, 53
Clindinne, ———, 59
  Joseph, 62
  Malli, 59
  Pieternelle, 60
  Walter, 60, 62
  Walteris, 59
  Wynty, 59
Coade, Lidia, 258
  Mary, 258
Coberly, Joseph, 263
Cocheau, Abraham, 23
  Jan, 23

Cocheron, Emeline, 113
  John, 121
  Nicholas, 113
  Selina Theresa, 121
Coddington, mrs., 124
  Ann, 124, 231
  David, 182
  Catharine, 199
  Catharine Helena, 130
  Elizabeth, 182
  Elizabeth Ann, 199
  Mary, 272
  Saml., 199
  Samuel, 126, 130, 136, 182, 191, 194, 231
  Samuel Franklin, 136
  Sidny Fitz Randolph, 120
Codington, Asher, 169
Codmas, Martha, 168
Coevert, Femmetje, 31
  Maria, 31
  Teunis, 29, 31
Cole, ———, 234, 238
  Abraham, 28-30, 245, 251, 255, 259, 262
  Abram., 260, 262, 264
  Ann, 23, 30, 34, 189, 251, 257, 258, 260, 262, 269, 272
  Anna, 36
  Catharine, 238
  Cathrine, 262
  Charity, 264
  Charles Perry, 209
  Cornelius, 268, 271
  Edward, 259
  Eliza, 189
  Elizabeth, 245
  Francis, 271
  Hannah, 251, 255, 259, 260
  Henry, 253
  Isaac, 259
  Jacob, 272
  John, 234, 258, 262, 271, 272
  John Bedell, 259
  Jonah Rodgers, 155
  Joseph, 235
  Margaret, 271
  Maria, 28, 32
  Martha, 245, 270
  Mary, 23, 35, 55, 167, 169, 262
  M. Elizabeth, 234
  Patience, 272
  Peter, 253
  Phoebe, 273
  Rebecca, 23, 29, 32
  Rebeka, 167
  Richard, 262, 268
  Sarah, 173, 232

Cole, Sarah Rodgers, 155
  Stephen, 257, 258 260, 262, 270
  Susan, 269
  Susan Ann, 209
  Susanna, 253, 260
  W., 155
  W., capt., 155
  William, 232
Colan, Cathrine, 81
  James, 81
Collon, Cath., 86
  Cathrine, 86
  David, 210
  James, 87
  Jas., 84-86
Collong, Rebecca, 171
Cologne, Mary, 271
Colon, ———, 186
  Ann, 103, 109, 112, 180
  Billetje, 177, 211
  Cath., 211
  Catharine, 75-78, 95, 100, 103, 106, 109, 165, 174, 211, 214
  Cathrine, 80, 87-90
  Daniel, 75
  David, 75, 81, 162, 237
  David Bennet, 162
  David M., 208
  Elizabeth, 76, 211
  Geo., 103, 210
  Georg, 81, 87
  George, 76, 81, 88, 90, 91, 93, 103, 165, 172, 210, 214, 215, 237
  Hannah, 90, 211
  Helena, 77
  James, 75-78, 80-82, 87, 88, 90, 175, 185, 210, 211
  James sr., 89, 90, 174
  James, mrs., 208
  Jane, 77, 180, 211
  Jas., 87
  John, 234
  Jonah, 78, 166
  Jonas, 211
  Margaret, 76
  Mary, 75-81, 95, 210, 214
  Mary Jane, 234
  Mary Magdalen, 77, 78, 210
  Peter, 75-77, 90, 91, 95, 177, 210, 211
  Rebecca, 211
  Rebekah, 77
  Sarah Ann, 162
Colong, Anne, 79
  Catran, 79
  Catharine, 79
  George, 79, 241
  Jeams, 79

Colong, Mary, 79, 241
Cool, Rebecca, 15
Coolter, Andru, 65
  William, 65
Conein, Janntye, 63
Conklin, John P., 209
Connelz, Mary, 155
Conner, Crowel Mundy, 128
  Dewitt Clinton, 146
  Elis., 93
  Elisabeth, 177, 211
  Elizabeth, 193
  Elizabeth Sophia, 131
  George, 216
  Jane, 230
  Richard, 94, 110, 128, 131, 189, 212
  Richard jr, 146
  Richd., 215
  Sarah, 212
  Sarah Lavinia, 214
  Sophia, 212
  William, 94
Conners, mr., 189
Connor, ——, 226, 231
  Abraham, Van Vechten, 105
  Adam, 251
  Ann, 175
  Anne, 73, 76, 210
  Anny, 251
  A. V. 231
  Cath., 200
  Catharine, 73-75, 107, 165, 179
  Daniel, 100
  Elizabeth, 74, 170
  George, 118
  Henry Augustus, 109
  James, Egbert, 134, 224
  Jane, 103
  Jeremiah, 251
  Mary, 87, 188
  Oscar Theodore, 121
  R., 103, 226
  Richard, vii, 73-75, 84, 87, 93, 97, 100, 103, 105, 107, 109, 111, 118, 121, 134, 179, 188, 189, 200, 210, 214, 224, 232
  Richard jr., 200, 222
  Richard, sr., 80, 107
  Richd., 84, 86, 107, 175
  Sara 74
  Sarah, 210, 222, 224
  Sarah Lovinia, 111
  Sophia, 84, 87, 93, 94, 113, 175, 200, 226
  Sophia Ann, 97
  Stephen Alexander, 107
  V. V., 231
Connors, col., 200

Conor, Cathrine, 83, 210, 241
  Elizabeth, 88
  Jonathan, 91
  Richard, 83, 88, 91, 210, 241
  Richard jr. 171
  Richd., 82, 94
  Sophia, 83, 88, 91
Conyer, Sarah, 273
Copes, Francis, 230
  John, 201
Cor——, Jacob, 58
Corbet. Amy, 37
  Anna, 13
  Isaac, 14
  Martha, 14
Corkin, Margaret, 249
  Patrick, 249
  Peter, 249
Cornelius, Valentine, 133
Cornon, Andries, 64
  Aront, 61
  Danal, 64
  David, 64
  Davit, 61, 63
  Peater, 64
Cornwell, Charity, vii
  William, vi, vii
Corron, Alfred, 145
  Joseph, 145
  Nicolas, 145
Corrsen, Maria, 51
Corsci, Cornelis, 53
Corsen, Catharina, 67
  Corneles, 58
  Cornelia, 52
  Corn., jr., 66
  Cornelius, 61, 64, 66, 67
  Cornelius, 52, 53
  Daniel, 55, 64, 171
  David, 61
  Elizabeth, 105, 170, 178
  Jacob, 51, 52, 57
  Jacob, jr., 57, 59
  Jannetje. 53
  John, 173
  Malli, 60
  Maria, 52, 53, 55, 57, 61
  Mareya, 59
  Mary, 67
  Marytje, 58
  Naile, 67
  Neelty, 59
  Neeltye, 55
  Nieltje, 52, 61
  Richard, 61, 67, 264
  Yannetye, 67
Corshong, Hery, 264
  Nancy, 264
Corson, ——, 271
  Alfred, 227
  Catharine, 199, 231

Corson, Cattriena, 62
  Daniel, 263
  Danl., 199
  Douwe, 63
  Elizabeth, 263
  George W., 204
  Leonard, 228
  Maria, 62
  Ragel, 63
  Richard, 204
  Richd., 180
  Sarah Ann, 199
  William Howe, 263
Corsse, Jacob, jr., 52
  Marytje, 52
  Suster, 52
Corssen, Antie, 15
  Antje, 49
  Beniamin, 15
  Benjamin, 18, 20, 27, 29
  Blandina, 16
  Blandyna, 18
  Catharina, 23, 25, 33, 38, 39, 48
  Christiaan, 10, 34, 37
  Christiaen, 13, 16
  Christjaan, 18
  Cornelia, 19, 20, 23, 29, 34, 37, 41, 45, 48, 51
  Cornelis, 15, 37, 38, 40
  Cornelius, 29, 31, 34, 37, 40, 43, 46, 48, 49
  Daniel, 46
  Elisabeth, 13, 16
  Elysebet, 18
  Jacob, 10, 11, 15, 19, 23, 27, 31, 39
  Jacob, jr., 43, 51
  Jacobus, 43
  Maria, 18, 29, 39, 40, 43, 44, 51
  Marie, 36
  Neeltje, 29, 37, 38
  Pieter, 31
  Rebecca, 27
  Suster, 10
Corsson, Johan, 11
Corszen, Antie, 11
Cortelyou, ——, 220, 226
  br., 161
  sr., 161
  Aaron, vii, 73
  Agnes, 75
  Amey, 85, 87
  Amy, 89, 91, 101, 107, 110, 180
  Charlotte Ann, 135
  Cornelius, vii, 73-76, 81, 85, 210, 214, 237
  David Hekkel, 141
  Eleanor, 73, 165
  Eleonore, 178

Cortelyou, Eliza, 114, 117, 120, 136, 140, 155, 178, 215, 220, 221
  Elizabeth, 73, 81, 83, 86, 88, 89, 93, 104, 107, 111, 112, 182, 184, 186, 228, 269
  Emma, 107, 222
  Eugene Augustus, 139
  Frances, 128
  George Adolph, 229
  Gertrude, Martha, 113, 115, 118, 182
  Gertry Martha, 88
  Hannah, 75
  Jacob, 74, 81, 83, 86, 88, 93, 95, 97, 102, 126, 128, 132, 170, 178, 182, 213, 220, 226, 230
  Jacob Winant, 132
  Jacomyntje, vii
  Jacques, vii, 76, 77
  Jacob, 135
  Josephine, 221
  Lawrence, 119-221
  Lawrence H., 136, 139-141
  L. H., 155
  Lockman, 129, 226
  Lorenz Hilliard, 91
  Maria, 129
  Martha, 74, 170
  Mary, 75, 76, 78, 132, 135, 168, 210, 214, 220, 230
  Mary Frances, 220
  Nelly, 129
  Peter, 73, 76, 85, 87, 89, 91, 95, 101, 107, 110, 119, 172, 180, 186, 222, 234, 271
  Peter Lochman, 95
  Sally, 112, 116, 132
  Sara, 73, 76, 92, 94, 95, 98, 102, 178
  Sarah, 75-92, 94-96, 100, 104, 106, 114, 241
  Sarah Ann, 87, 107, 110, 113, 119, 180
  Sarah L., 158
  Sarah Sprague, 214
  Simon, 75, 76, 78
  Theodore Hartman, 136
  Timothy Townsend, 77
  William Cuberly, 126
Cosie, Fellip, 18
Cosine, Anla, 270
Coteleau, ——, 49
  Debora, 24
  Dorothe, 24, 27
  Dorothea, 22, 25, 26, 28, 35, 47
  Geurtje, 22, 26, 35

Corteleau, Jaques, 24, 25, 27, 33
  Neeltje, 33, 43
  Pieter, 24, 27
Cots, Benjamin, 255
  Catrin, 255
  Daniel, 255
Coursen, Catharine Jones Martling, 125
  Cornelius, 120, 124
  Cornelius Van Name, 121
  Daniel, 125
  Daniel D., 121
  Danl., 186
  Eliza, 187
  Hannah, 216
  Jane, 186
  Maria, 183
  Mary, 189
  Mary Jane, 121
  Rebekah, 186
  Richard, 187
  Sarah Ann, 121
  Stephen Kittletass, 121
  Susan Ann Reed, 120
  William Blake, 124
Courson, Mary, 186
  Rebecca, 184
Cousine, Aletta, 165
Couwenhoven, Maria, 42
  Samuel, 42
Coyn, James, 158
Coyne, br., 161
  sr., 161
  Beatus, 235
  Harriet, 163
  Harriet Matilda, 156
  James, 156, 163
  Margaret, 163
Cozine, Elizabeth Ann, 231
  Hannah M., 235
  James Edward, 144
  Mary Priscilla, 149
  Peter, 144, 149, 174, 198
Craddock, Thomas, 167
Craig, ——, mrs., 235
Crain, Easter, 268
Craven, Christina, 28
  Esther, 31
  Jacobus, 28, 31, 32
  Neeltje, 31
  Thomas, jr., 31
Crawbuck, Godfrey, 126
  James Franklin Beattey, 126
Creage, Elisabet, 40
Creaven, Anna, 23
  Jacobus, 23
Creed, Elizabeth, 268
  Ellender, 268
Creven, Cobus, 11, 16, 19

Creven, Elsie, 11
  Gillis, 19
  Jacobus, 21
  Johannes, 16
Cribbs, Elijah, 97
  Martha, 104
  Richard, 97
  Sarah, 98
Cripp, T——, 233
Cripps, ——, 226, 228, 231, 233
  Anthony, 227
  Henry, 234
  J., 228
  James, 226, 230
  James, sr., 225
  Laurence, 169
  Wm., 231
Crips, ——, 215
  Anthony, 213
  Catharine, 190
  Catharine Fountain, 134
  Charity Butler, 134
  Charles, 228
  Elisabeth, 260
  Elisha, 214
  Eliza, 220
  Elizabeth, 111, 259
  Isaac Butler, 134
  James, 190, 271
  James Butler, 125
  John, 138, 256, 268
  Lawrence, 190, 215, 223
  Lenah, 214
  Lucy, 105, 108, 111
  Margrit, 256
  Martha, 108, 115, 118, 122, 170, 178
  Polly, 223
  Rachel, 111, 217
  Sally, 190
  Sara, 175, 259
  Susan, 215
  Thomas, 115, 269
  William, 125, 134, 138, 213, 259
  Willum, 256
Crocheron, ——, 238, 272
  ——, mr., 236
  Abraham, 51, 186, 255, 258, 265-267
  Ann, 128, 181, 182, 221, 264-266
  Ann Elizabeth, 117
  Benjamin, 266
  Catrine, 265
  D., 273
  Daniel, 51, 245, 258, 262, 265, 271
  David, 265
  Edm., 162
  Eleanor, 265
  Elezebet, 255

Crocheron, Elizabeth, 264, 267
  Fithee, 266
  Fithy, 265
  Frances, 161
  Frances Rebekah, 116
  Franklin Guyon, 121
  Geney, 261
  Henry, 255, 258, 260, 262, 265, 266
  Jacob, 169, 262, 264, 270
  James, 237
  Jane, 181, 266
  John, 116, 182, 186, 219, 258, 261, 265, 266, 270
  John N., 204
  Leah Stoutenborough, 162
  Lenah Araminta, 128
  Lucretia, 162
  Margaret, 181, 258
  Mary, 245, 261, 262, 265-267, 271
  Nancy, 239
  Nanne, 258, 262
  Nanny, 260
  Nathan, 204
  Nicholas, 116, 117, 121, 128, 181, 221, 245, 271
  Nicholas, jr., 109
  Patience, 194
  Reuben, 266
  Richard, 181, 239
  Sarah, 262, 265
  Sophia, 182, 266
  William Henry, 109, 116
Crochon, Abraham, 29
Crockeron, Judy, 187
Croese, Cornelia, 57
  Hendrick, 15
  Henrik, 29
  Neeltye, 55
Croesen, Abraham, 43, 44
  Adriaetie, 17
  Anna, 61
  Antje, 31, 37, 38
  Claesie, 53
  Cornelia, 46, 51, 52, 59
  Cornelis, 40, 41, 44, 48
  Cornelius, 48
  Femmetje, 36
  Gerret, 52, 53, 60
  Gerrit, 16, 17, 29, 36, 43-45, 51
  Hendereck, 52
  Hendrick, 20, 60
  Henrick, 29, 36, 37, 41, 43, 45, 48, 51
  Maria, 37, 41, 48, 52
  Neeltje, 41, 45, 50, 53
Croessen, Elisabeth, 15
Cropsy, ——, 188

Cropsy, Cornelius Cortelyou, 240
  Elizabeth, 240
  Ellen, 116, 119, 122, 218
  Ellen C., 219
  Ellen Connover, 188
  Harmon, 224
  Hermanus, 186
  Jacob, 240
  Jacob Rozeau, 186
  Martha Ann, 117
  Nich., 188
  Nicholas, 226
Crorse, Antje, 13
  Christjaen, 15
Crorsen, Cornelia, 59
Crorsse, Benjamyn, 19
Crorssen, Beniamin, 16
Crorsson, Benjamin, 18
  Blandyna, 18
Crosbun, Abigail, 268
Cross, Cornelius Vanderbilt, 136
  James, 227
  James Madison, 136
  John, 228
  William Harrison, 136
Crosse, Jacob, 10
Crossen, Jan, 15
Crouse, Henry, 182
Cruse, Lena, 179
Crusen, Maricha, 66
Cruser, Jane, 181
  Jemima, 181
  John, 181
Crusers, H.. 176
Crowel, Catharine, 269
Cubberly, ——, 240
  Ander, 262
  Ann, 269
  Henriette, 199
  Isaac, 199
  James, 161, 162, 271
  Joseph, 262
  Mary, 272
  Walter Inman, 161
  William Holland, 235
Cuberly, Ann, 129
Cummings, ——, mrs., 229
Cunow, Augusta Henrietta, 106, 108
Currant, Patrick, 178
Curshon, Daniel, 263
  Henry, 263
Curtis, Christopher, 77
  Eva, 77
Cusheron, Abraham, 246
  Jane Elizabeth, 246
  Johannah, 246
Cushon, Abraham, jr., 248
  Elizabeth, 248
  Jacob, 248

D

Dacer, Charcels, 65
  Marya, 65
Dacker, Mally, 63
Daille, Pierre, iii
Daily, Margaret, 166
Dangek, Andro, 64
  Samuel, 64
Daniels, Margareta, 48
  Margriet, 27, 30, 34, 36, 37, 40, 45, 49
  Margrieta, 36
  Nicholas, 184
Davis, Ebenezer, 188
  Elizabeth, 192
  Jacob, 189
  James, 124
  John, 124, 184, 189
  Maria, 237
  Paris M., 188
  Rachel, 188
  Richard, 188
  Sally, 184
  Sarah, 212
  Sarah Moore, 188
Day, Henry, 23, 29, 31, 33, 36
  Johannes, 48
  John, 37, 39, 48
  Maria, 33
  Petrus, 29
  Samuel, 23
  Simon, 36
  William, 39
Debaa, Hester, 62
debaa, Marya, 59
de Baa, Maria, 55
de Bo, Lowys, 19
  Lowys, jr., 19
de Bois, Louis, 11
de Camp, Bastiaan, 30
  Christina, 21
  Christoffel, 32
  Christyntje, 32
  David, 22
  Elsje, 25, 28, 32, 39
  Gedeon, 30
  Gideon, 22, 25, 35
  Hendrik, 22, 25, 32
  Laurens, 21, 22, 32
  Marytje, 21, 26
  Styntje, 34
De Camp, Christina, 25
  Elsje, 35
  Joh., 26
Decker, ——, 211, 227, 269
  col., 176
  mr., 183
  ——, mrs., 238
  Abm., 182, 191, 192, 195
  Abraham, 172, 176, 189, 190, 261

Decker, Abram, 262
  Alcy, 198
  Amanda Alvira, 141
  Andrew, 128, 130, 133, 198
  Andrew B., 194
  Angeline, 135
  Ann, 111, 140, 176, 194, 195, 197, 204, 217, 269, 270
  Barnet, 179, 187
  Barnet Depuy, 120
  Barnt, 180
  Cathalyntie, 14, 16
  Catharina, 17, 194
  Catharine, 112, 176, 182, 187, 189, 194, 197, 266
  Cathrine, 172
  Caty, 184
  Charles, 51, 262
  Content, 204
  Daniel, 180
  David, 194, 197, 227, 264
  Edward Egbert, 110
  Elisabeth, 170, 175
  Eliz., 197
  Eliza, 195
  Eliza Ann, 191
  Elizabeth, 119, 187, 197, 201, 217, 254, 256, 269
  Ellen, 187
  Ellen H., 183
  Elstye, 57
  Ephraim, 235
  Eva, 10, 51
  Febey, 254
  Frances, 240
  Freeman Degroat, 118
  Hanna, 92, 96, 101
  Hannah, 171, 179, 180, 190, 261
  Hannah Bedell, 266
  Isaac, 166, 269, 272
  Isaac Simonson, 119
  Israel, 66, 175, 189, 190, 252
  Jacob, 51, 179, 270
  James, 184
  Jane, 92, 94, 96, 99, 105, 106, 108, 190, 194
  Jane Eliza, 128
  Jane Maria, 109
  Jeseph, 194
  Johannes, 53
  John, 56, 106, 110, 112, 114, 116, 119, 174, 176, 177, 179, 191, 192, 194, 197, 198, 216, 217, 254, 256
  John Henry, 116, 216
  John Hilliard, 240
  Joseph, 141, 149, 266

Decker, Lawrence Hillyer Lafayette, 133
  Leah, 189
  Lidda, 264
  Lydia, 183, 184
  Mareytye, 60
  Margret, 173
  Maria, 196
  Martha, 192, 197
  Martha Ann, 202
  Mary, 180, 182, 191
  Mary Ann, 180, 182, 188
  Mary Elizabeth, 119
  Mary Frances, 112, 197
  Mathias, 176, 180, 194, 240
  Mathew, 109, 112, 252
  Matias, 264
  Mattheus, 10, 17, 57
  Matthew, 171, 180, 189, 261
  Matthias, 183, 268
  Meryan, 261
  Miriam, 252
  Molly, 61
  Moses, 120, 184, 268
  Nancey, 197
  Nanne, 254
  Nathan, 191
  Noah, 261
  Oliver, 119, 122, 182
  P., 204
  Patience, 128, 233
  Peter, 51, 53, 183, 240, 270
  Phoebe, 172, 261, 262
  Rachel, 190
  Rebecca, 184, 271
  Richard, 66, 118, 128, 135, 172, 182, 188, 198
  Richerd, 56
  Reuben, 196, 269
  Rubin, 256
  Sabina, 174
  Samuel, 184, 198
  Sara, 166
  Sarah, 66, 141, 172, 174, 175, 183, 270
  Sarah Ann, 114, 122, 140, 197
  Sarah M., 231
  Sarah Maria, 198
  Silvanus, 198
  Sylvanus, 271
  Theodore Hampton, 149
  Tunis Augustus, 128
  William, 180
  Williamson, 196
Deckker, Charles, 59
  Marya, 59
de Chene, Catlina, 20
  Francyntje, 23

de Chene, Jeroen, 20
  Maria, 20
de Chesne, Hierome, 21
De Conti, marquis, 258
De Coshorong, Abraham, 251
  Elizabeth, 251
  Nicholas, 251
De Decker, Abraham, 12
  Elisabeth, 14
  Johannes, 9
  Mattheus, 9, 12, 14
  Pieter, 17
DeForeest, Charlotte, 196
Deforest, capt., 115, 214
  John, 104, 219, 236
  Charlotte Jane, 115
  Phebe Ann, 104
De Forest, Ch., 101
  Cornelius Vanderbilt, 110
  Gerardus, 101, 224
  John, 101, 108, 110, 175, 236
Deforrest, capt., 114
  Charles Simonson, 122
  Gerardus, 118
  John, 122
  Julia Selina, 118
  William Hand, 114
De Forrest, Hugh, 214
  John J., 224
  Julia, 229
  Julia, Selina, 229
De Fries, John, 108, 110, 175
de Garemeaux, Jacob, 25
  Ann Catharina, 25
de Gramo, Agneta, 36
  Dirkje, 45
  Jacob, 31, 36, 42, 45
de Grameaux, Ab., 29
  Jacob, 29
  Matthys, 29
Degroat, Henry, 216
  John, 268
De Groat, Robert, 270
Degroot, Beelitye, 64
  Johannes, 52
  Pieter, 62
De Groot, Cattriena, 62
  Geertruy, 64
  Joh., 47
  Johannes, 41, 47, 49
  Lenah Ann, 142
  Pieter, 62, 64
  Robbert, 41
  Wm., 142
Dehart, Baltus, 55
  Catalyna, 55
  Edward, 67
  Jacob, 67
  Samuel, 58

De Hart, ——, mrs., 236
  Anna, 24
  Baltes, 54
  Cathalina, 14
  Catalyntie, 12, 14
  Catlyna, 31
  Daniel, 12, 14, 15, 17, 19, 21, 54, 55, 166
  Elisabeth, 17
  Jan, 24
  M., 236
  Margrietje, 24
  Matthys, 15
  Samuel, 19
  Saartie, 14
  Vereltje, 54
de Hart, Margrietje, 21
Deinmann, Carl Christian Frederick, 152
  Friderica Dorotea Cicilia, 153
De Jeen, Antoni, 14
  Michiel, 14
Dekker, Abraham, 46
  Catlina, 36
  Charles, 33, 35, 39, 43, 46
  Eva, 20, 39, 43, 44
  Johannes, 24, 33, 36, 39
  Magdalena, 43
  Maria, 20, 33
  Mattheus, 36, 46
  Matthys, 39
  Neeltje, 29, 43
  Pieter, 20, 24, 29, 30, 34, 36, 43, 46
  Sara, 34, 36
  Susanna, 29
  Zeger, 39, 44, 46
Dekkers, Catharina, 20, 22, 26, 29, 33
  Charles, 33
  Eva, 50
  Joh., 50
  Neeltje, 22, 24, 25, 33, 34, 39, 50
  Pieter, 22, 33
  Zeger, 33
Delaree, ——, 238
Demarest, Alfred H., iv
Dempsey, ——, 270
de Mersereaux, Jacob, 39
  Josue, 39
Demot, Marrityc, 64
Denice, Ann, 140
Denike, Samuel, 268
Dening, Raymond P., 228
Denis, Sarah, 28
Dennis, Mabala, 215
  Rachel, 169
  Thomas, 215
Dennys, Sarah, 165

Deny, Anna, 28
  Catharina, 28, 30
  Lydia, 28, 30
  Maria, 28
  James, jr., 28
Denyce, Ann, 132
Denys, Femmetje, 21, 28, 43, 44, 50
  Neeltje, 23, 26, 28, 32, 37, 42, 48
De Nys, Femmetje, 36
Denyse, Ann, 115, 126
  Denyse D., 186
Denysz, Femmetje, 23, 41
  Neeltje, 44
Depew, ——, 175
  Barnet, 175
  Niclas, 172
Depey, Peternel, 54
depu, Pieternelle, 58
de Pu, Barend, 52
  Johannes, 52
De Pue, Catharina, 16
  Jan, 11
Depue, Barent, 58, 62
  Johannes, 62
  Liesebet, 64
  Martha, 58
De Pugh, Abraham, 189
  Ann, 191
  Catharine, 189
  Daniel, 201
  Elizabeth, 203
  Else, 272
  John, 191
  Leah, 270
  Maria, 189
  Mary, 189
  Matthew, 191
  Nicholas, 189
  Sally Ann, 189
Depui, Maria, 120
Depuy, Lenah, 120
  Nicholas, 120
  Niclas, 172
De Puy, Ann, 191
  Cath., 191
  Eliza, 191
  Elizabeth, 191
  John, 191
  Israel, 191
  Nicholas, 191
de Puy, Barent, 57
  Elizabeth, 57
  Pieternalla, 57
  Susanna, 28, 35
de Riveaux, Jaques, 40
De Sceen, Katteleyn, 10
de Schweinitz, Bernhard, viii

De Silva, Elizabeth, 264
  Joseph, 264
  Joseph Griggs, 178
  Sarah, 264
  Susan, 178
De Silvee, Anna, 263
  Joseph, 263
de Sien, Antie, 15
De Syen, Catharina, 16
  Hieronymus, 16
De Wine, Lucas, 270
de Wint, Petrus, iii
Dey, Catharina, 23, 26
  Charles, 92, 96, 99
  Charles, mrs., 98
  Chas., 96
  David, 96
  Ery, 19
  Jan, 61
  Johannes, 19
  Lewis, 92
  Lydia, 23
  Maria, 13, 22, 29
  Mary, 96
  Rebeckah, 123
  Sara, 22, 23, 61
  Sarah, 216
  Simon, 13
  Uzal M'Ginny, 99
Deyoung, Peter, 165
De Young, Ann Elizabeth, 87
  Daniel, 76, 87
  Fanny, 87
  James, 76
D Grood, Elizabeth, 58
  Gerret, 59
  Johannes, 60
  Pieter, 58-60
Dimpfel, Elizabeth, 152
  George Louis, 152
  Louisa Julia, 152
Dine, negro, 186
Disosway, Thomas, 190
Dissasway, Ann, 196, 248
  Catharine, 248
  Cornelius, 248
  Israel Fitzrandolph, 135
  Israel O., 135, 196
  Israel R., 196
Dissossway, ——, 237
Dissosway, Catharine, 269
  Israel, 223
  Israel Fitz Randolph, 223
  Lucretia, 223
  Mark, 269
  Violetta, 269
Ditten, Richard, 198
Dittens, ——, 218
Dittmer, ——, 232
Ditton, ——, 234, 235
  D., 235

Ditton, Daniel, 207
Dixey, John, 270
Dixon, ——, 273
Dobson, Ann, 167
Doeller, Christine, 238
Doghety, Maria, 61
  Thomas, 61
Dominge, Ellen, 149
  Ellen Matilda, 149
  Raymond Augustus, 149
Domingo, Raymond A., 232
Donaldson, Jno. A., 234
Donats, Elizabeth, 173
Dongan, mrs., 256
  Elizabeth, 119
  Joanna, 272
  Richard, 257
  Thomas, 257
Donolly, Mary, 273
Dorlandt, Helena, 12, 57
  Jan, 12, 14
  Joris, 14
  Lambert, 12
Dorlant, Abraham, 31
  Anthony, 38
  Barber, 17
  Corn., 38
  Cornelis, 38
  Elsje, 20, 23-25, 30, 40, 48
  Eva, 23
  Harmpje, 23
  Isack, 18
  Jan, 17, 18, 23, 31
  Lambert, 23
  Lena, 13
Dorsee, Evo, 217
Dorset, Catharine, 79, 100
  Cornelius Cortelyou, 80
  Ellen C., 219
  Ellen Elizabeth, 127
  Ellen Maria, 196
  Isaac Lewis, 134
  John, 79-82, 86, 88, 89, 91, 92, 94-96, 98, 101, 102, 170, 175, 196, 218, 219, 241
  John, sr., 220
  John William Beatty, 218
  Margaret, 84
  Martha, 79-82, 86-89, 92, 94-96, 98, 100, 196, 241
  Peter, 88, 122, 127, 134
  Sarah, 82
  Susan Maria Mersereau, 122
Dorsett, mr., 121
  Amanda Elizabeth, 119, 217
  Catharine, 108, 113, 117, 176, 266

Dorsett, Eleanor Mary, 90
  Ellen, 217
  John, 85-90, 106, 108, 111, 113, 116, 119, 122, 176, 180, 188, 217
  John William Beattey, 122
  Marth, 180
  Martha, 85-91, 106, 108, 113, 176, 188, 216, 241
  Mary Jane, 116
  Peter, 136, 193
  Sarah, 108, 111, 180
Dorsitt, John, 83
  Martha, 83
Doty, Mary, 266
  Moses, 266
Doutey, Anne, 255
  Moses, 255
  Rachel, 255
Downes, ——, mrs., 226
Downs, Ann, 198
  John, 198
  Serena, 153
Doyle, Adam A., 192
  Elizabeth, 192
  Hugh, 169
  Robert, 192
Drageau, Margrietje, 50
  Maria, 45
  Marie, 34, 40, 48, 49
  Pierre, 9
Drake, Aaron, 187
  Anna, 264
  Anne, 172
  Benjamin, 259-262, 264
  Eliza, 272
  Elizabeth, 259
  Evelina A., 229
  Francis, 261
  Mary Ann, 200
  Rachel, 262
  Sarah, 259-262, 264
  William, 271
Drenkwater, Elisabet 37
  Margriet, 37
  Nathanael, 37
Dreyer, Carl Bruno, 154
  Frederick Adolph, 204
  Friederich A., 154
Drinkwater, Elisabet, 42, 45, 51, 54
  Hester, 40
  Margrietje, 42, 44
  Sara, 42
  Sarah, 44
  Sophia D., 223
Drisius, dominie, ii
Driskyl, Ann, 214
  Daniel, 214
Drummoncts, capt. 254
  Alexander, 254
  Mary, 254

Drummond, capt., 256, 258
  Ann, 249
  Daniel, 249
  Elexander, 249
  Jacobina, 256
  Susan, 256
  Susanna, 258
Drury, mrs., 98
  John, 98
  John Jeremiah, 105
  Joseph, 101, 214
  Susan Stillwell, 105
  William, 98, 101, 175
Dubaa, Maria, 56
Dubois, mr, 185
  Augustus, 247
  Catrin, 260
  Easters, 256
  Edward, 262
  Elis., 177
  Elisabeth, 186
  Esther, 246
  Hettie, 177
  John, 246, 256, 260, 262
  Margaret P., 177
  Maria, 53,
  Martha, 247
  Mary, 247, 256, 260, 262
  Lewis, 177, 260
  Margaret, 239
  Matthias, 260
du Bois, Esther, 41
  Louis, jr., 49, 51
  Marguerite, 41
  Martha, 51
  Samuel, 49
Du Bois, Lewis, 272
Duboys, Mary, 259
  Matthias, 259
du Cecoy, Dina, 27
du Chene, Anna, 24
  Cornelis, 24
  Francyntje 27
  Gerrit, 24
  Jannetje, 27, 41
  Michel, 25, 26
  Michiel, 24, 45
  Sarah, 40
du Chesne, Jannetje, 20
  Sara, 43, 51
  Sarah, 47, 49
du Chine, Sarah, 38
Due Seen, Machgyel, 18
  Valentyen, 18
Dugan, ——, 231, 232, 238
  Cornelius, 165
  Mary, 225
  Thomas, 234
Dungan, Abigail, 88, 266
  Abigail Simonson, 266
  Cornelia, 88
  Ruth, 93

Dungan, W., 93
  Walter, 88, 93, 266
Dungin, mrs., 87
  Abigail, 88
  Abigal, 86
  Sarah, 86
  Walter, 87, 88
  Walther, 86
Duke, Daniel, 263
  Loretta, 263
Dunham, mrs., 149
  Amos, 216
  Eve, 99
  Henry Roy, 99
  John, 166
  Lewis, 166
Dunn, judge, 216, 219
  ——, mrs., 216
  Ann, 83
  Ann Maria, 221
  Bittje, 83
  Dorothy Vanderbilt 226
  D. V., 226
  Edward, 225
  Isabella, 213
  John, 213, 218, 221
  John W., 219
  Margt. Eliza, 218
  Mary, 213, 221
  Robert, 83, 213, 220
Dupuy, Jacob, 250
  John, 245-247, 249, 250
  Leah, 249
  Ledde, 255
  Lena, 27, 29
  Liddy, 258
  Moses, 249, 255, 258
  Necolas, 255
  Nicholas, 247, 250
  Nicolas, 25
  Sarah, 245-247 250
  Susanna, 28
du Puy, Aaron, 50
  Barent, 50
  Catharina, 20, 27, 29
  Elisabet, 28, 33
  Elizabet, 39
  Elsje, 50
  Jan, 21, 22
  Johannes, 33
  Lena, 22, 25, 31, 32
  Mattheus, 33
  Moses, 43
  Nicolaas, 25, 29, 33, 39, 43
  Nicolas, 27, 34, 50
  Susanna, 21, 22, 31, 34, 39
Du Puy, Maria, 51
  Nicolaas, 24
Durant, Judith, 170
Durland, Gizeburt, 268

Durlant, Geisbertje, 54
Duringer, John, 152
  John Henry, 152
Durlyet, Maria Magdalena, 18
du Secoy, Anna, 27
  Dina, 29, 30
  Elisabet, 29
  Gabriel, 10, 30
  Israel, 27, 28
  Job, 28
  Johannes, 28
  Marcus, 10
  Susanna, 10
Dustan, ——, major, 225
  Harriet, Jean, 226
  Isaac, 228
  Oscar Fitz Patrick, 109, 213
  Sarah, 238
  William, 109, 213
  William, Saml., 225
du Tes, Susanna, 20
Duxbury, Ellis, ix
  judge, ix
Dye, Anne, 255
  Apha, 249
  Charles, 214
  David, 249, 255
  Elizabeth 255
  Jacobus, 14
  John, 214, 217, 218
  John David, 255
  Mary, 249, 255
  Rebecca, 215
  Sarah, 249
Dykeman, Eliza Cuszina, 113
  Gerardus, 115, 118
  Gerret, 113
  Mary, Ann, 115
  Rachel, 118
Dykman, mrs., 113
  Gerardus, 113
  Gilbert, 113
  Richard, 113

E

Earle, James, 227
Ebbet, ——, 228
  D., 228
Ebbit, David, 238
  Serena, 233
Ebbits, Ann Wright, 153
  George, 153
  George Patten, 153
  Harriet, 153
  Lucy, 153
Ecbers, Benyamen, 58
  Jacus, 58
Eden, Heinrich Jansen, 156

Eddy, Cornelius Cole, 201
Edmonds, William, vi
Egberszen, Jaques, 41
  Pieter, 41
Egbert, ——, 187, 216, 222, 223, 227, 228, 230, 231, 233, 234, 236
——, mrs., 225
  sr., 144
  A., 233
  Abm., 83, 86, 96, 98, 99, 102, 104, 107, 108, 160, 180, 193, 194, 198, 201, 202, 208, 217
  Abm., jr., 201
  Abm., sr., 198, 200
  Abr., 144
  Abraham, 75, 82, 86, 88, 89, 91, 93, 96, 97, 99, 102, 104, 107, 108, 171, 181, 183, 185, 189, 196, 212, 215, 221, 241, 257
  Abraham, sr., 114, 230
  Abraham Martino, 117
  Abraham Prawl, 109
  Abraham S., 150, 156, 202
  Abraham T., 229
  Abraham Tunis, 152
  Abrm., 149
  Abr. S., 147
  Adeline, 161
  Aletta, 130, 220
  Alfred, 226
  Ann, 80-89, 91, 93-99, 102, 105-112, 114, 116, 117, 119, 126, 160, 173, 177, 179-181, 183, 186, 194, 196, 198, 200, 201, 204, 210-213, 216, 221, 233, 241
  Ann Eliza, 198
  Ann Lavinia, 135
  Ann Martha, 193
  Ann Rebekah, 130
  Anna, 158, 159
  Anne, 73-75
  Annette, 235
  Annet Lake, 128
  Barney, 271
  Betsy, 219
  Barzillai, 119
  Benjamin, 104, 212
  C., 106
  Caroline Atkins, 139
  Cath., 212
  Catharina, 78
  Catharine, 73, 78, 107, 142, 154, 161, 205, 210, 212, 223, 269
  Catharine Ann, 137
  Catharine Hannah, 160

Egbert, Catharine Maria, 123, 147, 149, 157, 160, 202, 205
Cathrine, 210
Caty, 257
Charles, 102, 106, 110, 113, 115, 118, 215, 216
Charlotte Deforest, 144
Christiana, 215
Cornelius, 88, 90, 91, 98, 120, 123, 128, 132, 138, 145, 173, 188-190, 192, 198, 217, 223, 226
Cornelius Bird, 156
Cornelius Cortelyou, 79, 213
Corns., 205, 209
Corns., mrs., 200
Daniel Mersereau, 135
Edward, 74, 79-84, 86, 87, 93, 106, 126, 128, 133, 239, 143, 162, 168, 172, 174, 179, 198, 200, 206, 209, 211, 216, 217, 241
Edw., 80, 83
Edwd., 85, 174, 213, 230
Elis., 97
Elisabeth, 78, 138, 170, 198
Eliz., 87, 210, 212
Eliza, 123, 128, 133, 135, 146, 188, 192, 219, 223
Eliza Ann, 97, 114, 115, 150, 229
Elizabeth, 74, 78, 87, 89, 91, 94, 98, 128, 158, 177, 178, 206, 213, 241
Elizabeth Ann, 113, 215
Elizabeth Mary, 146
Elizebeth, 212
Ellen, 209
Ellen Simonson, 152
Emeline, 132, 160, 209
Ester Ellen, 139
Eugene Mortimer, 115, 220
Eupheme, 110
Frances, 168
Frances Lavinia, 126
Gertrude, 193
Gertrude M., 217
Hannah, 119, 198, 217, 222, 225, 236
Hannah Jane, 133, 139, 206
Hannah Mary, 119
Harriet, 198
Harriette, 116
Henrietta, 138, 147, 160
Henrietta Prell, 143
Henry, 94, 143, 222
Henry Edward, 216

Egbert, Hertje, 102
Holmes, 194, 227
Isabella, 221
Isabella Sarah Catharine, 118
Isabella S. C., 201
J., 231
Jac., 228
Jacob, 156, 207
James, 73, 78, 87, 91, 94, 96-98, 119, 165, 177, 178, 189, 195, 196, 210, 212, 213, 216, 217, 241
James, jr., 189, 217
James, sr., 111, 183, 184, 218
Jane, 101, 188, 212, 224, 225
J. Holmes, 226
Jane Louise, 132
Jas., 87
John, 73, 79-81, 83, 84, 86, 88, 90, 94, 96, 97, 115, 118, 123, 130, 134, 135, 138, 150, 156, 168, 173, 181, 183, 185, 190, 192, 200, 202, 205, 211, 212, 220, 222, 224, 226, 233, 237, 241
John, jr., 109
John, sr., 116, 193, 218, 219
John James, 102
John Merril, 146
John Simonson, 152
John V., 152, 157
John Vanderbilt, 111, 201
John William, 128
John Wm., 207
Joseph, 79, 96, 98, 102, 124, 151, 158, 188, 189, 194, 198, 212, 223-225, 237
Joseph Thomas, 124
Jno., 233, 234
Lemont Williams, 157
Letty Ann Lake, 126
Louisa, 145
Louisa Sidney, 152
Lucy, 80, 94, 101, 173, 192
Lydia, 118, 130, 147, 149, 156, 161, 163, 202, 205
Lydia Eliza, 130, 156, 158, 161
Madora, 149
Margaret Jane, 146, 201
Margrett, 217
Maria, 117, 119, 156, 184, 202, 212, 219, 232, 273
Maria Ann, 119
Maria Simonson, 156

Egbert, Marietta, 209
Martha, 183, 193
Martha Ann, 119, 196
Mary, 79-84, 86, 88, 90, 93, 94, 96, 97, 101, 102, 174, 181, 183, 210-213, 241
Mary Ann, 91, 117, 126, 139, 188
Mary Elizabeth, 139
Mary Jane, 112
Mary Josephine, 126
Mary Precilla, 122
Mary Van der Beak, 89
Moses, 78, 193, 210, 220, 257
N., mrs., 98
Nancy, 198, 233
Nicholas Depui, 120
Patience, 89, 111, 116, 121, 133, 186, 194
Peggy, 217
Peter, 115
Rachel Ann, 118, 234
Rebecca Maria, 202
Richard, 118, 230
Richard Edmund, 119
Sabina, 232
Sally, 87, 121, 128, 188, 195, 196, 220
Sally Ann, 215
Saml., 198
Samuel, 84, 112, 114, 116, 170, 183, 216
Samuel, jr., 219
Sara, 95, 102, 212
Sarah, 81, 102, 106, 110, 111, 113, 118, 131, 134, 174, 189, 193, 216
Sarah Adeline, 134, 207
Sarah Ann, 106, 191
Shirley Morton, 237
Stephen, 78, 86, 111, 117, 198, 212, 213, 215, 222, 235
Sussan, 113
T., 228
Thomas Holmes, 88, 146, 198
Thos. Holmes, 227
Teunis, 73, 94
Tunis, vii, 74, 75, 78, 83-87, 89, 93-95, 97, 102, 105, 107-109, 111, 113-115, 118, 122, 126, 132, 171, 174, 180, 183, 186, 191, 201, 212, 215, 217, 221, 225, 239, 241
Tunis, jr., 241
Tunis, sr., 216, 241
Tunis A., 196
Tunis J., 216, 220
Warren Alston, 114, 215

Egbert, Wesley, 151
  Wesly, 119
  William, 97, 128, 137, 139, 142, 193
  William St. Clair, 150
  Wm., 151
Egberts, Abraham, 257, 259
  Ann, 259
  Anthony, 259, 262
  Antony, 260
  Antye, 57
  Benjamin, 257
  Catharina, 50
  Catrin, 259
  Catrina, 53
  Catrine, 260
  Caty, 258
  Cornelius, 120, 160
  Edward, 91
  Eleanor, 260
  Elener, 262
  Elizabeth, 257, 259
  Jacobus, 23
  Jacus, 53, 57
  James, 258
  John, 258, 260
  Maria, 50, 51, 55, 56
  Martha, 260
  Mary, 259, 260, 262
  Moses, 259
  Reuben, 259
  Sarah, 91, 259
  Theunis, 12, 15, 17
  Tunis, 260
Egbertse, Abraham, 57, 59
  Abram, 53
  Egbert, 23
  Elisabet, 53
  Hester, 59
  Isaak, 23
  Johnnes, 54
  Teunes, 54
  Tunis, 57
Egbertsen, Abraham, 15, 17, 23, 27, 47
  Barent, 58
  Catharina, 49
  Egbert, 15
  Elisabet, 27
  Jacobus, 23, 26
  Jaques, 47
  Johannes, 23
  Maria, 23
  Teunis, 20, 26, 58
Egbertsz, Jaques, 37, 44
  Susanna, 44
  Theunis, 20
Egbertszen, Egbert, 27
  Jaques, 37
  Johannes, 27
  Nicolaas, 37

Egbertzen, Elizabet, 49
  Jacobus, 28
  Jaques, 30, 49
  Johannes, 28
  Laurens, 30
Eggers, Adelaide, 151
Eghmont, Corn., 39
Egmont, Altje, 19
  Christoffel, 32
  Cornelis, 16, 19, 25, 32, 35
  Cornelius, 28
  Femmetje, 25
  Zeger, 28
Ehrhardt, Catharine Christina, 157
Eidam, Elizabeth, 154
  Daniel, 154
Eisele, R., 237
Eldridge, Mary, 168
Elesen, Bastjan, 18
Elis, Sara, 59
Eliza, 181
Elland, Eleanor, 158
Ellas, Cornelus, 61
Ellens, Charles, 21
  Johannes, 21
Elles, ——na, 59
  Aagtje, 35
  Basteaan, 59
  Basteyaan, 55
  Bastejan, 54
  Bastiaan, 22, 29, 30, 32, 35, 40
  Catharina, 30
  Cornelius, 32
  Hendrikje, 22, 25, 30
  Henrikje, 35
  Maria, 55
  Sara, 40, 54
Ellis, Abraham, 67
  Basteaan, 64
  Bastiaan, 39, 42
  Catrina, 57
  Cattriena, 61, 64
  Cornelius, 64
  Egye, 61
  Garret, 67, 190
  Mary, 190
  Saara, 64
  Sara, 61, 64, 65
Ellison, William, 166
Ellwein, John, 79
Elmwood, John, 197
Elnesly, ——, 176
Els, Geesje, 26
Elston, ——, 271
Elsewarrt, Antje, 53
  Mareitje, 53
  Wellim, 53
Elten, Hester, 200
Emmons, William E., 209
Emmot, John, 193

Enyard, Abraham, 85
  Daniel, 78
  Elias, 76
  Elisabeth, 77
  Elizabeth, 210, 241
  Jemima, 76-78
  Mary, 85
  Mary Ann, 180
  Mathias, vii, 76, 180
  Matthias, 172
  Nicholas, 76-78, 85
  Sarah, 180
  Susanna, 78, 241
  Sussanna, 173, 210
  Timothy, 76
  William T., v
Erzer, Jäkle, 204
  Margaret, 204
Escord, Andre, 36, 39
  Daniel, 37
  Esther, 36
  Maria, 39
Essig, Johannes, 137
  Maria, 137
Etsch, Carl, 153
Ettlinger, Adolph, 156
  Louis, 156
Ettwin, John, 82
Eulner, Catharine, 158, 206
  Valentine, 206
Everse, Matteis, 65
Everson, Mary, 270
Exbersen, Susanna, 17
  Tunis, 17
Exjard, Elisabet, 52
  Mathies, 52

F

Faas, Jannetje, 28, 30
Facker, Catharina, 34
  Johan Henrich, 34
Falkenborgh, Maria, 56
Fall, George A., 202
Fardon, Aaron, 193
  Eliza, 219
  Isaac, 217, 219
Farrow, Catharine Elizabeth, 161
  Ida Lucretia, 161
  Lucy Ann, 161
  Samuel, 161
Ferhmann, Jacob, iv
Ferris, John, 169
Feust, Fredericka Carolina, 156
Fey, Doratha, 205
Fialan, Daniel, 65
  Hanry, 65
Field, chaplain, x, xi
  mr., 263
Finauf, Adelaide, 144

Fink, John D., 208
Fischt, Jane F., 238
Fisher, Anne, 58
   Johann, 150
Fitchet, Jane, 168
Fitzgerald, Margret
   Eliza, 218
   Mary, 197
   Michael, 218
   Sarah, 149
   Thomas, 197
   Wm., 197
Fitzinger, Deborah, 205
Fitz Patrick, Margaret, 204
Fitz Randolph, ——, 225
   Hartshorn, 217
Flager, Constance Maria, 144
   Henry, 144
   Isabella, 144
   John Walter, 144
Fleming, mr., 234
   D., 234
   Eliz., 167
Fletcher, gov., viii
Flinn, Roger, 170
Flitcher, Ann, 175
Folager, ——, 239
Folkertzen, Folkert, 31
Foot, Eliza, 187
Force, Marytje, 38
Foret, Liesabet, 63
Fortunate, John, 167
Fountain, ——, 226, 227, 232, 233, 239
   mr., 199
   ——, mrs., 226
   Abraham, 227
   Abm., 180, 227
   Anthony, 38, 170, 176, 177, 213, 214, 247
   Anthony, jr., 194
   Anthony, sr., 240
   Antony, 172
   Antje, 38
   Catharine, 229, 272
   Charles, 247
   Clarissa, 201
   Cornelius, 170
   Eliza, 194
   Elizabeth Ann, 137
   Else, 184
   Gideon, 234
   James, 197
   Jane, 106
   John, 176, 179, 181, 185, 199, 272
   John V., 231
   Leonard, 137, 197
   Louisa, 201
   Mary, 99, 102, 109, 137, 175, 176, 197, 226

Fountain, Nancy, 194
   Peter, 171
   Susanna, 169, 247
   Vincent, 171, 176, 179, 184
   William, 213, 229
   Wm., Austin, 234
   Wm., H., 183
Founten, Antoni, 62, 63
   Antony, 65
   Cornelus, 65
   Johannis, 63
   Maragrietye, 63
   Nensy, 62
Fowler, ——, 217
   Abigail, 217
Foy, Francis, 249
   John, 246, 249, 251
   Mary, 246, 249, 251
Frazur, Lewis, 168
Fredericks, Ann, 150, 153
   Ann (Nancy), 156
   Nancy, 156
Freegard, ——, mrs., 236
   Ellen, 208
Freeland, Michael, 269
Freelant, Metje, 53
Freeling, Rich., 180
Freeman, Bernardus, 25
   Gager, 165
   Gertrude, 197
   John, 192, 197
   Mary, 197
   Mary Elizabeth, 206
   Smith B., 206
Frende, Carl Aguste, 137
   Mary Blanche, 137
Frettert, Frederick Jacob, 158
   Jacob, 158
   Magdalena, 158
Fries, Maria Hetwig, 198
Fritz, George, 149
   Hans Jorg, 141
   Henrietta Elisabeth, 149
Frome, Mary, 268
   Nathaniel, 173
   Ploney, 268
Froom, Daniel, 172
Froome, N., 176
Frost, dr., 256
   Caroline, 223
   Elizabeth, 258
   John Thomas, 256
   Matilda, 223
   Robert, 24, 28
   Samuel, 223, 233
   Samuel, mrs., sr., 232
   Tamer, 258, 261
   Thomas, 258, 261
   Tomagine, 256
   Usselton, 28
   William Errell, 261

Fugel, Adam, 141, 143, 147, 150, 153
   Catharine, 150
   Hans Jorg, 141
   John, 150
   Maria Catharine Barbara, 147
   Michael, 143
   Nathan, 153
Futton, Isabella Forker, 214

G

Gaelledet, Maria, 57
Gage, Jonathan, 165
Gahner, Gallus, 140
Gaines, ——, 235
   Wm., 235
Galmer, Catharine, 157
Gambold, br., vi
   H., 165
   Hector, vii, 71, 76-79
Gans, Henry, 146
Garamaux, Jacob, 33
   Metje, 33
Gardner, Myles, 167
Gareau, Jean, 20
Garebrantz, Elener, 65
Garretson, ——, 216, 233, 270
   mrs., 132
   Abraham, 127, 130, 132, 133, 135, 193, 219
   Abraham Crocheron, 135
   Ann, 106, 167
   Catharine, 177, 218, 229
   Cornelius, 229
   Edgar Eugene, 133
   Elisabeth, 177
   Eliza, 218, 219, 227, 231
   Hendrick, iv
   Henry, 190
   Henry Davis, 130
   Hermanus, 127, 219
   Jacob, 194, 229, 269
   Jacob, sr., 228
   Jacob Herman, 158, 206
   James, 189
   James B., 206
   Jane, 271
   Jane Elizabeth, 206
   John, 168, 177, 193, 218, 224, 273
   John, jr., 216
   Maria, 177, 216
   Mary Ida, 158
Garrettson, ——, 235, 236
   mr., 236
   Abraham, 143
   Edwin, 238
   Hiram, 236

297

Garrettson, Jacob, 235
  James B., 234
  John, 160, 180
  John Jacob, 143
  Margaret Ann, 160
  Maria, 203
  Mary Elizabeth, 160
  Wm. H'y Smith, 160
Garribrance, France, 67
  Nailtie, 67
Garrison, Ann, 97, 100, 103
  Aulchie, 66
  Charles, 247
  Christopher, 74, 255
  Daniel, 247, 252
  Doroth., 80
  Elener, 255
  Elisabeth, 168
  Elizabeth, 241
  Esther, 268
  Febe, 255
  Hannah, 166
  Jacob, 247
  John, 66, 170
  Margaret Ann, 203
  Mary, 74, 247, 252
  Nicholas, v
  Phebe, 74
Garritson, col., 239
  Ann, 112
  Betsey, 84, 85
  Elisabeth, 211
  Eliz., 86
  Elizabeth, 83, 86, 87, 91
  Frances, 92, 95
  Gertrude, 170
  Hendric, 239
  Hendrick, 211
  Henry, 84, 172
  Hermanus, 93
  Jacob, 85
  James Birkby, 86
  John, 83-84, 93, 94
  Lambert, ix
  Mary, 83, 218, 221
  Phoebe, 172
Gasquoine, ——, 229
  H., 229
Gates, ——, 238
Gauthier, Andrew, 91
  Thomas, 91
Gebhardt, Godfried W., 157
  John Godfried, 157
Geffers, Mary, 260
Geibert, ——, 237
Geiser, Johannes, 149
  Louis, 149
Gendron, Magdalaine, 49
Gennens, Mary, 14
  Sara, 14
George, Catarine, 262
  Elleanor, 262

George, Joseph, 262
Gerbrants, Frans, 37
Gerbrantsz, Elisabet, 38
  Frans, 38
Gerd, Eliza, 153
Germond, ——, 232
Gerrand, Thomas, 169
Gerrebrans, Christeyaan, 64
  Neeltye, 64
Gerrebrats, France, 52
  Frances, 52
Gerresen, Abraham, 53
  Elizabet, 52, 53
  Johnanes, 54
  Nicklas, 52
  Nicolaes, 53
  Susanna, 53, 54
  Zeger, 52
Gerretse, Elizabet, 58, 59
  Elizabeth, 55
  Hester, 59
  Jannetye, 60
  Susanna, 58, 60
  Yannetye, 61
Gerretson, Annatje, 62
  Annatye, 63
  Johannis, 63
  John, iv
Gerrissen, Seger, 9
Gerrits, Aaltje, 22
Gerritse, Susanna, 57
Gerritsen, Zeger, 30
Gerritson, Abraham Crocheron, 88
  Anaatye, 63
  Annaetje, 65
  Cathrina, 33
  Cathrine Conor, 81
  Eliz., 89
  Elizabeth, 80-82, 88-90, 241
  Johannis, 64
  John, 80-82, 84, 88, 90
  Maragrietye, 64
  Nicolaas, 33
  Richard Conor, 82
Gerritsz, Charles, 21
  Lambert, jr., 21
  Magdalena, 21
  Zeger, 34
Gerritsze, Nicolaas, 41
Gerritszen, Elisabet, 44
  Lea, 47
Gerritz, Antje, 30
  Lambert, jr., 25
  Nicolaas, 25
Gerritze, Zeger, 40
Gerritzen, Abraham, 28
  Blandina, 51
  Catharina, 28, 29
  Christopher, 40
  Cornelis, 48

Gerritzen, Daniel, 9, 48
  Elisabet, 39, 43, 46, 50
  Elizabet, 42, 47
  Grietje, 9
  Isaac, 40
  Lambert, 9, 15, 39, 43
  Lambert, jr., 28
  Lammert, 9
  Nicholas, 40
  Nicolaas, 35, 43, 49, 51
  Susanna, 35
  Zeger, 28, 43, 49
Gerritzon, Jan, 38
  Nicolaas, 38
Gerrtbratse, Daniel, 55
  Frans, 55
Gewan, Elisabet, 50
  Jenne, 48, 49
Gibett, James, 142
  James Augustus, 142
Gibson, A. C., 225
  Elizabeth, 86
  Hugh, 86
  Sarah, 86, 177
Gifford, Mary, 272
Gilbert, ——, 227
  Abbey Ann, 134, 135
  Abby Ann, 130, 219, 220
  Elizabeth Frances, 139
  Hannah Jane, 121, 135, 219
  James, 121, 124, 130, 134, 135, 139, 219, 220, 236
  James Thomas Steward, 124, 220
  Maria, 134
  Sarah Ann Matilda, 130
Gildersleave, ——, 225
Gillesby, Grace, 200
Glascou, Jannetje, 33
Glascow, Jannetje, 38, 47
Gleave, Marya, 23
Glendinen, Cathrine, 173
Goddard, Kingston, xi
Goepp, Marie Ottilie, 155
Gold, Catharine, 252
  Jan, 46
  John, 45, 46, 249, 252
  Katharine, 249
  Marytje, 45
  Peter, 252
  Tryphena, 167
Gontz, Louis, 141, 200
Goodheart, Christopher, 185
  John, 185
  Sophia, 185
Goodman, John, 268
Goodyear, ——, 233
Goolder, Abraham, 11
Gouns, Jannetje, 53
Gowen, Margrietje, 53
Grace, Elizabeth, 268

Graham, Augistin, ix
Grameaux, Catharina, 21
  Jacob, 21
Gramo, Jacob, 20
  Johannes, 20
Grandine, ——, 272
  Catharine, 178
  John, 245
  Lewis, 245
Granger, Franca, 252
  Frances, 258
  William, 167, 252, 258
Grasbeek, Susan, 254
Gray, Abraham, 28
  Isaak, 28
Graz, Anna Maria, 204
Greegs, Anna, 27
  John, 29
  Maria, 32
  Martinus, 22
  Pieternelle, 25
  Thomas, 22, 25, 27, 29, 31, 32
Grey, George, 168
Griffin, Benjamin, 204
Griffis, Hannah, 247, 268
  John, 247
Griffith, Arthur, 245
  Hannah, 245
  John, 245
Griffiths, Peter, 268
Grimma, Martha, 169
Grondin, Jean, 41
  Pieter, 41
Grover, Barzillai, 266
  Christine, 266
  William, 266
Grunert, F. E., viii
Guebet, ——, 227
Guihon, Daniel, 84
  Henry Garritson, 84
  Phebe, 84
Guineau, Louis, 38
  Susanna, 38
Guion, Adrian, 269
  Ann, 113, 116, 117
  Catharine, 271
  Daniel, 117
  Elizabeth, 117
  Harmanus, 272
  Hermanus, 190
  James, 272
  John, 218, 271
  Margaret, 272
  Mary, 269
Gummert, C., 206
  Henriette Rosalie, 206
Gulledet, Elisee, 49
  Esther, 49
Guthrie, Eliza, 91
Guyon, ——, miss, 232
  Abraham, 90
  Addra, 272

Guyon, Ann, 109, 121, 221, 262
  Ann Elizabeth, 181
  Cornelius, 95, 273
  Cornelius D., 209
  Daniel, 88-90, 92, 95, 99, 113, 175, 181, 185, 211, 217, 221
  Danl., 99, 103, 109, 175
  Elis., 103
  Eliz., 99
  Elizabeth, 103, 109
  Elizabeth Clawson Young, 99
  Frances, 88-90, 181
  Francis, 211
  Harry, 199
  James, 175, 262
  James, jr., 199
  John, 167
  Peter, 165
  Richard Conor, 89
  Sara, 92
  Sophia Catharine, 99
  Susannah, 262

H

Haagewout, Catriena, 63
  Geertruy, 64
  Necclos, 64
  Neeltye, 63
  Neety, 65
  Peter, 65
  Pieter, 64
  Wynant, 65
Hacher, John, 271
Hafte, Benjamin, 36
  Katje, 18
Haften, Catharina, 26
  Jacob, 25
  Johannes, 25, 26
Hageman, Louis, 204
Hagen, Francis F., viii, 71
Hagewout, Aaltje, 20, 22-24, 30, 35
  Aeltie, 13
  Agbert, 57
  Annaetye, 60
  Derckie, 15
  Dirkje, 26
  Egbert, 13, 15, 34, 62
  Elizabeth, 78
  Geertie, 16
  Geertje, 20, 23, 26
  Geertruyd, 44
  Grietye, 62
  Harmpje, 20, 24-27, 31, 35, 37, 42
  Jacobus, 40
  Jan, 24
  Lea, 30, 31, 35, 37, 40, 42, 55

Hagewout, Leah, 47
  Leea, 53
  Margreta, 48
  Mary, 78, 79
  Neeltje, 18, 37
  Neeltye, 59, 60
  Nicholas, 79
  Nicklaas, 60
  Nicolaas, 23
  Peter, 78, 79
  Pieter, 16, 18, 19, 23, 26, 27, 31, 34-37, 40, 41, 44, 48, 59, 60, 62
  Pieter, jr., 16
  Pieter, sr., 15
  Rachel, 24, 35
  Sara, 53
  Stephen, 78
  Treintje, 53
  Trintie, 51
Hagewouyt, Catharina, 55
Hale, Wm. W., 208
Halle, Abm. Herman, 223
  Abraham Herman, 134
  Eugene Benhornean, 134
  Lafayette Mathias, 223
  La Fayette Matthias, 134
  Sarah, 134
Halstead, Susan, 273
Halsted, Elizabeth, 253
  John, 253, 273
Hamersly, Thomas, 91
Hand, Patrick, 230
  Phebe, 92, 97
Handlin, Elizabeth, 167
Hansby, Abraham, 232
  Ann, 232
Hansen, Hans, 22
Hanszen, Isaak, 46
  Jeams, 12
  Symons, 46
Hapenny, Davis Carel, 209
Harcourt, Daniel, 103
  Richard, 103
Harmer, Thomas, ix
Hartman, br., 136
  mrs., 112
  Eliza C., 126, 189, 194, 196
  G. A., 71, 111, 112, 183, 184, 214
  George A., viii
  Isabella Forker, 214
  Isabella S., 111
Harris, Abraham, 257, 261
  Margret, 257
  Rachel, 261
Harrison, mr., 207
  Mary Ann, 207
  Thomas, 205

Harry, negro, 185, 273
Harvey, R., 223
  Sophia D., 223
Harzan, Ann, 183
  Cornelius, 183
Harzen, Jacob, 183
Haste, Benjamin, 36, 39, 43
  Jacob, 36
  Johannes, 39
  Katje, 18
Hasten, Benjamin, 30
  Catharina, 26
  Johannes, 26, 27, 30
Hately, Richard, 169
Hatfield, Deborah, 173
  James, 196
  John, 173
  Sarah, 196
Hatsche, mr., 205
  Elizabeth Georgiana 152
  George, 152
  John, 152
Hattof, Anna, 156
Haughabout, Betsey, 186
  Clarisse, 221
  Ellen, 191, 194
  Hannah, 183
  James, 221
  John, 195
  Maria, 214
  Mary Ann, 195
  Peter, 183, 191
  Peter Nicholas, 221
  Rachel, 183
  Winant, 191
Haughawout, Dorcas, 222
  Elsie Jane, 196
  Nicholas, 222
  Rachel Ann, 222
Haughwort, Aletta, 81
  Eleonora, 91
  Mary, 81, 210
  Peter, 81, 210
Haughworth, Eleonore, 95
Haughwout, ——, 178
  Betsy, 145
  Daniel, 195
  Edward, 270
  Eleanor, 212
  Eleonore, 99
  Elizabeth, 270
  Esther, 195
  Francis, 181, 195
  Hester, 181
  Isaac Minton, 222
  James, 222
  Maria, 117
  Mary, 181
  Matthias, 181
  Nicholas, iv, 222
  Peter, iv, 165

Haughwout, Sarah, 222
  Susan, 159
  Winant 222
  Wynant, 181
Haugwout, Danniel, 65
  Egbert, 65
Hauseman, John, 84
  Martha Swaim Butler, 152
Hausman, Catharine Ann 153
  Isaac, 153
  James, 154
  Theodore Adam, 154
Hazard, Robert, 237
Heady, Catharine, 266
  Hester, 266
  William, 266
Heal, Eliza Swift, 164
  Emma, 164
  Peter, 164, 209
Heath, C., mrs., 229
  Cath., 239
  Eliza, 193
  John, 239
  Joseph R., 193
  Simon A., 193
Heckel, Elizabeth, 119
Hedding, Salome, 174
Heereman, Annaetje, 60
  Anne, 58
  Jannetye, 56
Heermans, Apollonia, 41
  Margrietje, 41
Heeveman, Anna, 55
Hegeman,, Alida, 45, 49
  Annatje, 53
  Catharina, 21, 24, 28, 31, 37
  Isaak, 21
  Jan, 28
  Maria, 28
Hegemans, Catharina, 22
Heheman, Aeleda, 67
Heilaken, Aafje, 49
Hekel, Eliza, 139
Hekkel, Eliza, 141
Helpertsse, Marytje, 19
Helpets, James, 19
Hemmium, Catharine, 167
Henderson, Jane, 118
  Richard, 270
  Uriah, 272
Hendricksen, Catharine, 208
  Elena, 13
  Hendrick, 13
  Tryntie, 9
Hendrickz, Ryk, 19
  Symon, 19
Hendrickzen, Elisabeth, 9
  Femmetye, 9
  Marytie, 9

Hendrickzen, Ryck, 9
Henly, Margaret, 167
Henricks, Jan, 20
  Ledy, 20
Herman, Anna Pauline, 140
  John Gottlieb, 140
Hero, Hannah, 82
  Jeremy, 82
  John, 82
Herod, Mary, 269
Herrington, Betsey, 186
  Eliza, 186
  William, 186
Hervan, Cornelis, 29
  Jaques, 26, 29
  Sara, 26
Hester, Rachel, 105
Hetfeath, Susanna, 51
Hetfeel, Susanna, 20, 24, 29, 30, 33, 34, 36, 43
Hetfield, Benjamin, 268
  Susanna, 46
Hetherington, James, 204
  William, 204
Hetseel, Susanna, 20, 24, 29, 33, 34, 36
Heusler, Barbara, 144
Hevler, Christopher, 166
Heyer, ——, miss, 232
Hibbets, Euphemia, 140
  Peter, 140
Hibbits, Oscar, 229
Hicks, Emma Ann, 199
  Sarah, 199
Hildreth, Will. H'y, 238
Hill, Alice, 165
  Anzell, 187
  David, 220
  Elizabeth, 220
  Ephraim, 187
  Sarah, 187
Hilliard, ——, 178, 240
  Abraham, 249
  Amy, 95, 186
  Ann, 251
  Anna Maria, 86
  Dinah, 249
  Francis, 261
  Hester, 251
  John, 187, 251
  John, jr., 249, 261
  Lawrence, 251
  Mary, 249
  Merrel, 187
  Nathaniel, 251
  Sarah, 86, 249-251
  Simon, 250
  William, 86, 249
Hillicker, John, 270
Hillird, Ester, 246
  Francis, 246
  John, 246

Hilliyard, Amey, 172
Hillyar, John, 261, 263
  Mary, 261, 263
Hillyer, Abram, 254
  Anne, 254
  Larrance, 254
  Lawrence, 273
Hilton, Alexander Stewart, 162
  Cornelia, 160
  Edward Banker, 160
  Ellen, 162
  Henry, 160, 162
  Henry Graham, 160
  Josephine, 160
  William McMurray, 160
Hilyear, James, 268
Hilyer, Ann, 257, 263
  Elizabeth, 257
  Emm, 263
  Lawrance, 257
  Lawrence, 263
  Margret, 263
  Mary Ann, 196
  William, 263
Hinslif, Mary, 166
Hirschle, Heinrich, 158
  Peter, 158
Hitchcock, Edward, v
Hoegel, Margaret, 204
Hoelten, Barbara, 57
Hofte, Feitie, 14
Hogelant, Aaltje, 25, 29, 50
  Cathrina, 38
  Daniel, 28
  Dirk, 25
  Elisabet, 28
  Elisebet, 18
  Jenneke, 25
  Joh., 21
  Marritje, 25
Holden, Adaline, 146
  Mary, 141
Holland, Henry, x
Holmes, ——, 240
  Ann, 197
  Eliza, 272
  Jane, 124
  Johannes, 34
  Joseph, 28
  Lucy, 168
  Margaret, 176, 197
  Mary, 97, 168, 173, 183, 190, 212, 270
  Obadias, 28, 31, 34
  Sally, 272
  Samuel, 197, 271
  Susanna, 31
  Thomas Charles, 202
Holzhalb, Bertha, 156
  Edward, 156

Hoogelandt, Christophel, 56
  Cornelia, 56
Hoogelant, Aaltje, 21
  Derck, 18
Hooghland, Catharina, 16, 27
Hooghlandt, Jores, 9, 12
  Marytie, 9
Hooghlant, Aaltje, 24
  Catharina, 29, 32, 34, 40
  Elisabet, 23, 24
Hoogland, Maria, 22
Hooglant, Aaltje, 22, 23, 25, 34, 52
  Catharina, 22, 26
  Johannes, 25
  Marritje, 28
  Marrytje, 24
Hoolten, Barbara, 56
  Barbera, 58
Hooper, ——, 217
  Abraham, 175
  Clement, 46
  Elisabet, 32, 42
  Elizabeth, 270
  Marth., 185
  Martha, 32, 35, 184
  Philip, 46
  Rachel, 46
  Sarah, 171
Hoppe, Christina, 21, 25
  Paulus, 21
Horsfield, Mary, vi
  Timothy, v, vi
Horton, William Henry, 207
Houghabout, Maria, 113
Houghwout, Daniel, 66
  Isaac, 66
  Mary, 66
  Nicholas, 66
  Peter, 66
  Susan Ann, 150
  W——, 66
Houlte, Barbera, 52
Houlten, Barber, 63
Houltje, Barbara, 53
Houseman, ——, mrs., 235
  Ann, 270
  Damy, 270
  Hannah, 91, 270
  Harriet, 208
  Isaac, 273
  Maria, 239
  Mary Elizabeth, 238
  Naatje, 98
  Sarah Amelia, 209
Housman, ——, 135, 152, 213, 225
  Aaron, 184
  Abm., 179, 190

Housman, Abraham, 121, 133, 190, 216
  Alfred, 143
  Ann, 184, 200
  Benjamin, 126, 131, 133, 192, 195, 213, 215, 224
  Caroline Houghwout, 163
  Catharine, 214
  Catherine, 133
  Diodema, 185
  Edward, 194
  Edward Perine, 215
  Egbert Haughwout, 159
  Eliza, 133, 183
  Elizabeth, 66, 121, 199, 223
  Hannah, 139, 142, 195
  Hester, 190
  Isaac, 153, 179
  Jacob, 179, 195
  James, 154
  James Edward, 131
  Jane, 179
  John, 150, 163
  John William, 126, 205
  Jno., 159
  Joseph, 164, 207
  Joseph Egbert, 133
  Judith, 194, 195
  Letty, 192
  Lydia, 164
  Margaret, 124, 130, 192
  Margarett, 190
  Maria, 151, 194, 202
  Martha, 269
  Martha Jane, 150
  Martha Swaim Butler, 143
  Mary, 133, 167, 195
  Mary Elizabeth, 164
  Mary Louisa, 133
  Naatje, 173
  Nancy, 66
  Nathan, 194, 199
  Ord., 172
  Peter, 66, 215
  Polly, 121
  Richard, 143, 194, 195, 199, 225, 229
  Sally, 183
  Sarah, 208
  Susan, 200
  Susan Ann, 163
Howell, Edward, 260
  Elisabeth, 253
  Elizabeth, 260
  James, 253, 255, 260
  Jams, 253
  John, 255
  Lezebeth, 255
  Richard, 253
  Susanna, 253

Howland, mr., 264
Hudson, John, 270
Hughes, Barney, 143, 145
  Barry, 255
  Catharine, 251
  Ellen Jane, 145
  George W., 227
  George Washington, 143
  James Cubberly, 225
  Martha, 251
  Matthew, 251
Hughs, Ann, 166
  John, 167
Huisman, Antje, 52
  Baarent, 65
  Elisabet, 53
  Johannes, 53
  Johannis, 65
Hulsebas, Albert, 156
  Gesina Carolina, 156
Hulsebus, Albert, 205
Hulten, Barbara, 61
Humphreys, ——, mrs., 233
  Asa, 230
Humphry, Joseph A., 200
Hunter, gov., iii
  Jane, 178
  Robert, ix, x
Hus, Cattrena, 63
  Mary Miglen, 63
  Matteus, 63
Hutmacher, Gertrud, 206
Hützel, Christina, 153
Huysman, Aart, 39
  Abraham, 50
  Anna, 21, 33, 56
  Antye, 59
  Catherina, 55
  Dirk, 47
  Jemynna, 56
  Joh., 30
  Johannes, 21, 25, 33, 36, 39, 42, 44, 47, 49, 50, 55, 56
  Maria, 49
  Margareta, 42
  Pieter, 36
  Rachel, 25
Hyde, ——, 238
  Emmett W., 202
Hylliard, Ester, 245
  John, 245

I

Immet, Christina, 26
Imyard, Nicholas, 268
Ingham, John, 170
Ingraham, Eliza Margaret Rider, 100
Ingraham, Eliza Margreth Rider, 212
  Elizabeth, 98, 100, 212
  George W., 98
  George Washington, 98, 100
  Geo. Washington, 212
Iniaart, Antje, 21, 23, 28, 31, 32
  Carel, 23
  Catharina, 50
  Gilles, 43
  Gillis, 11
  Jan, 11
  Mathys, 44
  Matthys, 35, 39, 42, 43, 46, 47, 50
  Susanna, 46
  Trintie, 11
Innes, Jane, 224
  John, 166
  Martha, 224
  Mary, 224
Innis, George, 220, 222, 227
  John, 222
  Martha, 220
Inyard, Elizabeth, vii
  Matthys, 55
  Nicklaes, 55
Irving, Theodore, xi
Itrockelf, Hendricka, 9

J

Jack, 175, 273
Jackel, Jacob Fried'k, 154
  Magdalena Rosina, 154
Jackle, Emma Amalia, 146
  Eva Maria, 146
  Jacob Fred., 146
  Jacob Frederick, 146
  J. L., 226
  Maria Catharine, 146
Jackson, Daniel, 187, 189
  Delia, 194
  Elisabeth, 23
  George William, 133
  Hannah, 193
  John, 133
  Margaret, 272
  Mary, 133
  Thomas, 187
  William, iii
  Wm., 66
Jacky, Magdalen, 196
Jacobs, Augusta, 229
  Wm. W., 229
Jacobsen, Ann, 81
  Anne, 76
  Cathrine, 82
  Christian, 76
  Hilletje, 81-83
Jacobsen, John, 81-83, 92
  John Christian, 83
  John Vandeventer, 76
  Maria, 92
Jacobsmyer, Anna, 154
  Johann Christian, 154
  Joseph, 154
Jacobson, ——, 222, 223, 232, 235
  Abr., 231
  Abraham Van Deventer, 99
  Ann, 76, 95, 98, 100, 103, 106, 109, 112, 174
  Anne, 75
  Bedel, 122
  Bedell, 96, 122, 127, 218, 222
  Cath., 200
  Catharine, 75, 120, 130, 136, 182, 189
  Christian, 75, 76, 165
  Christian, capt., vi
  Cornelius, 223
  Cornelius Van deventer, 90
  Elisabeth, 213
  Eliza, 86, 120, 125, 127, 191
  Elizabeth, 76, 170, 223, 231, 239, 240
  Elizabeth Amelia, 129
  H., 100
  Helletha, 221
  Hellethan, 109
  Hellethay, 196
  Hellethey, 112
  Hillethay, 90
  Hilletje, 84, 86, 88, 103, 106, 174, 190, 191, 194
  Hilletje Sleik, 88
  Israel, 191, 236
  Israel B., 129
  Israel Bedell, 88
  Israel Van Devender, 218
  Israel Vandeventer, 122
  J. Chr. 107
  John, 84, 86, 88, 90, 96, 103, 104, 106, 108, 109, 129, 170, 174
  John jr., 214
  John Bedell, 127
  John Christian, 107, 179
  John V. D., 93, 99, 120, 112, 179, 182, 187, 190, 191, 194, 196, 214, 217, 221
  Louisa, 200
  Lucretia, 108, 135, 196
  Maria, 120, 127, 190
  Mary, 129
  Mary Luisa, 107

Jacobson, Matilda, 104, 194
  Nancy, 115
  Peter, 84
  Sarah Ann, 218
  Warren Alston, 122
Jacobus, Rulof, 167
Jacobusz, Gerrit, 31
  Rachel, 31
  Tryntje, 31
Jacques, Isaac, 272
Jaddin, Martha, 14
Jager, Anna Maria, 34
Jakle, Carolina Louise, 140
  Jacob Frederic, 140
James, 180
Janance, Susanna, 268
Janer, Elizabeth, 183
Jannance, William, 268
Jans, Antje, 21
  Jacob, 13
  Jacobus, 13
  Neeltje, 21
  Sarah, 13
Jansen, Aeltje, 18
  Anna 28,
  Beletye, 18
  Cornelis, 23, 26
  Hendrick, 15
  Jacob, 10, 11
  Jacobus, 10
  Jean, 206
  Jean mrs., 206
  Johanna, 11
  Johannes, 18
  Marytie, 15
  Tyes, 18
  Tys, 15
  Wyntie, 11
Janssen, Elisabeth, 33
  Jan, 33
  Mary, 33
  Thomas, 33
Jansz, Auke, 25
  Cornelis, 20
  Fytie, 12
  Henrik, 21
  Isaak, 25
  Johannes, 21
  Maria, 19, 20
  Matthys, 24, 27, 28
  Neeltje, 21
  Rachel, 27, 36, 39
  Thomas, 19
  Thys, 19
Janszen, Albert, 38
  Belitje, 36
  Cornelis, 29, 32, 37
  Elsje, 37
  Esther, 38
  Femmetje, 44
  Hendrick, 21

Janszen, Henricus, 48
  Henrik, 35, 36, 38
  Henry, 31
  Jan, 37
  Lambert, 9
  Maria, 32
  Matthys, 21, 41
  Nathanael, 44
  Rachel, 37
  Sara, 29
  Thomas, 33
  Willem, 44, 48, 50
  Winnifret, 9
  Wynant, 41, 50
Janz, Aeltie, 13
Janzen, Aafye, 9
  Jacob, 9
  Lambert, 9-11
  Reyne, 10
Jaques, Caroline, 191
  David, 66
  Elizabeth, 66
Jay, Mary Elizabeth, 202
Jeacocks, William, 166
Jeirnee, Ann, 263
  John, 263
  Martha, 263
Jemison, Sarah E., 229
Jenkins, Thomas, 207
Jenkinson, Mary Ann, 203
Jennance, Eleanor, 260
  Sarah, 260
  William, 260
Jennens, Aentje, 53
  Jan, 53, 55
  John, 55
  Lammert, 54
  Sara, 54
Jenner, Anna, 67
  John, 57, 67
  Sarah, 57
  Willem, 57
Jenners, Aeltye, 58
  Anna, 58
  Elsye, 60
  Joh., 60
  Lambert, 56, 268
  Maria, 56
  Marya, 56
Jennes, Elsje, 45
  Jan, 20
  John, 24, 45
  John jr., 46
  Lambt., 45
  Sara, 24
Jennings, ——, 97
  mrs., 98
  James, 214
  James Lambert, 217
  Jane, 120, 123, 185, 270, 271
  John, 101, 176, 214, 217

Jennings, Lambert, 185
  Mary, 185
  Rachel, 98, 101, 104, 120, 123, 134, 191
  William, 101
Jennins, Catharine, 168
Jennius, Aentje, 53
Jenoure, Antie, 67
  Lambert, 67
Jewet, Zenophon, 170
Jewson, Nancy, 240
Jinnings, Alice, 171
  Rachel, 174
Jinnes, Antye, 59, 60
  Willem, 60
Johannesz, Marytje, 25, 27, 30
Johannis, Jannetje, 36, 39 43
John, negro, 184
  Daniel, 248
  Hannah, 248
  Jacob, 248
  Margaret, 248
  Moses, 248
  Rees, 248
Johnsohn, Henry, 252
  Rachel, 252
Johnson, ——, 45, 222, 228, 240, 273
  miss, 208
  mrs., 185
  Aaron, 185
  Abner, 174
  Abraham, 253, 270
  Addria, 195
  Albert, 38
  Andrew, 132
  Ann, 250, 259, 266, 273
  Anna, 55, 266
  Anna Maria, 151
  Anthony, 195, 273
  Casparus, 36
  Catharine, 270
  Charity, 175
  Charles, 105
  Charles Garrison, 79
  Clarisse, 221
  Charlotte, 164
  Cornelis, 178
  Cornelius, 105
  Cornelius Vanderbilt, 265
  D., 228
  Daniel, 185
  David, 261, 270
  Dowa, 259
  Edward, 133, 135, 139, 142, 163, 187, 195
  Edward M., 160, 162
  Edwd, jr., 194
  E., 142

Johnson, Eleanor, 79, 255, 256, 258
　Eleonor, 87
　Eleonore, 97
　Eliza, 239
　Eliza Ann, 130, 135
　Elizabeth, 174, 195, 254
　Elizabeth Secord, 163
　Eneas, 46
　Ephraim, 195, 271
　Esther, 46
　Eva, 46
　Fanny, 195, 203
　Frances Ann, 207
　Francyntje, 41
　George, 254, 255, 258, 260
　Hannah, 268
　Henricus, 49
　Henry, 250, 254, 256
　Hetty, 217
　Isaac, 268
　Jacob, 186, 256, 270
　James, 166, 187, 191, 239, 245, 250, 252, 266, 272
　Jane, 162
　Jane C., 209
　Jasper, 258
　Jesse, 272
　Johannes, 47
　Johannis, 38
　John, 61, 151, 160, 240, 270
　John Edward, 139
　Johnneton, 62
　Judith, 170
　Leah Elizabeth, 162
　Lewis, 270
　Margaret, 160, 162, 163, 185, 259
　Maria, 46
　Mary, 46, 110, 195, 220, 245, 250, 253, 259-261, 270, 273
　Mary Catharine, 132, 133
　Mattice, 260
　Nanne, 254, 255
　Nanney, 258
　Nath., 178
　Nathanael, 49
　Nathaniel, 55, 79, 254-256, 258, 265, 269
　Nelly, 265
　Nenne, 55
　Niers, 41, 51
　Peter, 184, 217, 222, 268
　Peter Augustus, 132
　Phebe, 191
　Phoebe, 239, 273
　Pieter, 61, 62
　Rachel, 250, 253, 256

Johnson, Richard, 121, 126, 130, 132, 142, 184, 191, 218, 221
　Richard Taylor, 121, 218
　Robert J. C., 204
　Samuel, 191
　Sara, 46, 48, 51
　Senne, 55
　Sophia, 106, 110, 114, 117, 118, 122, 129, 132, 133, 136, 140
　Suffiah, 260
　Susan, 218, 221
　Susanna, 273
　Thomas, 36, 46, 47, 260
　Tunis Van Pelt, 126, 221
　Wenne, 56
　William, 127, 164, 238, 260, 272
　William Henry, 127
　Winant, 258-261
　Wynant, 55, 271
　Wyntje, 45
Johnston, Bedell, 184
　Clara Holden, 146
　Dower, 250
　Eleanor, 207
　James, 250
　Mary, 250
　Richd, 185
　Robert, 146
　Robert Clyde, 146
　Thomas, 185
Jones, ——, 232
　Abigael, 58
　Abigail, 26, 45, 48
　Abm., 182, 193, 195
　Abraham, 253, 260, 269, 272
　Alice, 195
　Ann, 179
　Barent, 184, 258
　Barnet, 182, 196
　Catharine, 179
　Catrina, 53
　Daniel, 173, 184, 196, 263
　Eduard, 20, 22, 26, 29, 33
　Edward, 258, 260, 261, 263
　Elce, 263
　Eliphalet, 167
　Elisabet, 43
　Eliza, 272
　Elizabeth, 193, 196
　Elsy, 193
　Isaac, 57
　Isabella M'Lean, 130
　J., 179
　Jan, 54
　Jane, 172, 195, 271
　Jene, 253
　Johannes, 46

Jones, John, 39, 43, 46, 48, 51, 57, 253, 263, 272
　Julia Ann, 130
　Lucretia, 51
　Margaret, 269
　Margrit, 261
　Maria, 39
　Martha, 258, 260, 261, 263
　Martha ——, 182
　Mary, 182, 184, 263
　Mateus, 53
　Mathias, 179
　Mattheus, 22
　Matthias, 130
　Obadiah, 263
　Presilla, 195
　Rachel, 48
　Robert M. H., 205
　Susanna, 44, 46
Jons, Susanna, 53
Jonson, Rebecka, 63
Joons, Abraham, 60
　Jannetye, 60
　Maria, 62
Joreszen, Harmen, 12
　Neeltie, 12
Jorissen, Cornelis, 11
　Harmen, 13
　Neeltie, 11
Jorusen, Harme, 18
　Neeltje, 18
Journay, Jean, 22
Journeay, Ann, 258
　John, 174, 258, 272
　Joseph, 273
　Martha, 258
　Mary, 270
　Nicholas, 167
Journey, ——, 177
　Albert, 165, 247
　Elizabeth, 252
　James, 254
　John, 246, 247, 249, 251, 252, 254, 256
　Katharine, 251
　Martha, 246, 247, 249, 251, 252, 254, 256
　Mary, 256
　Nicholas, 246, 266
　Robert, 173
　William, 249
　Wm., 273
Joyce, Benjamin, 85
　Mary, 85
　William, 85
Juessen, Eefye, 59
　Joseph, 59
Julin, Catharine Maria Stewart, 148
　Hanna Ann Elizabeth, 143
　James Thomas, 142

Julin, Sarah Jane, 148
  William, 148
  Wm., 142, 143
Junor, David, rev., v
Jurcks, Jannetje, 53
Jurk, Jannetye, 63
Jurks, Catharina, 36
  —ety, 59
  Jan, 25, 28, 32, 36
  Jannetye, 55, 57
  Jannitje, 61
  Johanna, 25
  Pieter, 28
  Rachel, 32
Jurnee, John, 260
  Martha, 260
  Richard, 260
Jurriaans, Lea, 37
Jusen, Nanne, 263
Juwson, Enne, 56
  Joseph, 55, 56

K

Kadlitz, Cora, 162
  Elizabeth, 162
  John, 162
Kadmis, Joris, 62
Kanon, Abraham, 51
  David, 60, 61
  Jan, 51
  Maria, 51
  Marytye, 61
  Sara, 60
Karbet, Isaac, 12
  Maria, 12
Kasper, Thomas, 23
Katmus, Jenneke, 60
  Joris, 60
Kaus, Heinrich, 153
Kebel, Catharina, 155
Keen, Jesse, 167
Keetch, Abigail, 215
Keisham, David, 271
Kelly, Frances, 169
Kempton, ——, 237
  Matilda L., 239
Kenison, Elizabeth, 186
  Stacy, 186
  Stacy D., 186
Kennedy, Duncan, 168
Kerin, Terence, 263
Kerr, Elizabeth W., 236
Ketchum, ——, mrs., 137
Ketteltas, mr., 180
  Louisa, 158
  Stephen, 171
Ketteltass, Catharine, 165
Kettletas, Audra, 267
  Ann, 227
  Elizabeth, 267
  Mary, 227
  Peter, 227

Kettletas, Stephen, 227, 267
Keyes, ——, 237
Kierstede, Jacobus, 32
  Johannes, 28
  Lydia, 30
  Samuel, 23, 28, 30
Kiesele, August, 152
  Eliza Anna, 152
  Emilie, 152
  Lilia Augusta, 152
  Louisa, 152
Kilburn, Margaret, 235
King, ——, 211
  John, 211
  Mary Ann, 130
  Nancy, 130
  Rachel, 123
  William, 272
  William Henry, 130
Kingston, Elizabeth, 268
  John, vi
  Polly, 183
  Sarah, 268
Kink——, Hehanna, 63
Kinsey, ——, mrs., 230
  Abbey Ann, 135
  Cathrine, 172
  Charles Cortland, 227
  James P., 228
  John, 237
  Mary Ann, 172
Kinsy, Abby, 139, 148
  Abby Ann, 145, 195
  Benjamin, 195
  John, 195
  Susan Ann, 195
Kip, F. M., iv
  Maria, 29, 34
Kirby, Thomas, iv
Kirch, Carl Sebastian, 164
  Christine, 164
  John Henry, 164
Kirtche, Elizabeth, 148
  Henry, 148
  John, 148
Kissam, M. A., 227
  Samuel, 227
  Thomas M'Auley, 227
Kitch, Abigail, 111
  Hannah, 111
Klac, Henne, 64
Kleeve, Henne, 62
Kleinknecht, Theodore, 164
Klerre, Henne, 62
Kliestin, Ann Rosina, 93
Kneeland, Mary, 199
Knief, Rebecca, 155, 204
Kniep, Rebecca, 151
Kniper, John Herman, 152

Knoch, Johanna Henerika Juliana, 155
  Johan Heinrich, 155
Knoesel, Catharina, 164
  Christian, 164
  Salome, 164
Knox, George W., 203
  Sarah, 212
  Anna Maria, 155
  Reinhart, 155
Koebel, Catharine, 207
Kollman, Maria, 149
Koninge, Jans Geritt, 203
Korneman, Margareth, 204
Korse, Lysbet, 15
Korsen, Benjamyn, 19
  Blandyna, 18
  Jacob, 61
  Liesabet, 61
Korson, Maria, 61
Korsse, Blandyna, 12
Korssen, Benjamin, 18
  Benyamen, 18
  Chrystiaan, 12
Korszen, Christiaan, 12
Koss, Jane Eliza, 202
  Wm., 202
Kouwenhoven, Samuel, 44
Krankheit, Jacobus, 22
Kranisch, Louisa C., 140
Krapf, Conrad, 226
Kreven, Annetye, 11
  Jacobus, 11
Kribbs, Elisha, 171
Kroese, Antye, 55
  Claesye, 56
  Cornelis, 15
  Gerret, 56
  Gerrit, 15
  Neeltje, 56
Kroesen, Cathareyntje, 17
  Cornelis, 13
  Cornelya, 18
  Dirrick, 9, 17
  Gerret, 10, 19
  Gerrit, 12, 17
  Henderyck, 9, 10, 15
  Hendrick, 11, 13, 16, 18
  Maritje, 9
  Marytje, 19
  Neelje, 15, 58
  Neeltie, 12, 16
Kroeson, Abraham, 64, 65
  Cornelia, 61
  Cornelius, 64
  Geertruy, 63, 64
  Gerret, 63
  Johannes, 65
Kroessen, Cornelis, 13
  Derck, 9, 10, 12
  Henderyck, 13

Kroessen, Hendrick, 12
  Nickasa, 9
Krohm, John, 201
Krumdick, Dorothea, 153
Kruse, Elizabeth, 66
  John, 66, 168
Kruser, Henry, 188
  John, 188
  Miami, 188
Kruzer, Henry, 220
Kurrlin, Christina Frederika, 199

L

Laacerman, Isak, 63
  Nattenal, 63
Laackman, Maria, 13
Laakerman, Nettenel, 62, 63
  Susanna, 62
Laarens, Jacob, 57
  Jan, 57, 58
  John, 58
Laarns, Antye, 59
  Catharina, 60
  John, 59, 60
Lackerman, Catharine, 270
  Mary, 271
  Richard, 272
  Samuel, 269
  Sarah, 270
Lackes, Maria, 22
Lacreman, Abraham, 257, 260
  Ann, 257
  David, 257
  Elisabeth, 260
  Isaac, 256, 257, 260-262
  Jacob, 260
  Joseph, 262
  Margaret, 257, 260
  Margret, 261
  Martha, 257, 260, 262
  Mary, 260
  Matthew, 260
  Sarah, 260
  William, 260, 261
Ladeleer, Alice, 251
  Benjamin, 251
  Jacob, 251
Lafarge, ——, 235
  Caroline, 208
  Catrine, 262
  Charles, 262
  Elizabeth, 262
Laferge, John, 190
Laforge, ——, 231, 272
  Adrian, 250
  Adryong, 250
  Catharine, 265, 266, 271

Laforge, Charles, 250, 266
  Cornelis, 260
  David, 247, 248, 260, 265, 266, 273
  Dorcas, 190, 272
  Eliza, 272
  Elizabeth, 250, 269
  Henry Seguine, 266
  Jesse, 179
  John, 272
  Mary, 247, 248, 260
  Peter, 267
  Rachel, 247
La Forge, Adriaan, 20
  Catharine, 192
  David, 21, 191
  Elisabeth Ann Dongan, 119
  Jannetje, 20, 22
  John, 191
  Peter, 119
Laforsie, David, 16
Lageler, Marie, 26
  Marya, 22
  Nicolas, 29, 30
Lake, ——, 232, 234, 235
  ——, mrs., 228, 231
  Abraham, 40, 169
  Adriana B., 226
  Adriana Britton, 143
  Alida, 271
  Altie, 67
  Ann, 201, 270
  Anneke, 148
  Annette V., 200
  Arthur, 226
  Barent, 259
  Barnet, 190
  Barnt, 181
  Bettsy, 214
  Cath., 190, 217
  Catharine, 120, 123, 128, 132, 138, 145, 190, 193, 197, 218, 226, 267, 272
  Clace, 67
  Cornelius, 270
  Daniel, 172, 175, 197, 199, 200, 216, 222, 263, 264, 272
  Daniel W., 189
  Danl., 202
  Eliday, 264
  Eliza Jane, 188
  Elizabeth, 92, 94, 99, 105, 107, 112, 115, 172
  Ellen, 113, 115, 118
  James, 232, 234
  James S., 199
  John, 179, 199, 228, 229, 264
  John G., 143

Lake, Joseph, 40, 67, 143, 174, 175, 183, 195, 198, 199, 201, 218, 226, 233, 261, 267, 271
  Joseph, jr., 229
  Lanah, 272
  Margaretta M., 202
  Margaret, 263
  Maria, 183
  Martinus S., 197
  Mary, 188, 195, 258, 259-262
  Mary Ann, 128, 137, 151, 193, 195
  Mary Elizabeth, 139
  Mary Gifford, 143, 226
  Patience, 254, 267
  Polly, 190
  Richard, 188, 269
  Sabina, 232
  Sally, 271
  Sara, 166
  Sarah, 264
  Susan, 273
  Violetta B., 226
  William, 76, 190, 240, 258, 259, 261, 262, 264
Lakeman, Abraham, 27
  Elizabeth Johnson, 264
  Esther, 26, 30, 45
  Isaac, 264
  Jane, 264
Lakerman, Abrah., 24
  Abraham, 251
  Elizabeth, 251
  Esther, 29, 45
  Isaac, 256, 267
  Isak, 41
  Jane, 267
  Louis, 41
  Margrette, 267
  Mary, 263
  Sara, 24, 29
  Sarah, 251
  Susannah, 263
  William, 263
Lamb, Catharine, 204
Lambert, Elizabeth, 264
  John, 152, 264
La Mes, Maria, 22, 25, 32
Lange, Friedrich, 153, 205
  Fridrich, 205
  Sophie, 150, 230
Larance, William, 262
Larns, John, 65
  Richard, 65
Laroe, Aeltye, 11
La Roue, Catharina, 27
  Matthieu, 27
Laroy, Blandyena, 11
  Syemen, 11
Larrance, Mary, 268

Larrens, Anne, 253
　Elizabeth, 253
　Mary, 253
　Richard, 253
Larzalere, Ann, 273
Laselier, Nicolas, 45
Latimer, ——, mrs., 231
　Elizabeth, 206
　John, 206, 230
Latoret, Liesabet, 63
Latorett, Catrin, 268
La Torett, Polly, 271
Latorette, David, 265
　James, 265
　Mary, 265
Latouretta, Martha, 272
Latourette, John, 267
　Susannah, 267
La Tourette, Daniel, 35
　David, 33, 40, 41, 43, 45, 273
　Elisabet, 47
　Esther, 36, 40
　Henricus, 40
　Jaques, 40, 43
　Jean, 33, 36, 40
　Marie, 23, 36, 40, 45
　Marie Susanne, 45
　Pierre, 35, 40, 45, 47
　Susanna, 34, 38, 44, 47
Latteret, David, 246
　Elizabeth, 246
　James, 246
Latterete, Mary, 171
Latterette, Elizabeth, 248, 251, 257
　James, 248, 251, 257
　John, 249, 253
　Mary, 249
　Sarah, 248, 251
　Susannah, 169, 249, 253
Lattorette, David, 259
　Elizabeth, 259
　Francis, 259
Laurence, Mary, 256
　Richard, 256
　Susanna, 256
Lautoret, Elizabeth, 262
　Henry, 262
　James, 262
Lawrance, John, 54
　Willem, 54
Lawrence, ——, 207
　Anna, 34
　Catherine, 65
　Elizabeth, 248
　Francis, 250
　Leggett, 246
　Mary, 190, 226, 245, 246, 248, 250
　Richard, 245, 246, 248, 250
　Sarah, 245

Lawson, Reinhalt Wesley, 237
Lawtoret, Elezebet, 255
　Elizabet, 253
　James, 253
　Jams, 255
　John, 253
　Johnaton, 255
Lawtorette, David, 256
　Catrin, 256, 259
　Elisabeth, 259
　Elizabeth, 259
　Elzebeth, 256
　James, 259
Laza——, Catharine Louise, 117
　John, 117
Lazalyear, Benjamin, 261
　Elsey, 260
　Jacob, 260, 261
　Richard, 260
　Sarah, 261
Lazaryear, Johanna, 257
　Nicolas, 257
　Sarah, 257
Lazeleer, Alice, 249
　Jacob, 249
　Nicholas, 249
Lazeleere, Alice, 247
　Daniel, 247
　Jacob, 247
Lazelier, Catherine, 50
　Esther, 50
　Nicolas, 45
Lazilier, Catherina, 48
　Nicolas, 26
Leaforge, David, 167
Leak, Joseph, 46
　Maria, 46
Leake, Joseph, 168
　Thomas, 20
Lean, Jacob, 46
　John, 48
　Richard, 46, 48
Leating, Anna Mary, 151
Lecount, Katharine, 246
　John, 246
Lee, Elizabeth, 210
Leeck, Abraham, 13, 14, 17
　Joseph, 13
　Margariet, 14
Lefarge, Dorcas, 265
　Martha, 265
　Peter, 265
Leforge, James, 272
Lefurde, Catherine, 171
Legier, Cornelius, 211
Legrange, Mary, 169
Leibert, Eugene, viii, 71, 164, 209
　Sarah, 164

Leiser, Ernest Franz, 142
　Hetwig, 142
　Philip, 142, 198
Leisk, Antye, 55
　Thomas, 55
Leiting, Meda, 145
Lemory, ——, 219
Lemphy, ——, 218
Lenting, John, 229
　John, sr., 231
　Meda, 142, 147, 198, 203
Lennert, William L., viii
　Wm. L., 71
Lentz, George, 196
Leonard, ——, 100
Lerns, Danal, 63
　Fanny, 63
　John, 62, 63
　Mareia, 63
　Necclos, 62
Leroy, Sara, 22
Le Roy, Sara, 25, 32, 34
Lesalyear, Benjamin, 256
　Nicolas, 256
　Sarah, 256
Lesck, Jan, 10
　Jeems, 10
Lesher, Samuel, 195
Levando, Adolph, 155
　Elisabeth, 155
　Joseph, 155
Levering, bishop, v
Lewis, ——, 211, 237, 271
　——, mrs., 231, 240
　Ann, 226
　Billetje, 172; 177, 211
　Billijah, 86
　Catharine, 134
　Catharine Rachel, 136
　Daniel, 167
　David, 247, 269
　David Colon, 90
　Eliza, 122, 127, 134
　Elizabeth, 256
　Francis, 254
　Freelove, 268
　Hannah, 91, 95, 211
　Henry, 204
　Isaac, 177, 271
　Israel, 258
　James, 84, 86, 88, 90, 113, 133, 171, 180, 200, 211, 217, 218, 227, 250
　James Colon, 90
　Jane, 88, 211
　Jonathan, 240, 245, 247, 249, 250, 252, 256, 258, 260, 262
　Joseph, 262
　Katharine, 249
　Marg., 99
　Margaret, 223

Lewis, Mary, 84, 180, 218, 245, 247, 249, 250, 252, 254, 256, 258, 260, 262
  Mary Jane, 204
  Phoebe, 260
  Rebecca, 84, 86, 88, 90, 180, 199, 211
  Rebecca Jane, 147, 200
  Rebekah, 211
  Sally Ann, 113
  Sarah, 245
  Sarah Ann, 218
  Sarah Maria, 136, 140, 147
  Susan, 270
  Tenaton, 254
Leyning, Samuel, 268
Lezier, Cornelius, 90
  Eleonor, Maria, 88
  Jacob, 88, 90
  Sarah, 88, 90
Ligget, Hendrik, 24
Limner, Mary, 165, 210
  Owen, 210, 241
Lingelbach Marie, 203
Lining, John, 256
  Nanne, 256
  Samuel, 256
Lipincott, Mary, 139
Lion, John, 42, 45
  Maria, 45
  Neeltje, 42
Lisk, ——, 214
  Abraham, 175
  Anastace, 257
  Catlyntje, 64
  Elisabet, 33, 36
  Elizabeth, 245, 257, 270
  Jacob, 35
  John, 35, 166, 207, 214, 245, 247
  Marget, 245
  Margriet, 40
  Martha, 54
  Mary, 247
  Maryya, 51
  Matthew, 257
  Moses, 257
  Sara, 38, 50
  Tam, 51
  Thomas, 38, 40, 50, 247
  Tomas, 54
Lisse, Catlyntje, 64
Littell, ——, 226, 236, 237
  judge, 226
  ——, judge, 236
  Ada Louisa, 235
  Ada Louise, 159
  Alexander, 159, 161, 162, 206, 239
  Ann Maria, 221
  Clara Adelaide, 162
  Derric, 222

Littell, Dunn, 237
  Emma Laura, 161
  Eveline P., 228
  Hannah Jane, 162
  Henrietta, 228
  Jane, 161
  Margaret Eliza, 237
  Mary Eliza, 237
  Rebecca, 228, 235, 236
  Richard Dumont, 236
  Richd., 228, 235
  Richd. D., 221
Little, ——, 216
  ——, mrs., 222
  Emilie Teresa, 218
  Emma West, 235
  Margaret Eliza, 218
  Richard D., 218
Livingston, mr., 67
Locker, Phoebe, 174
  John, 183
Lockerman, Ann, 172
  Elizabeth, 173
  Mary, 171
Lockman, ——, 233
  miss ——, 234
  Abraham, 196
  Betsy, 188
  Catharina, 196
  Elizabeth, 208
  James, 205
  Jane, 188
  Joseph, 181, 188
  Richard, 196
Logier, Jacob, 211
  Sarah, 211
Lohmyer, Margareta, 205
Long, Abraham, 170
  Jacob, 167
Loper, Lewis, 271
Lorton, Sara, 31
Loskiel, George Henry, 93
  Mary Magd., 93
Loskilla, Geo. Henry, 92
Lossier, Jacob, 172
Lot, Elisabeth, 17
  Engelbart, 17, 19
  Pieter, 19
  Louisa, 183
Love, Jane, 165
Loveridge, William, 199
Lovet, Edmund John, 131
  Elizabeth, 131, 133
  James Henry, 133
  John, 131, 133
  William Thomas, 131
Lozier, ——, 223
  mrs., 112
  Amanda Augusta, 119
  Catharine Eliza, 116, 215
  Edward, 221
  Eliza, 215, 223

Lozier, Ellen Maria, 116, 187
  Elmira, 129
  Henry Cruse, 99, 212
  Jacob, 95, 99, 102, 116, 125, 129, 187, 212, 215, 223, 224, 228
  Jacob jr., 119
  John, 228
  John Beatty, 102
  Mary Ann, 125, 223
  Sarah, 107, 111-113, 212, 233
  William, 95
Loziers, Edward, 92
  Jacob, 92
Lubers, Nancy, 152
Luby, Henry, 235
  Julia, 160, 162
  Mary Elizabeth, 162, 238
  Thomas, 162, 206
Luckenbach, Augustus, 194
  Samuel, 194
  Sarah, 194
Luckert, John, 209
Ludlow, Ezra, 273
Lueders, Eleanore, 164
  Sarah, 164
  Thomas, 164
Lunt, Matilda, 158
Lutten, Thomas, 10
Lutz, Catharina, 140
  Christiana, 140
  Johann Martin, 140
Luyster, Willempje, 27
Lydle, Ann Fredericks Pierson, 150, 153
  Benjamin, 150, 153, 156
  George Washington, 153
  Gilbert Osborne, 150
  Josephine, 156
  Mary Elizabeth, 150
  Wm. Wallace, 150
Lynch, mrs., 256
  James, 196
  James Livingston, 196
  Rachel, 196
  Thomas, 256
Lysk, Isaac, 79
  John, 79
  Sarah, 79

M

M., Pieter, 58
Maar, Johannes, 63
Maarlin, Hendrick, 15
Maarling, Cattriena, 65
Maas, John, 235
MacDaniel, Catrine, 263
  Daniel, 263
  Dunkan, 263

MacDaniel, James, 268
Machgielzen, Johannes, 10
  Neeltie, 10
Mackeleen, William, 24
Mackelien, Maria, 25
  William, 25
MacKenzie, Eneas, ix
Macklean, Maria, 56
Mackleen, Carel, 53
  Elisabeth, 46, 53
  Mary, 59
Macklies, Cornelis, 17
  Eytie, 17
  Jan, 17, 19
Macky, Ann, 75
  John, 75
  Joseph, 75
Maclain, ——, miss, 233
  Cornelius, 232
Macleen, Maria, 62, 65
MacSwan, Daniel, 257
  Elizabeth, 257
  Sarah, 257
Madden, John, 229
Maerling, Aeltje, 62
  Cattriena, 62, 63
Maertlings, Johannes, 56
  Pieter, 56
Magels, Johan, 12
Mahkin, John Daniel, 208
Maines, mrs., 208
  David Wooley, 148
  William, 148, 201
Mains, Elizabeth Virginia, 150
  Wm., 150
Makings, John, 213
Makleen, Cherles, 58
  Willem, 58
Maklies, Eytie, 16
  Jan, 13, 16
  Margriet, 13
Mallen, Sarah, 203
Mallett, Elizabeth T., 209
Mambru, Lady, 43
Mambrut, Lady, 35
  Sarah, 32, 35, 37, 41, 45, 49
Manbrut, Lady, 29
Mandeveil, Aaltje, 22
Manee, Abram, 266
  Isaac, 266
Manez, Abraham, 22, 28, 38, 40, 43, 47, 49, 51
  Antje, 40
  Catherine, 47
  Maria, 43
  Marie, 31
  Pieter, 28
  Petrus, 38
  Rachel, 49
  Sara, 51

Mangels, Jannetje, 41, 46
Mangelsen, Jan, 16
Manin, Pierre, 26
Mann, Barbara, 137
  Christian, 137
  Mary, 168
Manne, Peter, 272
Mannee, Abm., 273
  Wm., 273
Maral, Maccy, 65
Maree, Jacob, 207
Marel, Anna, 63
  Geertruy, 64
  John, 63
  Marya, 63
Margaret, 175
Maria, negro, 186
Mariez, Maria, 31
  Pieter, 31
Marks, ——, 231
  Hezekiah, 166
Marlin, ——, 225, 272
  Ann, 78
  Anna, 67
  Anne, 77
  Barent, 12, 13
  Benjamin, 77, 78, 225, 270
  Catharine, 270, 272
  Francis, 272
  John, 77, 272
  Nauche, 269
  Peter, 78
Marlyngh, Isack, 18
  Pieter, 18
Marsac, Catharine Eliza Sassenberg, 128
  George Adolphus Hartman, 120, 123
  Harvy Washington Edgar, 134
  Henry, 104
  Mary, 123, 132
  Mary M., 191
  Michael, 101, 104, 120, 123, 128, 134, 174, 191, 196
  Olivia Ann, 196
  Olive Ann, 101
  R., 101
  Rachel, 128, 196
Marsack, Harvey, 97
  Mary Margaret, 98
  Michael, 97, 98
Marsero, Denil, 64
  Jacob, 59
  John, 64
  Josewa, 59
  Mareya, 59
Marsh, ——, 96, 117, 214, 237, 239
  Ann, 108, 127, 177, 180
  Christopher, 177

Marsh, Elizabeth, 245
  Henry, 245
  Jennet, 177
  Joannah, 245
  John, 96-98, 175, 177, 270
  John F., 239
  Joseph, 273
  Lewis R., 177
  L. R., 239
  Margaret, 239
  Ralph, 177
  Rhoda, 177, 214, 239
  Richard, 216
  Richd, 180
  Robert, 177, 214, 239
  Saml, 272
  Sarah, 180, 216
Marshal, Abraham, 258
  Abram, 260, 262
  Alice, 269
  Cathrine, 273
  Elizabeth, 256
  John, 245, 260
  Martha, 245, 262
  Mary, 258
  Rachel, 258, 260, 262
  Sara, 47
  Sarah, 256
  Susannah, 245
  Thomas, 256
Marshall, Ann, 270
  Experience, 171
  Frankey, 248
  John, 171, 248, 250
  Katharine, 248
  Margaret, 248
  Martha, 248
  Rachel, 177
  Sarah, 248, 250
  Susannah, 248
  Thomas, 248, 250
Marssero, John, 65
  Marya, 65
Marston, Cornelius, 190
  Deborah, 190
  John, 190
  Matilda, 190
Marteling, Aeltje, 53
  Annatje, 54
  Barent, 54
  Johannes, 53
  Maria, 54
  Peter, 53, 54
  Peter, sr., 53
Marteno, Annatje, 54
Martin, ——, 228
  rev. mr., 216
  Abigail, 180
  Ann, 256
  Benjamin, 180
  Charles, 216
  Chauncy St. John, 147

Martin, Georg Cortelyou, 147
  Hamilton, 256
  John, 111
  Moses., 196
  Nancy, 196, 232
  Nathaniel, 108, 111
  Nathaniel H., 180
  Oliver, 196, 233
  Oliver R., 144, 147
  Oliver Rollin, 144
  Ol. R., 228
  Rachel, 256
  S., 228
  Sarah, 147
  Sarah Ann, 144
  William, 237
  William Heard, 108
Martineau, Susan, 237
Martino, miss ——, 228
  mrs. 121, 123
  Abraham, 87, 121, 124, 128, 216, 222, 226, 228, 232
  Angelina, 226
  Ann, 82, 96, 99, 102, 104, 107, 171, 176, 212, 216, 217, 226
  Anne, 73
  Benajah, 89, 92, 96, 171, 180, 190, 211
  Benijah, 87
  Benjah, 210
  Benjamin, 85, 87, 92, 211, 214, 215
  Catharine Hanna, 99, 212
  Cathrine, 210
  Cornelius, vii, 95, 237
  Charity, 81
  Elen., 176
  Eleanor, 194, 212, 222
  Eleon., 177
  Eleonor, 81-83, 87, 89, 102
  Elisabeth, 177, 180
  Eliz., 85, 89
  Elizabeth, 73, 81, 87, 102, 178, 189, 210, 228, 241
  Elizabeth Merrell, 124
  Elizebeth, 212
  Ellen Maria, 128
  Ellenor, 221
  Gabriel, 96, 190
  Hanah, 85
  Hannah, 73, 87, 89, 210, 211
  Jane, 81, 82
  John, 81-83, 170
  Maria, 128, 194
  Mary, 89, 210
  Nancy, 228

Martino, Peter, 91
  Raymond, 121, 222
  Rebecca, 171
  Sarah, 73
  Steph., 176
  Stephan, 82, 83, 89
  Stephen, vii, 73, 81, 82, 87, 91, 95, 99, 177, 178, 194, 210-212, 215
  Stephen, jr., vii
  Stephen Vanranssalear, 216
Martinoe, Benajah, 75, 213
  Elisabeth, 165
  Eliz., 212
  Elizabeth, 75
  Mary, 165
  Naatje, 211
  Nancy, 185, 189
  Rebekah, 186
  Stephen, 75, 212
Martinse, Elizabeth, 184
Martling, Aaltje, 30
  Abraham, 186, 188
  Ann, 185, 187
  Anna, 26
  Barent, 26, 29, 37, 40, 263
  Benjamin, 192
  Benjm., 185
  C., 160
  Cath., 187
  Catharine, 188
  Daniel, 185
  Dorcas L., 196
  Dorcas LaFarge, 207
  E., 160
  Eliza, 122, 125, 133, 192
  Eliza Catharine, 190
  Elizabeth, 161, 162, 185, 192, 196, 208, 213
  Garret, 194, 198, 224
  Gertrude, 191
  Harriet, 209
  Isaac, 26, 40
  Isak, 30
  Jane, 188
  Johannes, 40
  John, 187, 188, 190
  Marritje, 22, 30
  Mary Ann, 135, 224
  Mary Elizabeth, 135, 158, 206
  Peter, 196
  Pieter, 55
  S., 208
  Sarah Catharine, 131, 296
  Stephen, 131, 135, 194, 198, 206, 208, 224
  Stephen Martling, 160
Martlingh, Isaac, 22

Martlingh, Marietje, 32
  Marretje, 37
Martlinghs, Aaltye, 57
  Anna, 56
  Barent, 57
  Jannety, 57
Martlings, Aaltje, 37
  Aeltye, 55
  Barent, 24
  Catharina, 44
  Debora, 27, 57
  Marytje, 20
  Pieter, 20, 24, 27, 44, 55
  Petrus, 20
  Mary, 180
Mascire, Josua, 55
  Rachel, 55
Mashel, Elcy, 254
  Sarah, 254
  Thomas, 254
Masjero, Josua, 52
Mass, ——, 223
  Francis, 223
  Lydia, 223
Massalaar, Annetye, 64
Massero, Josua, 60
Mateeus, 56
Mattes, Rosanna, 121
Matthias, mrs., 235
Maurer, Catharine, 195
  Jacob, 155
  John Jacob, 155
Mayhew, ——, 239
McBride, Catharine, 169
M'Cauly, Hamilton, 115
  Robert Thompson, 115
McClean, Charles, 57
  Jannetje, 57
  Mary, 57, 270, 272
McClennent, ——, 224
  mrs., 224
  William, 223
McClyman, Elizabeth, 216
  Louisa, 216
  William, 216
McClymer, Joseph, 199
McClynen, Sarah, 234
McClynnon, ——, 227
  Joseph, 227
M'Cullagh, John, 177
McDavit, Sarah, 272
M'Dewil, Rosetta, 203
M'Ginnis, Mary, 92, 96
M'Ginny, Marry, 99
McIntosh, Charles, 191
  Elizabeth Letitia, 128
  Harry Augustus, 123
  John Williams, 132
  Margarett, 191
  Mary, 128
  Stephen, 123, 128, 129, 132, 191
McKay, John, 269

McKee, John, 203
McKeese, mrs., 134, 135
McKensie, Eneas, ix
M'Kinlay, John, 102, 111
　Lydia, 111
　Lydia Jane, 111
　William, 102
　Wm., 102
M'Kinsay, Colens, 115
　Hannah, 115
　John, 115
McLaughlin, James, 191
McLean, ——, 215, 231, 233
　Ann, 222
　Anna, 236
　Charles, 61
　Charles, mrs., 226
　Cornelius, 222
　James, 213
　James Potter, 213
　Joseph, 203
　Lake, 213
　Magdalene, 171
　Maria, 61
　Mary Ann, 213
　William, 215
M'Lean, mrs., 102
　Charles Simonson, 102
　Isabella, 105
　James, 109
　James Potter, 109
　Joseph Lake, 105
　Lydia Ann, 102
　Magdalen, 97
　William, 102, 105
McLees, Rebecca, 199
McLeland, George, 168
McLymon, Benj. D., 239
McLynnon, Sarah E., 238
McNab, Rebecca, 144, 147, 200
McSwaim, John, 222
　Sarah, 227
McSwain, Catharine, 250
　Samuel, 250
　Sarah, 250
　Vincent, 228
McSwine, Mary, 213
　Sarah, 213
Meade, Richard, 273
Mecereau, All lada, 65
　John, 65
Mechleen, Cherls, 62
　Cttriena, 62
Medcalf, ——, 231
Medes, Elizabeth, 165
Meerling, Abraham, 17
Meerlings, Aeltje, 60
　Abraham, 58
　Antye, 60
　Barent, 60
　Benyaman, 60

Meerlings, Debera, 60
　Pieter, jr., 58, 60
Meertlings, Barent, sr., 58
Mellington, mr., 108
　Ann Eliza, 105
　Joseph, 105, 108, 111
　Joseph Henry, 108
　Lena Cripps, 111
Menee, Peter, 193
　Polly, 193
　Sally, 193
Mer——, Catharina, 58
　Pieter, 58
Mercereau, judge, 191
　Becke, 260
　Cornelia, 139
　Daniel, 116, 260, 261
　Elizabeth, 173, 187
　Ellen Maria, 116
　Gitty, 273
　Jane J., 199
　John, 262
　Joshua, 157, 187, 200, 224, 273
　Josua, 199, 258, 260
　Ledy, 256
　Lidde, 261
　Lucretia, 224
　Lydia, 261
　Margret, 173
　Maria, 224
　Mary, 258, 260
　Peter, 258, 260, 262
　Rebecka, 262
　Rebekah, 258
　Sarah, 258, 261
　Sarah Jane, 203
　Sary, 256
　Stephen, 166, 187, 256, 258, 261
　Stephen jr., 261
　Stephen Henry, 157
Mercereaux, Garret, 67
　Jacob, 67
Merchen, Mary, 20
Merel, Annaetye, 63
　Geertruy, 62
　Mareytye, 62, 63
　Susanna, 61
　Tammas 63
　Tammes, 64
Merl, Catrina, 61
　Elisabet, 24, 25
　Lambert, 24
　Richard, 23-25, 30
　Susanna, 30, 41
Merlengh, Barent, 18
Merlin, Abraham, 88
　Benjamin, 213
　Cathrine, 88
　Jane, 96, 98, 102, 212
　John, 88, 172

Merling, Altye, 64
　Antye, 65
　Isaak, 20
　Jannitye, 65
　Pieter, 65
Merlingh, Henderyck, 18
Merlings, Johannes, 60
Merrel, Abraham, 260
　Ann, 195
　Anna, 62
　Catharina, 56, 60 117
　Catrina, 53, 54
　Eliza, Ann, 117
　Elizabeth, 190
　Elsje, 15
　Elsje, 12
　Geertruy, 54
　James Hatfield, 197
　Jan, 51, 54
　John, 62, 190
　Jonathan, 117
　Lafayette, 117
　Lambert, 260
　Nanne, 268
　Richard, 13, 17
　Richart, 12, 13
　Sara, 54, 63
　Sarah, 197
　Seimon, 54
　Susanna, 54, 60
　Tabitha, 260
　Thomas, 197
　William, iv
Merrell, ——, 119
　Abm., 190
　Abraham, 188, 192
　Ann, 188, 190, 192, 261, 269
　Anna, 56, 58
　Annatje, 53
　Catharina, 58
　Catharine, 192
　Edward, 190
　Elce, 258
　Elisabet, 53
　Eliza, 192
　Elizabeth, 188
　Geertruyt, 58
　John, 58, 66, 190, 192
　John T., 192
　Johnaton, 256
　Jonathan, 119, 202, 219, 262
　Lafayette, 219
　Lambert, 254, 256, 258, 261, 262
　Magdalen, 192
　Maria, 202
　Martha, 193
　Martha Lavinia, 119
　Philip, 58
　Richard, 53, 193, 254
　Susanna, 58

311

Merrell, Tabita, 261
  Tabitha, 254, 256, 258, 262
  Thalata, 258
  Thalita, 256
  Thomas, 66, 192
  William, 269
Merrels, Jonathan, 131
  Julia, 131
  Maria, 131
Merril, ——, 43
  Abraham, 102, 177, 269
  Ann, 269, 272
  Annatie, 48
  Anney, 65
  Betsy, 270
  Catharina, 31, 48, 50
  Chatarina, 59
  Cherrity, 65
  Elisabet, 44
  Elizabeth Ann, 146
  Geertruyd, 33
  Hennis, 65
  John, 33, 178
  John, jr., 46, 48
  Jonothon, 184
  Lena, 177
  Mahala, 102
  Margareta, 49
  Maria, 228
  Martha Levinia, 152, 202
  Mary, 40
  Neeltje, 46
  Nence, 53
  Nicolaus, 37
  Philip, 31, 34, 37, 44, 46
  Phillip, 34, 40
  Richard, 40, 48, 49, 184, 185
  Sarah, 178
  Susanna, 31, 51, 53
  Susanne, 50
  Tabitha, 185
  Thomas, 48, 49
Merrile, Catharine, 140
Merrill, ——, 213
  Abm., 182, 213
  Abraham, 182, 189
  Anna, 61
  Antje, 57
  Catharine, 179
  Egbert, 182
  Eleonor, 182
  Elisabeth, 198
  Elisabeth Ann, 198
  Elizabeth, 182
  Elstye, 57
  Frances, 179
  Jan, 61
  Johannes, jr., 67
  Johannis, 57
  John, 57, 179, 182

Merrill, John T., 198
  Joida, 57
  Magdalen, 67
  Maria, 189
  Mary, 182
  Richard, ix, 57, 66
  Wyntie, 61
Merrit, Sarah, 272
Merry, Harriet, 226
  Julia, 230
Mersereau, ——, 217, 223, 271
  mr., 206
  mrs., 105
  Ann, 194, 266, 267, 270
  Charity, 247
  Cornelia, 131, 132, 142, 267
  Cornelius, 168
  Daniel, 129, 187, 194, 200, 266, 267, 271
  David, 148, 197
  David M., 200
  Elisabeth, 166
  Elizabeth, 197
  Ellen, 129
  Henry, 269
  Jacob, 194, 271
  Jane, 270, 272
  John, 167, 168, 247, 272
  John Edward Winant, 129
  Joseph, 176
  Joshua, 223, 236
  Josua, 257
  Maria, 223
  Marieta Gifford, 148
  Martha, 168
  Mary, 257
  Pati, 257
  Patience, 269
  Peter, 197
  Rebekah, 240
  S., 158
  Sophia, 235
  Stephen, 187, 272
  Stephen, jr., 217
  Susan, 266
Mersereaux, Daniel, 41
  Elisabet, 35, 41, 44, 48
  Estienne, 37, 43, 45, 51
  Harmanus, 66
  Jacob, 66
  Jean, 40, 41
  Johannes, 43
  Joshua, jr., 66
  Josua, 36, 40, 44
  Josue, 36, 40, 43, 51
  Maria, 41
  Mariamne, 45, 47
  Marianne, 35, 40
  Marie, 33, 36, 37, 40, 43, 45, 46, 48

Mersereaux, Martha, 33
  Paul, 36, 41, 48
  Peter, 66
  Richard, 51
Merserue, Paul, 67
Mertlings, Barent, 58
  Barent, jr., 58
Meserow, Charity, 251
  John, 251
  Lowrance, 251
Meshereau, Francis, 251
  Paul, 251
Mesier, James, 234
Mesker, Abraham, 16
  Evert, 11, 17
  Harmen, 11, 16
  Hendrickie, 11
  Johannes, 11
  Mattheus, 17
  Neeltie, 11
Meslur, Abram, 18
  Angenetye, 18
Messeker, Appolonia, 20, 32
  Apolonia, 23
  Eva, 20
Messiel, Charles, 21
  Elisabet, 21
  Marytje, 21
Mesy, Robert, 166
Meszelaar, Antje, 32
Metcalf, ——, 228, 229, 231
  Richard, 228, 238
Metchel, Eesse, 54
  Elsse, 54
  Lodewik, 54
Metselaar, Aafje, 22
  Abraham, 22
  Johannes, 22
  Lodewyk, 22
Metselaer, Abraham, 17
Metsger, Caty Rook, 112
Metzelaar, Aaghje, 33
  Cornelis, 28, 32
  Cornelius, 29
  Geertruyd, 35
  Harmpje, 26, 27
  Johannes, 26-28, 32, 33, 35
  Johs., 26
  Lodewyk, 29, 32
  Pieter, 20, 26, 27, 29, 33
  Sara, 32
Metzelaer, Abraham, 16, 17
  Agnietie, 16, 17
  Jacobus, 17
Metzger, Charles, 120
  M a t t h e w William Reeves, 120
Meyer, Simon, 168
Michan, John, 257
  Sarah, 257

Michau, Elizabeth, 258
  Mary, 258
  Paul, 258
Michaux, Ann, 254
  John, 254
  Sarah, 254
Micheau, Ann, 271
  Elizabeth, 269
  John, 259
  Paul, 252
  Mary, 252, 259, 272
  Sarah, 259
Michel, Anne, 43
Middelzwa, ——, 41
Miers, Derick, 187
  John, 187
  Mary, 187
Milbourn, Francyntje, 49
  Thomas, 49
Milburn, Lidde, 268
Milers, Mary, 19
Miller, ——, 218
  Aaron, 66
  Abraham, 135
  Abraham E., 137
  Catharine, 141
  Constantine, 98
  Elisabeth, 37, 220
  Elizabeth, 113
  George, 228, 234
  George Albert, 137
  Hendrick, 66
  Henry, 85, 86, 91, 113, 168, 172, 181, 218, 220, 221, 239, 241
  Isaac, 214, 227
  Jane Anna, 135
  Jean, 31
  John, iv, 27
  Joseph, 117
  Mary, 27, 85, 210, 241
  Mary Ann, 117, 221
  Thomas, 85, 113, 117, 181, 214, 218
  Winant, 113
Millington, Elizabeth, 199
Mills, ——, 227
  Eliza Ann, 148, 229
  Gilbert, 234
  Gilbert Tunis Egbert, 150
  Jeremiah, 187
  John, 146, 148, 150, 187, 227
  John Newell, 116
  Mary, 116, 146
  Mary Elizabeth Vanderbilt, 148
  Moses, 116, 187
  Moses Newel, 146
  Varnum Slocum, 207
Milton, miss, 207

Mitchel, Abraham, 173, 268
  Anna, 45
  Anne, 51
  Cathrine, 172
  James, 168
  Joannis, 58
  Lewis, 58, 192
  Mary, 82, 84, 178, 214, 268
  Peter, 82, 84, 173, 179, 192
  Rachel, 268
  Sarah, 192
  Susan, 179
  Sussanna, 82
Mitchell, Harmentye, 57
  John, 86
  Lewis, 57, 190
  Mary, 86, 104
  Peter, 178
  Rachel, 185
  Susan, 104
  Susanna, 166
Moehring, Frederick, vii
Moelich, Charles Frederick, 153
  Charles Lewis, 153
  Elizabeth Augusta, 153
Moellich, Eliz. Augusta, 233
Moering, sr., 83, 91
  C., 89
  Chr., 89
  Christina, 89
  Christine, 87-89, 90
  Frederic, 80, 82, 87
  Frederick, 71, 170, 172
  Mary Salome, 80
  Salome, 81-83
Moor, Daniel, 251
  John, 251, 252
  Larans, 252
  Mary, 251
  Nathaniel, 263
  Richard, 265
Moore, ——, 222
  Ann, 184
  Ann Maria, 87
  Cath., 93
  Catharine, 83, 184, 185, 189, 192
  Catherine, 90, 93
  Catherine Morgan, 90
  Cathrine, 87, 89
  D., 273
  Daniel, 89
  David, xi, 123, 127, 131, 192, 217, 222, 269
  David Mercerau, 93
  Elizabeth, 100
  George Washington, 131

Moore, James, 83, 87, 89, 90, 93, 95, 100, 184, 185, 189, 192, 233
  Jane, 144, 201
  John, 95, 273
  John Henry, 127
  Joseph, 171
  Mary, 222, 228, 252
  Plinkel Fleeson Glentworth, 217
  Richard, 233
  Richard Channing, xi, 269
  William Augustus, 123
  Wm., 207
More, Anne, 39
  David, 238
  Elisabet, 41
  Frankje, 37
  Hanna, 48
  Hilletje, 41
  Johannes, 45
  John, 250, 265, 266
  Laurens, 41, 43, 45, 49
  Mary, 250, 265
  Peter Vanpelt, 266
  Rachel, 49
Morgan, ——, 174, 211
  ——, mrs., 224
  Abraham, 39
  Ann, 169
  Annatje, 48
  Cath., 176
  Catharine, 264, 267
  Catherine, 182
  Catrine, 265
  Charles, 31, 39, 41, 43, 46, 246, 264, 265, 267
  Charles, jr., 34
  David, 264
  Debrough, 252
  Elisabet, 30
  Eliza, 272
  Eliza Ann, 194
  Elizabeth, 246, 268
  Jesse, 176, 252
  John, ix, 246, 252, 265
  Magdalena, 34
  Maria, 31
  Mary, 33, 172, 176, 182, 184, 267
  Pieter, 37
  Sara, 41, 46, 50, 51
  Thomas, 30, 34, 37, 42, 46, 48, 50
  William, 174, 182, 268
Morgen, Abraham, 9
  Adam, 12
  Elyner, 10
  Eva, 12
  Francyntye, 10
  Jarels, 10, 13
  Margrietye, 10

Morgen, Martha, 9
  Mary, 10
  Sara, 10
  Sarah, 13
  Thomas, 9, 10
  Tyssen, 10
Morgin, Eva, 11
Morgon, Fransintye, 62
Morrel, John, 172
  Joseph, 251, 253
  Martha, 253
  Marthe, 251
  Mary, 253
  Thomas, 251
Morrell, John, 255
  Joseph, 255
  Martha, 255
Morris, Catharine, 141
  Elizabeth, 146, 224, 227
  Ira K., i.
Morse, Francis, 178
Mortimer, bro., 104
  rev. mr., 187
  sr., 104
  Benj., 104, 105, 112, 184
Moserow, Baules, 67
  Paules, 67
  Tousseway, 67
Mosier, mrs., 229
  Charles, 229
Mossero, Elisabet, 52
  Josua, 52
Mott, mrs., 212, 221
  ———, mrs., 227
  Appalian, 85
  Applican, 85
  Appolona, 82
  Appolonia, 176, 178, 181, 185
  Appolonia Skerrit, 101
  Deborah, 185
  James, 82, 85, 104, 181, 185, 214, 269
  Jas., 85
  Jemima, 41
  John, 178
  Mary, 104, 110, 181
  Samuel, 82, 212
  Stephen, 104, 178, 214, 221
  Susanna, 85
  Sussanna, 85
Mount, Alicia Ann, 124
  Isabella, 124
  Joseph, 124
Mourits, Cornelia, 15
Mozier, ———, 223
  mr., 223
Müller, Catharine, 155, 204
Mundy, Ellis, 191
  Joshua, 191
  Phebe, 191
Murphy, Charles, 169

Murray, Mary, 174, 203
Mushereau, Charity, 247
  Frances, 247
  Francis, 249
  John, 247, 249
  Martha, 247
  Paul, 247, 249
Mussantine, Laforge, 239
  James, 192
  John, 192
  Margaret, 192
Myers, Anna, 155
  Elizabeth, 66
  Richard, 66

N

Neat, Ann, 145
  D., 145
Neats, Ann, 151, 154, 203
  Di., 142, 151
  Dy, 203
  Elizabeth, 151, 203
  John Richard Shelton, 142
  Lester Palmer, 151
  Sarah Frances, 151
  William, 142
  William, sr., 230
  Wm., 142, 151, 203
Nedicker, Elizabeth, 195
Nedwell, Ann, 233
Neefies, Cornelis, 9, 11
  Metye, 9
Neefjes, Aaghje, 29, 32
  Cathryna, 22, 26, 28, 32
  Johannes, 22, 30
  Joris, 22, 26, 28-30, 32
  Margarietje, 26
  Maria, 26, 27, 29, 33
  Neeltje, 27, 31, 36, 43
  Pieter, 27, 29, 30
  Sara, 22, 28, 30, 32, 35, 39, 40, 42
  Tryntje, 27, 29, 33, 35
Neeftjes, Joris, 17
Neefye, Saara, 64
Neefyes, Sara, 55, 59
Neftjes, Antje, 19
  Eechtje, 19
  Johannes, 19
  Jorius, 19
Neisser, br., vi
Neterman, Margarita, 154
Neul, Dirkje, 20
  Henrik, 23
  Johannes, 20, 23, 24, 26
  Margareta, 26
Nevius, Aagie, 15
  Cornelis, 14, 15
  Eechie, 14
  Gerrit, 15
  Jan, 16

Nevius, Johannes, 13, 15
  Joris, 14-16
  Margarietie, 16
  Marytie, 16
  Tryntie, 15, 16
Newland, Susan, 169
Newman, mr., 162
  Edward, 268
  W. H., 160
Nichols, Elisabeth, 165
Nicoll, John, 270
Niel, Anthony, 78
  Jacob, 78
  Mary, 78
Niewenhuisen, Elisabeth, 17
Noble, ———, 159
  mr., 209
  Abr., 146
  Abraham, 182, 200, 234
  Amanda, 238
  Catharine, 148
  Catharine Ann, 146
  Catharine Eliza, 201
  Daniel, 86, 182
  Edmd., 201
  Esther, 182
  Geo. Edward, 238
  Hetty, 217
  Maria Jane, 156
  Thomas, vi
  William Po., 200
Noe, Margret, 255
  Mary, 255
  Peter, 255
Norby, Sara, 32
North, Cath., 239
Nyts, Carel, 50

O

Oakley, Frances, 146, 233
  Jesse, 185
  Margaret, 94, 98
  Margret, 172
Oakly, Eliza, 271
  Fanny, 273
  Frances, 143
  Margreth, 95
  Mary, 270
Obedye, Elysabet, 20
Oblenis, Henry, 222
Oblinis, Albert, 220
  Eliza, 220
  Henry, 220
Ochs, Johanes, 205
Oehlmann, Anna Maria, 208
Oelmann, Mathew, 164
Oenaert, Annetje, 19
  Cornelius, 19
Oerter, William H., viii

Ogg, Elexander, 247
　Margaret, 247
　Mary, 247
Ogle, ——, 237
Ogles, Abigail, 170
Ohl, Heinrich, 152
Oldfield, ——, 231
　Egbert, 152
　George, 152
　John, 152, 202
Olfer, Pieternel, 53
Oliver, Donckin, 13, 14
　Anneke, 25
　Anneken, 20
　Elisabeth, 166
　Margarietie, 13
　Mary, 14
　Peternella, 57
　Petronella, 27
　Pieternella, 58
　Samuel, 27
　Susanna, 20
Olivier, Catharina, 20
　Samuel, 20
Ollefer, Nieltje, 54
Olmstead, John Hull, 205
Osborn, Mary, 225
Osborne, mr., 221
Ostrander, Nathaniel, 237
Oym, Louisa Antoinette, 205

P

Pachtman, Charles, 230
Packer, Hetty, 271
　Lydia, 272
　Maria, 273
Pailyon, Elsye, 58
Palmer, Ann, 168
　Elizabeth H., 151
　Mary, 186
　Sarah, 167
Papst, Ernst, 203
Para, Maria, 26
Paraal, Aron, 18
　Haron, 18
Paraels, Altje, 19
Parain, Francyntje, 23, 27
　Sara, 46
Pardee, mr., 218
Parein, Elisabeth, 22
　Francyntje, 35, 36, 38
　Marie, 42
　Sara, 43
Parelee, Abraham, 259
　Ann, 259
Pareyn, Daniel, 22
　Sara, 22
Parker, ——, 233
　Ann Eliza, 197
　Ann M., 230
　Benjamin, 256, 260, 270

Parker, Ellen, 197
　Ephraim, 260
　Jonathan, 168
　John, 256
　Mary, 192, 256, 260
　Nathaniel, 192
　Sally, 192
　Sarah, 271
　Thomas, 165
　William, 197
Parkinson, mr., 186, 193
　Christopher, 172
　Leonard, 215
　Mary Jane, 215
Parlee, Abraham, 262
　Ann, 272
　Catrine, 262
　Hannah, 269
　Henry, 167
　Isaac, 271
　Martha, 262
　Mary, 273
　Patty, 271
Parley, Abraham, 246, 248
　Barnt, 246
　Mary, 246, 248
　Peter, 248
Parlie, Eduard, 45
　Jean, 45
Parlier, Petrus, 51
　Pierre, 51
Parliez, Anne, 39
　Jean, 48
　Marie, 48
　Pieter, 48
Parra, Marytie, 9
Parrat, Marritie, 9
Past, Loco, 21
Pateman, Ann Caroline, 135
　Hannah, 135
　Joseph, 135
Paterman, Hannah, 134, 135
　Joseph, 134, 135
　Lydia, 134
Paterson, Mary, 168
Patke, Auguste, 206
Patterson, ——, 232, 233, 235, 238
　George, 238
Pattons, E., mrs., 201
Paulus, Cornelius, 188
　Jesse, 188
　Sophia, 188
Pauwelzen, Jannetie, 9
Payne, Jasper, vii, 71, 73
Pearce, Jns., 158
　Mary Jane, 158
Pearson, Jemima, 107
Peat, Hannah, 134
　Joseph, 134

Peat, Lydia, 134
Peck, Thomas R. G., iv
Peckman, ——, 224
　H., 224
Peestnet, Jannetye, 60
Pelec, Christina, 102
Peljoung, Elsje, 52
Pels, Christian, 113
　Christiana, 106, 110, 118
　Christianne, 115
Penhart, Martha Elisabetha, 155
Penhooren, Geertruyt, 57
　John, 57
Penny, Charles, 245, 246
　Daniel, 245
　Dorothy, 245, 246
　Elizabeth, 246
　Hannah, 245
Pennycant, Sara, 103
Pepperill, Hanna, 175
　Isaac, 268
Pereyn, Henry, 250
　Margret, 250
　Susannah, 250
Periene, Daniel, 80
　Lucia, 80
　Sara, 36
Perine, ——, 218, 224
　Abm., 183
　Abraham, 75, 255, 267, 269
　Ann, 210, 252, 272
　Catharine, 74-79, 85, 92, 95, 98, 100, 103, 105, 114, 119, 173, 185, 187, 192
　Catharine Elizabeth, 206
　Charles, 81
　Corn., 175
　Cornelius, 187, 188, 240, 272, 273
　Corns., 205
　Daniel, 74, 79, 80, 168, 210, 241
　Edw., 180
　Edward, 187, 189, 248, 267, 269
　Edwd., 240
　Elias, 74
　Elizabeth, 76, 171, 210
　Emma Elizabeth Cortelyou, 129
　H., 235
　Hannah, 255, 256, 273
　Henry, 129, 133, 248, 252, 255, 256, 270, 271
　James, 78, 83, 85, 89, 90, 210, 213, 214, 224
　John, 81, 147, 218, 222, 224, 225
　John E., 200

Perine, Joseph, 79
  Lenah, 185, 187
  Lucy, 79, 80, 210, 222
  Lucy Ann, 224, 225
  Magdalen, 187
  Margaret, 270
  Margaretta, 183
  Margret, 252
  Martha, 80
  Mary, 28, 81-83, 165, 213, 267, 269
  Mary Matilda, 133
  Mathias, 77
  Miranda, 266
  Patience, 240, 267
  Peter, vii, 74-78, 80-83, 168, 210, 225, 266, 269
  Peter, jr., 85
  Peter Razeau, 267
  Richard Taylor, 147
  Sally, 267
  Sally Ann, 197
  Sarah, 82, 183
  Sarah Ann, 157, 200
  Silas, 83
  Simon, 190, 205
  Susan, 248
  Susan Ann, 147, 188
  Susan G., 205
  Susanna, 80
  Sussana, 82
  Sussanna, 81
  William, 266
  William Oscar, 222
Perkins, Dr., 205
  Mary E. B., 205
Perrine, James, 89
Perry, ——, mrs, 223
Personet, George, 41, 46
  Jannetje, 41
  Johannes, 46
Peter, negro, 241
Peters, Abigail Ann, 103
  John, 103
Petersen, John Henry, 208
  Margaret, 203
Peterson, Eliza, 193
  John, 114
  Mary Ann, 114
  Sally, 185
  Sarah, 114
Pethman, Daniel, 259
  Heletie, 259
Petman, Catrin, 262
  Daniel, 262
  Hilletie, 262
Petit, Charles, 39
  Elisabet, 39
Pew, ——, 178
  Eliza, 272
  Mary, 178
  Sarah, 175
Pfohl, Louisa T., 230

Pforr, John, 203
Phanot, James, 120
Pharo, Samuel, 206
Phillipel, Maria, 54
Phillips, John, 209
Phillipse, Mary, 55
Phoebe, 273
Phrol, Sarah, 172
Pierson, Ann Fredericks, 150, 153
Pikkering, Ule Catharina, 50
Pikkerling, Ule Catharina, 38, 41
  Ule Catharine, 47
  Ule Cathrine, 44
Pillion, Catharine, 265
  John, 265
Plessing, Augustus, 152
  Emilie, 152
Plummer, Rebecca, 268
Pollard, John, 273
Poillon, Abraham, 269
  Adrian, 269
  Ann, 247
  Catharine, 43
  Catherine, 45
  Catline, 41
  Elsje, 50
  Francis, 252
  Jacob, 267
  James, 252
  John, 247, 252, 267, 270
  Judith, 167, 247
  Margaret, 267
  Marget, 247
  Margret, 247, 252
  Maria, 41
  Marie, 47, 49
  Mary, 247
  Peter, 252, 266
  Sarah, 210, 247
  Susanna, 270
Poilyon, Elsje, 57
Pollion, Elizabeth, 246
  James, 266
  John, 246, 266
  Marget, 246
Pollon, Elizabeth, 261
  John, 259
  Margret, 259, 260
  Margrit, 261
  Peter, 259-261
Pollworth, James, 143
  Peter, 143
  William, 143
Polon, Adder, 256
  Catrin, 263
  Francis, 256
  James, 256
  Margaret, 263
  Peter, 263

Possel, Jan, 9
  Thomas, 9
Post, Abraham, 52, 64, 67, 182
  Adriaen, 56
  Claartye, 62, 64
  Claerty, 59
  Claertye, 58, 60
  Clara, 56
  Experience, 179, 186
  Francis, 171, 179, 186, 196
  Garrit, 186
  Gerret, 54
  Gerret jr., 56
  Gerrit, 55, 61, 64, 65, 173, 182
  Gerrit sr., 59
  Jannetye, 62, 64
  Johannes, 52, 55, 56, 59
  Klaart, 62
  Lea, 65
  Leya, 59
  Maria, 64
  Mary, 182
  Marya, 64
  Miriam, 67
  Newton, 186
  Peter, 179, 186, 237
  Pieter, 64
  Sarah, 196
  Susan, 237
  William Francis, 196
Potter, Mary Ann, 109
Poulse, Franscyntje, 59
  Frntcintye, 61
Poulson, Francyntje, 55
Powel, Elisabeth, 262
  Mary, 262
  Nenney, 268
  Thomas, 262
Praal, Aaltje, 22
  Aaltye, 61, 63, 64
  Abraham, 10, 49, 61
  Alida, 61
  Anna, 23
  Antie, 12
  Arent, 9, 39, 44, 46
  Arent jr., 10, 23, 24, 30
  Arent C., 9
  Aron jr., 14, 17
  Beniemen, 65
  Beniemin, 61
  Elisabeth, 17
  Henderske, 46
  Henricus, 44
  Isaac, 14, 56
  Johannes, 22
  Johannis, 65
  Maragritye, 56
  Maria, 13, 14, 26, 39
  Mary, 11, 14
  Marya, 65

Praal, Pieter, 9, 10, 12-14, 22, 30
　Sara, 20, 30, 36
　Willem Jorisze, 39
Prael, Aeltje, 60
　Aeltye, 61
　Aentie, 18
　Altye, 55
　Aront jr., 18
　Isaak, 59
　Isack, 55
　Lowies, 59
Pral, Isaak, 53
　Petrus, 53
Prall, ———, 271
　Abraham, iv, 66, 67, 128, 220, 269
　Abraman, 67
　Aletta, 135
　Ann, 176, 198
　Benjamin, 166
　Catharine, 196
　Daniel, 270
　Edward Beattey, 128
　Edward Beatty, 220
　Giddy, 198
　Henrietta, 201
　Henry, 151, 203
　Isabella, 220
　John, 272
　Mary, 65
　Peter, 66, 169
　Sabina, 232
　William Henry, 151
　Wm., 201
Praul, Abigail, 185
　Abm., 184
　Abraham, 193
　Aletta, 115
　Alfred Cortelyou, 117, 217
　Benj., 239
　Benjamin, 191, 193
　Catharine, 217
　Charlotte, 108
　David, 108, 113, 117, 176, 216, 217
　Edwin Theodor, 114
　Elisabet, 185
　Elizabeth, 239
　Ellen, 239
　Emeline, 113
　Henrietta, 111
　John, 178
　Maria Ann, 116
　Peter, 185
　Sara, 178
　Tunis Augustus, 109
　William, 109, 111, 114, 116, 216
Praull, Ann, 101
Prawl, Aletta, 109
　Catharine, 105

Prawl, Danl, 181
　David, 105
　Sarah Ann, 105
　William, 181
　Wm., 109
Pray, Elizabeth, 273
Presser, Pieter, 19
　Valeteyn, 19
Pretch, Benjamin, 246
　Esther, 246
　James, 246
Pretchet, Ester, 249
　James, 249
　William, 249
Preyer, Andries, 28, 32
　Anna, 27, 49
　Catharina, 44
　Celia, 23, 26-28, 31, 32, 38, 44
　Celitje, 41
　Jacob, 28, 31-34, 42
　Jannetje, 37
　Johanna, 33
　Johannes, 27, 32, 37, 41, 42, 44
　Pieter, 42
Price, mrs., 188
　Benjamin, 193
　David, 193
　Elias, 193, 195
　Esther, 193
　Hannah, 126, 128, 133, 138, 143
　Hester, 195
　Jacob, 36
　Lucy, 169
　Margaret, 189
　Peter, 168
　Ruth Ellen, 193
Prickett, Catharine, 271
　Elizabeth, 179
　Harriet, 186
　Sarah, 179
Priester, Henry, 168
Prince, Mary, 227
　Robt., 227
　Samuel, 233
　Wm. Robert, 236
Prine, Ann, 257, 260
　Edward, 257, 260, 265
　Fanny, 266
　Hannah, 256
　Henry, 253, 256, 257
　James, 256
　Joseph, 228, 257
　Mary, 257, 266
　Naomi, 256
　Peter, 253
　Sarah, 257, 265
　Supfiah, 256
　Susanna, 253
　William, 266

Pritchet, Isaac, 268
Pritchett, Harriot, 271
Proll, Catharine Mary, 100
　Jacob, 100
Prue, Elias, 183
　Esther, 183
　Hannah, 216
　Jacob, 36
　Mary, 192
Pryor, Andrew, 190, 273
　Andries, 57
　Catharine, 179, 271
　Catharine Maria, 190
　Elizabeth, 190, 273
　Jan, 57
　John, 192
　Lanah, 273
　Mary, 272
　Susan, 192
Pu, Johan, 10
Pue, Elisabeth, 12
　Johan, 12, 16
　Moses, 16
Puelyon, Elsye, 62
Puillon, James, jr., 227
Pugh, Lenah, 184
　Nicholas, 184
　Sarah, 166
Puy, Martha, 39

Q

Quinty, Anthony, 229

R

Racey, Bessie, 237
Racy, ———, 229
　Charles, 229
Radfort, John, 268
Radlitz, Ada Medora, 163
　Elizabeth, 163
　John, 163
Raff, Rosina, 152
　Rossina, 204
Ral, Anna, 27
　Antje Mangels, 20
　Catharina Mangels, 21
　Francyntje Mangels, 23
　Fytje, 51
　Hans, 37
　Jan, jr., 51
　Jan Mangels, 22
　Maria, 27
Rall, Meria, 32, 37
Ralley, Ann, 245
　Franky, 245
　Henry, 245
Ralph, Abraham, 55
　Benyamen, 56
　Eleanor, 271

Ralph, Elizabeth, 58
  Joseph, 55, 56, 58, 270
  William, 270
Rambel, Ann, 170
Randal, ——, 229
  John, 229
Randolph, ——, 230, 233, 235
  mr., 217
  ——, mrs., 236
  Elizabeth, 182
  John, 199, 230
  Samuel, 270
Rapp, Ros., 150
Rappeneker, Anton, 164
Rathon, mr., 85
  mrs., 85·
  Catharine, 85
Rathyen, mr., 154
  Ann, 149
  Anna, 149, 150, 228
  Henry, 146
  J., 204
  John, 143, 146, 149, 150
  Mathin, 143
Raymond, Henry C., 207
Rea, Lydia, 102
Reacy, mr., 200
Reader, Cath., 164
  Christopher Vroome, 164
  George L., 164
  George Lewis, 209
Rece, Ellen Elizabeth, 161
Rednor, Peter, 166
Reed, ——, 228
  Harriott, 189
  Susan P., 228
  William, 167
Reilly, Susanna, 263
  Terrence, 263
Reiners, Anna, 150
Reinke, A. A., 157, 206
  Abraham, vii
  Amadeus, viii
  Amandens A., 161
  Clement L., 161
  Edward Jacob, 161
Rengaten, Catharine Friederica, 137
Reso, Geertruy, 60
  Jacob, 60
Resoo, Catriena, 61
  Jacob, 61
Resor, Jacob, 54
  Susanna, 54
Resszeau, judge, 219
  Polly, 219
Reuter, Louise Johanna Catarina, 152
Reyerse, Adrian, 77
  Catharine, 77, 79

Ryerse, Lewis, 77, 79
  Richard, 79
Reyerson, Catharine, 78
  Lewis, 78
  Phebe, 78
Reyken, Elesabet, 17
  Elisabet, 17
  Reick, 17
Reynolds, Silas, 271
Rezeau, Sarah, 268, 269
  Susan, 269
Rgt, Jenny, 64
Rhine, Mary, 137, 138, 140, 202
Rice, br., vi
  mrs., 202
  Lydia, 144
  Owen, vii, 71, 73
  William H., viii
  Wm. Henry, 71
Richards, ——, mrs., 238
Richardson, Charlotte Jane, 207
  Ellen, 205
  Margret, 58
  William, 58
Richau, Anna Maria, 23
  Antie, 16
  Daniel, 12
  Isaack, 13
  Jacob, 12
  Johannes, 12-14, 16
  Mary, 14
  Paul, 12
Richaud, Anna Maria, 32
  Catharina, 25, 30
  Catline, 36, 39
  Elsje, 37
  Isaac, 36
  Johannes, 32, 37
  John, 24
  Lea, 24
  Rachel, 32
Richgau, Johannes, 9.
Rickeman, Albert, 251
  Katharine, 251
  Mary, 251
Ricken, Pieter, 11
Rickerte, Elizabeth, 241
Rickow, Anne, 168
  Hezekiah, 165
  Reuben, 166
Rider, Anthony, 93
  Mary, 93
Riders, Anthony, 93
  Mary, 93
  William, 93
Ridgway, Caturey, 167
  Elizabeth, 169
Rigga, Abraham, 54
  Ragel, 54
Riker, Eliza, 271
Rineo, Elizabeth, 268

Rinke, A. A., 71
Rinslard, Sophia, 206
Ripley, ——, 236
Rives, ——, 227
Robbins, Mary, 195
  Nathaniel, 195
  Susan, 195
Robin, Thomas, 241
Robins, Else, 273
Robinson, ——, 231
  Mary, 272
  Thomas, 165
Rodgers, Lucy, 184
  Sarah, 155
Roe, John, 273
Roff, Catharina, 181
  Frances Louisa, 148
  Francis Louisa, 154
  Joseph, 181
  Louisa, 151, 157
  Mary, 233
  Susan Ann, 181
Rogers, ——, 230
  Jacob, vii, 71, 74
  Ogden M., 238
  O. M., 230
Rokere, Christina, 140
Rol, Antje, 33
  Catharina Mangels, 35, 45
  Fitye, 59
  Hans, 33
  Jan, 43, 57
  Jan, jr., 43
  Jan Mangels, 48
  Marytje Mangels, 42
Roland, rev. mr., 264
Roll, Marytje, 44
Rollens, Charles, 58
  Philip, 58
Rolph, Abraham, 66
  Abrm, 66
  Cornelia, 53
  Joseph, 53
  Larance, 254
  Mary, 254
  William Roberson, 254
Rome, Charity, 138
Romer, ——, 232
  Ann, 141, 199, 201, 229
  Catharine, 219
  Catharine Ann Elting, 159
  Charity, 136, 141, 143
  Charity Guyon, 195
  Eliza, 139, 142, 197
  Elizabeth, 146, 168
  Emeline, 136
  Emma Jane, 159
  Fanny Ann, 136
  Isaac, 159
  Isaac Parlee, 129
  J., 129

Romer, James, 129, 136, 139, 141, 147, 149, 175, 195, 197, 199, 201, 202, 219
  James, jr., 140
  James, sr., 140
  James Isaac, 140
  John, 134, 136
  Joseph, 144, 201
  Joseph Lake, 129
  Margaret Jane, 129
  Mary, 149, 195, 197, 202, 225
  Mary Ann, 134
  Mary Elizabeth, 147
  Mary Louise, 129
  Mary Matilda, 159
  Sarah, 208
  Sarah Jane, 140, 144
  Sophia, 166
  Thomas Simpson, 147
Romeyn, widow, 100
  Sarah, 100
Rondshaler, br., 138
  A., 71, 137
  Ambr., 138
  Edward Henry, 138
Rondthaler, Ambrose, viii
Rook, Amos, 120, 214, 226
  Catharine, 120
  Caty, 112
  Eliza Ann, 112
  Frederick Moehring, 214
  George, 214
Rooke, Amos, 87, 89, 91, 168, 219, 241
  Cathrine, 89
  Frances, 212
  Frederick, 89
  Martha, 89, 219
Rooks, A., 101
  Amos, 97, 101, 112
  Frances, 97
  Francis, 174, 211
  Martha, 97
  Martin, 112
  Mary, 101
Room, Mary, 200
Roomer, Andrew, 269
Roose, Jacob, 53
  Weintje, 53
Root, ——, 232, 234
  Elliott Aymar, 158
  Geo. M., 159
  George, 234
  George M., 158
  Pierre Vanderbilt, 159
Roper, Elizabeth, 259
  Isaac, 259
  Jemima, 259
Rose, Catharina, 164

Roseau, Jacob, 50, 51
  Petrus, 50
  Susanna, 51
Roseaux, Pierre, 43
  Susanna, 50
Rosen, Gerrit, 20
  Nicolaas, 20
Rosenthal, Theodor, 204
Ross, Daniel, 169
  Mary, 126, 201
  William, 190
Rotben, Anna, 146
Rothfus, Christina, 150
  John, 150
Rotsen, Anna, 143
Row, Mary, 36, 21
Rowland, John H., xi
Rozeau, Elizabeth, 186
  Hosea Alexander, 176
  Mary, 176
  Peter, 176
Rudinger, Augusta Caroline, 137
Rudmeyer, Abraham, vii
Ruebottom, Ann, 91
Ruede, Charlott Elizabeth, 140
  Charlotte Elizabeth, 144
Ruppinger, Catharine Friederica, 137
  Johann, 137
Rus, Mary, 21
Russel, Mahala, 215
Rutan, Sara, 31, 34, 39, 41, 43, 46
Ryck, Marytje, 19
Rycke, Abraham, 14, 16
  Arme, 19
  Femmetie, 11
  Jacob, 19
  Pieter, 11, 19
Rycken, Abraham, 14
  Femmetie, 10, 13
  Hendricus, 10
  Isaac, 16
  Johanes, 10
  Johannes, 13
  Pieter, 10, 11, 14, 16
  Weyntie, 9
Ryckszen, Ryck, 11
Ryers, Arris, 234
  Orris, 183
  Sarah, 183
  Terrence R., 183
Ryerse, Adriaan, 62
  Cathrine, 80-82
  Lewis, 80-83
  Luwes, 62
Ryerss, Catharine, 172
  Cathrina, 241
  Cathrine, 241
  Lewis, 241

Ryersz, mrs., 184
  A., 66
  Adrian, 210
  Aris, 66, 67
  Cathrine, 210
  David, 67
  Hannah, 66
  Lewis, 241
  Sarah, 214
Ryerze, Lewis, 165, 182
  Orris, 182
  Sarah, 182
Ryke, Aabram, 17
  Abraham, 17, 20, 25
  Bennetie, 17
  Elysebet, 17
  Femmetje, 20
  Harmpje, 23
  Johannes, 17
  Judith, 22
Ryken, Abraham, 17
  Femmetie, 13
  Henricus, 21
  Lena, 15
  Ryk, 13, 15, 16, 21
  Sofia, 16
Rykman, Albert, 29, 34, 38
  Rebecca, 34
Ryt, Jacob, 27
  Maria, 27
Ryte, Maria, 51

S

Sabel, mr., 206
Saddler, Ann Eliza, 145
  Augustus, 145
  Mary Elizabeth, 145
Saffin, Aaron, 181, 187
  William, 181, 187
Sal, ——, 181
Salbacher, Bertha, 156
  Jacob, 156
Sally, 180
Salter, James, 185
Sam, 180
Sandars, Hanna, 63
  Ragel, 63, 65,
  Richard, 63, 65
  Sara, 65
Sanders, Eliza, 127, 130, 133, 135, 143, 193, 219
  Else, 130
  Elsie, 132
  Peter, 193, 228
  Sarah, negro, 189, 273
Saran, 180
Sargent, Mary, 172
Saul, 183
Saunders, mrs. ——, 227
  Peter, 168
  Sarah, 169

Savary, Peter, 268
Sayler, Ragel, 54
Sayles, Maria, 208
Scales, Thomas, 203
Scarret, ——, 270
  Appolonia, 269
  James, 265, 267
  John, 269
  Mary, 265, 267
  Susanna, 170
Schaber, Margaret, 226
Schade, Catharina Elizabeth, 208
Scharlach, Heinrich, 204
Scharot, Mary Elizabeth, 132
  Thomas, 132
Scharret, Benjamin Gryon, 114
  James, 112
  John, 114, 116
  Joseph, 118
  Mary, 114, 116, 184, 197
  Mary Ann, 117
  Peter Swaim, 116
  Richard, 117, 197
  Susan Ann, 197
  Thomas, 118
Scharrit, Daniel, 112
Scharrot, ——, 216
  Appolonia, 185
  Augustus Eugene, 119
  Charity, 216
  Hannah, 185
  James, 185
  John, 119, 185, 189
  Mary, 189
  Mary Ann, 216
  Richard, 216
  Richard, jr., 216
  Susan Ann, 185, 189
Scharrott, Martha, 225
  Thomas, 225
Schenck, Benjamin, 270
Schenk, Holmes, 240
Scherret, ——, 214
  Catharine, 214
  Catharine Eliza, 212
  Esther, 106
  Frances, 212
  James, 106
  John, 212
  Thomas, 214
Scherrets, John, mrs., 113
Schiegel, Alke Marg., 150
  Christian, 153
  Gesine, 145, 153
  Johan Chr., 153
  Kissine, 148
Schilman, Sara, 30
Schilmans, Sara, 20
Schinnis, John, 62
  Susanna, 62

Schlect, Catharine, 152
  Elisabeth, 149
  Johannes, 204
  John, 150, 152
Schmidt, doct., 204
  dr., 154
  Augusta Henriette, 154
  Auguste Henriette Wilhelmina, 204
  Carl Henry, 155
  Cath., 152
  Catharine, 145, 148, 150
  Catharine Christiana, 145
  Catharine Margaret, 158
  C. C., 234
  Elisabeth, 157
  Elisa Barrett, 141
  Elizabeth, 152
  Emma, 155
  George, 144
  George Sommers Marks, 150
  Jacob Edward, 148
  John, 157, 206
  Jno., 158
  Louis, 141
  Magda., 144
  Magdalena, 144
  Margareth, 200
  Martin, 139, 141, 144
  Paul, 141, 145, 148, 150, 152, 155
  Sophia, 139
Schmit, Catharina, 50
  Johan Adam, 50
Schneider, Anna Emilia, 149
  Clara Catharina Margareth, 203
  Jacob, 149, 203
  Maria Clara, 149, 203
Schoenberg, Eliza, 152
Schout, Ary, 21
Schouten, Adriaan, 23
  Adriaen, 15
  Ary, 23
  Marytie, 15
Schultzebach, Terresia, 133
Schumacker, Johanna, 203
Schuman, Alvina, 164
Schutzenbach, Teresa, 138
Schuyler, Jan, 44
Schweinitz, mrs., 206
  B. E., 145, 205
  Bernard E., 71, 154
  Paul Bernhard, 155
Scobe, Ann, 252, 262
  Elexander, 252
  Elisabeth, 262
  William, 252, 256, 262

Scobey, John, 259
  Liddie, 259
  Nanne, 259
  William, 259
Scoby, Alexander, 257
  Ann, 257
  William, 257
Scott, Eleanor, 239
  Mary Caroline, 227
Seabrook, Patty, 272
Seaman, ——, 222
  Ann Elizabeth, 127
  Barnt, 189
  Benson, 120, 125, 127, 191, 222
  Elizabeth, 191
  Henry John, 125
  Jane, 272
  John, 272
  Julia, 120
  Wm., 191
Seawood, Elizabeth Frances, 154
  Eva Harrison, 151
  William B., 203
  Wm., 154
  Wm. B., 151
Sebering, Catharina, 25
Sebring, Eliza, 179
  John, 179
Seely, Mary, 187
Sefurde, Catherine, 171
Segain, Catharine, 251
  James, 251
  John, 251
  Sarah, 251
Segan, Else, 249
  Elsie, 250
  Jacob, 249
  James, 249, 250
  John, 249
Segang, Ann, 273
  Barnt, 273
  Elizabeth, 270
  Hery, 271
  Hetty, 272
  James, 269
  Mary, 271
  Stephen, 270, 272
Seghong, Elisha, 250
  John, 250
  Sarah, 250
Segoin, John, 168
Segoine, Elizabeth, 66
  John, 66
Seguime, ——, 218
Seguin, Dorcas, 39
  Jaques, 32, 35, 42, 43
  Jean, 32, 35, 39, 42, 43
  Jonas, 32
  Sara, 35
Seguine, ——, 231, 236
  judge, 193

Seguine, Abraham, 183
  Catharine, 167, 267
  Catrin, 255
  Catrine, 260
  Elizabeth, 273
  Ells, 246
  Elsie, 250
  Henry, 180, 214, 220, 238, 249, 267
  H'y, 236
  Jacob, 267
  James, 246, 249, 250, 255
  John, 180, 181, 183, 185, 260, 267, 268
  Katharine, 249
  Lydia, 134, 138, 183, 185, 202
  M., 205
  Margaret, 267
  Margrette, 267
  Mary, 185
  Patience, 238
  Rachel, 180, 183, 229, 273
  Sally Ann, 214
  Sara, 260
  Sarah, 246
Seguyn, Caty, 252
  Henry, 252
  James, 252
  John, 252
  Sarah, 252
  Steven, 252
Seibert, Paulina, 207
Seidel, Charles Fr., 106
  Dorothea S., 106
Seimensen, Geertruy, 53
Seimesen, Anatje, 53.
  Weintje, 53
Seisema, Meda, 203
  T. O., 203
Sekinger, Eva Maria, 154
Selenf, John, 183
Selif, Peter, 165
Selle, George, vii, 71, 74
Selyns, dominie, ii
Semson, Jan, 18
  Sande, 18
  Tabeta, 18
Senne, Amalia S o p h i e Matilda, 150
  August, 145, 153, 205
  August Ernst Wilhelm Christian, 153
  Charles Henry Augustus, 145
  Christian, 231
  Diedrich F r i e d r i c h Christian August, 153
  Dietrich, 153
  Ernst, 145, 148, 150, 153
  Friedrich, 153
  Gesiene, 150

Senne, Heinrich August, 205
  L o u i s a Margaretha Christiana, 148
  Louise, 150
Senseman, Edwin T., viii, 164
  Lucinda Eliz., 236
  William Ormsby, 164
Sep, Margreta, 54
Sequin, Lydia, 123
Sequine, ——, 218
Seym, ——, Palli, 58
Seymense, Jenneke, 58
  Palli, 60
Seymensen, Elybet, 17
  Willem, 17
Seymerson, Abilgale, 85
  Elizabeth, 85
  Isaac, 85
Seymonse, Antye, 61
  Christoffel, 61
  Daniel, 60
  Maria, 56
  Sara, 60
  Seymon, 56
Seymore, ——, 209
Seymourson, Ann, 210
  Bernard, 210
  John, 88
  Ruben, 88
  Sarah, 88
  Sussanna, 172
Shaber, Catharine Margaretha, 137
  Johann T., 137
Shaddock, Joseph, 185
Sharman, Fredrik, 36, 39
  Jacob, 36
  Thomas, 39
Sharot, Mary, 132
Sharp, Elizabeth, 181
  James, 181
  Samuel, 264, 273
  William, 264
  Wm., 181
Sharret, John, 184, 208
  Mary, 184
  Susan Ann, 184
  William, 199
  Wm., 205
Sharrot, ——, 217, 219, 229, 231, 232, 235-237
  ——, mrs., 238
  Abm., 200
  Abraham, 123, 124, 130, 192, 237
  Alfred, 124, 154
  Benjamin H o u s m a n, 124
  Catharina, 127, 194, 217
  Christiana, 194
  Cornelia Frances, 233

Sharrot, Daniel, 232
  David, 127, 232
  David Mercereau, 139
  Eliza, 126
  Elizabeth, 131
  Hannah, 214
  James, 123, 219, 224
  James, jr., 219
  James, sr., 193, 217, 218
  Jeremiah, 124, 127
  John, 122, 124, 127, 187, 192, 194, 228, 240
  John D., 208
  John Davis, 126
  John William, 125
  Joseph, 131, 132, 139, 142, 238
  Joseph Willson, 132
  Lenah Ann, 124
  Lucretia, 194
  Lucy Ann, 218
  Maria, 187
  Martha, 126
  Mary, 192, 195, 217, 229
  Mary Ann, 130, 207
  Milvaise, 231
  Polly, 187
  Richard, 123, 217
  Richard, sr., 193, 219
  Sarah, 200
  Stephen, 122
  Susan Ann, 124
  Thomas, 122, 126, 154, 202, 207, 232
  Washington, 127
  William, 218
  William Henry, 131, 203
  Wm., 229, 231, 236
Sharrott, Abraham, 161
  Agnes, 235
  Agnes Caroline, 157
  Benjamin Guyon, 237
  Benjamin T., 237
  Catharina Eliza, 142
  Cornelia Frances, 157
  Hannah Jane, 161
  James Wilson, 157
  John, 144
  Jno. William, 161
  Mary, 142
  Richard, 236
  Susan, 124
  Thomas, 149, 164
  Thomas Howard, 149
  Thos. Jeff., 226
  William, 225
Shaw, Charles Henry, 201
  George, 263
  Mary, 263
Shay, mrs., 221
  Henry, 101, 219
  Odissa, 101, 176
Shelling, Barbara, 156

Sherer, ——, mrs., 238
Sherret, Richard, senr., 241
Shields, Ann, 190
  Catharine, 190
  Thomas, 190
Shingles, George, 173
Shum, Catharine, 147
Shuttleworth, J o s s e l y n, 272
Sibell, Benjamin, 181
  John, 181
  Sarah, 181
Sicking, Eva Maria, 140
Siebern, Barnt., 194
  Thomas, 221
Sielof, Blandiena, 61
  Pieter, 61
Siersema, Frederick, 150
  Frederick Henry, 231
  Henry, 150
  John, 147
  John Theodore, 147
  Meda, 150
  Phoebe Ann, 145, 227
  Theodore, 150
  Theodore Onnis, 198
  T. O., 145, 147
  Unitas, 226
Siersina, MarianneEmily, 142
  Meda, 143
  Theodore O., 142
  T. O., 143
  Unitais, 143
Sikkel, Abraham, 47
  Claasje, 47
  Elisabet, 47
Sikkels, Ariaantje, 41
  Elisabet, 41
  Zacharias, 41
Sikkelse, Elizabeth, 60
Silberhorn, Christian, 207
Silof, Daneel, 62
  Danel, 64
  Elsye, 62
  Saartye, 62
Silva, Joseph, 268
Silve, Elizabeth, 256
  Nanne, 256
Silvester, Ann, 246
  Elizabeth, 246, 248, 249
  Francis, 248
  John, 246, 248, 249, 268
  Martha, 249
  Sara, 249
Silvy, ——, 216
  Eliza, 102
  Elsea, 178
  Frances, 216
  Hester, 97, 100, 189
  Jane, 105
  Joseph, 102, 256

Silvy, Richard, 97, 100, 105, 189
  William, 100
Simerson, Alice, 165
Simes, Johan, 16
Simesen, Catrina, 54
  Cristfel, 54
  Cristofel, 52
Simsembach, Aaltje, 38
  Jan Philip, 38
Simeson, Catharine, 165
  Stofel, 63
Simessen, Aert, 14
  Antie, 14
  Barent, 15
Simesson, Isaak, 11
Simon, 180
  Catherina, 46
  Thomas, 46
Simons, Catharina, 26
  Christoffel, 50
  Wyntje, 39, 49, 50
Simonse, Maria, 62
Simonsen, Aert, 14
  Geertruy, 12
  Hans, 14
  Jeremyah, 58
  Margrett, 190
  Simon, 58
Simonson, ——, 118, 269
  ——, miss, 236
  Aaron, 173
  Aart, 67
  Abbey Ann, 193, 219
  Abby Jane, 130
  Abigail, 198, 246, 248
  Abigail Ann, 101
  Abm., 194
  Abraham, 66, 101, 176, 197
  Ann, 79, 121, 124, 128, 181, 190, 192, 193, 260, 261, 266
  Art, 67
  Arthur, 186, 188, 194, 271
  Audra, 267
  B., 100
  Barent, 79, 170
  Barnet, 100, 101, 105, 107, 119, 122, 182
  Barnt, 219, 220, 223, 246, 248, 268
  Benjamin, 161, 163, 207
  Blandena, 53
  C., 206
  Cath., 201
  Catharine, 152, 157, 197, 207, 230, 269
  Ch., 228
  Charles, 97, 100, 108, 236
  Charles, sr., 232
  Charles M., 227
  Charles Mc., 233

Simonson, Chas., 100, 214, 234
  Chas. V., 229
  Christopher, 67
  Cornelia, 191
  Cornelius, 97, 225
  Daniel, 189, 235
  Daniel D., 130
  Ecford Webb, 163
  Eliza, 205
  Elizabeth, x, 67, 134, 135, 158, 183, 198, 245, 267
  Elizabeth Hilliard, 101
  Ellen, 152, 157, 188, 201
  Emeline, 204, 225
  Emma Josephine, 234
  Francis, 260
  Hanna, 101
  Hannah, 119, 182. 192, 268
  Hans, 53
  Helen Melissa, 161
  Hylah, 108
  Isaac, x, 67, 130, 198, 220, 235, 268, 269
  Jacob, 267, 269
  James, 194, 204, 209
  Jane, 90, 96, 105, 135, 137, 193, 219, 234
  Jemima, 168
  Jeremiah, 181
  Joannah, 122
  Johannis, 67
  John, x, 66, 152, 157, 177, 189, 191, 192, 194, 201, 205, 206, 239, 245, 248, 260, 261, 266, 269, 271
  John Beatty, 79
  John G., 206
  John King, 225
  Joseph, 182, 183, 188, 193
  Josephine Vanderbilt, 228
  Lavina, 181
  Lena, 99
  Magdalen, 271
  Margaret, 166
  Margarett, 197
  Margret, 90
  Margrietye, 62
  Margrit, 67
  Maria, 165, 191, 232
  Mary, 100, 108, 115, 120, 123, 182, 188, 194, 214, 218, 225, 227, 236
  Mathias Decker, 96
  Nancy, 191
  Nathan Runnek, 220
  Nellie, 184
  Ort, 246
  Patty, 216
  Peter, 269

Simonson, Phebe, 189, 191
  Phebe Ann, 100
  Rebecca, 182, 183
  Rebekah, 188, 193
  Reuben, 90, 96, 99, 101, 105, 106, 108, 119, 190, 193, 219, 226
  Sarah, 100, 182, 188, 220, 223, 234
  Sarah A., 228
  Sarah Adeline, 163
  Sarah Ann, 223
  Sarah Eliza, 130
  Silas, 181
  Sophia, 217
  Stephen Bedell, 266
  Susan, 186, 234
  Susannah, 194
  William D., 202
  William Gosen, 214
  Wouter, 67
Simonsse, Simon, 52
  Van Pelt, 52
Simonsz, Isaak, 36
Simonze, Geertruida, 61
  Maria, 61
Simonzen, Aert, 12
Simonzon, Antie 12
Simorson, Elizabeth, 26
  Isaac, 263
  John, 263
Simoszen, Aert, 12, 15
  Simon, 12
Simson, Jane, 268
  Petrus, 22
Sinclair, J. H., iv
Sinning, Conrad, 206
  Martin, 206
Sinnis, Elsye, 61
  John, 61
  Lammert, 61
  Merya, 61
  Wellem, 61
Sinseman, Edwin T., 71
  E. T., 162
Sips, Isa, 50
  Ite, 50
Sisk, John, 183
  Peter, 183
  Sarah, 183
Skane, Matthew, 43
  Pieter, 43
Skarret, Patty, 199
Skerret, ——, 178
  mrs., 92
  Ann, 88-90, 181
  Appolonia, 176, 178
  Catharine, 176
  Christiana, 105
  Elizabeth, 81, 82, 87, 89, 177, 212
  Hannah, 82
  James, 90, 181

Skerret, James, jr., 88, 89
  John, 81, 84, 92, 98, 103, 105, 173, 211
  Joseph, 173
  Maria, 92
  Maria Martha, 211
  Mary, 81, 82, 84
  Rachel, 84
  Richard, 82, 84, 87, 174, 176-178, 212
  Ruth, 87
  Susan, 174
  Thomas, 82, 178, 199
  William, 82, 88
Skerrett, Hanna, 174
Skerrit, ——, 94
  mr., 86
  mrs., 97, 100, 103
  Abraham, 85, 110
  Anna, 85, 94, 97
  Appolonia, 101
  Cath., 99
  Catharine, 101, 103
  Catharine Elizabeth, 97
  Elizabeth, 84, 85, 102
  Eve, 99
  Frances, 101
  James, 94, 97, 103, 175
  John, 95, 97, 174
  John Garritson, 94
  Joseph, 98
  Lucy Ann, 95, 104
  Martha, 104
  Mary, 84, 85, 101, 103
  R., jr., 110
  Richard, 84, 85, 86, 110, 181
  Richard, jr., 100
  Richard, sr., 84
  Richd, jr., 84
  Susan, 175
  Thomas, 100, 104, 108
  William Crips, 108
Skinner, Letta, 168
  Joannah, 268
Skirmen, Abraham, 65
  Alizabeth, 65
  Peggy, 65
Slack, Ann, 249, 252
  Barney, 167
  Barnt, 270
  Elizabeth, 269
  Jacob, 269
  John, 249, 252, 269
  Katharine, 249
  Margaret, 271
Slact, Francis, 262
  John, 262
Stager, Sophya, 55, 56
Slecht, Barent, 12, 13, 30
  Catharina, 23
  Cornelia, 23
  Cornelis, 13

Slecht, Elisabet, 47
  Henrik, 23, 26, 30, 32, 34, 35, 37, 38, 46
  Hilletje, 26
  Jacob, 32
  Jan, 35
  Johan, 12
  Johannes, 23, 47
  Maria, 23
Slechts, Hylletie, 12
Slect, Barent, 261
  Elizabeth, 261
Slegt, Catharine, 166
Sleight, Cornelius, 182
  Henry, 169
  Jacob, 182
  Jane, 182
Slinsby, John, 268
Slot, Eva, 49
  Maria, 25
Smack, Annetie, 12
  Johannes, 12, 15
  Leendert, 12
  Leenert, 10
  Martin, 239
  Marytie, 15
  Sara, 10, 239
Small, Adam, 197
  Jacobina, 139, 197
  Margaret, 197
Smart, John, 272
Smith, ——, mrs., 237
  Abel, 82
  Adam, 168
  Andrew, 273
  Ann, 146, 200
  Anna Mar., 106
  Catharina, 110
  Cathrine, 170, 251
  Christian, 215, 250
  Christina, 269
  Christopher, 251
  Danl., 198
  Eleanor, 165, 166
  Emeline, 197
  Elizabeth, 82, 170
  Ester, 250
  Esther, 169
  Frances, 229
  Frances Louisa, 207
  Henry D., 106
  Hester, 251
  Hetty, 240
  Isaac, 250
  James, 221
  Jeremiah, 230
  John, 262
  John W., 225
  Maria, 57
  Mary, 221, 261, 262
  Mary Elizabeth, 221
  Ruth, 273
  Samuel, 82, 171

Smith, Sarah, 230, 264
  Sarah Ann, 230
  Susannah, 261
  Thomas, 232
  William, 261, 262, 264
  William Henry, 208
Smitt, Christian, 254
  Hester, 254
Smyet, Casper, 11
  Maria, 11
Smyt, Tammus, 17
Snedicker, Brasilla, 238
  Mary, 232
Snedieker, Abm. I., 197
  Isaac V., 197
  Sarah, 197
Snediker, ——, 236
Sneeden, ——, 232
Sommers, George, 150
  Lavinia, 157
  Robert, 143, 157
  Robert Gray, 143
  Susan Ann, 143
Soner, Anna Maria Clara, 154
  Andrew, 154
Sotten, Jan, 11
  Thomas, 11
Spangenberg, bishop, vi
Spann, Mary, 168
Spear, Violetta, 143
Spears, Claushea, 171
Spicer, Ann Eliza, 160
  Diana, 160, 208
  Jane, 160
  Matilda Catharine, 160
  Thomas, 160
Spier, Baay, 26
  Sytje, 26
Spong, Francis Maybury, 220
  Mary, 220
  Robert, 220
Spragg, ——, 226
  Andrew, 271
  J., 226
  Jacob, 271
  Mary, 73, 268
Sprague, ——, mrs., 234
  George W., 198
  John H., 201
  Sarah M., 231
Spree, Caty, 63
  Edwort, 62
  Willim, 62, 63, 65
Spries, ——, 222
  Johann, 133
  John, 222
Sprong, Barnabas, 80
  Citie, 80
  Jane, 80
Squier, Mary E., 207
Squire, John, 223

Mary Louisa, 223
  Stephen, 193
Squires, Martha, 227
  Sarah, 273
  William, 177
Staat, Maria Margareta, 50
Staats, Abraham, 12, 23
  Agneta, 20, 22, 23
  Agnietje, 25, 28, 32, 36
  Anna, 23, 25, 28, 31, 37, 40, 44, 48, 49
  Annaatie, 13
  Annetye, 10
  Antje, 19, 23, 24, 30
  Catharina, 13, 15-17
  Catryna, 18
  Cornelia, 9, 22, 24, 28, 30, 31, 34, 35, 45
  Edmond, 13
  Elisabeth, 17.
  Elizabeth, 15
  Isaak, 12
  Jan, 13, 18, 23, 25, 33, 38, 39
  Jannetje, 29, 30, 33, 35, 37, 39, 44, 48, 51, 52
  Johan, 9-11, 13, 15-17
  Kathareina, 9
  Magdalena, 30, 34, 37, 42, 48, 50
  Maria, 22, 31, 43
  Marytie, 51
  Neeltje, 20, 25, 33, 40, 41
  Pieter, 9, 13, 15-17
  Rabecca, 57
  Rabecka, 52
  Rebecca, 11, 34, 37, 38, 45, 52
Stackhouse, Joseph, 167
Stacy, ——, 228, 231
  mr., 228
Stebs, Mally, 64
Steker, Maria, 158
Steel, John, 231
Steers, ——, 230, 239
  Charles, 229
  F., mrs., 234
  John, jr., 229
  Thomas, 229
  William, 230
Stephens, Susan, 273
Stephenson, ——, 229
  Richard, 200
Stevens, John, 272
Stevenson, Mathew, 172
Steward, ——, 223
  mrs., 103, 117, 121, 123, 130, 134, 201
  widow, 143
  Abraham, 223
  Abraham M., 194
  Anthony, 225

Steward, Anthony Y., 135
  Archibald Douglas, 135
  Hannah, 194
  Mary, 135, 225
  Sarah Elisab., 225
  Sarah Jane, 143
  Thomas, 114, 194, 215
  Thomas, mrs., 114
Stewards, mrs, 115
Stewart, Abraham, 145
  Alexander, ix
  Anthony, 142, 144, 148, 151
  Anthony Y., 139
  George Anthony, 148
  Julia Ann, 142
  Mathias Burger, 145
  Mary, 142, 144, 148, 151
  Mary Alina, 151
  Samuel, 144, 227
  Sarah Elizabeth, 139
  Sarah Jane, 111, 142
  Thomas, 111
  William Thomas, 142
Stibs, Willem, 31
Stile, Isabella, 231
Still, Edward, 269
Stillewel, Frenck, 9
  Joachim, 58
  Richard, 58
  Thomas, 9
Stillewil, Annaetje, 60
  Thomas, 60
Stillwel, Antoni, 62
  Mareia, 64
  Rabecca, 53
  Tammes, 62
Stillwell, Abm., 175
  Abraham, 114, 132, 219
  Ann, 175
  Catharine Ann, 114
  Daniel, 258
  Elias, 57
  Geertje, 40
  Hettee, 256
  Hiram, 207
  Ida, 48
  Jeremiah, 253, 256
  John, 208, 235
  John William, 132
  Jos., 101
  Lenah, 271
  Lucretia, 122
  Mary, vii, 113, 258
  Nicholas, 110, 111
  Peter, 219, 253
  Rebaco, 256
  Richard, 258
  Sarah, 213
  Susan, 105, 114, 117
  Susan Ann, 147
  Thomas, 57
  William, 181

Stillwell, William W., 201
  Yetty, 253
Stillwill, Frances, 215
Stilwel, Anna Cathrina, 21
  Rachel, 13
Stilwell, ——, 129, 216, 234
  Abm., 189
  Abraham, 116, 128, 169, 175, 181, 214-219, 225, 232
  Ann, 175, 181, 253
  Anne, 165
  Araienty, 253
  Ariaentie, 251
  Catharina, 48
  Catharine, 214
  Charity, 117, 175
  Daniel, 22, 35, 41, 47-50, 174, 189, 195, 213, 214, 216, 219, 220, 234, 251, 253
  Elias, 32, 35
  Elisabeth, 94
  Eliza, 220
  Elizabeth, 174, 195, 220
  Esey, 251
  Frances, 85, 87, 98, 102, 241
  Francis, 108
  Francyntje, 41
  Gitty Ann, 218
  Hannah, 195, 213, 214, 234
  Harriet, 229
  Henry, 214
  Henry Edward Perine, 116
  J., 231
  Jan, 22
  Jaques, 49
  Jeremiah, 253
  Joakim, 170
  Johannes, 22
  John, 213, 268
  Jos., 101
  Joseph, 83, 215, 217, 218
  Joshua, 175
  Katharine, 251
  Lucretia, 126
  Margaret, 158, 162
  Maria, 61
  Marietta, 218
  Mary, 46, 128, 169, 175, 218, 276
  Nic., 272
  Nicholas, 85, 92, 108, 214, 251
  Nickolaas, 57
  Niclas, 91
  Nicolas, 46, 94, 241
  Richard, 46, 50
  Sally, 133
  Samuel, 268

Stilwell, Sarah, 129
  Sarah A., 157
  Sus., 98, 101
  Susan, 101, 103, 110, 113, 175
  Susan Ann, 145, 155
  Susanna, 83, 98, 215
  Susannah, 251
  Thomas, 29, 32, 223
  Thom's, 229
  Willem, 22
Stilwil, Eleyas, 60
  Jan, 59, 60
  Joachim, 59
Stilwill, Abraham, 184
  Caty, 184
  Charity, 123
  Gitty, 184
Stockdale, Charity, 229
  Sarah, 238
Stodhoff, Catharine, 199
Stol, Johanna, 21
Stoll, Jacob, 148
Storer, Daniel, 168
Story, Celia, 107, 110, 112, 115, 123
  Susan, 273
Stout, Mary, 213
  Sarah, 66
Stoutenborough, Anthony, 245, 250, 251
  James, 250
  John, 245
  Mary, 245, 250, 251
Stoutinbura, Anthony, 253
  Mary, 253
Strickhousz, Elisabet, 37
Strickland, Eleanor, 167
Strockelf, Hendricka, 9
Struss, Gerd., 205
  Metha, 205
Stryker, Cornelius, 20
  Gerritje, 20
  Jannetje, 20
  Peter, iv, 67
Stuart, Hannah, 213
  Sarah, 167
  Thomas, 213
  William, 213
Styversant, Christian, 67
  Samuel, 67
Sugan, Catrin, 255
  John, 255
  Sary, 255
Sullivan, Dennis, 195
Summers, ——, 229
  Albert, 145
  Elizabeth, 209
  Emily Etta, 161
  George James, 147
  John, sr., 230
  Robert, 145, 147, 155, 161, 229

Summers, —— S., 158
  Susan, 161
  Sylvester, 155
Sumsenbach, Christoffel, 41
  Jan Philip, 41
Sutlif, David, 215
  Penina, 215
  Valentine, 215
Sutten, Thomas, 10
Swaim, ——, 226
  Catharine, 92, 94, 97, 100
  Dinah, 174, 185
  Dorothy, 216
  Elizabeth, 271
  George, 234
  George, Abraham, 146
  Harry, 187
  John, 185, 197, 201, 222, 269
  Lenah, 124, 127
  Maria, 124
  Martha, 143, 152, 185, 197, 226
  Martha Ann, 127, 220
  Martinus, 185
  Math., 226
  Mathias, 146, 201, 227
  Matthias, 269
  Mary, 116, 127, 269
  Mott, 223
  Susanna, 171
Swaime, Benjamin, 66
  Dorothy, 97
  Matthew, 66
Swain, Martha, 138
Swame, Abraham, 254
  Albert, 17
  Johannes, 17
  John Rolph, 254
  Magyel, 17
  Mary, 254
  Willem, 17
Sweem, Anna, 21, 26, 27, 29, 30, 33, 35, 40
  Annetie, 13
  Anthony, 21, 33, 36
  Anthony Thysz, 21
  Antie, 16
  Barent, 11, 13, 39, 42, 51
  Benyamen, 56
  Catharina, 27, 58
  Cornelius, 26
  Elisabet, 26, 28
  Elisabeth, 11, 12, 14
  Elizabeth, 56
  Geertruyd, 48
  Helena, 46, 51, 58, 59
  Isaak, 59
  Jannetje, 35
  Joh., 36

325

Sweem, Johannes, 13, 14, 16, 17, 19, 22, 27, 28, 35, 36, 42, 50
  Johannes, jr., 21
  Johannes sr., 22
  John, 65
  Lea, 21, 32, 36, 40
  Leah, 27, 29, 38
  Lena, 33, 35, 39, 43, 46
  Lysabet, 19
  Lysbet, 21, 25, 28, 39
  Magdaleen, 11
  Magdalena, 14
  Maria, 12, 22, 30, 33, 34, 36, 39
  Martha, 16, 17
  Marya, 29, 65
  Marytje, 38, 50
  Mateis, 53
  Mathys, 59
  Matthew, 43
  Matthias, 45
  Matthys, 11, 21, 35, 45, 56, 58
  Rachel, 21, 36
  Sara, 61, 65
  Tys, 16, 48, 50
  Willem, 22, 26
Sweems, Anthony, 21
  Jacobus, 21
  Jan, 20
  Joh. 21
  Johannes sr., 20
  Maria, 25
Sween, Matthys, 10
  Saraatie, 12
  Thys, 12
Sweens, Antoni, 12
  Neeltie, 12
Swem, Martinus, 54
  Matheus, 60
  Maties, 53
  Matties, 54
Swift, ——, 220, 238
  mrs., 164
  Caroline, 237
  Eliza, 220
  Emma, 160, 209
  Eugene, 208
  Isaac, 125, 131, 134, 136, 160, 220
  Isaac B., 230
  James Bodine, 134
  Jeremiah, 136
  John, 237
  John William, 125
  Margaret, 229
  Margaret Elizabeth, 131
  Mary, 237
  Sarah, 160, 237
Syloy, Hester, 83
  Oliver Taylor, 83
  Richard, 83

Sylva, Cornelius, 225
  Joseph, 166
Sylve, Richard, 269
Sylvy, Frances, 187
  Hester, 187
  Jas., 179
  Joseph, 177
  Juliana, 179
  Richard, 187
  Susan, 179
Symensen, Aert, 19
  Christoffel, 19
Symenson, Aart, 62
  Abraham, 63
  Daniel, 63
  Fransintye, 62
  Johannes, 55
Symensse, Wyntye, 56
Symerson, Barnet, 86
  Daniel, 87
  Dorothy Barnes, 87
  Elizabeth, 87
  Isaac, 87, 171
  Phebe, 86
  Ruben, 86, 87
  Rubin, 172
  Sarah, 87
  Williga, 172
Symesen, Aentje, 18
  Aert, 18
Symeson, Daneel, 61
  Eevert, 63
  Jenneke, 65
  Johennis, 61
  Marretye, 63
  Rem, 63
  Symon, 61, 63
Symessen, Aron, 14
  Barent, 10, 11, 14
  Johannes, 11
  Wyntie, 10
Symons, Aaltje, 50
  Aart, 27, 30, 34, 36, 37, 40, 45, 48, 49
  Anna, 27
  Annatje, 46
  Antje, 44
  Barent, 32, 36
  Catharina, 30, 44
  Cornelius, 40
  Daniel, 30
  Geertie, 48
  Geertruyd, 25, 48
  Hans, 46, 49
  Isaak, 24, 43, 45
  Isak, 46
  Jeremias, 24
  Johannes, 25, 44, 46, 48, 50
  Maria, 49
  Susanna, 34
  Symon, 46, 50

Symons, Wyntje, 20, 33, 36, 42, 44, 47
Symonse, Christoffel, 55
  Hans, 58
  Jannetye, 57
  Symon, 55
  Wyntye, 58
Symonsen, Art, 53
  Symen, 53
Symonson, Abigail, 93
  Abraham, 174
  Antye, 64, 65
  Barent, 64
  Charles, 174
  Christophel, 56
  Cornelis, 64
  Elizabeth, 56
  Geertruy, 64
  Hannah, 94
  Hetty, 94
  Jacob, 94
  Jane, 92
  Johannes, 65
  John, 211
  Johnnis, 64
  Maria, 64
  Nicholaes, 56
  Reuben, 92, 94, 211, 241
  Ruben, 95
  Sara, 63
  Symon, 56, 63
  Wyntye, 55
Symonsse, Johannes, 52
Symonssen, Barent, 20
  Maria, 20
Symonsz, Aart, 25, 48
  Anna, 48
  Antje, 31
  Barent, 20, 23
  Cornelia, 44
  Geertruyd, 33
  Isak, 27, 31
  Maria, 27, 37
  Marritje, 34
  Martha, 39
  Simon, 41
  Symon, 31, 33, 34, 35, 37, 39, 41, 44, 48

T

T., Aeltye, 58
Tabor, Jesse, 167
Tucker, 165
Taege, —— mrs, 238
Tailor, Aaltje, 27
  Abraham, 20, 24, 27, 31, 37
  Ephraim, 37
  Pieter, 31
  Rachel, 24
Talbot, John, ix

Taler, Alezebeth, 255
  Henry, 255
  Judith, 255
Talor, Abraham, 15
  Abram., 19
  Altje, 19
  Ephraim, 15
  Ephrum, 15
  Margriet, 15
Tayler, Harmentje, 57
Taylor, ——, 241
  mr., 176, 209
  mrs., 116
  —— Squires, 177
  Abraam, 17
  Abraham, 25, 26, 35, 42, 188
  Abram., 268
  Amantica, 251
  Ann, 267, 271
  Arriantie, 251
  Benjamin, 267, 270
  Catharine, 188
  Chas. mrs., 232
  Daniel, 252
  Elizabeth, 92, 95, 99, 103, 159, 162, 171, 187, 211, 245, 246, 260
  E., 200
  Edward, 121
  Edward R., 235
  Elisabeth, 218
  Eliz., 179
  Emeline, 163
  Ephraim, 268
  Esther Pamela, 267
  Fanny, 267, 270
  Frances, 262
  Guda, 252
  Henry, 251, 252, 257, 259, 262
  Hester, 97, 100, 189, 269
  James, 231, 251
  John, 188, 246, 259, 267, 272
  Josephine Adelaid, 163
  Jude, 259
  Judith, 169, 252,, 257
  Liddy, 262
  Maregriet, 17
  Martha Ann, 185
  Mary, 168, 235, 268
  Oliver, 187, 260, 262, 267
  Olliver, 262
  Olly, 268
  Peter, 252
  Richard, 174
  Sarah, 187, 260, 262
  Thomas, 245, 246
  William, 163, 209, 257
Teague, Margery, 168
Teeler, David, 55
  Rachel, 58

Teeler, Samuel, 55
Teitus Aeltje, 52
Telburgh, Johannes, 17
  Pieter, 17
Teller, Sarel, 19
Tellers, Aerjaenje, 19
Telston, ——, 169
Tenbroeck, Phoebe Ann, 207
Tenbrook, sr., 93
  Henry, 93
Ten Eik, Margrietje, 22
Ten Eyk, Margaritje, 28, 31, 33, 37, 42
Tenicke, Samuel, 252
Tenor, negro, 185
Terret, Mary, 174
Terrils, mr., 273
Teunisse, Lena, 10
  Nies, 10
Teyszen, Barent, 9
  Maghdalena, 9
Thatcher, Charles, 188
  Elizabeth, 188
  Grace, 188
Thealer, Jan, 9
  Ephraim, 9
  Margrietie, 9
Theunissen, Jan, 14
  Mary, 14
Thiebault, John F., 231
Thistle, —— mrs., 236
  Samuel, 234
Thomas, negro, 181, 186
  Elizabeth, 196
  Hagar, 191
  Thomas, 196
  William, 196
Thompsen, John C., 195
  John E,, 195
Thompson, ——, 271
  mr., 115
  Alexander R., v, 161
  Ellenor, 197
  Evelina, 197
  Harriet Matilda, 156, 158
  J., 143
  James, 136, 138, 141, 143, 195
  John, E., 221
  Joseph Lake, 141
  Louis, 215
  Margaret, 115, 270
  Mary Elizabeth, 136
  Peter, 197
  Robert, 195
  Samnel L., 209
  Samuel, Lewis Ryess, 138
  Susan, 195, 217
  William, 209

Thomson, Mary, 248
  Phoebe, 172
  Samuel, 248
  William, 248
Thorn, Ann, 166
  Catharine, 168
  Emily Augusta, 225
  William, 168
Thorp, Abigail, 41
  E,, 79, 80
  John, 41
  Margreta, 41
  Timothy, 41
Thorpe, E., vii, 71
Thum, Catharine, 141, 143, 153
  Christina, 141
  Ferdinand, 141, 197, 199
  Jacobina, 141
Thun, Ferdinand, 139
  Margaretha, 139
Thyssen, Anthony, 10
Tiboux, —— mrs., 228
Tiebout, Marytje, 42
  Teunis, 42, 44
Tietelo, Hieronimus, 16
  Stieven, 16
Tilburgh, Mettje, 20
  Pieter, 20
Tillier, William, ix
Timolat, Henry N., 207
Tites, Aaltje, 30
  Cornelis, 26
  Jannetje, 43
  Sara, 32
  Syrah, 26
Tites, 30, 32, 33
Titesz, Teunis, 51
  Tites, 51
Titsoer, Metie, 17
Titus, Aeltje, 54
Titusz, Antje, 45
  Maria, 36
  Marytje, 47
  Syrah, 39
  Tites, 36
  Titus, 39, 45, 47
Tocet, Susanna, 53
Toers, Aaron, 20
  Judith, 20
  Pietertje, 20
Tom, 181, 182
Tompkins, Daniel D., iv
Tompson, ——, mr., 228
Tonpet, Henrietta V., 228
Tooker, Ann Matilda, 127
  John, 120
  John M., 191
  John N., 127, 190
  Julia Eliza, 120
Torrance, Alfred, 156
  Daniel, 156

327

Torrence, Elliot, 230
Totten, Charity, 254, 257, 258
  Ephrahim, 257
  Joseph, 254, 272
  Lavina, 174
  Letitia, 272
  Mary, 258
  Rachel, 272
  Silas, 254, 257, 258
Toupet, ——, 229
Touppet, E. Louisa, 230
Tourneur, Benjamin, 34
  Woodhul, 34
Townsend, ——, 228, 229, 237
  mr., 228
  E., 237
  Henry V., 235
  John, 196
  Sarah, 196
  Willlam, 196, 233
Trot, Thomas, 166
Trott, Thomas, 268
Truxton, Sarah, 273
Tubbs, Frances, 197
Tucker, Abraham, 215
  George, 230
  Phebe, 185
Turner, ——, 226
  Eliz. A., 207
  Jeremiah, 195, 228
  Judith, 195
Tuthill, Ann Jane, 183
  Elizabeth, 183
  Israel, 183
Tyaden, Jhns Jansen, 205
Tylborgh, Jorius, 19
  Pieter, 19
Tyler, Rachel, 57
Tysen, Catharine Adeline, 208
  Cornelia, 67
  Emeline C., 208
  Harmen, 208
  Harriet, 233
  John, 66
  John, jr., 66
  Jno., jr., 67
  Louisa, 237
  Mary, 169, 178
  Raymond, 208
Tyson, ——, 212, 233
  Abraham, 184, 196
  Edwin, 205
  Elizabeth, 228
  Hannah, 195
  Jane, 205
  John, 167, 199
  Margaret Ann, 194
  Mary, 196, 212
  Peter, 196
  Richard, 184, 199

Tyssen, Cornelis, 10
  Elisabeth, 10

U

Upton, Mary, 177
Usselton, Sara, 24, 28
Utely, br., vi
  Richard, vii, 73, 74
Utley, Richard, 71

V

Vachereau, Susanna, 270
Valkenburgh, ——, 59
Van, Phoebe, 270
Van ——, Sara, 54
  Seimen, 54
Van Allen, ——, mrs., 230
Van Amen, Saertie, 18
  Symon, 18
Vanamour, David, 173
Vanbilt, Hannah Maria, 144
  Phoebe Jane, 136
Van Boskerk, Fytje, 51
  Jannetje, 37, 40, 43, 46, 48, 49
Van Brakel, Maria, 39
  Matthys, 36, 39
  Rachel, 36
Van Brunt, Catharina, 35, 39, 42, 45, 49, 51
  William, 269
Van Campen, Aeltie, 16
  Arent, 17
  Christina, 14
  Elsie, 16
  Gerrit, 18
  Giedie, 16
  Gydeon, 18
  Gydon, 19
  Hendrick, 13, 14, 16, 18
  Johanes, 18
  Johannes, 12, 14, 16, 17
  Lammert, 14
  Laurens, 13
  Martha, 12
  Mary, 14
  Marytie, 16, 18
Vance, James Wadsworth, 224
  Oliver, 224
  Sarah, 224
Vancleaf, Cornelius, 262
  Elisabeth, 262
  Hester, 262
  Martha, 257, 261
  Mary, 261
  Mattho, 253
  Sarah, 261
Van Cleaf, Daniel, 240, 253, 257, 261

Van Cleef, mrs., 193
  Anletchy, 187
  Beniamin, 17
  Cornelius, 47
  Daniel, 187
  Isebrant, 17
  Jacob, 186, 187
  Jan, 47
  Johannes, 16
  Letty, 187
  Martha, 187
  Sofia, 16
Vanclef, Benjamin, 255
  Marta, 255
Van Clef, Daniel, 251, 255
  John, 251
Vancleif, Sarah, 269
Vancleve, Nicolas, 174
Van Clief, D., 273
  Mary, 270
Van Cott, James, 197
Van Crampens, Louwerens, 19
Van de Bilt, Hilletie, 15
  Jacob, 15
  Rem, 15
Vandel, Peter, 269
Vandelip, Dennice, 253
  Elias, 253
  Martha, 253
Vanden Bergh, Geesie, 16
  Rut, 16
Vanderbeak, John, 211
  Mary, 211
Van der Beak, Mary, 89
Vanderbeck, Doritje, 54
Van Derbeck, Jan, 54
Vanderbeeck, Burger, 64
  Conradus, 64
  Liesabet, 64
Van der Beek, Dorothea, 35
  Jan, 22
  Jaques, 28
  Lena, 47
  Martha, 28
  Rem, 22, 25, 28, 35, 47
Vander Beek, Sophia, 22
Vanderbilt, ——, 215, 231-234
  capt., 231
  Aaron, 115, 118, 120, 123, 130, 218
  Ann Amelia, 164
  Benjamin Simonson 120, 218
  Betsey, 192
  C., 97
  C., jr., 106
  Catharine, 77, 223
  Catharine Ann, 138
  Catharine Juliette, 136
  Cecilia, 202

Vanderbilt, Celia, 195
  Charles Henry, 163
  Charlotte, 101, 104, 108, 110, 114, 115, 118, 122, 175, 196
  Christian Ann, 112
  Corn., 112, 136, 156, 175
  Corn., sr., 118
  Cornelia, 64
  Cornelius, 74, 75, 89, 92, 97, 99, 106, 118, 122, 124, 129, 130, 132, 133, 136-138, 140, 174, 184, 192, 195, 202, 220, 221, 223, 225
  Cornelius, jr., 110, 112, 114, 117, 125, 221
  Cornelius, sr., 114, 122, 214
  Cornelius E., 233
  Cornelius Egbert, 139
  Cornelius Jeremiah, 129
  Cornelius Taylor, 130
  Corns., 203
  Dane Ellenwood, 231
  Dorothy, 73, 76
  Edw., 138
  Edward, 90, 117, 119, 126, 139, 188, 198, 202, 205, 233
  Edward Ward, 141
  Eleanor, 74
  Eleonora, 92
  Eleonore, 178
  Ellen, 123, 144, 221
  Ellen V., 202
  Emily Elmira, 117
  Elijah Rhine, 137
  Eliz., 110
  Eliza, 130, 148, 164, 221
  Eliza Ann, 144, 202
  Elizabeth, 84, 90, 106, 107, 110-113, 144, 180, 188, 195, 211, 219, 221
  Elizabeth Ann, 117, 161
  Ethelinde, 110, 136
  Eva Louisa, 163
  Frances Lavinia, 124
  Frederick Putnam, 224
  G e o r g e Washington, 132, 140, 223
  Hanna Maria, 149
  Hannah Maria, 119, 198
  Henrietta, 164
  Hester Maria, 205
  Hetty, 150, 215
  Hetty Maria, 125, 202, 220
  Isaac, 115, 231
  Isabella, 108, 111, 113, 115, 118, 122, 126, 132, 144, 180, 213, 215, 221, 224

Vanderbilt, Jac., 238
  Jacob, 73, 75, 77, 95, 97, 103, 130, 144, 169, 210, 211, 218, 224, 234, 264
  Jacob Ellis, 226
  Jacob H., 144, 195
  Jacobus, vii
  James Oliver, 146
  Jane, 89, 184
  John, 73, 84, 90, 92, 94, 95, 99, 103, 105-108, 111-113, 116, 120, 123, 233, 141, 144, 147, 163, 164, 180, 187, 188, 192, 195, 196, 202, 203, 211, 221, 225, 228
  John, jr., 107, 110, 112, 115
  John, sr., 218, 219, 222, 230
  John E., 205
  John Edward, 126
  John R., 202
  John William, 164
  Joseph, 74
  Leena, 64
  Lydia, 207
  Lydia Ann, 140
  M., 206, 208
  Margarett Metcalf, 130
  Maria Louisa, 122
  Mary, 73-75, 97, 100, 130, 149, 154, 174, 202, 214, 225
  Mary Alicia, 133
  Mary Ann, 198, 233
  Mary Clara, 164
  Mary Elizabeth, 118
  Neiltje, vii
  Nieltie, 210
  Oliver, 74, 84, 110, 112, 138, 141, 146, 164, 208, 215, 220, 223
  Phebe, 74, 89, 92, 97, 98, 101, 110, 144, 174, 175, 184
  Phebe Jane, 106
  Phoebe, 232
  Phoebe Jane, 136
  Presilla, 196
  Priscilla, 147
  Rachel, 264
  Richard Taylor, 107, 219
  Robert, 264
  Sarah, 92, 116, 119, 122, 125, 137, 138, 141, 163, 164, 187
  Sarah Ann, 110, 144, 196
  Sarah Catharine, 123
  Sarah Elizabeth, 122, 203
  Sarah Louisa, 138
  Sophia, 112, 118, 124

Vanderbilt, Sophia J., 156
  Thomas, 172
  Vettje, vii
  William H., viii
  William Henry, 114
Van der Bilt, Antje, 30, 46
  Charlotte, 83
  Cornelius, vii, viii, 42, 80, 81, 83, 84, 87
  Elizabeth, 83, 86
  Essabel, 86
  Femmetje, 23, 24, 26, 30
  Hilletje, 23
  Jacob, vii, 23, 25, 26, 28, 32, 37, 42, 44, 48, 81
  Jacobus, 28
  Johannes, 37
  John, 83, 86, 171
  Magdalena, 32
  Mary, 80
  Phebe, 80, 81, 83, 84, 87
  Rem, 17
Van Derbilt, Jacob, 66
Van der Bosch, Laurens, 111
Van der Hoef, Gerrit, 49
  Hendrick, 49
Van der Hoeve, Johannes, 35
Van der H o e v e n, Anthony, 40
  Cornelius, 26
  Elisabeth, 33
  Joh., 21
  Johannes, 26, 29, 30, 33, 40
  Lea, 21, 29
  Susanna, 24-26
V a n der H u v e n, Johannes, 14
Vanderlip, Boude, 256
  Mary, 256
  Thomas, 256
Van der Schure, F e m metje, 31
V a n deventer, Abraham, 75
  Ann, 165
  Elisabeth, 170
  Elizabeth, 75
  John, 210
  Mary, 75
Van Deventer, Cornelius, vii
  Geertruyd, 28, 30
  Geertruydt, 27
Vandick, Ann, 251
  Catharine, 251
  Zachariah, 251
Vandike, Ann, 247
  Jacob, 247
  Zacharias, 247

Vandr Bilt, Antje, 24, 26, 27, 31
Femmetje, 48
Van Dusen, Daniel, 270
Vanduser, Abraham, 116
  John, 116, 119
  John Vanderbilt, 119
Van Duser, Abraham, 184
  Ann, 187
  Daniel, 187, 221
  Daniel C., 221
  Ellen, 221
  Isaac Housman, 122
  Jacob Taylor, 125
  John, 122, 125, 130, 187
  Louisa, 221
  Oliver Vanderbilt, 130
  Sarah, 130, 203
Vanduzer, Abraham, 148, 154
  Abrm., 151
  Elisabeth Ann, 141
  Eliza Ann, 151, 154
  Ellen Louisa, 151
  Eveline, 154
  Isaac, 154
  Isaac Oliver, 154
  Jacob, 154
  Jacob mrs., 146
  John, 141, 151, 154
  John Housman, 154
  John V. Junr, 148
  Margaret, 154
  Mary, 154
  Peter Winant, 154
  Sarah, 148, 151, 154
  Sarah Catharina, 148
  Sarah Elizabeth, 148, 151, 229
Van Duzer, Abraham, 157, 161, 163, 202
  Ann Lyle, 161
  Anna M., 158, 159
  Daniel Clyde, 159
  Daniel Theodore, 137, 138, 224
  Edward Vanderbilt, 161
  Eliza Ann, 163
  Elizabeth, 163
  Elizabeth Ann, 157
  Emma, 237
  Evelina, 231
  George, 236
  Henry Carey, 163
  Isaac, 157, 159, 163
  Isaac H., 203
  Jacob, 141, 157, 158, 159, 162, 163
  Jacob Theodore, 157
  John, 137, 138, 157, 202, 203, 224, 229
  John Jacob, 157

Van Duzer, Lilian, 159
  Margaret, 157-159, 162
  Margareth, 163
  Mary, 157, 159, 163
  Mary Emma, 157
  Mary Louisa, 141
  Percival, 162
  Peter W., 231
  Peter Winant, 157
  Priscilla, 163
  S., 157
  Sarah, 158, 159, 168, 202, 224
  Sarah E., 231
  Wm. Oliver, 158
Van Dyck, Annetie, 9
  Hendrick, 9
Van Dyk, Catharina, 35, 39
  Cornelius, 45
  Elisabeth, 28
  Henricus, 25
  Jacob, 35, 39, 42, 45
  Lambert, 25, 28
  Tryntje, 35
  Zacheus, 42
Van Dyke, John, 272
Van Engelen, Ahasuerus, 13, 26
  Elisabeth, 47
  Rachel, 13, 39, 43, 44, 46, 48, 51, 57
  Ragel, 54
Van Gelder, Anna, 41, 49
  Annaatje, 44
  Henricus, 49
  Lena, 44, 48, 50
  Sophia, 49
Van Hoorn, Antje, 30
  Jan, 30
  Jannetje, 24, 30, 42, 47, 49
  Neeltye, 60
Vanhoren, Neeltye, 62
Vanhorne, Jacob, 98
  Sarah Egbert, 98
Van Houten, Abraham, 178
  Janneke, 50
Van Kleef, Isebrant, 15
  Jannetie, 15
Van Lawa, Dina, 50
  Henrik, 26
Van Leeuwen, Dina, 44, 46, 48
  Frederyk, 22
  Hendrik, 22, 35
  Lena, 35
Van Naame, Sara, 61
Van Name, Aaron, 182, 186, 197
  Anna, 26
  Cath., 182

Van Name, Charles, 197
  Cornelius, 186
  Deborah, 197
  Edward, 113
  Eliza Augusta, 118
  Johannes, 33
  John R., 204
  Mary, 182
  Michael, 113, 118, 182
  Moses, 182
Van Namen, Aaron, 20
  Anna, 22, 30, 32, 40
  Antye, 62
  Aron, 56, 57, 59, 62, 65
  Dina, 29, 40
  Engelbart, 13, 14
  Engelbert, 21, 26
  Evert, 12, 13, 20, 24
  Helena, 60
  Incres, 54
  Jenneke, 46
  Jenneken, 24
  Joh., 26, 37, 40
  Johannes, 19, 21, 31, 40
  Joseph, 13
  Maria, 20, 26
  Michael, 115
  Moses, 30
  Mosis, 65
  Pieter, 19
  Rachel, 59
  Rebecca, 26
  Sara, 16, 24, 26, 29, 31, 43, 54
  Sartje, 18
  Simon, 16, 30, 36, 39
  Sophia, 115
  Symon, 18, 20
Van Namer, Mary, 169
Van Namur, Aaron, 179
  Ann, 186
  Cornelius, 186
  David, 173
  Elizabeth, 169
  Frances, 179
  Mary, 179, 182
  Michael, 182
  Moses, 169, 182
Van Nes, Anna, 31
  Isak, 31
Van Nieuwenhuysen, Johannes, 19
Van Norman, Mary, 174
Van Pe, Antje, 38
Van Peldt, Anna, 67
  Antony, 57
  Kadlyna, 51
  Maria, 57
Vanpelt, Abraham, 196
  Ann, 196
  Antye, 64
  Barber, 64

Vanpelt, David, 196
  Derckye, 55
  Elizabeth, 79
  Jeams, 79
  John, 65
  Maria, 52
  Mary, 65
  Peater, 64
  Sara, 63, 64
  Simon, 52
Van Pelt, ——, 59, 225, 226, 232
  Aart 26
  Abm., 109
  Abraham, 99, 102, 109, 176
  Abrm., 226
  Aeltie, 10
  Aeltje, 17, 18
  Aert, 16
  Alice, 77
  Altje, 18, 19
  Amy, 99
  Ann, 79, 183, 210
  Anna, 58
  Annetie, 9
  Antje, 33, 40, 46, 47, 49, 53
  Antony, 29, 34, 38, 44, 47, 58, 65, 250, 252, 258
  Antye, 55
  Aron, 178
  Barbara, 57, 66, 272
  Blandina, 20, 30-32, 34-40, 45, 47, 51
  Blandyena, 11
  Cathalyn, 14
  Catharina, 16
  Catharine, 121, 125, 187
  Cathrine, 173
  Catlyna, 55
  Catlyntje, 21, 22, 24, 30, 38, 40, 50, 54
  Charlotte, 183
  David, 63, 183, 271
  Derckie, 16
  Derkje, 54
  Dirkje, 47
  Elezabeth, 255
  Elizabeth, 58, 177, 192, 256-258, 260, 271
  Elsje, 42, 45, 50, 52
  Feeby, 250
  Francis, 250
  Franky, 268
  Georg, 87
  George, 184, 187, 204, 215, 229, 258, 270, 272
  George Washington, 131
  Grietje, 47
  Hanna, 175

Van Pelt, Hannah, 262, 268
  Helena, 38
  Hendrick, 9, 10, 21, 24
  Henrik, 31
  Jacob, 12, 14, 16-20, 22-24, 26, 30, 32, 35, 61, 182, 187, 255, 257, 258
  Jacomyntje, 24, 25, 27, 33
  James, 256
  Jan, 9, 11, 12, 14-16, 18, 21-25, 29, 34, 35, 38-42, 44, 45, 47, 50, 52-58
  Jan, jr., 54
  Jan Teunis, 12
  Jane, 77
  Jane R., 209
  Jannetje, 53
  Jannetye, 59
  Jennie, 57
  Johannes, 11, 13, 14, 16-19, 21, 22, 25, 30, 34, 40, 53, 57
  John, iv, 62, 66, 79, 131, 136, 170, 184, 186, 210, 230-232, 249, 250, 252, 253, 256, 258, 260, 262
  John Christopher, 131
  Joost, 16, 18, 19, 47, 48
  Joseph, 256, 260
  Judy, 79
  Lena, 39-41, 208
  Maragrietye, 56
  Margaret, 191, 249, 250, 258, 271
  Margret, 252, 253, 256, 262
  Margrit, 260
  Maria, 12, 23, 26, 29, 33, 36, 41, 43, 45, 52, 55, 61
  Marritie, 9
  Mary, 87, 184, 249, 255, 257
  Mary Elizabeth, 136
  Marya, 21, 61
  Marytie, 16
  Marytje, 31, 37, 45
  Moses, 177
  Nenne, 14
  Nieltje, 54
  Peter, 87, 126, 131, 173, 183, 184, 186, 187, 191, 192, 199, 204, 234, 250, 258, 271
  Peter I., iv
  Peterus, 58
  Petrus, 18, 50, 61
  Petures, 52
  Phoebe (Feeby), 250
  Pieter, 12-20, 22, 27, 31, 40, 47, 56, 57, 63, 175

Van Pelt, Rachel, 59
  Richard, 173
  Richd., 192
  Saartje, 38
  Safya, 59
  Samuel, 14, 18, 56, 58, 182
  Sara, 13-15, 19, 21, 25, 38, 48, 50, 52, 53, 56, 63, 65
  Sarah, 56, 102, 165, 171
  Sarah Ann, 182
  Sartje, 19
  Seymon, 53
  Simon, 13, 16
  Susan, 121, 126, 136, 191, 221
  Susanna, 38, 54, 57, 62, 252, 258
  Susannah, 250
  Symon, 47, 51, 57, 58
  Teunis, 30, 34, 40, 45, 48, 49
  Theunis, 9, 260
  Tony, 39, 41
  Treintje, 52
  Tunis, 131, 250
  Willem, 17, 47
  William, 52, 77, 169
Van Ranst, Peter, 40
  Sara, 40
Van Santen, Josua, 11
  Stoffel, 10, 11
Van Santvoord, Corn, 28
  Cornelius, 22, 28, 40, 48, 50
Van Santvord, Johanna, 52
Van Schayk, Margaretha, 25
Van Schuere, Catharina, 61
Van Schuren, Chathrine, 67
Van Schuure, Catharina, 56
  Catrina, 52
Van Sekelen, Elisabeth, 52
Van Seuren, Catrina, 54
Van Sheure, Catharina, 55, 61
Vanscice, Cathrine, 250
  Charles, 250
  Joseph, 250
  Sarah De Hart, 250
Vansise, Sara, 165
Van Syle, Lydia, 167
Van Tilburgh, Dirkje, 21, 25, 29, 31, 33, 36, 42, 45
  Henricus, 34
  Pieter, 24, 34
  Willem, 24

Van Tuil, Abraham, 10, 13
　Elena, 13
　Geertruyt, 10
　Isaack, F., 10
　Otto, 63
Van Tuyl, Ab., 36
　Abraham, 13, 23, 41, 43-46, 50, 51, 53, 56
　Anna, 27
　Antje, 24
　Catharina, 24
　Catharyntie, 13
　Denys, 41, 45, 50
　Femmetje, 50, 53
　Geertruyd, 29, 36, 43-45
　Helena, 40, 41, 44, 45
　Isaac, 13
　Isaack, 24, 29, 46
　Isak, 45
　Jan, 45, 46
　Johannes, 49
　Machiel, 51
　Neeltje, 45, 50
　Otto, 23, 56, 60, 63
Van Vleek, Henry, vi
Van Voorhees, Femmetje, 27
　Jacobus, 31
　Jan, 31, 36, 37, 43
　Jan Stevens, 27
　Koert, 28
　Neeltje, 43
　Roelof, 36
　Willempje, 27
Van Voorhes, Maria, 49
　Roelof, 49
Van Wagene, Gerrit, 15
　Hendrik, 60
　Johannes, 57
　Marregrietye, 60
Van Wagenen mr., 203
　Annaetye, 60
　Annatje, 61
　Antje, 50, 54
　Catharina, 60
　Cornelus, 54, 56, 60
　Hendrick, 61
　Manes, 60
　Maragrita, 56
Van Wageninge, Jacob, 37
Van Wageningen, Jacob
　Gerritsz, 47
　Jacobus, 42
　Lea, 42
Van Wagenne, Cornelis, 62
　Hendrik, 62
　Johannes, 62
　Lena, 62
Vanwinkel, Eghye, 65
Van Winkel, Aaghje, 37
　Aaltje, 48

Van Winkel, Daniel, 37, 44, 48, 49
　Elias, 169
Van Wogelom, Adriaan, 17
　Adriaen, 13, 15
　Cristina, 53
Van Woggelom, Abraham, 41
　Adriaan, 38, 40, 41
　Ary, 27, 32
　Blandina, 14
　Christina, 38, 40, 42, 43, 49, 50
　Cornelius, 39
　Douwe, 29, 30, 35, 39, 51
　Hilletye, 41
　Jan, 33, 38
　Jan, jr., 14
　Jan Staats, 35
　Zuster, 29
Van Woglom, Annatje, 54
　Antje, 52
　Arey, 18
　Arie, 54
　Crestina, 52
　Douw, 19
　Douwen, 52
　Jan, 18
Van Woglum, Anna, 27
　Andries, 31
　Ary, 23, 26-28, 31
　Catharina, 48
　Christina, 48
　Douwe, 27, 48
　Hilletje, 23, 24, 29
　Johanna, 23
V. Duzer, Ann, 184
　Daniel, 184, 236
　Debora, 102
　Julia, 236
Vechten, Catharyna, 19
　Gerrit, 10, 14
　Jan, 14
　Johan, 19
　Magdaleentie, 14
　Maghdalena, 10
　Nicolaes, 14
Veghte, Cornelia, 17
　Gerret, 18
　Gerretye, 57
　Gerrit, 26
　Gerritje, 26, 30, 31, 42, 47
　Henrik, 34
　Jan, 17, 18, 24, 28, 30, 31, 34, 35, 45
　Jannetje, 30
　Nicolass, 45
Veghten, Jan, 22
　Jannetye, 56
　Johannes, 22

Veldtman, Geertruyda, 61
　Jan, 55, 61
　Jannetje, 61
Velein, Ludwig, 203
Veltman, ——, 59
　Geertruyt, 57
　Hendereck, 52
　Hendrik, 52, 59
　Jan, 53, 57
　John, 63
　Maria, 53
Ven Pelt, Sara, 61
Verbeck, John Renatus, 96
Verkerk, Mayke, 37
Verschuur, Cathrina, 50
Vesey, William, viii
Vetyto, Petrus, 18
　Steven, 18
Vielen, Antje, 20
　Cornelis, 9
Vile, Antje, 24
　Blandina, 20, 27, 29
　Elisabet, 39
Vilen, Antje, 24, 27
Villette, Judith, 89
　Taylor, 89
Vincnant, Zedick, 171
Vleereboom, Tryntje, 30, 31
Vlierboom, Catharina, 21
　Catharyna, 25
　Jannetje, 34, 40, 43
　Tryntje, 31, 39
Vliereboom, Tryntje, 44
V. Name, Dina, 37
V. Namen, Sara, 26
V. Namur, Maria, 183
Vogler, William H., viii
　Wm. H., 71
Voke, Christopher, 264
　John, 264
　Mary, 264
Voorhis, Julia Palmer, 206
　M., 206
　Mary, 202
　Mary Elizabeth, 149, 154, 202
Vooris, Howard, 137
　Julia Parmer, 137
　Mary, 137, 138
　Mary Elizabeth, 137
V. Pelt, Sally, 183
　Samuel, 183
Vredenburg, ——, 231, 232
Vreeland, Derrick, 67
　George, 188
　Jacob, 67, 188, 208
　James, 162, 208
　Jas., 160
　Jennie Martling, 162
　Rebecca, 188
　Wilhelmus, ix

Vreelant, Jannetje, 37, 44, 49
  Metje, 50
  Michiel, 50
Vreland, Helmig, 60
  Jannetje, 60
  Johannes, 60
Vrelandt, Jenneke, 51
  Magiel, 51
Vrelant, Helmis, 62
  Helmog, 60
  Jannetje, 48
  Jannitye, 62
  Machgiel, 62
Vrielandt, Metje, 51
Vrome, Rachel Ann, 235
Vroom, ——, 214
  Catharine, 160, 209
  Christopher, 151, 188, 202, 209
  Eliza Taylor, 164
  Elizabeth, 209
  Elizabeth S., 164
  George W., 164
  Georgiana, 228
  Mary, 188
  Richard Blake, 209
  William V., 202
Vroome, ——, 238
  sr., 154
  Alb., 208
  Albert, 163, 208
  Ann Eliza, 154
  Carolina, 163
  Catharine, 163
  Christian, 67
  Christian, sr., 66
  Christopher, 152, 158, 161, 162, 239
  Elizabeth, 66
  Gar., 238
  Garret, 161
  Garrett, 206
  Garrit, 151
  Garry, 158, 161
  George, 159, 162
  Georgianna, 147
  Lewis, 238
  Louis Taylor, 162
  Lenora Walker, 159
  Lydia, 163
  Maria, 163, 239
  Maria Ann, 159
  Maria Louise, 149
  Martha Jane, 163
  Mary Ann, 152
  Mary Anna, 158
  Peter Houseman, 239
  Sarah Elizabeth, 161
  Will., 163
  William, 157, 161, 163
  William White, 67
  Wm., 147, 149, 154, 158

Vroome, Wm. Emmett, 157, 234
V. Santvoord, Anna, 25
  Corn., 23, 25, 31, 37, 44
  Jacoba, 37
  Maria Catharina, 23
  Staats, 31
  Zeger, 44
V. Tuyl, Abraham, 28
V. Woggelum, Christina, 33, 35, 51
  Douwe, 31, 33
V. Woglom, Beelletje, 54
Vyle, Pieter, 11

W

Waacker, Ledey, 9
Wade, br., vi
  Eleanor, 272
  John, vii, 71, 73
Wadsworth, Elisabeth, 197
  John, 197
  Mary, 197
Wagener, Adam, 141, 199
Waggelom, Suster, 55
Waglom, Caroline, 162
  Jan, 13
  Margaret Anna, 158
  Peter Anderson, 158, 162
Waglon, Catharine, 245
  John, 245
Waglum, ——, 170
  Abraham, 269
  Andres, 246
  Catharine, 269
  Elizabeth, 246
  Jane, 269
  John, 273
  Joshua, 270
  Mary, 273
  Nelly, 246
Wagner, Clara, 154
Wagstaff, Agnes, 232
Wait, Ann, 239
Wakeham, ——, mrs., 231
Walderon, Jacobus, 49
  Joseph, 49
Walker, ——, 232
  Jacob, 197
  John, 197
  Maria, 197
Waller, Catherine Elizabeth Burgher, 129
  Charles, 129
  Jocelyn, 225
Walls, Ann, 263
  George Nathaniel, 263
  James, 263
Walter, Anna Catharina, 155

Walter, John, 149
Walters, Sara, 44
Wandel, Charity, 171
  Danl., 220
  Jane, 175
  John, 169
  Mary Elizabeth, 220
  Mathew, 266
  Peter, 191, 266
  Sarah, 191, 266
Wandell, Ann, 193
  Daniel, jr., 206
  David, 206
  Elisa, 230
  Henry D., 233
  Julia, 237
  Peter, 235
  Peter S., 230
  Peter S., jr., 238
  Philip, 237
  Sarah, 234
  Sarah Ann, 207
Wappelrie, Elisabeth, 9
Ward, mrs., 141
  Ann, 169
  Anne, 74
  Charity, 74
  Elisabet, 24, 27
  Johanna, 171
  Maria, 208
  Sara, 167
  William, 74
Warner, Edmund, 168
  Julia C., 207
Warren, Catharine, 120
  James, 173
  Joshua, 120
  Phebe Ann Glazier, 120
Waters, A., 254
  Ann, 126
  Elizabeth, 167
  Helen, 122
  John D., 122, 126
  William, 122
Wauterzen, Jan, 9
Web, Aaltje, 30
Webb, Mary, 249
  Richard, 167, 249
Weber, Francesca, 158
Webs, Aaltje, 26
Weeb, Alchey, 264
  Noyche, 264
  Richard, 264
Weed, ——, 236
  ——, mr., 236
Weidenmiller, Caroline, 149
Weidmuller, Carl Heinrich Christian, 153
  Caroline, 151
  Heinrich, 153
Weliams, Maria, 52

Wels, Lambert, 12
Welsh, Richard, 235
Wendel, Aletta, 75-77, 210
  Anne, 76
  Anne Mary, 75
  Charity, 76
  John, 75-77, 210
  Thomas, 77, 210
  Walter, 191
White, ——, 225
  Catharine L., 204
  Erskine N., iv
  George, 197
  Isabella, 236
  Jane, 197
  John, 123, 171, 197, 214, 215
  John C., 236
  Mary Louise, 130
  Nancy, 185
  Pinkney, 236
  Rebecca, 215
  Rebekah, 130
  Richard, 123, 130, 225
  Richd., 215
  Sara, 166
  William, 212
Whitehead, ——, 232
  Elias, 209
Whithead, John, 24
Whitman, Susanna, 29
Whitsworth, ——, 225
  John, jr., 225
Whitworth, John, 225
Whrite, Andrew, 261
  John, 261
  Juda, 261
Wians, ——, 232
Widsworth, Elizabeth, 137
  John, 137
  Margaretha Ann, 137
  Mary, 137
Wilhelm, Johann, 199
Wilhelmin, Leonhart, 195
Willemsen, Antie, 16
  Hendreck, 17
  Hester, 53
  Ragel, 53
Williams, B., 199
  Benjamin Y., 199
  Catharine, 199
  Hester, 267
  John, 167, 267
  Lamont, 205, 235
  Maria, 52
  Rebecca, 267
  Stephen H., 201
  William, 171, 219, 267
Wilmot, Thomas, 48
Wilson, Abraham Noble, 146
  Grace Noble, 148

Wilson, James, 204
  Margaret, 168
  Robert, 184
  William, 146, 148
Winant, ——, 188, 229, 230, 233
  Abraham, 177, 248, 258
  Ann, 248, 252, 265, 267
  Charity, 262
  Charles H., 226
  Christian, 259
  Cornelous, 255
  Cristyan, 255
  Daniel, 252, 254, 265
  Danl., 230
  Elizabeth, 258, 262
  George, 259
  George Henry Tyson, 147
  Hannah, 262
  Isaac, 262
  Jacob, 195, 263
  Jeremiah, 182
  Johannah, 263
  John, 182, 262, 263
  Lizabet, 254
  Mark, 225
  Mary, 126, 128, 248, 258, 265
  Peter, 255, 259, 262, 265, 267
  Rachel, 254
  Sarah, 182
  Simon, 182
  Susannah, 252, 267
  William, 147, 179, 201
  Winant, 265
  Wm., 229
  Wm., sr., 234
Winants, Abraham, 254
  Catharine, 267
  Cornelas, 254
  Cornelia, 267
  Cornelius, 267
  Mary, 254
Winet, Ann, 189
Winnens, Daniel, 250
  Rachel, 250
Winnett, Charles Henry, 207
Winning, Ann, 129
  Ann Louise, 129
  George William, 129
  William, 129
Winnings, Isabella, 193
  William, 193
  Wm., 193
Winsor, mrs., 204
  George, 204
Winter, Abadia, 36
  Elizabeth, 268
  Frans, 22

Winter, Geertje, 31, 35, 50
  Jan, 39, 42
  Jesias, 39
  Margreta, 36, 39
  Maria, 42
  Obadia, 35
  Obadiah, 50
  Obadias, 22, 28, 31
  Rebecca, 50
  Susanna, 39
Winters, Elizabeth, 216
  Susanna, 20
Wisselpenning, Gerritje, 26
Wolby, mr., 209
Woersman, Marie, 33
Woertman, Maria, 31, 34, 35, 37, 41, 44
Wogelom, Jan Pieterszen, 9
Woggelom, Blandina, 12
  Johan, 12
Woggelum, Blandiena, 10
  Christyntien, 12
  Grytie, 9
  Hilletje, 36
  Johan, 12, 15
  Suster, 15
Woglom, Peter, 186
  Simon, 186
Woglum, Hilletje, 23, 28
Wohlfahrt, Friderika, 204
Woinat, Corn., 34
  Cornelis, 24
  Hendrikje, 24
Wolf, Anna Maria, 149
  Charles, 164
  Maria Eliz., 236
Wolfe, Sarah, 197
Wolfen, Maria, 141
Wolly, Elihu, 165
Wood, ——, 219, 226, 233
  mr., 176
  Abbey Ann, 219
  Abraham, 183, 252, 266
  Abraham Aston, 103
  Abraham S., 208
  Agnes, 163
  Alice, 264, 265
  Ann, 180, 193, 264, 266
  Barbara, 233
  Bradley, 163
  Cath., 184
  Catharina, 127
  Cathrine, 186, 187, 214, 267
  Charles, 272
  Charles D., 193
  Cornelis, 266
  Daniel, 185
  David, 191

Wood, Deina, 188
  Demah, 188
  Edward, 160, 205
  Elce, 263
  Eles, 265, 266
  Elias Marsh, 108
  Elisabeth, 250, 263
  Elizabeth, 117, 163, 167, 173, 181, 191, 203, 213, 246, 257, 262, 263, 268, 271
  Emeline, 136
  Emily, 226
  Emmeline Hillyer, 107
  Eve, 252
  George, 246, 250
  George Colon, 109
  Henrietta, 151
  Isaac, 270
  Israel, 192
  Jacob, 165
  Jacob Clendenne, 106
  James, 104, 110, 144, 158, 180, 183, 191, 193, 219, 226, 252, 263, 264, 266, 271
  James B., 151
  Jane, 184
  Jannetje, 31
  Jemima, 268
  Jesse, 273
  John, 167, 188, 189, 193, 205, 233, 246, 255, 257, 259, 261, 264, 270, 272
  John Grondain, 257
  Joseph, 180, 264
  Margaret, 257, 271
  Margaret Ann, 113
  Margareth Ann, 198
  Margret, 255, 261
  Martha, 175
  Mary, 80, 98, 166, 181, 193, 194, 198, 254, 255, 257, 260-262, 264, 265, 267
  Mary Ann, 144, 145, 159
  Mary Augusta, 160
  Moses, 100, 103, 106, 109, 112, 175, 214, 234
  Nancy, 218, 264
  Obadia, 35
  Patience, 263
  Peter, 107, 110, 113, 180, 198
  Phoebe, 271
  Polly, 217
  Richard, 41, 254, 257, 267, 270
  Richard Webb, 80
  Richd., 184
  Ruth, 183
  Ruth Mary, 100

Wood, Saml., 219
  Stephen, 31, 35, 41, 80, 104, 108, 117, 165, 166, 176, 180, 185, 188, 218, 260-266, 270
  Stephen Lawrence, 264
  Steven, 35
  Susannah, 266
  Timothy, 170, 181, 187, 257, 264, 268
  Vincent, 266
  William, 192
  William Barber, 266
  William Henry, 158
Woodland, J. A., 207
  John E., 208
Woods, Cath, 200
  Joseph, 239
Woodruff, David, 268
Woodward, Isaac, 271
  Mary Elizabeth, 202
Wouters, Antie, 15
  Antje, 24
  Benjamin, 15
  Cornelis, 10
  Jacob, 10, 15
  Lambert, 13
  Sara, 13
Wreath, Isabella, 102
Write, Hannah, 264
  John, 259, 263, 264
  Jude, 259
  Judy, 264
  Mary, 263
Wright, ——, 271
  Cath., 183
  Catharine, 180, 188
  Elizabeth, 188
  George W., 203
  Hannah, 271
  Henricus, 37
  Henry, 37
  Jacob, 33
  Jean, 268
  John, 260
  Joshua, 180
  Judah, 185
  Judith, 260
  Mary, 183, 271
  Polly, 185
  Susan, 201
  Susanna, 33
  Thomas, 183, 188, 273
Wunsch, Frederick, 204
Wyllemit, Maritje, 17
Wynand, Francis, 174
Wynandts, Pieter, 23
  Wynandt, 23
Wynant, ——, 271
  Abm., 273
  Ann, 270
  Catharine, 270, 272

Wynant, Cornelis, 28, 32, 35
  Cornelius, 35
  Daniel, 181, 271
  Elisabet, 28
  Elizabeth, 180, 269-271
  Frances, 181
  George, 180, 270
  Hannah, 273
  Isaac, 270
  Jane, 270, 271
  Jesse, 180
  John, 270
  Lanah, 272
  Maria, 32
  Mary, 181, 269-271, 273
  Mary Ann, 270
  Moses, 271
  Patty, 270
  Peter, 269
  Pieter, 16, 32
  Sarah, 181
  Wynant, 35
Wynants, Abraham, 30
  Antje, 45, 46
  Daniel, 36
  Catharina, 23, 26, 30, 32, 34, 35, 37, 39
  Cathrina, 46
  Cathryna, 32, 38
  Cathryntje, 38
  Geertje, 41
  Jacob, 34
  Johannes, 42
  Johannis, 38
  Peter, 32
  Pieter, 23, 24, 36, 39, 41, 42
  Wynant, 30, 34, 36
Wynantse, Pieter, 12

Y

Yarrel, Thomas, vii, 71, 74, 75
Yates, Abraham, 40
  Joseph, 40, 218, 248, 268
  Martha, 248
  Sarah, 248, 272
Yeates, Abraham, 246
  Joseph, 246
  Sarah, 246
——yellard, Ann, 268
Yennes, John, 64
  Mareya, 64
Yerks, Mary M., 203
Yocom, Thomas S., xi
Yoons, Eva, 63, 64
York, negro, 241
Young, Ann, 267
  Charles, 200
  Elisabeth, 175

Young, Elizabeth Clawson, 99
George, 267
Mary, 109
Thomas, 267

Z

Zeller, Elizabeth, 166
Zeluff, Daniel, 268
  Sarah, 268
Zielofs, Blandina, 56
  Pieter, 56
Zikkel, Elisabet, 47, 49
Zilkens, August, 204
Zimsenbach, Philip, 50
Zinzendorf, count, vi
Zorn, Esther Ruth Eliza, 164
  Georgiana, Theodora Jacobina, 164
  John Theodor, 164
Zumsenbach, Christina, 44
  Hanna, 47
  Johan Philip, 44, 47
Zutphen, Abraham, 33, 34, 38, 42
  Antje, 38
  Jannetje, 42
  Maria, 34
Zweem, Johannes, 19

www.ingramcontent.com/pod-product-compliance
Lightning Source LLC
Chambersburg PA
CBHW050614300426
44112CB00012B/1504